THE LAND OF THE PERUMALS

THE LAND OF THE PERUMALS

OR

COCHIN, ITS PAST AND ITS PRESENT

FRANCIS DAY

GYAN

Published by

Gyan Publishing House
5, Ansari Road
Daryaganj, New Delhi-110002
Phone: 011-47034999, 9811692060
E-mail: books@gyanbooks.com

Distribution Network
gyanbooks.com
India, USA, Canada, UK, Australia

ISBN: 978-93-7169-315-8 (PB)

First Published, 1863

2nd Impression 2025

Printed at: Gyan Press, Delhi.

THE LAND OF THE PERUMALS
Author: FRANCIS DAY

THE LAND OF THE PERMAULS,

OR

COCHIN, ITS PAST AND ITS PRESENT.

BY

FRANCIS DAY, ESQ., F.L.S.

H. M. MADRAS MEDICAL SERVICE,
CIVIL SURGEON BRITISH COCHIN, AND MEDICAL OFFICER
TO THE GOVERNMENT OF HIS HIGHNESS THE RAJAH OF COCHIN.

What can he tell who treads thy shore?
No legend of thine olden time,
No theme on which the Muse might soar
High as thine own in days of yore.

MADRAS:

PRINTED BY GANTZ BROTHERS, AT THE ADELPHI PRESS,
21, RUNDALL'S ROAD, VEPERY.

1863.

To

GEORGE PEARSE, Esq., M. D.

Honorary Physician to H. M. and

Late Director General, Madras

Medical Establishment.

These pages are dedicated, as a slight testimony, to the worth of one, who after a long Indian career, retired from the Service, carrying with him, the sincere attachment of his friends, the gratitude of his numerous patients, and the best wishes of the Members of the Medical Service, over whom he had so ably presided.

PREFACE.

DURING a residence of a few years in Cochin, the facts were collected, from which the following pages have been compiled.

Owing to the kindness of G. Ballard, Esq., the present Collector of Malabar, permission was obtained, for the perusal and employment of official documents, which proved of great assistance.

H. H. the Rajah of Cochin, and S. Menone, Esq., the Dewan, most obligingly afforded information, upon many subjects connected with the Native State. Great assistance was also received, from the late lamented General Cullen, who for nearly twenty years, ably held the post of British Resident, and was intimately acquainted with the people, their manners, customs, and laws.

C. D'Albedÿh'll, Esq., Judge of the Appeal Court of Ernaccollum, was good enough to translate the Memorials of the Dutch Governors of Cochin, and some of their Secret Records, which give an insight into the policy of that nation, and their relationship with the neighbouring native States.

Thanks are due to Conrad Vernéde, Esq., for his assistance in obtaining personal intercourse with Namboorie Brahmans, and other Hindus, with the view of facilitating enquiries into Hinduism, as it now exists in the Cochin State. G. Garthwaite, Esq., Inspector of Schools, obligingly Romanized the Indian words, for the Index: whilst many other officials and friends afforded their assistance, to all and each of whom, thanks are here offered.

Owing to the civility of Messrs. Smith Elder and Co., some old books on Malabar, now out of print, were procured in London, and proved of great assistance, with reference to the early history of this portion of Malabar.

The following are the principal works referred to, in the ensuing pages :—

Herbert's *Travels*, 1665. Purchas, *His Pilgrims*, 1625. Tavernier's *Travels*, 1676. Travels of two Mahomedans in the 9th century. Voyage of Captain Walter Peyton to India, in 1615. Stavorinus's *Voyage to India*, 1777.

Faria's *Portuguese Asia*. Notes concerning the factory of Cranganore, from the Journal of Roger Hawes. Phillips' *Account of Malabar*, 1717. A voyage round the world by Commodore Roggewein, in 1721-1723. Sonnerat's *Voyages and Travels.* Cope's *Voyages and Travels*, 1754. Hamilton's *New account of the East Indies.* Paolino de St. Bartholomeo's *Travels*, 1800. Ormes *History of Industan.* Kerr's collection of Voyages and Travels, 1824. Discoveries in India, from 1497 to 1505, by Herman Lopez de Castaneda. Dr. Francis Buchanan's *Journey through Mysore, Canara, and Malabar*, 1807. Memoirs of Dr. Claudius Buchanan, 1817. Forbes's *Oriental Memoirs*, 1834. Elphinstone's *History of India.* Taylor's *History of India.* MacFarlane's *History of India.* Mill's *History of India.* Wilk's *History of Mysore.* Asiatic Researches. Calcutta Reviews. Madras Journals of Literature and Science. Journals of the Asiatic Society. Records of Travancore and Cochin. &c., &c.

CONTENTS.

ERRATA.

Page 1	line 2	from bottom	for "Horsley"	read	"Arthur."
„ 3	„ 5	„ „	omit "Pilla."		
„ 17	„ 5	„ „	for "ro"	read	"to."
„ 58	„ 12	„ „	„ "forms"	read	"reforms."
„ 66	„ 11	„ „	„ "1762"	„	"1785."
„ 66	„ 2	„ „	„ "1762"	„	"1785."
„ 78	„ 4	„ „	„ "August	„	"April."
„ 123	„ 3	„ „	„ "are"	„	"is."
„ 156	„ 6	„ „	„ "1795"	„	"1793."
„ 236	„ 8	„ top	„ "1567"	„	"1657."
„ 269	„ 16	„ „	„ "may"	„	"might."
„ 305	„ 5	„ „	„ "a Namboorie"	read	"a married Namboorie."
„ 320	„ 2	„ „	„ "Choties"	read	"Choghutties."
„ 446	„ 21	„ „	„ "he"	„	"it."
„ „	„ 22	„ „	„ "his"	„	"its."
„ 496	„ last		„ "karagurta"	„	"kanagurta."
„ 503	„ 14	„ „	„ "rubripimus"	„	"rubripinnis ?"
„ 504	„ 12	„ „	„ "voalis ?"	„	"ruallagoo ?"
„ 521	„ 6	„ bottom	„ "Tricopterœ"	„	"Trichopterœ."
„ 538	„ 15	„ „	„ "lightly"	„	"tightly."
„ 545	„ 18	„ „	„ "Vetla"	„	"Vetta."

N. B.—Besides the above, there are a few typographical errors in some of the names.

CHAPTER I.

TOPOGRAPHY OF THE COCHIN STATE.

General Description—Its Divisions—Legendary origin of Tripoonterah—Legendary division of Islands—Curious Pilgrimages—Travancore lines—Trichoor Fortifications—Verapoly—Devil's Mouth—Alwaye—Buildings—Water Communications—Back-waters—Rivers—Reservoirs—Roads—Mountains—Geology—Mineral Productions—Harbours—Narrikal Mud Bank.

THE Native State of Cochin may be called a Province of Malabar, situated on the Western Coast of Hindustan, and lying between the 9th and 11th degrees of North latitude, and 75th and 77th of East longitude. It is bounded on the West by the Ocean, on the North by British Malabar, on the South by the Native State of Travancore, and on the East by the long line of mountains known as the Western Ghauts. It contains (including Chittoor) 1,131 square miles, of various descriptions of territory.

The Cochin State encircles several portions of Travancore, and one large town, known as Cochin, in latitude 9° 58' N., and longitude 76° 18' 30" E., the property of the British Government: whilst its own district of Chittoor is itself surrounded by British territory. The State is divided into Kunneeanúr, Cochin, Cranganore, Kodachayree, Mukundapurum, Yainamakul, Thaullapullay, Trichoor, Chaylayekurray, and Chittoor.* Excluding this last division, it consists of hills and low-lands: these latter being from fifteen to twenty miles in width, and stretching from the ghauts to the sea-shore. The low-lands are divisible into two portions, a long sandy or *maritime* territory, from two miles to

* Many of the following measurements, and other information, are taken from the excellent *Official Reports* of *Lieutenants Connors* and *Ward;* M.S.S. of the Surveyor General's Department: also M.S.S. records of the *Dutch Government of Cochin:* the report of *Dr. Francis Buchanan,* 1800: *Lieutenant Horsley,* 1810, *and Assistant Surgeon Oliphant,* 1834. M.S.S. Alterations and additions have been made, to bring them up to the present time.

a few hundred yards in width, on the west face of which lies the sea, whilst its eastern side is bounded by the backwater, sometimes two miles wide, but more commonly a few hundred yards. This maritime territory is intersected by the openings of the Cranganore river at Ayacotta, and the Vypeen river at Cochin. One-third of this tract is covered by water, and more than half the rest by cocoanut trees : it is essentially the land of the fishermen, and along it went the only road low caste men might use in olden times: here very few Brahmans and no Namboories will reside, unless attached to a palace or a pagoda.

The remainder of the low-lands, or the *plains*, are the portion lying between the backwater and the hills : which, instead of being sandy, are more commonly either alluvial, or composed of laterite, and intersected in many places by rivers. This portion of the State is more holy than either the maritime or hilly districts.

The *Hilly* portion, or the Ghauts, are nearly covered by magnificent jungles, mostly upon a granite formation. Here the tiger and cheetah, the bear and the elephant, dispute with man his claim to be the lord of the forests.

Kunneeanúr is the division to the south-east, of a triangular figure, having a circumference of about 55 miles, and comprehending a superficies of 63¾ square miles, but little outlying spots pertaining to it, increase its size to 80¾. The aspect of this district is varied, and its capacity very great : it presents a series of minute chains of steep slopes, much overgrown with thick stunted jungle, whilst about one-third is cultivated. The intermediate vallies and flat surfaces have nearly two-thirds under cultivation, half being rice, and the other cocoa-nut plantations.

This division contains five sub-divisions, *(Proverties)*, of about equal size, including detached places, viz., Kunneeanúr, Neendacurray, Nettúr, Ernacollum, and Vullarapullay, comprised in 99 villages. The whole contains about 23,000 productive trees. The most remarkable place is Tripoonterah *(Teereepuneythoray)*, the principal residence of H. H. the Rajah, and nine miles east of Cochin. Though denominated a fort, and surrounded by a moat and wall, with gates at each entrance, it may be said to be incapable of offering resistance to a foe.

"In the distress which followed the great war,* a Brahman "came to Khristna and Arjuna, complaining of the loss of his nine "children. Khristna was silent, but Arjuna hearing the Brah-"man's wife was likely soon to become a mother, guaranteed the life "of the forthcoming infant, even by himself, if necessary, entering "the fire as a sacrifice to Yama, to save its existence. Khristna "rebuked Arjuna for his rash promise, and then took him to Vai-"cont'ha, where the Brahman's nine children were found seated in "Luchsmi's lap. They were brought back to earth in a celestial "car, and descended at Tripoonterah, which was set apart as a holy "place, in the fifty first day of the Cali-yuga."

Once a year, ten days before the Ohnam, (about the middle of August,) the Rajah goes in state, wearing his star, and attended by all his native officials, from one palace to the other. This feast is called the *Uttum Chumium*, Mal. or that of "star decorating." It is said to be held in commemoration of the day when the first Cochin Rajah entered into possession of his Malabar dominions.

The palace (*Colgaum*,) is a curious pile of old buildings, entirely of native architecture: its small windows, narrow stairs, low passages, and confined yards, are very differently formed to European ideas of comfort. In some, rooms, doors, and large glass windows, have evidently been introduced at a later date, than the erection of the building. A guard is stationed at the gate, within which no low caste person may enter. A covered passage reaches from the palace to the gateway, but a screen or scarlet curtain prevents any passer-by from being able to gaze within. The entrance hall is square, and leads directly into the room where the Rajah daily transacts business and receives visitors. At one end is a swinging silver cot and an almirah full of books, whilst pictures adorn the walls. On the opposite side of the road is a handsome reception hall, built by the Dutch, consisting of two very fine rooms, of elegant proportions, and well lighted by means of large glazed windows.

In the immediate vicinity of the palace is a small bazaar *(Pilla)*, into which no person below the rank of a Nair may enter. (Native Christians are admissible.) There is also a pagoda having a fine tank and a large Ootooparrah where any Brahmans, should tney

---

* *Mackenzie Manuscripts*, Book No. 3. Countermark 896.

desire it, may be gratuitously fed; another is also situated close to the Fort. A Church stands outside, in which the Roman Catholics and Syrians officiate at different times, and about two miles to the south is a hill upon which the Rajah possesses a bungalow.

The Christian Church mentioned as being exterior to the walls is sixty feet long, and twenty-five wide. About one-third of its length is enclosed by a railing or screen. The ceiling is divided into little squares, in which angels' faces are represented: at the altar is a large frame, with paintings in its various compartments, intended to illustrate New Testament scenes. There is a large cross in front of its west entrance, and close by a box for the reception of alms for the poor: near to this is a stone font, and holy water in a recess by the door. About one mile from Tripoonterah, at Curringacherry, is a Syrian Church dedicated to St. George, within which may be seen a representation of "God the Father;" there are no images, but several crosses. At the west entrance is a place for receiving alms of rice or oil.

Kunneeanúr is the largest sub-division, and contains a small palace as well as a pagoda: scattered over the northern portion of this sub-division are several small bazaars: in that at Mulienthwrutti is a large, square Church. The Proverty (sub-division) of Nettúr, lying along the borders of the lake, is rich in cultivation, gardens, and inhabitants. The Candenaad Church is much decorated, and about one mile from it is that of Diamper, or Udiamper, where Menezes held his celebrated Synod. A picture of Sir F. Drake long graced its walls, placed close to the cross. Another remarkable one was a woman confessing her sins, and the devil crouching at her elbow.

Ernacollum (*Yernacollum*) is perhaps the most important sub-division, and it is in a great degree the seat of the Native Government. Here is the Dewan's (*Prime Minister*) Cutcherry, where the records (not at Tripoonterah) are kept. The Judges of the Court, the Commercial Agent, and other Officials, also transact their business here. On a line with the Cutcherry, to the north, is the Jail where half the prisoners are kept, and a little further on the Rajah's Hospital, raised by *Rama Vurmah*, Rajah of Cochin. The original building was constructed in 1848, and opened on August 14th of that year: again it was enlarged in 1851, and again as well as being tiled, in

1859.* All these edifices face the backwater, from which they are divided by a road and a slight expanse of grass.

The backwater, dotted with islands, is here nearly two miles across: whilst sea-wards, or to the westward, is the town of Cochin; a little to its north is perceived the opening of the Vypeen river, with Vypeen itself, nearly imbedded in trees. To the W. N. W. is the Island of Balghatty (*Ponyekurra*), on which is a bungalow, where the British Resident lives when at Cochin, and on the summit of one of the highest trees is a flag staff, from which floats the British ensign, when H. M.'s Representative is present. A short distance to the rear of the Ernacollum Cutcherry is an upstairs durbar room, rarely made use of: it is a fine building, of modern construction. There is a Travellers' Bungalow, also a straggling village and bazaar, containing rather a large population, who are mostly Christians, (many of them being fishermen,) but Jews and Konkanies also reside there. There are two Roman Catholic Churches, one for Europeans and Eurasians, and the other for natives: although close together, one is said to be situated at Korruthullay, the other at Unjikaimul (meaning literally "five nobles," or chieftains holding landed property). These names are said to be derived from five petty chiefs, all of whom, in ancient times, had a share of Ernacollum.

Vullarapully is a highly cultivated, populous, and beautful little territory, lying along the northern bank of the Purreeaar river, which nearly surrounds it. This is a portion of the Allungaad district, obtained by the Travancore Rajah about 1762, at which period this small spot was retained, and on it stands the palace of one of the eldest Tumbarans, or Ladies of the Cochin Rajah's family. Passing up the Purreeaar river, above the much frequented sanitarium of Alwaye, is Sherwurrah, where the Cochin Rajah has just completed a handsome palace, close to the remains of a former one. It is situated on the brow of a low slope that overlooks the stream. Not far distant is a Christian village and Church: and near to this stands a pagoda of some note, in the vicinity of which the Swinging Festival (*Thoo-*

* In the first eleven years 2,008 *in-patients* were treated and dieted within this hospital, and 9000 received advice and medicine as *out-patients*. Out of those treated, 123 died.

kum, Mal.) is annually celebrated: when deluded Hindu devotees imagine they are propitiating the deity by having hooks passed through the skin of their backs, and thus being swung around.

Farther up the river is Maliatur, with its hill of the Cross (*Crucemah.*) It is considered by natives miraculous, that the timid wild ibex, from the neighbouring forests, come to this rocky place, where unmolested by all, they are regarded with wonder, and treated with kindness.

The *Cochin* division of the State is a maritime district: stretching along the coast for twenty six miles. It includes an area of 62¾ square miles, nearly 17 of which are under moist cultivation, 21 are covered with water, and the remainder by magnificent topes, gardens, and villages. This portion of the country, cursed by the Brahmans, as fit only for outcastes, and unsuited for their priestly race, unless Konkanies, those compelled to attend a pagoda, or serve in the Rajah's Palace, is singularly happy in its natural productions, perhaps no portion of the globe is richer in useful vegetation: whilst the fish in the sea and backwaters are innumerable. Here no tiger or wild beast can assail the inhabitants, very few Mammals, with the exception of jackalls and otters, having ever been seen along these sandy islands. It is sub-divided into Cochin, Sherria Anandapooram, Vypeen, Muluacaad; and these again into forty four portions termed Mooriesor villages.

The Cochin sub-division, commences from the Vypeen river, and lies south of British Cochin: whilst to its east is the Island of Vendoorty, two miles in length, and believed, according to tradition, to have been divided from the Island of Balghatty (*Ponyekurra*), which is now more than a mile distant, by only a small stream.

It is asserted that a cocoanut leaf fell into this stream, when a woman, from each Island, rushed forward at the same time and seized it: both held on, but at last the Vendoorty female let go, and the Island of Ponyekurra at once drifted away from its previous neighbour Vendoorty; the names of these Islands refer to this legend. Ponyekurra, meaning "came on this side," and Vendoorty, "left on that side."

This Island of Vendoorty in the time of the Portuguese formed a portion of the endowment of the Cathedral of St. Cruz, situated in the town of Cochin. The Dutch probably sold it to the Rajah as, according to their records, it belonged to them in the year 1753: but not when Cochin fell to the British. It contains a Christian population and a Roman Catholic Church opposite the Canal, leading to Tripoonterah.

The town of Cochin will be described in the Chapter on the English: it includes part of the Culvetty village, and the Muttencherry bazaars, although the greater portion of the latter are in the Native State. Close to Jew's Town is the Rajah's Palace, one of the two most important which belonged to him, when Europeans first arrived. About A.D. 1550 the Portuguese built him the present edifice or a great portion of it, as probably additions and alterations have been made since that period.

Sherria Anandapooram is the most southern sub-division of the Cochin districts having a larger proportionate quantity of land under wet cultivation than either of the other three proverties.

Vypeen, or Baypeen, (*Waipey*) extends from the river, which divides it from Cochin, to the Cranganore or Ayacotta opening. Its most southern portion is British territory: its most northern now belongs to Travancore.

In 1743, "the Paliat Achen, or free Rajah,* had a residence at "Chenotta (*Chennamungalum*), close to Cranganore, and was the "*free lord* of the Island of Vypeen," (with the exception of some gardens and lands situated at its southern extremity, opposite to Cochin, which belonged to the Dutch East India Company;) "and "some time previously he had become the ruling sovereign of "Manacotta and Mooloorcurra, lying above Chetwye: also his "rights extended over the old kingdom of Williar Wattalta, above "Parda, which was hardly more than a name." The Paliat Achen is represented as "fifty years of age, who speaks little but thinks well."

The meaning of the word Vypeen is, "a place which has arisen from a swamp:" and there is an era, called the *Poothoo Veppoo*, or new Vypeen, corresponding to A. D. 1341. *Paoli* gives a legend

---

* *Dutch Government Records,* 1743: but still, the Paliat Achen appears to have been in some respects a vassal to the Cochin Rajah and his hereditary Minister.

to the effect that in that year the Vypeen river found its exit in the sea and Vypeen was formed : but such is impossible, as the river and the *Sinus Colchious*, or large expanse of backwater, are mentioned by *Ptolemy*, and other writers, as existing anterior to their time. It is remarkable that the era of *Colum*, or Quilon, which has been asserted to have originated at the building of that city, is proved by the *Mackenzie M.S.S.*, to have reference only to a great religious festival, when water suddenly filled the tank. The era of Poothoo Veppoo, which *Paoli* mentions, as used in the Narrikal Church, may very possibly refer to the origin of the first Christian Church, built on the swampy, but sacred, island of Vypeen. Certainly, according to the Kerula Ulpati, the land from Vypeen to Narrikal, in this year was first taxed, as being in a fit state for cultivation, which it was not previously.

Beyond Vypeen is Cruz Mirabile or the Wonderful Cross, a small wooden Church on the banks of an estuary, formed by the backwater and erected there after the ancient Church became submerged. There is a sandy ridge to its south, now frequently only 65 feet wide, over which the sea occasionally breaks when the S. W. monsoon continues strongly, for some time before the freshes are well down: people have often been apprehensive of the formation of a new opening here, which might cause the overflow of all the low inland paddy fields, besides ruining the Cochin out let. Various reasons have been assigned for the name of this Church; one being, that here the Portuguese cross was planted, as a symbol that they claimed sovereignty over the country; and another, that St. Thomas landed here, and reared the cross himself. The next village is Malliapooram (*Mully paugum*,) to which pertains a flag staff of the Cochin native Government, and a Master Attendant. A sandy ridge near, is known as " the old bar," and probably a river once found its exit here. At 2¼ miles distance, W. N. W., is the pagoda of Yellumgunnapullay, celebrated for an annual festival held there: whilst 1¼ miles to its north, is Narrikal (*Nharica*), a Christian village, consisting of a street running east and west, terminated by a church. A small palace and pagoda are situated to the north. The sea is here smooth through the entire year, owing to a " mud bank" that breaks the force of the waves.

There are several other small villages of no note, until Palliport (*Pallipuram*, or *Mannapaad*) is reached. Here is a holy pagoda, where trials by crocodile ordeals took place, after the prisoner had been sworn before the idol. Just to the north of this is a ditch dividing the Cochin territory from the British and that of Travancore, this ditch is probably a remnant of the "Travancore lines." The ground from here to the Ayacotta opening was purchased along with the Cranganore fort, from the Dutch, by the Travancore state. In 1743 this territory, as already observed, was under the free lord Paliat Achen. The Cochin State claims it as theirs, but it is also said to have formed a part of Paroor, when that State fell to the share of Travancore in 1763, but they did not obtain possession of this outlying place, because the Dutch held it as their own. To the north, and close to this ditch, is the Palliport Lazaretto, or Leper asylum: it and the grounds on which it stands, are British property. Originally a Portuguese building, erected as a Syrian College in 1587, it was turned by the Dutch to its present use. The number of patients they maintained there for the last fifty years of their rule, averaged less than ten: now there are usually, above forty. Next to this is a fine church, where the feast of the "Virgin Mary" is annually held with great pomp: it is said that an oil painting of her floated over the sea, and appeared off the shores of Palliport. A short way to the north is a comfortable house, and close to it a small octagon tower, built by the Portuguese, to command the neighbouring backwater: within this building is a well of good water.

The Muluacaad sub-division is composed of ten small islands in the backwater, most of which are under wet cultivation. The British Residency, as already stated, is situated on Balghatty (*Ponyekurra*), one of the ten, 2⅛ miles from the Cochin flagstaff. The position of this house is delightful, and its construction very superior: whilst from its upstairs verandah a most picturesque view is obtainable. About these islands, multitudes of ducks are reared, which find a ready sale in Cochin. Ramanthoorty, or Candle island, was formerly a great resort for smugglers, but is now rented by the Rajah's Government. Moorakumpard is another island in the backwater, the property of a Native: or rather the water was so, where the land now is. He has for twenty years the right to any portion where the water does not exceed the depth of a ky-kole, or a boatman's bamboo, of about three fathoms' length. He sub-lets any part to whoever will undertake to fill it in: the amount of space is one thousand koles, by 400 : for which he pays ten rupees yearly rent, and at the termination of each 20 years, it is to be re-adjusted according to the produce of the ground.

The *Cranganore* (*Kodungaloor*) division has been the scene of most momentous changes in times gone by: here the Jew and the Christian obtained footings and founded towns before the Portuguese landed in India. Here the Government of the Permauls was held, here it flourished and decayed. On this spot the Portuguese fort was raised in 1523, and they contemplated at first making it the seat of their chief power in Malabar. Here fell the Portuguese might to Dutch prowess, whilst Cochin still continued in their possession. Here the Dutch had to sell* their fort and territory to a Native Prince, before the British would fire a shot, to hold back the victorious Tippoo. Now it is a ruin, mouldering in the dust, with but one solitary tower overhanging the broad expanse of the river, which rolls on slowly, but deeply, beneath. Its old moat is the resort of the crocodile and paddy bird, and its once well used streets resound no more to human tread. The solitary stranger, perhaps, disturbs a snake in his path, or an owl in the dense overhanging trees, but rarely a mortal will meet his eye. Cranganore fort is utterly and entirely deserted.

The line of the Rajahs of Cranganore (the Native town of this name is some considerable distance from the site of the fort,) who are Schatriyas, is still extant: they found their claim to this territory as having been granted to their family by Shayrum Permaul, the chief of whose guard was their ancestor. Their right to regal authority they have long been forced to waive, either before the superior power of the Cochin Rajah,† or that of the Samorin.

* In the *Dutch Records* for 1743, it is expressly stated: the Cranganore territory owed obedience to the Dutch Company, and was not under the Rajah of Cochin. That they obtained this territory by a treaty of peace made with the Samorin, December 17th, 1717, but they allowed the line of the Cranganore Rajahs to continue as their vassals.

† The Rajah of Cochin, in 1792, unsuccessfully laid claim before the British Commissioners, to the whole island, called by Europeans, Chetwye (*Manapuram*): which consisted of three small territories, Cranganore to the south, Paponetty or Ayroor in the centre, and Chetwye to the north.

Cranganore fort is N. N. W. 18 miles distant from Cochin. This territory comprehends an area of 18¾ square miles, and is well covered with cocoanut plantations and rice lands, though some portion is merely a sandy tract. It contains a celebrated pagoda, dedicated to Bhagavadi, where there is a door apparently of stone, but fixed in a half-opened position. A tradition is attached to this and believed in by both Hindus and Christians, which asserts that St. Thomas and Bhagavadi held a discussion at Palliport, about the respective merits of the Christian and Hindu religions. Arguments waxed warm, and Bhagavadi considering it best to cease further discussions, decamped, and jumping across the Cranganore river, made straight for the pagoda. St. Thomas not to be outdone, rapidly gave chase, and just as Bhagavadi got inside the door, the Saint reached its outside, and setting his foot between it and the door post, prevented its closing: there they both stood, until the door turned to stone, one would not allow its being opened, nor the other permit its being shut.

At this pagoda the feast of *Baranee* is held in the middle of March, when the Nairs and other Sudras offer up cocks to Bhagavadi, beseeching immunity from severe diseases during the succeeding year. Near it is another pagoda, to which the Konkanies and the higher castes resort for devotional purposes. The number of devotees who come long distances to Cranganore is remarkable: even the road to eternal bliss in some portions of Travancore is said to pass through this temple.* A large pagoda sacred to Iuppen, the Hindu deity of the country, stands on a hill near Cottayam: in it the Hindu god Iuppen, and the Mahomedan Bawa, are alike objects of adoration, as it is asserted they are bosom friends, living in the same place. From this the pilgrim proceeds to St. Andrea, near Allepey, on the sea coast, where having bathed, prayers are offered at this Christian shrine, for St. Andrew is said to have been a bosom friend of the other two: finally he proceeds to Cranganore, where his wanderings are completed.

* In the *Dutch records* it is stated that Cranganore is deemed specially sacred, on account of its having been built whilst Puresu Rama was on earth. At Trichoor it is said the name *Kudungaloor* is merely a corruption of *Kodi* (a crore), *lingum* (the Indian Phallus), *oor* (country). In the Kodungaloor, or Cranganore pagoda, are numerous figures of the lingum.

There is a fine upstairs Cutcherry at Cranganore, (the native town) situated in front of the pagoda, which no low caste man may approach. There is also a good bazaar. The road towards the south leads to a palace of the Cochin Rajah, which is about one mile distant.

Stretching between Cranganore and Chetwye, the island is divided into three small States, Cranganore to the south, Chetwye to the north, and Paponetty or Ayroor or Belanga in the centre. In 1743 the ruler of Ayroor was nephew to the Cranganore Rajah, both were stated " to be poor princes, without any power. Ayroor " was taken from the Samorin by the Dutch, in 1717, and settled " upon the Company, as were the lands of Trikonetty, Aeraltoo, Aral-" tapala, Moodele, Coonattoo, and Pootenbare, which last six districts, " comprising 18½ villages, were given by the Extra Councillor General " in Chief, Willem Backer Jacobsz, as a present to the Rajah of " Cochin." Subsequently by desire of the Batavian Supreme Government, they were resumed : but in accordance with fresh orders, contained in a *Secret letter* from Batavia, dated July 4th, 1740, they were restored to that Prince.

The ***Kodachayree*** division consists partly of ***plains*** and partly of ***hills***, and is of a most irregular form. Its eastern side is bounded for twenty miles by the Shallacoodee river, separating it for much of this distance from the Iddiara and Naithoad hills, belonging to Travancore, which last State also possesses sovereignty over the Allungaad district, which bounds it for about twenty miles on the south. Its arbitrary lines of demarcation from other districts, and also from the Tunnalapuram talook of British Malabar on its east, are too complicated to define. It comprises 342 square miles of country, and is divided into four Proverties, Kodachayree, Paulathingul, Thaulaycaad, and Koruttee.

Kodachayree is one of its largest sub-divisions, not one twentieth of which is under cultivation. In the Dutch Government records for 1743, it is stated, " the lands of the Kodachayree petty Kaimul " lie between Paroor, Cranganore, the Cochin territory, and the " ghauts, and annually yield 125 candies of pepper, whilst the best " cardamoms come from that place : but that, and the wax, are in " the hands of the Jesuits, who are located at Ambalacatty, and their

" Chief is designated Archbishop of Cranganore, his residence being " half a mile from Pootencherra, in the Cochin territory." Up to 1706 this Kaimul had been under the Samorin, he then shook off his authority, and joined himself to the Cochin faction.

Amongst its few villages (about 13) is seen the remains of a small fort, once the residence of a family which exercised sovereign sway over this part of the country, and whose descendants as private individuals still live in the neighbourhood.

Shallacoodee is the chief place in this sub-division: here the officials reside, and the Rajah has also a small palace. It is a great satisfaction to find a comparative absence of the rattan and allied climbers, in these jungles. The small Ceylon leech is here a great pest to the traveller. Shooting, especially for bison, is very good. The Mulchers (a tribe of hill people) assert that in the depth of the forest there is an enormous tiger, of a white or cream colour, and having yellow stripes: it is reputed to be most ferocious, and its destruction much desired.

A few miles from Shallacoodee is Angamale, formerly the seat of the Syrian power in Malabar. Tippoo laid this town waste and destroyed the churches, but that dedicated to St. George was subsequently restored. On the banks of the backwater stands Tekkah Paroor, and on the opposite side is a cross which, tradition asserts, was erected by St. Thomas. This Church was built in 1712.

Paulathingul is still more mountainous than Kodachayree, whilst only a seventeenth part is under cultivation. It comprises eighteen villages, most of which lie along its western boundary, or that farthest from the ghauts. This district is much infested by elephants, rendering cultivation difficult; other game also abounds. From its forests, a large amount of timber is felled.

Thaulaycaad possesses thirteen straggling villages. It was formerly a wealthy district, but during the present generation its opulence has vanished, owing to its trade having declined. There is good inland navigation as far as this district. The town of Auwuttatoor, with its large pagoda, is said to have been one of the 32 divisions into which Malabar was formerly divided.

Koruttee is the most southern Proverty of the Kodachayree Division: containing twenty villages, and is also the most populous, one-half being under cultivation. The most celebrated place within its limits is Armanuddee, where there is a well known pagoda.

The military frontier of Travancore includes a large portion of the Cochin territory, and passes through the southern part of the Kodachayree district. The celebrated Travancore lines were not of any considerable strength: they occupied the greater part of the crests of a series of slopes, which were comparatively open, and not remarkable for elevation or steepness. They commenced at Yellungayree to the eastward of which the hills were supposed to afford some defence: they then extended twenty four miles to the westward, and terminated at Jacotay—a name which was occasionally employed to designate the whole work. The latter consisted of a rather strong embankment and parapet of earth: the whole measuring at the highest part above fifteen feet, but the elevation was not always the same: the ditch was, generally speaking, about half that depth, and two or three feet broad. An Abattis, composed of a bamboo hedge, was planted, which, in some places where it has been carefully preserved, may still be seen flourishing. Along its inner side ran a broad and level road, and scattered along this at irregular intervals were forty-two small works. The greater part of these walls have now been levelled by the rains. Tippoo, when he attacked them, first turned the eastern extremity, which was no very difficult task; but a panic occurring amongst his troops, they were compelled to retreat, and for months he was kept outside, what he termed, "that contemptible wall."

The *Mukundapuram* division encloses an area of fifty-two square miles, but twenty-three and a half more belonging to it are situated in detached places. Its western portion is most fertile, especially along the banks of the Kodungaloor (Cranganore) river; but little waste ground is found in the low lands, where cocoanut groves abound, whilst one-third of the district is under rice cultivation. It consists of four sub-divisions, Arreepaulim, Mahapoorcaunum, Mookundapooram, and Poodoocaad, to which may be added Paddhanutoulum. Within its limits, including its detached portions, are fifty villages, of which Irinyalacoday is the principal, containing many Christian inhabitants, and a pagoda, considered peculiarily holy, which the Christians are prohibited from approaching. A market is held at this place every Saturday.

The *Yainamakul* division lies south west of Trichoor, separated for about ⅔rd of the distance by the lake, and for the remainder by a small stream. It contains an area of about sixty six and a half square miles, but nearly a quarter of this is occupied by the lake, and a quarter of the remainder is under cultivation. The eastern portion is uplands, the western, cocoanut plantations; the greater part of the land between the sea and the lake is cultivated. It has four Proverties, Yainamakul, Payringoatucurra, Ooraghum, and Arrumboor.

Pallypuram is a beautiful little spot of territory belonging to the Rajah of Travancore, who obtained it amongst the Paroor lands: it has a range of low bare topes, the most elevated of which is crowned by a pagoda. It lies on the borders of a narrow arm of the lake, which forms its northern limits. Pallypuram itself is merely an ancient pagoda, shaded by an immense banyan tree.

The *Thaullapully* division contains an area of 71¼ square miles, and consists of a succession of minute chains of hills, or rather slopes, one-fourth of which is under cultivation. It is sub-divided into four Proverties, Kunumkulumcurray, Choondul, Yecaul, and Chengaullycotay, which include ninety four villages. Thaullapully in 1743* was divided amongst four chiefs termed Ainecootty, Poonatoor, Manna-Colam, and Kacattoo: the last died away, and the territory passed into the hands of the other three. The Ainecootty Nambuddy was driven from his country in 1690, by *Hendrick Adriaan Van Reede,* who made it a present to the Samorin, who privately resold it to its former ruler for 40,000 gold fanams. In 1743 it was under the Rajah of Cochin, but the people were said to be very fickle in their allegiance, and to be one day in favour of the Cochin Rajah, and the next of the Samorin. The Poonatoor chief owed allegiance to the Samorin, but was considered equally inimical to him and to the Rajah of Cochin: he carried on an intrigue with the French at Mahi for three years, in hopes that they would enable him to shake off the Samorin's yoke. Manna-Colam was divided in its allegiance between the Samorin and the Rajah of Cochin, and caused considerable trouble.

Kunumkulumcurray may be considered the capital of the district, and is one of the largest Christian towns in this part of Cochin: it

* *Dutch Government Records of Cochin* M.S.S.

is situated both on the summit and the declivity of a low hill, which is crowned by churches: amongst which at no great distance is that belonging to the Protestant Mission, the foundation stone of which was laid on March 26th, 1856. An English school, five vernacular schools for boys, and one for girls, are attached to the Mission. A distant view of this town gives a more favourable impression than is realized on a nearer approach. It contains about four hundred houses of a better class, two-thirds of which are inhabited by Syrians, and the remainder mostly by Romo-Syrians. This town was formerly surrounded by a bamboo hedge, and had two gates, which have either decayed or been destroyed. There is a good bazaar, all the ordinary produce of the surrounding country is procurable, as well as many different kinds of cloths and plenty of grain, some of the neighbouring British districts are supplied from this bazaar. A Travellers' Bungalow and a Tannah are found here: but the Cutcherry is at Kukkaad.

Yecaul is a large scattered village, the temple of which prettily caps the summit of a low isolated rock. Chemmunthulthay has a handsome pagoda, and a population consisting almost entirely of Brahmans.

Mooloorcurry, also called Irunaad, is a small district, containing an area of 26¼ square miles. In 1743 it was a free lordship, lying close to the Samorin's territory: it is said* to have been in the possession of the Achens of Mannacode, but wrested from them by the Paliat Achen,† Dewan of Cochin, who retained it until 1809, when, on his rebelling against the British, it was assumed by the Rajah of Cochin, and transferred by him to the Thaullapully division. From that period the Paliat Achen's family have been pensioned out of the funds arising from it. This territory is divided in the centre by a low chain of hills, covered in places by small jungle: it is pretty fairly cultivated.

The *Trichoor*, or Trichoowapayroor division, has been subject to many disputes, and in 1815 permanent marks were erected, defining its boundaries from those of the two neighbouring Achens. This division contains a superficial area of 169 square miles, one

* Lieutenant Connors' and Ward's *Report*.

† *Achen* now bears the signification of *Saib* in other parts of India.

fifth of which is cultivated with paddy; dense forests are found in this district, and some of the lake is also within its limits, the surface of which in the month of August is covered with the beautiful blossoms of the sacred lotus, the seeds are eaten and considered delicacies by the natives.

The large town of Trichoor is of great antiquity and sanctity, said to have been founded by Puresu Rama, the sixth incarnation of Vishnu. It has always been remarkable for its splendid pagoda, and college fcr the education of Namboorie youths. It is encompassed by a ditch and earthen rampart, having parapets of the same material, which were erected in 1794, having an elevation of from 7 to 13 feet, and a breadth of about 15 feet, with a ditch along the outside from 2 or 3 feet deep, to 10 or 12. On its west face it is 2,485 yards in length: on its east, 1,925: its north, 3,190: and on its south, 2860: giving a circumference of 4½ miles. The Rajah's palace may be called the citadel of Trichoor, and is 310 by 200 yards: it has some bastions, is entered by two strong gateways, and might be a sufficient defence against cavalry. As the lines, or outer fortifications, have never been completed, it is probable that either a want of funds, or a conviction of the inutility of the undertaking, induced the Rajah to discontinue it. It was evidently constructed to fortify the place against the Mysoreans, should they again descend on that portion of India; and its commencement may have been partly suggested by the British Commissioners, who, in 1793, advised the native Princes to shake off their allegiance to the Mysoreaans, if possible. Most of the Christian population reside in a long street, near the Romo-Syrian Church. On the highest portion of the town stands the largest pagoda, with fine entrances—north, south, east, and west: the gateways have a great deal of carving about them, with pent roofs. The building is an exceedingly picturesque object. There are good roads running along its four sides, and near it are several streets of Putter, or Potie Brahmans, who are almost entirely devoted to mercantile pursuits. Should low caste persons dare ro intrude into the west end of the town, amongst the residences of the higher castes, they are liable to receive a good beating, and usually get it.

The Rajah's palace is a rather commodious upper storied building, partly of European architecture: it is situated on a gentle elevation, commanding a fine view of a picturesque country, in which a person accustomed to the sea coast is struck by the dearth of cocoanut trees, and the vast increase and luxuriance of the jack and banyan. The Residency, not far distant, is by no means a good building, it was formerly the private house of a conservator of forests, from whom it was purchased by the Sirkar.*

The small pagoda of Wurrukanadu is situated on a low eminence, and surrounded by a high wall, which conceals it from prying eyes: a number of small temples are crowded within the sacred enclosure. The four turrets, marking its four entrances, are reputed to have each been built by a different prince, namely, the Rajahs of Cochin, Palghat, Calicut, and Travancore. It is surrounded by a grove of teak trees, whilst it is imbedded in, and partly concealed by, the thick foliage of the wide spreading-banyan. Here also stands the sacred College, where Namboorie Brahmins, who are to be ordained for the ministry, learn to meditate for years in silence and solitude. In the month of May a large feast is celebrated, and votaries swarm into the place. Elephants assist in the ceremonies; and disputes, and even affrays, often occur, as to which idol has the right of precedence: in former times swords were frequently drawn and blood shed, before this question of rank could be settled.

Trichoor has a Zillah Court and a large Jail as well as a District Tannah. Supplies can here be readily procured by travellers. A Captain's Detachment of two companies of sepoys from Quilon is stationed here, which gives off a small guard to Ernacollum, and another to Tripoonterah. The official residence of the Officer Commanding was formerly the bathing bungalow of the Rajah of Cochin, who thus employed it until the tank beneath was desecrated by the Mahomedans, who killed cows and threw them into the water: since which the house has been too polluted for any but a European or a very low caste native to live in; but now, as the troops have been increased to two companies, the Dewan purposes charging rent for this *polluted abode*, so it is to be hoped that it has recovered its caste. Another house has lately been built for the Lieutenant. The spot now occupied by the barracks is said to be the site of the house for feeding Brahmans: and the small building

* The Cochin *Native Government.*

around which the sepoys clean their arms of a morning, was the centre of a holy pagoda.

There is an English school here, supported by the Rajah, but inferior to that attached to the Protestant Mission, which has both boys and girls as boarders. There is also a very large Protestant Church situated on a rising hill, near the high road, a little way out of Trichoor, it was commenced in 1840. Two Travellers' Bungalows are also in Trichoor, one near the canal, in which persons either going or coming by backwater usually take up their abode: and the other in the centre of the town, but more fitted for travellers by land, not being so far from the road.

Trichoor is a place of considerable trade; and a great quantity of cotton cloth is manufactured there. All the rice and grain from Palghat must also pass through this town, on its way to Cochin. The principal market day is Friday. The disease called Elephantiasis rarely exists so far inland as this station, but leprosy is very prevalent. From June to January cabin boats can go from Trichoor to Cochin, a distance by water of fifty-two miles: whilst nearly all the year round cargo boats can proceed by that route, but should the water be low, passengers and goods may travel to Kurriapudnam, by land 21½ miles, where there is a good bungalow, whilst it is about half way to Cochin.

The two large Christian villages of Arnaatcurray and Ooloor are near the Trichoor lines: the former S. W. one mile, and 1,100 yards: the latter S. E., 3¼ miles. It is curious to ride through these Christian villages about the time of their evening prayers: no one is stirring in the streets, and no sound is heard, save the voices of the various households raised in prayer. The village of Paununjayree is situated 7½ miles E. N. E. of Trichoor, in the midst of hill scenery, on the eastern skirts of this village is a pagoda now in ruins, but still bearing the name of Gooroonaden Umblum, and very celebrated in the annals of Malabar. Close to it is Putticaad, where a Travellers' Bungalow stands on the side of the road from Trichoor to Palghat. This place was formerly remarkable for the number of robberies committed on travellers. The robbers came down in the woody pass, seized their booty, and rapidly decamped.

It is now a celebrated place amongst sportsmen, as large game is found in abundance, within an hour's walk of the bungalow. It is necessary to take a guide, as a European is very liable to lose his road in these forests, and in that case would probably never be heard of again. The Botanist, and Zoologist, would find his time fully occupied here amidst the most beautiful scenery, and the greatest variety of animal and vegetable life, amongst which numerous species of magnificent trees and ferns flourish in rich profusion. This district contains many large villages.

The *Chaylayekurray* division is a frontier one, divided from Malabar by the Pooneear river: it contains an area of 167¼ square miles, about 25 being under wet cultivation, and 12 with dry grain: thirty miles of it are plain slopes, the remainder hills and forests. It is divided into the Proverties of Chaylayekurray, Pullianoor, Mutchat, and Moneduthecottay, containing 47 villages. Warrukkunchairy is about 8½ miles from Trichoor, on the road to Sheranoor. There is a small neat palace on the south bank of the river, and also an Ootooparrah about 1¾ miles to the N. E. of this. At the foot of the high hill of Uggumalla is a stone, on the road to Pullaynoor, at the temple in which place a yearly festival is held to the household deity of the Rajahs of Cochin, who are unable to attend it because unless crowned (which they now never are) they cannot pass this stone.

The *Chittoor* division is insulated by the British Talooks of Malabar and Coimbatore. It is 15 miles in length from north to south, and has a medium breadth of eight miles, with an area of 118 square miles; eleven being of wet cultivation, fifteen of dry, and about ten of plain slopes.

Although the whole of the Cochin State has now been mentioned, two places belonging to Travancore require notice, which once formed portions of Cochin.

Passing up the river towards Alwaye is *Verapoly*, the seat of the Carmelite Mission in these parts: it is situated on the left bank of the river, 9 miles N. E. of Cochin, about a hundred yards from the river's edge, and only slightly raised above the level of the tide. A number of cocoanut trees partially conceal its massive walls. The buildings occupy a large space of ground, and the Church was commenced about the year 1673, when the island on which it now stands was destitute both of houses and cultivation, and formed a portion of the territory of the Rajah of Cochin. The building consists of three straight piles of masonry, all of which (excepting the Church) are two or three stories high: their extremities face the river's bank. A passage along the centre, from north to south, forms a communication between various parts of the structure. The Church is situated at the northern end of the building, and is a miniature representation of St. Peter's at Rome. It is perhaps the most exquisite little building in this part of India. In its various chapels are rude emblems of saints, and pictures of rather a primitive description.

At the southern extremity of the building, at its east end, is a school where about twenty native scholars reside, divided into two classes. Their appearance gives the impression of extreme contentment. Their school rooms are large and airy, and their cots are ranged along the sides of the same apartment, serving as seats by day, and couches by night. The books from which they are educated are either in the Latin or Malayalim tongues. At the eastern end of the same pile of buildings is the refectory, the upper room being appropriated by the Vicar and the other Europeans: and the lower by the native Clergy, who also live in this range.

There does not appear to be any distinct library, but the Vicar Apostolic, or Bishop, possesses some excellent works, and others especially those written by the Carmelite Friars, may be seen in most of the rooms. Some Protestant works are scattered about, labelled "heretical," but they do not appear to be prohibited.

The Bishop and the European Carmelites are dressed in suits of a chocolate colour, the native Clergy in black, and those under training in white. Their mode of life appears very simple, and the effect produced on the native mind is no doubt good.

The private rooms of the Bishop are nearly as plain as the rest of the building. Altogether a visit to this place gives an impression that these men could only leave their country and their friends to toil in comparative poverty amongst strangers, and lay their bones in a foreign land, under the firm conviction that their cause was a righteous one. The amount they receive from Europe is said to be only 12,000 francs a year, or about five thousand Rupees, with which they have to support all their establishments, assisted partly by their congregations.

Not far from Verapoly, on the way to Alwaye, and close to the margin of the same side of the river, is a cavern, termed "*the devil's mouth*:" it is about three feet high, but is said to be so full of snakes and bats, that no one will venture to explore it.

A few miles beyond Verapoly is *Alwaye*, situated about twenty miles from the town of Cochin, and about two miles below Sherwurrah, already mentioned, in the Ernacollum division. It stands on the banks of a river, and is usually reached by boat, although there is a road leading to it from Ernacollum. It is a tract of considerable size dotted with about twenty bungalows, to which during the hot months of April and May, many persons retire, both to escape from the heat of Cochin, and enjoy the bathing. The European houses are on the banks of the river, the natives form encampments upon the sands: some persons even remain there all the year round. The water is believed to have medicinal virtues, and to remove the ill effects of prickly heat, boils, and even to reduce elephantiasis, or rather this disease is not indigenous as far inland as this fertile spot, where coffee grows luxuriantly, and the pepper vine flourishes. Cochin is supplied with drinking water, either from Alwaye or from a place opposite Verapoly. Much of the butter also is obtained from this district: the natives here make good baskets, and a variety of pretty little children's toys of basket work: besides umbrellas, (*kodas.* Mal.) of palmyra leaves.

This appears to have been the sanitarium of Cochin, from the advent of Europeans to India: being mentioned as such, both in the time of the Portuguese and the Dutch, who probably used the same primitive style of bathing houses, as are now in existence, viz., bamboos fixed into the water at intervals, with mats tied round them, from which a covered passage of the same materials leads up to the house. The sands of the river are excessively fine and smooth. An observatory was kept up here by the Rajah of Travancore: and there is a Traveller's Bungalow, of an inferior description: as well as a Residency, of which the less said the better. The banks of the river are rather high and embellished with most beautiful trees, that in the hot months are often covered with blossoms: whilst magnificent butterflies and birds of gorgeous plumage, are seen in every direction. This stream which is apparently both very gentle and shallow, has unhappily been the scene of several fatal accidents to Europeans whilst bathing; as at a short distance to the south there is a rock, around which are some holes in the bed of the river.

In the Cochin State the number of *remarkable buildings* is exceedingly small, such as there are, generally are dedicated to religious purposes, and have been already named: the remainder may be summed up as follows. There are some old ruins, the remains of pagodas, near the old Fort of Cranganore, also in ruins, and one spot is pointed out as being the residence of the Permauls, when they were governors of Malabar. At Irinyalcoday is a temple, the chief of which is a sunnyassie, who must be nominated from certain families. He enjoys considerable immunities, and when he goes out, is preceded by a lamp and sword, and has all the insignia of supreme authority. He acknowledges no superior, and will reside in the presence of no Prince. He watches over the temple, superintends its ministerial and lay concerns, sees to its revenues, and overlooks its expenditure.

The Ootooparrahs have already been several times mentioned. In some places a portion of the pagoda is used, in lieu of erecting a separate building. They were originally instituted for pilgrim Brahmans, and even now a rule exists, that unless detained by sickness, no one may take more than two days' food in the same establishment. In Travancore there are many more of these Ootooparrahs than in Cochin, for no Namboorie Brahman will reside in the former State although the Rajahs have in vain tried by every means in their power, to induce them to do so. But the caste of the reigning family (Nair) is too low to suit the bigoted arrogance of these Namboories, who consequently prefer living in the dominions of the Schatriya Prince of Cochin where however they are not nearly so pampered. Many of the pagoda lands have been assumed by the State, which in this case undertakes the expenses of the establishments, but not quite in the style desired by the Brahmans. One Namboorie has been induced to raise an Illum at Cottayam, in Travancore, which is giving great offence to others of his caste. This is probably the first of them who has settled in this State. The villages of foreign or Potie Brahmans, are called *Agrarums*, or

Gramams, and are built in straight streets. The Namboories, or Brahmans of the country, and the Nairs, live in detached houses, surrounded by gardens, called collectively Désas.

The *means of communication* are of two kinds, by land and water, for the backwater in the Cochin State takes the place of roads in other parts of India. The rivers are in places sufficiently deep for boats to pass along. The backwater from Chetwye at the extreme north of the Cochin State, to its southern limits, runs parallell with the sea, from which it is only divided by a sandy slip of ground: communications exist between them at Chetwye, Ayacotta or Palliport, and Cochin, these three places being the respective openings of of the backwater, the Paroor river, and the Alwaye river, so called from the places they pass in their course, or at that where they debouch into the sea as the Ayacotta or Cranganore, and Vypeen. There are many minor streams as well as these large rivers, which take their rise in the ghauts and flow down to the ocean, carrying with them an enormous quantity of debris, and such a large body of water that during the monsoon time the sea itself, for at least two miles from the shore, possesses no saline taste. The sandy. islands dividing the sea from the backwater appear to have been formed by the action of these enormous streams, flooded with the freshes of the S. W. monsoon, and laden with deposits from the ghauts, meeting at their outlets the full force of the ocean, which at this period lashes the shore most violently. The rivers flow towards the west, the sea beats from the west, the former bring down mud, the latter throws up sand, and thus islands have been formed : as they have increased in size, and obstructed the course of the rivers, these last have opened a little lower down each year, and in this manner the present maritime portion of Cochin has arisen from the sea. It is curious to observe recent marine shells, far in the interior of the country, buried in the laterite in vast quantities.

The Backwater, besides extending itself north and south, sends off numerous branches and many sub-divisions. In some places it is shallow, especially in the northern portion of the Chetwye branch, but between Cochin and Cranganore, and between the former place and Allepey, about thirty miles to the south, it is at all times navigable, for both cabin and cargo boats. From Allepey towards Quilon it becomes shallower. But from the commencement of the S. W. monsoon, or the beginning of June, this large expanse of water is navigable throughout its whole extent. It is affected by the flood tides twice in every 24 hours, when it rises about two feet and flows (excepting during the monsoon, when the rapidity is according to the amount of the freshes) at the rate of about 2½ miles an hour: but it cannot in any portion be called sluggish. For carrying cargo, canoes are preferred, which, drawing only about three feet of water, are adapted to all seasons of the year. These canoes are sufficient to protect produce from the deleterious effects of either sun or rain, being furnished with a convex bamboo roof, covered with mats of split bamboos or cadjans. The water is salt (excepting during the monsoon time,) and mostly muddy; whilst the bottom is slimy, the banks low, and the shores generally either one long range of splendid cocoanut plantations, or else a succession of paddy fields.. In some places, more especially to the south of Cranganore, houses and villages are dotted along its banks, often nearly hidden by the trees: whilst at intervals the white and picturesque fronts of numerous Roman Catholic and Romo-Syrian Churches are perceived. At one spot near Cochin seven Catholic Churches may be seen at the same time, as well as the Protestant one.

Channels and canals open communication between the backwater and various parts of the interior of the country, or join two backwaters together. To the south there is one connecting the backwater with Tripoonterah. At Yeddacochi a branch of the backwater strikes into the interior, where it divides south and west, forming a broad shallow lake, the sides of which are cultivated: this is connected by channels with other places.

The Poonany river, called in the north the Bahrahdum, passes along the southern border of the little district of Mooloorcurray, its banks are high and steep; whilst the Pullianoor, after running in a curve of nine miles, discharges itself into an estuary at Poonany. The Yelliaut rises in the hill Kudrapauree: flows N. N. W., eleven miles west of Chaylayekurray, and then joins the Poonany.

The Sheranoor river rises in the Vellany Hills, and runs for four miles in a rocky channel: it is then joined by some others, which increase its size, and timber can be easily floated down from thence as far as Puchypauree, where large masses of rock appear in the stream and obstruct the passage. It passes for twenty miles through the Trichoor district.

The Veycoor river emerges from vallies in the north of the Trichoor district, through which it runs for nine miles and three quarters; it is made use of in irrigation.

The Warrukkunchairy river rises in the Kudrapauree hills, and runs eight miles and a half along the Yainamakul division. Near Muhnium it divides: the largest branch joining the Cranganore river, up to which spot it has a sandy and gravelly bed. The tides influence it as high as Kurriavanoor, where a bank is thrown across to bar their farther entrance.

The Shallacooddee river runs a course of nearly seventy miles, but until within eighteen of its mouth, it flows through a wild and mounrainous country: as it gets into the plains, however, houses and cultivated spots of land may here and there be seen, dotted along its high banks, which decrease in elevation as it approaches the sea. It is navigable as far north for cabin boats, as Shallacooddee, excepting in very dry weather, when the traveller must land at Marlie, half way between Cranganore and that place, and then proceed by land: canoes can go eighteen miles further up, but beyond this is the Adrampully cataract, having a perpendicular fall of eighty feet, and forming a fine spectacle in the monsoon time.

The Paroor river divides at Alwaye, and its branches become so intricate, that description would fail satisfactorily to explain its course. Near Cranganore, its main branch having passed Paroor, divides into several, one of which flows in conjunction with other streams under the cliff, on which the remnants of the old fort still stand. The depth of the stream just here is forty feet, but it rapidly shoals: and from thence may be computed at about a quarter that depth.

The Kaychayree river rises at the foot of some hills, and after a course of twenty-seven miles through the Thaullapully district, it pours its contents into the lake. During the monsoon time its waters are made to irrigate certain lands by means of dams: were their construction superior, the gain to the cultivator would be immense, whilst the cost could but be trifling. This river is only navigable a short distance from its mouth.

The Yainamakul has a deep sluggish current, influenced by the tides, and is always navigable. Its banks are high and its bed slimy. During the rains its waters are fresh, but at other times salt.

The Poodoocaad river passes for some distance through the Kodachayree district. Its steep banks are overgrown with forests, but its stream is shallow, although in the rains timber can be floated down it for a considerable distance.

In the Chittoor district the Annamullee flows fifteen miles through the forest, and the Colungode defines the limits of Nemary for two miles and a half more.

There are many other smaller streams, some with names and some without: but all rising in the ghauts or hilly ranges, and flowing westward towards the sea. In a country intersected by water like the Cochin State, large tanks are not required, and do not exist, but smaller reservoirs might be enumerated by thousands. In the hotter and drier inland spots, hollowed trees and granite basins are kept full of water under sheds for the use of cattle: and some may even be seen on the high roads.

The *roads* with their passes and defiles, and the *hills* and *forests* next claim attention. The principal road runs parallel with the sea coast; from Cranganore it passes northwards to Chetwye, and on to British Malabar: whilst to the south it joins a similar road in the Travancore State, going through Cranganore, Palliport, and Cochin. There are ferries at each of the rivers; and for the conveyance of horses and carriages, a wooden platform, with raised railed sides, is placed upon two boats lashed together, and termed a Jungar. There is a ferry from the Cranganore side of the backwater to the mainland: and another short one to Kurriapudnam, where a good Travellers' Bungalow is situated on a fine raised piece of ground. This road passes northwards through Kurriavanoor, (10½ miles distant,) where there is another excellent bungalow: from thence to the large town of Trichoor, 10 miles further on, where it joins the main road to Palghat: passing through Putticaad (8¾ miles from Trichoor,) where there is a good bungalow. This is throughout an excellent road, and the greater part of the way it is planted along its sides with trees, most of which are cashew nuts, banyans, and cocoanuts, with here and there maroti trees and talipot palms. It is, generally speaking, flat, and in some places sandy and heavy: all the streams are bridged over, and at Kurriavanoor, where the river is crossed, there is a large wooden bridge. From Trichoor to Putticaad the road is not so good, and beyond this it becomes decidedly worse.

From Trichoor N. N. E. to Shoranoor (18 miles distant,) where the railway station is, the road passes through Warrukkunchairy (eight miles and a half), where there is no bungalow, but the Cutcherry may, if necessary, be occasionally used as one: it is in every respect a most undesirable room to remain in. The road in this part is covered with very fine banyan trees. Sheranoor is ten miles farther on, and the road runs through rather a jungly tract. At that place a new bungalow was erected in 1862, and a magnificent granite bridge is being built across the wide but shallow river, in order to connect the Rajah's territory with the railway, a branch of which it is proposed shall be continued over this new bridge to Trichoor: should persons be found willing to sink their money upon a scheme, which will greatly facilitate travelling, and form an easy mode of transit for the comparatively small amount of traffic in that direction. If the Overland steamers ever stop at Cochin or its vicinity, a line will then be necessary, not to cease at Trichoor, but to be carried on to Kurriapudnam, following much the direction of the present road, only adopting a shorter course.

From Warrukkunchairy a road branches off to the west to Kununkulum: another direct from Trichoor to the same place, passing N. N. W. through it. There is a bungalow not far from the house and Church of the Protestant Mission. There is also another road from Kununkulum, S. W. joining the sea road, already mentioned, a little above Chetwye.

The inland road of olden times runs nearly parallel with the seashore one, commencing in the south at Quilon it passes up to the Mavillicurray, and on due north to Cottayam, from whence it proceeds in a very circuitous direction to Kulashayakaruh Mungalum, where it is again carried on north to Tripoonterah: here it divides into three, one continuing north, to Allungaad, from thence through Paroor, and joining the sea road at Cranganore. The second or N. E. branch terminates at Perrumbaloor: the third goes to Ernacollum, about three miles before reaching which it sends off a branch to Verapoly.

From Ernacollum to Alwaye a road proceeds N. E., it is not a good one, being constantly encroached upon: from Alwaye it extends east to Perrumbaloor, where, turning to the south east, it passes on to Kodhamungalum, and along the base of the ghauts to the S. S. E.

Another road requires mention, which passes to the east from Allungaad through Shewurray above Alwaye, where it suddenly turns to the north through Kodachayree, Koruttee, and Shallacoodie, direct to Trichoor: it is not adapted either for riding or driving.

Amongst the routes mentioned, Europeans (with but few exceptions,) only travel along the following, taking the town of Cochin as a centre. To Chetwye, by water direct. To Trichoor, during the rains, by backwater, the whole way: or by water to Kurriapudnam, and from thence on by road through Kurriavanoor. From Trichoor to the railway at Sheranoor, by land through Warrukunchairy. From Trichoor to Palghat, direct through Putticaad. But if the traveller intends proceeding in a bandy he has a very bad stage before him to Wuddakunchairy, for in the depth of the forest, far removed from all chance of assistance, is a rocky bit of ground, with large pieces of stone in the road and on each side of it. The bungalow at this place is unhealthy to sleep in from the feverish locality in which it is situated. Wild elephants may not unfrequently be encountered in this road, rendering it dangerous. From Trichoor to Kunnunkulum by the direct road. The other roads are useful to sportsmen, but unadapted to easy travelling. Southwards of Cochin travellers proceed to Allepey or Cottayam, by water.

The *Mountains* of Cochin are entirely confined to its eastern frontier and the Chittoor district. In the Kodachayree division two-thirds of it, as already mentioned, is hilly and mountainous, and amongst these ranges stands Paundymoodee, or Asses' Ears, a name which well describes the appearance of its two conical summits, from the top of which the other hills appear like plains. From this an immense ridge runs east and west, the extremities being terminated by the Coombunchayree and Paullapully hills. The elevation is very great, and the sides precipitous, measuring thirteen miles to the valleys beneath. The Thaullapully district, although containing no large hills, is full of asperities: particularly in the southern part, where the slopes though low, fall with great rapidity. The amount of brushwood and timber is very small.

The Western portion of the Trichoor district exhibits a succession of waving, champaign, uplands, with beautiful and varied scenery; whilst the eastern part is mountainous and woody, the forests commencing a few miles east of Trichoor, and the ramification of the Paullapully hills appearing on its south-east. At the pass termed Koodrancotay to the east of Putticaad the ridges of Vellanymala and Moodumala unite: the first has the greatest elevation, and its wooded summit spreads into a flat table-land, nearly half a mile broad: its north and west sides are steep and well wooded. Poneduthumala and Ponemala, are low ridges to the north of an inferior height, presenting the appearance of a green wall, their summits are rocky. There are many ranges of hills, all portions of the western ghauts, from whence come much of the timber and bamboos, with which the various markets are supplied: this subject will be referred to under the head of Botany.

In the Cochin district there are some slopes covered by low stunted brushwood, and many fruit trees, but no good timber. Around Kurriapudnam and its vicinity the amount of brushwood is very great, and the sportsmen will find it well stocked with hares: much the same may be said of the slopes in the Yainamakul district.

The outlying division of Chittoor has an uneven surface, but no very high hills; the Mutchat range runs S. E. from Uggamala to a distance of nine miles, from thence its slopes branch off on both sides. Most of this district is overrun with forests, which however yield very little valuable timber, but the axe of the planter is at work: one coffee plantation has been commenced, and others appear likely to follow. There are said to be two thousand serpent groves in this district, which are all objects of veneration to the Hindus.

The *Geology* of the country is difficult to define. The sandy tract near the sea has already been alluded to, as formed by the action of the rivers, when antagonistic to the waves of the sea during the monsoons: one bringing down alluvial deposit, the other throwing up sea sand. The alluvial territories in the State are evidently merely the debris of the hills and forests, washed down by the monsoons, and deposited in the low lands: but on either sides of most rivers and at raised spots, the laterite (*Buch.*) comes into view: it is commonly called the soap stone from its appearance; the itch stone, from its roughness and darkness of colour, due to long exposure to the air: and the brick stone, from its employment for building purposes. It is a species of indurated clay, in which both animal and vegetable exuviæ are said to have been found; near Alwaye, even iron spear heads and axes have had the credit of having been obtained from it. Whilst in Kurriavanoor and other places, numerous species of pure white quartz are seen, in some of which nodules of iron ore are occasionally found. The presence of quartz in laterite has been regarded as a reason for believing these formations to be due to the decomposition of primitive rocks, this quartz being the only portion remaining of its primary component parts. Laterite has been well described by *Buchanan*, as diffused over the country in immense masses, without any appearance of stratification. It is full of cavities and pores, and contains a very large quantity of iron, in the form of red and yellow ochres. Whilst excluded from the air, it is so soft that it can readily be cut by any iron instrument: it is dug up in enormous masses and cut into the required form with a trowel or small axe. It becomes in time as hard as a brick. *Dr. Cole* gives its varieties as follows:—" sometimes it is " very hard, compact, and heavy: highly ferruginous, of a deep red " colour, penetrated in all directions by sinuosities, containing the red " and yellow earths: some masses are nearly half composed of the " white lithomargic earth, which renders it very crumbling: other " varieties exhibit a pisiform structure, numerous rounded pebbles " being united together by a yellow clayey cement, this seems of re- " cent origin. Again, in many superficial situations, it is a mere gra- " vel, possessing very little coherence, and apparently formed from " the debris of the laterite itself: the pebbles composing this gravel " still exhibit the structure of the red conglomerate of sandstone, and " of the ochrey iron ore." One variety is of a light colour, having pinkish white, or yellowish streaks or mottles of various shades, running through it: this is the kind most commonly employed for building purposes. It is cut out in the form of bricks, in the quarry, and becomes very hard if exposed to the air for a few months. It should properly be kept for a year before being used, but not longer, as it is liable to become rotten.

Laterite is found of various consistencies, from that of the hard black coloured stone, which has been exposed for some time, to that of soft clay, in which wet cultivation is carried on, and from the mud of which, excellent tiles, bricks, and chatties, are made; as the rains eat oval holes into laterite bricks they are generally chunamed, but as chunam blackens by exposure, buildings become of a dirty colour on their S. W. sides. Where the hard laterite is found near the surface of the earth, the ground is rendered very unproductive. The plains in the hot months are like sandy tracts, with very little, or rather no grass; when ridden over they reverberate as if caverns were beneath. On this formation many forms of animal life do not thrive: the guinea worm does not exist, and the tape worm is also unknown. Here trees are often stunted in their growth, but in localities where moisture accumulates and decomposes its substance, some species occasionally thrive.

Beneath the laterite is granite, or allied geological formations. It is found on the top of some hills, and more rarely on their sides. In many places the soil around the bases of the mountains is a dark permeable rich earth, in which timber grows abundantly. Wherever flat surfaces occur on the sides of the hills, their decomposition and debris afford materials for the growth of trees and other vegetables.

The *Mineral* productions of this fertile, agricultural, and timber producing country, are comparatively few: or perhaps more correctly speaking, but few have been discovered. Gold is found in small quantities in the sands of the Cranganore river near the ruined fort, but at present is not known any where else in the territory. Old Portuguese authors mention its having been collected along the sea shore, even opposite Cochin. The sands of most of the rivers appear as if gold dust were present in enormous quantities: their beautiful yellow glitter is sufficient to deceive any casual observer, whilst even the quartz contains iron in small golden coloured nodules, which give it something of the appearance of auriferous quartz. But unfortunately, the little flakes of floating yellow substance are merely golden mica without one trace of the precious metals; this mica extends up the coast, certainly as far as Cannanore, but there the silver variety partially takes its place. Yellow mica may be found in small flakes on the summits of hills, where there is no laterite; its glitter may be distinguished in the black alluvial deposits in the river banks, in their sands, and on the dusty roads.

Iron is not now worked in the Cochin State, but it has been in days gone by: several old furnaces for obtaining it from laterite are in existence at Sheranoor. From the appearance of the pipes, a considerable amount was procured. In the Chittoor district it has also been obtained. It is found in masses or veins, in the substance of the laterite.

Though various authors have attributed "cat's eyes," beryls, and several species of precious stones to Malabar, the Cochin State can lay claim to be the native country of but few.

Salt is not at the present time manufactured, though such was attempted some years since on one of the islands close to Cochin. The amount obtained from the salt pans was insufficient to repay for the labour expended.

The *Harbours* and sea-board of the country still remain undescribed. The mariner would be venturesome indeed, who brought his vessel near the shores of Cochin during the violence of the S. W. monsoon, or from the beginning of June to the middle of August. The roll of the sea and the violence of the winds are then too great for vessels to beat about on this unsheltered coast, unless the seasons prove unusually mild, or there should be such a place as the Allepey mud bank to run into. There is no indentation of the shore worthy the name of a harbour, and only two outlets of rivers, viz., at Cochin and Palliport, respectively; elsewhere vessels have to lie in an open roadstead. During a violent storm in May 1859, all the vessels lying outside Cochin had a most narrow escape: some slipped, eventually all got safely away.

The harbour of the town of Cochin is the most important in this part of India, and is a very excellent one: consisting of the wide river, which having a straight course of little more than half a mile, divides Cochin from Vypeen with a width of 680 yards opposite the flag staff. This river forms a connecting channel between the sea, and a large expanse of backwater of sufficient size and depth, to contain more vessels than are ever likely at any one period to visit the place. The bar is about 1¼ miles from the shore at the mouth of the river. It is a very narrow ridge* of sand extending in a semicircular direction, from the shoal water off Vypeen point to that off Cochin point.

* Lieutenant Taylor's *Official report*, H. M. surveying vessel *Bheema*.

Although this is all literally speaking "bar," the bar proper, or deepest part of this ridge, is an arc of a circle, the chord of which is 600 yards, and its versed sine about 100 yards. At the lowest water, on the shoalest part, there is a depth of 13 feet : and the extreme rise and fall of the tide is 3 feet, generally not above $1\frac{1}{2}$. The ridge at this depth (13 feet) is broader (i. e. from E. to W.) in some places than at others. The best channel is 100 yards wide, and its cross section not more than 10 yards ; but in some spots so narrow that it is frequently missed in sounding for it. It must not be supposed that it is here meant that when the amount of water covering the bar is 13 feet, vessels with that draught can enter without bumping, as the dip of the wave makes a difference. About 11 or 9 feet at times can only pass over in perfect safety.

The cause of these bars is the ocean swell and the ebb tide, by which also, according to their relative strength, their direction is determined. The tidal wave, *Lieutenant Taylor* points out, comes from the N. W., whilst the ebb tide finding an exit to the same direction, occasions the shallows off Vypeen. The alluvial deposits brought down by the freshes have a tendency to accumulate on the bar.

One of the requirements of the port, or rather of the mercantile shipping,† is a steam tug, to tow vessels in and out, and also to be employed when its services are not otherwise required, in working a steam rake, or dredge for the purpose of deepening the bar. The sea is now carrying away the S. W. extremity of Vypeen, and it is feared that if the bar is not deepened, the great body of the freshes will pass more and more to the N. W. Should a channel form here, the bar will inevitably become more or less silted up, and in time it may be impassable for all but small vessels. Such a consummation need not be expected, at least for many years, as a century since the water on the bar was 14 feet. The currents shift continually, and the set now against the Vypeen side of the river, may, before another season has passed over, be against the Cochin bank.

---

* It cannot be supposed that increasing the depth of the bar, so as to permit larger vessels to enter the Cochin river, will increase the amount of produce shipped from the port. Any one who has seen the British harbours along the Western Coast, must be persuaded Cochin is far superior to any of the others.

The tides are very irregular, not only with respect to the stream of the ebb and flood, but also to their rise and fall. The flood stream occasionally lasts four hours, yet with an absolutely imperceptible rise in the water. The average amount of water on the bar, at night time, is 15 feet.

The entrance to the Cranganore or Ayacotta river, at Palliport, is very intricate, and only small native crafts enter. But south of it is a mud flat, stretching a little to the south of Narrikal, a large village, five miles by sea north of Cochin. The distance from the backwater to the sea shore is about ¾ of a mile, along a sandy road, leading through the village. There is little to add to the description given of it by the Dutch *Admiral Stavorinus* in 1777, who stated that a reef existed at the mouth of the Cranganore river, at its north side (now, owing to a new opening having formed, being at its south side). This stretches out to sea about ¾ of a league, forming a harbour or place protected by mud banks, and into which vessels may run with safety during bad monsoons, and lie there secure in 20 or less feet of water, almost without cables. This soft mud partially prevents the roll of the sea, which breaks its force upon its circumference, and is totally imperceptible as the land is approached, the place appearing more like a fresh water lake. The mud flat is now said to extend for half a mile south of Narrikal, and to the north for about four miles. The smoothest portions of the sea are between the villages of Narrikal and Nairumbalum, 1½ miles to its north : W. N. W from Narrikal the sea at soundings less than 3 fathoms, invariably retains its stillness : between 3 and 5 fathoms there is a slight swell. To the south of Narrikal the mud bank is narrower, and the deep water and stillness nearer the shore. To the north, the soundings* are shallower and the water smooth further out to sea.

During the S. W. monsoon the swollen rivers of the Western Coast, loaded with alluvial matter, rush impetuously towards the sea. Should any obstruction occur at their outlets, deposits are occasioned, as at the Cranganore and Quilon rivers, where mud banks have so arisen. Whether this impediment to these alluvial deposits being carried out to sea is *merely* owing to the action of the waves being

* Master Attendant's *Official report*, 1862.

directly antagonistic to the course of the river, or whether other causes are also in operation, may be questioned. For the formation of the Narrikal mud bank, a reef of rocks formerly existed (the Ayacotta reef) at the mouth of the Cranganore river, which long prevented the divergence of the course of the stream to the northward, as invariably occurs in all those of the Western Coast. This reef is now on the southern side, owing to the stream having taken a circuitous direction behind it.

The whole of the long islands (the maritime districts of Cochin,) between the sea and the backwater are evidently alluvial deposits brought down by the river, and sand washed up by the sea. The direction of these mud banks being the same as the long islands, and the character of the soil nearly identical : the same cause may fairly be considered as giving rise to both. Though Narrikal, as being the point nearest Cochin, has given its name to this mud bank, the density of the sea increases proceeding northwards. The mud becomes very thick and black, and large pieces of flat hard flakes of it are perceived lying on the shore, about one mile north of Narrikal, where they have been thrown up by the sea. Passing onwards still towards Cranganore, at Nairumbalum, a large bank of the same substance is found, of from 6 to 10 feet deep, evidently brought down by the river, which continues supplying this mud harbour, with deposits.

Every little stream and gully forms an excellent diminutive representation of the large rivers, bringing down alluvial matter. On making sections of the sand, layers of it are found alternating with those of dark mud : the larger the stream, the thicker the various layers; no gases arise from the water, and no oily matter (as suggested,) floats upon it. It is simply the action of the sea, which prevents the subsidence of the mud, for as soon as placed in a still vessel, it sinks.

The mud feels unctuous and sticky, but is not gritty, unless mixed with the sand. It is of a very dark greenish colour, and has but a slight odour. Under the microscope it shows "very minute angular "fragments of quartz, the largest hardly visible without a lens: this is "the sand. *Secondly*, Foraminiferous shells, of the genus Rotalia, and "a few fragments of larger shells. *Thirdly*, Diatomaceœ, of which

" were discovered species from upwards of 20 genera. *Fourthly*, a few " spicules of sponges and corals, very minute : and some amorphous " matter, which was not destroyed after long boiling in strong acids." On a more elaborate enquiry* the mud was found to be very tenacious and resistant of pressure, like a stiff piece of jelly : and it is supposed that, acting like an immense spring, it yields to the pressure of the waves, that the water thus loses its force and becomes quiescent : whilst the mud expanding is prepared for a fresh encounter. An examination into its composition resulted in the discovery of sixty-two species, belonging to 30 generæ, of the class Cryptogamia, and sub-group Diatomeœ.

The Allepey mud bank, about 30 miles south of Cochin, in the Travancore State, is much largerthan that at Narrikal. This bank has evidently shifted, and is still shifting gradually southwards : thus between 1693 and 1723, it moved three miles to the southward : from 1723 to 1825 it had again moved on 15 miles, or at an average of nearly one mile in eight years. It does not appear at the present time to be progressing so rapidly.

---

* *Madras Journal of Literature and Science.* New Series, No. XII, page 264, by Lieut. Mitchell.

CHAPTER II.

THE NATIVE STATE OF COCHIN.

Legendary origin of Malabar—Brahmanical Government—Foreign Governors—Origin of Cochin Rajahs—Legendary division of Malabar—Arrival of Portuguese—Arrival of the Dutch—Wars with the Samorin, and Rajah of Travancore—Hyder Ali—Tippoo Sultan—Battle of the Travancore lines—British treaty of 1790—Intrigues with the French—Nair disturbances—Laws of succession to the Musnud—Ancient and Modern laws—Revenue.

THE Native State of Cochin appears to have formed a portion of the ancient kingdom of Keralam, the name of which was derived from *Veera Keralam*, the first Prince who ruled over it: *Keroolem*, the son of Iayenthen, grandson of Indra, and Son-in-law of Veruma: or the Sanscrit word *Keram*, a cocoanut. The monarch may have been known as the "king of the cocoanut country," that species of palm, growing to perfection along the whole extent of its fertile coast.

Keralam, or Parasu Ramah's territory, Malayalam, (*Mala*, hill, *Ala*, sea): the country below the Sukhein, or Western ghauts, is bounded on the north by the river Chandraghiri, in latitude 10° 30′: and extends as far South as Cape Comorin. It has been by some authors considered as forming one of the fifty-six districts of the Bharata division of Hindustan.

The origin of Malabar, according to Hindu tradition, may be traced back to the time of Parasu Ramah, (the sixth incarnation of Vishnu,) who, it is asserted, after destroying the Schatriyas, was seized with remorse concerning the blood he had shed, and wishing to offer an atonement, made his territories a present to the Brahmans. He then proceeded to Kailasa, and recounted his adventures to *Paramayswaren,* entreating that god, to grant him another kingdom:

but he, unable to meet his wishes, advised his applying to the god of the sea. Accordingly having proceeded to the southern extremity of India, accompanied by Subhramanien, they there consecrated a small spot of territory, and imagining the presence of a Virgin goddess, worshipped her under the name of *Canniya Coomaury*, (the words being almost synonymous and signifying, "Virgin girl.") Subsequently, the place received the same designation, which was gradually corrupted into "*Cape Comorin.*"

The sea god, Weruma, (pronounced Veruma,) thus invoked, soon appeared: and on hearing Parasu Ramah's request, granted him land, as far as he could throw his Chuckram, (disc, or axe,) across the sea, promising that the water should recede, up to the spot, where it should fall. Parasu Ramah then exerting all his strength, threw his Chuckram, in a N. W. direction, for a distance of about 1,500 miles (so states the *Kerala Ulpati)* in length, and 150 in breadth!

The gods then directed Parasu Ramah, to build 24,000 *Chutrums*, (temples), promising, that so long as charities were continued to Brahmans, they would reside in the country, and preserve it from harm. Vishnu then presented him with his *Chuckram*, assuring him, that whenever he was invoked by that weapon, he would personally appear. Parasu Ramah then proceeded northwards, and as directed, built houses and temples for the Brahmans, and at Trichoor,* he consecrated the image of Siva, calling the place *Thrisivamayru*, a word derived from, *Thri*, a syllable often affixed to the names of Hindu Deities, *Siva*, the god, and *Mayru*, or Meru, the sacred mountain.

Parasu Ramah then proceeded to the river Khristna, and shortly afterwards returned, accompanied by a Brahman, his wife, and eight sons, all of whom he located at Trichoor. The father he made the head of all the Malabar Brahmans, giving him the title of Yogiyar: whilst to the eight sons, he presented eight villages, over which he installed them as Lords, and where they subsequently resided.

Next he went to the district of Tanjore, whence he brought another Brahman, with his wife and sons. The father of this family, was installed as Wadiyar, (spiritual preceptor,) over the temple

* A large town in the Cochin State.

Parasu Ramah had built at Trichoor. He made various journeys to other localities, sometimes obtaining treasure, and sometimes Brahmans, for this new country: and, thus he was enabled to people 24 Gramams, or villages. He next procured Schatriyas, Sudras, and Hindus of all the Castes, including carpenters, and labourers, as well as seeds of plants, and grains. All appeared to be going on well; Parasu Ramah was quietly governing, under the personal direction of the gods, when the Brahmans began to return to their Native lands, carrying away with them, the riches they had accumulated. To obviate this emigration, Brahma having visited Keralam, gave the Inhabitants a new language, termed "Malayalim," appointing certain ceremonies, and directing that all the people of Keralam should wear the Cudumi, on the forepart of the head; he likewise instituted other changes. After Brahma had left, Ganesha made some further changes, in the manners, and ceremonies: the principal of which were, that the eldest son only (of Brahmans) should marry, and that those of this superior caste should only wear one Poonool, or sacred string, worn by the twice born classes, across the left shoulder, and meeting like a belt, over the right hip.

Parasu Ramah ordained that all Brahmanee women should carry with them an umbrella, whenever they stirred out of doors, to prevent their being seen, by those of the male sex. That a Sudra servant girl should go before them: that they should be well covered by a large cloth, but should wear, neither ornaments, nor jewels.

The whole of Keralam being peopled, it was given to the Brahmans, by Parasu Ramah, to be kept exclusively for the support of Temples, and religious establishments, To this day, Malabar is distinguished, as the *Kerma-Bhoomi*, or "land of good works, for the expiation of sin."

Another version is, that having obtained the land from Veruma, as described, and peopled it with Brahmans: before long they returned to their Native countries, asserting the new country was too full of snakes to be safe, and too swampy to be healthy. A fresh set of Brahmans were then despatched there, and directed to propitiate the reptiles by worship: whilst to set a mark upon this new race, Parasu Ramah seized each one by the hair of his head, and hurled him over the mountains into Malabar. The consequence of this rough procedure was, that the unshaved lock on the top of the head *(cudumi)* was dragged forward half way to the forehead; in which position it is still worn by this class of Brahmans, distinguishing them from all others.

Shortly after this period, Parasu Ramah visited Malabar, and requested some of the chief Brahmans, to give him a small piece of ground, on which to erect a hut for his own residence. And on his request being refused, he cursed the whole tribe, and prophesied that however great and holy they might consider themselves, they would in reality, be a degraded race, to the end of time.

He then retired to the Western Ghauts, but subsequently becoming tired of a solitary life, he assumed the form of an ascetic, and proceeding to Veruma, implored the gift of a small piece of land, extending only as far as he could shoot an arrow over the sea. The request was granted, but Veruma being soon afterwards informed by some Brahmans who his late visitor had been: became alarmed, and repented his promise; but as he could not break it, he prevailed upon the *god of death* to assist him in thwarting Parasu Ramah.

The time fixed upon, for shooting the arrow arrived: but the *god of death* having changed himself into a white ant, had, during the previous night, eaten two-thirds through the bow string, consequently the arrow was not discharged, as the string, when pulled, snapped asunder. Parasu indignantly declared that his inveterate and revengeful enemies, the Brahmans, had been concerned in this occurrence, and decreed, that to the end of time, the souls of any of them who died in Keralam, should be transmigrated into the bodies of asses. He forthwith retired to the Ghauts, where he is believed still to be watching over the Western Coast, and at long intervals appearing in some terrible form, to affrighted travellers.

The Brahmans now established an aristocratic form of government under chiefs: but each wishing to be independant of his neighbour, dissensions, and their results, the insecurity of life and property ensued.

About B. C. 68, a great congress was held, when the rulers of Keralam agreed, that they would send to Chera* for a *Permaul,* or Governor who should rule over them for twelve years, at the end of which period, he should retire from public life : the most approved mode of doing which was by cutting his own throat on a scaffold erected for that purpose. After having joined in a great farewell feast, this tragedy, enacted in view of the assembled guests, completed the entertainment. His body was then burnt, and the post refilled. These governors were bound to observe certain Brahmanical regulations, and in matters of doubt the decision of the Brahmans was final.

The term Cheramal Permaul, or Cheraman Perumal, which merely signifies "a governor from Chera," has been erroneously considered, to mean a family who ruled Malabar, when in truth it was simply an official designation. In olden times the country was always called "*Cheraman lokoun*" or Cheraman's country.

Rejecting Hindu traditions, it appears most probable, that the ancient rulers of Keralam were dispossessed by a Brahman named Parasu Ramah, who invaded the country, and that when he died, the Chiefs divided the territory amongst themselves, until, in consequence of disagreements, they found it necessary to send to Chera for a Governor, whom all would agree to serve under, whilst he himself was bound down by certain restrictions.

The Brahmans without doubt divided themselves into two sects, the worshippers of Varahou, (the incarnation of the Boar,) and those of Sharabou (the incarnation of the Bird,) and these distinctions are even now partially maintained. These two divisions had each two *Talis,* or species of "Councillors or Secretaries of State:" these four were located at Cranganore, where the Governor also resided. Besides these, there were other petty Talis in various places. In the course of time the power of the Permauls augmented, whilst that of the Talis gradually dwindled into insignificance. Many of even these titles, were given to nephews of the Permauls, thus still further increasing their power.

* Chéra is stated by *Elphinstone,* to be a small State between the territory of the Pandyas, (Madura) and the western sea : comprehending Travancore, part of Malabar, and Coimbatore. It is mentioned by Ptolemy, and may have existed at the commencement of our era. It was subdued and divided in the 10th century.

In this manner a species of hereditary nobility was formed, and when the Rajah of Anagoomty was preparing to invade Keralam, many distinctions and mottoes were conferred, amongst which the Cochin Chief had that of Raveeloke Sharajay given him: this occurred, A. D., 325* (351 ?) The last Permaul, is stated by Zeirreddien Mukhdom to have been of the Vysia or Sudra caste, and called *Shukerwutty*, or *Chuckerwutty*. But this statement is generally received with incredulity.

All the Permauls do not appear to have been desirous of terminating their rule in self-destruction, some retired for life to a pagoda—a custom subsequently adopted by the Samorins. Finally, *one* Governor arose, who set the authority of the Kings of Chera at defiance, refusing to resign his Government: but the then Rajah *Kishen Rao* was not disposed to give up his power over Malabar without a struggle: so at the head of an army he marched to dispossess this recusant Permaul, whom he defeated and compelled to take refuge in the Ghauts. The people had soon cause to regret the change of masters; and when Kishen Rao had firmly established himself at *Tiruvanji Collum*, a place now in the Cochin State, close to Cranganore, the Namboories (Malabar Brahmans) considered it time to effect a revolution in favour of their friend Cheraman Permaul, (as he is commonly called.) One of their Chiefs therefore went to see Kishen Rao, and owing to his high rank and sacred character, readily gained admission to his presence. The wily Brahman flattered and caressed, and after a short time gained permission to introduce to the king, a few friends of the same priestly caste. One day whilst engaged in conversation, they availed themselves of a favourable opportunity, and murdered Kishen Rao. Great confusion ensued, during which Cheraman Permaul regained the sovereign power. A native Prince, in laying his claims before the British Commissioners, in 1793,

---

* It is very difficult to ascertain anything respecting the accuracy of these very early dates, even when they relate to European history. *Thomas Cana* certified that he *saw* the last of the Permauls alive in the year 345, whilst on a reference to the Brahman College at Trichoor, an answer was received, which corroborates his statement asserting that Cheraman Permaul ascended the Musnud about March 24, A. D. 341, and reigned 36 years and four months: but the date of May 378, is then given as that, at which he was last seen: making the length of his reign 37 years and two months.

to a small tract of land, pleaded that it had been presented to his ancestors, by Cheraman Permaul as a reward for murdering Kishen Rao.

Some believe that the last Permaul was permitted to be Governor for thirty-six years, at the end of which time he retired, and was induced by the Majains, commonly known as Jains, A. D. 378, (352 ?)* to proceed to Mecca, at which place many of that faith were established: carrying on a trade with India, which, in subsequent centuries, fell into Moorish hands.

From this last Permaul, or Governor, whose name has been variously given as Sheo Ram, Shermanoo, Permaloo, and Cheraman Permaul, &c., all the present Rajahs, Chieftains, Nobles, and Landholders, assert that their ancestors received grants either of territory, nobility or estates.

Malabar had scarcely been portioned out, when an Erary, or person of the caste of cowherds,† arrived from Poondra, on the banks of the Cauvery near Errode in the Carnatic: and claimed his share of the kingdom. He reminded Cheraman Permaul that his independence was achieved, owing, in a great measure, to his assistance, and that of his brothers. The Prince replied, that he had little left to bestow, excepting his own palace, which, with the ground lying around it, and leading to the sea beach, he had retained, that he might leave the shores of India still the monarch of the soil on which he stood. But he presented him with his sword, (kept to this day by the Samorin's descendants, with the greatest reverence,) bracelets, and sovereignity over as much land, as a cock could be heard crowing from a neighbouring temple, completing the transfer by placing a gar-

---

* See an account by *Kookel keloo Nair* in an interesting paper in the *Madras Quarterly Journal of Literature and Science.* Referring to this subject the writer observes that the Jains, or Bhuddists, " as a people, were settled in " Arabia, and many visited Malabar; the original name was Mahajain, and " became in time corrupted to Magains, or Magans. The Hindus through mis-" take call the Mussalmen also Bhuddists, and from this arose the idea, that " the last of the Permauls became a Mahomedan."

† The gowlees, (cowherds,) in the Deccan, appear to belong to the same race as the people of Malabar, and have Canarese and Malayalim words, mixed up with the Mahratta.

land round his neck, and sprinkling it with otta of roses.* He then gave him the title of *Samorin*, or Lord over the other Rajahs, leaving him to acquire his authority over them, and extend his territory, as he could.

The ancient name of the town of Calicut, whence Cheraman Permaul is said to have embarked, has escaped record, but the native name for it, at the present time, is *Cozee-cota*, a contraction of *Cozee-cooghee-cota*, the fort from whence the cock crew.

Another version is, that Cheraman Permaul, tired of sovereignity, divided his dominions amongst his Chiefs and friends in the following manner:—giving the northern portion to the Rajah of Colastria: that part immediately south of this to the Samorin, or Samoory Rajah: from thence as far as the Travancore State, to the Rajah of Cochin: and that lying to the extreme south, to the Rajah of Travancore.

The Dutch Government Records state that Cheraman Permaul, after dividing his territories, retired for life to the pagoda of *Tiruvanji Collum*. In the Dutch Road book, dated 1742, quite a different version is given of the origin of the four great Rajahs of Cochin, Colastria, Calicut, and Travancore, and one which appears by no means unlikely to be correct, viz., that the first, or Rajah of Cochin, only was a Schatriya: the others were Sudras: that the first was the son of the sister of the last of the Permauls, and consequently the rightful heir: whilst the other three were merely his own children, who, according to the laws of Malabar, could not be his heirs, all inheritance going through the sister's children. Thus, if the last Permaul's wife were a Sudra, this would account for the Samorins, the Rajahs of Colastria, and those of Travancore, all being Sudras.

Sixteen lesser kingdoms of the first rank, were placed under the authority of Kaimuls, who possessed the power of deciding, in cases of life and death, regarding their own subjects; these posts were given to the friends of the Permauls, and comprehended Repelim, Porca (Chambagacherry), Teckencoor, Quilon (Coilam), Culli Quilon (Kayencoilam), Berkencoor (Wadacancoor), Arangolla (Walluanatty,)

* This appears to have been an ancient symbol, of the gift, or transfer of property.

Tannoor (Bettette), besides many others, (apparently of lesser size), such as Cranganore, Ayroor (Iroor), Mangatty, Paroor, &c. There were also still smaller districts, the rulers of which had no power over the lives of their subjects. The superior Rajahs (such as the Rajah of Cochin) considered these Kaimuls their vassals, merely holding land as feudatories, whilst they, on the other hand, did not always remain faithful to one Prince, and only obeyed orders when it suited their convenience to do so. The smaller States were again subdivided, and so on "ad infinitum," until it became a proverb in Malabar, that "though two steps might be made in one territory, a third must "pass the boundary." The claims of the four superior Rajahs to sovereignty, appear to have been founded in justice, if Cheraman Permaul had the right to invest any one with such authority. But as Kaimuls merely held their lands by the same tenure, they would hardly have argued its illegality. In those days, right existed by the force of the sword, and appeals were unknown, except to arms.

The early history of the Cochin Rajahs is involved in obscurity: their lives seem to have been passed in warfare, either attempting to extend their territories at the expense of their weaker neighbours, or defending themselves against those who were stronger, in which they were assisted by the Kaimuls or subordinate petty chiefs, who in their turn, expected assistance, against more powerful neighbours.

Little can be collected respecting this country prior to the arrival of the Portuguese, A. D. 1500, when the Rajah evidently, under the impression, that their assistance would enable him to check the increasing power of the Samorin, gave them a friendly reception as will be detailed in the next chapter. For the Samorin had entered into an alliance with the Moplahs, who had given him material assistance against the Cochin Rajah, by which he had defeated him on several occasions. On the arrival of the Dutch, in 1663, they found the Rajah, kept a State prisoner by the Portuguese, and a Ranee (his aunt,) governing the kingdom, who appears to have been devotedly attached to the Portuguese nation.

The Dutch Governor of Cochin, *Jacob Lobo*, about 1678 speaks of "the Cochin Rajah, with his four kingdoms of Porca, Berkencoor, Mangatty, and Paroor," and observes that by adoptions and deaths he had obtained the territory, stretching to within half a (Dutch) mile, of the town of Cochin. *Van Gollenesse* in 1743, speaks of "the Cochin Rajah and his four states," mentioning the same as were detailed by Jacob Lobo, 65 years before.

In the year 1715, the Samorin perceiving that the Dutch had either become lukewarm, respecting their ally the Cochin Rajah: or else were unable to protect him, over-ran and conquered a portion of his territory. From this period the dissensions connected with the State, became so mixed up, with the history of the Dutch, that an account of them must be deferred, until speaking of that nation.

On October 15th, 1753, the Cochin Rajah met the Dutch Ambassador at Mavillicurray, where they attempted to negotiate a lasting peace with Travancore, but the Dutch had to attend to the interests of the Company and therefore left the Rajah to make his own terms; and although peace was agreed upon, it was of short duration. The Cochin Rajah was induced by the chiefs of Teckencoor, Wadacancoor, and other places, to assist them in throwing off the yoke of the Rajah of Travancore, who had annexed their territories. Accordingly, some thousands of Nairs from Cochin, in conjunction with those of Teckencoor, the Coddacherry Kaimuls and other great personages, marched to Porca, to attack the Travancore troops. But they were completely routed, and the second Coddacherry Kaimul, the young Paliat Achen, and one of the chief Ragiadoors (Province Governors, Tahsildars) of Cochin were made prisoners. Travancore then seized the whole of the Porca district, along the sea coast, nearly as far as Cochin: and it was remarked at this time by the Dutch Commandant, that "the Rajah is in great danger of losing the whole of his territory," and in 1756, he also reports, "Travancore since 1753, has "conquered Teckencoor, Wadacancoor, Porca and the greatest portion of Cochin, including Culli Quilon, Quilon, Attinga, Martha "and Peritally."

The Travancore Rajah undoubtedly intended to annex any territories he could conquer. Many of these little States, although perhaps not at that time, paying tribute to Cochin, certainly had been vassals to that Rajah.

In 1755 the Samorin again invaded the Cochin State, and attacking the Island of Chetwye, drove in some Dutch outposts, and over-ran a portion of the Cochin territory. He was joined by a number of petty Princes, and gradually possessed himself of most of the Cochin State.

In 1757 it was agreed between the Rajahs of Cochin and Travancore, that as the Chembagacherry and Wadakencoor chiefs, had combined against Travancore, and given that Rajah much trouble : he should be allowed to reimburse himself, out of their revenues, for his expenses ; and that the Cochin Rajah, should not interfere, or have any intercourse with these Princes, who nevertheless were permitted to reside at Trichoor.

The Rajah finding that he could gain no assistance from the Dutch, against the Samorin, sent an embassy, to his old enemy, the Rajah of Travancore, whose General, a Fleming, named *Eustachius de Lanoy*, was considered at that time, the most successful commandant in South India. He had 10,000 Nairs under him, whom he had disciplined as regular Infantry, and double that number as irregular foot, but no Cavalry.

The following was the agreement then entered into, between these two Princes. "The Cochin Rajah, having requested the assis-"tance of the Travancore Rajah, to drive the enemy away, and *to* "*extend his territories, as formerly:* namely, to Pookaitha on the "west, and Chitatu on the east : as also to recover for him, all "those lands, which he had in Walapanaud district, has agreed to *give* "*up to Travancore*, that portion of Carapooram, lying to the south "of Pamba Azi (Andar-azi), and north of Allepey, with the ex-"ception of Andicadow Chellana, and Combalum : and also to "give up the Paroor, and Allungaad districts : and has also agreed, "that one-half of the revenues of the reclaimed lands, which are to "be collected by the Cochin officials (with the knowledge, and super-"vision of those of Travancore) shall go towards defraying the ex-"penses of the Travancore army, as long as its presence may be re-"quired in those parts : and that if the army pushes into Walapa-"naud, all that part of the district, which is the Samorin's, shall "become Travancore property."*

* *Cochin Sircar Records M. S. S.*, dated December 26th 1761.

The Travancore Rajah, now erected works on a strip of land, commencing opposite Cranganore, and extending to the Ghauts; which it was anticipated would be a check upon any future advances of the Samorin. Whilst, just flanking their western extremity, were the Dutch Forts, of Cranganore, and Ayacotta or Azi-Cotta, (the mouth of a river, and a Fort). From ten to thirty miles, of the Cochin State, lay to the northwards, and exterior to these lines: although by far the largest portion was on the south, and within them.

This treaty was satisfactorily concluded, for the Samorin's troops being divided into three portions, one at Cranganore, one at Paroor, and the third at Verapoly: the Travancoreans attacked them suddenly, and routed them with great slaughter. In 1762 the provisions of the treaty were fully carried out, and the following year with the same assistance, the Rajah was enabled to take part of Chowghaut; whilst about the same period Maprana and the Mangatty lands also fell to him; the two last territories lie to the South of the river Innemaka, and formerly belonged to a Nambiar, from whom the Samorin took them, and in 1717, made them over to the Dutch: who in returning to the Cochin Rajah the lands he had lost to the Samorin, retained Maprana, which they let out to the old Nambiar, for 4 lasts of paddy annually, (16,000 Dutch pounds). It was again retaken by the Samorin in 1753, and now it was by the assistance of the Travancore Rajah, again annexed (in 1763) by the Cochin Rajah, and the Nambiar deprived of all authority. The Dutch Government then demanded, that the Nambiar should either be replaced as their tenant, or that the Rajah should pay them the stipulated rent; the last course was agreed to.*

The power of *Hyder Ali* about this time became known in Malabar; and the Rajah of Palghaut, (part of whose possessions had been taken in 1758-59 by the Samorin,) applied to Hyder for assistance, agreeing in return to become his vassal. In 1760-61 Hyder's

* In 1762, the Rajah of Cochin, mortgaged the Coosipully lands, lying north of Vypeen, to the Dutch, for Rs. 15,000, in order to meet the expenses of the small army, which in accordance with his agreement with the Rajah of Travancore, had been equipped for the field against the Samorin. If these lands were not redeemed by the Rajah before September, the Dutch were to collect the revenues.

troops relieved him; Hyder and the Samorin now continued negotiating on various subjects until 1766, when the former at the head of his victorious Mysore army, swept down into Malabar, and possessed himself of the entire country from Cannanore, to the Cochin territory, when the Rajah of the latter State, agreed by the advice of the Dutch, to pay to Hyder a sum of Rs. 200,000 and eight elephants, if he would not invade his territory.

In 1772 several disputes occurred between the Dutch and the Rajah of Cochin, respecting the boundaries of their respective possessions. The Dutch claiming the whole of Muttencherry as theirs by right, and apparently with foundation, as their territory extended one mile south of Jews' town. The Dutch Commissioners however gave in, judging it advisable to await a more favourable opportunity to enforce their claims, probably aware, that power was then on the Rajah's side.

Previous to this, as already mentioned, the Rajah of Travancore, had erected a long earthen wall, thirty miles in length, from Palliport, along a great portion of the Cochin State on a slip of land ceded to him by the Cochin Rajah: and in 1775, this wall which had been constructed fourteen years previously, was improved: and the ground at Palliport belonging to the Dutch, was purchased by the Rajah of Travancore. These works checked the advance of the Mysoreans, and saved two-thirds of the Cochin State from invasion. But Sirdar Khan, the Mysore General established his head quarters at Trichoor, and demanded eight lacs of rupees from the Cochin Rajah as a gift, on which this prince sent ambassadors to Seringapatam, to treat with Hyder personally: when it was finally settled, by his being obliged to give 4 lacs of rupees as a nuzzer, and 4 elephants; and to enter into an agreement, to pay an annual tribute of Rupees 120,000. The Rajah of Cranganore, was also compelled at this time, to give Rupees 120,000 as a nuzzer: and a tribute of Rupees 20,000 yearly. After satisfactorily concluding these arrangements, Sirdar Khan moved off to the north.

The atrocities of the Mahomedan invaders, soon alarmed all the Natives of Southern India; Prince after Prince, Chief after Chief, and thousands of their followers, fled to Travancore: and the forcible conversion of Hindus, created terror in the minds of all.

None were safe, even Ambassadors were forcibly compelled to join the Mahomedan sect, and the victims of self-destruction, might have been counted by thousands. Agreements respecting money were violated, as although the tribute remained the same, large gifts were frequently enforced: whilst the Rajah of Cochin, was obliged to maintain 1,000 troops at Calicut for Hyder, to coerce the Nairs.

In 1786, the Rajah of Cochin, and the first prince of Travancore, met at Muttencherry:* and remained in conference six days, upon these Mahomedan atrocities: and a fortnight subsequently, a second interview was held.

August 13th, 1790, the Rajah died of small pox, and was succeeded by his younger brother, *Virôlam Tamburan,* a proud, brave man, who was exceedingly oppressive to merchants, in and around Cochin. He appears to have been greatly influenced by Mysore councils, and caused two of the overseers of the Temple, *Tirumala Davossam,* to be put to death, for refusing to deliver up its treasures, into his hands. He plundered the bazaars, and informed the Dutch, that he was determined to rule all the Pagans himself, and that they were only there to trade, and not to govern. The Dutch then attacked him in his palace at Muttencherry, retook his plunder, and compelled him to retire to Tripoonterah, from whence he was scarcely ever permitted to move.

In 1789, Tippoo swept through Malabar, to punish the Nairs who had risen in arms against him, three thousand men preceded this merciless tyrant, and his own body-guard numbered 30,000. Many of his victims were hung, even mothers with their children around their necks: others, were dragged to death by elephants: no mode of execution was too terrible, no torture too great, to satiate his fiendish vengeance. Churches were plundered, and the roofs of all places of worship blown off: whilst Hindu, and Christian women, were compelled to accept Mahomedan husbands

* The next meeting between members of these two Royal houses, occurred on January 16th, 1862, when the Rajah of Cochin, received the First prince of Travancore, at his Palace, at Muttencherry; after the return of the latter, from a visit to Madras.

No Hindu was allowed to wear the lock of hair on his head. The rack and starvation, were used as instruments of conversion: and those obstinate unbelievers, who refused to be convinced, by these persuasive arguments, were put to death.

Cochin at this time, was the only State in Malabar, at peace with Tippoo. The latter now ordered the Rajah to meet him, but he having had that honour the previous year, declined a repetition. Tippoo on this, became suspicious of his fidelity: whilst he on his side, was alarmed at a report, that the Mysorean army, was on its road to convert, or otherwise exterminate, all the Hindu population.

Tippoo now made the existence of the barrier wall, a cause of complaint as it divided him, from two-thirds of his vassal state of Cochin, and consequently obstructed his passage thereto; and gave the Rajah of Cochin orders to claim it, as being on his territory. He also complained, that Nairs, and others, fleeing from his power, obtained refuge in Cochin: therefore as the Rajah would not obey his summons, he determined to fetch him by force, and made preparations for assaulting the Travancore lines.

Between July and November, 1788, upwards of 30,000 Brahmans, including their families, escaped from the Calicut districts, into Travancore.

In 1789, Tippoo commenced his march from Coimbatore, with 20,000 regular infantry, 10,000 spearmen, and matchlock men; 5,000 horse, and 20 guns.

The troops of the Rajah of Travancore, were received into the Dutch Forts of Cranganore, and Ayacotta, and the Rajah applied to the Madras Government for assistance. The English had not calculated on the left flank being thrown on the Dutch Forts, and two battalions were marched to assist the Rajah of Travancore, but only on his own lines.

So the Forts of Cranganore, and Ayacotta, were sold by the Dutch to the Rajah of Travancore, a transaction which gave rise to much discussion, as although the Dutch had taken them from the Portuguese in war, the Rajah of Cochin claimed the ground on which they stood, asserting that its transfer to Travancore, without his consent, was illegal. But on the other hand, as the political existence of the Cochin State, depended on this transfer, it was considered a case of necessity, and carried out on the law of expediency. It was finally sanctioned by the Madras Government, in 1790.

On the night of December 28th, 1789, Tippoo had established his camp, six miles to the Northward, of the principal gate of the lines.

Leaving most of his forces to manœuvre at day-break before them, he marched with 14,000 Infantry and 500 Pioneers, by a circuitous route, and guided by a Native of the country passed round their right, or East flank: believed by the Travancoreans, to be inaccessible.

At day-light, the guards on the walls, saw the Sultan's army, amongst which shone the bright uniform of his body-guard. But Tippoo was then nine miles away, and at day-break, had turned the lines, with very feeble opposition. Having advanced three miles along them, on their inner side: he commenced making a road, by levelling the rampart, into the ditch: which was about 16 feet wide, and 20 deep.

But the Pioneers were tired, and the work difficult, so Tippoo continued his advance along the rampart, the enemy retreating before him, until at last they made a stand, in a small square building, employed as a magazine, and storehouse; and having drawn a small gun inside, they poured grape upon the advancing Mysoreans.

Tippoo ordered up a new corps, and directed them to take the place, at the point of the bayonet: but just as they were advancing, a party of 20 Travancoreans, poured in a close fire, killed the officer commanding, and caused a panic. The panic became a rout, and the day was lost. The Sultan was carried away in the rush, the rear became the front, and the troops broke over the rampart, into the ditch, to escape, and here 2,000 men are said to have perished. The Sultan fell with the rest, and was lamed for life; his bearers were trodden to death, and his seals, rings, and ornaments, fell to the lot of his enemies, clearly demonstrating his own narrow escape.*

* The Hindus assert, that Tippoo's defeat, was a dispensation on him, for his cruelty in the Annimallis. Knowing that the destruction of a female elephant, is considered one of the worst violation of Hindu laws, for the preservation of animal life, he practised it. Female elephants were chained to the ground by their forefeet, and the Sultan then tried, how deeply he could cut with his sword, through the necks of the poor animals. He then ordered Mussalmen, and lastly even Brahmans, to take their turn, in the amusement. Ganesha was no doubt incensed, and retribution followed.

Tippoo, deeply mortified and enraged, reached his tent in a common dooly, and swore he would not quit the spot, until he had stormed "that contemptible wall." He called in detachments, ordered siege guns from Seringapatam and Bangalore, and for three months and a half, remained awaiting the necessary materials, for making the attack. In April these arrived, and rendered opposition impossible. A series of approaches were made, the ditch was filled, and a breach effected, of nearly $\frac{3}{4}$ of a mile in extent. On his appearing before Cranganore, the garrison fled, but the leading fugitives being put to death, the remainder returned. Tippoo then tried to menace the Dutch, and make them surrender Cranganore: when Col. Hartley, with one regiment of Europeans, (British), and four of Natives, who arrived from Bombay and elsewhere, deeming the post untenable, it was abandoned on the night of May 7th, and occupied by the Sultan the next morning. The Travancore troops, retreated to their own country, and Cochin was open to the advances of the merciless Tippoo, who determined at the head of his army, to demolish the lines, for which purpose he set apart six days. The Sultan himself set the example by striking the first stroke with a pickaxe, courtiers and chiefs followed the fashion, and followers of every denomination were obliged to assist in this work of destruction. The money changer was compelled to leave his hoards, the shopkeeper his goods, to help in breaking down the inanimate wall. Whole regiments of soldiers were marshalled up for this purpose, and some long breaches made.

A little before this time, Tippoo established a second Mysore Collectorate at Trichoor, desecrating the Hindu places of worship, as well as both the public and private schools, inside which, cows were slaughtered to pollute them, the bodies of some of them being afterwards flung into the tank, behind the bathing house of the Rajah of Cochin. He also seized a petty Hindu chief, and numerous others of that persuasion, and forcibly converted them to Mahomedanism.

Trichoor being now established as his head quarters in the rear, and the Travancore lines having been broken through, the Mysorean Army on April 15th, 1790, had extended their outposts as far as Verapoly, the monastery of which was taken by them, and everything they could find either plundered or destroyed. Tippoo, himself with his main body, had reached Alwaye, when he received the astounding news, that *Lord Cornwallis*, at the head of an English army, was rapidly advancing on Seringapatam. No time was to be lost, and collecting all his forces, he immediately left, to protect his captial. The Travancore general, reported him as flying from his valorous Nairs, and regretted he could not overtake him, and sweep him from the earth: but in the mean time, he had the satisfaction of feeling, that he had driven him out of the country!

In April, 1789, the great league between the English, and the Native States of Malabar, was entered into. The latter stipulated to pay the same rate of tribute to the British, that they had done to Tippoo, and to become their vassals, provided the English would recover their dominions, and in future protect them from foreign invaders. On September 26th of this year, Chowghaut was taken by the British forces.

There is no need to follow the course of events here, Tippoo succumbed to British arms, and the Dewan of Travancore, was permitted to make the final settlements, with the native Princes. The Cochin state amongst other places, was ceded to the English, as Tippoo stated, it had been his territory. At Trichoor he had established a Cutcherry, nominated Collectors of the Revenue, over that portion of Cochin exterior to the Travancore lines, and exercised other rights of sovereignty.

It is unnecessary here to describe the awful retribution, to which Tippoo's followers were subjected. Vengeance had long waited, so when it came it was of the most cruel description. The desecrators of the Hindu temples, appear to have been treated the most severely: the tardiest, and most painful deaths, even roasting, or burning by a slow fire, were commonly practised. A chieftainess, on being reproached as one of the foremost in these deeds of vengeance, replied, "those impious monsters, burnt the temples in which our forefathers prayed, and cast out and broke in pieces, the images of our gods which had been objects of adoration from the remotest antiquity."

About September 1790, a treaty to which there is no date, was entered into between the Rajah of Cochin, and the English Government, in which the former promised to throw off allegiance to Tippoo, and become tributary to the East India Company instead;

who on their part, agreed to assist him, in recovering the land wrested away by Tippoo, in 1789, the said Rajah paying a tribute for the first year, of Rupees 70,000 for the second year 80,000, third 90,000, and the fourth 100,000, the same to be continued every year subsequently, in equal quarterly payments. It was expressly stipulated, that he was only to be tributary for those lands, which should be recovered by the British from Tippoo Sultan, "*and with which the Dutch East India Company have no concern,*" and over which he agreed, that the English East India Company shall be for the future acknowledged sovereigns.

By the end of 1791 all the Native States of Malabar had fallen into British hands, and at the treaty of Seringapatam, dated March 16th, 1792, the districts of Calicut and Palghaut, were ceded to the British.

The English Commissioners, in their able report* on Malabar, in 1793, stated that they had concluded their agreement with the Cochin Rajah, who was to pay two lacs of Rupees a year, for the whole of his country, whilst he was repossessed of that portion, taken from him by Tippoo in 1789-90: but many disputes arose, respecting various places, as the Rajah claimed those, taken from him by Hyder Ali, and even other possessions, which his ancestors had lost, upwards of a century previously. In some instances he had a show of right, in others none at all; it appeared probable, that he was at this very time, in correspondence with Tippoo Sultan: and it was discovered, that he had forbidden his people on pain of death, to give the British any information.

The Rajah remained in possession of all his rights, subject to the control of the company, in case of persons complaining of oppression: whilst a British resident was appointed, one of whose duties was to enquire into any case, which might be brought before him.†

---

* *Report of the Commissioners,* dated Ayacotta, October 11th, 1793.

† The various *British Residents* of Travancore and Cochin, have been as follows:—*Col. Macauley,* 1800, until March 1810. *Col. T. Munro,* 1810, to January 1819. *Col. S. McDowall,* 1819, died in November 1820. *Col. D. Newall,* February 1821, until May 1827. *Col. Morison,* 1827 to December 1829. *Lieutenant Colonel E. Cadogan,* (acting) 1829, to June 1834. *T. A. Casamaijor,* Esquire, 1834, to January 1836. *Colonel Fraser,* 1836, to 1838. *Captain Douglass,* (acting,) 1838, to November 1839. *Lieutenant Colonel T. Maclean,* 1839, died in July 1840. *Lieutenant General Cullen,* 1840, to January 1860. *F. N. Maltby, Esquire,* 1860, to May 1862. *W. Fisher, Esquire,* 1862.

It was considered unwise, to attempt introducing British laws and regulations, which were quite insufficient to curb a population, the members of which, walked about, not merely armed, but with their weapons drawn in their hands, ready for immediate assault or, defence, as the interest or passion of the moment, might dictate.

In the beginning of the present century, French councils appear to have been predominant, with the Rajah of Cochin : and in 1802, some persons from the town of Cochin, presented H. H. at Tripoonterah, with a picture of Buonaparte. As the head of this deputation was a Dutchman, and one suspected, or rather known, to be in communication with the French, and surreptitiously supplying them with cargoes of rice, at the Mauritius, a close scrutiny was kept, upon all that occurred. The Dewan now became very troublesome, interfered considerably with British subjects, and even went so far as to arrest several, within the Company's limits.

At the termination of the year 1808, a bitter feeling against the English, appears to have arisen in Travancore : the Dewan of that State, being hostile to British rule, and having acquired such power over the Rajah, that he was kept almost in a state of bondage : the subsidy was left unpaid, and the directions of the Resident, for disbanding some of the Rajah's troops, disregarded. He also appears to have made arrangements, with the Government of Cochin, to assist him in his machinations. No animals could be obtained by the British troops for slaughter, and attacks were made both on the town of Cochin, and the British Cantonment of Quilon. In January 1809, a boat containing bullocks for the troops, was seized near Quilon, and the unfortunate Peon in charge murdered by the natives, as a warning to others, to deter them from attempting to bring in cattle.

Preparations were now made for war, and the troops were directed to annex the Cochin state, and imprison the Dewan of Travancore. But on February 7th, 1809, the Cochin Minister, or Paliat Achen, sued for pardon, promising to surrender all arms, with the exception of two small guns, and five hundred muskets, which were only to be retained, to do honour to the Rajah : and also agreeing, to increase the subsidy, to Rs. 276,037 annually.

He was then ordered to resign his administration, and proceed to Bombay. This he promised to do, but went to Trichoor instead, from which place he was obliged to be conveyed to Bombay by force. After the installation of the new Dewan, Kuniye Krishtnen Menon, a fresh treaty was entered into: all Fortresses, and Military stores, being handed over to the British. But the state still continued unquiet, the new Dewan was restless, and appeared influenced by the same hostile counsels, that had ruined his predecessor. Constant disputes occured, between the Rajah who was friendly to the British, and the Dewan: whilst the whole country was in a discontented, turbulent state.

The Dewan was in consequence removed, and his duties under taken by Col. Munro, the Resident, until a trust-worthy successor could be found. The Rajah was perfectly satisfied with this arrangement, and stated his conviction, that it was the only one capable of restoring order, and reducing the country to tranquility: adding, that he had passed his time in reading the Shastras, and in meditation: that now his days were drawing to a close, and he felt, that he was incapable of personally undertaking these onerous duties: whilst the next in succession, was too young and inexperienced, to do so. He was consequently convinced, that committing his country, temporarily to the care of the British, was only an act of justice to his subjects, whilst at the same time, it was gratifying to himself.

The Resident at once commenced retrenchments by reducing his own allowances, and those of the other European officials: many forms were introduced, especially amongst the unscrupulous and extortionate revenue Collectors: whilst the Brahmans who were eating up the finances of the country, were shorn of some of their emoluments The British government, on August 16th, 1814, gave up all control over Christians, residing in the Cochin and Travancore states: in order that in future, there should be no distinction between them, and their fellow-subjects, as it appeared that there existed, a jealous and antagonistic feeling against them, occasioning many disputes whilst the under Officials treated them harshly, whenever they had an opportunity. As a matter of conciliation to the Christians they were allowed to lay any complaints before the Resident, and Christian Judges were appointed to all Courts of justice. Unfortunately this excellent arrangement, which has acted so beneficially, was met by the Christians in a very hostile spirit: they refused to either submit to the Rajah's authority, or to pay their taxes, and frequent riots and disturbances ensued.

In 1818, the subsidy was reduced to two lacs, with the proviso, that should this sum not be forthcoming at the appointed time, the English are at liberty to annex the country: giving the Rajah and his Family, Rupees 35,000, and one fifth of the surplus revenue: from that period, uninterrupted harmony has prevailed.

His Highness *Rava Virmah* * the Moota Tumbaran, (the designation by which Cochin Rajahs are known,) the present Rajah, ascended the musnud, on May 5th, 1853, when twenty-five years of age.

The succession descends in the female line, the eldest nephew by the sister's side, being the heir to the musnud. Should there be none. such, the eldest female Tumbaran, ascends as Regent, until the birth of a son in the family. Females may be adopted, to carry on the line of succession, should there be any danger of its extinction The members of the present Royal family, are as follows:—*Sisters* of the Rajah, H. H. *Coonjee Amah* Tumbaran, born in 1814. H. H. *Coonjee Pillah* Tumbaran, born in 1822. H. H. *Coonjee Kava* Tumbaran, born in 1832, and H. H. *Mungoo* Tumbaran, born in 1839.

Nephews and Heirs, H. H. *Rama Wurmah*, Ellia Rajah of Cochin, born May 11th, 1835. H. H. *Veera Kerala Wurmah*, first prince, born in 1845. H. H. *Rama Wurmah*, second prince, born in 1848. H. H. *Veera Kerala Wurmah*, third prince, born in 1850. H. H. *Rama Wurmah*, fourth prince, born in 1852. H. H. *Ravee Wurmah*, fifth prince, born in 1853. H. H. *Veera Kerala Wurmah*, sixth prince, born in 1854, and H. H. *Ravee Wurmah*, seventh prince, born in 1859.

The Rajahs of Cochin, for the last three centuries, have been as follows. *Veera Kerala* died 28th April, 1549: Rajah and two Princes slain in a battle with the Samorin January 27th, 1565: the

* In olden times, the Cochin Rajah, had the token of unlimited power carried before him: consisting of the branch of a cocoanut tree, the lower end of which, was bound with a bandage, leaving the top quite free. Petty Princes, if subject to any higher authority, were obliged to have the branch bound at each end.

next Rajah, killed in battle at Poodiakavoo, February 10th, 1565: A Rajah, (who went to Benares,) died May 3rd, 1601: *Veera Kerala,* died April 25th, 1615: *Ravi Virmah,* died September 30th, 1624: the next at Cochin, July 11th, 1637: his successor at Trichoor, February 2nd, 1645: the succeeding one, at Irinyalacooday, July 4th, 1646: *Veerya Arya,* at Cochin, January 27th, 1665: the next, on June 1st, 1697: his successor at Tirroovullah, November 22nd, 1697: the next at Trichoor, October 25th, 1722: another, on April 19th, 1742: *Rama Vurmah,* died at Cooreckaad, January 7th, 1746: the next, at Tripoonterah, January 1st, 1750: the next, at Cochin, August 16th, 1760: his successor, at Tripoonterah, September 24th, 1775: the next of small pox, August 13th, 1790: *Virolam* Tumbaran about 1798: *Rama Vurmah,* died at Trichoor, September 28th, 1805: *Rama Vurmah,* died at Vellarapully, January 14th, 1809: *Veera Kerala,* died at Tripoonterah, August 6th, 1828: *Rama Vurmah,* died at Tripoonterah, November 8th, 1837: *Rama Vurmah,* died at Irinyalacooday, 31st May, 1842: *Rama Vurmah,* died at Trichoor, July 10th, 1851: *Veera Kerala,* died of small pox, at Benares, February 22nd, 1853*.

The reign of His Highness, *Rava Virmah,* the present Rajah, has been marked by a series of reforms; the general prosperity of his subjects, is now nearly on a level with that of the people residing in the neighbouring British possessions. He has also shown his wisdom, in not adopting the English abolition of compulsory labour, a law doubtless very beneficial, in large towns like Calcutta, Madras, and Bombay; but hardly suited to the wilds of Malabar, where combination takes the place of competition.

The laws for the Administration of Justice, have since 1833, been much the same as in the British territory: perhaps in some cases not quite so tardy in obtaining decisions: but in others, especially criminal proceedings, dragging over a long and weary course of time. The prisoner awaits his sentence, sometimes for years, and then at last meets the doom of death; such protracted misery, is happily unknown in the British territories. A singular custom has

* The above list, is compiled from one furnished by T. Shungoony Menon Esq., the *Dewan of Cochin.* Adoption occurred A. D. 1689 according to the *Dutch records* of Cochin.

prevailed from olden times of never putting either women or Brahmans to death; no matter how horrible a murder, or even a series of them they may have committed, they escape with perpetual imprisonment, as their heaviest punishment. In prison, the difference between those who are confined for murder, and others, is; that the former, have irons on their arms, as well as legs.

The ancient laws respecting judicial cases, now obsolete, are interesting, from being entirely the result of Native legislation, and carried out by Native officials: a short summary of them is therefore given. Hindus were formerly tried, according to the laws laid down in the Shastras; Mahomedans, by those in the Koran; and Christians by persons of their own creed. The Hindus being the most numerous class, and that of the ruling powers, are referred to in the following account :—

Courts of Justice, were nominally open at all hours, and on most days, being only closed on some few holidays. The evidence of women, slaves, and persons of infamous character, was inadmissible. Chogans being comprehended under the designation of slaves, the evidence of what is now the largest proportion of the community, was then unavailable. The laws were founded, on the dogmas of the Brahmanical faith, and no independent code appears to have existed. Questions involving religious, or moral differences, were judged by a council of Brahmans, with the High Priest at their head: the Rajah also had a seat with them, and the last vote.

The *Adigarhi* or local Magistrate, at times made a circuit, attended by four soldiers: and punished, certain minor offenders on the spot. Cases of a more heinous description, were tried in a species of Court of Justice, in the house of the Magistrate, which was invariably near a temple, some of the Brahmans being always members of the Court: here cognizance was taken, of all civil and criminal affairs, except those against the laws of caste, and morality. These Courts were under the supervision of the Northern, and Southern Lieutenants, (*Karriakars*) of the Kingdom, who acted according to orders received from the Rajah through the head Karriakar. Robbery was rather rare offence, but falsehood, and perjury, so common, that torture was frequently found necessary, *to induce witnesses to state the facts, or prisoners to confess their crimes.*

The most heinous offences, and hardened offenders, were punished by death. If the criminal were a Nair, persons of his own caste, had the privilege of despatching him: if, of a lower station, that office fell to the executioner, and was almost invariably effected by hanging.

Death was decreed, for slaying a man of a higher caste, killing a cow, committing treason, exciting insurrections, or wounding so severely as to draw blood. The same sentence was passed on any low caste man, who should form a fugitive connection, with the wife of a Brahman: on any person robbing either a temple, or the Rajah's treasury; committing great, or highway robbery: breaking into houses, or being guilty of petty larceny, for the third time. Murderers, if of low caste, were either hung, or suspended by *a hook through the chin.* No sentence of death was put in execution, until the culprit had himself acknowledged its justice : but if he took too long in reflecting on the subject, torture was employed to convince him.

Should a murderer have absconded, the corpse of the victim, was burnt inside the house of the former, whose relations had to provide for the family of the dead, during the period of mourning, which lasted about a fortnight. The murderer was now outlawed, and every one who met him, was justified in slaying him.

Nairs were not always subject to the above laws. If a Nair killed any person, of a lower caste than himself without the Rajah's order to do so, he was fined Rs. 400, and was obliged to promise, not to commit a similar offence, or in case of doing so, to suffer death without a murmur. If he wounded another, he had to pay his expenses, until he was cured : but if two persons were both wounded when fighting, each had to maintain himself.

Next to the punishment of death, that of slavery, was the most severe. It was principally reserved for females, reprieved from execution. Should the conduct of a Brahmanee woman, have been light with a low caste man, she was tried by Brahmans, and if found guilty, became the Rajah's slave. A low caste woman, allowing any improper intimacy with a Brahman, was sold to the Moplahs.

Incorrect Brahmanee women, were punished, by loss of caste : as also, were Brahmans, for theft, or eating with those of inferior caste: and though they were, and still are permitted to form fugitive connections with Nair women, and act as Fathers to their families: they were not, neither are they now allowed to form intimacies, with those of a lower grade.

Minor offences, were less severely sentenced: thus, the penalty for petty thefts, was the restoration of the article, and a certain number of lashes on the back. The extent of the punishment, being increased, according to the number of times, the offence was committed; in some instances, mutilation of a finger, or a hand, was inflicted. The Rajah of Cochin, in 1793, reported, that in his State, "if any one commit a small theft, he is to be kept for six "months, or a year, in confinement: after being so exemplarily "punished, and a fine taken from him, a little of his flesh, or his "nose, is cut off, and he is set at liberty."

At one period, drunkards, and persons who sold arrack, opium, or bhang, were condemned to lose their property. Smugglers, especially of pepper, were punished by the loss of their noses and ears; but at the end of the last century, this sentence was commuted to imprisonment. Probably these evaders of the revenue, carried on the same system, as the smugglers of the present day: who, in British Cochin, are divided into three strong gangs: one of which, always proceeds by the sea: another by the backwater: and a third by land. They first endeavour to pass by bribery, and consequently are rarely obliged to resort to force. It appears, that during the last eighty years, Natives in this part of India, have been impaled alive, for selling cows to Europeans.

All matters of a religious nature, were determined by a council of Brahmans: as were also subjects relating to marriages, the settlement of daughters, and every species of offence against caste; as well as hatred, enmity, assaults in which blood had not been drawn, and quarrels between parents and children. In some of these cases, in which decision was no easy matter, the parties occasionally submitted to trials by ordeal.* These were of several kinds, and will be described, amongst the *manners and customs.*

* A late Governor of Madras, about 1860, when making a tour of the Presidency, was expected at Tanjore. The Brahmans accordingly met, and agreed to petition, that *trials by ordeal* should be re-established, such being a part of

When a person was to be arrested for debt, the Judge sent an official, who drew a circle on the ground with a stick, around the prisoner, charging him, in both the Rajah's name, and the Judges', not to quit it, until his creditor was satisfied, either by payment or security. Breaking this circle, was punished by death, or outlawry If this plan for enforcing payment did not succeed, a sharp stone was placed on the prisoner's head, and heavier ones continually piled above it, so that in time, if he refused to satisfy the claim, his skull was broken in, and death ensued. If the debtor were inside his house, a wand of green twigs, was placed in the door way, or bushes of green shrubs, were fastened to a stick, and secured on the door, which precluded any one from crossing the threshold.

The Judicial Department at the present time is composed as follows:—for *Civil Justice*, one 1st Judge, a Hindu: one 2nd Judge, an European: and one Shastry. There are two Zillah Courts, one at Ernacollum, the other at Trichoor: the composition of each of which is the same. Though a European or Eurasian, always enters as 2nd Judge, he is eligible for promotion to the higher post: but in that case, the office of 2nd Judge must be held by a Hindu. There are two Moonsiff's Courts, one at Chittoor, the other at Angikaimul.

Criminal Justice.—In police cases, the Dewan is Chief Magistrate, and the Talook Tassildars are Police Officers. Should the crime have been a serious one, the case is referred to the Zillah Criminal Court, which is empowered, to inflict corporal punishment to the extent of 36 stripes with a rattan, or to fine as high as the sum of Rupees 200; and also, to take security, to the amount of Rs. 500, for one year. Any cases believed to merit heavier punishments, than the above, are committed to the Sessions' Court at Ernacollum, which is presided over by one of the 2nd Appeal Court Judges. Here they have power to inflict 48 stripes, to imprison for 7 years with hard labour, and to take security for good conduct for three years, to the amount of Rs. 500. The Sessions' Court can refer cases to the

---

their religion: and a proclamation had stated, that the various religions were to be exercised without restraint. Checking ordeals, had therefore been a hardship, under which their religion was still suffering, and consequently an injustice: and they prayed for the removal of the prohibition on them. Subsequently other councils prevailed, and the petition was not presented.

Appeal Court, when they are tried by the two Judges, and the Shastry. The power of this Court is unlimited, but no heavier punishment than 14 years' imprisonment, can be carried out, without the sanction of the Rajah, and sentences of death, must be also confirmed by the British Resident, acting under the orders of the Government of Madras. There are two jails, one at Ernacollum, and the other at Trichoor; and they each, generally contain, about eighty prisoners.

Slavery had been from the earliest ages, an institution, both in Travancore and Cochin, and was only abolished in 1854. It is not improbable, that many of these miserably debased slaves, are still unaware of the change in their condition, and do not understand that they cannot now be legally sold as cattle, or made over with the estate, upon which they work. " This measure was never at-" tended with any advantage, even to the poor slaves, for whose " benefit the concession was intended. Deprived of even the most " distant contact with their high caste proprietors, and prevented " from appearing in places of public resort, they are confined by " force of circumstances, to their swampy fields, on a level with the " brute creation. To such a class, freedom is no boon." In 1854, there were 6,589 slaves in the Cochin State, or including soil slaves, above fifty thousand, more than one-sixth of the entire population.

In course of time, the revenue has considerably changed, wherein, the reforms of the Mahomedan conquerors, have no doubt effected much good. To prove a sovereign right over a territory, it is necessary to bring evidence, that the person has received, "either customs, " or Poorespandrum, (the essential attributes of dominion in Mala-" bar,) for the country." Previous to the Mussulman invasion, the Brahmans and Nairs, were the only landowners, and large landholders in Malabar, with the exception of the Rajahs, who had some estates for their maintenance, and certain religious establishments were likewise thus provided for. The revenue of the Malabar Rajahs, was not at first a fixed one, as they called upon their vassals for military service. A land tax was unknown. Extraordinary emergencies called for extraordinary contributions, but these were rarely exacted, except to meet a foreign invader.

As times rolled on, another system gradually supervened; the Rajahs levied from the lands, (exempting those belonging to the temples, and to Brahmans,) a settled revenue in money, or kind, equal to one-fifth of the produce. They also received the crops from the crown lands, and the customs on trade, and import and export duties: as well as fines for offences, and protection money, or a kind of black mail, levied on the subjects of neighbouring Princes: also the estates of all (with the exception of Brahmans,) who died without heirs: and a species of poll tax, upon the living. Presents had also to be given, at the two great festivals of Ornum and Vishoo. All precious metals or stones which might be discovered were claimed as *Royalties*, as also elephants when alive, or their tusks when found dead. Cardamoms, teak, jack and blackwood trees: ebony, bamboos, honey, and wax: the skins of tigers, the fins of sharks, and the wrecks of stranded vessels. In the territories of the Samorin, (but whether also in Cochin is unknown,) a certain share of the estates of all who died, went to the crown.

At a still later period, another plan was enforced, and in addition to the articles named as Royalties, and the presents received at the feasts of Vishoo and Ornum, about half the crops from the land, were claimed as the property of Government. The farmer received his rice for seed, and the produce was considered to increase ten times: five and a half shares of which went to the cultivator, or tenant, and the remaining four and a half were divided between the Government, and the Brahman landlord, the first having two-thirds, the latter one-third. In betel-nut, pepper, cocoanut, and jack fruit, the cultivator had only half: because there was not much trouble in looking after them.

In 1762* the Rajah of Cochin levied duties on the following scale, around the Fort of Cochin: one-eighth of cocoanut, and fruit bearing trees: three-tenths of the paddy; the cocoanut trees were estimated at two poothens, (one anna, eight pie,) rent: betel-nut trees at a quarter of a poothen; jacktrees at eight poothens: but this was not paid upon freehold property, which was untaxed. There were great complaints, that the Revenue Officers exacted too much, whilst they on their part declared that they could collect nothing. The

* According to a treaty, between Mr. Van Angelbeck, Governor of Cochin and the Rajah of Cochin, dated, October 11th, 1762. *Government Records of Cochin.* M. S. S.

Rajah also claimed tolls on the backwater, upon rice going into Cochin, for which purpose he had chowkies at Angikaimul, Vypeen, Balghatty, and Paloorte: but produce which had once paid custom, was exempt from further toll.

Hyder for the short time his people held Trichoor, and the surrounding territory, would allow no land to go untaxed, not even those set aside for the maintenance of the temples, or other places of worship. Tippoo in his turn, followed the same course, and subsequently destroyed all pepper vines, and cocoanut trees, as he believed, such a proceeding would keep away European merchants from Malabar. This wanton destruction, was carried to such an extent, that in the Calicut district, in 1793, not one pepper vine in fifty, was found standing, and the destruction of cocoanut trees, had also been enormous.

About the year 1778, large tracts of land were cleared, reclaimed and planted by private persons, in the Cochin State: they holding, the ground rent free, until the trees began to bear, when a small ground rent was imposed: because according to the Hindu laws of Cochin, it is wicked to part with land entirely, excepting to a Brahman. This was continued until 1793, when the Rajah after consultation with the Dutch, on the best means of raising money, to pay his subsidy, placed a tax of 12½ per cent. on the produce of the trees, and 30 per cent. on that of rice cultivation. In 1802, money was again urgently required, and the Rajah resumed all these lands, which however owing to the indifference of the officials, and the damage often wantonly perpetrated, by the late owners, soon again became waste: consequently it was judged advisable, to re-farm them out, at a lower rate, than in 1793.

After a time, the *Sircar*, or Native State, found that it was a loser, by receiving rent in produce, as in the event of bad seasons, it obtained nothing; so a fixed amount, payable in money, was determined upon, computed according to the productiveness of the land, and the value of the rice. In 1858, a revision of the value of the measure of rice, was made, the cost of which had much risen: this increased the revenue, by 20 per cent.

The land revenue, of the Cochin State, for forty-eight years, or from 1812 to 1859-60, has risen from 320,000, to Rupees 474,147.

There is one curious exemption from house taxation, a Brahman cannot be taxed for the dwelling in which he resides.

Up to the year 1836, transit duties were levied upon all articles, which passed from one Talook to another : a most irritating system, both to Merchants, and Travellers, and consequently obstructive to trade, Chowkies were placed in all directions, and Peons stationed in them, to examine the boats : they levied a species of black mail on the boatmen, and detained them as long as they liked. This injudicious tax was abolished, and in 1847, the Customs were exclusively frontier and sea-duties : whilst British produce going from one British possession to another passed toll free. The yearly revenue of the Cochin State from 1800 to 1811 was four and three quarter lacs of rupees : to 1821, seven and a quarter : to 1831, seven and a half : to 1841, seven and three quarters : to 1851, nine : and to 1859, nine and a quarter.

The largest source of revenue, were the monopolies, consisting of tobacco and salt : the latter of which, was originated in 1810. Cardamoms and pepper are so little cultivated, that monopolies on them have never realised sums in Cochin, as in the Travancore State. The chief monopolies therefore consist in the purchase of tobacco and salt, which are disposed of, at advanced rates to the people.*

Many little vexatious duties, have been swept away. In 1847, that on the second crop of paddy, which amounted annually to Rs. 9,676 was given up, as also some other small imposts : the selling price of tobacco was reduced one-sixth, and also again another sixth in the year 1852. Amongst the items of expenditure, there is one which appears curious : viz., that for feeding Brahmans, but this is regarded as a religious duty. The expenditure for public works, [excluding the last three years,] has been annually as much as half a lac of Rupees.

In 1840, when General Cullen became Resident, the Revenue from all sources was 7 lacs. The cocoanut trees increased, and the productions of the country augmented so much, that no additional burthens were required, and taxes could be remitted. On his retirement in 1860, after a most prosperous administration, the revenue was 9

* Whilst these pages were going through the Press, the tobacco monopoly was abolished, August 15th, 1862 : and a license tax, imposed in lieu of it.

lacs, whilst a reserve of ten lacs, had accumulated in the Government securities.

It is unnecessary to enumerate the various reforms which have successively been instituted. At Ernacollum, a small English School for 40 boys has been established, another at Trichoor for 20, and a third at Muttencherry for the Jews. There are six vernacular schools maintained by the Sircar in different Talooks, irrespective of about 300 private ones. Hospitals have been erected; and subscriptions to charities have formed a part of the policy of this enlightend state. A Conservator of Forests, has been appointed, and lands let for coffee plantations. A road was completed a few years ago by the Rajah, at the expense of the State, to connect Trichoor with Palghaut, so that cotton could be brought down to Cochin for export, from the Coimbatore district, and screws were erected by traders in the town for preparing it for shipment. This road was then continued from Trichoor to Kurriapudnam, about 20 miles of Cochin, and from whence water communication is open at all seasons.

Following up improvements to the present day: the Rajah with the desire of advancing the interests of his country, has drawn out his investments, and is making a noble bridge at Shoranoor, to connect his territory with the railway. The Ghauts will no longer be a barrier between Cochin and the rest of the world, and with the increased facilities of mingling with their fellow-men which will be afforded the people of this state, it is to be hoped, that many local customs may soon pass into oblivion, and only be found amongst the records of things gone by.

CHAPTER III.

THE PORTUGUESE IN COCHIN.

Early voyagers to India—Bartholomew Diaz—Don Vasca deGama arrives at Calicut—Visits Samorin—Returns to Europe—Cabral takes a fleet to Calicut and bombards the town—Sails to Cochin and establishes a factory—De Gama returns, acts most inhumanly at Calicut—Proceeds to Cochin—Fort erected at Cochin—Pacheco Governor—Brutality of Gonzalo Vaz—Albuquerque's wars—First Minister of Finance despatched to Cochin and disastrous results—De Gama returns to Cochin where he dies—DeSousa reduces the pay of the Military, so they refuse to fight—Dutch begin to appear in India—Government employ and honours publicly sold—Dutch take Cochin.

In the middle of the fifteenth century, Europeans began to speculate on the existence of unknown lands, and enquire into the produce of distant climes. Rewards stimulated the adventurous, America and other regions were discovered, and inexhaustible wealth appeared within the grasp, of which-ever nation should prove boldest in the search. There was one peninsula reputed to possess fabulous riches, its shores were believed to be rolling in gold, its hills to be enriched with precious stones, and its land everywhere yielding pepper, ginger, and other valuable spices: this wonderful region was India, said to be peopled by a dusky and effeminate race, who though timorous of strangers, were ready to barter, their rich natural and artificial productions, for simple inexpensive articles of European manufacture. Columbus believed that India could be reached by steering westward, but his maps were rather in error, respecting longitude, and it has been asserted, that whilst in search of it, he stumbled on America.

In this emulation for discoveries, and thirst for gain, which suddenly seized on the nations of Europe, Portugal bore a very prominent part, whilst its king Henry, stood pre-eminent amongst the Princes of Christendom, his greatest ambition being to open a route to India by sea, with which view he spared neither trouble, nor expense: but, although the various expeditions sent out by him, made many discoveries along the coasts of Africa, he was not destined to obtain the object of his wishes. About the year 1486, John II, who had added to his other titles, that of, "Lord of Guinea," applied to, and obtained from the Pope, a grant of all countries, lying to the East, which should be discovered by the Portuguese, or even by any other nation. All Christian Kings and Princes were prohibited from intruding on such lands, which were bestowed by his Holiness, in perpetuity, on the Portuguese, who were directed to place a stone cross, six feet high, on any spot they might discover: whilst to prevent mistakes, it was to be engraved with the name of the discoverer, and the arms of the reigning King.

The first Adventurer who achieved any great result, was *Bartholomew Diaz*, who in 1486 succeeded in rounding the southern extremity of Africa, which he designated "the Cape of Storms." But whilst congratulating himself, upon the honour and glory to which he should attain, as the discoverer of the long wished for route to India, the prize eluded his grasp, for owing to a failure of provisions he was compelled to return.

The Monarch's hopes were greatly raised, on hearing of this partial success, and he consequently changed the name of "the Cape of Storms," to that of "the Cape of Good Hope."

Another expedition was forthwith planned, and volunteers called for, from all the sea-port Towns; but various causes, prevented its being carried into effect, until ten years later.

A suitable Commander was during this time nominated, in *Don Vasca de Gama*, who was appointed Admiral and General of the Expedition. He was a man of noble birth, whose indomitable will knew not fear, whose opinion brooked not control, besides being justly celebrated, for his courage, and experience, on the seas.

The Squadron under De Gama's command, consisted of three vessels; the Angel Gabriel, the San Raphael, and a Caravel; besides a provision ship, which accompanied them only as far as a place subsequently known, as St. Blaze, where she was burnt, and the provisions, distributed amongst the other vessels. The complement of the fleet, consisted of 148 men. This expedition occasioned great excitement, it was regarded by many, as tempting Providence; and it's total annihilation, confidently predicted.

But Vasca de Gama, was not a man to be deterred by such prognostications, he took leave of the King, and accompanied by the Captains of the other two vessels under his command, Paulo de Gama, and Nicholas Coello, he left Lisbon for the place of embarkation. They were preceded by some monks, of "Our Lady of Belem," chanting prayers for their safety, and followed by crowds of the inhabitants, weeping, and lamenting the departure of relatives, and friends, whom they considered doomed to certain destruction.

On July 8th, 1497, this little fleet, destined to immortal fame, bore away from the shore. The Cape De Verd Islands, having been appointed as the place of rendezvous in case of separation.

Bartholomew Diaz accompanied the Squadron, in a small Caravel, until August 3rd, when he returned, to report progress to the King. On November 20th, the Cape was safely doubled. About this time very stormy weather was encountered, on which the sailors and the pilots mutinied, and demanded an immediate return to Portugal. The officers, however, stood by De Gama: the ringleaders were seized and ironed, when the remainder submitted, and the fleet proceeded on its voyage. On March 25th, they arrived at St. Blaze, where the provision ship was destroyed.

In March 1498 at Mozambique, a pilot was procured, to take the fleet across to India, but he carried it to Bombaza, with the intention of delivering the Christians, into the hands of the Moors. Fortunately, however, at the entrance of the barbour, the Admiral's ship ran aground, and the pilot dreading a discovery of his villainy, jumped overboard, and swam to a Moorish vessel, which was lying at no great distance from the Fleet. This first aroused De Gama's suspicion of treachery, and being determined to know the truth, without delay, he commenced torturing some Mozambique Moors, whom he had on board, and at length extorted a confession from them, by pouring boiling hog's lard upon the most sensitive parts of their bodies: in the mean time, the remainder of the prisoners, threw themselves into the sea, and managed to effect their escape. The crews then joined in singing the "Salve Regina," in gratitude for their wonderful deliverance from almost certain destruction, at the conclusion, of which, the sick are said, to have miraculously recovered. When the flood tide set in, De Gama's vessel floated off, and the fleet sailed away, reaching Melinda, on April 21st; where they were hospitably received by the King, who provided them with a pilot, to take them to Calicut. They again set sail on April 21st, and on May 18th sighted India, anchoring before Calicut, on May 20th, 1498.

The enthusiasm of the crews, at the sight of the long wished for shores was unbounded, and festivity and rejoicing, were the order of the day. It was not long however, before several boats arrived from the shore, filled with fishermen, curious to ascertain, from whence came these strange looking vessels, and with what object? Whilst De Gama and his companions were equally astonished, at the appearance of the nut brown Natives, whose scanty clothing did not, they thought promise a rich population.

Calicut was at that time, the principal town on the Western Coast of India, and the residence of the Samorin, the King of the spice country, who although, a Hindu, was reputed to be an extremely tolerant Monarch, permitting the free exercise of all religions, in his territory. It was also the principal place of resort, for Merchants from Arabia, many of whom had settled there, and were carrying on a flourishing trade, in spices, and other valuable commodities.

The Samorin was a very wealthy and powerful prince, who boasted of being able to bring 30,000 men into the field, at a day's notice, and 100,000 in three days. De Gama on leaving Portugal, had been permitted to carry with him, some condemned convicts, with a view of employing them if necessary, on any dangerous enterprises, in which he did not like to peril the lives of his own men. He now ordered one of these felons, to return with the fishermen, in order to see what reception Europeans might expect, from the Natives. On landing, the convict was immediately surrounded by the inhabitants of the place, who were eager to gaze at one of these strange unknown foreigners, who had so unexpectedly visited their shores. As they could not understand his language, but supposed him to be a Moor, they took him to the house of some Merchants from Tunis, one of whom named Bontaybo, immediately recognized him as a Portuguese, and exclaimed in Spanish, "*D***l take you, what brought you here.*"

On learning that they had come by sea from Portugal, "in search of Christians and spices," he was greatly astonished, and inclined to be very sceptical, asking, why, if this route really were practicable, other nations had not also availed themselves of it? But at length becoming convinced of the truth of the convict's statements, he returned with him to the fleet.

On reaching the Admiral's ship, Bontaybo saluted him with these words, "good luck! good luck! many rubies, many emeralds! Thou "art bound to give God thanks for having brought thee, where "there is abundance of all sorts of spices, precious stones, and "many other riches of the world."

On hearing these good tidings in the Spanish language, the sailors are said to have shed tears of joy. A long conference then ensued, between the Moor, and De Gama, respecting the Samorin, the country, trade, &c., which determined the latter on immediately despatching an embassage to that prince, reporting his arrival, and soliciting an interview.

Bontaybo undertook to act as Interpreter, and two Portuguese accompanied him to the Monarch, who was then at Ponany. They were graciously received by the Samorin, who appeared gratified at receiving an embassage, in the name of a Christian King, of such a distant country, soliciting his friendship and alliance. He listened attentively to the account of their voyage, and dismissed them with a message to De Gama, to the effect, that he heartily welcomed him and his people to his dominions, and would be happy to see him whenever he pleased. He also sent a Pilot, to bring the vessels safely into the harbour, at a place below Calicut, called Pandarane (Beypoor?) but the Admiral deemed it more prudent, to anchor his fleet outside the bar at that place.

The Cutwal of Calicut, with many of the nobility, and principal persons of the State, assembled with 200 armed Nairs, ready to escort De Gama, to the Samorin: but the Admiral excused himself for that night, from accompanying them. He then called a council of his officers, and communicated his intention of visiting the Samorin on the following day. But they were all, especially his brother, very averse to his perilling his valuable life, amongst those of whose real disposition towards him, he knew nothing; pointing out, that in the event of his being murdered, none of them would ever succeed in returning to Europe, and that the benefits of their great discovery would be lost.

But De Gama's resolution was not to be shaken, and he indignantly replied to their remonstrances, "What! shall we return to "Europe, having merely accomplished the voyage, and anchored off "the shores of India? Shall we after having been invited to visit "the prince, sneak away like cowards, without spices, or any other "proofs, of our great success? No! If I fall, it is the will of God: "if I return not in three days, set sail, and steer for Europe."

Accordingly on the following day, he landed with his Interpreter, Secretary, and ten others, leaving strict orders, that during his absence no one should on any pretext, be allowed to board either of the vessels. The boat which took them to the shore, was gaudily decked with flags, and had a well armed crew. Orders were issued, that a fully manned boat, should lie near the shore, until De Gama's return, to keep up communications with the fleet: and that Paulo De Gama, should temporarily assume the post of Captain General. On landing, they were received with great respect by the Cutwal, and others.

De Gama, and the Cutwal, then got into Tonjons, and started for Calicut, stopping half way for refreshments, where the party partook of boiled fish, rice, ghee, mangoes, and figs. They then embarked in two vessels lashed together, (evidently a jungar:) on their way, they stopped at a Pagoda, into which they were admitted, believing it, as they asserted, to be a Christian Church: they allowed the Brahmans, to sprinkle them with holy water, and to mark their foreheads with sandal wood, and they then prostrated themselves before the idols which they mistook for rude representations of the Virgin Mary and other Saints. But one of the party more scrupulous than the rest first called out, "If these be devils, I worship not them, but God!"

At Calicut, they entered another Pagoda, and again worshipped the images! an immense crowd had assembled to see the strangers, and at one time entirely barred their progress. But at this spot they were fortunately met by the Cutwal's brother, with 3000 Nairs who conducted them on to Calicut, preceded by every description of noisy music, trumpets, drums, and horns, varied by occasional discharges from a camel gun. They reached the palace at 5 P. M.

At the entrance they were received by some of the chief men, who conducted them through four courts, at the gate of each of which, ten Peons were stationed, armed with silver mounted staves. At the last entrance, they were met by the chief Brahman, and after having embraced him, were ushered into the Samorin's presence. On their admission, the pressure of the mob, to obtain a sight of the King, became so great, that many persons were trodden to death. The hall in which they were received, was of a semi-circular form, surrounded by seats, raised one above another; the floor was covered with a carpet of green velvet.

The Samorin, who was of advanced years, and tall in stature, was reclining on a low couch, covered with a cloth of white silk, embroidered with gold, and placed on a dais or raised part of the floor: over his head, was a rich canopy. He wore a cap adorned with precious stones and pearls; with jewels in his ears, and a jacket of fine white muslin, with buttons of large pearls, the button holes of which were worked with gold thread. His dress, or lower cloth, reached from the waist to the knees, his fingers and toes were covered with jewels, and his arms with rich bangles. On a table close by, stood a shallow gold basin on a gold stand, containing betel for him to chew with the nut of the areca palm, &c., during the reception. On the ground was a gold spittoon for his use, and near him, a gold fountain for water. All natives whilst in his presence, held their right hands before their mouths, lest their breath might pollute the monarch.

De Gama on entering, made three very profound salaams, as did also his suite. He was then requested to seat himself on the steps of the dais: and water was produced, for the party to wash their hands in, but some of them being thirsty, drank the pure fluid. The Samorin then sent for figs, and fruit, for them to eat, and laughed most immoderately at them whilst so engaged, on which De Gama becoming nettled, declined entering into any conference, unless conducted into a more private room. Consequently, the Samorin, De Gama, the chief Brahman, the betel server, and the Interpreter, withdrew into an inner apartment, where they had an amicable conversation, and agreed upon an alliance of friendship between Portugal and Malabar.

The next day, De Gama who was much elated by his apparent success, decided on sending the Samorin the present he had brought for that purpose, viz., four scarlet cloaks, six hats, four branches of coral, and twelve boxes each containing seven brass vessels, a chest of sugar, two barrels of oil, and a cask of honey. The Cutwal who had been asked to look over these various articles, before their presentation, enquired on seeing them, whether De Gama intended to insult the Samorin, by such a trivial offering, almost the whole of which, could easily be purchased in the Bazaar,* and informed him that nothing but gold could be presented, and that all strangers admitted to the honour of an interview, gave gifts proportioned to their rank, and importance. De Gama pleaded, the uncertainty in which he had been in, of ever reaching India, as the reason why, he had not brought costly gifts from his King, and promised that on his return, this should be remedied, by an immediate despatch of valuable and princely presents. But the Cutwal was not to be appeased, they parted in anger, and were never after reconciled.

The Moors were far from being gratified by the Samorin's reception of these European interlopers, being well aware, that should the Portuguese establish a trade with India, their profits would rapidly diminish. This conviction was strengthened by a prophecy current amongst them, that a vessel would come from a far country, bringing the conquerors of India, the destroyers of the Mahomedans, and the enemies of the Hindus. They accordingly assembled in consultation, on the best means of frustrating De Gama, and decided on representing to some chief officers about the Samorin, that De Gama was merely a pirate and no ambassador, and by his having attacked vessels, during his voyage to India, clearly proved his object was not peace and friendship. They bribed the Cutwal to assist them, and he in conjunction with some others, laid the matter before the King, who was very much perplexed, as to the best course to pursue.

De Gama was now kept waiting two days, before the Samorin

* It is certainly a curious coincidence, that all these articles, are now procurable in any Bazaar; and probably were so, at that time, whilst they do not much resemble European gifts.

would grant him a second interview, and even then was detained for three hours, before he could obtain an audience, from which ten out of his twelve followers, were excluded. The Samorin then demanded a present, but appeared satisfied with De Gama's explanation, merely requesting the gift of a gilt image of the Virgin, from the Admiral's ship: which however he declined parting with. He was then desired to show his letters, and produced two, one in Arabic, and the other in Portuguese, to the effect, that the King of Portugal, being anxious to form a treaty of friendship and alliance, with the Samorin, had despatched his dearly beloved, Vasca De Gama, to negotiate it. The translation of these, caused rather a better feeling and De Gama received permission, to go on board his vessel, to bring specimens of his merchandize.

But various impediments were still thrown in his way, and he was detained at Pandarane, unable to procure a boat, as the Cutwal demanded, that he would order his ships, closer in land, when he would be allowed to depart: but this he firmly declined doing, and hostile intentions towards him then became very apparent. He was detained a prisoner for two days, at the end of which time, the Cutwal sent on board, for some of the merchandize, which he was anxious to see, and De Gama, leaving two Factors on shore, to look after the goods, was permitted to return to his vessel, which he determined not again to quit.

The Portuguese found they could not sell their goods, as the Moors effectually prevented the Natives from buying, besides which they openly insulted them, and on seeing any of them, contemptuously spat upon the ground, saying, "Portugal, Portugal," but no notice was taken of their enmity. On March 10th, De Gama sent the Samorin a present, of a number of scarfs, and corals, by his Factor: with a message, stating, that he intended returning to Europe very shortly, and would be happy to take an Ambassador, from the Samorin, to the King of Portugal. But he refused to receive, or even to look at the present, and gave orders under penalty of death, that no intercourse should be held with the strangers. But on August 19th, six of the chief men, came by stealth on board the Admiral's ship, accompanied by fifteen followers: they were all detained as prisoners, and offered in exchange, for the two Portuguese on shore. This plan succeeded, and the latter were sent on board the next day, with a letter from the Samorin, to the King of Portugal, which was written, or rather engraved on an ollah, (leaf), and was as follows: "Vasca De Gama, "a gentleman of thy house, came to my country, of whose arrival I "was very glad. In my country, there is abundance, of cinnamon, "cloves, pepper, and precious stones. The commodities I wish to pro- "cure from your country, are silver, gold, coral, and scarlet." The headmen were then sent back, and with them a stone pillar, the mark of Portuguese possession, and sovereignty: but as the merchandize had neither been returned, nor paid for, the fifteen Natives, were retained as hostages for it. Bontaybo now come on board, and stated that he had been kept in prison, under the impression that he was a Portuguese spy, who had been despatched to India, to give an account of its riches. He stated that he feared to reland, lest he should be put to death, so De Gama offered him a passage to Europe, which he gladly accepted. De Gama shortly afterwards sailed up the coast, and from thence to Portugal, carrying the fifteen natives with him. He reached Belem in September, 1499. Only fifty men, returned alive from this expedition.

De Gama was loaded by his delighted Monarch with rewards and honours, and permitted to bear the Royal arms of Portugal, placing at their foot two *Does*, called "Gamas" in Portuguese, and also given a pension of 300,000 reas annually. Whilst the King assumed, or was granted by the Pope, the title of, "Lord of the conquests, and navigation, of Ethiopia, Arabia, Persia, and the Indies."

The discovery of the Cape route, effected momentous changes, in mercantile affairs. Previously, spices and other productions, had been conveyed from India, and elsewhere, in the East, by the Arabian gulf, to Bussora, from thence to Damascus, and eventually to the Port of Beyrout, in Syria, where they were purchased, and carried to Europe, by merchants, who were principally, Venetians, or Genoese. Another route was, by the Red Sea, Cairo, and Alexandria. Subsequently, when the Portuguese had become the predominant power in the East, the Sultan of Egypt, finding his revenue decreasing, threatened to destroy the Holy Places in Jerusalem and elsewhere, if the Moors who traded with his country, were molested.

In the following year, Pedro Alvarez Cabral, was despatched

from Portugal, with ten ships, and two Caravels, carrying 1,500 men, besides 20 convicts, to establish a factory, by fair means if possible, but otherwise to carry fire and sword, into the country. Some of those who had sailed with De Gama, accompanied him: and Bartholomew Diaz, commanded one of the vessels, and five Friars of the order of St Francis, accompanied the fleet.

Cabral received secret orders, that if he succeeded in negotiating with the Samorin, he was to endeavour to induce him to banish the Moors from his dominions. On March 5th, 1500, the sailors embarked, Cabral was presented with a royal banner, which had been blessed by the Bishop of Visen, and a cap which had received the Pope's benediction; thus armed, on the 9th, the fleet commenced their voyage. On May 24th, they encountered a sudden tempest, near the Cape of Good Hope, and four vessels foundered, with all hands on board: but on September 13th, the remainder of the fleet, arrived off Calicut. Cabral then despatched a deputation to the Samorin, of one European, and four Natives, the latter being some of those carried away by De Gama, but as they were fishermen, *(mucuas,)* and consequently low caste men, the Samorin could not receive them.

Cabral then demanded, that hostages should be sent on board, to obviate any treachery, in case he wished to land, and named the Cutwal, and a chief Nair, as the most suitable persons: they, however, declined the honour, but on other hostages being furnished, Cabral landed, with thirty officers, and men.

An interview then took place, at which, rich presents were exchanged, and a treaty of friendship, "as long as the sun and moon should endure," was entered upon.

About this time, a vessel from Cochin, of 600 tons burden, passing the Port, the Samorin requested Cabral to capture it: which he succeeded in doing, but subsequently restored it to the Rajah of Cochin. A factory was soon established at Calicut, in which seventy Europeans were located. Cabral however found, that he still progressed very slowly, having only succeeded in loading two vessels with pepper, in two months. The Moors appear to have effectually prevented the Portuguese, from obtaining any large supply, of this valuable condiment.

Cabral at length became very impatient at the delay, and informed the Samorin, that he must immediately receive lading for his vessels as he was anxious to return to Europe; complaining that the Moors had been served to all the spices, thus precluding his procuring any.* The Samorin hesitated and appeared embarassed how to act, and Cabral with a view to hasten his decision, on December 17th, attacked and seized a Moorish vessel, which was loading in the harbour, on which the Moors on shore became greatly excited, and besieged the Factory, slaughtering 50 of the Portuguese, in sight of their countrymen, who however, could render no assistance: the remaining twenty contrived to escape, by swimming off to the ship's boats, which were lying as close to the shore, as was safe.

Cabral demanded satisfaction for this outrage, but not receiving any, he bombarded the town, killing 600 of the inhabitants; and then seized ten of the Samorin's vessels, to pay for the merchandize left on shore, which was valued at 4000 ducats: some of these ships contained merchandize, and on board one of them, were three elephants, which were killed, and *salted* for the voyage! Having thus revenged himself, Cabral sailed for Cochin, protesting, that in Calicut, the people could not be trusted, and that truth and honour were alike unknown. It appears on the other hand, that Cabral was hasty, and perfectly regardless of the sacrifice of human life: being quite ready to slaughter Moors and Nairs, indiscriminately, with or without provocation, and with no expectation of doing any good.

On December 20th, 1500, the fleet arrived at Cochin, and a Syrian Christian, Michael Jogue who was a passenger in one of the vessels, (for the purpose of visiting Rome, and afterwards proceeding to the Holy land,) was despatched on shore accompanied by an European, to visit the Rajah, Trimumpara, who received them, in a very friendly manner, and sent a message to Cabral, that he might either purchase spices for money, or give merchandize in exchange for them, as was most convenient to him.

Cabral was in every respect, much pleased with the Rajah of Cochin, who although, much less wealthy than the Samorin, and con-

* In those days pepper was a monopoly, and only procurable from the Government Factors.

sequently not living in so much state, was greatly superior to him in every other respect being honest in his dealings, and intelligent and truthful in his conversation.

Cochin at this time, was described as a long low sandy Island, covered with cocoanut trees, and divided by a deep river, a quarter of a mile broad, from the neighbouring Island of Baypin, or Vypeen. Passing up this river for half a mile, a wide expanse of backwater appeared, which extended for about 100 miles, north and south.

The town of Cochin, was small, and situated close to the river, and in it was the Rajah's palace, (where Muttencherry now stands,) by no means an imposing edifice, and badly furnished. A few Moors resided there, and possessed better houses than those of the Native population, which were merely composed of mats, with mud walls, and roofs thatched with leaves. At this period, no buildings were allowed to be constructed of stone or brick, and tiled, excepting Temples and Palaces: but Moorish merchants were permitted, to surround their dwellings with stone walls, for the security of their merchandize.

The Rajah suggested, that to avoid any misunderstanding, and to create mutual confidence, it would be best for him to send Nair hostages on board the fleet. This was accordingly done, the Nairs being exchanged for others, every morning and evening, as they could not eat on board, without violating some religious rules. An alliance of friendship was signed, and the Portuguese promised Trimumpara, at some future date, to instal him as Samorin, and to add Calicut to his dominions. A factory was then given the Portuguese, in which seven factors were placed, to sell their merchandize. The Rajah allowed them a guard, and permitted them to sleep within the walls of his palace. One night, this factory caught fire, which of course was attributed to the vindictiveness of the Moors, but no injury appears to have resulted.

Whilst Cabral was at Cochin, he received deputations from both the Rajahs of Cannanore, and Quilon, inviting him to visit them, and promising to supply him with pepper and spices, at a cheaper rate than he could obtain them at Cochin, but their offers were politely declined. Two natives also paid Cabral a visit, and requested a passage to Europe, stating that they were members of a large

Christian community, residing at Cranganore, *(Kodungaloor,)* about 20 miles north of Cochin, in which some Jews of little note, were also located.

Just as Cabral was preparing to leave Cochin, on January 10th, 1501, a fleet belonging to the Samorin, carrying 1500 men, was descried off the harbour. The Rajah immediately sent messengers, to inform the Portuguese, of the appearance of the enemy, and to offer them any assistance they might require. But the Calicut people held off, and had evidently no wish to come to an engagement. On the following day, finding that they did not attack, Cabral chased them, but was overtaken by a violent storm, which carried him out to sea. He did not subsequently return to Cochin, but put into Cannanore where he received on board an Ambassador from the Rajah of that country, to the King of Portugal. From thence he proceeded to Europe, carrying with him the hostages, whom he had forgotten to land.

Thus was Cochin first visited by European vessels, filled with Portuguese, who after their recent capture of the Rajah's vessels, apprehended retaliation but instead met with nothing but kindness, and hospitality, as well as every assistance in obtaining lading for their ships. Cabral in return, unfortunately, but as he asserted accidentally, carried off the Nair hostages to Europe, leaving his Factor and people on shore, without any attempt, either to provide for their safety, or re-convey them to their Native land. But they were taken every care of by the Cochin Rajah, and subsequently honourably returned to their friends.

As the number of vessels lost in these first expeditions, counterbalanced the profits, the King of Portugal proposed, that merchants should trade to India in their own vessels, on the following terms: namely, that 25 per cent. of the profits should go to the King, and the trade in spices remain wholly in the hands of Government officials, who were to decide upon all Mercantile transactions, even to the necessary expenditure for factors. It is hardly requisite to observe, that no persons came forward to avail themselves, of this extremely liberal proposition.

The next Portuguese navigator or rather buccaneer, who arrived in Cochin, was John de Nueva, who was despatched from Portugal, in March 1501, in command of four vessels. The King supposing all difficulties with Calicut amicably settled by Cabral, ordered De Nueva, to leave two of these ships, at Sofala, and to proceed with the remaining two, to Calicut: in case he met with Cabral, he received instructions, to obey him as General. At St. Blaze, he found an old shoe, hanging from the branch of a tree, which contained a letter, from Pedro de Tayde, giving an account of what had lately occurred at Calicut, and also of the friendly dispositions, of the Rajahs of Cannanore, and Cochin. It was thought best on receiving this information, to take all four vessels on to India, as the whole force did not exceed eighty men. Nueva anchored at Anchediva, in November, and from thence proceeded to Cannanore, where he was amicably received by the Rajah, who offered him lading for his vessels. This Nueva declined, until he had consulted the Factor at Cochin, whilst *en route* to which place, he attacked and captured, a Moorish vessel, opposite Calicut. On his arrival at Cochin, the Factor came on board, and informed him, that although the Rajah was naturally extremely indignant with Cabral, for having carried away his hostages, and departed without bidding him adieu: he had nevertheless, treated him and the other Portuguese, who were left in his territory, in a friendly manner.

Being apprehensive, lest their enemies, the Moors, might attempt to massacre them, the Rajah had even lodged them in his own palace, and had provided them with a guard of Nairs, to protect them when they went into the town. He also stated, that the Moors had persuaded the Native merchants, to refuse to exchange their pepper, for Portuguese merchandize, and that therefore ready money would be required for all purchases. Nueva being unprovided with this, returned at once to Cannanore, but found that owing to the machinations of the Moors, it was as necessary there, as at Cochin. He now quite despaired of procuring lading for his vessels, but the Rajah of Cochin when informed of his dilemma, at once became his security, for 1000 cwt. of pepper; 450 of cinnamon; 50 of ginger; and some bales of cloth. Whilst lying off this place, on December 15th, about 180 vessels, filled with Moors, arrived from Calicut, with the intention of attacking the Portuguese fleet. The Rajah immediately offered Nueva any assistance in his power, this was however civilly declined, and all the ordnance at the command of the Portuguese vessels, was speedily brought to bear on the enemy. By this means, a number of their vessels were sunk, and the remaining Moors were too much discouraged to continue the action. Owing to the generosity of the Rajah, the Portuguese ships were soon loaded, and Nueva departed, leaving his European merchandize for disposal in Cannanore, under the charge of a Factor, and two clerks. Before sailing, he received an embassy from the Samorin, offering excuses for his previous conduct, and promising to give hostages, if he would proceed to Calicut, and there load his vessels. To this message, Nueva vouchsafed no reply.

The king of Portugal, on learning the treatment which Cabral had received from the Samorin, was extremely indignant, and determined to exact further retribution. Vasco de Gama, was therefore despatched from Lisbon, on March 3rd, 1502, in command of an avenging squadron of fifteen vessels, being followed a short time subsequently, by his cousin Stephen de Gama, with five smaller ships.

When opposite Calicut, De Gama attacked, and captured a vessel belonging to the Moors, and having transferred all their merchandize to his own fleet, he confined the crew beneath the hatches, and then set fire to the ship. In a state of desperation, these unhappy men, forced their way out: many leaped into the water, and were drowned: but the remainder, were recaptured, and barbarously burnt alive. The children had previously been removed, they numbered about twenty, and Vasco de Gama, determined to devote them all, to the monastery at Belem, to which establishment he presented them. Subsequently he captured many Malabar sailors, and threatened their immediate execution, unless the Portuguese merchandize, and prisoners, were returned within a very short period. On this not being acceded to, the Natives were hung, and their hands and feet, sent to the Samorin. De Gama tortured messengers, executed Ambassadors, and his deeds were a blot in the annals of a Christian nation, and a disgrace to the name of humanity, over which it would be well could a veil be drawn. The fleet now sailed for Cannanore, where a treaty of friendship, and commerce, was concluded with the Rajah, and a Factory established. Having loaded some of his vessels at this place, and the remainder at Cochin, De Gama proceeded to Calicut, on his sanguinary mission, and he bombarded the town. He then returned to Cochin, having left Vincent De Sodre, with six fully armed vessels, to protect the coast. An interview, with the Rajah then took place, at which De Gama demanded the following stipulations :—that there should be a fixed rate at which pepper, and other merchandize, should be delivered to the Portuguese ; that they should be permitted to raise factories, and storehouses, and be the only nation so favoured. The Rajah hesitated in giving a decided assent ; De Gama became very angry, and embarked in his boat for the fleet. The Rajah however, knowing his vindictive temper, and apprehensive that he might perhaps serve Cochin, as he had lately done Calicut, followed him quickly in a small boat, and entreated him to write down his requests, when they should be all acceded to. The blame of the misunderstanding, was laid on the stupidity of the Interpreter, and the interests of Portugal and Cochin, were discovered to be identical. De Gama now being pacified, returned on shore, where he presented the Rajah, with the following tokens of friendship from the King of Portugal: a gold crown set with jewels, a gold enamelled collar, two richly wrought silver fountains, two pieces of figured arras, and a splendid tent: all of which were accepted with great satisfaction, although the utility of most of the articles, was unknown. After having signed a new treaty, as well as the agreement required by De Gama : the Rajah entrusted him, with a handsome present, for the King of Portugal. A Factory was now established at Cochin. The Rajah made only one stipulation, which was, that no cows should be slaughtered in his dominions: this he said, was a capital crime by his laws, and could not be permitted; he regretted having to allude to so painful a subject, but he had been informed, that several of these revered animals had been killed for the European sailors. De Gama promised that this should not again occur, and when a few days subsequently, three Moplahs, [Mahomedans, or Native christians,] offered beef for sale, he immediately delivered them up to the Rajah, who had them hanged, for committing such a heinous offence.

Whilst at Cochin, De Gama received a message from the Samorin, entreating him to return amicably to Calicut, when the merchandize, &c., should be restored. De Gama acceded to his request, although strongly dissuaded from venturing by his Officers. But when off Calicut, instead of the friendly reception which he hoped for, his vessel was attacked by 34 of the Samorin's fleet, and must certainly have been destroyed, had not de Sodre unexpectedly appeared, with his cruizing squadron. The enemy then quickly dispersed, and De Gama returned in safety to Cochin. The Samorin now finding himself foiled in his stratagems, and defeated whenever he attempted open hostility, became alarmed at the secure footing, which the Portuguese had apparently obtained in Cochin. He therefore wrote to the Rajah, requesting their expulsion from the town, and that they should in future, be refused either admission, or lading for their vessels. In return for this favour, he promised the Rajah, his eternal friendship, and compliance with all his wishes.

In reply, the Rajah of Cochin nobly stated, that the Christians were his friends, and had always treated him as such; that he had signed a treaty of friendship with them, and to break his word, would be a cowardly, and dishonourable act, and one which he could never be guilty of. He also informed the Samorin, that he favoured trade with any nation, and could refuse protection to no merchant, who did not infringe the laws of his country.

The Samorin on receiving this reply, was extremely indignant, and despatched another letter, still more emphatically urging his former requests upon the Rajah. This however proved as ineffectual, as the first, the Rajah positively refusing, to break faith with the Portuguese.

It is worthy of remark, that the Rajah delicately refrained, from making any allusion to this subject, when conversing with the Portuguese. Whilst his noble conduct, in remaining unmoved, both by the persuasive arguments, and vindictive threats of the Samorin, was apparently actuated, only by the strict integrity of his views, with regard to what was right, and honourable.

Before leaving Cochin, De Gama received a deputation, from the Syrian Christians of Cranganore, who stated, that in consequence of the oppressive conduct of the heathen towards them, they were anxious to place themselves, under the protection of the King of Portugal. In testimony of their sincerity, they delivered their rod of justice into De Gama's hands: it was of a red colour, tipped with silver at both ends, and had three bells at the top. He dismissed them, with many promises of assistance, and protection.

The fleet sailed from Cannanore, for Portugal, where it arrived, September 1st, 1503. De Gama on his arrival was received with great honour, and created, *Lord of Videgueyra*, and, *Admiral of the Indies.*

The Samorin on learning De Gama's departure, determined to coerce the Rajah of Cochin: and collected an army of 50,000 Nairs at Ponany, about sixty miles north of Cochin. Many of the nobility, and chiefs of the Cochin State, now earnestly advised the Rajah to give up the foreigners, and not allow his country to be desolated, for persons of whom he knew nothing. But the Rajah rejoined, that whilst he had life, his treaties should never be violated, nor his honour tarnished, by the massacre, or even persecution of defenceless men, who had been confided to his protection. Hostilities were then prepared for.

At this time, Vincente de Sodre, arrived at Cochin, with his coasting squadron, and was requested to remain, and afford the Rajah any assistance in his power. But apathy, or cowardice, rendered him averse, to join in the approaching struggle; so, framing some frivolous excuses, he sailed away, and left the Rajah, and his subjects, to fight their own battles.

The Samorin, who had been joined by many treacherous Chiefs of the Cochin State, now harangued his army, contrasting the friendly way in which the Moors had behaved for the previous 600 years, with the conduct of the Portuguese, whom he designated pirates, and robbers, and accused of having attacked him without a cause, and in revenge for imaginary grievances, plundered and destroyed his vessels, and executed his ambassadors. He added, that the Rajah of Cochin, although well aware of the truth of these assertions, had notwithstanding the requests sent him to the contrary, given these foreigners refuge in his dominions, and was therefore one of their accomplices: so he must be deprived of his kingdom, and his sanguinary friends of their lives.

The Samorin's brother, Nambeadarin, then rose; and urged the impolicy of the present proceeding, which he asserted, originated with the Moors, who dreaded the loss of their trade. He added, that because the Rajah of Cochin had received the Portuguese, as he would any other merchants, who wished to trade with his country, surely that was no reason why he should be punished in so severe a manner, especially as the Rajahs of Cannanore, and Quilon, had also desired the advantage of trading with these foreigners.

But all arguments were unavailing. The Astrologers were requested to name a fortunate day for the commencement of the enterprise, and the Samorin marched with his army to the Island of his ally the Rajah of Repelim, eight miles from the town of Cochin.* On March 31st, he entered the Cochin territory, and attempted to force a passage by the Ford, near Cranganore, but was repulsed by 5,500 Nairs, who were entrenched there, under the command of Naramuhin, the heir apparent. Being foiled in this endeavour, the Samorin now determined to attempt stratagem: he accordingly bribed the Cochin paymaster, to oblige the Nairs to return to the Town, to receive their daily rations, and then taking advantage of a time when most of them would be absent, he attacked Naramuhin, who after a protracted resistance, was at length overpowered, and slain along with two of the Rajah's sons, and nearly all his men. On hearing this disastrous intelligence, the Rajah fell fainting from his seat, and was at first believed to have expired.

An universal panic now prevailed, and many of the principal inhabitants of the Town, fled in consternation. The Portuguese proposed removing to Cannanore, but this the Rajah would not hear of: declaring, whilst he lived he would protect them, even were he to lose his kingdom in attempting to do so. The Nairs now became most urgent, in their demands for the death of the foreigners, and had they not been under the immediate protection of the Rajah, would certainly have massacred them all.

The Samorin again made overtures for peace on the same terms as before. Thus the Rajah was beset on all sides, but still he withstood, alike, arguments, entreaties, and threats. On receiving his reply, the Samorin ordered the whole country to be laid waste, with

* Repelim is known as Eddapully or Ellengaloor, and is in the Cochin State.

fire and sword. Being informed, by two Milanese lapidaries,* who had deserted to him, of the panic prevailing in the Town, he immediately marched thither. The Rajah at the head of his troops, defended the place for some time, but at length, after having been wounded in one of the engagements, he was overpowered by numbers, and obliged to withdraw with the remnants of his force to the Island of Vypeen, opposite Cochin. All the Portuguese, with their property, accompanied him.

The monsoon now commenced, and the Samorin after burning Cochin to the ground, retired to Cranganore. He left a strong detachment on the Island of Cochin, with orders to throw up entrenchments for their defence.

Fortunately on September 20th, 1503, Francisco de Albuquerque, with six sail, arrived at Cochin, when the enemy fled in extreme terror to Cranganore. Albuquerque was received with every demonstration of joy. The Rajah even wept on embracing him, assuring him, that his only wish to be restored to his dominions, was, that his subjects might be convinced that he had acted honourably. Albuquerque, knowing that the Rajah's finances, owing to the war were in a very impoverished condition, presented him with 10,000 crowns, thanking him at the same time, in most complimentary terms, for his protection of the Portuguese. The Rajah then re-entered Cochin in triumph; and on the same day, the Samorin's troops were attacked by the Portuguese, and easily routed: they appeared quite disheartened, and demoralized. Two days afterwards, they were again defeated, at the Island of Charanaipin, and at the close of the engagement, Albuquerque knighted several of his Officers, who had particularly distinguished themselves.

On the following day, the Portuguese attacked and captured Repelim, which was given up to plunder. The Rajah now wished for peace, being averse to seeing his country devastated, and his subjects slain: but Albuquerque was of opinion, that the Samorin, and

* These lapidaries constructed more than 400 guns for the Samorin, in whose service they continued, until the year 1506, when they were both murdered as traitors, by 200 Nairs, and Yogees. However, they sold their lives dearly, as they are said to have slain six of their assailants, and wounded forty more, before being finally overpowered.

his allies, had not been sufficiently punished, and therefore determined to continue his aggressive measures.

He, however, took advantage of the high favour which he enjoyed with the Rajah, to request permission to erect a Fort at Cochin, close to the edge of the river, for the protection of the Portuguese factory, in the absence of their vessels. This the Rajah readily granted, and even stipulated, that he should be allowed to supply the materials at his own cost; which he accordingly did.

The foundations were laid, on September 26th, 1503. It was constructed in the form of a square, each face being eighteen yards long, [probably this is a mis-print, for one hundred and eighty,] with bastions at each corner, on which ordnance was mounted. The walls were composed of trunks of cocoanut trees, firmly fixed into the ground, and bound together by iron hoops, and large nails. Earth was rammed in between the two rows of timbers, and the whole was surrounded by a wet ditch.

The Rajah sent workmen to construct the Fort, but Albuquerque ordered all the Portuguese to assist. On September 30th, Alonso de Albuquerque arrived from Portugal, with three vessels under his command, and as his crews joined those of his cousin, in the business of erecting the Fort, it was very speedily completed.

The following morning, it was with great pomp and solemnity, christened "Manuel" after the reigning sovereign of Portugal. Albuquerque accompanied by all his people then marched round it in procession, headed by the bands of the squadron, whilst the Fort Vicar bore aloft the crucifix, under a canopy, upheld by the Captains of the fleet. The Fort was then blessed, and consecrated, by the celebration of mass, in a small wooden church, dedicated to St. Bartholomew, which had been raised within it.

The war was now resumed, and carried on principally with the Rajah of Repelim. The Samorin exerted himself to the utmost to prevent the Portuguese, being able to obtain pepper, and spices, at Cochin: in hopes, that these odious foreigners, finding their trade destroyed, would leave India. Consequently being unable to procure lading for his vessels, Alonso de Albuquerque was obliged to seek it at Quilon, where he determined, that if not immediately supplied with what he required, to declare war against the Rajah, and obtain it by force. But he was amicably received, and easily procured spices, &c., for his vessels. He also obtained permission to build a factory, and established a Commercial Depôt, leaving there a Factor, two Clerks, an Interpreter, two Friars and some others in charge, after which he then returned to Cochin.

The fleet finally sailed for Europe, on January 31st, 1504. Duarte Pacheco having been previously appointed Commandant, was left, with four vessels, ninety able bodied men, and all the sick, to protect the Rajah of Cochin. As much ordnance, and ammunition, as could be spared, was also given him.

On the voyage home, Francisco de Albuquerque's vessel, and another, were separated from the Fleet, and never heard of again. Several other vessels, were subsequently lost.

From the time of De Gama's second visit to India, the Portuguese in virtue of the sovereign rights they claimed, obliged all vessels, to give them a manifest of their goods: and they also appear, to have indiscriminately plundered and burnt, any belonging to the Moors. At the present time, they would doubtless have been regarded as legalized pirates, whose destruction would be beneficial to trade, and justified by the law of nations.

The Moors, naturally wished to quit Cochin, which was now ruled by their most virulent enemies, but Pacheco positively refused them leave, and also warned them, that any who attempted to escape, would be hanged. A strict blockade was now maintained by the Portuguese vessels, and no one permitted to leave the place without a pass, or enter without being searched: whilst all passers by, were stopped and examined. Incursions were continued into the neighbouring territories, and plunder and slaughter, mistermed "glory," appear to have been of common occurrence.

The Samorin now again determined to try his strength, against the Portuguese, so Pacheco decided, on defending the passage of the river, at Chetwye, forty miles north of Cochin. He accordingly started for this place, on April 16th, 1504, with his own people, and 500 Nairs, leaving only 49 men in the Fort at Cochin, and 25 in one of his vessels. The Samorin being alarmed at his approach, proposed peace: but Pacheco declined all overtures, observing, that as the Samorin had wished for war, war he should have. On receiving a second message to the same effect, he bastinadoed the messenger, and returned him to the Samorin, with a challenge, to come and avenge the insult if he dared.

The next day the forces met, and a battle ensued, in which the untrained troops of the Samorin were routed. It was with difficulty that they were induced to advance; at the first volley they wavered, and at the second fled in terror. A series of skirmishes were subsequently of daily occurrence, in all of which the Portuguese obtained the advantage. This so disheartened the Samorin, that he retired into religious seclusion, with many of his Brahmans, and chief men. Some Nairs being suspected of an attempt to assassinate Pacheco, were arrested, and two of them hanged, after having been first nearly flogged to death. But this created great consternation among the Rajah's troops, of the same caste, who remonstrated with Pacheco on the subject, informing him, that though in extreme cases, their laws permitted the execution of a Nair, by those of their own caste, they did not allow him to be flogged, as that was an insult to their caste and contrary to their religion, debarring him from the performance of certain necessary religious rites. In fact so much disturbance was created, that the remaining prisoners were spared. And as this appeared a good opportunity of paying the Rajah a compliment, without any expense or trouble to himself, Pacheco sent the men to the Rajah, with a message to the effect, that though they had purposed attempting his life, he would not take theirs, but left them to be dealt with, according to the well known clemency, and justice, of their own Sovereign.

Many of the Allies, and principal Chiefs, subject to the Samorin, were now extremely anxious to make terms with the Portuguese, amongst whom was the Rajah of Repelim, who alarmed for his country, and himself, proposed to enter into a treaty. He at the same time sent Pacheco a present, of a large quantity of pepper. An alliance between them was then entered into, being apparently the first, formed between the Portuguese, and any petty Indian Prince.

Many of the Moors of Calicut, now finding their trade at that place quite destroyed, came to Cochin, and settled there: by this means, its importance greatly increased. Towards the end of the year 1504, Suarez de Menezes arrived from Portugal, as commandant of the fleet. Shortly afterwards, when he was at Cannanore, a Portuguese boy who had been a prisoner of the Samorin's, since Cabral's time, was sent to him by that Sovereign, (who had emerged from his retirement) to endeavour to negotiate a peace, and to entreat Suarez to visit Calicut, when all the prisoners should be delivered up to him: whereas if he refused, they would all be immediately executed. Suarez therefore, in the hope of rescuing the unfortunate Portuguese, who had been in the Samorin's power for so long, determined to proceed thither, where he anchored on September 7th. He however, refused to make any terms, until the two Milanese lapidaries, who had deserted from Cochin, were given up to him.

In the meantime, he sent messages to the prisoners, urging their escape to his vessels, as quickly as possible. But this the Samorin took care to prevent, by having them strictly guarded. Suarez after waiting several days, and finding that the Samorin had no intention of sending him the deserters, whom he demanded as a preliminary step, to any treaty, decided on cannonading the town. After doing it much injury, he sailed away for Cochin, where he arrived on September 13th.

He was received with great honour by the Rajah, to whom he delivered many valuable presents, from the king of Portugal: with complimentary messages, and thanks for his protection of the Portuguese, with all of which the Rajah was much gratified.

The Samorin now made great preparations, for acting on the defensive, against the Portuguese, during the time their fleet remained in India, determining on its departure, to continue hostilities against the Rajah of Cochin.

Suarez advanced to Cranganore, where the Samorin had stationed himself, with his Army. Having captured the town, he ordered it to be burnt, and the work of destruction had already commenced, when some Syrian Christians, inhabitants of the place, came and entreated him to desist, representing that within the city were several Churches dedicated to the Virgin, and the Apostles, which would be destroyed. The conflagration was therefore stopped, but not until much mischief had been done. On his return to Cochin, Suarez knighted several of his Officers.

Suarez after this engagement, received overtures from the Rajah of Tannoor, who requested permission to become a subject of the King of Portugal. Many Moorish merchants, also left the cities of Calicut, and Cranganore, and returned to Mecca; resigning an Indian trade, which had latterly proved unremunerative.

The fleet sailed from Cochin, for Europe, on December 27th, leaving Manuel Telez de Vasconelles, as Captain General, with three vessels, and 100 Soldiers to guard the coast of India. The Rajah was greatly disappointed, that Pacheco who was a great favourite, did not remain to protect him, instead of Vasconelles. At parting with the former, he offered him many handsome presents, thanking him at the same time most warmly, for having so valiantly defended him from his enemies. Pacheco however declined the presents, assuring the Rajah, that he had only performed his duty, and therefore must be excused accepting any reward. He however, consented to carry a letter from the Rajah, to the King of Portugal commending him to his Sovereign's favour, and commenting on his conduct in high terms of praise.

Suarez, when returning to Europe, being driven near Calicut, attacked the fleet there, and is stated to have captured 17 vessels, and put 2,000 men to death. Owing to this severe loss, the Moors now completely deserted this place, and the Samorin was too much disheartened, to carry out his hostile intentions against the Rajah of Cochin for some time subsequently.

Towards the close of the year 1505, Don Francisco de Almeyda arrived in Cochin, from Portugal with eight vessels, all that remained out of a fleet of twenty two, carrying 1,500 soldiers with which he had left Europe. Half these vessels were to return to Portugal, with merchandize. At Anchediva he had built a fort and left a garrison of 80 men as well as two ships. He came to India as "Viceroy of all the Indies," being the first who had ever borne that title.

The various *Portuguese Viceroys of India* have been as follows: *Don Francisco d'Almeida*, A. D. 1505. *Alphonso d'Albuquerque*, 1509. *Lopo Soares d'Albergaria*, 1515. *Diago Lopes de Siqueira*, 1518. *D. Duarte de Menezes*, 1521. *D. Vasco de Gama*, 1524. *D. Henrique de Menezes*, 1525, *Lopo Vas de Sampaio*, 1526. *Nuno da Cunha*, 1529. *D. Garcia de Noronha*, 1538. *D. Estevao da*

Gama, 1540. *Martim Alphonso de Souza*, 1542. *D. Joam de Castro*, 1545. *Garcia de Sá*, 1548. *Jorje Cabral*, 1549. *D. Alphonso de Noronha*, 1551. *D. Pedro Mascarenhas*, 1554. *Francisco Barreto*, 1555. *D. Constantino de Braganca*, 1558. *D. Francisco Coutinho*, 1561. *Joam de Mendonca*, 1563. *D. Antam de Noronha*, 1564. *D. Luiz de Attaide*, 1568. *D. Antonio de Noronha*, 1571. *Antonio Moniz Barretto*, 1573. *Rui Lourenco de Tavora*, 1576. *D. Diogo de Menezes*, 1576. *D. Luiz d'Attaide*, 1578. *Fernam Telles*, 1580. *D. Francisco Mascarenhas*, 1581. *D. Duarte de Menezes*, 1584. *Manoel de Souza Coutinho*, 1588. *Mathias d'Albuquerque*, 1590. *D. Francisco de Gama*, 1597. *Aires de Saldanha*, 1600. *D. Martim Alphonso de Castro*, 1604. *D. Fr. Aleixo de Menezes*, 1607. *Andre Furtado de Mendonca*, 1609. *Rui Lourenco de Tavora*, 1609. *D. Teronimo d'Azevedo*, 1612. *D. Joam Coutinho*, 1617. *Fernam d'Albuquerque*, 1619. *D. Francisco de Gama*. 1622. *D. Fr. Luis de Brito*, 1627. *D. Miguel de Noronha*, 1629. *Pedro da Silva*, 1635. *Antonio Telles*, 1639. *D. Joam da Silva Tello de Menezes*, 1640. *D. Filippe Mascarenhas* 1645. *D. Vasco Mascarenhas*, 1652. *D. Rodrigo Lobo de Silveira*, 1655. *Antonio Mello de Castro*, 1662.

Almost the first piece of intelligence, Almeyda received on his arrival, was, that the factor and others, left at Quilon, had all been murdered by the Moors.* He, therefore, dispatched his son Lorenzo, with six vessels to that place, giving him orders, provided he could obtain lading for his vessels, to ignore all knowledge of the massacre, but that if spices, &c. were refused him, he was to take ample vengeance for the murder of his countrymen.

Lorenzo found a fleet of twenty-four Calicut vessels, awaiting his arrival, and an engagement ensued, in which they were all routed. He then rejoined his father at Cochin. Almeyda had received instructions from the King of Portugal, to crown Trimunpara, Rajah of Cochin, for which purpose he had come provided with a golden diadem, richly adorned with jewels. But as Trimunpara had previously become a religious recluse, and abdicated in favour of his nephew Nambeadora, Almeyda transferred this honour to him,

* Almeyda commenced the Cannanore Fort in 1505, whilst on his way to Cochin. He left Lorenzo de Brito, with 150 men, and two vessels to defend it.

and with great pomp, and solemnity, placed the crown on his head.

About this time, an earthquake, and total eclipse of the sun, having occurred, the Astrologers predicted the certain annihilation of the Portuguese power in India,* and advised the Samorin again to try his fortune in battle. Whilst he was making active preparations for recommencing hostilities, an unfortunate circumstance gave him the opportunity of inducing the Rajah of Cannanore to break his alliance with the Europeans, and engage in warfare against them.

Gonzalo Vaz meeting with a richly laden Moorish vessel, not far from Cannanore, plundered and scuttled her, totally disregarding, a Portuguese pass produced by the Moorish Captain, and the crew having been first sewn up together in a sail, to avoid discovery, were thrown overboard. Unfortunately, one of the bodies floated on shore, and was identified, as that of the nephew of a wealthy merchant of Malabar. The subject was then laid before the Rajah of Cannanore, who was justly indignant, and was prevailed on by the Samorin, to aid him in expelling foreigners, whose own passes were of no avail, and who slaughtered and plundered, not only their enemies the Moors, but any other Merchants, whom they were able, making themselves the terror of the seas, and the curse of the mainland.

As the author of this atrocity could not be discovered, the blame fell upon Lorenzo de Brito, who commanded the Fort at Cannanore, and he was consequently besieged by the Rajah. But receiving reinforcements from Cochin, he was enabled to hold out, until relieved by De Cunna, who so intimidated the Rajah, that he sued for peace, which was granted, on terms very advantageous to the Portuguese.

About this time, the Sultan of Egypt, sent a large fleet, to oppose the Portuguese in India. And the two forces meeting at Chaul, the Portuguese sustained a disastrous defeat, in which Lorenzo de Almeyda* was slain, along with many others.

In the same year, 1508, Alphonso de Albuquerque arrived at Cochin, with orders to supersede Almeyda, who was directed to return to

* Almeyda proposed to punish the Sultan of Egypt in a stupendous manner, that was never realized, viz., plundering Mecca and Medina, and subsequently desolating Egypt, by diverting the Nile, across Nubia, and Abyssinia to the Red Sea!

Portugal, in one of the trading vessels. But the latter declined to obey, until he had avenged himself on the Sultan. A controversy now arose, and Albuquerque retired into private life in Cochin; whilst Almeyda proceeded on his intended expedition against the Turks.

At the commencement of the following year, he returned to Cochin, after having defeated his enemies and captured the colours both of the Sultan, and his Admiral Meer Hoossain, which re-established the prestige of the Portuguese name, in the Indian seas.

On entering Cochin in triumph he was met by Albuquerque, who even before he had laid aside his robes of State, requested him to resign the Government, pursuant to the Royal orders. Almeyda replied that after having taken off his heavy robes, there would be sufficient time to discuss the matter. On mature reflection Almeyda decided to retain the Office of Viceroy, and on his intimating this decision, disputes became so irritating, that he made Albuquerque a prisoner, and sent him to Cannanore, where he was respectfully treated by Lorenzo de Brito. The Rajah of Cochin sided with Albuquerque, and even delayed supplying lading for two homeward bound vessels, until he should be installed as Viceroy.

In November 1509, a large reinforcement arrived from Portugal, under the command of Marshal, Don Fernando Coutinno, who was invested with extraordinary powers, for settling any disputes which might have arisen. He therefore, carried Albuquerque with him to Cochin, where he forthwith installed him as Viceroy. Almeyda fitted up a ship most gorgeously for his passage to Europe, but when completed, Coutinno refused him permission to sail in her. In November, Almeyda finally departed for Europe, the Natives predicting, that such a brute would never pass the Cape. But they were mistaken, for he rounded it in safety, and scoffingly observed to an attendant, "*Now God be praised, the witches of Cochin are liars!*" But he had not long cause for exultation, for on the succeeding morning, he landed with a party of 150 men, to obtain water for his vessel, when his cupidity was aroused, by the sight of a drove of a cattle, tended only by children. Having surrounded them, he observed, "these cattle shall serve us as food, and "these children shall be made a present, to our Lady of Belem." But the owners of the cattle, and the parents of the Children, rapidly assembled, armed with sharpened sticks, hardened in the fire, with which they fiercely attacked the Portuguese, fifty of whom miserably perished, and amongst them the first Viceroy of the Indies, thrust through the neck by a stake.

During the Vice Royalty of Almeyda, the Portuguese claimed the whole of the East as theirs, in accordance with the Papal Bull. To this demand the Native Princes of India declined submitting, consequently feuds were of frequent occurrence, and almost every cargo was purchased with blood.

Albuquerque with 3,000 troops attempted to take Calicut, on January 2nd, 1510, but was repulsed, and Coutinno slain. He then entered into an alliance with the pirate Timoja, and appeared off Goa at the end of the same month. The garrison surrendered without a blow, but on the appearance of a large force, Albuquerque was obliged to evacuate the place. He subsequently retook it, but was again compelled to leave it, but finally recaptured it, in November of the same year. He then laid the foundation of a Fort, and intended raising a magnificent monument, in honour of all the Officers and others, engaged in this glorious enterprise. But so much quarrelling ensued, as to whose name should be placed first on the tablet, that they all petitioned, that the face of the stone might be turned downwards, which was accordingly done.

Albuquerque wishing to form an European colony at Goa, now obliged many of the Portuguese, to marry native women. He also commenced the formation of a Native army. In 1512, the Samorin becoming alarmed at the power of the Portuguese, entered into an alliance with them, and permitted the erection of a Fort, at Calicut. In the following year he sent an embassy to Portugal,* and at the same time, Albuquerque transmitted some captives taken in

* The Ambassador became a Christian, and was knighted, by John III of Portugal, he was Christened "John of the Cross." On his return to Calicut, he was banished from the Court in disgrace, as a renegade from the religion of his fathers. In 1532 he joined the Parravars and at the head of a deputation of them came to Cochin, imploring the assistance of the Portuguese, against the Moors. All the embassage, (85 souls) turned Christians. A Portuguese fleet was sent to their relief when 20,000 of them immediately consented to be baptised; ten years subsequently, Xavier organized a church for them.

war, as a present to the King. Albuquerque's renown had now spread far and wide, and many of the surrounding Princes, were most anxious to form treaties of friendship with him, and sent Ambassadors for that purpose.

In 1515, Albuquerque was superseded by Soarez, and received orders to return to Portugal, Diego Mendez, and Diego Pareira, were sent out at the same time, one as Governor of Cochin, and the other as Secretary to the Viceroy. Both these men had been previously despatched to Europe, as criminals by Albuquerque, who appeared quite heart-broken, at receiving such ungrateful treatment from his country, for whose benefit he had done so much. He was ill at the time, and observed, "It is now time for me to take "refuge in the Church, having incurred the King's displeasure for "the sake of his subjects: and their anger, for the sake of the "King. Old man! fly to the church, your honour requires that "you should die, and you have never yet omitted anything, in which "your honour was concerned." He wrote to the King, concluding his letter, as follows:—"The affairs of India will answer for themselves, "and me." He shortly afterwards proceeded to Goa, where he expired of grief, on December 15th, 1515.

Albuquerque was one of the best, and bravest, of the Governors, who had ruled Portuguese India. He augmented the revenues, by lowering the duties: and by justice at sea, he raised the maritime trade. He combined the character of a financier, with that of general, and was a favorite with all classes. At his death, he was universally mourned, even by the independent Native Princes. His ungrateful Sovereign, lost in him a true hero, and an unselfish man. At his tomb, his countrymen, whilst bemoaning their own wrongs, frequently called on God to revenge his,—consequently his remains were transferred to Lisbon, in spite of great opposition from the inhabitants of Goa.

Portuguese Historians, designate Pacheco, Francisco de Almeyda, and Alphonso de Albuquerque, the founders of their Indian empire. The first by his valour, and the fiery heat of his actions, was said to have melted, both the arms, and the riches of the Samorin: the second, filed and polished the acts of the first, with his own sword, and that of his brave son, reducing the insubordinate to obedience, and humbling the Egyptian Sultan: whilst Albuquerque, the Financier, Politician, and General, added to its ornaments, the three precious jewels, of Goa, Malacca, and Ormuz.

At the close of the year 1515, Soarez arrived from Portugal, as Viceroy of the Indies. He was accompanied by a fleet of thirteen vessels, carrying 1,500 soldiers, many being men of rank who were in hopes of finding some means of restoring their fallen fortunes. The new Viceroy, was far from rivalling the popularity of his predecessor, at Cochin, his disposition was cold, and reserved: and his conduct, especially disagreeable to the Rajah, who had been accustomed to the amiable affability, of Albuquerque. The nephew of the latter, finding it impossible to get on amicably with Soarez, returned to Portugal.

Immediately after his installation, Soarez started on a tour of inspection, through the Portuguese possessions in India. His first measures were very unpopular, as he superseded all the Captains, and Governors of Forts, and substituted favourites of his own.*

In 1517, Alcacova was sent out, as Surveyor of the King's revenue, a species of Official, known as *Minister of Finance*, who was a constant check on the Viceroy, and greatly curtailed the almost unlimited power he had previously enjoyed. This led to great dissensions between them, especially as the *Financier* was inclined to exceed his authority. At length, finding he could do nothing, he returned to Europe, where he made loud complaints of the maladministration in India.

From this period, the controlling powers at home, listened to any charges emanating from India, against the Governors, and Commandants: and consequently, frequently annulled the orders of the local authorities, who in their turn became disgusted, and directed their energies, more towards amassing private wealth, than acquiring honour, and respect, for their country, and its laws.

In 1518, Diego Lopez de Sequeira, the discoverer of Malacca, superseded Soarez, who left for Portugal with nine ships. Under Soarez, the honour of the Portuguese name rapidly sank. Already

---

* About the end of the year 1515, the Portuguese proceeding from their Fort at Malacca made their first voyage to China. This was the commencement of a direct trade between Europe, and the Celestial Empire.

the Native Princes, viewed with suspicion a foreign race, who claimed all their territories, as a gift from the Pope, [a potentate, whose name they knew not, and whose authority they did not recognise;] and who erected stone pillars, and subsequently pointed them out, as signs of sovereignty. It was asserted, that "the period had "now commenced, when the soldiers no more followed the dictates "of honour, when those who had been Captains became traders, and "rapacious plunderers of the innocent Natives;" "command became a "shame, honour a scandal, and reputation a reproach;" every petty Governor, followed laws of his own making; justice, and order, were set at defiance: and to crown all, non-official adventurers, spread terror at the rapacity of the foreigners. Soarez retained the Viceroyalty for three years, but his successor was as bad as himself, and massacres of the Natives, (unworthy the name of battles) were o daily occurrence.*

In 1521, Sequeira, who was now Governor, wintered at Ormuz, sending his nephew Alexius de Menezes, to Cochin, with full powers to conduct the Government, during his absence, the homeward bound fleet, were therefore despatched by him and the other duties of the office carried on. In this same year, the Samorin believing, that in the absence of the Viceroy, he might have more chance of success, against the Rajah of Cochin, again attacked him, but was easily routed.

In 1521, Don Duarte de Menezes, succeeded Sequeira, who at once left for Portugal. Menezes followed the example set him by Soarez, and deposed all the commandants of Forts, electing officers of his own choosing, to their appointments.

In 1524, the celebrated Don Vasco de Gama, returned to India: it having been represented, that the preceding Governors, had lent themselves to great abuses. His vessel was accompanied by 13 others, having 3,000 troops on board. Whilst at sea near Cambaya, and in a dead calm, the ocean suddenly commenced tossing so violently, that the people gave themselves up for lost: but De Gama, knowing that it arose from an earthquake, exclaimed, "Courage, my "friends; the sea is only trembling for the fear of us!"

* In 1517, the first Portuguese factory in Ceylon was established.

The Viceroy having gone to Cochin, found the Portuguese possessions there threatened by the Samorin, who however was at once scared away, by the terror of De Gama's illustrious name. Pirates were compelled to abandon their trade, owing to the vigour now imparted to the Government.

Unfortunately De Gama's rule was short, as on the night of December 25th, 1524 this celebrated man, the discoverer of the Cape route, expired, after being only three months in India. Whatever his private virtues may have been, in public life, he was vindictive in his animosities, fiendish in his punishments, blood thirsty in his councils, and unfeeling in his actions: but withal, a bold and skilful navigator, fearless in danger, and regardless of self. He perished in a fit place for such a hero, in an eastern city, where Europeans had first permanently settled, amongst a race differing from them, in language, complexion, and creed. In a State, where violence had hitherto not been meted out, in revenge for imputed treachery. In a land noted for its natural productions, its spices, its oils, its gold, and its precious stones.

His funeral although princely, was hardly worthy of such a man; thirteen years subsequently, in conformity with his own expressed wishes, and those of his Sovereign, his remains were removed to Portugal, where they rest amongst the famous and noble, of that formerly great and enterprising nation.

Before De Gama's death, he sent for Lope Vaz de Sampayo, the Official next in rank to himself in Cochin, and stating that he felt his end approaching, he appointed him his temporary successor, and delivered into his hands, an envelope sealed with the Royal Arms of King John III of Portugal, and having the following superscription. "To remain unopened, until, (which may the Al-"mighty forbid,) Don Vasco de Gama, Viceroy and High Admiral "of the Indies, shall have departed this life."

After De Gama's demise was certified, the Head Officials of Cochin, met in the principal Church, where Sampayo now Provisional Viceroy, broke the seal of the document entrusted to his care. It was found to contain the nominations of three successive Viceroys. The first appointed Don Enrique de Menezes, as De Gama's immediate successor. The other two were, un-read, re-sealed, and deposited in safe keeping.

On the following morning, Sampayo dispatched a letter to Goa where Menezes then was, to inform him of De Gama's death, and his nomination as his successor: on receiving which, he immediately left for Cochin, and assumed the reins of Government.

At this period the Samorin again became very troublesome, and besieged the Portuguese Fort at Calicut. The Garrison was reduced to great distress, but subsequently receiving reinforcements from Cochin, the Nairs were beaten off, and forced to retire. As this Fort was not considered of importance, equivalent to the amount of expenditure and danger incurred in its maintenance, it was evacuated and blown up.

In February 1526, Menezes expired at Cannanore. He left a paper detailing the mode of Government, which he advised should be adopted after his death. This was unfortunately lost, but he was believed to have named the Governor of Goa, as his Provisional successor.

The second royal nomination was now opened, when it was found, that Pedro de Mascarenhas, was appointed to fill the vacant office, but as he was away at Malacca, it was decided to open the third paper, and Sampayo next in rotation, was appointed acting Governor, after taking an oath to deliver up charge to Mascarenhas, on his arrival in India.

But having held the keys of power for several months, Sampayo did not feel inclined to resign them. On learning that Mascarenhas might shortly be expected in Cochin, he assembled the council, who according to his wishes, decided that Mascarenhas was not to be installed as Governor. Sampayo sailed for Goa, leaving Alphonso Mexia in charge of Cochin, with strict orders to carry out the decision of the Council, and permit no assumption of power by Mascarenhas, who on landing unarmed, was attacked and wounded by Mexia. He retreated to his vessel, and immediately sailed for Goa, to seek some explanation from Sampayo, of this extraordinary reception. On his arrival, he was arrested, and retained in irons, until reference had been made to Portugal. On the decision arriving from Europe, it was found, that Mascarenhas was recalled, and Sampayo confirmed in the Government.

In October 1529, Nunho d' Acunha landed at Goa, as Viceroy. He entered the city with much pomp and ceremony, but shortly afterwards left for Cochin, stopping "en route" at Cannanore, where Sampayo came on board, and formally resigned his office: but on his wishing to return to the town, Nunho refused him permission, informing him that he was a prisoner, and must proceed to Cochin, to answer any accusations which might be made against him. A proclamation was then issued, calling on all who had any complaints to make against the late Governor, to bring them before the present one, who was anxious to redress all grievances. Sampayo protested against this proceeding, alleging that in India, and especially in Cochin, it was quite unnecessary to assemble people by the sound of a trumpet, to make false accusations against Government Officials. Sampayo was imprisoned, and all his effects, sealed up and sent to Lisbon to the King. When taken into custody, he made the following remark to an Officer, "tell the new Governor, "that I formerly imprisoned others, he imprisons me, but I can "foretel, that one will arrive, who will imprison him." To this Nunho replied, "I may be imprisoned, but I will never deserve it, and Sampayo does." The latter was subsequently sent to Europe, in a worthless vessel, with only a few attendants, and barely sufficient provisions for the voyage.

He landed at Lisbon in irons, and for two years was confined in a dungeon in the castle, in company with the Visier of Ormuz. He was then tried for his unjust treatment of Mascarenhas, and sentenced to forfeit all his allowances as Governor, to pay Mascarenhas a compensation of 10,000 ducats, and to be banished to Africa. He however escaped into Spain, where he denaturalised himself, and then wrote to the king, saying, that he had left an ungrateful country, which had rewarded his deeds with ingratitude, and his honourable actions with dishonourable treatment: that henceforth as a Spaniard, he would endeavour to blot out the slur cast upon him, as a Native of Portugal. The King consequently reversed his previous decision, and Sampayo returned to his Native country.

Nunho commenced his Vice-royalty, by endeavouring to conciliate all parties, especially, the Rajah of Cochin, who had been much annoyed by the conduct of his immediate predecessors, and whom he found kept as a prisoner in his own palace, and like every other Prince in alliance with Portugal, a victim to injustice and oppression. He redressed grievances, and by governing with justice and impartiality, restored the trade and prosperity, of Portuguese India.

About 1531, the Samorin finding the Portuguese power increasing, became really anxious to conclude a peace with them, and presented them with a piece of ground at Chaul, on which to build a Fort. The Sultan of Guzerat, and the Emperor of Delhi, being at war, the Portuguese agreed to assist the former, provided Diu was made over to them; this was acceded to, but a disagreement subsequently arose about some of the terms, and in 1537, a meeting was arranged, between Nunho and the Guzerat monarch, Bahadoor Shah.

Mutual distrust prevailed, and therefore the conference was held in boats. But notwithstanding this precaution a disturbance arose, and the Sultan met with a violent death; some assert that he was shot by the Portuguese, others that he was only stunned by an oar, and subsequently dispatched by a halbert. At any rate, a long and disastrous war resulted.

In 1533, all Governors of Forts, and dependencies, in Portuguese India, were ordered to take an oath of obedience, to the Governor-General. In November 1538, Nunho was relieved by Don García de Noronha, who treated his predecessor in a most insulting manner, and even refused him a vessel in which to proceed to Europe, obliging him to hire a merchant ship for that purpose. Nunho's mind became much depressed, at the unworthy treatment he received, and still more so, at what he anticipated might be in store for him, when he arrived in Portugal; the prophetic words of Sampayo, appeared never absent from his mind, and he died on his homeward voyage, with his last breath desiring, that his body should be thrown into the sea, and not be conveyed to his ungrateful country.*

In 1539, a peace was concluded with the Samorin, which lasted

* Paichi Marcar a powerful Moor of Cochin, sent forces to the assistance of Bhuwaneka Bahu, VII, a Ceylon King, to aid him against the Portuguese, but they were intercepted and dispersed. In 1540, the Samorin in conjunction with this same Moor, sent further assistance to the same Ceylon King. Paichi Marcar's head, and those of his chiefs, were finally made a present to the Portuguese, by their obliged friend the Ceylon King, who thus purchased peace for himself.

for thirty years, greatly to the benefit of both the contracting parties. On the death of the Viceroy, which occurred at Goa, to the great joy of all classes in India, Martin Alphonso de Sousa, was found to be nominated as his successor, but as he had departed for Portugal, the next on the list, Don Stephano de Gama, the son of the famous Don Vasca, succeeded to the Vice-royalty, in April 1540. Well aware of the false accusations to which his position would expose him, and perceiving the exhausted state of the treasury, he had his private fortune publicly valued, before taking up the appointment. He founded the College of Santa Fé at Goa, for the instruction of converted heathen youths, and appointed the Vicar General, Michael Vaz as first Rector.

In 1542, Don Martin Alphonso de Sousa, arrived at Goa, as Governor-General, and with his fleet, on board the "Quilon," was the celebrated Francisco Xavier, one of the first of the society of Jesuits, and it would have been well, had his example of earnest zeal in the propagation of Christianity, and the welfare of the heathen, been followed by his successors. The profligate manners of the Portuguese, had been strongly represented to the King of Portugal, as causing much injury to their advancement in India, and preventing the Natives from embracing Christianity, and he learnt to his surprise and sorrow, that Christian slaves, were frequently sold to heathen masters, who compelled them to change their religion for idolatry. At this period, the worship of idols, was tolerated at Goa, where the Brahmans were very insolent. The Rajah of Cochin confiscated the property of any of his subjects, who became Christians, and Xavier found that the idolatrous princes made martyrs of them by violent persecution, and the Portuguese Officials, by their disgraceful conduct, caused many to apostatize Christian purity had not been introduced by Europeans, but on the contrary, they had adopted the vicious customs of the heathen. Xavier's preaching, and his Christian example, first caused a beneficial change.

De Gama's successor arrived in the dead of the night, and sent at once, desiring him to deliver over charge. Indignant at being aroused from his bed for such a purpose, he sent back a message, which was neither conciliatory nor polite. De Sousa's first action was to diminish the pay of the soldiers, this caused much discontent, and the next time they went into action, they declined obeying an order to advance, saying, "the rich gentry might march if they "would, but that they only came to make up by plunder, the pay of "which they had been unjustly deprived." De Sousa taunted them, with being unlike their brave ancestors; to which the mutineers replied, that, "the men were the same, but the Governor was changed, "and that their conduct was the result, of his decreasing their pay, "to enable him to give gratuities, to those who knew better how "to beg favours, than to deserve them." De Sousa subsequently became celebrated as a great Pagoda robber. In 1545, he was obliged to resign his command, as the Native Princes, formed a confederacy against him, and his own people hated him, in consequence of the reduction of their pay, and other unpopular acts.

His successor Juan de Castro, was a most meritorious Governor, under him justice was equitably administered, and commerce protected. The Portuguese may be said in de Castro's time, to have reached the summit of their Eastern power and glory. He died in 1548, and left the following record of his countrymen. "I dare not govern "India, by men who are so changed from truth and honour. "The Portuguese entered India, with the sword in one hand, and "the crucifix in the other: finding much gold, they laid aside the "crucifix to fill their pockets." When his effects were examined, three rials and a bloody scourge, were all that could be found. Gracia de Sa succeeded him, but died suddenly in July 1549: during his brief rule, Jesuit Missions to the East were established by Xavier. De Sa was succeeded, by George Cabral.

In 1550, the Samorin and the Rajah of Pimienta, attacked the Rajah of Cochin, who was assisted by 600 Portuguese, under the command of Francisco de Sylva, the commandant of the Fort at Cochin. In the engagement which ensued, the Rajah of Pimienta was killed, but his men subsequently rallied, and De Sylva and fifty of his troops were slain. The Samorin at the head of 14,000 men, then marched towards Cochin, but was kept in check, until the Governor-General Cabral arrived, which he did shortly afterwards, at the head of 6,000 Portuguese, and 40,000 Nairs, belonging to the Rajah of Cochin: just as he was about attacking the enemy, Cabral received orders to desist, from all military operations, by Don Alphonso de Noronha, who had in the meantime arrived from Portugal, to supersede him. A legislative council was now instituted, which greatly curtailed the authority of the Viceroys. In February 1550, a town near Cochin was attacked by 8,000 Nairs, but they were repulsed by the Portuguese, who lost fifty men. Pirates were about this time very troublesome, frequently attacking the Portuguese vessels. On their complaining to the Samorin, he advised them to punish them, if they could.

About this time, the Portuguese built the Rajah of Cochin a palace at Muttencherry, which they presented to him. In 1557, at the request of Sabastian, King of Portugal, one of the Churches in Cochin, called St. Cruz, or Santa Cruz, (*Holy Cross*) was raised to the dignity of a Cathedral, by Pope Pius IV, and a Dominican elevated to the post of Bishop.

A succession of Governors now followed, of whom there is little to record, as the Portuguese possessions were at that time in a state of comparative tranquillity. It seems to have been the rule, for each Governor-General to quarrel with, and malign his predecessor, frequently sending in charges against him to the King: some of them left India as prisoners, others died of grief, and most in a forced retirement.

In 1560, Don Constantine de Braganza was Viceroy; he fitted out an armament against the people of Jaffna in Ceylon, to revenge the persecutions to which the Native Christians were subjected. It was accompanied by the Bishop of Cochin, who before the town was assaulted, performed mass, and granted numerous plenary indulgences for those soldiers who should fight valiantly, and a general absolution to all who should fall. The tooth of Bhudda was now captured, and the king of Pegu fruitlessly offered a fabulous price for its ransom. The Civil and Military powers wished to accede to his terms, in order to replenish the exhausted treasury. But the Priests forbad it, the tooth was placed in a mortar, ground to powder, then burnt, and the ashes strewn over the sea.

In 1564, during the Viceroyalty of Don Antonio de Noronha, Cannanore was beseiged by Nairs, but they were driven off by the Portuguese, who adopted the inhuman revenge of cutting down

40,000 cocoanut trees. They appear frequently to have punished the Natives in this way, thereby entailing great suffering upon many innocent persons, as these trees constituted their principal means of subsistence. It is remarkable, that when Native states waged war on each other, these plantations were regarded as sacred, and never injured.

In 1567, the great poet Camoens, (who sang the praises of Cochin in verse,) having served sixteen years in India, without obtaining anything worthy of his acceptance, although he had been promised much, was desirous of returning to Portugal: the Governor, however wished to retain him in India, and therefore imprisoned him for an imputed debt of 200 ducats, but his friends came forward, and paid the amount, when he sailed safely away. Even to the present time, his Luciad is highly admired in Cochin, by those of Portuguese descent.

About this time, a merchant of Venice, Cæsar Frederick, visited Cochin, and has left an account of the trade, which was then carried on. It consisted principally of pepper, ginger, cinnamon, (this must have been the Cassia) areca, and coir. The pepper is stated to have been of an inferior description, unripe, and full of dirt, in consequence of the price paid for it being fixed at a low permanent rate. Any person who married and settled in Cochin, received some office or employment, according to his trade. The married citizen paid no duty on sugar, or silk, but on all other articles, 4 per cent. to the Rajah of Cochin, who charged duty according to the valuation placed by the owners, on their own articles. The bachelors paid 8 per cent. on everything, to the King of Portugal.

In 1571, the Portuguese possessions in the East, were divided into three portions, designated India, Monomotapa, and Malacca. The Viceroy of India, Don Antonio de Noronha, returned from Lisbon, with a fleet carrying 4,000 men, one half of whom died of sickness on the voyage. He was of a very avaricious disposition, and declined allowing the new Governor of Malacca, Barreto, the money required for the Government. Barreto, consequently refused to go there, and sent a complaint to Portugal. The Government of which country, despatched Francisco de Sousa to Goa, with a sealed packet, which he was directed to deliver to the Archbishop, before he visited the Governor. This packet was opened in the Archiepiscopal church, and publicly read by a common crier, when to the general astonishment and indignation, it was found that the Home Government, without waiting for any justification which the Governor might have to give, had on the sole complaint of Barreto, superseded him, and given his appointment to his accuser. Barreto was succeeded, by Don Diego de Menezes, in 1576.

In 1577, the Jesuits at Cochin, published a translation of Giovanni Gonsalvez's book on Christian worship, [*Doctrina Christiana*] in Tamil, and other works appear to have been printed for the use of the Fishermen, on the pearl fishery coast. In 1578, they printed the *Flos Sanctorum* in the same characters.* In this year Spain having subdued Portugal, Indian affairs became less attended to, and the Portuguese date their decline from this period. Five years previously, Mesquita having been directed to seek satisfaction for an insult offered to a Portuguese vessel, scoured the coast of Malabar, seizing many Native vessels, the crews of which he sewed up in their own sails, and deposited in the ocean. The relations and friends of the victims, travelled from place to place, exhorting all to rise and revenge their murdered countrymen, and a solemn league was then formed, to extirpate the Portuguese from India; war commenced in 1580, and was carried on with disastrous effects, for some time. The confederates consisted of the Samorin, the Rajahs of Guzerat, and Acheen, and some other princes. It is needless to enlarge upon the many engagements, and desperate fighting, which ensued, as it did not extend so far south as Cochin. The confederated Princes, were eventually defeated by the Portuguese, and peace established.

In 1581, Don Francisco Mascarenhas, came out as Governor of India, being the first appointed by the Spanish authorities. In 1584, he was superseded by Don Duarte de Menezes, who on arriving at Cochin, found that the Portuguese had seized the Rajah's customs house, and refused to restore him the duties there levied. He entered into an accommodation, and matters re-assumed their old footing. Menezes died in May 1588, and was succeeded by Emanuel de Sousa Coutinno. In 1590, Mathias de Albuquerque, who had been greatly

* In 1679, at Ambalacate, on the Malabar coast, they published a Tamil Dictionary, written by Father Antonio de Proenza.

beloved as an Indian officer, came out as Viceroy, and was so haughty and arrogant, that he rendered himself detested by all.

In 1594, a bull arrived from the Pope, called "the bull of Crusade," "commanding the Portuguese to reduce the infidels of the country, to the faith, by force of arms." This device was only a new pretext, to sanction the plundering of Pagodas, which were the repositories of Hindu treasures.

In 1597, Vasco de Gama's grandson, became Viceroy, and the same year news arrived, that two Dutch vessels had rounded the Cape, and appeared off the Coast of India. Orders were immediately issued, to attack them wherever they could be found, one was destroyed, and the other wrecked. But on the following year, a fleet of eight vessels left Holland for India, each with eight hundred men on board, and three years' supply of provisions. Admiral Van Nec, commanded the expedition, which succeeded in establishing a trade at Amboyna, as well as a Factory at Baroda.

In 1598, Cuneale Fort was attacked, by the combined forces of the Samorin, and the Portuguese,* but they were defeated, and 300 Europeans slain. However, on the following year, it was surrendered on the promise, that the lives of the Garrison should be spared; but when the Rajah of Cuneale landed at Goa, with 40 men, the latter were torn to pieces by the mob, and the Rajah and his Nephew publicly beheaded, by the order of the Viceroy, because it was asserted, that he had taken the title of "Defender of the Mahomedan "faith, and conqueror of the Portuguese."

In 1599, the famous Don Alexis de Menezes, Archbishop of Goa, landed in Cochin, where he was received in great state, by the Governor, the Bishop, and all the officials. The Town Council immediately assembled, when Menezes called on them to begin manifesting their zeal for the Christian faith, by reducing the Mahomedan fortress of Cuneale, which he designated a nest of pirates. He soon commenced his visitation amongst the clergy, and the Synod of

* The Samorin was induced to join in an alliance with the Portuguese, his old enemies, against the Rajah of Cuneale, as the only effectual means he had of punishing one, who had taken upon himself, the titles of, *King of the Malabar Moors*, and *Lord of the Indian seas*, and who had also cruelly ill-treated a Nair, and dared to cut off the tail of an elephant!

Diamper, (the death blow to the Syrian Church for nearly 100 years,) was shortly afterwards convened. Subsequently he unsuccessfully attempted the conversion of the Rajah of Cochin, and immediately afterwards, raised the Rajah of Porca, to the rank of a Prince, and by conferring on him the title of "*Brother in Arms to the King of Portugal.*" This gave great offence to the Rajah of Cochin, the only Maha Rajah in the neighbourhood. About this time, the Samorin first permitted the Portuguese, to erect churches, and forward the christian religion, in his territories.

In 1600, De Gama was superceded by Ayres de Saldanna, the former was so universally detested by his countrymen, that they even destroyed the statue of his celebrated grandfather, which had been erected at Goa. An effigy of the late Governor, was hung at the yard arm of his own vessels, and even the fowls he had provided for his voyage, were poisoned. Twenty years afterwards, he returned as Viceroy.

In 1607, the Portuguese who were suffering reverses in their contest with the Dutch, learned that two English vessels had arrived in India, they attempted to take them, but were unsuccessful, and the ships reached Surat in safety.* In this year also, the celebrated Alexias de Menezes, Archbishop of Goa, became Viceroy. From this period, little of note occurred in Cochin, from 1619 to 1622, Herman de Albuquerque who was Viceroy, at that time never once received any letter of instruction or information, from the Court of Spain, though attacked by the Dutch, as well as by the English and Natives at Ormuz, from which they were finally expelled: they obtained no assistance from Europe, but were left to fight their own battles as they could.

About this time the Government at Madrid, directed the Governor to dispose of all Civil and Military appointments by public sale, in order to raise money for the support of his Government. The title of Don was sold for a few hundred dollars, and all who could raise the money availed themselves of the honour. A silver plate was

* Moens in his Memorial says, "the Samorin made a contract with Admiral "Peter Willem Verhoeven, under date 16th November, 1608, when he was "compelled by that Admiral, to besiege the town of Cochin, which was in the "hands of the Portuguese."

taken by the Governor on which was the person's name, with the title of Don prefixed to it: this H. E. bound with his own hand to the individual's forehead, and ordered him to rise Don ——. Enormous sums were thus collected. Subsequently the Dutch sold this Portuguese title cheaper, and 50, 25, and even 10 dollars were received as an equivalent for the honour. In 1627, the Bishop of Cochin, Don Luis de Brito succeeded to the Viceroyalty, but died twenty months afterwards. When the patents of succession were opened, it was found that Don Lorenzo de Cunha, was appointed Civil Governor of India, and Nunno Alvarez Pereyra, to the Military command. This entailed great dissensions, as there were two of the latter name, who were thought equally eligible for the appointment. It was finally settled, by its being recollected, that one was a Don, the other was not, whilst no title was mentioned in the patent.

In 1639, whilst the Archbishop of Goa was acting Viceroy, some Dutch ships sailed up to Goa, and destroyed the Portuguese vessels, lying there: in the succeeding year, Portugal having shaken off the Spanish yoke, more attention was paid to Indian affairs: but it was too late, the time of their triumphs had gone by, and the glorious prestige of the Portuguese name, had departed for ever. From this period, their power rapidly declined, divided councils led to divided actions, and defeat consequently ensued. Although individually they were still the same brave and gallant race of soldiers and sailors as their forefathers had been, suspicion of the Government in Portugal, engendered suspicion of that in the East, and Officials knowing that they themselves would be judged harshly, appear to have meted out to others, the same amount of justice they anticipated for themselves.

Persons having purchased their ill paid Government appointments, became grasping and mercenary, not probably so much for the love of money, as for the necessity of obtaining it for their expences: for in those days, Cochin was a gay city, and the common saying was, "China is a good place to make money in, and Cochin to spend it at." The style of living and the pay were consequently incompatible, and helping themselves was a necessity. The whole nation was groaning under priestly dominion, a dominion which set the Bishop's mitre before the King's crown, and the Church before the State, and woe to that Governor, who should dare to disobey the mandate of a priest. This people who aimed at an Empire in India, both spiritual and temporal, at wholesale conversions effected by conviction, bribery, fraud, or violence, who considered no expenditure too large to effect their object, whose self-love had alienated all friends, and injustice created many enemies, were now on the eve of resigning their authority to others.

Another power was now to become predominant in the East, another race was to try their hand at supremacy, and another religion to be introduced. The Portuguese had become objects of aversion to their old allies, the Princes of Cochin, as they had deposed the Rajah, and created his Aunt, the Ranee.

The Dutch beginning to dislike the interference of the Mogul, and others at Surat, wished to establish a settlement on the coast of Malabar, where they might be territorial sovereigns, as well as traders, without being subject to the rapacious exactions of the Mahomedan Government, or the neighbourhood of their successful rivals, the English. Cochin appeared a suitable spot, so they determined to try and dispossess the Portuguese, and occupy it themselves.

In 1661, the Dutch entered into an agreement with the Paliat Achen, hereditary Chief minister to the Cochin Rajah, to assist them in their schemes. "When the Dutch planned the conquest of "the coast, he (the Paliat Achen) materially assisted, and met Van "Goens, 12th March 1661, in a friendly manner, and entered into "an agreement, the purport of which was, that as the Portuguese "and other enemies had deprived him of his lands, he would place "himself entirely under the protection of the Dutch, who were to res-"tore him by force to his territories, whilst he was to obey them "in all things. This agreement was dated the same day on board the ship *De Muscaatboom*.* The Dutch troops appeared on the northern side of Cochin, at Vypeen, where Van Goens fixed his head quarters at the Bishop's house, and strongly fortified the Roman Catholic Church. Leaving 800 men to garrison it, Van Goens re-embarked the remainder of his force, and landed on the southern side of the town. The Rajah of Cochin now openly asserted, that he and the Dutch had entered into an alliance.

* Moens' Memorial. *Dutch Government records.*

Van Goens seized a church to the south, and made it his head quarters. He then attacked the Ranee's Palace at Muttencherry, and after a struggle, succeeded in taking it, and making the Ranee a prisoner. On the following day, the Dutch attacked the fort of Cochin, but the Officer commanding the storming party was killed, and they retreated in confusion. Regular approaches were now opened, but the old Portuguese spirit showed itself, and the garrison bravely defended themselves for several weeks, when the Rajah of Porca, came to their assistance, with 6,000 Natives, and the Dutch determined to retreat.

In the dead of the night, they accordingly embarked in silence. When the morning broke, the Portuguese were amazed at finding their enemy's camp abandoned. A Jew had sounded the hours as usual, thereby effectually deceiving them, and proventing any sally on their part. Seven hundred men were left in the entrenchment at Vypeen. This year Tangicherry fell to the Dutch.

As the Jews had favoured their enemies the Dutch, the Portuguese considered it necessary to punish them, to prevent the recurrence of such conduct, and therefore immediately on the siege being raised, they plundered Jew's Town of almost all it contained, attempted to destroy the synagogue, and carried off the Pentateuch, which was subsequently in 1668 recovered uninjured.

The absence of the Dutch was but temporary. In 1662, Cranganore fell to them: on October of that year, they returned to Cochin under Hustart, but were vigorously met by the Portuguese, who in vain attempted to prevent their landing. The head quarters of the Dutch were fixed at the convent of St. John, the destruction of which had been unsuccessfully attempted by the garrison. In November, Van Goens with a large number of troops, joined the besiegers, but the garrison bravely determined to stand a siege.

In December, the Rajah of Porca, arrived with a large native force at Ernacollum, and threw supplies into the Fort. It was therefore determined to attack him. The natives under Portuguese Officers, met their foes most gallantly, and drove them back with great loss, and the Dutch were compelled to bring up fresh troops before the Porca Contingent could be routed.

But the Portuguese still held out, so the Dutch with the assistance of the troops of their ally the Rajah of Cochin, and the Paliat Achen, determined on storming the Fort, and for eight days and nights, were enabled to keep up a succession of assailants, the troops being relieved every three hours. A remnant of the glorious valour of the early Portuguese, appears to have animated this little band of their descendants, in so long maintaining such an obstinate defence. At length when the Portuguese Commandant Pierre de Pou, found that no assistance could reach him, that his Native allies had forsaken him, and had joined the new European power, that provisions were becoming very scarce, and all were worn out, with fatigue and anxiety; he capitulated, and the Dutch became masters of Cochin, on January the 8th, 1663.

Four hundred Topasses who were not included in the terms of the capitulation, " on discovering the omission, and knowing the cruel " and licentious character of the Dutch soldiery in India, drew up " close to the gate, at which the Portuguese were to march out, and " the Dutch to enter, declaring that if equally favourable terms were " not granted to them, as to the Portuguese, they would massacre " them all, and set fire to the town." It was deemed advisable to accede to their demands, and subsequently some of them, even enlisted in the Dutch service.

At this period the English had a factory in Cochin, but the Dutch on taking possession, ordered them to leave forthwith; they accordingly withdrew to Ponany.

The day after the capitulation, a frigate arrived from Goa, bringing the information that peace had been declared between Holland and Portugal. The Portuguese naturally felt very indignant, at the deception practised upon them, but the Dutch excused themselves by saying, that they had retaliated in kind, the trick played on them a few years previously at Pernambuco in Brazil, by the Portuguese.

Thus fell the Portuguese power in Hindustan, and though the cruelty of its rulers, their breaches of faith, and negation of the rights of others, cannot be extenuated, still the times in which they lived may be pleaded as some excuse, and their loss of empire as an atonement.

It has been usual of late years, to draw comparisons between the Portuguese and Dutch, highly detrimental to the former nation, it is questionable whether facts support such conclusions. The Portuguese language is spoken in every town of note, and many villages, from Bombay to Cape Comorin: the language of their successors has disappeared. The Romish religion yet flourishes, the Dutch converts as a rule, have seceded to Rome. The former nation has indelibly left her mark upon the people, the influence of the latter has vanished as a passing cloud.

A Portuguese priest at Goa, being vauntingly asked by one of the newly dominant power, "when do you imagine the sway of my "countrymen will melt away like that of yours in India?" "As soon" he replied "as the wickedness of your nation, shall exceed "that of my people!"

CHAPTER IV.

Origin of Dutch power in India—Wars with Portuguese—Political acts in Cochin—Dutch Governors—Dutch Clergy—Reduction in the size of Cochin Fort—Disputes with Samorin—Chetwye Fort—Van Imhoff arrives—Attack on Travancore—Pepper treaty and consequent decline of Dutch power—Samorin invades Chetwye—Hyder sends friendly letter—Hyder arrives at Cannanore, and foretels British supremacy in India—Proposes offensive and defensive aliance with the Dutch—Dutch supply Hyder with arms and Elephants—Hyder demands free passage to Travancore—Mysoreans take Chetwye, relief frustrated—Dutch propose alliance with Hyder, who declines—Tippoo—English Commissioners—Rajah of Travancore attempts annexing Dutch Quilon—English attack Cochin—Capitulation—Dutch become prisoners of War—Dutch institutions.

The Dutch who in 1663 became masters of Cochin,* commenced their trade and settlements in Hindustan, long subsequent to the Portuguese. At the latter end of the sixteenth century, *Philip of Spain* prohibited commerce between Holland and Lisbon, which obstructed the people of the former country from obtaining Indian spices, which they had previously procured through that channel.

About the year 1595, the first Dutch fleet appeared in the Indian seas, in search of those condiments they were unable to purchase elsewhere. A Dutch merchant named *Houtman*, having been confined in Lisbon for debt, acquired much information respecting the Eastern trade, of which he transmitted a full account to his countrymen, then engaged in their struggle against Spain. His observations attracted so much notice, that a subscription was raised to liquidate his debts, on which he returned to his Native land, where in 1594, he assisted in the organisation of the *Dutch East India Company*, which in the course of the next year, commenced despatching ships to Hindustan.

---

* Cochin in the *Dutch Records*, is said to have been called Perimbaddapu, and before the advent of the Portuguese, to have formed a portion of Repelim.

The Naval battles in the Indian seas, between the Dutch and Portuguese, were constant, and on the whole disastrous to the vessels of the latter nation. As the Dutch supremacy became more manifest, and their trade augmented, territorial possessions on the continent of Hindustan, became a necessity to them. In 1604, a truce for 12 years was concluded, between Spain and Holland, one article of it recognised the right of the latter, to share in the Commerce of India. Still the vessels of the rival powers, always fought when they met.

The first place at which the Dutch established themselves, was on the Western Coast at *Cambaya*, as early as 1617 : within 50 years, this station was abandoned as unsuitable, together with those of *Brodera*, and *Chircees*, both of which had been taken possession of in 1620. At *Ahmenabad*, the Mahomedan Capital of Guzerat, they founded a factory in 1618, and retained it until 1744, but as it proved unremunerative, it was then evacuated, leaving only a few Natives, as tenants until more propitious times, should enable them to return and reclaim it.

The Dutch possessions in *Persia*, established in 1622, as well as their other factories in connection with them, or near the Western Coast of India, were subordinate to *Surat*, until 1633, when the former were placed directly under the Supreme Government of Batavia. *Vingorla* factory was established about 1655, but there were resident Dutch merchants there, as early as 1641. The Portuguese having in 1640, shaken off the Spanish yoke, in 1646, entered into a treaty with the Dutch, in which it was stipulated, that the latter were to have free access to the ports of the former until 1656, and also to be received as friends in all their settlements, whilst each were to retain the conquests they had made.

In 1667 the various factories, and possessions in Malabar, and on the Western Coast, including those of *Quilon, Culli-Quilon, Cranganore, and Cannanore*, were placed under the *Cochin* command, that fortress having become the seat of their chief power in India. The reason why the Dutch desired territorial sovereignty, has been alluded to in the previous chapter. Cochin formed a good position, where no Native powers could molest them, and having failed in their attack on Goa, in 1660, they succeeded in taking Cochin, in 1663.

The Dutch power being now firmly established in Cochin,* they turned their attention, to removing everything they considered obstructive to their rule, their religion, or their convenience. After the town had been plundered, all property both public and private, was sequestered by the Dutch Company. Any inhabitant who wished to leave the place, was permitted to embark for Goa, the remainder were obliged to take an oath of allegiance to the new power. The fort and houses were left standing as before; but the streets were re-named. The Romish Churches, with the exception of the Cathedral of St. Cruz, or Santa Cruz, were destroyed, as the latter was required as a store house, more especially for sugar from Batavia, and cinnamon from Ceylon: as well as nutmegs, cloves, iron, copper, cordage, rice, pepper, and other articles; its tower was used as a flagstaff. The church of the Franciscans, was employed for the celebration of the services of the Dutch reformed religion.

The Dutch Government soon commenced entering into treaties with the neighbouring Native States. On March 22nd, 1663, a treaty † was concluded with the Rajah of Cochin, who consented to become their vassal, and by which according to Article IX, "all "Christians were placed under the protection of the Dutch Company, "the article stating, that all are under the jurisdiction of the Com- "pany, and should any be guilty of misbehaviour, he is amenable

* Most of the *Dutch Government records of Cochin*, numbering many hundred volumes, are still extant in the Cutcherry. Some are effaced by time, and more mutilated by insects. Owing to valuable translations kindly made, by *C. D'Albedyhll, Esq.*, and the use of those effected by a former Collector, (*Oliphant,*) much of the text of this Chapter has been compiled from Official sources, hitherto unpublished. Each Dutch Governor left a *Memorial* for his successor, which detailed the history of his administration, &c., likewise a *Diary* was kept, in which all important, and many unimportant events were registered. There were also the "letter received" book, and the "letter despatched" book. The "Secret resolution record" the translation book of all letters from the neighbouring Rajahs, the Judicial, and Orphanage records, the Trade books, and many others.

† The treaties between the Dutch and the Rajah of Cochin, were dated, March 22nd, 1663: February 25th, 1664: February 23rd, 1674: May 21st, 1678: May 9th, 1681: April 6th, 1698: February 14th, 1772: October 11th. 1785. But there were also agreements in writing, and other verbal ones, all considered binding on the Rajah.

"to the Company's laws. By a subsequent treaty, dated February "25th, 1664, also article IX, it was stipulated, that those Christians "who reside in the Rajah's territory, shall obey and perform their "obligations to that Government, as the Heathen do."* Deputies were despatched to the Rajahs of Quilon, Culli-Quilon, and other petty states, and treaties of friendship and trade entered into.

Within the fortress of Cochin, Roman Catholics were debarred from the exercise of their religion: whilst their priests were banished, and warned not to enter its precincts in their canonicals. No lay professors of that creed, were allowed to sleep within its walls, or hold any office under the new Government, until they had taken an oath, that they renounced not only their king, but their creed: and thus a number of hypocrites were gained over, that the other Churches no doubt were well rid of. All the Roman Catholics who did not apostatize, left Cochin, and refused to have any mercantile transactions with its new rulers. The Governor soon perceived that an error had been committed, and unless some remedy were discovered, Cochin bid fair soon to have only the garrison and the officials as inhabitants. A compromise was effected with the Roman Catholics, and the church of Franciscans was returned to them, but before the long disputes arose, charges and counter-charges were made, so another arrangement became necessary. It was then agreed that no Roman Catholic Church was to be made use of inside the fort, but the members of that communion had permission to erect a new one at Vypeen, and to remove to it any of the internal fittings from the church of the Franciscans, they might desire. On that island, the church now standing was consequently erected, and dedicated to "Our Lady of Hope," in it, the Altar and the old screen, from the Franciscan church, may (it is asserted) still be seen. The office holders were to be Europeans, Portuguese, Eurasians, and their legitimate descendants.

Cochin was taken by Hustaart, who on departing to attack Cannanore, left two Commissioners in charge **Peter de Bitter* and **Charles Valkenburg*, subsequently in the same year **Ludolff Colster*, was nominated as its first Dutch Governor, *Hendrick Adrian Van Reede*, held this office, from 1673 to 1677. *Jacob Lobo*, 1677 to 1678.

* Memorial of Governor Moens. *Official Records* M. S. S.

Marten Huysman, 1680 to 1681. *Gulmer Vorsburg*, 1684 to 1686. *Isaac Van Dielen*, 1687 to 1693. *Swaardekroon*, to 1698. *Peter Coesaart* (acting) 1698. *Magnas Wichelman*, 1698 to 1701. *W. Moerman*, 1705 to 1709. *Barent Ketel*, 1709 to 1716. *T. Hertenberg*, 1717 to 1724. *De Jong*, 1724 to 1731. *A. Maten*, 1731 to 1735. *J. S. Van Gollenesse*, 1735 to 1743. *Siersma*, 1743 to 1748. *C. Stevens*, 1748 to 1750. *Le Haye*, 1750 to 1751. *C. Cunes*, 1751 to 1757. *C. De Jong*, 1757 to 1761. *G. Wayerman*, 1761 to 1764. *C. Breekpot*, 1764 to 1769. *C. L. Senff*, 1769 to 1771. *Adrian Moens*, 1771 to 1781. *Van Angelbeck*, 1781 to 1793. *Van Spall*, 1793 to 1795.†

It is worthy of note, that in the Dutch fleet was a Clergyman, who, according to *Governor Moens*, was "the first Protestant who preached "in Cochin: his name was *Doctor Anthonius Scherius*, who came with "Admiral Kigklof Van Goens, and who after the town was taken on "the 8th of January, 1663, held public service on the 23rd of that "month." The following are the list of the Clergy, as given by *Moens*. *Dr. Henricus Wallius*, 1663, died 1665. *Dr. Philip Baldœus*, January 28th 1664, left soon after. *Dr. Jacobus Maxwez*, and *Dr. Bartholomeus Heynen*, arrived November 1664, left January 1665 for Ceylon. *Dr. Balthazar Obiede Meter*, February 1665, died in March. *Dr. Marcus Mazius*, 1666, suspended and sent to Batavia, April 1675. *Dr. Johannes Casearius*, February 1669, left commencement of 1677. *Dr. Rudolphus Meerland*, December 1676, left February 1692. *Dr. Gerardus D. Oude*, February 1692, left March 1700. *Dr. Gosuinus Hupperts*, February 1700, ordered to leave April 1705. *Dr. Philippus Gooting*, 1705, to February 1717. *Dr. Cornelius Petrus Schrevelius*, January 1717, died in May. *Dr. Jacobus Canter Vischer*, December 1717, left for Batavia, 1723. *Dr. Petrus Paulus Van Breen*, November 1723, to November 1726. *Dr. Walerius Nicolai*, November 1726, died April 1736. *Dr. Johannes Philippus Wetzelius*, March 1738, left in April. *Dr. Godefridus Johannes Weyerman*, January 1739, left in April. *Dr.*

---

† The above list of *Dutch Governors*, with the exception of those with * before their names, are compiled from such official letter books as could be deciphered. The dates given, are in accordance with the first and last letter of each, that could be discovered.

Johannes Scherius, January 1740, died August 1746. *Dr. Mathias Wermelskircher*, February 1747, soon left, returned February 1748, and March 1749, there being no resident Clergyman in Cochin. *Dr. Hermanus Grieser*, 1750, left the same year. *Dr. Carel Sezilles*, March 1758, left 1761. *Dr. Peter Cornelisz*, January 1761, and was present in the town at its capture by the British, in 1795. He officiated in the place until about 1802. *Dr. Bastian Jansz*, came April 1763, to study Portuguese, and left February 1764.

The Dutch found that territorial sovereignty in Cochin had many disadvantages and expenses, which they were not subject to when traders in a foreign state; and Ludolf Colster had to allay the irritation caused by the violent measures of the two Commissioners, his predecessors. On December 21st, 1663, the following notification was issued in the fortress, "that until further orders, the people of "Cochin shall be unmolested in the enjoyment of their property, "and the revenue from the date of this order, shall be collected ac-"cording to the letter of the King of the Netherlands.".

The fortress was too extensive for a small garrison, whilst it could not be decreased, and without fortifications, no town would have been safe in such a situation. Troops had to be maintained at Quilon, Culli-Quilon, Cranganore, Cannanore, and subsequently at Paponetty, Chetwye, and other places. In fact the forces were kept at rather too large a number, for Malabar to pay its expenses, and return a profit. Mr. Swaardekroon, in his *Memorial on the Malabar Coast*, in 1698, says, "it is to be regretted that the Company "carried so much sail here in the beginning, that they are now de-"sirous of striking them, in order to avoid being overset."

In 1680, the destruction of the forts of Cannanore, Cranganore, and Quilon, was agitated, in consequence of the expence of maintaining them, and the little profit derived. But the Supreme Council of Batavia,* finally decided, that an attempt should be made to give Cannanore back again to the Portuguese, in exchange for Macao, which was a loss to that nation. Cranganore, and Quilon, were also offered for sale. The subject was transmitted to the King of Portugal, but no arrangement was effected.

* Secret orders, of Supreme Government of Batavia. *Cochin Records.*

In 1680, it was resolved, that the fortifications of Cochin, Cranganore, Cannanore, and Quilon, should not be kept up, and also that reductions should be effected, in both the Civil and Military establishments; the total European force proposed to be maintained, was 455, as well as 200 Militia. This resolution owing to various causes, remained unacted upon until the year 1697, when the walls of Cochin had become so ruinous, that something was obliged to be done, so it was therefore directed that, that fort should be reduced one half. At Cannanore and Quilon, only one tower was to be left standing in each place, and at Cranganore merely the exterior works: whilst all Military out-posts were to be withdrawn, excepting those at Paponetty, Porca, and Culli-Quilon.

In rebuilding on a reduced scale the fort of Cochin, care was taken to leave the streets standing. There were seven strong bastions, named respectively after one of the United Provinces. Some of the principal streets were designated as follows, according to an old plan still extant: de Linde straat, *Lime tree street:* de Heere straat, *Gentleman's street:* de Peeterceelie straat, *Parsley street:* de Bree straat, *Broad street:* de Smee straat, *Smith's street:* de Osse straat, *Ox street:* de Burgen straat, *Citizens street:* de Kalven straat, *Calf street.*

The *Topazes*, and *Moondoocars*, were drilled as Militia, each of these having a Captain, or Commandant, over them, to settle trivial disputes, whilst the Fishermen were used as Coolies. They received no pay, but were expected to work, in return for the protection granted them, and were greatly oppressed by the Headmen, a system connived at by the Government.

The only vessels to be kept up, were one small yacht, two sloops, and three row boats; and as the rigorous system of revenue stations, which had been established along the backwater, was a great expence, and created much irritation amongst the Natives, without a corresponding amount of remuneration, it was decided to be too harsh, and directed to be immediately discontinued. At this time, no vessels were permitted either to enter, or leave the Cranganore river, which compelled all traffic, to pass under the Cochin fort walls.

The Dutch Cochin fort, according to Stavorinus, was nearly semi circular, and about a mile and a half in circumference: on the land side were six large bastions, and a cavalier to the eastward: an irregular work on the water side, a substantial loop holed wall terminating at its eastern extremity in a ravelin, before the cavalier: a wet ditch ran round these works, whilst before it was a covered way, and glacis.

The north, or river side, was defended by batteries, whilst a stone wharf, or more properly speaking a plain wall, was erected on the river face, which served two purposes, to protect its banks from the threatening effects of the freshes, and also for a landing place. Either its construction was very faulty, or the materials were inferior, as in 1821, much of it had fallen in, and extensive repairs were deemed necessary: this may however have been in some degree due, to the current of the river setting in against it.

The sea, or west face, was protected by a ravelin, the east by morasses and a strong wall, and the west by walls and a wet ditch. There were three small gates, one to the west the Bay-gate, another to the east called the New-gate, and one on the north the River-gate. Along each side of the wider streets, and ramparts, were Portia trees, *Thespesia populnea*, left by the Portuguese, and under their grateful shade, the inhabitants of an evening lounged or promenaded. A small but elegant, public garden, was kept up inside the fort, and a larger one near the Governor's house: in the vicinity of which, the richer classes possessed Bungalows. There were also others, on the neighbouring Islands.

The pieces of artillery in the fort, consisted of 95 of iron, six of brass, and two mortars. Five hundred and thirty Europeans,* and thirty-seven Natives, were considered a sufficient garrison. This reduction in power, caused the Dutch to fall considerably in the estimation of the Natives, and they became but little feared by the surrounding people.

The principal buildings within the fort, were the Commandant's house, on the north west bastion, and the only one built on the Dutch model. The governor's house, was half a mile to the south, divided from the fort by a long sandy plain. There was an hotel at which

* The European troops maintained in Cochin were rarely above one quarter or a third Dutch: the remainder were composed of English and French deserters, renegade Germans, and similar broken down adventurers, who came for the purpose of mending, or making their fortunes.

the Dutch paid a rupee a day, for board and lodgings, and persons of other Nations two rupees: this was yearly farmed out by the Government.

The Governor of Cochin, was subordinate to the Supreme Council of Batavia, and if not a member of the Batavian administration, his title was that of Commandant. The Town Council consisted of, the Second who was a senior merchant: the Fiscal, the chief of the Military, the Ware-housekeeper, the *Dispensier* or Purveyor, and all the Junior Merchants, (not tradespeople, but Government Civilians,) who might be in the settlement, either in or out of office. The Council had a Secretary, generally a junior merchant, who also held the post of Malayalim translator. The chief of the Military had the title of Major, the Commandant of the Artillery that of Captain-Lieutenant.

At the commencement of the eighteenth century, the Cochin Council became involved in disputes with the Samorin, respecting their rights as heirs of the Portuguese. The quarrels were thought to have been fomented by the English, whose settlement of Bombay, the Dutch had unsuccessfully attacked in 1673. Again in 1696, the English at Anjengo, burnt the Dutch factory there, asserting it had given cover to one of their enemies.*

In 1701, war with the Samorin commenced, and continued in a desultory manner, until 1710, when a truce rather than a peace was concluded. Governor *Moens* traced all the Dutch troubles in Malabar, to the Cochin Rajah, whom he asserted, they had to protect against the Samorin. Four years subsequently, another dispute arose respecting a piece of ground at Chetwye, which was claimed by both the Samorin and the Rajah of Cochin: whilst the latter prince, made it over to the Dutch, the Rajah of Ayroor was also a consenting party to this arrangement, and they agreed forthwith to commence erecting a fort at the mouth of the river, which was declared to be from henceforth, the boundary of the Samorin's territory.

The Samorin, acting under the advice of the English Resident at Tellicherry, sent sepoys disguised as labourers, to enter the Dutch service, for the purpose of carrying stones and mortar for building

* Amongst the Dutch records of Cochin, of 1790, there is a decision, that the English fort at Anjengo shall be destroyed.

the fort. These men were directed to take their opportunity, to lie in ambuscade amongst some neighbouring bushes, and overpower the enemy.

Two Dutch Lieutenants had at that time charge of the works, and were one evening playing at dominoes in the temporary guard room, about half a mile from the fort, whilst the troops were sauntering about enjoying the cool of the evening, and the sentinels not dreaming of danger were inattentive, when they were suddenly overpowered, and the half built fort taken. The officers rushed up with the few men they could collect, but one of them was killed advancing, and the other considering success impossible, drew off the remainder of his forces, and embarked for Cochin: but before leaving, he had the mortification of seeing the English flag, waving over the unfinished fort. On his arrival at Cochin, he was tried for negligence, and shot. The Samorin's people removed the Dutch guns, and demolished the walls of the Chetwye fort.

Councillor Willem Bakker Jacobtz, at the head of 4,000 European and coloured troops, then took the field, recovered the fort of Chetwye, and took Paponetty, a few villages in which district had previously been pawned to the Samorin. The war was terminated in 1717, when the latter was compelled to rebuild the walls of the Chetwye fort; to pay a large sum towards the expenses of the war, and also to promise to give seven per cent. for all pepper that should hereafter be exported from his country. His territories south of Chetwye, were confiscated, and divided between the Dutch and the Cochin Rajah. On April 10th, 1717, the Dutch flag was first hoisted at Chetwye.

The Supreme Government of Batavia, found that in 1721, the expenses of the Cochin command exceeded the receipts, and strongly urged their representatives there to desist from keeping up a continual warfare, and to endeavour to live peaceably with their neighbours. It was also directed, that should the Samorin attack their ally the Rajah of Cochin, they were to remain strictly neutral, as on account of the enormous expenses they had been put to, in fighting the Rajah's battles, all such support must now be withdrawn, and the sovereignty over, quarrels amongst, Native powers must be settled by the Natives themselves. But it was found, that the English managed to foment dissensions for them, and whatever peace councils might preach at a distance, prudence forbad those on the spot from carrying out.

In October 1733, Itchara Pataree, a Ragiadoor of the Rajah of Culli-Quilon, sent express by his master, and accompanied by two of the Cochin Rajah's friends, called upon the Dutch Governor, A. Maten. He stated that the Rajah of Travancore, was making great preparations to attack Culli-Quilon, on the 16th of that month, and was also trying to persuade the Teckencoor and Porca princes, to join in the war. Assistance was therefore most urgently wished for from the Dutch, and the Cochin Rajah. But Governor Maten replied, that the cause of these troubles was owing to the Rajah of Culli-Quilon, having without any provocation, invaded the Marta territory. He continued, that he could give no assistance, but as the chief of Peritally had refused leave to the Travancoreans to pass through his country, to attack Culli-Quilon, they had better join their forces to those of the Peritally Chief.

Two days subsequently, two Ragiadoors, of the 3rd prince of Berkencoor, came on an embassage, requesting the Dutch and the Rajah of Cochin, to mediate between himself and the 2nd prince. The Rajah had been murdered by the latter, who had seized the Government. The *Diary* of these times, is full of details, of the lawless state of Malabar. On February 4th, 1734, Kelloo Menon, was sent by the 2nd prince of Mangatty, to inform the Governor, that Tottachery Tallichanoor of Peradbiddy, had been murdered in the Trichoor Pagoda, by his nephew, because he was about to permit the Cochin Rajah, to appoint the princes of Chialoor, as Governors of Peradbiddy. By the entry on March 4th, 1734, it appears, that there was a division in the Cochin State, for the Cochin Rajah and the Chief of Paroor having quarrelled, the Ellia

---

* Mr. Swaardekroon, a former Governor of Cochin, who was Governor-General of Batavia, from 1718 to 1725, procured the coffee plant from Mocha, and after paying a very high price for what was first produced (15 rix dollars, *per* 125 pounds weight,) he further encouraged its growth by every means in his power. In 1753, 1,200,000 pounds weight were furnished from Cheribon, as much from Jaccatra and the Preanger lands: in 1768, from Jaccatra and the Preanger lands, 4,465,500 pounds weight of this were produced.

Rajah of Cochin, chose to join the Paroor troops. On March 28th, the Rajah intimated to the Governor of Cochin, that he had directed his troops to attack Paroor, and kill the 2nd prince.

In 1734, the Travancore Rajah, made himself master of the fruitful pepper kingdoms of Peritally, and Elleda Suruwum, which a few years previously, had been united, owing to the demise of one of the Rajahs, without leaving a nearer heir than the neighbouring prince. On its seizure by Travancore, the Royal family were confined, and the Rajah died in prison, in 1736. One princess only escaped, by taking refuge in Teckencoor.

In 1738, the Angria pirates, who were at that time the terror of the seas, attacked the Dutch ship *Noord Wolfsbergen*, and the yachts *Zeelands Wolvaaren*, and *Magdalena*, the two last fell into their hands, after three days' hard fighting. The ship escaped, and brought the intelligence to Cochin. All vessels captured by these pirates, were taken to Gheria.

In 1739, Mr. Van Imhoff, the bitter enemy of his opponents, and a most intolerant Governor, came from Ceylon, to examine into, and report upon, the Cochin accounts. On his arrival, the increased and constantly increasing power of the Travancore Rajah, was pointed out to him. This prince acting apparently under English, or other hostile councils, was very unfriendly to the Dutch company, and Van Imhoff considered, that some steps ought immediately to be taken, to curb his arrogance, and curtail his power: whilst the pecuniary difficulties of the Company, required adjustment.

It was considered necessary, to compel the neighbouring Rajahs, to deliver the full amount of pepper which they had contracted to supply, and at the stipulated prices, and should they refuse to act up to their agreements, to ravage their states with fire and sword. It was also suggested, that if the plan adopted in their colonies, were instituted here, it would instil terror, and produce a good effect; namely, making one or more of the most refractory Rajahs, or their heirs prisoners, and sending them to Batavia.

The curtailment of the Travancore power, was no doubt a subject well worthy of attention at this period, but as they were without sufficient forces at hand to command respect, it would have been more judicious, had the Cochin council waited for re-inforcements from Batavia. The troops in Cochin at this time, consisted of 462 infantry, and 23 artillery: this included 158 Europeans, and 191 Topasses, supplied by Van Imhoff from Ceylon. Matters were regarded as too serious to admit of delay, and it was believed the neighbouring petty princes would join in the onslaught, if there was a good watchword for the war. The cause of the princess of Elleda Suruwum or Ellertoo Sooroopum also designated Peritally was taken up, and a protest sent in 1740, to the Rajah of Travancore, against his retaining her territory. It is said Imhoff himself carried this message, and not succeeding in his mission, became exceedingly angry, and threatened an invasion of the Travancore territory. The Rajah replied, that doubtless he might do so, but there were forests into which he could retire in safety. Imhoff retorted, that "where Travancoreans could go, Dutch could follow." The Rajah then broke up the conference, by sneeringly observing, he had been thinking some day, of invading Europe.

Negotiations having thus failed, in 1741, the princess was forcibly re-instated, in the regency of her kingdom. The Dutch obtained a large farm at Airoor or Iroor, about 3 Dutch miles from Quilon, and also Bichoor in the Berkencoor country, where they erected a strong redoubt, (these were abandoned at the peace of 1742.) Again the Travancore forces took the field with great success, every Dutch outpost in Travancore falling before them: they then attacked and defeated the Allied forces, on which the princess fled to the Cochin State for refuge, and the Dutch pensioned her at two rupees five annas, (daily it is to be hoped.) During the war in 1742, the Dutch fort at Quilon was attacked by 6,000 of the best of the Travancore troops, but it was so well defended, chiefly by the Nairs, under their old Rajah, Achootha Barrier, that the enemy were obliged to retire. Advantage was taken of this occurrence, a peace proposed, and a truce entered upon. It was remarked to the Supreme Government, that the peace would probably be lasting, as Travancore funds were running very low.

During this campaign, the people of the countries of Peritally, and Elleda Suruwum, behaved in the most cowardly manner, "their motto apparently being," according to the Dutch Governor's report, "that one who is dead cannot come to life again, consequently "their first duty was to be careful of themselves, and act according "to whatever circumstances best suited their individual cases."

The Dutch by the end of October 1742, had taken Killimanoor, and were ready to make a dash at Attingal, still they had been considerable losers, and both parties appear to have become tired of hostilities. The Travancore Rajah concluded a peace with the Signatty or Rajah of Culli-Quilon, at Manattoo, in September, when the latter agreed to give one elephant, and Rupees 1,000 a year for 4 years, and to cede much of his country to Travancore. At the termination of this affair, the Travancore Officials, gave those of the Rajahs of Cochin and Teckencoor to understand, that their master had a great desire to come to terms with the Company, and ordered them as they valued his friendship, to try and bring it about. But these mediators had no wish to assist with their services, although the Dutch exhorted them to do so. After three months, (in December,) the Cochin Council determined to act for themselves, without their Native Allies, and to address the Rajah of Travancore direct: he seemed willing to agree to terms, and sent his officials, the Delwah, and Coochu Moossadoo, to Mavillicurray, whilst the Dutch despatched Ezekiel Rabbi, and Silvester Mendes, the Captain of the Topasses. Within the expiration of a month, (January,) affairs were so far completed that some members of the Cochin Council, were about to proceed to Mavillicurray for the purpose of concluding the business, when the Travancore Officials, suddenly gave them to understand, that His Highness had changed his mind, consequently if they wished to effect any arrangement, they must go to Trivandrum.

The conference was broken up, and it was decided to prepare for war. On this Travancore re-opened negotiations, the parties met at Paroor, (near Quilon), and the affair was nearly closed, when it was again broken off. A third conference held at the same place, ended in a similar manner. The Dutch continued these negotiations, without expecting any good result, but simply to gain time, for obtaining instructions from Batavia.

Cochin affairs were such a source of anxiety, at this period to the Supreme Government of Batavia, that when Commandant *Golonesse*, in 1742, in a letter to them, was induced to maintain that Malabar was one of the most important possessions of the Dutch company:

the Governor-General *Mossel*, bitterly replied, "I am so far from "being of your opinion, that I rather wish the ocean had swallowed "up the coast of *Malabar*, an hundred years ago."

Constant changes were occurring about this time, in the various petty Native States. About 1739, when the Rajah of Quilon died, his country became blended with that of Culli-Quilon, whose Rajah was also prince of Pannapully. His troops numbered about 15,000, and he received a yearly subsidy of 500 fanams, for the destruction of wild beasts, which it is observed his troops efficiently performed, and that they were more adapted for guards, or for the defence of walls, than for hostile engagements in the field.* In 1742, the Samorin troops 1,000 strong, invaded the Cochin Rajah's territory, but withdrew when the English protested.

Wars with Travancore, and negotiations for peace, continued for several years, until at last the following treaty was proposed by that State, and conditionally accepted with modifications at Cochin, it was finally sanctioned by the Batavian council, in an order dated October 18th, 1748. Again difficulties were raised, and it was not until August 15th, 1753, that peace was finally concluded. By it the Dutch bound themselves in future, to follow a *strict peace policy*, to keep clear of all disputes, and never again to resort to force, except in self-defence. Governor *Moens* in later years, severely commented upon this treaty, observing, "the system of Government entirely changed from this time."

The ninth article of this treaty, entered into with the Rajah of Travancore, and signed on the above date, stipulated, that the Dutch "shall recede from all engagements, which they may have "entered into with the other Malabar princes, whom the King of "Travancore might choose to attack, and on no account interfere "in their disputes, afford them assistance or shelter, or in any re-"spect raise any opposition to the enterprises of the king."

* In 1740, October 13th, the Dutch entered into an alliance with the Rajah of Repelim. It was under the four following heads. 1st, that he was to deliver up all his pepper to the Company. 2ndly, to stop and punish all smugglers in that article. 3rdly, to give up all deserters. The Company binding themselves to protect him, provided he entered into no wars, without obtaining their consent.

Thus the Dutch threw over their Native Allies, and pledged themselves to leave them all to the mercy of Travancore. Had the treaty ended here, it might have been charitably surmised, that it had been wrung from them in consequence of disastrous defeat: but unfortunately, the concluding portion shows that a pecuniary motive, was also at work, as it agrees, to make a yearly present in money to Travancore, to supply its Rajah annually on payment, with various kinds of warlike stores and ammunition, to the value of Rupees 12,000, whilst they were to receive 1,500,000 pounds of pepper, at Rupees 13 per every 100 pounds, with any other production his state yielded: and 10000 pounds more, out of the territories *to be conquered*, at 11 Rupees for every 100 pounds. Certainly giving up their former Allies to an ancient enemy, and providing arms to subdue their former friends, for the sake of gaining 4 annas, or six-pence on every 25 pounds of pepper, was an inglorious act.*

At the private interview at Mavillicurray, between the Cochin Rajah and the Dutch Ambassador on one hand, and the Travancore Rajah on the other, the Dutch unsuccessfully attempted to have a clause inserted, that should the Rajah of Cochin, or the Chetwye island be attacked by Travancore, such was to be considered equivalent to a declaration of war. A promise was however obtained,† that the Rajah of Travancore, "would live in friendship with the "Rajah of Cochin, provided he gave no cause to the contrary." The Cochin Rajah had then to make what terms he could for himself, and the two princes agreed to continue in friendship, but ended in open enmity, and soon went to war, without any interference from the Dutch, excepting useless protestations. Subsequently finding the Travancore army was annexing all the territory to the south of the

---

* This pepper treaty was ever after a source of irritation, and Van Angelbeck alludes to the subject in his memorial to his successor, in 1793. The Rajah never appears to have furnished the quantity he promised, and Commissioners were continually being sent to Trivandrum to remind him, at last it was only by agreeing to raise the price to Rupees 115 a candy, that they obtained any; in 1790 none was furnished, and a higher price demanded, which Van Angelbeck refused to give. Sometimes Travancore declared the Dutch ought to have none, as they were assisting their enemies: afterwards that they were engaged with the Mysoreans; anyhow, the treaty does not appear, to have brought either credit, or money to the Dutch.

† Memorial of *Commandant F. Cunes*, dated, December 31st, 1756.

town of Cochin, Governor Cunes addressed a letter to the Rajah, in which he pointed out, that the Dutch limits extended for two miles South of Cochin, and he trusted that they would be respected.

In 1749, Angria's piratical fleet, consisting of seven grabs, and six galleys, ap peared before Cochin, but sailed away without attempting anything. In 1754, they attacked three Dutch vessels, the *Wemmenum* 50 guns, the *Vreede* 36 guns, and the barque *Jaccatra* 18 guns. The first two took fire and blew up, the last fell into the hands of the enemy. This piratical power, which was subsequently destroyed in 1756, by the British Commodore James, aided by a Mahratta contingent, had originated from a fleet kept up by the Mogul, under an Admiral termed the *Sidee*, for the protection of Mahomedan ships, when trading between India, Persia, and Arabia, from the attacks of both pirates and Portuguese. In 1757, Gheria was given over to the Mahrattas, who became no less dreaded by the Dutch, than their piratical predecessors had been.

From this period the prestige of the Dutch rapidly declined: the petty princes soon discovered how their interests had been given up to Travancore in the treaty of 1753, and they turned to the Samorin for assistance. The Samorin found that he could insult the Dutch with impunity, as although they sent remonstrances, these were unsupported by physical force. Therefore, daily becoming bolder, he retook Paponetty or Ayroor, and obliged the Dutch to retire to Cranganore, with the loss of eight pieces of Artillery.

In 1755, and the following year, the Samorin with some thousands of Nairs and Moors, again advanced, and invaded the country around Cranganore; they strengthened themselves at Paponetty and threw up earth works at Tripoonatty, had posts at Madilagaum, and made palisades at the river, closing the passages, and preventing supplies reaching the Dutch garrison at Madilagaum. The officer in command of this outpost, withdrew his men to Cranganore, and thus augmented the force in that garrison, by 140 men. The Samorin princes, with 5,000 troops, advanced close to the Cranganore fort, and over-ran the Paroor territory, apparently with the intention of subsequently attacking the Dutch. Great alarm was felt for Cochin, as the garrison at this period, only consisted of 138 Europeans, and 75 Topasses: so some Natives were enlisted, and applications made to Ceylon for reinforcements, but there were none to spare. The Dutch then requested the neighbouring Rajahs of Chetwye, Ayroor, and Cranganore, all residing on the island of Chetwye, to stop the Samorin's further progress, as they were destitute of troops in Cochin. But these princes, suspicious of a foreign alliance, from which they had rarely obtained any advantage, declined. The Rajah of Paroor and the Samorin became great friends, the former furnishing the troops of the latter, with supplies.

Stavorinus observes, that the petty princes, perceiving the Dutch no longer protected them against Travancore, had recourse to the Samorin, whom they persuaded to enter into hostilities against the Company, imagining that if they were obliged once to take up arms, matters would eventually come round, according to their wishes. Even the Rajah of Travancore on being applied to by the Dutch, quietly rejoined, "that he had told the Samorin's Ambassadors, that they ought "to advise their Sovereign to stop." But the Travancore Rajah was suspected of being a looker on, with the expectation that the Dutch would be compelled to beg his assistance, and then he could carry out his schemes of conquest.

The Samorin now finding, that he was becoming very powerful, and all the petty princes were flocking to his standard, or offering him aid, proposed to the Dutch, that they should enter into an alliance, and attack their mutual enemy of Travancore. On October 18th, 1756, a Jew, Ezekiel Rabbi, was sent by the Samorin, to offer to the Dutch 2,000 candies of pepper yearly, if they would join in a league against Travancore. The Cochin Council replied, that as soon as their lands which he had taken were restored, they would treat upon this subject, but the basis of the treaty must be the old one of 1717, with the addition of a few articles: whilst in the intermediate time, Travancore was sounded, as to whether she would assist the Dutch against the Samorin, as it was deemed advisable to discover, what terms either party would give, before deciding upon which to join. Governor *Cunes* remarks, in a letter to Batavia, "should Travancore refuse to join us, it becomes the "more urgent, that your Excellencies should furnish sufficient forces, "to enable us to assume a commanding position, merely to over-awe "these Malabar Chiefs, and thus to continue on the terms of most "intimate friendship with Travancore, without the slightest room "for any misunderstanding: and I must also add, that should the "Samorin give an opportunity for a renewal of friendship with "him, on reasonable and honourable terms, it is advisable to at "once close with them." Then follows an apology, for having been compelled to go to war, but the Samorin had been permitted to continue his aggressions as long as possible, having been only met by protests, and the consequence had been, that he became more and more exacting. The Cochin Rajah at this period, held no intercourse with the Dutch, probably being indignant, at their not joining him against Travancore.

Before long, news arrived, that the Samorin intended to pass down his troops, by water, from Paroor to Porca, and the Dutch wrote to the Rajah of Travancore, advising him to look to it. The latter despatched 200 additional Nairs to Porca, but remarked, that were he to attempt to drive the Samorin out of Paroor, a larger force would be needed, than he felt disposed to send into a foreign State. At this time secret information was received, that the Danes who had a factory at Calicut, were assisting the Samorin, with powder and lead, as well as seven Artillerymen.

Casparus De Jong became Commandant in the commencement of 1757, and in his *memorial*, dated, March 7th, 1761, observes, that he found everything in confusion. Paponetty and 8 Dutch cannon were in the Samorin's hands, Chetwye was invested on the land side, the enemy had built a stone fort at Poolicurra 1½ miles from Chetwye, and another at Madilagaum, where cannon were mounted, whilst he had staked the river and placed guards at Pootencherra, in order to prevent communications with Chetwye.

In 1757, three hundred European, and seventeen hundred coloured troops arrived from Batavia, and De Jong was enabled to act more vigorously; in the succeeding year, the obstruction in the river at Pootencherra was broken through, Chetwye fort was relieved, and the Samorin's troops routed in every encounter. The Samorin had wished to regain the Sovereignty over the whole island of Chetwye, whilst the Travancore Rajah quietly looked on, until the Dutch solicited his assistance, when he took the opportunity of extending his conquests, under the pretence of assisting the Company.

The Samorin now perceived symptoms of a storm lowering over his own country, for ominous whispers began to be heard in Malabar, that Hyder Ali wished for sovereignty over the Western Coast. The Dutch power was increasing, and the Travancore Rajah appeared as if he were about to join them, so in this year (1758) the Samorin concluded a peace, though the treaty was left unsigned, because as De Jong remarks, that concluded in 1717, remained in full force, whilst this new one was rather detrimental to the Company's reputation. The terms were as follows :—

The stone fort at Madilagaum and the watch places at Chetwye, and Pootencherra were to be razed, and the captured cannon returned to the Dutch, who were likewise to be re-instated in the possession of their settlement at Madilagaum with the lands and gardens pertaining thereto. The 18½ villages which had been taken from the Cochin Rajah, were to be restored to the Dutch, and the Samorin was to pay 65,000 rupees, for the expenses of the war.

De Jong observes, that in the treaty of 1717, the Samorin was to have paid the expenses of the war 10,625 rix dollars, but it was six years before it was received. He now paid 35,084 rupees 4 annas, on account of the 65,000, and ceded three islands opposite, Palliport, which the Dutch were to retain until they had re-imbursed themselves for the expenses of the war not already paid, from these islands they obtained from ten to twelve thousand rupees yearly. In 1773, when Hyder came into Malabar, the accounts were still unsettled, whilst he claimed the whole of the Samorin's territory. But as these islands had never belonged to Hyder, the Cochin Council decided to retain them, until they should be reclaimed by the Samorin.

De Jong denominates the Rajah of Travancore a dangerous neighbour, who had annexed and was then (1761) in undisturbed possession of, the kingdoms of Culli-Quilon, (including Quilon), Porca, Teckencoor, and Berkencoor, besides Attingal, and Travancore. The treaty of 1753, with the Rajah of Travancore, article 29, stipulated that all the Dutch subjects and vassals, in the island of Chetwye, should remain free and unmolested, but fears were now entertained, that he contemplated adding these lands to his dominions. De Jong apprised the Rajah of Travancore, what he considered the limits of the Dutch territory around Quilon and Cochin, but little notice appears to have been taken of his communication. So he addressed another letter, affirming that Castella, two miles south of Cochin, was the Dutch boundary, within which he requested no acts of hostility might take place, as the inhabitants were under the protection of the Dutch, but that the Travancore Rajah might within those limits, hold the same rights over the people that the Cochin Rajah had previously possessed, because he conceived that he had fairly acquired this, by the fortunes of war. He continues his memorial, by remarking to his successor, that there is nothing to prevent the Travancoreans driving the Cochin Rajah out of his palace at Muttencherry, annexing the land up to the walls of the Cochin fort, making their vassals and merchants his subjects, and seizing the river and land customs duties. Their people at Quilon were he asserts then treated by the Travancoreans like slaves, whilst the Paliat Achen, the Kodachayree and two other Kaimuls, were either prisoners in the hands of Travancore or treated as such.

The Travancore Rajah who had agreed in the treaty of 1753, to supply the Dutch with pepper at a certain rate, now refused to fulfil his contract, and informed them that they were no longer a sovereign power, but merely a number of petty merchants, and that if they required spices, they must purchase them at the market rates.*

---

* In 1757, *Commandant de Jong*, addressed some *secret considerations* to Batavia. He observes, that the principal object of the Dutch company, in expelling the Portuguese from the Western Coast of India, was in order to become the possessors of the pepper-trade, exclusive of every other nation. But the bad faith of the Malabar princes, and the competition of European rivals, caused them much disappointment. Their competitors bought pepper as they required it, always paying the market rate, or a little above it, whilst the Dutch insisted upon the performance of the contracts at a low fixed rate, and that no pepper should be disposed of, until they were served. The contracts mention no *fixed rate*, but only speak of the *market rate*, as the rule to be adhered to. The Dutch designated all trade with other parties contraband, and frequently brought Military force to check it, this was expensive, and the Malabar command was almost invariably in debt.

In his *memorial*, he gives his opinion, that monopolies in this article, did not exist before the advent of the Dutch, and were illegal combinations of the rulers, as he hints for defrauding the people. The Portuguese obtained it he remarks, from the Rajahs, but they only acted like brokers, between the owners

In 1762, the Travancore Rajah having defeated the Samorin, in the cause of the Rajah of Cochin, re-instated the latter in part of his dominions. He also opened Allepey which he had taken from Cochin, to foreign trade, greatly to the loss of the Dutch, who refused to permit such being done, some years previously, when their leave was asked by the Rajah of Porca: giving as a reason, that they should possess no check, upon the exportation of cinnamon and pepper.

The treaty of peace between the Dutch and the Samorin, had not in 1762 been completely fulfilled, there still remained Rupees 16,000 due to the former, so the island of Moothoocoonoo, (taken from Paroor,) was mortgaged to them for that amount, and if unredeemed in two years, was to become Dutch property. Travancore disapproved of this transaction, and laid claim to the island, on behalf of the Rajah of Cochin, according to the treaty with that state, dated 1761, (see page 48) matters thus remained, until 1766 or 1767, when troops were sent from Cranganore, to hold forcible possession of those lands. Subsequently both the Travancore and Cochin Rajahs, repeatedly asked permission, to build a strong fort there, as a boundary to the Jacotay lines, but were invariably refused.

In 1762, Hyder Ali suddenly made himself master of Bednore, and fortified that town, as well as Onore, Barcelore, Bekkenore, and Mangalore. He was assisted* by the Portuguese, who allowed their officers to take service under him. The Dutch at this period had factories at Barcelore and Mangalore, but he did not interfere with them. He applied to the Governor of Cochin *(Wayerman)* for one thousand muskets, on which they were promised and written for to Batavia, but the Supreme Government disapproved of this course, and declined furnishing them. Hyder subsequently moved towards the north: and the arms he could not procure from the Dutch, were furnished by the French.

---

of the pepper, and the Portuguese Government. When competition arose, monopolies were by degrees introduced, but such a power does not exist in the laws of Cheruman Permaul, by which the rulers of Malabar are bound, and from which they cannot deviate, without the consent of their subjects. This was a cause, why the Rajahs and Chiefs, feared to prevent smuggling, as they were well aware, of the illegality of the system of monopolies.

* *Governor Moens'* memorial to his successor, 1781.

Breekpot was installed as a Governor of Cochin in 1764, and shortly afterwards received a letter from Hyder Ali, in which he expressed his hopes, that he and the Dutch would continue friends, and proposed their again sending a Resident Factor to Barcelore, to reopen the trade, in forwarding the success of which, he promised to use his best exertions. Breekpot despatched a polite answer, and stated that the Company did not wish to extend their trade at present, but that as soon as they had resolved on doing so, they would gladly avail themselves of his friendly offer. A short time previously, the Cannanore establishment had been reduced, and now some more of the ammunition, weapons, and goods, were transferred to Cochin, in accordance with orders formerly received from Batavia. The fort had been directed to be destroyed, but as it was reported in good order, well laid out, capable of defence by a small body of troops, and advantageously situated for trade, it was determined to allow it to remain. But instructions were given, that if Hyder Ali offered a good sum for it, it was to be sold to him, with a proviso, that a Dutch President should be permitted to live and trade there, both house rent, and tax free. Subsequently in 1771, this fort was purchased by the Ady Rajah, or as he was commonly styled, the Sultan of the Laccadives.

Breekpot found that directions had been received, to destroy fort William at Chetwye, and build a warehouse instead, but his predecessor Wayerman, had refused to obey what he termed, "a most impolitic order." He pointed out, that it was a necessary frontier fort, and therefore he merely reduced the establishment. In 1765, Breekpot decreased the number of guns, from 42 to 22, and in the January following, sent an Engineer, to estimate the amount it would cost, to break down the fort, and build a warehouse. Time was lost, the monsoon set in, and nothing was done. In 1767, again strict orders were received from Batavia, to destroy the Chetwye, Quilon, and Cranganore forts, but owing to the presence of the Mysoreans, the orders could not be obeyed. Wayerman had been directed to blow up Cranganore fort, but he replied, that if he did so, all the houses within it must share the same fate, whilst the cost of breaking it down by manual labour, would be excessive. He reduced the establishment from 67 to 40 men, with 14 guns. This Governor asserted, that Cranganore was the key to North Malabar, and its destruction would be suicidal. Breekpot further decreased the garrison, by 8 men. In the year 1767, owing to the great peculation in the Government money in Malabar, a large sum had to be written off, to make good the deficiencies.

On February 18th, 1766, Hyder had arrived within nine miles of Cannanore, and the Commandant of that fort, reported to Cochin a month later, that although Hyder had ordered any Nair, or other Hindu, to be put to death who wore the topknot of hair on his head, *(cudumi,)* he had been so civil to their possessions, and dependants, that not a cocoanut had been picked from one of their trees, nor even a leaf abstracted. On March 15th, the crafty Mahomedan visited the Dutch commandant, H. Kroonenberg, at Cannanore, treating him most courteously, and inviting him to his camp at Cherkil. On his accepting the invitation, he placed him by his side on his own elephant, and at 3 P.M. they reached the camp, where he was consigned to the care of Nawab Ali Raza Khan, from whom he gleaned the following particulars, viz., that Hyder preferred the Dutch to all other European powers, and would grant them favours, he would show neither to the English, nor the French. Subsequently, Ali Raza Khan further informed him, that Hyder had been heard to say, "the English are masters of the whole of "Bengal, of the greatest part of the Coromandel Coast, they are trying to get Malabar under them, and have it in contemplation to "send an expedition to China. What then will remain for us to "do, but to submit to them? I clearly foresee and assure you, that "unless a change takes place within two years, the English will be "masters of all India. I know well my friend," continued Ali Raza Khan, "that Hyder does not see things dimly, and he will "sacrifice everything to prevent this coming to pass. He is a brave "soldier, and if his life be spared, he will succeed."*

Governor Moens, in his Memorial, states, that Dutch Commissioners at Hyder's request, met him at Calicut, in April 1766, when they enumerated the titles by which they held their factories, and right to trade, under the Samorin: they also informed him, that the Rajahs of Cochin and Travancore were their Allies, and trusted he

* *Dutch Government records of Cochin.* M.SS. dated, March 1766.

would not molest them. His replies may be summed up under the following heads, made in the form of propositions by him.

1st. That he was anxious to form a treaty of friendship with the Dutch Company, and would allow them to purchase the produce of his country: but they in their turn, were required to furnish him with what he had need of, in the form of articles and goods.

2ndly. That if the Dutch Company required assistance for the purposes of defence, he was willing to furnish them with 30,000 land forces, and his fleet: but that he should expect the co-operation of their vessels of war.

3rdly. That should he again return towards the south of the Malabar coast, the Dutch Company must provide him with 1,000 Europeans, whose pay and expenses he would defray.

4thly. That he was willing to allow the Company to keep the Chetwye lands, and as regards permitting the Rajah of Cochin to remain unmolested, that he would do so out of respect to the Company, though he had a longing for that pepper producing country, but that he was unable to guarantee anything respecting Travancore. That whenever he purposed proceeding southward, he required a free passage through the territories both of the Company and the Cochin Rajah, he on his side guaranteeing the inhabitants against losses. He also stated, that he had not yet made up his mind, when he should advance towards the south.

5thly. That he was ready to give the Company more lands.

6thly. That he would allow the Company to trade freely as far northwards, as his power was established, or might hereafter be.

7thly. That the Dutch might replace their establishments at Barcelore, and institute others at Ponany and Calicut."

Moens continues, that it appeared Hyder was anxious to enter into an offensive and defensive alliance with the Dutch, and he even wrote a letter to this effect, which was addressed to the Supreme Council at Batavia. The Cochin authorities replied, that they were unable to answer his requests, which had been at his desire submitted to the Supreme Council: still they flattered him with delusive expectations. Hyder, however, was not to be imposed upon, and modified his promises, especially regarding the Rajah of Cochin, which he said must be conditional, as he expected him to contribute towards the expenses of his wars: and he offered to enter into a like arrangement with Travancore. His demands were, 4 lacs of rupees, and 8 elephants from the former Rajah, and 15 lacs with 30 elephants from the latter, in default of receiving which, he proposed paying a visit to those countries.

The Governor of Cochin transmitted these requests, to the respective Princes. The Travancore Rajah replied, that he was unaware that Hyder went to war to please him, or in accordance with his advice, and was consequently unable to see the justice of his contributing towards his expenses. Besides he continued, he was a tributary to the Nawab, Mahomed Ali, and could not afford to be a vassal to two powers at the same time: still he would give a considerable sum of money, provided Hyder Ali would re-instate the Rajah of Colastry, and the Samorin, in their dominions. He also asserted, that the dispossessed Princes were prepared to contribute, and boldly concluded, that towards such an object, the Dutch Company ought to subscribe largely. The Rajah of Cochin replied, that he left his affairs in the hands of the Company, and trusted that whatever conclusions were arrived at, the Colastrian and Calicut Princes, would regain their dominions.

The Dutch Governor feared to send such answers to Hyder, and instead of despatching to him a Commissioner, wrote to say, that he had communicated his terms to Batavia, Travancore, and the Rajah of Cochin, and trusted all would be arranged in a satisfactory manner. On July 20th, the Travancoreans, who appear to have entertained less hopes of a peaceful solution than did the Dutch Governor, commenced extending their lines, to within the range of the guns of Cranganore fort, and on to the territory of the Cranganore Rajah. The Dutch fearing to offend Hyder, sent notice to the Travancore Rajah, that he must cease his work, and that no armed Nairs belonging to his State could be permitted within their (the Dutch) limits. Only a month previously, (June 14th) the Commandant of the Cranganore fort had called upon the Cranganore Rajah, and complained that he had permitted the Samorin's family, and armed followers, fleeing from Hyder, to take refuge in his country. He "also pointed out to him, that according to a lawful contract between him "and the Honourable Company, all the land from Chetwye to Cran-

"ganore, was under the overseership of the Company, and also that "His Highness and his whole country were under the protection "of the Company: that therefore his request to send away the Sa- "morin's family and followers, was not unreasonable, and that here- "after, His Highness must abide implicitly, by the good advice "given him by the Company." The Rajah acquiesced, and promised obedience in future.* On the 22nd when the Samorin and his followers returned, they were desired to retire. The Dutch Officer commanding Quilon, reported on May 22nd, that "our competitors "the English, have sent from 70 to 80 men, and 500 fire arms, to the Travancore Rajah."

In October (1766), it was rumoured, that Hyder intended to invade Travancore: but he delayed his movements, and on the following January receiving information, that the Mahrattas and the Nizam were about to attack Mysore, he hastened back to the protection of Seringapatam. Governor Moens wrote on November 16th, 1766, to the Officer Commanding Cranganore, directing that no Konkanies, Moplahs, or black Jews, were to be permitted to proceed northwards, unless they had passports, as it seemed probable they wished to join Hyder Ali.

On February 20th, 1767, Hyder's fleet of 28 sail, came into the Cochin roads, and two of them even entered the river, and anchored close under the wall. Their Admiral stated, that they were in pursuit of the Mahratta fleet. The next day they left for the north. In March the following year, many of these vessels were captured by the English Squadron. In 1770, the Mahratta fleet, consisting of 30 sail, came into the Cochin roads, reporting that they were friends, wishing to make a treaty, and asking to be allowed to anchor close to the town wall. Permission to do so was granted them, but they did not avail themselves of it. After remaining 18 days, and virtually blockading the place, they sailed northwards.

When *Moens* became Governor on April 2nd, 1771, he found the defences of Cochin in a very dilapidated state, there was no covered way, or glacis, the ditch was nearly dry at low water, and only knee deep at high water, the breast works were broken down, and the

* *Official report to the Governor of Cochin.* M.SS.

wheels of the gun carriages appeared above the walls. In two places the town was particularly weak, near the bastion termed "Gelderland," and that designated "Holland," which were not far distant from one another, here no ditch existed, and that part of the fortifications was almost defenceless, for the guns were worn out, and their carriages rotten. On a representation being made, he was permitted to make a deep and good ditch encircling the fort, execute repairs, and form a covered way and glacis, whilst a fair show of cannon were planted on the walls. These necessary repairs were completed in 1778.

Moens left a most elaborate Memorial for his successor, consisting of 553 pages in Manuscript, it is still in excellent preservation, and comprises a very much fuller account than those of any of his predecessors. The reason for this increased amount of information, was an order sent in 1777 by the Supreme Government of Batavia, for answers on the following subjects. A short account of the country and the nations inhabiting it, with a Map if procurable. The form of the native Government. The most common words in their language, and the characters employed by them in writing. Some of their books. A summary of their manners and customs, especially with reference to births, marriages, and burials. Their modes of agriculture, how they prepare and work in metals. Their plan of computing time, and their knowledge of astronomy. An account of the seasons, with remarks on the heat, cold, and barometrical variations. A description of the animals, plants, and minerals. Rare animals and birds were directed to be forwarded in arrack. Plants to be sent between two pieces of paper, with their leaves, blossoms, and fruit. Minerals in their ore, with a statement of how, and where they were procured. A strict enquiry was to be instituted into all herbs, plants, roots, or other natural productions, employed by the natives for the cure of diseases, or any other purpose. Any useful vegetable productions, such as roots, plants, herbs, the bark, leaves, or fruit of trees, were directed to be forwarded to Batavia.

In 1772, the disputes between the Rajah of Cochin and the Dutch, had become rather ominous, as the former was naturally indignant at the way in which he had been treated by the latter. A convention was then held, to settle these differences; one subject agitated, was the right of the Dutch to collect the revenues around Cochin. The following terms were finally agreed to, by the Dutch Governor. "From this day forward, as long as the Government of Cochin "exists, I do cede and transfer, unto you and your descendants, the "right of collecting the income from Muttencherry and Chellye, "(two suburbs of Cochin.) To collect the farms and customs of "Amaravady (also a suburb of Cochin,) and to conduct the affairs of "Muttencherry, Chellye, and of the Konkanies and their temple."* But there was the following understanding, "that the Rajah shall "impose no new demands upon the Konkanies, that they shall have "full liberty to complain to the Dutch Governor if aggrieved, and "that the Rajah shall not interfere in any matters of the temple, "without the knowledge and consent of the Company."†

It is necessary to observe, that the disputed ground, had in olden times been the esplanade of the fort, which was made over to the Dutch by the Cochin Rajah in 1663: but the treaty does not state, whether as a gift with the right of sovereignty over it, or merely as a loan. In 1791, the Rajah loaded the Konkanies also called Canareens with new imposts, this was resisted by the Cochin Council. The English are said to have espoused the Rajah's side but he eventually gave way, and admitted the right of Dutch protection over the Konkanies and Christians.

Giving up these rights must have been a great trial to the Dutch, as they had guarded them most jealously ever since 1663. In this year the Cochin Council reported to Batavia, that the French had massed 7 or 8,000 troops at the Mauritius, the object of which was unknown. But they thought an increase to the Cochin garrison was desirable with as little delay as possible, as the Dutch forces on the Malabar coast at that time, amounted to merely 607 persons, of whom 332 were Europeans, but some were invalids. The next year, their forces consisted of 640 men, of whom 360 were Europeans, and a few months subsequently, a further augmentation of 150 Sepoys was made.‡

---

* *Dutch Government Records* M.SS.

† *Memorial of Van Anglebeck*, 1793.

‡ The amount of pepper received in Cochin, between March 31st 1771, and the middle of April 1772, was 1,494,407 pounds: or 161,333¼ pounds less than the previous year.

Matters with Hyder Ali up to that period had taken no definite turn, the Dutch Council trusted to some fortunate accident, obviating the necessity of a decision, whilst he was awaiting a favourable opportunity to invade Travancore, without doubt counting upon the active, or at least passive friendship of the Dutch and the Cochin Rajah. At any rate he may have fairly anticipated a free passage, in accordance with his communication to the Commissioners in 1766. In 1773-74, he swept down into Malabar, the Samorin again became a fugitive, and attempted to take refuge with the Cranganore Rajah. But the Dutch Governor ordered him instantly to depart, so he embarked in a Native craft for Travancore, with which Rajah alone, he appears to have been safe in his forest encircled cities. In this year the Travancore Rajah as a matter of courtesy, handed over to the Dutch, three native Christians, who were under sentence of death, for killing a cow: in return, he asked for arms, promising payment for the same.

In October 1775, the Dutch supplied Hyder with elephants, as well as fusils from Ceylon, which they landed at Negapatam. The Dutch Factor at Calicut apologized for the fire-arms being of an inferior description, but promised to send to Europe for better. The elephants he observes, were the best procurable, and he hoped they *would answer the purpose for which they were intended.* He continues by complaining of the extortions of Hyder's agents at Calicut, and the excessive demands they made on the Dutch vassal the Rajah of Cranganore. He also observes that he has had the pleasure of sending Carpenters and Ironsmiths to assist in the construction of the Mysore fleet now being built: and concludes by wishing Hyder, health, a long life, and success in his undertakings.

In 1776, Hyder sent a letter, accompanied by handsome presents, and demanded a safe passage through the territories of the Dutch Company, for the purpose of attacking Travancore, in accordance with his demands in 1766, at Calicut. But although a former Governor *(Breekpot,)* had been profuse in his promises to Hyder, so long as distance divided them, the present one *(Moens,)* was afraid of giving a favourable reply, as he had no instructions from Batavia. Hyder considered this excuse as an evasion, and certainly with a show of reason, as he could hardly believe that the Governor had been waiting ten years for an answer from Batavia, as to the manner in which his advances were to be met, and now the time to act had arrived. Highly incensed by this conduct, Hyder then threatened the annihilation of the Dutch Company, and Sirdar Khan was directed to advance with 10,000 men, and over-run the Travancore territory. In August of that year, he had invaded the northern portion of the Cochin State, taking amongst other places the Fort of Trichoor, but his further advance was checked by the Travancore lines.

The Dutch now congratulated themselves on the disappearance of the Mysoreans, but a letter soon arrived from Sirdar Khan, in which he claimed the Chetwye territory, on the plea that it had formed a portion of the Samorin's dominions, wrested from him by the Dutch, who had promised to return it after a certain period. That time having elapsed, and Hyder being now by right of conquest the successor to the Samorin, the Cochin Council were requested to give up the lands, which they declined doing. On October 9th, Sirdar Khan crossed the Chetwye river near Poolicarra, a little to the north of the Dutch Fort, and took possession of the custom's house, making a prisoner of the writer who was sent to him as the bearer of a message. The Mysore forces now divided into two bodies, one of which proceeded southwards towards Paponetty, from whence the Dutch Resident retired into the Cranganore fort, taking with him the Company's treasure. Sirdar Khan now threw up strong works at Paponetty, and despatched a letter to the Governor of Cochin, stating that Hyder Ali considered that he had met with a premeditated insult from the Dutch Governor, who had given no decided reply to his letter. Still he wished to be friends, but a free passage for his troops towards Travancore, was essential: and were such refused, it would be considered equivalent to a declaration of war.

Governor *Moens* replied, that he was glad to understand that the Mysoreans wished to be regarded as friends, and he should feel obliged by their evacuating the Dutch territory, and not allowing their people to approach the Cranganore fort. But before his reply could reach its destination, Sirdar Khan attempted to surprise this fort, on October 11th, but failed. He then wrote another letter, stating that having taken the lands of Paponetty, he should feel obliged by the accounts for the last 20 years, being forwarded. He also demanded the territory, the Dutch Company had received from the Samorin, in 1758, as well as a Nuzzer, and a free passage towards Travancore.

Without sufficient troops to hold their own by force, surrounded by Native States, outwardly friendly but secretly hostile, attacked by the Mysoreans, and awaiting instructions from Batavia, *Moens'* position was a very difficult one. A common danger it was true, bound the Cochin and Travancore States to the Dutch, but it was feared that they did not possess sufficient forces, to afford any effectual barrier against the advance of the Mysore troops. Still *Moens* considered it advisable, to sound the dispositions of the two Rajahs, so wrote and informed them, that he was ready to commence offensive operations against the Mysoreans, but he first required a categorical answer, as to how far he could depend upon their support: he also proposed a plan, on which all would have to act in concert, against the common enemy. The Rajah of Travancore replied, that he had entered into an alliance with the Nawab of Arcot, and the British, in which it had been stipulated, that he was only to act on the defensive, and not to be the aggressor, otherwise he would receive no aid: so he regretted being unable to join the Dutch, except for defensive measures. Should the Mysoreans advance on his territory, British and Arcot troops were promised for his assistance.

Urgent requests were despatched to Ceylon for more troops, as there were only 200 effective soldiers present, and the safety of Cochin itself was now endangered, for it was ascertained, that a fleet consisting of one 3 mast ship, six 2 mast grabs, and twenty well armed gallivats, were preparing at Calicut, to take troops by sea past Cranganore, to the island of Vypeen. It was suspected that the Ayacotta fort, would be first attacked, and should it fall, that Cranganore would be besieged from the south, whilst Sirdar Khan invested it from the north. An armed sloop was placed at the entrance of the Cranganore river, and two armed merchant ships, further out to sea, to cover the coast. The Rajahs of Travancore and Cochin improved the lines which commenced from the rear of the Ayacotta fort, and were carried along the southern bank of the river towards the ghauts. The Cranganore and Ayacotta forts were strengthened, the first and most important by having a retrenchment thrown up under its guns, and the latter by being repaired.

Some Travancore Sepoys were now sent to Ayacotta, which the Mysore troops prepared to attack. But unwilling to come to blows, the Travancoreans retired to their own country, fortunately at this critical time, a Dutch detachment arrived by sea, and consequently the Mysoreans retreated. A strictly defensive policy was now decided upon, for fear of giving offence to the British and the Nawab of Arcot, but in November as a further reinforcement had arrived, the Dutch considered themselves strong enough to become the aggressors.

The Mahomedans had invested Chetwye, the garrison of which place sent a message to Cochin, representing that they could not hold it much longer, so Governor Moens now determined to attempt its relief. Provisions and ammunitions having been packed in casks, 180 men embarked in the ship Hoolwerf, having some small boats in tow, for the purpose of landing the men and stores. On the same afternoon, November 11th, they arrived before Chetwye, but the surf being high, the wary Mahomedans had the satisfaction of perceiving, that they delayed landing until the next day. A chosen band of Sirdar Khan's troops were told off, and in the dead of the night placed in ambuscade close to the beach, where the landing was most likely to be effected, and in silence awaited the disembarkation of their prey.

The morning dawned, and the Dutch having examined the shore, could see no vestige of an enemy, all appeared perfectly quiet, and they congratulated themselves on surprising Hyder's troops. The landing commenced, the first boat upset, but the troops waded to the beach with their loaded muskets wet, and their ammunition of course spoilt. Suddenly the ambuscade rushed out, and finding advance impossible, the Dutch retreated in good order to the beach: but their boats were gone, and the terrified Native boatmen, were pulling quickly away from the scene of strife. Some of the Detachment were killed, and the remainder obliged to surrender themselves prisoners of war.

The Europeans were disheartened, and abandoned the attempted relief, whilst the Mahomedans were greatly elated, and the fort of

Chetwye was compelled to capitulate on the 13th, one condition being, that the garrison should be permitted to retreat to Cranganore, a promise which was of course broken. The prisoners were plundered of everything, even to their very clothes, and with the women, children, and slaves, were sent to Calicut. From thence the Military were despatched loaded with chains to Seringapatam, where all took service with Hyder, excepting the Commandant of Chetwye and the Resident.

The whole of the island including Chetwye, Ayroor or Paponetty, and the territory of the Rajah of Cranganore,* (excepting the Dutch fort,) all of which were tributary to the Dutch, now succumbed to Hyder's General: but he found his further advance, impeded by the Travancore lines. The Cochin Council now decided upon still further strengthening the Cranganore fort, and on not again breaking up their troops into detachments.

On January 9th 1777, the answer to Hyder's letter arrived from Batavia, and with it the customary presents, which with an apologetic letter from the Governor of Cochin, were forwarded to Hyder's camp. On February 25th the Commandant and Resident of the Chetwye fort, arrived in Cochin, from Seringapatam, and informed Governor Moens from Hyder, that most of the prisoners, including the women and slaves, were set at liberty, (some soldiers were induced to remain in Hyder's service,) and that they were commissioned by Hyder to say, that he was still anxious to enter into a treaty of friendship with the Company, upon which subject he would shortly write. Hyder's letter disowned Sirdar Khan's proceedings, and stated that he had only despatched him into the sandy country, to enquire after some of the Samorin's lands: that he had no unfriendly feeling towards the Dutch, and whilst returning the prisoners, trusted all matters of dispute between them would be rapidly and amicably settled.

Hyder Ali in a secret correspondence, became very pressing to

---

* The Dutch appear to have been generally kind to their allies, when fugitives; thus in May 1777 the Rajah of Cranganore, was granted Rupees 50 a Month: the eldest Payencharry Nair, Rupees 30: and from September 1777 the Prince of Cartamana, Rupees 40 a Month: the same to be continued, so long as they remained faithful.

carry into effect his former propositions, for entering into an alliance with the Dutch. He now reduced his requirements to 400 European Infantry, and 100 Artillerymen. Governor Moens evaded this application without declining it, and held out hopes which were never carried into effect. He foresaw that neutrality with the English and Travancore must cease, should he join Hyder. The Dutch council also wished to prevent the Travancore Rajah, who was becoming alarmed at Hyder's increasing power, from forming too intimate relationship with the British, so they tried to induce him to believe, that from Hyder he had nothing to fear.

It is evident in *Moens'* memorial, that he plainly foresaw the course events would take, and it is no less clear, that he hated but feared the British, and admired but dreaded the power of Hyder. Had this ambitious and capable Dutch Governor of Cochin, been at this period possessed of sufficient troops at his own disposal, untrammelled by Batavian orders, there can be but little doubt, he would have joined the Mysoreans. Had he done so, Travancore must have fallen, and the Cochin state would have become a desert. Then who could have foretold, what course events on the Western coast would have taken? probably the result would have been far different, from that which fortunately for the British and the Natives, a few years subsequently, closed the annals of anarchy in Malabar.

Again Moens hoped for peace, especially as it was rumoured, that Hyder had enough to do with the Mahrattas: but the English were accused of again raising the question, respecting the right of the Dutch over the Chetwye lands, which were asserted to belong to the Samorin. It the meantime the Mysore forces proceeded northwards, to quiet the Nairs, but previous to their departure, they strengthened the fortifications of Chetwye. The Samorin now returned to his country, and in conjunction with some Moplahs, gave great uneasiness to Hyder's troops, but failing to repossess himself of Calicut, he retired to Travancore.

On January 8th, 1778, the Dutch planned an expedition, to recover their lost ground. They stormed and took the Cranganore Rajah's palace, which had a garrison of 300 men, and pursued the enemy to Paponetty. The succeeding day, the Dutch forces reached

Bellapattoo, and on the evening of the third day arrived before Chetwye. At once the guns began to play upon the fort, and continued all that night, and throughout the next day. On the third day, they unsuccessfully attempted to storm, the attack was continued seven days, but the enemy commencing to assemble in force on the opposite side of the river, the Dutch were obliged to retreat to Cranganore, on January 19th, with the loss of some guns. On the morning of March 3rd, the Mysoreans attacked the Cranganore palace, with 3,000 men on foot, 150 horse, and 4 guns. After 10 hours' fighting, the Dutch retired to the Cranganore fort, with the loss of 6 men.

In March, the Dewan of Travancore came to Cochin, to have an interview with Governor Moens, who pointed out to him, the necessity of preventing Cranganore from falling into the hands of Hyder, and urged that it was to the interest of the Travancoreans to join the Dutch, as they were running a risk of losing their country, whilst the Dutch could only lose a little strip of territory, which Moens hinted might even be avoided, should he join the Mysoreans.

About this time, Hyder who was now most indignant with the Dutch, was obliged to go to war with the English* and the Nawab of Arcot. On his way, he found time to plunder the Dutch storehouse at Porto Novo, and make a prisoner of the Resident.

Now, Moens commenced cautiously opening his favourite scheme, and wrote to Hyder respecting an offensive and defensive alliance with him. But Hyder refused to listen to his overtures, and gave him to understand, that as soon as he had leisure, he would turn his arms against the Dutch. Finding such to be the case, the Cochin Council had only to await the bursting of the threatened storm, and in the meantime they assisted the Travancore Rajah, by occasionally sending competent persons, to examine the Travancore lines.

Moens, when handing over charge to Van Angelbeck in 1781, enumerated nine islands (including Vendoorty,) as well as 69 gardens and pieces of land, which were then the property of the Dutch. He observed that they had 42,089 fruit-bearing cocoanut, and other trees: 4,507½ parrahs of fields, and 19,716 salt pans. He advised attempting to exchange the outlying farms, and thus consolidating

* Hyder engaged Lally to ass ist him with some French troops in 1779.

their territory, but suggested, that it was unlikely the neighbouring Rajahs would agree. The next best plan he considered to be, to sell all that they could, as they were a constant source of quarrels, especially those places situated in Travancore. Hyder had it appears, offered to purchase Cranganore,—it is not mentioned when,—but probably from the Commissioners in 1766.

On December 30th, 1793, Van Angelbeck retired, and it is unfortunate that his successor, to whom he addresses his Memorial, had been 26 years on the coast. He consequently assumes, that he is acquainted with the various transactions of the last thirteen years: and this renders his remarks upon many of the stirring events which occurred during this time very brief, whilst some of them he does not even allude to. It appears that during his tenure of office, the island of Vendoorty became the property of the Rajah of Cochin, and other bits of land were likewise disposed of either to him, or to the Travancore Rajah. He observes that the island of Vypeen, with the exception of, its northern portion termed Palliport, and the town of Vypeen at its southern extremity, at this period (1793) owned the Cochin Rajah as its lawful Sovereign, but the Paliat Achen still held several villages, as the Rajah's vassal.

In 1783, the Rajah of Chetwye, was peaceably re-instated in his dominions by the Dutch, when they retook the place from Tippoo's forces: but in the following year, orders arrived from Batavia, to return this territory to Tippoo, Hyder having died in December 1782. It appears that in November 1784, the Dutch and the Mysoreans were on friendly terms, as there is a letter from Arazada Beck Khan, Governor of Calicut, dated November 18th, in which he informs the Governor of Cochin, that he is despatching some articles down the coast in a Dhoney, and requests that the Dutch will direct the boatmen to return as soon as possible.

In 1785, the power of the Rajah of Cochin having increased, and as he was irritated against the Latin Converts, who had possessed peculiar privileges, a new agreement was entered into with the Dutch Government of Cochin, to the effect, that these Christians were henceforth to pay a tax to the Rajah, which was to be collected by their own head man, but should he refuse to realize it, the Dutch Government were to do so. But the Dutch were still to exercise jurisdiction over them, in Civil and Criminal matters. The Rajah, however, did not long agree to these terms, many of the people were dispossessed, and even turned out of his dominions. Sometimes to save appearances, he allowed them a trifle for their land, but they suffered the most cruel persecutions. The Dutch at this time, claimed jurisdiction over 36,000 Christians, but they could not protect them: expostulations were futile, and force they were unable to employ.

In 1787, the Cochin Council were again alarmed, by the approach of the Mysore army. For Tippoo marched to Calicut, to "improve "the morals, and realize the revenue." He issued a Proclamation, stating that the poor Malabars, were more shameless in their immorality, than the beasts of the field, and that unless they forsook their sinful practices, and lived like the rest of mankind, he would in accordance with his repeated vows, honour them with Islam.

Matters now appeared ominous for South Malabar. On April 16th, the Danish Commercial Agent arrived from Calicut, and reported that Tippoo at the head of a large army, had arrived at that place, and destroyed the Danish factory. In May (1788) it was rumoured, that 1,000 Infantry, and 30 Cavalry, were leaving en route for Cranganore: Tippoo remaining, to complete the demolition of the Calicut fort, and erect another at Wapoor. The Travancore Rajah writing on the 31st of that month, stated that the Cochin Rajah had met Tippoo at Palghaut, on the 26th. These two Rajahs held a conference on June 4th, at Anna-nada, north east of Cranganore, the Cochin King had been directed, to introduce two of Hyder's Vakeels, to the Rajah of Travancore, and they were expected with some presents on the 11th,* some correspondence occurred between Tippoo Sultan and the Dutch, with reference to Hyder's old wish, of entering into an offensive and defensive alliance with them: but

* To give an idea of the presents which were exchanged, between the Dutch Governor, and the Rajah of Travancore, the following is inserted. Van Angelbeck wrote to the Rajah, September 30th, 1795, stating that he is transmitting the following things, which he trusts His Highness will accept as a proof of the Company's friendship. Two flasks of Cinnamon oil: two flasks of Clove oil: one case of Cloves: one piece of red Velvet: four pieces of Satin: one Carboy of rosewater: two reams of gilt edged paper: one pound of red sealing wax: and four bundles of quills.

many of the letters appear to be missing. There is one dated September, 1788, in which it is stated, that Tippoo's Sepoys will shortly be at Cranganore, to assist the Dutch against Travancore, and the writer who is at Calicut, ends by saying, "time will show, if he "(Tippoo Sultan,) really wishes to assist us, or is merely serving "his own interests."

In 1789, Tippoo is said to have requested the Cochin Rajah, to treat with the Dutch on his account, for the purchase of the fort of Cochin, as he understood they had expressed a wish to sell it, together with Cranganore, and Ayacotta: but negotiations did not terminate as Tippoo desired. The British encamped three Corps in the rear of the Travancore lines, and declared that any attack upon them, would be considered equivalent to a declaration of war: at the same time, Mr. Hollond, the Governor of Madras, intimated to the Rajah of Travancore, that if he were the aggressive party, the British would afford him no assistance.

The Dutch now consulted with the Travancore authorities, on the best means of either keeping the Mysore army at bay, or of involving the British in the coming struggle: so a sale, which had been talked about for the previous two years, was at once carried into effect, and in August, Cranganore and Ayacotta became Travancore property. At first the sale was disapproved of by the Government of Madras, as well as by Lord Cornwallis the Governor-General, as it was believed these places were situated within the territories of the Rajah of Cochin, but it was proved, that the lands had been taken by the Dutch from the Portuguese, and had consequently been in the possession of Europeans nearly 3 centuries, during which period neither rent nor tax had been levied on them by any native power.

In October, Tippoo's army was encamped near Paulghaut, in December the Travancore lines were attacked as has been described, (p. 53.) and immediately subsequently Cranganore also fell, it having been evacuated on the previous night. Tippoo's General, Lally completed its demolition, which the English pioneers had commenced, previous to evacuating it. The next year Tippoo's troops were again driven away, but whilst in the Cranganore territory, they committed terrible devastations.

The Dutch had now discovered the insecurity of alliances with the

Mysoreans, they had seen the Portuguese spurned, and their territory annexed by Hyder, as the only thanks given them for their assistance in 1762. They had perceived the French insulted, because their troops were not more in numbers: and they had personally been received with supercilious arrogance, when they really attempted to join with Hyder and Tippoo. True, their own deeds will not bear much scrutiny, but they were a Mercantile body, whose objects were peaceful trade, not devastating wars, they consequently invariably joined the strongest party, or whichever they believed would best forward the ends they had in view. When war with Tippoo was imminent, they had just had a misunderstanding with that Prince, whilst the rising power of the British was evident to the most superficial observer.* They offered the Bengal Government to join their forces to those of the English, an offer politely, but decidedly declined. They then furnished Travancore with artillery men and cannon, to assist in the defence of the lines.

Van Angelbeck in his Memorial, enters slightly into the British contract of 1790 with the Rajah of Cochin, when the former placed the latter in sovereignty of certain lands, external to the Travancore lines, of which the Mysoreans had previously dispossessed him. He observes, that when those transactions were nearly completed, the Government of Madras, gave the Cochin Council notice respecting them, in a letter dated June 1st, 1790, and requested to know what engagements existed, between the Rajah and the Dutch, as they hoped to avoid doing anything, which might subsequently interfere, with the good understanding that existed between the two Companies. Mr. George Powney had been directed to ascertain these particulars, and the Madras Government, trusted that the Cochin Council would assist him.

Van Angelbeck states, that he did not deem it advisable, to let Mr. Powney know what their engagements with the Cochin Rajah really were, but the following article was inserted in the treaty, which he, (Mr. Powney,) signed with the Cochin Rajah.

* April 26th, 1790, Colonel James Hartley, arrived in Cochin, as Commissioner, from the British to the Dutch, he remained until September 1st, when he left in the Beagle, a 12 gun vessel. Dutch Commissioners Cellarius, and Eversdyck left Cochin, as Agents to the Rajah of Travancore, on August 12th and returned on September 4th.

"That owing to a treaty which exists between the Dutch Com-"pany, and Rama Wurmah Rajah of Cochin, the Governor in "Council of Madras, not wishing to enter into any engagements, "which might be detrimental to existing arrangements, between "those parties. *It is resolved,* that Rama Wurmah shall become "tributary to the English East India Company, only in respect to "such districts or places, as are above enumerated, and are at pre-"sent in the possession of Tippoo Sultan, and with which the Dutch "East India Company have no concern. For those lands, the said "Rajah shall pay tribute to the English East India Company."

Van Angelbeck, appears to have been quite as jealous as his predecessor, of English interference, and warns his successor, to be careful not to permit them to intermeddle in the affairs of the Cochin Rajah's lands, which remained under Dutch protection, "for," he continued, "if they are allowed to insert their little finger in the "affairs of these regions, they will not rest until they have managed "to thrust in the whole arm."

Many instances he says he could adduce, of the British having interfered, the most glaring of which was, that Mr. Duncan the English Commissioner, requested to see the original agreement, made between Mr. Powney and the Rajah of Cochin, respecting the land beyond the Travancore lines, as well as that which was entered into between Hyder Ali and the Cochin Rajah. The Rajah replied, he had no objection to produce them, but the Dutch Governor's consent must be first obtained. The next morning, a box was brought locked to Mr. Duncan, and he was informed, that in it were the treaties, and that Van Angelbeck held the key of the box. Mr. Duncan was much vexed at this proceeding, but passed it off by sarcastically remarking, "Well, Sir, the Rajah places much "confidence in your great kindness, but it occurs to me, that he in "this instance misuses it, by forcing upon you the trouble of "unlocking a box."

In August 1792, Governor Van Angelbeck applied to Colonel Hartley at Chetwye for assistance, who informed him that he would comply with his request as early as possible, but the expenses of the troops must be borne by the Dutch. Van Angelbeck returned for answer, that he only required one regiment of Europeans, and another of Sepoys, stationed near Cranganore to cover the Coast: and although it was true their immediate presence would be for the protection of Cochin, still this would tend towards the security of the English possessions, and it was therefore reasonable that each Company should bear its own expenses. Colonel Hartley again wrote to say that the troops had been sent in accordance to the Dutch requisition, and therefore if they remained, they must bear the whole of the expenses: to this no answer was returned. Van Angelbeck observes to his successor, that Colonel Hartley was unable to decide any such question, and should the Bombay Government demand the expenses, he advised him to employ the same line of argument, and if unsuccessful, to gain time by stating the necessity of applying to both him (Van Angelbeck) and Batavia.

Van Angelbeck observes, that the greatest causes of dissension they have experienced, with the Rajah of Cochin, have been on account of the Christians, more especially respecting the inland Roman Catholics. The Syrians or St. Thomas's Christians, whom he says are termed Moplahs, were not under their protection, but the Moondoocars or Roman Catholics, including the Latin Converts, were so.

The Roman Catholics he observes, had baptized vast numbers of Heathen vagabonds, who had consented to this course to escape the punishments which their crimes deserved, consequently there was much justice in the Rajah's complaints. The extent to which each Governor could interfere depended very much upon his personal influence with the Rajah. A fertile source of complaint was killing cows, which the Native Government frequently protested against. This Van Angelbeck had ineffectually attempted to check, but observes, every nation and religion, must be governed by their own customs and laws. In disputes with the Rajah, he advised Van Spall to give him immediate redress, to lose no time in affording justice, and without delay to comply with his demands whenever they were reasonable: and that nothing should be demanded from him, unless a sufficient Military force were at hand to back all just requests.

Van Angelbeck draws especial attention, to the annexing policy of the Rajah of Travancore, whom he observes, without doubt was trying to filch away their possessions in Quilon. The following is a summary of his observations. The Rajah and his Ministers, were continually oppressing the inland Christians, who were under their protection, and some who had taken refuge in Quilon were even not safe. The inhabitants of Quilon had been from 1663, the Company's subjects, and were governed without the least interference of the Rajah of Travancore, whose subjects they had never been, as after the Rajah of Quilon died, they came under the rule of the Signatty, or Chief of Culli-Quilon.

At first the Rajah of Travancore claimed from the fishermen, 10 chuckrams, (a small coin 28½ to a rupee,) and 3 fish annually, not because they were subjects of the Signatty, but because they extended their fishing excursions opposite his territory. Whilst any of them who were married in the Roman Catholic Church at Moondacara, situated in the Travancore limits, were obliged to pay a fee of ten chuckrams.

After Travancore annexed the Culli-Quilon territory, the fishermen paid 30 chuckrams annually for every large net, and 15 for each small one, and this was the origin of the so-called poll-tax. Dutch officials collected it, whilst the Travancore officials had to apply to them for the amounts. By degrees the Travancore revenue officers commenced interfering within the limits of Dutch Quilon, and the Commandant there, *Kosier*, was of that lazy temperament, that he took no notice, and thus the inhabitants became partially governed by Travancore people.

Subsequently much trouble was occasioned in wresting Quilon from Travancore, but it was finally settled in 1788. A conference was held in October of that year, at Mavillicurray, when the Rajah observed, many of his subjects had taken up their abode in Quilon, and were he to give them up, he should be a pecuniary loser: it was promised, they should be turned out, and it was agreed:

1st.—That the remaining inhabitants, shall submit to no increase of the obligations to which they were formerly subject.

2nd.—That the taxes will be collected by Dutch officials, who shall pay the amount into the Rajah's treasury.

3rd.—That the Rajah's officials shall interfere no more, in the affairs of Dutch Quilon.

The limits of the Dutch town still exist, and it is natural to ask, *how, and when, did Travancore obtain Quilon?* Certainly they are now in possession of it.

It will be necessary here to diverge a little from Dutch, to present history. A person of high rank in the Travancore State, lately suggested that the British Government should make over to Travancore, Tangicherry close to Quilon, and Anjengo a few miles to its south. It does not appear that this is proposed for the people's benefit, but for the purpose of preventing smuggling.

It might be good policy to follow *Moens'* advice, and consolidate scattered possessions, were the British in the same relationship to Travancore as were the Dutch, but isolated spots along the coast may again be some day required. Travancore can have no claim upon Tangicherry, first Portuguese, subsequently Dutch, and now British, it was in European hands before Travancore forces ever crossed the Quilon river, or annexed the territories of Quilon and Culli-Quilon. In 1809, Tangicherry was useful to the British, here troops were landed during the Nair riots, not to be met by a hostile, but by a serviceable, willing, and Christian British population.

Van Angelbeck concluded his memorial, by adverting to the numerical strength, and duties of the soldiery to be maintained in Cochin. He remarked upon the resolutions in February and September 1793, to reduce the Garrison to 600 men, which he considered impolitic, as the French might interfere, nevertheless, if such a course should be directed by the Supreme Government, he advised the following to be kept up, viz., 550 Infantry, 50 Artillerymen; the former to consist of 2 Companies of Europeans, 1 Company of East Indians, and 1 Company of Sepoys, and the Artillery to be formed of 30 Europeans, and 20 Natives. He concluded by dividing them into the proportion of officers and men he deemed sufficient for a Company, and in this detail demonstrated, that every soldier would have 8 hours sentry duty daily, which he pithily remarked "was as much "work as he supposed could be obtained out of them." His arrangement left 63 Europeans, 14 East Indians, and 14 Sepoys for the sick report, absence, and irregular duties.

Owing to Governor Van Spall having been made a prisoner of war by the British, he left no memorial of his rule, for the use of his successors. During the period of his tenure of office, but few stirring events occurred in Cochin, still evidently a great struggle, not only on the Malabar Coast, but also in Europe, was impending over the Dutch.

On January 8th, 1795, the French Republican Army crossed the Waal in force, and the Stadtholder fled to England. It is needless to detail the well known events of European history, the Republicans were received as deliverers, and Jacobinism spread : whilst to crown the Dutch disasters, their fleet in the Texel, was captured by a body of French Cavalry !

The scene now shifts to England, from whence on March 3rd, 1795, directions were transmitted from the India House, to seize the Dutch possessions in the East, in order to prevent their falling into the hands of the French, as well as to retain them for their legitimate Sovereign. The following proclamation was enclosed, signed by the *Stadtholder*, at Kew, February 7th, of the same year : and addressed to all Governors, and Commandants of stations,—"We "have thought it necessary to write to you, that his Britannic Ma-"jesty's troops shall be admitted, and take possession of the forts "in our Colonies, and that they are to be considered as the troops, "of a kingdom in friendship, and alliance, with their High Mighti-"nesses, in case the Colonies should be summoned by the French."

A short time previously to this, private information had been received, that *Mr. Van Spall*, the Governor of Cochin, was laying in provisions, for the purpose of withstanding a siege, which he anticipated from the British, and that he had applied to the Cochin Rajah, for assistance. The *English Commissioners*, wrote to the Rajah, stating that they had received this intelligence, and warned him to give the Dutch no assistance, but on the contrary to impede them in every way in his power. This course he faithfully promised to pursue, as being tributary to the British.

On July 23rd, Major Petrie marched from Calicut to the frontiers of the Dutch settlement, in command of the two flank Companies, of H. M. 77th Regiment, and a battalion of Native Infantry. He was ordered if possible, to obtain a peaceable entrance, in which case, the Governor and Council, were not to be molested, and all private property, and the rights of individuals were to be left unaltered, the British troops merely remaining to deter the French from landing. *But, in case admission were refused,* Major Petrie was directed to watch the place, and await the arrival of a siege train, when he was to storm the town, giving no prize money, but seizing the stores for Government use. Negotiations proved useless, as the Governor refused to admit the British troops.

Mr. Stevens, the Senior Civilian on the Coast, thought that possibly some misconception might have arisen, between Major Petrie, and Governor Van Spall: and therefore went personally to Cochin, and in conjunction with Major Petrie, held a conference with the Governor, on the night of Setember 6th. The latter, at once agreed to deliver up the fort peaceably, but stipulated, that he must first obtain the concurrence of his Council. On the following day, he is said to have prevaricated, and consequently negotiations were suspended. This did not materially delay the final downfall of the place, as on September 10th, a reinforcement left Tellicherry, to join Major Petrie, consisting of the remainder of the 77th Regiment, the 5th N. I., 1 Company of Artillery with 6 six pounder field-pieces, 6 eighteen pounder battering cannon, 6 twelve pounder iron guns, two 8 inch mortars, with tumbrils, provisions, &c. The whole of this was safely landed, about one mile to the South of Cochin.

On the night of October 19th, finding negotiations useless, a shell was fired from one of the eight inch mortars, which alighted upon the Commandant's house.* It now became apparent, that force would be employed, and the Governor well aware, that Cochin was not in a position to resist an attack, re-opened negotiations. But Major Petrie, feeling that the time for treating the Dutch Garrison as allies was passed, now viewed them as enemies: and aware of his strength, accepted Mr. Van Spall's propositions, after first modifying them, as will be seen in the following Preliminary Articles, which are taken from the original documents.

Propositions in Dutch.	*Answers in French.*
The Governor in Council of Cochin, proposes to Major Petrie,	The Garrison of Cochin will be prisoners, and the Fort given over

* The Military report respecting the capture of Cochin is at present not to be discovered. *Mills,* in his "History of British India," states it was taken after "a great resistance." See Vol. VI. page 69.

of the 77th Regiment, and Commanding the Detachments, of the King's, and East India Company's troops, to surrender this place, on the 20th of this month, and requests at the same time, that all hostilities may cease.

to his great Britannic Majesty, to-morrow noon, at twelve o'clock, at which time, the Bay-gate, and the New-gate, shall be delivered over to such detachments, as Major Petrie will order to take possession of them.

ARTICLE 1ST.

The Officers of the Garrison, and the Military, that have defended Cochin, will with all the honours of war, march out from the Bay-gate, together with their arms, baggage, flying colours, beating of drums, and lighted matches, as also two cannon, with their appurtenances.

ARTICLE 1ST.

The Garrison will march out as requested, and lay down their arms on the Esplanade, when they must return back, as prisoners of war.

ARTICLE 2ND.

All Officers, and Soldiers, which are of the Garrison of Cochin, will with as little delay as possible. be transported either to Batavia, or Ceylon, at the expense of the English Government, in English vessels.

ARTICLE 2ND.

Cannot be granted; about the Garrison, it will be disposed of, as the Commander-in-Chief may deem proper.

ARTICLE 3RD.

The said Officers, and Soldiers, will take with them all their effects, without their being liable to any search. Their servants, and slaves: whilst those that are married, will likewise be at liberty, to take their families with them.

ARTICLE 3RD.

Allowed, excepting with respect to *slaves*, a name unknown in the British dominions.

ARTICLE 4TH.

The Governor, the Members of Council, and all the servants of Police, and Trade, Churchmen, Military and Naval, and other servants, in the pay of the Dutch Company, as also all the Inhabitants of Cochin, either Europeans, or Natives, will be at liberty to hold their persons, and property, moveable and immoveable, merchandize and other effects, without being therein molested, or obstructed, on any account whatsoever.

ARTICLE 4TH.

All private property will be sacred.

Article 5th.

Among the foregoing, is also understood, regarding the liberty of the Factor, and Resident of Porca, J. A. Scheits, who is now employed here, in keeping the Company's mercantile books, and he must be allowed to return to his station, to resume his office.

Article 5th.

A reasonable time will be allowed him, to settle his affairs, but he must be considered as a prisoner of war.

Article 6th.

The Governor, the Members of Council, and all the servants of Police, and trade, the Churchmen, and further servants in pay, will be at liberty to take their families, male, and female, slaves, and also their possessions, either to Batavia, or Columbo, and they will be granted thereto, at the expense of the British Government, the necessary ships, and transports.

Article 6th.

This is replied to, in the 2nd Article.

Article 7th.

The funds belonging to the Orphan College, and the Poor House, will not be confiscated, or seized upon, they being money of Orphans and the poor.

Article 7th.

The funds mentioned in this article, will belong to his great Britannic Majesty, in so far that he will appoint persons over them, for their management.

Article 8th.

All Officers, and servants, Civil and Political, of the Company, who may wish to remain at this place, as private individuals,shall be granted the protectionof the British flag.

Article 8th.

All the Inhabitants, who are willing to remain, and to take the oath of allegiance to his great Britannic Majesty, will in every respect, be treated as British subjects.

Article 9th.

All mercantile articles, ammunitions, artillery, goods, arms, provisions, and other articles, which belong to the Company, and are found at this place, will faithfully be made over, according to a specific statement, to the Commissaries that will be appointed to receive them, and the specified list, will in duplicate, be duly delivered to Major Petrie.

Article 9th.

Everything mentioned in this article, will be faithfully delivered over to such persons, as Major Petrie will appoint hereafter, to dispose thereabout, agreeably to the direction of his great Britannic Majesty.

ARTICLE 10TH.

The fortifications, the Government House, all Magazines, and other public buildings, belonging to the Company, will be kept as they are at present, and not be demolished.

ARTICLE 10TH.

Regarding the Fort of Cochin, and all other public buildings, they will be disposed of, as the Commander-in-Chief, or the Commanding Officer, will think proper at the time.

ARTICLE 11TH.

The free exercise of the reformed religion, as usual in the Dutch Church, where Divine Service is performed, will be permitted.

ARTICLE 11TH.

Allowed.

ARTICLE 12TH.

The Convent at Verapoly, and all other Romish Churches, as also the Heathen Temples, will receive the protection, that they have hitherto enjoyed, under the Dutch Company.

ARTICLE 12TH.

The British Government, every where, protects religious exercises.

ARTICLE 13TH.

All Topazes, (half castes,) and Inland Christians, as also the Banians, Silversmiths, Painters, Washers, and Shoe-makers, who are subjects, and vassals of the Dutch Company, will retain their property, and also all privileges, and protections, which they always had enjoyed, of the said Company.

ARTICLE 13TH.

Answered, in the 4th and 8th articles.

ARTICLE 14TH.

All Documents, Charters, Resolutions, and other papers, belonging to this Government, will without any search being made of them, be delivered over to the Governor, Mr. Van Spall, in order to be carried with him, wherever he may be removed to.

ARTICLE 14TH.

All Public Documents, and Papers, must be delivered over to persons, appointed to receive them, but Mr. Van Spall will have authenticated vouchers, of those which may in any way concern himself, during his management of Cochin.

ARTICLE 15TH.

No one will occupy the Government House, during (his) Mr. Van Spall's stay at Cochin, but he will remain in it, unmolested.

ARTICLE 15TH.

Answered, in the 2nd Article.

Article 16th.

In case of any English Deserters, being found in the Garrison of Cochin, they will be pardoned.

Article 16th.

All Deserters, will absolutely be given over.

Article 17th.

All Public Papers, Notorial, or Secretariat deeds, which may in the least, be to the security of the possessions, belonging to the Inhabitants of this place, will be respected and preserved, in the hands of those, who hold that Office, in order to be made use of, whenever required.

Article 17th.

Answered, in the 14th Article.

Article 18th.

The Auctioneer of the Town, the Sequester, and the Curator, (Trustees), will be supported, in the recovering of all outstanding money, and be therein protected, by the usual Officers of Justice.

Article 18th.

All inhabitants, who remain in Cochin, will be subject to British Laws.

Article 19th.

After this capitulation shall have been signed, the New-gate shall be made over to an English Detachment, of 50 men, to which an equal number of Dutch Soldiers, shall be added, to whom it will be charged that no Dutch Soldier may go out, and no English one may rush in, and the next day all the gates will be taken possession of by the English troops, and the Garrison of Cochin will retire to a certain place, and remain there until their departure for Batavia, or Ceylon, laying down their arms, as usual, with the exception of the officers commanding them, who will retain their swords.

Article 19th.

The Gates of the Fort of Cochin, will be taken possession of, by a Detachment of British troops, tomorrow noon, at 12 o'clock. The Garrison will be lodged, as conveniently as the circumstances will allow, until it can be disposed of, thereabout, agreeably to the second Article. The Officers may retain their swords.

Article 20th.

All servants of the Company, the Police, Military, Navy, and others in pay, will be supported by the English Government, until

Article 20th.

Major Petrie is of opinion, that he has not the power to enter into such an agreement, on account of the Honorable Company. The last

they are taken in English vessels, to the place of their destination, either Batavia, or Columbo.

part of this article, has been answered in article 2nd.

ARTICLE 21st.

All sick, and wounded, now in the Hospital, are to be treated, and maintained, by the English Government.

ARTICLE 21ST.

Allowed.

The fulfilment of all the above stated articles, and the manner of capitulation agreed to, are to be faithfully observed and signed respectively, by Major Petrie, the Governor Van Spall, and the Council of this place.

19th October, 1795.

(Signed) J. L. VAN SPALL,
(„) P. J. DECAN,
(„) I. A. CELLARIUS,
(„) I. H. SCHEIDS,
(„) A. LUNEL,
(„) C. VAN SPALL.

Major Petrie consents to a cessation of Arms, until 4 o'clock in the morning, at which time, Mr. Van Spall should declare, whether or not he will accept the aforementioned articles of capitulation.

11 30 P.M. 19th October, 1795.

(Signed) G. PETRIE,
Major, 77th Regiment,
Commanding.

No succours could be expected, and the Dutch Garrison were therefore obliged to agree to the above terms, and surrender Cochin, becoming thereby, *prisoners of war.*

The Dutch Institutions of Cochin, were copied from those of Batavia. The constitution of the Town Council, has already been mentioned.

No European whatever could reside in the place, or embark in trade without enlisting, and covenanting to serve the Dutch for five years, but on certain payments, he was exempted from all duty, except to repel actual invasion, or on emergent occasions. Thus all the white inhabitants were Military, and under Military orders, an excellent plan for preventing their causing trouble to Government.

Merchants carried on their business very comfortably, Captains of ships were not allowed to buy anything from the Natives directly, but obliged to apply to one of the European Factors, who in their turn contracted with Native merchants, for the delivery of certain articles at a given price, on board ship. But the European Factor being the recipient of the money for the goods, and the Native merchant being paid only on the receipt of the articles on board ship, the profits were made without much difficulty, or much outlay. Their greatest trouble appears to have been, in receiving imports, and when dealing with residents in the place.

Their laws were nominally the same for Europeans and Natives, but in reality they were very different, according to the religious persuasions professed by their dark subjects. By the side of the warehouse, or Cathedral of Santa Cruz close to the river, stood a large gallows, whilst another was perceptible about ½ a mile distant, on a low Island, known to this day as "Gallows' Island," a place now only employed as the receptacle for the corpses of paupers. It was rarely that Europeans were executed by hanging, but Military executions by shooting, occasionally took place.

Native Christians were divided into two parties, the Moondoocars or persons who wore white cloths and puggeries, and Topasses who were dressed in hats and drawers, each division being under a Captain, or Commandant who was accountable to the Governor of Cochin, for their conduct.

Moens states, that, "on the taking of Cochin there were many " Topasses here, and along the Coast, who were the descendants of " the Portuguese. Some were slaves who had been given their free- " dom, others were the offspring of native women, with whom their " masters had formed temporary alliances. After the Portuguese " left the place, they assumed the surnames of their masters. Prior " to 1663, they had a bishop of their own, and a Cathedral within " the town of Cochin. When the Company took the place, they " came under their protection, and were allowed the exercise of their " religion. They were placed under a Captain and four Ensigns, " as well as other subordinate officers." He also states that during his tenure of office (from 1771 to 1781), "450 of them, were drilled " once a month, to learn the use of arms."

If an European killed a slave, whether by an accidental blow, or otherwise, he was severely punished, but rarely by death. The law laid down was, that slaves might be corrected by their masters, in any way short of causing death. To obviate the chance of an exasperated master, giving a fatal blow, there was an official, who amongst his other duties, received complaints against slaves, and on payment caused them, if males to be beaten before their master's door, if females within his house.

Slaves* were purchased in large numbers, no enquiries were made respecting whence they came, and their lives are said to have been as vicious, as their transactions were abominable. The practice of slavery commenced in the time of the Portuguese.

As a rule the slaves do not appear to have been treated badly, but when any very grave offences were proved against them, they were unmercifully punished. Impalement, and more rarely the nail torture, and that by fire or water, were employed.

Impalement being a refinement of cruelty, of more an eastern than an European character, an account of the Dutch method of practising it, may perhaps be interesting. In olden times it was a common Malabar punishment for theft.

An iron spike was thrust through the criminal's skin, in the lower part of the back, where a cross cut had been previously made for its insertion: then the point of the spike was guided by the executioner's finger, so as to bring it out at the neck or shoulder, carefully avoiding injuring any large arteries, or vital organs, as such would afford the poor victim speedy relief. The lowest extremity of the spike was then made fast to a wooden post, which was raised perpendicularly, and fixed into the ground, and thus the culprit was supported, partly by the iron spike under his skin, and partly by a small bench, placed underneath his feet, and raised about ten inches from the ground.

Tortured by thirst but denied water, scorched by the sun but denied shade, devoured by insects but refused any means of keeping them away; his miserable existence, terminated in a lingering death, that in some instances was protracted for three days. A shower of rain was hailed as the greatest blessing, as it caused the wound to mortify, and death rapidly ensued.

As the Dutch never broke criminals on the wheel in Ceylon, it

* Report says, that the Church was occupied as a slave godown, on special emergencies, and that in the week days, when the sacred edifice was not required for religious purposes, it was employed to keep these unfortunate creatures in, who had usually been carried off by the Moplahs, and sold to the Dutch, who shipped them to Ceylon, Batavia, the Cape, and other places.

appears probable that this horrible punishment was also unknown in Cochin. The substitute for it, *Wolf* says, was breaking their thighs with an iron club.

There was an Orphanage for the reception of illegitimate children and orphans of the poorer classes. They were taught various trades, and the boys when at a suitable age, were generally draughted into the army, and the girls respectably married.

A jail also existed, as well as a Spin-hays, or house of correction for disorderly women. In the *Diary* of 1790, there are the following entries, February 13th, a Moor woman taken by the Patrols, this day sentenced to be whipped and imprisoned for 2 years. March 20th, the Christian prisoner Barki Chowry was this day tortured.

The pay of the various officials, was no criterion as to their emoluments, which were augmented by numerous perquisites. Thus the Dutch Commandant, or Governor of Malabar, received the following. All foreign ships and sloops entering the river,* with the Governor's permission, either for the purposes of trade, or otherwise, paid for anchorage, viz., from 1½ to 2 masts, rupees 160 to the Governor, but if from 2½ to 3 masts, rupees 200.

The Shawbunder likewise received Rs. 10. Persons on receiving leave to build a Bombara, or Dow, paid rupees 100 to the Governor, rupees 50 to the Second in Council, and rupees 25 to the Shawbunder.

On the sale of all private Merchandize, 1 per cent. went to the Governor, who also received 5 per cent. on the value of all timber exported, 1 per cent. on that of all coprah, 1 rupee for every thousand cocoanuts, the same on every bale (consisting of 80 pieces) of Colechi cloth, one fanam on every choadna (16 quarts) of cocoanut oil, 4 rupees on every last of nelly (paddy), and 8 rupees on each last of rice.

A Bombara or Dow leaving Cochin, paid rupees 44 to the Governor for its passport; a shibar, botilla, or pattimar, of one mast rupees 11; and a maldive rupees 10. On issuing passports to country crafts, ships, and sloops, the following fees were paid; for vessels of 25 candies rupees 10, to the Governor: of 40 candies rupees 12: of 60 candies rupees 14: of 80 candies rupees 16:

* Dutch, *Government Records*. M.SS.

of 100 candies rupees 18: and for every additional candy, the Secretary received rupees 2. A munchew, and other small vessels paid from rupees 3 to 3½: the endorsement of a passport was rupees 3: pattimars and dhonies bringing letters, or passengers, required no passport.

In 1785, Van Angelbeck, the Governor of Cochin, complained to the Rajah, that his Ragiadoor was claiming fees from a vessel that wintered in the river, near the Moor bazaar. The Rajah replied, that in the agreement of 1772, the right of levying fees, upon vessels anchoring within his limits, certainly was omitted, but such had been a mere oversight, as it was a well known, and old established custom. That he always had, and always should levy them as follows, viz: A ship rupees 150: a Bombara or Palla, rupees 40: a large Almeida, rupees 12; a small one, rupees 8. Should the vessel belong to a foreign merchant, and he desired to winter in the Rajah's territories, the Captain had to give in addition, a piece of cloth worth rupees 25 for every ship: a piece of taffety worth rupees 12 for every Bombara or Palla: whilst the Captains of Almeidas and other small vessels, had to present offerings in accordance with their size.

Every one had a certain percentage of whatever passed through his hands, from the Cashier, to the Auctioneer, always paid by the person who received anything from the Company, or paid anything to it. Persons bringing Slaves, paid so much a head for their certificates to the Secretary. Fishermen gave eight pounds of fish daily. The owners of country vessels with gram, or provisions, a branch of 100 betel leaves, and two rolls of jaggery sugar, and so on.

The Governor was of course a great personage, and was always received with much State. As late as 1775, it was usual for the congregation in the churches, to stand up on his entrance, no matter at what period of the service it occurred. All carriages were drawn up on one side of the road, and pedestrians stopped when he passed, whilst the same marks of attention, were paid to his wife and family.

Forbes mentions having occasionally resided in Cochin for several weeks at a time, during the latter part of the Dutch rule, and states, that, "it was a great place for trade, and presented a striking "contrast to Goa; a harbour filled with ships, streets crowded with "merchants, and warehouses stored with goods from every part of

"Asia, and Europe; marked the industry, the commerce, and the "wealth of the inhabitants."

He subsequently adds, that he "always received the kindest attention from the Governor, and the principal inhabitants, whose "tables were furnished with hospitality, and graced with politeness, "their houses and gardens displayed the national cleanliness, and "neatness."

At the Governor's house, "three female slaves, neatly dressed, "attended each of the guests, before the dinner was put on the "table; one of them held a silver basin decked with flowers "to contain the water, which another poured upon his hands from a "silver vase, and a third offered a clean napkin on a salver. At "the English tables, two servants attended after dinner, with a "gindy, or cover of silver, on white copper, the former was adorned "with fresh coloured flowers, stuck in a perforated cover, to conceal "the water which was poured from the latter, over the hands of "each guest."

The taxes in Cochin were numerous, but insufficient for the expenses of the place. All vessels passing along the backwater, paid taxes at Cochin, Palliport, Cranganore, Paponetty, and Quilon: whilst tolls were exacted on all liquors, metals, food, or slaves, imported or exported: 12½ per cent. on the produce of trees: and 30 per cent. on that of some of the land: even the fishermen were charged for the right of using nets.

A curious custom prevailed, in that, when the Rajah of Cochin, or those who were not subjects of the Dutch Company purchased land, the new proprietors did not become subject to Dutch laws and taxes. Van Angelbeck on leaving, draws his successor's attention to this, and advises that none but those who take the oath of allegiance should be permitted to possess lands within their limits. The Rajah of Cochin had purchased many farms, and this gave rise to disputes. Van Angelbeck says he offered him 50,000 rupees for his house and garden out of town, but for the good of the Company he had sold it to Van Spall for 40,000.

It might be expected, that with these taxes, no one had ground rent to pay, but such was not always the case. Land held by descendants of old Dutch families, Native Christians, or by the Teroo Mala

Davossum, or Konkanee temple, was rent free. The remainder was leased for 10 or 20 years, to servants or dependants of the Factory, at the expiration of which term, it was put up to public outcry, for a similar period: and the *Records of the Dutch Government* inform us, that the inhabitants of Cochin, "paid annually certain sums of "money, for the purpose of repairing lights placed in several streets, "and keeping the drains in order."

The policy of the Dutch, was the same in all their possessions, and contemporary authors in Ceylon declared it to have been narrow-minded and grasping. The Kandeans came to the conclusion, that their gods delighted in human blood. By compounding a system of harshness, rewards, and punishments, they attempted to convert all classes to their religion. They insulted the heathen idols on principle, and to a certain extent trampled on the native customs, but perhaps their disavowal of treaties, and abandonment of their Allies, occasioned them the most injury in Malabar. Their campaigns were deficient in the brilliant dash of those of their Portuguese predecessors, and they were in fact owing to circumstances over which they had personally little control, more merchants than Statesmen or soldiers, and more occupied with commercial business than with their own honour.

The failure of the Dutch policy should be a warning to other nations, not to permit either their Civil or Military officers, to enter into commercial speculations. The soul of commerce is gain, which should never be a motive power with an official in his public capacity. His salary should be sufficient for his wants, his pension for his retirement, and his savings for his children. An under-paid class of officials is a curse to a country, a dissatisfied one a nuisance, and a satisfied one a blessing.

CHAPTER V.

THE BRITISH IN COCHIN.

Origin of British trade to India—English East India Company—Treaty with Samorin—Course of events on the Western Coast—Hyder—Tippoo—Cession of Malabar to British—Slave Trade—Capture of Cochin—Disturbances—Allepey Massacre—Institutions of Cochin—Revenue—Judicial—Police—Marine—Orphanage, and Friend-in-Need Society—Medical, and Scholastic Institutions.

The historical portion of the last Chapter, concluded with the termination of the Dutch rule in Cochin, when that fortress was captured by the troops of the English East India Company, instead of being peaceably occupied, as would have been the case, had Governor *Van Spall* and his Council, obeyed the order of the *Stadtholder*. Expelled as factors by the Dutch, the British now returned as conquerors, and since their advent, Cochin has undergone many changes. In its Council Chambers, Government Councils are no longer held: its political power has passed away: and it now fills a place, to a certain extent commensurate with the value of its Commercial exports. It will be necessary to revert to the commencement of the British rule in India, and to allude to various circumstances, which have had more or less particular, or general bearing, upon their assumption of power, on the Western Coast of Hindustan.

English merchants at first traded to India, in Portuguese vessels, and received a reasonable amount of protection, from the sailors of that nation. But in time, they refused to admit the right of the Portuguese, and subsequently of the Hollanders, to monopolize the route to India, to the exclusion of other European Nations. Then the British trade with Hindustan commenced, and in 1591, their first fleet, consisting of three large ships, under the command of

Captain Raymond, and in 1596, three more, under *Captain Wood*, attempted to reach India, but were unsuccessful.

On December 31st, 1600, the *East India Company of London*, consisting of 216 merchants, presided over, by George, Earl of Cumberland, was incorporated by Royal Charter. At first this Company attempted merely to trade with India, but finding themselves treated as enemies, by both the Portuguese, and Dutch, they were obliged to arm their vessels in self-defence: subsequently they built factories, and protected them, first by walls, and afterwards by forts. In 1639, they applied to *Sri Ranja Rajah*, of Chandragheri, for a piece of ground: and he granted them permission, on March 31st of that year, to erect a fort at Madrasnapatam, which was forthwith commenced, by *Mr. Francis Day*.

In 1608, Captains Hawkins and Keeling, who arrived at Surat from England, obtained leave to sell the goods they had brought, but were prohibited from founding a permanent settlement, until they had received permission from the Mogul. In 1615, Captain Keeling, with three English vessels, arrived at Calicut, where he was informed, that the Samorin was absent besieging Cranganore, but was desirous of seeing him, and entering into an alliance with the British. The small fleet consequently sailed for Cranganore, where the following agreement was concluded.

"UNDERECON CHEETE, *great Samorin, &c., to James*, King of "Britain, &c. Whereas your servant and subject, William Keeling, "arrived in my Kingdom, at the port of Cranganore, in March 1615, "with three ships, and at my earnest solicitation, came ashore to see "me, there was concluded by me, for my part, and by him for the "English nation, as followeth:

"As I have ever been at enmity with the Portuguese, and propose "always so to continue: I hereby faithfully promise, to be and "to continue, in friendship with the English, both for myself, "and my successors, and should I succeed in capturing the "fort of Cranganore, I engage to give it to the English, to possess as "their own, together with the island belonging to it, which is in "length along the sea coast, nine miles: and three in breadth: and "I propose to build thereon, a house for my people, to the number "of one hundred persons.

"I shall hereafter endeavour, with the aid of the English, to con-"quer the town and fort of Cochin, which formerly belonged to my "crown, and kingdom: and shall then deliver it to the English, as "their own; provided that the charges of its capture, be equally "borne by both parties, one half by me, and the other half by the "English Nation. And in that case, the benefit of the plunder thereof, "of whatsoever kind, shall belong half to me, and half to the Eng-"lish. And thereafter, I shall claim no right, or interest, in the "said town, precincts, or appurtenances, whatsoever.

"I also covenant for myself, my heirs, and successors, that the "whole trade of the English, in whatever commodities, brought in, "or carried out, shall be entirely free from all customs, imposition, "tax, or other duty, of any quality, or description.

"To these covenants, which the shortness of time, did not permit "to extend, in more ample form, I, the Samorin have sworn to per-"form, by the great God whom I revere, and not only for myself, "but my successors; and in witness thereof, I have laid my hand "upon this writing, &c." The Samorin's sign manual, consisted in placing his extended hand, over the written, or more properly speaking, the engraved ollah, or palm leaf, on which most deeds were executed.

The Samorin in forming this alliance, appears to have been actuated, by a wish to obtain European assistance, against the Portuguese: and this treaty, offers Cranganore, and the whole island on which it stands, as far as Chetwye, to the British: as well as Cochin which he asserts, was formerly his own, and which he promises to make over, as soon as captured. Captain Keeling, much to the Samorin's annoyance, declined remaining with his vessels, to join in the attack on Cranganore: but left ten Englishmen, who after the war was over, were to found a factory at Calicut. Amongst these was Mr. Stamford, a gunner, who being of a convivial disposition, one evening imbibed rather too freely, and was picked up, by a foraging party of Cochin Nairs, who delivered him to their allies the Portuguese: subsequently, he was conveyed as a prisoner to Cochin. The remainder of the party, were so badly treated at Calicut, that they were glad to escape, on any terms.

As the naval power of the English increased, their encounters with their enemies became both more frequent, and sanguinary. They were in almost continual warfare with the Portuguese, generally also with the French, and although sometimes in alliance with the Dutch, as often their deadly foes. But after the year 1663, the Portuguese power in India declined so rapidly, that they became no longer feared. The *French East India Company,* was established in 1642, more with the object of territorial aggrandisement, and military renown, than for the mere purposes of trade: but on April 5th, 1761, they finally succumbed to the British, when not a flag of that nation was recognized, not a single fort acknowledged their supremacy, not a Sepoy owed them allegiance; and although they possessed factories at Surat, Calicut, and some other places, they had not a single agent in Bengal; and the English East India Company were able to turn their arms on other foes. It is true, that the French rose subsequently, in Hyder's and Tippoo's favour, and that some of their Settlements were restored to them; still they never afterwards acquired sufficient power, to become a source of anxiety to the English East India Company.

In 1708, the English obtained a grant of the fort at Tellicherry, from the Colastry, or Cherical Rajah, and eleven years subsequently, a disagreement occurring between the former and the Coringotte Nair, they carried on a successful war against him, and it was enacted,—that henceforth the English were to enjoy the exclusive right to the pepper produce of his country, free of all duty. In 1722, the same privilege (with a reservation in favour of the Dutch alone) was conceded by the Cherical Rajah throughout his still extensive country. Three years subsequently, the Rajah of Cartinaad allowed them the pre-emption of all pepper and cardamoms, grown in his territory; and in 1759, the Rajah of Cotiote, concluded a similar treaty. Thus, British power, and influence, rapidly extended itself in Malabar: and the heads of the Tellicherry factory, mediated between antagonistic States, settled differences amongst rival Rajahs, and appear to have been consulted, respected, and feared, by all the chiefs, residing within the limits of the ancient Colastrian kingdom.

In 1751, the English concluded a treaty, with the Rajah of Bednore, and acquired permission to establish a factory at Onore, with freedom to trade throughout his dominions: this occasioned a temporary cessation of intercourse with the Rajah of Cherical, who was then at war with the Bednore Rajah. But in 1757 another treaty of offence and defence was entered into, between Mr. Hodges, the senior British merchant, and the Cherical Rajah, from whom the English obtained in 1761, "the further important privilege, of "collecting on their own behalf, the customs duties, and tolls, within "their own territories, for the small consideration, of a fixed quit "rent, of 21,000 silver fanams, or Rs. 4,200 per annum, to be paid "to his Government. In addition to the foregoing, he and the other "Rajahs, had by this time, successively and separately, yielded up "their rights, to all wrecks, or strandings, of the Company's ves-"sels, or property; an article, which with the customs, or merchan-"dize, constituted two of the most inherent, and acknowledged, ro-"yal rights, of the Malabar Princes, of that period."*

In 1766, Hyder descended a second time into Malabar, and possessed himself of the country, from Cherical to the Cochin State. In 1768, the English and Hyder went to war, when the Nairs reinstated themselves, in their various possessions, and retained them until 1773-74, when Hyder again descended upon the northern portion, and re-established tribute over these various princes, sending *Sree Nawas Rao*, through Palghaut, into the southern division.

The Samorin at this time, committed suicide, in consequence of the treatment he received from Hyder. It was the custom of the former to maintain twelve hundred Brahmans in his palace, and until they were fed, he fasted. No Mahomedan ever had an audience with him, as he never condescended to address a word, to a disciple of Islam. Hyder Ali sent him his compliments, and requested an interview: this the Samorin declined, and only consented to see his head Brahman. Hyder imagining that a little fasting, would bring him to a knowledge of his helpless position, sent rice on the following day, for only five hundred Brahmans: on the second day, for three hundred: and on the third day, for one hundred: after which, no food was allowed to pass. The Samorin fasted three days, and then set fire to his palace, and perished in the flames, as did also some of his women, and three Brahmans; the remainder succeeded in

* M.SS, *Report of Commissioners*, to Lord Cornwallis. 1793.

escaping. On this, all the princes of the Samorin's family fled to Travancore, and Hyder's authority was established in Malabar.

Many of the Rajahs felt aggrieved with the English, for not having joined them, especially the Cherical Rajah, and when the English and French were at war, in 1778, this Rajah, in September, marched his troops to Mahé, to assist the latter people in its defence. In the following month, some of Hyder's forces also joined the French, as he was indignant that persons escaping from his power found an asylum at Tellicherry.

In 1779, the Cherical Rajah, obstructed provisions from being carried into Tellicherry, and his out posts commenced firing at the British workmen. The chiefs of the three petty principalities, subordinate to Cherical, (the Rajah of Cartinaad, the Chief of Irvenaad, and the Nair of Coringotte) gave private information to the authorities of Tellicherry, and a small revolution was organized: the English supplying them with stores and ammunition, and they in return giving coolies, wood, and charcoal, which enabled the British to reduce Mahé, on March 17th, 1779. But Hyder sent a re-inforcement, and these Chiefs were obliged to escape from the country. The Cherical Rajah, in 1779, commenced hostilities against the English, and being joined by Sirdar Khan, besieged Tellicherry, but finding that the Mahomedans were not acting faithfully, the former withdrew his forces in January 1782, and proceeded to Arcot, to lay his complaint before Hyder, who forthwith arrested him for not having paid his tribute. *Major Abingdon*, seeing this defection, made a sortie, slew Sirdar Khan, took the Rajah of Coringotte, (who led the besiegers,) prisoners, and dispersed their army. The British were now in a position, to reward those Princes who had been friendly to them, and punish those who were hostile. The unfortunate Cherical Rajah, who was always on the wrong side, now joined the British under General Matthews, but in 1783, Tippoo came down, and made the General a prisoner, and at the same time deprived the Rajah of Cherical of his dominions. At the final peace of 1784, it was stipulated that no Rajahs should be punished by Tippoo, on account of their friendship with the British, during the late war: but in the enumeration of them, the Cherical Rajah was omitted. Each Rajah, however, was to make his own terms, with

Ashed Beg Khan, a native of the Carnatic, who was appointed by Tippoo, Commandant of Malabar.

In 1788, Tippoo returned to the Western Coast to punish both the Hindus, and Moplahs, who had risen against his authority. On his arrival, he summoned all the Rajahs of Malabar to his presence, but with the exception of the Rajah of Cartinaad, all feigned sickness. Tippoo stated his ardent desire, to prove to all Hindus, the truth of the Mahomedan religion, and trusted that his endeavours to that effect, would be forwarded by the Princes of the country: but his invitation met with no response, so he then demanded twelve lacs of rupees as a gift. In March, or April, the following year, he took possession of the French outposts at Mahé, tearing down the flag of his most Christian Majesty.

About the middle of this year, Tippoo who was at Coimbatore, organizing an attack on the Travancore State, sent orders to his new Dewan at Calicut, to circumcise all Brahmans, as an example to the lower castes, whom he hoped would at once join the new religious sect. If they still held out, and refused to become Mahomedans, they were to be compelled to eat beef; this order was carried into effect, in July of that year, and horror, and consternation, spread throughout the length, and breadth, of Western India. All who were able to do so, fled to Travancore: thousands committed suicide, and the flames of rebellion spread far and wide. Even some Moplahs, joined in an attack on Calicut, and Lally was despatched to break up the siege, this he effected, but he could not subdue the universal hostility of the population.

Many petty Rajahs, and even the Beebee of Cannanore, asked leave to take refuge in Tellicherry. Tippoo on hearing of this, dared the English to receive them, and they consequently adopted a middle course, and allowed the refugees to pass through their territories, to reach the Travancore State in peace. Tippoo before long encamped near Tellicherry, and forcibly converted many Hindus: and also caught the new Rajah of Cherical, who came to make his obeisance, and informed him that the same argument, which had been employed to the lower classes of Hindus, would be applied to himself: on hearing this, he sent orders to his family, to flee to Travancore, promising them, that he would never die a recreant to his father's faith: and then committed suicide.

All the petty Hindu Rajahs fled, and it was evident, that they anticipated assistance from the British, who on their side could not stand idly by, and see their fellow creatures murdered by thousands, because they had been born of Hindu parents. These disturbances, interfered considerably with the English trade. A treaty already alluded to, was then concluded, in which the Cochin Rajah joined, and by the end of 1791, all the Malabar country, had fallen into British hands. The amount of the various tributes, was settled generally, at half what had been exacted by Tippoo: whilst English troops were promised to defend the country from foreign invasion, and domestic strife. The first Rajah who paid his tribute, however, returned home, and shot himself.

The division of the country, and the settlement of the legality of the claims, of the various Rajahs, and Chieftains, over the territories under them, was a very difficult task. The Brahmans and Nairs, wished to have their lands again, rent free: but the Mahomedan plan of assessment, being considered the fairest for all parties, as Military tenures would no longer be necessary, (the British troops being sufficient, for the protection of the country) it was continued unchanged, excepting as regarded the amount. The Hindus now wished to retaliate on the Moplahs, and the discord, oppressions, and murders, which ensued, were very difficult to check: for the petty Rajahs considered it no crime, to put a Moplah to death. On December 20th, 1792, all articles excepting pepper, were thrown open to public trade.

One of the horrors of Malabar, which the British first endeavoured to put an end to, was the kidnapping of children, by gangs of Moplahs, who sold them to the supercargoes of European vessels, more especially to the French at Mahé, and the Dutch at Cochin. Numbers of poor innocent children, were thus entrapped, and carried away, to pass the residue of their lives, in hopeless slavery. It was enacted, that all stealers of children, or persons engaged in this traffic, should be scourged and fined: but even this, did not put a stop to this infamous trade. The English Government, then wrote to that of the Dutch in Cochin, requesting them to abolish the practice of buying children for slaves: but they declined, stating that they realized large sums of money by it! When Cochin was taken, almost every servant in the place was found to be a slave.

On October 19th, 1795, the British Troops under Major Petrie, arrived before the fortress of Cochin, and failing to obtain an entrance, threatened to open fire upon the town. Acting under the orders of the Stadtholder, they had at first endeavoured to obtain an amicable footing, and to make no changes in the Government of the Town. But finding this impossible they determined to adopt other measures as their entrance was necessary to prevent it from falling into the hands of the French.

The Council of Cochin in this emergency, unable to hold the place, but still unwilling to deliver it up, acted in a very injudicious manner; the town was consequently obliged to capitulate, and the Inhabitants became prisoners of war.

In December 1796, those who were desirous of returning to Batavia, were sent to Bombay, and the following year they received permission to proceed to Batavia: but many preferred returning to Cochin, and in 1804, so great was their distress, that they were compelled to petition Government, for pecuniary assistance, and were then all pensioned for one year more, on the understanding that by the expiration of that period, they were to have left India, or at all events, to have forfeited all right to further assistance. But as usual, when the time had elapsed, the English East India Company relented towards those who remained, and even up to the present day, some of the Dutch in Cochin, are receiving pensions.

The Dutch Courts of Justice, and many of their institutions, which will be referred to further on, were left unaltered for some time: as although they worked badly, it was considered by the Governor in Council by no means improbable, that this place might eventually be restored to the Dutch, and therefore no reforms were commenced, until after this question had been finally settled.

The British Resident of Travancore and Cochin, at first took up his quarters, in the house now employed as a Cutcherry, whilst the town was of course garrisoned by British troops. The Government garden was divided into two portions, half being given to the Military, and half to the Civil powers: and this division was continued, until after the Nair riots, in 1809, when not being kept up, part of it was rented out.

The Rajah of Cochin, appears not to have been best pleased at the change of European Governors in Cochin, although the Dutch supremacy had become extremely irksome to him. It has already been stated, that obtaining evidence from the people of the State of Cochin in 1793, was almost an impossibility. Had the British shortly after the taking of the town, examined the records of the Dutch government, many of their decisions, respecting the claims of certain neighbouring States, to territory, could never have been given. In 1799, it was reported, that the father, and brother, of the vicar of the churches of Edapilly, and Earanakollata, had been confined in two separate tiger cages, at Trichoor, from October or November 1797, for one year and ten months, by order of the Cochin Rajah: that for the whole of that period, they were kept loaded with irons, and were not released from their dens, until the evening of August 15th, 1799, when on pretence of being required to proceed to Tripoonterah, they were let out but immediately murdered, and buried. Two other brothers, had previously escaped, one to Trevandrum, and the other to Calicut. This was one of many cruel acts apparently inflicted, on the supposition, that the parties, had given information to the British.

Government finding that the outbreaks, and disturbances, constantly arising in the Cochin State, and generally over Malabar, extended even into the Town of Cochin, re-imposed in that town and territory the regulation, of July 22nd, 1793, "that no guns, muskets, "matchlocks, or other firearms, tulwars, or swords of any description, nor any bows and arrows, shields, balls, powder, ammunition, "or anything coming under the head of warlike stores, (excepting "for the use of Government,) should be imported" into Cochin, or exported from it, on any account whatsoever. The secret memorandum stated that this was enacted, "in order gradually to discountenance, and extinguish, the spirit of independence, and depredation, "so tenaciously cherished amongst the southern Moplahs, and "other similarly disposed persons, by depriving them of the means "of indulging in it." Saltpetre, and sulphur, were no longer allowed to be sold, excepting on a pass signed by the Magistrate, and no more was permitted to be imported, unless disposed of to Government Officials.

In 1802, amicable relations between the English authorities, and the Rajah of Cochin, appear only to have existed outwardly, whilst the Dutch prisoners of war, took advantage of this unpleasant feeling, and presented Napoleon's portrait to the Rajah. It was never ascertained, whether any letter accompanied the gift: but the Rajah's people became very insolent, and even went so far, as to arrest British subjects within British limits: the garrison was consequently directed, to "strictly exclude all the servants "of the Cochin Rajah, from the British territory, lying around the "Town."

On October 6th, 1803, secret orders were sent to Cochin, to prepare for foreign invaders, (the French) and directing the garrison, that immediately an enemy was perceived anchoring before the town, it must be evacuated as untenable: all the inhabitants were to be removed to the interior, should the boats of a hostile fleet approach the shore: whilst all country boats were to be removed, or destroyed: cattle driven away: and provisions rendered useless. As troops could not be spared, in sufficient numbers to garrison Cochin, and enable it to resist an European force, it was decided that the fort should be blown up: this was carried into effect and ere a month had elapsed this Fortress had ceased to exist. Many of the Government buildings, also shared the same fate: and thus Cochin, after having been an important Military strong-hold, for three centuries, dwindled into a mere mercantile port.

Disturbances in the Rajah's territory, rumours of rebellion, and the encroachment of the Dewan on the British power: gave the authorities, and troops, sufficient employment for some time. In 1808, the Travancore Dewan openly commenced war against the British, and the Paliat Achen, or Cochin Minister, favoured his views, and seconded them as far as he was able. Cochin then became the scene of an atrocious attempt to murder the British Resident, *Colonel Macaulay*, who had with him, a guard of only about 25 sepoys.

On December 29th, 1808, at half-past 2 A. M., nearly six hundred armed sepoys, belonging to Travancore, arrived at the southern side of Cochin: and rushing to the Resident's house, then occupied by

Colonel Macaulay, at once obtained possession, and destroyed everything they could discover, including all the Public Records, both of the Magistracy, and Revenue. They searched every where for the Resident, but he was enabled to escape, with his escort of sepoys, and got on board a Pattimar. The jail was broken open, and the prisoners set loose: consternation, and fear, were so universal, that no resistance was at that time attempted.* But by the evening, many of the Travancoreans, had become perfectly intoxicated, and a body of one hundred coolies, and police, were sent to arrest, as many as they could, and made a few captures.

Troops were sent for from Quilon, and preparations made, to resist a second attack, which was anticipated. The officials of the Cochin Government, had on January 10th stopped all provisions from entering Cochin, and on the 12th, 2,000 armed men in the pay of the Rajah, were reported as collected a little to the north of the town on the margin of the backwater, with 5 guns, mounted on the banks: whilst about three Malabar miles to the south, 1,000 armed Travancoreans, were in readiness, to advance.

Col. Macaulay, feeling his insecurity at Cochin, embarked in the grab *Snow*, taking with him the treasure, and also the men, of H. M. 12th foot. He lay off Cochin, in hopes that should reinforcements arrive, he might be able to land the few men with him, who alone, were insufficient to defend the place, but might be serviceable, in conjunction with other troops. Many of the inhabitants, removed to Calicut. But on the following day, matters did not appear so serious, and accordingly, the Resident and his escort re-landed.

About this time, twelve European soldiers, and thirty-three sepoys, were proceeding from Quilon to Cochin, and the sick wife of Colonel, C—— took advantage of the escort, and the presence of an Assistant Surgeon, to accompany them. When they had arrived half way, as far as Allepey, and had reached the narrow canal, the sepoys wished to land, and cook; the natives on the shore, who appeared friendly, enticing them to do so. No suspicions were entertained, the soldiers arms were lying unloaded in the bottom of the boats, and the rowers were all on shore: the sepoys then

* *Official Report to the Judge of Malabar.* Government records. M. S. S.

landed, but perceiving treachery, they called out, to warn the Europeans: but it was too late, a rush was made from the banks, and the whole party was overpowered. A horrible scene then ensued, the prisoners' hands were tied behind them, after which, they were most unmercifully beaten, then their eyes were destroyed, and they were finally put into sacks, and drowned in the canal. The only person spared, was the lady, as it is considered illegal, in this part of the country, to put a woman to death, under any circumstances, and thus one alone survived, to give an account of this horrible tragedy. On this spot, British justice executed the Dewan's brother, who appears to have assisted the murderers. But the Dewan himself escaped this fate by flying to an inland pagoda, where he died of his wounds.

On January 21st, 1809, the Nairs had advanced so close to Cochin, that they broke into the house of the late Dutch Governor, and plundered it, as well as destroyed his garden. On the 25th, the Travancoreans again attacked Cochin, but this time the troops were ready to receive them, and barricades had been thrown up across the principal streets. The enemy, however, advanced from the eastward, instead of from the south, as had been anticipated. In their course, they set fire to, and burnt the Custom's house at Muttencherry, and murdered several Christians. The Muttencherry bridge was broken down, but this was probably done by the troops, to check the enemy's advance. They came on with their guns adorned with crimson shoe flowers, *Hibiscus rosa sinensis*, sacred to Siva, and the gods of Blood. They did not, however, approach with any bravery, and were without much difficulty, forced to retreat, many being taken prisoners. It was deemed unadvisable, to call out the Dutch Militia.

The rioters continued hovering about Cochin, and on February 28th, again paid the late Dutch Governor's house, an unwelcome visit. The cruizer *Lively*, Lieutenant Gilmore, commanding, arrived from Bombay, to assist against the enemy, but grounding opposite the Muttencherry Palace, during some operations there, the officer commanding her, fearing she might fall into hostile hands, had her blown up.

It was now time, for the British power to put forth its strength, and rejecting further pacific measures, to pour troops into the country. In 1809, *secret* orders were received in Malabar, for forces to advance, open communication with the Quilon subsidiary brigade, and act in conjunction with it. But should they experience any resistance, they were directed to seize the Cochin State, and confiscate it to the British. A proclamation was then issued, offering friendship, or war; and the first, as previously detailed (page 57) was accepted. The Paliat Achen, became an exile, his family title of "hereditary Prime Minister to the Cochin Rajah" passed away, and another succeeded to his post; whilst efficient measures were organised, to prevent a repetition of such disturbances.

Near Cochin, in the Travancore district of Paroor, and in Ayroor and Chandroor, the Native Christians, in the month of March, created great disturbances, and British troops had to be quartered in those places, and it was also deemed necessary, to station two armed Pattimars at Cranganore. In April, the Native Christians in the Cochin State, sent in a petition, representing the ill-treatment to which they were subjected, by the Rajah's officials. It was now considered advisable by the Resident, to take forcible possession of the Palace at Muttencherry, which was effected by a party of sepoys, on April 11th. Troops were kept constantly moving about the country, a Captain's guard was stationed at Tripoonterah, and a Lieutenant Colonel's at Allepey, matters soon began to quiet down, and by the middle of October, most of the outposts were withdrawn to Quilon and Cochin.

Military operations since this period, have not been necessary, the town of Cochin was, by the convention of 1814, ceded to the British: otherwise the peaceful times, which have succeeded to its former eventful transactions, afford but little historical matter to record. A small guard is kept over the Dewan's Cutcherry, at Ernacollum, and another at Tripoonterah. In 1860, the last vestige of the military occupation of Cochin ceased, the few sepoys who up to this time had been stationed there, were withdrawn, their hospital turned into a police office, their barrack and magazine being handed over to the latter force, and their lines pulled down and destroyed. Now no troops are seen in Cochin excepting those passing through, or guards of honour, for the purpose of attending at Durbars, or for other professional purposes.

The *institutions* of Cochin, have gradually changed, from their Dutch form, to that which exists in other portions of the British possessions: but it is strange, that some persons still fancy, that their houses and lands, are not amenable to taxation, because the terms of the Capitulation, state, (Article 4th) "all private property will be sacred," forgetting that it also declares that the inhabitants will be amenable to British laws.

In 1847, a permanent ryotwarry system was introduced by *Mr. Conolly*, and a quit-rent imposed. In many of the leases, no redemption clause exists: they are subject to a revision of rent, every twenty years. The amount of land, outside the fort, exceeds 13,000 acres.

The following* shows the *Collection* in rupees, during the last 5 years in Cochin: but it must be observed, that in 1861, the taxes to pay for the mutinies in Bengal, of 1857, were imposed.

	1857.	1858.	1859.	1860.	1861.
Collections on landed property	19,122	18,145	17,902	17,073	16,324
" " Abkary farm	6,150	6,150	6,150	6,150	6,150
" " Vypeen ferry	815	815	815	815	815
" " Sea Customs	59,177	62,823	51,327	47,879	93,327
" " Salt	1,468	1,925	978	602	479
" " Stamped paper	3,215	4,040	5,465	3,760	5,330
" " Postage stamps	3,500	3,858	4,412	5,315	6,213
" " Post office	2,642	3,686	2,427	1,771	1,599
" " Telegraph	"	"	4,480	6,234	7,903
" " Hoondis, receipt stamps and bills of lading				"	1,937
" " Sundries as income tax		"	"	"	49,380

The various items, speak for themselves, and it is only necessary to observe, that the population in 1861, consisted of 11,449 persons, the revenue receipts were upwards of 189,457 rupees: or a rough average, of 16 rupees, or £1 12*s.* a year, on each individual, of every sex and age.

Civil, and criminal justice, was at first administered, according to the Dutch laws: and even some of their officials, were retained unchanged. In the year 1812, insecurity of life and property, had

* Return furnished by *Mr. Green*, Revenue Sheristadar.

become so great, that many respectable persons were obliged to leave their houses, and congregate within the town of Cochin, for without its limits, no woman or child was safe. A Zillah Court was established in 1812, and done away with in 1817, the records being sent to Calicut. In 1812, it was brought to the notice of Government, that children were being sold as slaves in Travancore, and this course was reprobated in the strongest terms, although it was not until 1854, that slavery was nominally abolished, in the Cochin and Travancore States, owing to the exertions of the British Resident, Lieutenant General Cullen,* who obtained the emancipation of 23,000 Government slaves, and an amelioration in the condition of those belonging to private owners.

* Whilst these pages were being printed, Lieutenant General Cullen, eminent as a scientific observer, and successful administrator, expired at Allepey, October 1st, 1862, regretted by all classes of the community. Rarely, if ever, has a European in Malabar been so beloved by natives; even after his resignation of the office of Resident his opinion was more regarded, and his favour more esteemed, than was that of his successor in the appointment. On his *retirement* all classes vied which should do him most honour, whilst the richer portions of the community strove to perpetuate his name. In Travancore, the natives presented him with an address and expressed their intention, "to "institute in manifestation of their gratitude and regard, one or two annual "prizes in his name to be open to subjects of Travancore only," and for this purpose they subscribed 2,500 rupees. In the Cochin State 6,000 rupees were raised to erect a Choultry at Vaylum Thavalum for the accommodation and refreshment of wearied travellers, which was to bear his honoured name.

The late Rajah of Travancore wrote him a most complimentary letter, from which the following extracts are taken. "Your name is associated in our "memory with many important and interesting events, the most conspicuous "of which, is the provision made through your powerful intercession, for the "continuation of the line of succession to the musnud of Travancore: an "event which nothing can erase from the memory of myself, family, and "the whole country, and for which we cannot adequately feel grateful.

"To preserve the memory of your name in our country, and as a token of "our esteem and regard towards you, we intend to establish a scholarship in "your name, in my free-school here, and for eventual admission into the "Presidency University, for the support of which, myself, and other members "of my family have individually contributed funds for its endowment."

The Rajah of Cranganore, the Syrian metropolitan, the chief of the Mahomedans, the Jewish Rabbi, each headed addresses of regard to the outgoing Resident. The Namboorie Brahmans, and the heads of the Thiroomalla Devasom shenay pagoda, likewise presented addresses to him on his retirement.

For some years, Cochin has only had a Sudr Ameen's Court, under the control of the Judge of Calicut, to whom all decisions must be referred. This appears sufficient for the wants of the place. Civil cases under 10,000 rupees, can be tried here. The number of civil suits which have been instituted during the last five years, are as follows:—*

1857	Remaining 187	Filed 147	Decided 157
1858	„ 177	„ 203	„ 161
1859	„ 219	„ 256	„ 173
1860	„ 302	„ 226	„ 314
1861	„ 214	„ 264	„ 365

Thus a civil case on an average, is not kept waiting above one year, before obtaining a decision.

Criminal Justice, has been remodelled, especially as regards the various castes and sects, who were formerly under the control of the Dutch, and subsequently under that of the English. In 1814, it was decided, that of the castes amenable to British laws,† "Wunnears, and Tuttans, remain subject in all cases, to the authority of the Judge, and Magistrate of Cochin, within the local limits of whose jurisdiction, it is understood that they principally reside. But with respect to the Canarese, and Konkanies, and White Jews, the jurisdiction of that Court, will be confined to civil cases, to the determination of disputes between them, and British or Dutch subjects, whilst in criminal cases, when the offence shall have been committed against the British Government, or British subjects, in the most extensive meaning of the term, they will also be amenable to its decrees." This it went on to state, was in accordance with the Dutch treaties. No Customs' chowkey, was to be permitted to be placed by the Rajah, in Muttencherry, which it was stated, would be a "real annoyance to the inhabitants of Cochin, did it exist." It was also decided, not to continue exercising any jurisdiction, over the Native Christians in the Rajah's territory, as such rendered them objects of jealousy to their fellow-subjects, and occasioned many and serious disputes.

Again in 1835, this question was re-agitated, and it was ruled by

* From a return furnished by the Joint Magistrate.

† Order by the *Governor in Council*, Madras, August 16th, 1814.

the Court of Directors, on June 1st, 1836, "that British subjects, "apprehended in British territory, on any charge of offence, committed within the possessions of any Native prince, are amenable "only to British tribunals. That British subjects, apprehended in "the territory, within which the offence is alleged to have been "committed, are amenable to the jurisdiction of the tribunal, established there. Subjects of the Native State, whenever apprehended, "are always amenable to the British Courts, for crimes and heinous "offences, committed within the British territory. That British "subjects, charged with heinous crimes, committed within the British territory, who may have taken refuge within the territory of a "Native State, are to be delivered up to justice, and *vice versâ*, with "respect to subjects of a Native State."

Criminal justice, during the last 5 years, has produced the following cases:

1857	Remained	0	New cases	195	Discharged	9
1858	"	2	"	147	"	19
1859	"	0	"	141	"	17
1860	"	1	"	93	"	11
1861	"	0	"	380	"	23
1857	Committed to Calicut			10	Convicted in Cochin	174
1858	"		"	10	" "	120
1859	"		"	10	" "	114
1860	"		"	5	" "	78
1861	"		"	9	" "	348

Natives do not appear to relish English *justice*, and it was an excellent rule, of the late Court of Directors, that all Magistrates were obliged to pass in the Native language. Persons ignorant of it, are the tools of their subordinates, and the puppets of their interpreters. More speedy justice, and less law, is the desideratum for India: and a large emigration of Lawyers from Europe, would be no blessing to Mofussil Courts.

The *Police Force* was organised in 1860, and since then, have discharged the duties of Cochin: time will show its capabilities.

In fixing the pay of the men, the first half of *Earl St. Vincent's* maxim, in regard to Naval officers, of "keep them poor, and they "will serve you well," appears to have been kept in view. There is one European Inspector, having 56 Natives under him.

The *Marine establishment* is under a Master Attendant, who supervises all duties, connected with the shipping: excepting, the "Registration of Vessels," which is one of the Joint Magistrate's offices. To this department, is attached a useful anchor boat, a Cutter, and a Report boat. Every vessel on its arrival, or departure from Cochin, is reported, in the usual form. A depôt of coals is kept, for the use of H. M.'s steamers.

The following shows the amount of tonnage, entered at Cochin, from May 1858, to December 31st, 1861.* It is only in the last named year, that the tonnage of vessels, that do not pay duty, has been registered.

	British tonnage.	Foreign tonnage.	Country coasters.	Small vessels free.
1858 from May 1st to Dec. 31st	12,416	919	10,957	Unregistered.
1859 the whole year	29,951	6,481	25,679	"
1860 " "	35,683	8,533	25,055	"
1861 " "	35,999	11,202	34,024	37,410

During the last three years, the average tonnage, amenable to Port dues, has been 70,869 tons. The year 1862, has been an unusual one, for late enactments, have almost closed the Port of Allepey, to commerce: and trade has consequently, been diverted to Cochin. The amount of tonnage, is not a correct index, of the business of the port: but this will be alluded to, more fully under the head of, "exports, and "imports." The registered tonnage, includes that of every vessel, which by stopping above 48 hours, or landing any portion of its cargo, or passengers, renders itself amenable to port dues. Steamers from Bombay come irregularly, once a fortnight, sometimes oftener. The "Licensed Pilot," was appointed "Government Pilot," in October 1860.

The *poor of Cochin*, next claim attention. In the time of the Dutch, an Orphanage existed, and so much has been incorrectly stated, concerning the Government *mismanagement* of this Institution, since 1795, that the official report is here given in full.†

* From a return, furnished by the Master Attendant.

† The following observation was printed and given publicity, amongst HISTORICAL NOTICES OF COCHIN. "One cannot wonder that poverty abounded

"When Cochin surrendered to the British arms, Major Petrie "made no alteration, in the Institution of the Orphan Asylum, it "was going on as under the late Dutch Government. The Pre "sident and members of the Asylum, always administered the funds "of the Orphans, while they remained under age. The money was "generally laid out, on mortgages of houses in the town, and two "collateral securities were taken by the College, for the money so "raised, at 6 per cent. per annum: from which, 4½ per cent. were "paid to the pupils, agreeably to their share in the Orphan treasury. "The remaining 1½ per cent. on the conclusion of their accounts, "(which was in August,) was divided amongst the President, the "members, and the Secretary. The President had the share of two "members, the rest was divided in equal proportions, amongst the "members, and Secretary. From this emolument, a messenger was "employed, at the pay of six rupees a month: and thirty-two rupees "paid to the Secretary for stationery for a whole year. Whoever "died intestate, the Secretary administered the estate of such persons, "assisted by two Members, deputed by the College for that purpose. "He, (the Secretary,) then acted as Auctioneer, receiving 4 per cent. "on the amount sold, and 1 per cent. was paid the messenger, who "acted as crier. The two members so employed, received each one "rix dollar a day. Such was the practice of the College, for many "years. If one of the parents died, leaving any children under age, and "the survivor wished to administer to their shares, the College could "never object to it: but it was necessary, that he, or she, who "wished to do so, should deliver into the College, within six weeks, "from the death of the testator, or testatrix, an inventory on oath, "of all the property; and give two or more sufficient securities for "the amount, which according to the tenor of the Will, such chil- "dren were entitled to, to be refunded them, when they attained "their proper age, boys 24, girls 21."*

"in a decayed Settlement like Cochin; and what we must regard (to say the least) "as the *inconsiderate* suppression of the Dutch Orphan House, with its ample "funds, must have increased the misery in many an indigent household." Unprejudiced readers may satisfy themselves, how far facts are in accordance with this assertion.

* *Cutcherry Records.* M.SS.

In 1832, when the foregoing report was made, most of the mortgagees, did not pay interest upon the monies, which they had received: whilst amongst the houses which were mortgaged as security for the repayment of the principal, some were in ruins, and consequently no rent was obtainable from them. Petitioners then requested the interference of Government, and that the affairs might be wound up, as some of the members of the College Board, it was asserted, were amongst the defaulting mortgagees. A Government Committee was therefore appointed, who acceded to the request of the Petitioners: and in 1836,* the funds as far as possible, were realised, and divided amongst those entitled to them.

The British when they first came to Cochin, did not institute, the present "Friend-in-Need Society," but a Poor-house was built, prior to 1820, by the exertions of the Resident, and the European community, most handsomely assisted by the Rajah of Cochin, who gave a donation for its erection, and also a subscription of one hundred rupees a month, to the poor. Up to the year 1855, this building was employed, as a residence for paupers, but it was then destroyed by a heavy monsoon: and Government subscribed two thousand rupees towards the erection of a more spacious one. The Rajah's subscription is still continued, and with the addition of Rs. 30 from the Resident and Dewan, and Rupees 70 from the inhabitants of the town, forms a fund, employed for the support of from 30 to 40 indigent persons, within the poors' house, and for assisting about 100, with outdoor relief, without reference, to their caste, creed or sex. For this, a Managing Committee was formed, in 1845, and rules were organized for its regulation.

A Civil Surgeon was attached to Cochin, in May 1817, and the appointment has been continued from that time: under him are two native subordinates, one stationed at the Dispensary, and the chief duties of the other lying amongst the Police, and the prisoners within the jail. There is also a Vaccinator, whose duty it is, to vaccinate persons in the place.

The Dutch do not appear to have kept up any Dispensary, for the civil population, but had extensive military hospitals, in which however, they very unwisely, made enormous deductions from the

* *Government order*, dated September 27th, 1836.

pay of the sick. Thus the soldier, or sailor, knowing that whilst he was on the sick list, his family if he had one, would be starving, continued his duties as long as he was able, and frequently only entered the hospital, to be speedily carried out a corpse. Some most interesting, and extraordinary revelations, on this head, with regard to Batavia, were published by Admiral Stavorinus.

The present Government Dispensary, was opened at the end of January, 1853, and the following are the number of admissions, that have taken place, during the last five years:

1857	Out Patients, admitted	4,711	In Patients, admitted	405
1858	„ „ „	4,673	„ „ „	337
1859	„ „ „	4,580	„ „ „	376
1860	„ „ „	6,347	„ „ „	415
1861	„ „ „	6,980	„ „ „	585

The schools in Cochin, are rather inferior; the Protestant free schools, are situated on the site of the old hotel, where the Dominican convent stood, in Portuguese times. They are under the supervision of the Missionary chaplain. There is also a school for boarders, opened in 1859, which contains about twenty boys and girls, the average cost of each, being about fifty rupees a year. The "Free schools" have a small endowment, arising from an old Church fund, and receives Government assistance.*

		Pupils.	Govt. aid.	Endowment.	Subscriptions.	Fees.
Boys' School established	1857	124	Rs. 384	275	30	92
Girls „ „	1853	46	„ 130	„	119	„
Vernacular „	1856	89	„ 6	„	211	15

Thus it will be seen, that the attendance in them is but small, Government aid for education in Cochin, which was received during the years under review (the last obtainable in Cochin,) was Rupees 520: and the funds raised from subscriptions, and fees, exclusive of the endowment Rupees 467. Government affords great assistance in India, in the form of "Grants-in-aid," toward schools, should parties be able or willing, to come forward with proper teachers, who can satisfactorily undergo the Government test. No doubt, there are some persons, who would like to see the old Dutch practice revived in Cochin, and taxes obtained from persons of all denominations, applied

* Report of *Director of Public Instruction*, for 1859 60.

exclusively to the support of Protestant schools.* Government without interfering, with the methods of teaching, where they give Grants-in-aid, adhere to the following principle in their own scholastic establishments. "As a necessary part of this policy, the Holy "Scriptures have been excluded from the course of teaching: "but the Bible has a place in the School-libraries, and the "pupils are at liberty to study it, and to obtain instruction "from their Masters, as to its facts and doctrine, out of "School hours, if they expressly desire it."* Bigoted indeed must be that man, who would deny instruction, because his creed alone is not taught, and intolerant that person, who would force his version of the sacred volume, to be read by those, whose spiritual teachers forbid it. Education surely must be necessary for the rising masses, before they can understand their errors: and the people must be taught to think, before they can be expected to be convinced by arguments. It has been remarked, that it is surprising, such scrupulous persons, as the above, should permit themselves, on any consideration, to receive money collected from such unhallowed sources, as taxes upon a Hindu and Mahomedan population.

In the preceding chapters, the political vicissitudes, through which Cochin has passed, during the last three centuries and a half, have been traced. Rising on the site of a native town, it became one of the first of the European fortresses in the east: diminished in size, and shorn of much of its splendour by the Dutch: its fortifications were finally destroyed by the British, in 1803. Though wanting in the interest of former days, still it possesses much to attract the notice of the passer by. Some of the Institutions of this port, have already been adverted to: it now remains to describe the place, as it at present stands.

The stranger visiting Cochin, arrives either by sea, or by the northern or southern branches of the backwater, the highway to Allepey and Quilon on the south, and to Trichoor and Chowghat on the north: there are no roads, or rather none deserving the name, by which a traveller can enter the town. Riding is almost out of

---

* *Lord Stanley's* despatch on education in India.

the question, and driving simply impossible: still palanquins can go to Ernacollum, but much delay and trouble is occasioned, in crossing over the backwater, to Cochin.

The view of Cochin from the roadstead, is by no means devoid of interest: far away inland, the scene is bounded, by high hills, the continuation of the western ghauts: whilst between these mountains and the sea, the country appears to be a flat, cultivated plain. The broad opening of the Vypeen river, is easily discernible: but not so the backwater, into which it expands. The island of Vypeen, on the northern bank of the river, seems a dense jungle, or rather grove of cocoanut trees, in which no houses are perceptible. The Cochin island, lying on the southern bank, is also covered with trees, from amidst which, churches and houses, are visible. The flag staff tower, the most conspicuous object amongst the buildings, first claims attention. This massive square structure, upon which a seventy-five feet mast arises, is the remains of the Cathedral of Santa Cruz. Apparently close to it, stands the large church of the Franciscans, whilst several houses, situated on elevated portions of the old ramparts, are distinctly discernible.

As the traveller by sea advances nearer to the river's mouth, the scene again changes: along either bank, are seen extraordinary Chinese fishing nets. The houses at Vypeen, soon become visible on the left hand, and after passing one larger than its neighbours, a white Roman Catholic church appears, thrown well back, and imbedded in cocoanut groves. Turning to the right, a house situated on a laterite rock, is first passed, and further on a small piece of green is seen, in the midst of which, stands the flag staff tower; any further view, is shut out, by quaint old houses, with their pent tiled roofs, appearing as if they had been bodily transported, from some old town, in continental Europe. Meanwhile the vessel glides on, several wharfs are passed, then some mercantile yards, and the backwater, expanding to a width of nearly three miles, on the banks of which, seven churches are visible, as well as the British Residency, about two miles away to the east, and the native town of Ernacollum, a little further to the south-east. The whole length of the river, is about half a mile, its width at the mouth about 800 yards, and opposite the tower a little less.

The river, or entrance into the backwater, divides the British territory, into two portions. The sea, or port limits, are marked by boundary pillars: one being a mile north of the northern entrance to the harbour, the other three miles to its south. But inland it may be said, that Vypeen is about 250 yards, of the most southern extremity, of one island: and Cochin the last mile and a half, of the northern extremity of the other. Thus the whole of the outlet, belongs to the British.

Cochin consists of that portion, within the limits of the old walls, about 800 yards across, and still called the fort: as well as, that which has sprung up exterior to them. Of the latter, the most important, are the Culvetty, and the first portion of the Muttencherry bazaars, which extend along the banks of the backwater, about three quarters of a mile, in an easterly, and south easterly direction, and then merge into the bazaars, in the Rajah's territory. Amaravady also possesses numerous houses, and a good sized bazaar.

The fort walls have been destroyed, but mounds of earth, the remnants of the old ramparts, exist in parts of its west or sea face, and also along a portion of its south and south-east fronts. Exterior to a portion of the old rampart, on the land side, is the fort ditch, part of which still remains in the form of a tank, some portion being employed for paddy fields, whilst the rest is a swamp.

British Cochin, is a flat sandy plain, raised only a few feet, above the level of high water mark. The whole of this range of long Islands, situated between the sea, and the backwater, appears like a sand bank, intermixed with alluvial deposits: although in some places, along the banks of the backwater, a substratum of clay, has been observed. Water is found, at from six to ten feet, from the surface: it is saline, probably from the amount of free percolation that occurs, owing to its proximity to the sea. The use of it for drinking purposes, appears to occasion that hideous disease, known as elephantiasis, or elephant leg.

Bishop *Middleton*, thus describes Cochin, in 1816: "it proved "to be in a condition, in all respects, sufficiently miserable: some "of the principal edifices neglected, and falling into decay: the "Dutch church shut up for want of a minister, the school in the "fort destroyed, the children left unbaptized, the sick unassisted, "and without the last consolatory offices: and a total apathy amongst "the inhabitants, respecting education, and religion."

This picture is happily at the present time quite inappropriate, as the town possesses a resident clergyman, a protestant school assisted by Government, another for the Roman Catholic children, and several private ones, a Government Dispensary, and a flourishing trade.

Amongst the most remarkable buildings, is the flag staff tower already several times alluded to, as being a portion of what in former days, was a magnificent Portuguese Cathedral: subsequently converted by the Dutch, into a storehouse for their merchandize: whilst the nave is believed to have been finally blown up by the British. The height, of this tower (now employed as a light house) is 61 feet 8 inches above the level of the grass. The light is shewn at an elevation of 67 feet above the tower, excepting during the S. W. monsoon, when it is placed at 32. On May 11th, 1809, at 6 P. M. a flash of lightning struck it, and split the mast and yards. Vessels whether anchoring, or merely passing, are signalled, and reported to Madras.

The present Protestant Church, is a massive pile of ancient buildings, capable of accommodating a very large congregation. It was erected by the Portuguese, for the Franciscans; and renovated, according to an inscription over the entrance, A. D. 1779. It possesses no beauty, and its length, extends across the northern end of the parade ground.* In 1817, a Chaplain was appointed to Cochin, but subsequently the Clergyman stationed at Quilon, paid periodic visits. In 1826, a Missionary settled in Cochin, but in 1839, ill-health compelled him to leave the place, and shortly afterwards,

* On the taking of Cochin, the following silver furniture was delivered up, as the property of this Church: 1 font, 1 plate, 2 bread dishes, 2 waiters, 1 funnel, 4 goblets, 68 cyphers and letters, 1 margin and 1 bell for the collecting purse, a small font, and the brass stand of an hour glass, apparently employed for regulating the length of the sermons, but the glass unfortunately is broken: the cyphers appear to have been used, for marking the hymns on a board. Besides these, there were various designations, for as many bags: so that subscribers, knew whether their money was given to the Leper-hospital, the orphanage, the widows, or the poor.

the Mission was removed to Trichoor. Again the Quilon Chaplain performed the duties, and continued to do so, until October 1852, when a Missionary Chaplain was appointed, for whom Government subscribed one hundred rupees a month, besides meeting most of the expenses. In May 1860, the first Missionary Chaplain left, and was succeeded in May 1861, by the present incumbent.

Inside the Cochin Church, on the flagged floor, are many very fine tomb-stones. Some in memory of Portuguese Roman Catholics, others of Dutch Protestants: some are covered with magnificent coats of arms, interspersed with death's heads, and cross bones: or figures standing in very Hinduised attitudes. It by no means follows, that these stones are placed over graves: in many places in Cochin, there are magnificent tomb-stones, at the door-ways of houses, or as coverings to drains, and in similar situations. Many of these were collected, (probably in 1816,) and the Church was reflagged. After the British captured Cochin, no interments were permitted within the Church.

The old *burial ground*, now closed, bears the date of 1724, on its gate-way. It is a small place crowded with tombs, of many curious forms and shapes. Broken trees and pillars, slabs and monumental urns, are seen in rich profusion: but most of the names of those reposing beneath, have been effaced by time, and all are hastening, with more or less rapid steps to decay: whilst to render the scene more desolate, rank grass, and the Indian heliotrope, (*Lantana mutabilis*), with its little scarlet flower, springs not only from between, but also from the sides and tops, of these mouldering monuments.

The *parade ground* is a nice little patch of green, in nearly the centre of the old fort, where the arsenal, and other buildings, are said to have stood: which not being required by the British, shared the fate of the town walls, in 1803. About 30 years since, the officer commanding, had the parade ground, very neatly planted with portia trees, many of them are now decaying, but it is a pretty spot, about 250 paces square, and having the old military (now police) buildings, situated on its eastern side. It is surrounded on three sides, by a good laterite road: a few trees planted with some little regard to appearance, and kept nicely trimmed, so as not to grow too high, would be a very great improvement.

The *Cutcherry*, is reputed to have been in Portuguese times, the residence of the priests, of the neighbouring ruined Cathedral of Santa Cruz. Many are the vicissitudes through which this building has passed. Here the Nairs broke in, and tried to murder the British Resident: since this period, it has been appropriated in the following manner:—"The lower rooms as prisons for criminals, some of the "upper ones as a jail for debtors. When troops were in the town, "it was a mess-house for the officers, the Fiscal otherwise resided "in it, and one room was set aside for the Magistrate, whenever he "should visit the place. When the troops were decreased, and a "mess-house no longer required, still the Magistrate of Malabar, for "a considerable period, retained his room there." At last it was decided to locate the Sudr Ameens Court at one end, and that of the Fiscal with the record-room at the other: the prisoners were placed in the centre, and the rooms surrounding the yard, on the ground floor, were appropriated to their use. This partition of the building, still remains in force: the portion occupied by criminals, is calculated to hold 60, allowing each 519 cubic feet of air. Solitary cells have been erected for Europeans, in which they are generally tormented by mosquitoes, and irritated by prickly heat.

The Government, or branch of the *Madras Bank*, was established in Cochin, in 1862, it stands at the north east corner of the parade ground. The *Government Telegraph office*, is situated at the south west corner of the same piece of green, it was instituted in Cochin, in 1859. The telegraph cables, having to cross several rapid rivers, and also being exposed along the line of the sea coast, to the full violence of the S. W. monsoon, occasionally fail, as might be anticipated. The *Government Post office*, is placed at the S. E. corner of the parade ground; whilst in Muttencherry, is the *Sircar Ungil*, or Rajah's post. There is a little *newspaper*, published in the town every Saturday.

A *Synagogue* of black Jews, or rather a house used by them for that purpose, is situated in the centre street, passing from the southern end of the parade ground, but there is nothing in it worthy of note.

The majority of houses within the fort limits, are of Portuguese construction, usually two storied with laterite walls, rarely parallel, and of an average thickness, of 2½ feet: they have tiled, pent roofs, with comparatively small windows, some of which are glazed in small panes, and all have strong wooden out-side shutters. Each window has a seat inside, on either hand, where the occupant can at his ease, observe all that is passing in the street beneath. The outside walls are of various hues, from white, to blue, yellow, or even red.

Superstition, peoples almost every house, with ghosts of various forms and shapes: even the Protestant Church, is said to be haunted by an old woman, who is sometimes seated disconsolately in one spot, sometimes in another, but most commonly on the sides of the old well close by, on the parade ground. On being approached, she is said to assume the shape of a pig, which on being pursued, disappears in the form of a number of small grunters.

The town is built in streets, running in a N. E. direction, which makes the rooms hot. The most objectionable style of houses, are those which partially enclose a square, within which is a garden, as in the monsoon time, they are thus rendered very damp.* During the wet months, grasses, weeds, and parasitic ferns, grow luxuriantly on the house tops, especially in localities protected from the full violence of the S. W. monsoon. In the hot weather, it all dries up, and looks like hay. Along either side of the streets, are stone drains, which were made by Government, in 1812, at a great expense: but unfortunately, many of the larger ones, are now rendered useless. Twice a year, the convicts clean out those, which have not been permanently destroyed, and they also keep the roads in tolerable order.

Strangers arriving at Cochin, would be struck by seeing European looking houses and streets, well beaten laterite roads, little patches of green never quite burnt up, and the open parade ground in the centre of the town.

There is not much space for driving; along the face of the river

---

* As a *Medical topography*, is incompatible, with the scheme of the present, work, it can only be observed: that it is unfortunately but too true, that "no "town of corresponding importance, possesses in so small a degree, appliances, "for the preservation of the public health, or where sewerage and drainage, "are so little attended to:" but these matters, are in no degree under medical control. Readers curious on these subjects, are referred to the first 3 volumes of the *Madras Quarterly Journal of Medical Science*, for the years 1860 and 1861.

is a road, that extends onwards through the town, passing the Protestant Church, the parade ground, through one street, by the native (formerly Scotch) Church, and the benches on the S. W. extremity of the fort, where it reaches the sea beach road. Here there is nothing to interfere with a good view of the ocean, which is only divided from the road, by a loose sandy tract: whilst on the left hand, are houses and cocoanut plantations. After proceeding about a mile, the limit of the drive terminates, near this point stands the new cemetery, and beyond are numerous small pools, in which the dhobies wash the clothes. Here the Amaravady road is joined, it leads back to the town of Cochin, between cocoanut plantations, and houses: first comes the Poor-house, a clean looking building, but almost hidden amongst the trees on the left, next a Roman Catholic Church, erected in 1834, with a pair of cross-keys carved in stone over the gate-way, further on is a Konkanie pagoda (see Chapter VII) to the right, here the road expands, and peepul trees are for a short distance, planted along both sides. Continuing in this direction, a blank wall on the left, defines the limits of an oil yard; another further on, that of the Government Dispensary, next to this is the compound of the Syrian Metropolitan, within which are the walls of an unfinished Church, long since commenced, but apparently never destined to be completed: skirting this, and leaving a large screw house on the right, the flag staff tower, again comes into view. In this course, there is not much to see, unless it be the vegetation, or the people, of whom large numbers are Topasses (persons wearing hats), who are of two classes, first, the regular, and irregular descendants of the Portuguese, and Dutch, inhabitants of Cochin: and secondly, those of the converted slave population. Every caste and creed, in other times, (and the Moplahs in the present day) purchased women and children, and converted them to their faith, this class, if Christians, dress as Eurasians, but are far inferior to the first.

There are many varieties of costumes, from the fully dressed native, who is clothed merely from the waist downwards, (the upper half of the body being provided for by a sacred string, and a little paint, or ashes,) to urchins with no clothing at all, or merely a bit of string. During the rainy months, the most frequented streets, have a strange appearance, as every native carries an umbrella, composed of leaves of the palm tree, mostly tarred. The pandalls, (bamboo mats nailed on to square wooden frames,) over the windows also look curious.

That portion of Cochin, which has the most Oriental appearance, is the bazaar along the side of the backwater, and although it is rather too fragrant to be pleasant, still it is curious enough to repay a stranger for the trouble of visiting it. The backwater lies along the left hand side, divided from the road, by a few mercantile, timber, and building yards. On the right are shops, where their owners are seated cross legged, ready to meet the requirements of customers. The calico merchant has handkerchiefs of all colours for sale: next is a crockery shop, where common bright coloured European ware, is seen standing by the side of bowls and scent bottles from China, and wooden spoons from Aden: a little farther on, are several carpenter's shops, where numerous brass bound boxes, are exposed for sale, called blackwood, although not really so, but only the rough jungle wood, *Cooroo Murradoo* Mal. which is of much the same colour.

When the ground near the Muttencherry bridge was let for yards, the inhabitants of the place remonstrated, alleging that during the time of both the Portuguese and Dutch, it was never enclosed: but kept as a spot, for depositing timber, ready for those who were building vessels, as well as for petty merchants, and duty was levied on the timber, and rent on the spot, whilst the vessel was being built.

On reaching the Muttencherry bridge, which crosses a sluggish canal, of extremely dirty water, boats are generally seen in the afternoon, bringing in fish, oysters, and vegetables for sale. On its further side the bazaar may be said, really to commence. On the left hand stands, first a Police Office, and then the British Custom's house, with these exceptions, shops are seen on either side of a narrow street, and before many of them, the salesman is seated on the ground, with his merchandize spread out around him. Here is the fruiterer, with piles of pumpkins, bandikyes, pine-apples, guavas, chillies, and other vegetable productions; whilst next door, there are live monkeys, of both black, and brown varieties, a mongoose or two, with parrots, loris, mynahs, and pigeons. Again there is an herbalist's, where the votaries of native drugs, procure the necessary ingredients, the smoker his tobacco, the opium eater his accustomed stimulus, the bhang consumer the dose which gives him such delicious reveries, and the betel chewer the leaf wherein he wraps pieces of chunam, with the nut of the Areca palm, which when in his mouth turns the saliva red, and leads the uninitiated European to labour under the impression that the surrounding natives are constantly expectorating blood. Another shop is piled with chatties made of baked red clay, and fire ovens of the same materials, most of which are manufactured near Alwaye. The petty Hawker seated by the side of the street, is loudly proclaiming the praises of his wares. On cumblies spread upon the ground before him, are strings of Brahmanee beads, true and false tortoise-shell combs, and boxes, brass or silver boxes in which to carry little coins, small looking glasses, bright beads, knives in red leather sheaves, English scissors, rusty nails, screws, common padlocks, &c.

The noise is very great, but this is no criterion of the amount of business transacted, as the rich man makes as much commotion about a *poothen* (10 pie) as if his existence depended on its being saved, and here the poor man, obtains his daily supply of food, and his clothing. All complain of their extreme poverty, whilst each endeavours, to over-reach his neighbour. About half a mile beyond, leaving the Arab and the Hindu, the Christian and the Jew, jostling each other, the stranger reaches a wide space, where on the right hand side, is a range of quiet looking shops, the verandahs of which are raised a little higher than usual, and here the din of the tin-man's, and copper-smith's hammers, are almost deafening: this is the goldsmith's quarter, and here a combination of Tuttans, money venders, and jewellers, reside: men who although desirous of leading their customers to suppose them so poor, that an anna more or less is of vital importance to their existence, have in reality within their dwellings, hoards of gold and silver ornaments, and precious stones. Here the numismatic collector, may frequently obtain rare, and valuable coins. This road continues past a white Roman Catholic Chapel, edged with black, and a little further on, reaches the Rajah's palace, and Jew's town.

Reverting to the town of Cochin in the centre street of the fort, or in the fort bazaar, which passes directly S. E. of the flag staff tower, are two or three Inns, which are made use of by sailors and others, but they scarcely deserve the name of Hotels. Here also are the best shops, for obtainining European articles: whilst those who are fond of animals, may procure a parrot, a monkey, or a mynah.

Vypeen is on the opposite side of the river, and but little is to be seen there, with the exception of a Roman Catholic Chapel, dedicated to "Our Lady of Hope," and erected in 1665 or 1666.* Its method of Church Government, during the last few years, has unfortunately given rise to many dissensions. Most of the congregation, wishing that the rules in force, from its erection to the present time, should remain intact: whilst on the other hand, the Bishop of Verapoly, is anxious to institute certain reforms, which are not quite approved of by the congregation. The Church is still said to contain, the screen from that of the Franciscans, which the Dutch permitted the Roman Catholics to remove.

The river half a mile in length, which divides Cochin from Vypeen, has been alluded to. The laterite wall, built by the Dutch, along its southern bank, fell down in 1821, owing partly to the inferior materials of which it was constructed, and partly to the setting in of the current in that direction: but in 1843, it again turned against the Vypeen side of the river, and between those two periods, many fruitless efforts were made to preserve its banks, only resulting in the walls being undermined by the sea, whilst wood was rendered useless, by the ravages of the wood boring insects. Again, the set of the river altered to the Cochin side, but owing to the laterite rock alluded to, as existing on the site of the late Dutch Governor's house, the town of Cochin is pretty well protected. Again, in 1857, the sea washed away a breadth of land, of between 90 and 100 feet, leaving Vypeen 2,500 feet wide, but after the termination of the monsoon, the sea receded nearly 200 feet: but the next year, it again encroached, and has continued to do so, every monsoon: but it generally recedes, in the subsequent fine weather. Some years since, probably about 1847, the sea washed up to the benches, situated, on a part of the S. W. corner of the old rampart, but it

* *Official Letter* from the Vicar, to the Magistrate of Cochin.

subsequently retired to its original limits. It is improbable, that any engineering, (unless at an enormous expense) would effectually preserve the banks.* The same difficulty was once found to exist, on the Ponany river, and a reward was even paid by Government, to a fortunate Engineer, who at the commencement of his work, was assisted by the current diverting in its course, he consequently obtained the credit of having saved the bank; but either before the money was paid, or immediately subsequently, the current returned to its old course, and the erection was at once undermined and destroyed.

Near the bank of the river, is the Traveller's bungalow, in which travellers can rest for two days at a time, one formerly existed over the river, but it has been obliged to be pulled down as insecure.

The Dutch kept up an Hotel, situated where the Protestant schools now stand, which was annually put up to auction, when the landlord covenanted to supply travellers at a fixed rate. This was continued under the British, until 1811, when the house had become rather ruinous, and the Hotel-keeper complained, that his expenses were not re-imbursed, or barely so, and it was consequently discontinued.

A number of beggars, flock into the town on Fridays and Saturdays, but more especially on the latter day, and are accustomed to receive weekly alms, from various benevolent inhabitants. It is curious that these are the two days, held by Hindus, as most fortunate for begging, and set apart for such, in many parts of India. The Dutch authorities originated this custom in Cochin, as on those days they permitted beggars to enter the fort, and on no others.

Cochin is pretty well supplied with articles of food, but there is no doubt, that the prices have very much risen of late years: this is considered a mark of the prosperous state of the place, and to a certain extent no doubt is so, but not entirely. The doing away of the price lists, by which those who chose to sell articles at a certain rate, could do so, has been a most serious loss to Europeans, especially to those whose pay has not increased, in proportion to the increased cost of living. There is now *no competition*, but a large amount of *combination*, for the purpose of raising the prices of all articles.

* From the *Official Records* in Cochin Cutcherry 1843.

The drinking water here, has been said to cause the frightful disease, known as elephantiasis, from which persons' legs, become sometimes as much as 21 inches in circumference, or even more. The Portuguese consequently obtained water from Alwaye, and this was believed to decrease the risk of incurring the complaint. The Dutch continued this plan, and supplied all their servants gratuitously, but charged other persons, ¼ of a rupee for a six gallon cask, delivered at their doors. The English also followed the same custom, but gave it gratuitously to almost every one : until the Military were removed, when they discontinued the supply.

Beef is rarely procurable, and even then is not very good. In the time of the Dutch, there was a licensed butcher in Cochin, who paid for being allowed to supply the town with meat at a certain price, he was permitted to kill beef: but there was also a regular beef butcher, and the sum paid by him for his license, was set apart, towards the maintenance of the Lepers in the Lazarretto, at Palliport; and the support of that establishment. The mutton is pretty good, the sheep are brought from Coimbatore, and Palghaut, as this climate does not suit them : goats thrive well : pork is easily procurable, but unless properly fed under European supervision is very unwholesome: whilst poultry is plentiful, and cheap. Fish can be obtained all the year round, of a fair quality, and appear rather superior, during the S. W. monsoon, than at other periods. Oysters abound, as do also prawns, and crabs, it is however advisable, to abstain from them in October, and the two following months, as at that period they are frequently prejudicial to health: bread is excellent, and vegetables are usually abundant.

CHAPTER VI.

CHRISTIANITY IN MALABAR.

Early Christians in Malabar—St. Thomas's arrival—Early Ecclesiastics—State in which Portuguese found the Syrian Church—Xavier—Menezes—Synod of Diamper—Jesuits announce themselves as Western Brahmans, and forge fifth Veda—Carmelites sent to Malabar—Dutch arrive—European Catholic Priests ordered to leave—Dutch try to dispose of congregations to Portuguese—Agree to permit Carmelites to return—English East India Company Officials make first attempt to introduce Missionaries to India—Trial to regenerate Syrian Churches—Virulence of disputes increase—Syrian Architecture—Dress of Clergy—Means of support—Liturgies—Fasts—Feasts—Marriages—Births—Burials—Protestant Missions—Court of Directors, advice to Missionaries.

In Malabar, from almost the commencement of the Christian era, a Church has existed, which to Europeans, has been amongst the wonders of the Eastern world. Those who have followed its ancient creed, have usually been denominated Syrians, because their tenets and principles of Church Government, are very similar to those obtaining amongst the Copts in Syria. The native appellation is, *Nasarane kai*, *Suriani Mopillas*, or *Marggacarer*, "people who have a law." In olden times they were called *Peishcára Brahmans*, owing both to the class from which they sprang, and to their being superior artificers, (Peishcars.)

A knowledge of Christianity, was in very early days, spread into distant quarters of the globe, partly owing to the persecutions directed against its exponents, which forced them to seek refuge in more congenial climes, where they might peaceably follow the practices of their religion, denied them in their native lands. It may also have partly arisen, from the eastern luxuries imported for the use of the Roman Citizens, for some of the merchants engaged in this commerce, may have been instrumental in the diffusion of the Christian faith.

It is not improbable, that in company with some of these Roman merchants, St. Thomas the apostle visited India, and the date generally given, is A. D. 52. It appears that he erected Churches in Aden, and Socotra, and subsequently proceeded to Hindustan: although, whether he landed on the western coast at Maliapore,* or Cranganore near Cochin, or at Maliapore near Madras, is very problematical, and at the same time immaterial. Jerome in the year 420, speaks of the Mission of St. Thomas to India, as a universally acknowledged fact. Whilst in the ninth century, Alfred the Great sent an embassy to his tomb in Hindustan: and Marco Polo writing about 1292, mentions this tomb as then in existence. Baldæus in 1662, gives an account of a stone pillar at Quilon, said to have been erected by St. Thomas; at the present time, a similar pillar stands there, and is stated to have been raised by the same person. It is highly venerated, by the Syrians, and others.

Governor *Moens*, in his memorial, states, that "the prevalent be-" lief is, that St. Thomas after labouring on the Coromandel coast, "went to Cranganore, and converted many: and also at Maliancara, "(near Palliport,) Cottecay, Repelim, Gekkomungalum, Ternetta, "and Tiroewangotta, (probably Travancore), built some Churches, "ordained two priests, and then returned to the Coromandel coast." The tradition amongst the Syrians is, that St. Thomas built seven Churches in Malabar, viz., one at Palloor near Chowghaut, still in existence: another at Cranganore, now destroyed: a third at Cottakareel, or Paroor still standing: as are also those at Cocamungalum or southern Paliapuram: at Quilon: and at Narannm: whilst the seventh at Shazaloo, near the famous Chowri Malla, has been destroyed by wild elephants.

St. Thomas is believed to have made many converts, especially the son of a native of rank at Cranganore, whom he ordained a Deacon. Subsequently he is said to have met with an accidental death at St. Thomas's Mount, (Maliapore, *the city of the peacocks*, now called St. Thomè,) near Madras, where a low caste man shooting peacocks, unfortunately killed the Saint. Marco Polo mentions being shown this spot at the Mount, in the 13th century. Even up to

* At Cruzmilagri, midway between Cochin and Maliapooram, is the spot pointed out by local tradition, as that where St. Thomas landed. But it is quite as probable, that, the Portuguese planted the cross in this place, in token of territorial sovereignty.

the present day, persons annually perform pilgrimages to this place, kiss the spot where he was slain, deposit their offerings, and repeat their prayers at the Apostle's grave. Another legend is, that he lived in a place where there were two caves, into which he retired for prayer and meditation. One day when thus engaged, a Brahman thrust a spear through the orifice which admitted the light, and inflicted a mortal wound, the head of the spear breaking off into the Apostle's body. He just managed to crawl into the inner cave, where he died embracing a stone cross. His Disciples subsequently found his body, and removed it for interment to a Church which he had raised.* Another legend states, that St. Thomas and Thaddeus, parted at Edessa, when the former accompanied a party of merchants first to Socotra, and from thence to Western India, where whilst he was paying his respects to the King of the place, a native struck him without any provocation: but this man subsequently going to draw water from a tank, had his hand bitten off by a tiger. He immediately ran back to the palace, to tell his misfortune, but was followed by a dog, carrying the hand in his mouth. St. Thomas was still in the royal presence, and taking the severed member, replaced it in its proper position, where it remained so firmly fixed, that even the mark of the join was quite imperceptible. The Apostle is stated subsequently to have gone, first to Calicut, then to China, and returning from thence through Thibet into India, to have ended his days at Maliapore near Madras.

It is very probable, that these converts made by St. Thomas, or St. Thomé Christians, as they are commonly called, were joined by others from Syria, who had heard of their existence. In the second

* Portuguese Historians affirm, that in 1547, when this cave was being cleaned out, the old stone cross was discovered, and on it many dark red spots resembling blood. Miracles did not cease here, for in 1551, it is stated, that when the oratory was being repaired, this stone was solemnly set up, and whilst the priest was reading the Gospel, it commenced turning black and shining, then perspired, and resumed its original grey colour, when the spots of blood came out clearer than ever. Ten years later, the hieroglyphics on the cross, were translated by a Brahman, into a short history of the Saint and his Converts, with an account of his death, and the erection of the stone, by certain Kings in commemoration of him. Before the year 1561, its being in a perspiration was considered a good omen, but since that period it has been a bad one.

century, Egyptian mariners carried tidings to Alexandria, of the Christians residing in Malabar, who traced their paternity in Syria to St. Paul, and owned the supremacy of the Patriarch of Babylon. Therefore they must have been here, at least one hundred years prior to the doctrines of Nestorius. It is by no means improbable, that the Jews who came to Malabar, divided themselves into two parties, one of which became Christians, and the other retained their ancient faith.* Nearly every account mentions Cranganore, as being the central place from whence both the Jews and Syrians spread. The Mahomedan author Ferishta, in his general history of India, says, "formerly before the rise of the religion of *Islam*, a company of "*Jews* and *Christians*, came by sea into the country of Malabar, and "settled as merchants. They continued to reside there, until the "rise of the Mussulman religion."

It has been asserted, that Cheramal Permaul, (whose rule ceased A. D. 378,) gave these sects extensive privileges, and a charter engraved on metal plates, in nail or triangular headed characters, in Malayalim, Canarese, Bisnagur, and Tamul. The witnesses were four Jews of rank, whose names are written, in old Hebrew characters. These tablets appear to have been lost in the 16th century, and were not recovered until about fifty years since, when owing to the exertions of Major Macaulay, then British resident of Travancore and Cochin, some plates, reputed to be the same, were found.

Thomas Cana is also said to have written the account of these people, anterior to his time, on copper plates, which were deposited in the Church at Tervalcarre, near Culli-Quilon, but were lost when the Travancore Rajah annexed this State. These privileges are said also to have been written on a stone in the Cranganore Pagoda, and this mistaken belief which is now universal in Malabar, is also mentioned by Governor Moens, nearly 100 years ago, as being then prevalent.

---

* *Paoli* says, "had they been originally Indians, why should they make use "of Chaldaic expressions, and not much rather words peculiar to the Malabar "and Sanscrit languages? it is therefore not improbable, that a considerable "number of Christians, went from Persia and Chaldea to India, and united "themselves to the small body of the original Indian Christians, whose ancestors were formerly converted to the Christian faith, by the Apostle Thomas."

After a time, as the power of these early Christians increased, they were able to throw off the yoke of their heathen rulers, and to raise a Chief of their own sect and creed. This line was continued, until one of their sovereigns being childless, adopted the son of the King of Diamper as his successor: which prince being subordinate to the Rajah of Cochin, the Syrians again fell under the Government of Hindus. It may well be said of them, that as soon as they obtained political power, their influence began to deteriorate.

In the commencement of the fourth century, at the council of Nice, one of the names subscribed is "Johannes," *Metropolitan of Persia, and the Great Indies.* Thirty years subsequently, Athanasius invested one Frumentius, a Syrian by birth, with episcopal authority in South India, where he proceeded with two kinsmen and became a martyr. One of his relations was subsequently made Secretary, and the other, cup bearer, to a Native prince, and on his death, they undertook the education of his son. They afterward, erected a Church, and one of them was installed as Bishop by Athanasius. The ophilus the famous Arian Bishop, visited India about A.D. 350.

Cosmas states, that in 572, Christian churches existed in Malabar and Ceylon, the Bishops being sent from Persia, where they were consecrated: the doctrines at this period, were those of the Nestorians,* for the Primate of Persia, was at that time subject to the Nestorian Patriarch of Seleucia. About 658, the Metropolitan of Mosul, declared that the churches in India and Persia, were in a declining state,† owing to the neglect of the Primate

* The term *Nestorians*, is derived from *Nestorius*, who was consecrated Bishop of Constantinople, A. D. 429. He acknowledged the *duality* of persons in the Saviour of the world, and that a worshipper might unite in his adorations, the persons and the natures, which he separated in his Creed.

† During the seventh century, the Moplahs oppressed the Syrians, so they retired from the Northern portions of Malabar, to the Cochin territory, choosing a head man or king. Subsequently owing to adoption, a Hindu prince ruled over them in temporal matters: when the Portuguese arrived, he was named *Beliarte*, Rajah of Diamper, and was bound to protect them against Hindus or Mahomedans, but being bankrupt, he applied to the Europeans for pecuniary assistance. The Christians were divided into two parts, the *Northern* or Samorin's party, denominated *Panircurra*, which included all

of Persia, stating that as he now refused to acknowledge the authority of Seleucia, the succession of Priest-hood had been cut off from India. Relying upon Apostolic succession direct from St. Thomas, the Primate of Persia, now considered the authority of the Patriarch of Seleucia, unnecessary: thus they continued, until A.D. 780, when the Persian party, again submitted to Seleucia, and Christianity flourished up to the year 920.

About A.D. 696, according to one authority, a Bishop of the Church of the Jacobites* arrived in India, from Alexandria: others again have argued, that this sect never came until A.D. 1663, after the Dutch took Cochin. From this period, most of the prelates of the Malayala Church, have considered themselves as dependent upon the sec of Antioch. Towards the close of the eighth century. Thomas Cana, believed by some to have been a wealthy Armenian merchant, came to Malabar: but whoever he may have been he appears to have obtained great power over the Syrians, who under his protectorate left the jungles, and settled down along the sea coasts. *Moens* says, "Assemanus believes that Mar Thomas was that Bishop, whom the "Nestorian Bishop Timotheus sent out about A.D. 800 to India, "together with some monks, out of the cloisters at *Beth-Abensi* "and that he was by birth a Maronite of Mount Lebanon, who "subsequently became a Bishop. Manuscripts state, that Mar Sa-"por, and Mar Peroses, came from Babylon, A.D. 829, and ob-"tained privileges from Changara Irawisri, Rajah of Culli-Quilon, "to erect Churches in his country."

Princes and tribes in the Northern portion of Malayala: and the *Southern* or Cochin Rajah's division, termed *Ciovarecurra*, which included the Princes and tribes in the South of Malayala. This division has been erroneously considered, to designate the descendants of the legitimate and illegitimate offspring of Thomas Cana, reputed to have possessed two wives, one a *Nairchee*, the other a *Chogan;* the offspring of the former settling in North, those of the latter in South Malabar. A third tradition is, that all the *Syrians* are descended from four distinct families, who at different times, settled in various places on the Malabar Coast.

* The name *Jacobite*, is said to have been derived, from Jacob of Uraha, (commonly known as Edessa, or Callirhoe,) who A. D. 656, was consecrated Bishop of Uraha, the Metropolis of Osrhoene, now called Ourfa, near the Euphrates. He restored the Syriac language to its original purity. His doctrines were that there was but *one will* or operation, in the *two natures* of Christ.

The Princes of Malabar, treated their Native Christian subjects well. They were given equal, or superior rank with the Nairs, and allowed to be governed by those of their own sect, in both temporal and spiritual matters. Their first king, is said to have been a convert from Hinduism. Prosperous times injured this Church, and its prestige began to decline from the tenth century, when they first had a king to rule over them, their royal authority passed into the hands of the heathen prince of Diamper, and the Portuguese found them in reality, governed by the Rajah of Cochin.

"In 1500," says *Governor Moens*, "four Syrian Bishops came to "this coast, named Mar Mardina, Jena Ally, Mar Jacob, and Mar "Thomas. * * In 1504, two Bishops wrote, and informed the "Patriarch, of the arrival of the Portuguese in Malabar: after these, "came, about A.D. 1550, another Bishop named Mar Abraham." Moens also observes, "there must have been Roman Catholics on "this coast, long before the arrival of the Portuguese, for it is well "known, that there was a Romish priest named Fre Jordan at "Tanna, and Salsette, but the date is unrecorded. Also, in A.D. "1320, there were in Persia four Franciscans, named Fre Thomas "de Tolentino, Fre Jacomo de Padua, Fre Demetrino, and Fre Pedro. "Doubtless, Vasca de Gama brought out many Priests, as it is well "known, no Portuguese vessel started for sea, much more so for a "long voyage, without having clergy on board." As early as 1503, Father Rhoterie, is mentioned as settled at Quilon.

When Cabral came to India, in 1500, he took away with him to Portugal, two brothers, who subsequently in Europe, gave an account of their sect in India. The Christians at Cranganore, in 1502, when Vasca de Gama was at Cochin, sent him a deputation, bearing the sceptre of their last monarch, and besought him to intercede with the Portuguese king, to become their ruler, and protector, as it was the custom of the country, that the head of each sect, should rule them in both temporal and spiritual concerns. They complained of being much oppressed by the Native princes, and that those who resided on Pagoda lands, were compelled to be present at the festivals of the Heathen Deities of the place.

On enquiries being instituted respecting this people, it appeared that their bible and prayers were in Syriac, which was to them an unknown tongue; that they practised Hindu rites of purification, attended Hindu feasts, used charms, consulted fortune tellers, and submitted to ordeals. Prayers to the Saints, and those for the dead, were customary, whilst they are said to have had monasteries. Of Rome they had never heard, her liturgies were not employed in their Churches, and transubstantiation was unrecognized.

At the head of the Syrian church was a Metropolitan, the inferior clergy were termed Catanars, who were divided into two grades, the senior corresponding to our presbyters, whilst the inferior were deacons. Besides these, they had their Malpans, or doctors. Clergy were permitted to hold secular offices, also to marry, whilst their wives took precedence in the Church, and were known by wearing round their necks a golden cross. Though governed in temporal cases by the Prince of Diamper, under the control of the Cochin Rajah, they were subject in civil, spiritual, and moral matters, to their Bishop of Angamale, Metropolitan of India. They paid a certain tribute, and had on some specified occasions, to bring a number of troops, armed and properly equipped, into the field.

All these Christians, says, *Paoli*, " in 1502, at which period Vasca " de Gama came a second time to Malabar, were Nestorians. Some " of them denied the Divinity of Christ, and could not endure " images, but on the other hand, they showed a greater reverence for " the holy cross. They had no other sacraments, than baptism, the " last supper, and the consecration of Priests. They believed that " the souls of the just, were not admitted into the presence of God, " before the final judgment, and that until that period, they were to " remain in Eden. They employed a kind of baptism quite different " from ours, (the Roman Catholic): and their Priests all practised " simony, as they dispensed the sacraments, merely for money. " Many of the poor people were not baptized, because they were not " able to pay the fees. The sacrifice of the mass, was established " according to the manner of the Nestorians. The wine which they " consecrated, was palm wine, (arrack): the host consisted of some " wheaten flour, mixed with salt and oil: and it was always let " down from a hole above the altar, when the priest was to bless it. " Mass was read every Sunday, but no person was obliged to attend " it. On Sunday evening, every one might eat flesh, on Wednesdays

" and Fridays they ate fish or herbs: on Shrove Sundays, there was " a general fast. Their holy water, the preparation of which was left " to the Sacristan, consisted of common river water, in which a few " particles of earth, brought from the grave of St. Thomas, at Malia- " poram, were dissolved. Their festival days began the preceding " evening, and ended towards evening the day following. During " that time, the shops were shut, and all labour ceased. Their " Priests were accustomed to employ excommunication, known under " the name of *Maharon*, and which is very severe against offenders."

The Syrians were much esteemed, the greater the number of them, a Native prince had in his dominions, the more he was feared by his neighbours, as they were said to be very faithful and trust-worthy. The men always went about armed, and were well trained in the use of weapons, their education being carried on in this science, from their 8th to their 25th year. They were the natural protectors of the silver-smiths, brass-founders, carpenters, and smiths. They united together when any infringements were made upon their rights, or one of them was subject to insult. A low caste man who struck a Christian, incurred the punishment of immediate death, or if exempted from this, he was obliged to carry a gold or silver hand (according to the rank of the affronted person,) to the Church, and there offer it up as a propitiation. In those days, Christians never touched a Sudra, nor even a Nair. Any of these castes, who refused to acknowledge their precedence, they were empowered to slay forthwith. Only Brahmans and Syrians, (besides Jews) might have covered porches before their doors, and travel on elephants, (a distinction otherwise accorded to the Royal heirs,) whilst they might sit in the King's presence, even on the same carpet, a symbol of an Ambassador.

In the year 1517, some Portuguese landed at Maliapore, near Madras, where they found several Christian Chapels, and a Moor informed them, that he had been miraculously cured of blindness, by visiting this holy place. Here he stated, his ancestors had been accustomed to burn a light in one of the Chapels, traditionally asserted to have been erected by St. Thomas, whose body was believed to lie within together with those of two of his disciples, and a converted Hindu king. An investigation was then commenced, and on digging near the wall, a stone discovered, which the Portuguese translated as follows :—" When St. Thomas built this Church, the " king of Maliapore gave him the duties, on all merchandize im- " ported, which was one-tenth." Going deeper, they reported the discovery of the body, with the spear head within it : also the remains of his disciples, and of the Native king, they observed that the bones of this last differed from those of the former, as *they were not so white !* On enquiry, they ascertained, that when St. Thomas landed, Maliapore now close to the sea, was twelve leagues from the coast, and that the Saint had predicted, " that when the " sea came up to the site of the city, a people should come from the " west, bringing with them, the religion he taught."

Besides these, there were many miraculous legends current, one of which was that a Brahman slew his own son, and charged St. Thomas with the murder, but the Saint raised the body to life, who forthwith acccused his father of having done the foul deed. On another occasion it was asserted, when St. Thomas required a certain piece of timber to be taken to his chapel, the combined strength of numerous men, and elephants, was insufficient to move it: on which he himself laid hold of it with both hands, and easily dragged it to the place of its destination. Russians who visited Syria, in A.D. 371, attested that St. Thomas died a Martyr in India, but that his body was subsequently transmitted to Edessa. This if correct, slightly militates against the Portuguese and Native accounts.

In 1541, the celebrated Francis Xavier came to India, he was most zealous in his efforts to convert the heathen around him, and presented his countrymen with a noble example of self-devotion, and perfect indifference regarding his own temporal welfare, when it interfered with the spiritual advantage of others. His mind appears to have been wholly engrossed by religious subjects, and efforts for benefiting the souls of his fellow-men, and with this view he attacked vice wherever he found it, and denounced the immorality and religious supineness of his countrymen, in indignant terms. He is said to have converted, or perhaps more properly speaking baptized, 700,000 Natives, and certainly it would be difficult to find one, more active, untiring, and zealous, in Missionary labours. He died in 1552.

About this period, the Inquisition which had previously been established in Goa, discovered that the Syrian Christians were heretical in their belief, and many came to an untimely end by its orders, Their Priests even forsook them, to scramble for the many tempting inducements of power, and pecuniary rewards, held out by the Portuguese, to lure them from their posts.

In 1545, Albuquerque, Archbishop of Goa, made proselization a State policy, and compelled his soldiers to marry Native females, who had been converted to Christianity. He sent a Franciscan Friar to Cranganore, to preach the Gospel, and before long erected a College at the same place, in which Syrian youths were instructed in the Latin rites and language. But when thay had become fitted to enter the ministry, the Syrians refused to admit the Romish form of worship, into their Churches. A second College was erected in 1587, for their instruction in their own language, on the Vypeen Island at Palliport, known as Vaipacotta, where the Syrian costume was allowed to be retained, and some of their rites observed. But still the Syrians refused to permit this new clergy to preach in their Churches, in which course they were fully supported by their new Bishop.

It now became evident, that all idea of converting these people to the Romish faith must be given up, or another course pursued, either of force or stratagem ; the former was adopted, and the Syrian Bishop Mar Joseph was made a prisoner, and sent to Portugal, from whence it was intended to forward him to Rome in order to afford him the benefit of instruction in Church mysteries.

But Mar Joseph was as great an adept at stratagem as his captors, and contrived to ingratiate himself so much with the Spanish Queen, that she permitted him to return to Goa, carrying letters patent from her, directing the Portuguese not to interfere with him, in the discharge of his ministerial functions, as he had promised to exert himself to the utmost, to bring his clergy and their congregations, over to the Romish See. But in the intermediate time, the Malabar Christians, or Syrians, finding themselves deprived of a Bishop, had written to the Patriarch at Babylon, to send them one, a request with which he had at once complied, by consecrating and despatching a Bishop named Abraham. But on Mar Joseph's return, dissension of course arose, as to which was head of the Church in Malabar. The greater part of the Syrians sided with Mar Joseph, who laid information with the Portuguese, against Mar Abraham, who was consequently arrested in Travancore, by emissaries of that nation, with the connivance of the Rajah. He was despatched to Europe, but the vessel owing to stress of weather, being obliged to put into Mozambique, he contrived to effect his escape, and reached Babylon in safety, where the Patriarch re-conferred on him, the title of Bishop of Malabar. But he, fearing that the Patriarch's power in Malabar, was less than that of the Portuguese, proceeded to Rome, and appealed to the Pope for assistance, promising to yield him most implicit obedience, and was accordingly confirmed by him in his appointment.

Mar Joseph in the mean time, considering himself firmly re-established in his See, again commenced preaching according to the tenets of his Church, which he had formerly abjured. On the Pope's being informed of this, he issued a bull for his arrest, in 1567, he was therefore captured and sent to Rome, where he probably died.

Governor Moens states, that " after the arrival of the Portuguese, " the Rajah of Cochin issued a strict order, against the Roman " Catholic religion being received : but A.D. 1560, this was cancell- " ed, and his subjects were permitted to embrace any faith they " liked best."

After Mar Joseph had been sent to Rome, Mar Abraham returned, but on the examination of his briefs, it appeared that he had prevaricated to the Pope, and he was therefore detained in custody, whilst inquiries were instituted. But not liking his position at Goa, he contrived to escape whilst the Friars were engaged in prayer, and reached his flock in safety, where he was joyfully received. But the Portuguese were determined to re-capture him, and issued orders to that effect.

Pope Gregory XIII on receiving a report of these proceedings, ordered a council to assemble at Goa, and directed Mar Abraham to attend it, sending him at the same time, letters of safe conduct. He obeyed, and satisfied the council, by again abjuring his faith, and swearing allegiance to the Pope. After which, he was allowed to return to his people.

But as soon as he reached Malabar in safety, he broke all his oaths, and taught the Syrian faith as formerly: writing a letter to say, that he had only abjured it through fear of the Portuguese, "who were over his head, as an hammer is over an anvil." His constant troubles appear to have affected his health, as he applied to the Patriarch of Babylon, for some one to assist him in his labours during his life time, and on his decease to succeed him in his office. His request was granted, and Mar Simeon arrived in Malabar. At first he was held in greater respect than Mar Abraham, whose repeated abjurations of his creed, had shaken the confidence of his flock, who could no longer be certain how long his religious tenets would continue unchanged.

But after some time, affairs went on less smoothly, Mar Simeon was impatient for the reins of power, and Mar Abraham tenacious of what he considered his rights, and at last the strife waxed so warm, that the two Bishops commenced fulminating excommunications against one another.

Mar Abraham now thought that the Latin Church might possibly assist him, so he denounced Mar Simeon to the Portuguese, as an enemy to their creed, and an intruder into Malabar. Upon which Mar Simeon was informed, that if he wished to succeed Mar Abraham, it was necessary for him to proceed to Rome, to have his title ratified by the Pope. He accordingly placed his Vicar Jacob in charge during his absence, and went to Goa, from whence he took ship to Portugal, and was never again heard of, but is believed to have expired under the cruelties of the Holy office, which was alike ignorant, either of toleration or indulgence, where heretics were concerned.

In 1590, the Archbishop of Goa, Don Matthias, summoned Mar Abraham to another council, but by this time he had no further need of the Portuguese, having got rid of Mar Simeon, he therefore refused compliance, and declared his adhesion to the rites of the Syrian Church. Five years subsequently, Pope Clement VIII despatched a brief to Don Alexis de Menezes, Archbishop of Goa, ordering him to enquire into the faith of the Malabar Bishop, and his flock. In the event of finding him disseminating heretical doctrines, he was directed to supersede him, and place a Vicar Apostolic of the Roman Catholic communion, over his Bishopric, and thus bring these congregations under the dominion of the Papal See.

Menezes found Mar Abraham guilty of everything laid to his charge, and it was discovered, anticipating that he would be deprived of his Bishopric, he had sent privately to Babylon for a successor. Orders were then despatched to the Commandants of every port, to arrest any Chaldean, Persian, or Armenian ecclesiastic, who had no pass from Menezes himself, or any person who might be suspected of being such, although under the disguise of mariners, mendicants, or any other class. At Ormuz the new Bishop was arrested, and subsequently several other ecclesiastics at various ports, disguised as mariners.

Menezes now determined on bringing the Malabar Church, under the control of the Roman Pontiff. A letter was then despatched to the Vicar Jacob, whom Mar Simeon had left in charge, inviting him to join the Roman Catholic faith, and holding out inducements of rich rewards and high honours, in case of his acceptance. But whilst negotiations were being carried on, Jacob died, and on this letters were sent to Mar Abraham and his Archdeacon, advising them to lose no time, in eradicating the errors of their Churches, and bringing them under the authority of the Pope. But they declined making any alteration, in the rites of their faith. In 1597, this versatile Bishop, Mar Abraham, died: on which Menezes nominated a Jesuit, Francisco, as Vicar Apostolic of the diocese. But subsequently it was judged advisable, to appoint George, then the Syrian Archdeacon, and the President of the Syrian College of Vaipacotta, as coadjutor, with Francisco as Bishop. But the Arch deacon refused to act with his two colleagues, and was therefore made the Governor of the Church, and strongly urged to sign the confession of faith, on which he demanded four months for deliberation. At the end of this time, however, he positively refused to accede, and assembled a synod of Syrians, and in their presence, swore always to defend and uphold their ancient faith: whilst they on their part, took an oath to protect him, from the power of the Portuguese. Conjointly they then issued a manifesto, declaring that in future no Catholic priest, should be allowed to enter within the precincts of any of the Malabar Churches, and that these congregations would acknowledge no Bishop, who had not been consecrated at Babylon.

Menezes now determined personally to inspect the Churches of Cochin, but was compelled to defer his visit until the following spring, as the petty Rajah of Paroor, was at that time at war with a neighbour. But he wrote to the Archdeacon to inform him of his intentions, the announcement of which was received with great alarm, as the Syrians were well aware, that if force were employed, they must succumb, especially as the Rajah of Cochin would assist the Portuguese. The Archdeacon consequently wrote a most submissive letter, promising to sign the confession of faith, provided it was brought to him by a Priest, who was not a Jesuit. A Franciscan Friar, accordingly was the bearer of it. The Archdeacon however on seeing it, refused to append his signature, and merely wrote to say, that he was a Catholic, and would believe whatever tenets were held by that Church. But as Menezes declined accepting such an evasive answer, the Archdeacon eventually signed the confession.

On December 27th, 1598, Menezes accompanied by some troops, embarked at Goa. On his arrival at Cochin, the Governor, and principal inhabitants, gave him a most brilliant reception. He then announced his intention of bringing over the St. Thomé Christians to the Catholic faith, and made enquiries of the Rajah of Cochin, as to whether he might depend upon his assistance. The Rajah was averse to the employment of force, but feared to run counter to the Portuguese, and therefore acceded to their wishes: Menezes agreeing to pay the sum of 30,000 ducats in gold, for the use of 50,000 Nairs, should their assistance become necessary.

The Archdeacon was ordered to repair to Cochin, and letters of safe conduct were sent him for that purpose. He assembled his Catanars,* or native clergy, and the principal persons composing his congregations, and consulted with them upon the best course to pursue: and it was finally decided, that the Archdeacon should attend Menezes' summons, accompanied by 3,000 well armed men, to protect

* Literally *Nair Priests*, or aristocratic clergy: the first syllable being of Syriac origin, the second a corruption of *Nair*, a Malabar name for a superior class of Sudras.

him against treachery. That he should temporize, and give way to Menezes in small matters, evading the most important, in hopes that the Portuguese Priest, would soon return to Goa, and that their long expected Bishop, would shortly arrive, to take the responsibility upon himself. But the latter was in prison at Ormuz, of which Menezes was aware, although they were not so.

The party accordingly set out, the armed men being commanded by two Malabar Chiefs. On his arrival at Cochin, the Archdeacon was conducted to the presence of Menezes, by the Governor. After a long discussion, a truce was agreed upon, and it was decided, that they should conjointly visit the Malabar Churches, and meet for that purpose on the following day, at the Syrian College of Vypeen. On arriving there as appointed, Menezes found that the Archdeacon had not come, so without waiting for him, he proceeded to the Church, dressed in full canonicals, and delivered an elaborate sermon, on "John x. 1, "he that entereth not in at the door," &c., representing that the true door of the sheepfold, was not through Babylon, but Rome. He informed them of the existence of purgatory,* denounced the Patriarchs of Babylon, as merely thieves and robbers, and concluded by declaring his intention, of holding a confirmation in that Church on the following day, and directed the whole congregation to attend, that they might be admitted into the true faith. Subsequently when present during the Syrian service, he found that the Patriarch was still alluded to in it, notwithstanding his exhortation to the contrary : so, determined to get rid of this objectionable person, he formally excommunicated him, and made the Archdeacon and the Catanars sign a paper to the same effect, which was affixed to the Church door.

The people now became greatly enraged, and could scarcely be restrained from avenging themselves on the Portuguese, but the Archdeacon and Catanars exerted themselves to the utmost, to keep them quiet, and enforce patience, urging that then they could

* At this period, the Romish Church acknowledged the seven sacraments, of baptism, confirmation, the eucharist, penitence, extreme unction, holy orders, and matrimony; the Syrians are said to have had only three, viz., baptism, the eucharist, and holy orders, and to have repudiated the idea of purgatory.

do nothing but dissemble, as the only way of preserving their faith from utter extermination, and that though they might pretend to be Roman Catholics, they were all willing to die martyrs for the Syrian faith, when the proper time to do so had arrived, which they thought was not just then.

The Portuguese governor now became alarmed for Menezes, and wrote to warn him of the exasperated state of feeling amongst the Syrians, recommending him to use a little more precaution, and proceed more gradually, and also suggesting that he was perhaps a little too despotic, and rash in his proceedings. But Menezes in reply assured him, that he was acting according to what he believed to be right, that therefore he felt no fear, and no compunction, for what he had done: and that he fully intended, visiting the whole of the Syrian Churches.

The Syriac Bishop generally resided at Paroor, and at that place the Syrians were more incensed against Menezes than at any other, and imbued with an intense hatred of the Roman Catholic creed. This they even carried to such an extent, that when two of the Rajah's relatives had visited Rome, they were not re-admitted into this State, as it was feared, they might have imbibed some of the tenets of the Latin Church. To this place, Menezes accordingly proceeded. On his arrival, he was met by only a few people, and on going to the Church, found it full of armed men, who appeared inclined to dispute his entrance. He therefore ordered his guard to return to the boats, fearing they might act hastily : and unattended, entered the Church in his canonicals. After blessing the congregation, he delivered a sermon to prove, that the only true faith was that of the Roman Catholic Church, and exhorted all to embrace its tenets.

He proposed confirming them all on the following day, but this they positively declined, not having been taught by their own Priests, that such was necessary. They advised him to return to Cochin at once, whilst he was in safety, and informed him, that even if their brethren at Vypeen, had allowed him to touch their heads, and those of their wives, they would not submit to such a disgrace. Menezes was quite undaunted by this, and proceeded to point out the advantages of confirmation, but finding that they only became more excited, and that he was doing harm rather than good, he rose and exclaimed, "I preach the doctrines of Christ and of St. "Thomas, believed in by all Christians, and in defence of which I "fear not to die." He challenged the Archdeacon (who was then present,) or any of those who were so bold at their midnight conventicles, to meet him in the broad light of day, and argue on their faith; when if possible, they would have an opportunity of refuting him in his reasoning, on the superiority of the Roman Catholic religion.

The Archdeacon left the Church, and presently returning with a few boys, insultingly told Menezes, to confirm these lads, as no one with more sense, would submit to such a rite.

Menezes, finding that he could effect nothing at Paroor, proceeded on his tour, to visit the other Syrian Churches, undeterred by the dangers, threats, and machinations, which surrounded him. At every step armed men followed him, determined to compass his death, but he contrived to evade them. The Archdeacon pursued the same route as himself, and entering the various towns first, effectually prevented the Archbishop from obtaining either a congregation, or a hearing. At length Menezes wrote to the Archdeacon again, inviting him and his Catanars to a conference, promising to meet them, and argue as friends, forgetting and forgiving all that was past. They answered his summons, accompanied by an armed force, to be employed either for their own protection, or the destruction of Menezes, according to circumstances. The Archdeacon first demanded, if he had not denounced their Patriarch as a heretic. Menezes replied "Before I answer you, tell me do you believe in "St. John's Gospel?" The Syrians exclaimed that they would rather die than deny its truth. "Then" said Menezes, "you will "find it there stated, that the word was made flesh and dwelt "amongst us: whilst all Nestorians, of whom the Patriarch of Baby-"lon is one, say, the word did not make itself flesh, but dwelt in "Christ as in a Temple." The Syrians could not reply to this, but insisted that Menezes should not attempt to confirm any more members of their faith, but in future conduct himself as a stranger, and not again interfere. He agreed to convene a Synod on a future day, at which he would meet them, and is said to have promised, that he would not in the intermediate time confirm any more Syrians: but this is probably an invention of the Archdeacon, as he continued confirming all who would submit to that rite.

The Archdeacon then sent letters to the heads of all his congregations, informing them, that Menezes' object was "to reduce the "Churches of Malabar to the See of Rome, and consequently the "Christians of St. Thomas, to the authority of the King of Portu-"gal." Menezes appointed a Synod to be held at Diamper, at which place the Syrian rulers had formerly resided. He repaired thither, sending to inform the Archdeacon that he intended holding a public ordination, and suggesting that his presence would be acceptable to him: but he refused to attend, and requested Menezes not to ordain any Syrian youths, unless they had been brought up in the College of Vypeen. But the Archbishop replied, that his duty to the Pope his master must be performed, and that he should ordain any whom he considered fit for the Ministry, without any reference, as to the College, or Seminary, in which they had been educated.

The Archdeacon then issued an order, forbidding any one under pain of excommunication, to be ordained by Menezes, who had no authority over the Malabar Churches, from which he called on all Catanars who had any regard for their faith, rigidly to exclude him. But before this edict was received, many had applied to be confirmed, and thirty-seven were ordained, subscribing to the Roman Catholic confession of faith, and swearing obedience to the Holy See.

Menezes then continued his tour, being received at different places in various manners, but on the whole the majority of the Syrians, do not appear to have met him in a hostile spirit. High mass was performed at Cartiarte, on Palm Sunday. He abolished the custom from which the Priests had hitherto derived their revenues, viz., the annual offerings presented at this season, and also attempted to introduce auricular confession. The Queen of this country, ordered him on pain of death to quit her dominions; but Menezes replied, "I have my work to perform, and until it is comple-"ted, I shall not leave. Compass my death if you deem such a course "good, but I feel assured, that God will avenge himself on my mur-"derers in the next world, even if the armies of Portugal are unable "to do so in the present, but remember that you have already felt "the power of the latter, should you act as you propose, you may "possibly feel it still heavier."

That night he held a Meeting of Catanars, and informed them, that he was quite tired of these constant disputes with the Archdeacon, and intimated his intention, of giving the appointment then held by him, to a man named Thomas Curian who was present. The Catanars pleaded that the Archdeacon was very young and inexperienced, and asked twenty days' grace for him to decide upon his future conduct, before he was thus superseded.

On Easter eve, the Syrians celebrated their *love feast*, and sent Menezes a double portion, which was graciously received. He appears to have been always ready, either to visit and console the sick, or to give money to assist the poor, he was therefore held in great esteem amongst the Syrians, for his kindness and charity, as well as for his piety and humanity. When he found the doors of Churches closed against him, he never employed force, but sending for the head officials, he quietly reasoned with them, and usually prevailed upon them to allow him to enter. The Rajah of Cochin sent orders to all Syrians in his dominions, to acknowledge and obey Menezes as the head of their religion, under pain of his heaviest displeasure.

The Archdeacon seeing that the Syrians were rapidly seceding from their ancient faith, and embracing that of Rome, sent a threatening letter to Menezes, informing him that if he did not cease his attempts at conversion, those who still remained loyal to their religion, would join together and murder him. To this the Archbishop immediately responded, by excommunicating the Archdeacon, as an enemy to the Pope, and one striving to stir up the Native princes to rebel against his authority. He also wrote him a letter, citing him to appear before the tribunal of God, to give an account of the souls that through his obstinacy, were then burning in hell, and answer for the crime of keeping them back from the Church of Rome, beyond the pale of which there was no salvation. On the receipt of this, the Archdeacon fainted with terror, and on his recovery, declared that he plainly saw, that now he must either submit or be destroyed: on consideration, he decided on the former course, and wrote to Menezes to that effect.

Menezes then drew up a deed of ten articles, which the Archdeacon signed, promising to abjure the Nestorian heresy, confessing that there was only one Christian law, agreeing to acknowledge the confession of Pius IV, to deliver up all the books in the diocese either to be amended or burnt, as might be deemed advisable, to acknowledge the Pope, and curse the Patriarch of Babylon. He also promised to receive no Bishop unless sent by the Pope, to obey Menezes as his prelate, to issue letters for a Synod to assemble at Diamper at which he himself was to attend, and after it to accompany Menezes in visiting the various Churches. This paper was signed by the Archdeacon at Vypeen.

On June 20th, 1599, the Synod of Diamper assembled at that place. Menezes was attended by the Governor of Cochin, the civil and military authorities of the garrison, and a strong force of armed men : he was met on his arrival by a number of Romish and Syrian Priests, altogether there were 153 Catanars present, eight of the most respectable of whom, with the Archdeacon, and four laymen, were nominated as a committee: to them Menezes submitted a decree, which he had composed for their consideration, and approval; and it met their unanimous assent. After High Mass, at which the choir from Cochin attended, the sessions began, and the various decrees were passed with scarcely any opposition, one of which was that Christians should refrain from touching persons of inferior caste, when in the company of high caste heathens,* but forbade all such scruples, when only Christians were present.

However there was one thing which they unanimously agreed in declining to give up, and that was the ancient custom of praying in the

---

* The four Roman Catholic castes, are at the present time, divided in the following manner. The first, the *Arawutnarleecar*, (or the community of sixty-four,) is said to have consisted originally of converted Brahmans and Nairs. The second, the *Moonootecar*, (or three hundred,) are the Latins, or Topasses, so named from wearing hats, and believed to have mostly sprung from domestic slaves. The third, the *Unutecar*, (the five hundred,) are considered to have originally sprung from Mucuas, or converted fishermen, and other low-caste people, they generally call themselves Moplahs. The fourth, the *Erunoortecar* (seven hundred,) are the descendants of the soil slaves. The Catanars or Priests are generally taken from the second, or fourth of these communities or castes.

Syriac tongue, declaring that they would rather sacrifice their lives, than pray in Latin. Considering that they were equally ignorant of both these languages, religion could scarcely be considered as being much benefited by the refusal. Menezes seeing that on this point they would not yield, conceded the question, as they had allowed all errors to be expunged from their liturgy; and so the Romo Syriac Priests continued to pray in the Syriac language, although very few amongst them, comprehended it in the smallest degree.

All married Priests who refused to leave their wives, were excommunicated, and the Romish sacraments established. Menezes then in order to place the Syrians more under the power of the Portuguese, advised the removal of their See from Angamale to the fortress of Cranganore; this was carried into effect in 1605. He visited the Syrian Churches throughout the country, and wherever he could find any Syriac books which he considered heretical, he committed them indiscriminately to the flames, and once at least whilst these sacred records were consuming, he headed a procession, which marched round the burning pile, chanting hymns in the praise of that God whom they believed themselves to be serving. For this wanton destruction, his name has been held in execration, but scarcely deservedly so, as there is no doubt that he was acting purely from motives of religious zeal, and his duty on such a point would be, not to regard the loss of valuable literature, when he considered it was more than imperilling the souls of numbers, perhaps dooming them, to eternal misery. Although such zeal might have been mistaken, surely it was commendable in a religious point of view.

At this time the news of the King's death arrived, and Menezes prepared to return to Goa, to celebrate high mass.* He accordingly

* About this time the Roman Catholics of Calicut, were thrown into a state of great excitement, by a play which was acted by the Syrians. The principal characters represented St. Thomas, and St. Peter, with St. Syriac as umpire. St. Thomas commenced by detailing an account of St. Peter and himself, showing how they were both disciples of our Lord, and that now his territories were infringed upon: that he claimed the East, the West was St. Peter's, and there he ought to remain. St. Peter replied, that he claimed all the world. The umpire St. Syriac decided in favour of St. Thomas, because the Christians of India, depended not upon St. Peter, but on the Patriarch of Babylon, whilst the Portuguese prelate he denounced as a faithless heretic, and decided that the decrees extorted by force at Diamper, were manifestly null and void.

assembled the Syrians, and informed them, that as they had now no Bishop, they ought to apply to the Pope to send them one, and inquired if there was anybody they particularly wished to be appointed to the vacant post. They replied that they would prefer *himself*, to any one else. A remarkable answer, considering the way in which *he is said* to have persecuted them. Menezes then promised them that if he could obtain the Pope's sanction to such a course, he would resign his Bishoprick, and live amongst them at Angamale: and to prove his sincerity, he transmitted his request to be appointed Bishop of the Syrian Church, resigning his See at Goa. But the Pope refused to permit this, and appointed Francisco Rotz a Jesuit, who was principal of the Syrian College, Archbishop of Cranganore. He was the first Latin prelate, who ruled over Malabar, and from that period the Syrians were under the See of Goa, many of the ancient names of their Churches were even changed.

Menezes returned to Goa on November 16th, 1599, where he found that he had been nominated Governor, the people received him most joyfully, and had prepared a triumphal arch in honour of his great victory over the Syrians: but he declined any public recognition of his services, remarking, "glory is due to God alone."

Governor Moens states, that in "A.D. 1600, this coast was placed "by Pope Clement VIII, under the Jesuit Father Franciscus Rotz, "a Spaniard by birth, as Bishop of Angamale, and in 1609 (1605?) "this title was changed for Archbishop of Cranganore, by order of "Paulus V, and in 1617, the aforesaid Bishop Rotz died. In 1609, "he proceeded to Verapoly, to settle some disputes between Bishop "DeSales, and the Priests: and he resigned his office as administra- "tor, to Vanischt, according to a subsequent order received from "the Pope. This Bishop had under him, four Latin Churches, "which were purely Romanists, viz., at Chattiatte, Verapoly, a cha- "pel at Muttencherry, and Perimani (on the Island of Vendoorty): "also 47 Syrian Churches, four of which for a time were under the "Archbishop of Pootencherra, or Cranganore, and two under the "Schismatics. Besides these there were many other Latin Churches "here."

In the year 1606, a Jesuit Mission was established at Madura under De Nobili, and then another phase of *Christian worship* was inaugurated, and one which has left an indelible mark of disgrace upon that order, in which "the end sanctifies the means." They infused Hinduism into the doctrines of Rome, and amalgamated the two, calling themselves *western Brahmans,* of a higher order than any in the east. They dressed and ate according to Brahmanical practices, conformed in every thing to their doctrines, and not content with this, actually *forged a fifth Veda,* as supplementary to the four existing amongst the Hindus. Idolatrous Hindu rites were amalgamated with Romish ceremonies, and before long their followers, (for they can scarcely be called converts,) numbered some thousands, surely it might have been affirmed with truth, that the Christians had become Hindus, not the Hindus Christians!

"In 1617, a Jesuit father, Heronimus Xavierre, a Spaniard, was "made Archbishop of Cranganore, but died the same year at Goa: "he was succeeded by a Jesuit father, Stephanus de Britto, (a Por-"tuguese,) in 1618, who died A.D. 1634, and in 1636, his post was "filled by father Jesuit Franciscus Garzia Mendez, who died at "Cochin A.D. 1659. From that period, the Churches were ruled by "the Vicar Apostolic, as Archbishop of Cranganore," *(Moens.)*

In the year 1619, a conclave of Roman Catholic clergy was held at Goa, when the question of the treatment of Brahmans who had embraced Christianity was raised, as they had refused to give up wearing the sacred thread. It was decided, that this Hindu mark of the twice born classes, was no badge of heathenism, but merely a mark of nobility, therefore there was no necessity for resigning it, when those entitled to wear it, became Christians. As the Jesuits had at this time even high, and low caste Churches, this decision might have been anticipated.

There were Jesuit Bishops of Cranganore, and one was present in that fortress, in 1662, when it fell into the hands of the Dutch. But the yoke of the Jesuits, had for some years become intolerable to the Malabar Christians, and they had determined on having a Bishop of their own, they therefore appointed their Archdeacon to hold that office, and wrote to the Copts of Egypt, the Patriarch of Babylon, and the Jacobites of Syria, requesting that a Bishop might be sent them.

In 1653-54, a person named Attila, or Mar Ignatius, who appears to have been a Nestorian, arrived as Bishop from Babylon. He was hated at Damascus, and his office taken from him for bad conduct, on which he fled to Alexandria, and the Prelate of that place, proposed that he should proceed to India. But the Portuguese arrested him near Cranganore, and showed a letter from the Patriarch, approving of the choice made by the Syrians, of Thomas as their Bishop, but under the most solemn injunctions, that he was neither to consecrate the oil, nor confer orders, and directing that four of the principal ecclesiastics should be associated with him, in the management of the Churches and their congregations. Thomas and his four co-adjutors took a solemn oath, to obey every direction contained in the letter. A meeting then took place at Diamper, to consider the best course to pursue with respect to this new Bishop, the majority were of opinion that it would be best to submit to the Jesuit prelate, it was finally determined to invite him to come amongst them, intending to make him prisoner, and hold him as a hostage for Mar Attila. But he was far too wary to trust himself in their hands, knowing that no faith could be put in their promises.

Mar Attila was carried a prisoner to the town of Cochin, by the Portuguese, on which twenty-five thousand armed Syrians, with the Archdeacon at their head, marched to within a mile of this place, from whence they sent messengers, demanding that Attila should be given up to them: but this was refused. A few days subsequently, Mar Thomas was consecrated to the office of Bishop, twelve Catanars officiating at the ceremony: from this time all confidence between the Syrians and the Portuguese was at an end. Whilst the Syrians were before Cochin, Attila in the dead of the night was conveyed on board a Galliot, which immediately sailed for Goa, where the Carmelite *Paoli*, says, he perished in the flames of the Inquisition.*

There is a tradition still in existence, that this Mar Attila was drowned in the Cochin river, by the Portuguese, when the Syrians came to attack the town. But as he is stated on excellent authority to have been burnt at Goa, it seems scarcely probable that he died in two different ways, at two different places, unless he had more lives than usually falls to the lot of mortals. Perhaps when embarking, he fell, or jumped into the river, from whence he was dragged out, and despatched to Goa, where "flammis datus interiit." The Syrians had a

Alexander VII hearing of this defection, and considering that it was to a great extent owing to the conduct of the Jesuits, and to their having displaced the native Catanars, to make room for creatures of their own : decided on sending some barefooted Carmelites, to supersede the Jesuits in Malabar, they arrived at Surat, in 1656. But the Jesuits who believed themselves the lawful Ecclesiastical masters of India, refused to admit them into their Churches.

They however reached Cannanore about 1567, and were warned, that they might expect great opposition from the Portuguese, and the Syrian Archdeacon, who shortly after issued orders, rigidly excluding them from admission into the Churches under his authority. But the Carmelites soon contrived to become friendly with the Syrian people, especially those in the South, although from the Jesuits they still encountered great opposition.

A meeting of the Malabar Christians was decided to be held at Repelim, on the fourth Sunday after Easter, in 1657, and the Carmelites were invited to join. The Syrians evidently cared very little who ruled over them, provided that the Jesuits did not. The Carmelites proposed, that Mar Thomas should be arrested, and sent to Goa, but the Archdeacon did not approve of this mode of procedure, as he was aware, that a very common maxim at Goa was, that "faith need not be kept with heretics." However nothing was finally decided on. Shortly after this, a second meeting was held, in which the Carmelites endeavoured to make some amicable arrangements, which might bring the Malabar Churches once again under the sway of Rome. But their proposals to that effect were decidedly negatived, as however informal the Archdeacon's consecration might have been, the Syrians wished to retain him in his office. Subsequently finding that Mar Thomas himself admitted the irregularity of his ordination, his congregations became doubtful, as to whether he really were a Bishop, and many in consequence of

carving, representing his martyrdom by drowning, which formed part of a shrine in the Church at Mavillicurray. They appear to have prayed before it, and treated it with superstitious reverence. But as Attila was not drowned, he can hardly be reckoned a martyr on that score, and as he had never been in India previously, the Syrians could not have had a very accurate idea of his religious attainments, or administrative capacity.

these scruples, returned under the authority of Rome, and even Catanars and whole congregations seceded in a body.

The Portuguese at Cochin now perceiving that Mar Thomas could "only be conquered by force," applied to the Hindu Rajah of Mangatty for assistance, which greatly alarmed Mar Thomas, and induced him to make a feint of submission, by writing to the Carmelites, addressing them as the Apostolic Commissioners, a title which he had previously refused to acknowledge. He also offered to obey them in everything, and to admit their authority.

A Council followed, at which deputations from twenty-four Churches met the Carmelites, and decreed that as Mar Thomas' ordination had been informal, it was consequently null and void. But Mar Thomas obstinately refused to accede to this decree, or to ratify any treaty of re-union with Rome. At a meeting subsequently held, at the Church of St. Thomas, near Cochin, it was decided, that Joseph de Santa Maria, should be nominated as Bishop of the See of Malabar, an election which was afterwards confirmed by the Pope, who on December 15th, 1659, consecrated him Bishop of Verapoly. He arrived in India, in April 1661.

The Carmelites now proceeded to Mangatty, to meet the deputation of the Churches, Mar Thomas also went there, where he openly insulted the Carmelites, and refused them seats before the assembled people. It was finally agreed, that until the arrival of the Pope's decision, one of the Carmelites should act as Pastor.

When the new Bishop, Joseph of Santa Maria arrived, he found that the Jesuit Bishop of Cranganore, Garzia, was dead, and had nominated as his successor, a Vicar General, who refused to acknowledge the new Carmelite Bishop. The assistance of the Inquisition was called in, and by its aid, his opposition reduced to submission. Mar Thomas had been very active in his exertions against the new Bishop, he wrote to the heads of the various Churches, informing them all, that Joseph's briefs were forgeries, as he had never really visited Rome, but was merely a Jesuit in disguise. Notwithstanding all opposition, fifty-two Churches recognized the new Bishop, and on the Native Princes' seizing on the revenues of some of the most refractory, the remainder followed their example.

A conference between Mar Thomas and the new Bishop was held, at the Court of the Ranee of Cochin, in the presence of her chief Officers, and numerous Brahmans, which concluded by all the Churches, acknowledging the authority of Rome. Mar Thomas having previously excommunicated all who had joined the Bishop's party, or should afterwards do so, now found himself left without friends, and meditated flight: but was frustrated by the inhabitants of Candenaad, who had been made responsible for producing him, whenever he was required, under penalty of an enormous fine. He appears to have been in communication with the Dutch, and in a great measure, to have depended on their taking Cochin.

When the Dutch possessed themselves of Cranganore, (where the Jesuit Archbishops resided,) it was the seat of learning, science, and religion, in Malabar. Here was a noble Jesuit College, containing a splendid library, whilst within the fortress walls, a magnificent Cathedral reared its stately head, and around it were the gorgeous and costly tombs of the Archbishops and Bishops, who had formerly held sway over this famous citadel. Beyond the walls at Palliport, was the College of the Christians of St. Thomas, for the instruction of youths of that persuasion, in the Syriac tongue.* This last building was subsequently converted into a Leper Hospital, and the masters and pupils removed to Changanacherry, which from that period they termed Vaipacottah.† The Carmelites subsequently, erected a seminary at Verapoly. Of the buildings within the fortress of Cranganore, no record now remains, as they were totally destroyed.

After the capture of Cochin by the Dutch, in 1663, all European Ro-

---

* History is silent respecting what became of the numerous Syriac books, the Dutch must have obtained at Cranganore; they do not ever appear to have been given to the world, and a long personal search, has proved their non-existence amongst the Dutch records of Cochin.

† It seems that after the advent of the Dutch, many institutions such as the above, on being removed to more secure territory in the Native States, took the names of their original stations with them. Consequently it does not always follow, that Roman Catholic stations which bear certain names at the present day, are the same places, which formerly in the time of the Portuguese bore those designations.

man Catholic Ecclesiastics, were ordered to leave the coast. The Carmelite Bishop, finding that he had only ten days allowed him before his departure, consecrated Alexander de Campo, as his Vicar Apostolic, and Bishop in heretical places. After which he excommunicated Mar Thomas, and proceeded to the town of Cochin, to answer a summons from the Dutch, which directed him, to attend on them at that place. He there made many ineffectual efforts to obtain the countenance of the new governing powers, and to induce them to sanction his remaining in Malabar, but contrived to instil them with aversion towards Mar Thomas and his party, as well as to prejudice them in favour of De Campo. He was naturally anxious for the welfare of a Church, for which he had done so much, and was at the same time irritated against Mar Thomas, who was evidently a bad man, who cared only for his own aggrandisement, and was indifferent as to the means employed to obtain it, provided he could keep himself secure, from the strong arm of the temporal powers.

When the Dutch were established in Cochin, the position of the various Christian sects, appears to have been as follows. The Syrians had at last partially thrown off that allegiance to Rome, which had been obtained from them, through conviction, bribery, fraud, or violence. The Jesuits had removed their ancient Bishopric of Angamale, into the Cranganore fort, where the head of their sect was Archbishop : but their violence had rendered them abhorred, and their frauds had caused them to be detested : they were now proscribed, but obtained an asylum in the Cochin State.

The barefooted Carmelites, had been sent by the Propaganda, to attempt to stem the rising storm : to alter the hatred against Priests, to affection for them : and by kindness, and conciliation to the wants of all, to endeavour to refasten the links of that Romish chain, that the violence of the Jesuits, had snapped asunder. The Carmelites were commencing to be favorably received, when the Dutch arrived; at this period a Carmelite Bishop partly ruled the Malabar Church, whilst the Syrian Bishop was a Negro unfavourably viewed by all, and in fact, a fugitive from his own Churches, his party were known as the *New Christians*, and lived mostly in the more hilly portions of the country. The Romish Church was divided into two, the Portuguese, and the Italian

Carmelites, who although hostile to one another, both compelled their communicants, to follow the liturgies of Rome, and obey her doctrines without reserve. There was likewise a subdivision of them, or the Romo Syrians, who differed in some minor points from the Roman Catholics, being permitted to employ the Syriac language in their Churches, and continue some of the Syriac rites, and their Priests were dressed in white, instead of always in black.

When the Dutch ordered all Romish Ecclesiastics to quit the country, they intended without doubt, when a more favourable season came round, to purge the Roman Catholic and Romo Syrian Churches,* of the errors of Rome, and the Priests of Portugal, as well as to bring them all into the bosom of the Lutheran Church. But that time never arrived, an hundred years passed away, and the new rulers still neglected them, and when a little more than another quarter of a century had elapsed, the Dutch sway had ceased, the Lutheran faith had passed by.

Next in succession over these Churches have been the British, who for about fifteen years took no notice of these ancient people; then suddenly it was discovered, that their doctrines though few in number, were pure, and essentially agreed with those of the Church of England. Missionaries were despatched to them, a College was erected, the Ranee endowed it, Churches were reared, when a misunderstanding occurred, the Syrians refused to continue acting conjointly with the Europeans, and it was then discovered, that they were idolatrous, and imbued to the core with the errors of Rome, and further connection was dissolved. It is a divided Church, containing much evil and good intermixed, but consisting of a people, no impartial person can view without interest, as well as being persuaded, of their immeasurable superiority over the surrounding Hindus. They appear to feel their importance, and to be proud of their ancient independence.

It has already been mentioned, (Chapter IV,) how the Dutch at first procured Converts, but how rapidly temporal retribution followed. The native (Roman Catholic) Christians, applied to the

* The Dutch never had the protectorate over the Syrian Churches, commonly known as the "Hill" or "New or St. Thomas' Christians," but they had over all the other Christian sects.

Cochin Rajah, for a piece of land, exterior to the Dutch limits, where they could erect houses for themselves, and worship in the manner they had been accustomed to. The Rajah acceded, they handed over to him a large sum of money, as a species of mortgage upon the ground, and having entered into possession, they were permitted to enact their own civil and ecclesiastical rules. The Dutch at first were more intolerant to Roman Catholics, than were the Hindu Rajahs, for they refused leave to the Carmelite Bishop Joseph, to remain on their coasts. Anticipating this order, a native Catanar, Alexander de Campo had been consecrated, to carry on the necessary work. The Dutch officials when ordering the European Priests to leave, raised no objection to De Campo remaining, as head of the Malabar Churches, concerning the affairs of which, they did not at this period much concern themselves. Had they considered it expedient that the Syrians should have again possessed their old forms of Church Government, surely Mar Thomas would have been encouraged, but the Dutch forbad him to enter the town of Cochin, and would hold no intercourse with him. Had the intention been to leave the Churches to choose for themselves, they would not have taken De Campo by the hand. In fact, they either cared nothing for the Syrians, or believing they were at that period friendly to Rome, they wished for political reasons, to exalt the Carmelites who were Italians, above the Jesuits who were mostly Portuguese, and therefore more to be dreaded. The Nestorian Bishop was consequently set aside, and the Carmelite star became in the ascendant, in the person of their pupil De Campo.

The European Romish Priests, do not appear to have thought lightly of deserting their flocks; some retired to the Samorin's territory, and attempted to treat with the Travancore Rajah, who was not very friendly to the Dutch, the ally of his enemy the Rajah of Cochin. Some Carmelites are said to have hidden themselves in thickets, and forests, where they lived in caves, or trees, supported by their flocks, and tended by their congregations.

The Dutch now perceiving the error they had committed, wished to induce the Roman Catholics to return, and communications between the Cochin Council, and the banished Romish Priests, assumed an official form. In 1673, Matthœus, had become so honoured by the

Dutch Governor, that he obtained leave for Priests to appear openly, and even no objection was offered, to the Cochin Rajah giving them leave to build a house at Chattiate, near Ernacollum. This Matthœus is the same eminent Priest, who was so useful to the Governor of Cochin, H. Van Reede, (also a good scholar,) in the preparation of his *Hortus Malabaricus.*

In this year, the Carmelites were permitted by the Rajah, to erect their present Church, at Verapoly, which was founded by Bishop Florentius, and dedicated to St. Joseph. This beautiful structure, (see page 21) is modelled after St. Peters' at Rome. Some unknown power, (perhaps the Dutch,) induced the Cochin Rajah, to yearly despatch an order to Verapoly, directing the Clergy there, to receive none of his subjects into the Catechumen's house, neither to baptize any. This letter was continued, for 30 or 40 years. The Travancore Rajah a little later, threatened death, or imprisonment, to all high caste Hindus, who might embrace the Romish faith, and loss of property to all Sudras. He even carried his threat into execution, and had the Nair head of a family, shot at Arampulli, for refusing to renounce this faith, which he had recently embraced.

In 1680, an attempt was made,* to sell back to, or exchange with Portugal, the stations where the Roman Catholic religion had taken such hold, retaining Cochin for the purposes of trade. The Dutch appear to have valued these congregations, higher than did the Portuguese, so the sale was not effected.

Dissension marked the internal state of the Malabar Churches, and disunion reigned almost supreme. After the accession of Gulmer Vorsburg, as Governor of Cochin, in 1684, a series of cruelties marked the treatment of all of the Roman Catholic creed. At last, an arrangement was come to, and the Home Council perceiving nothing could be done with the Malabar Churches, neither would the Portuguese purchase them, permitted Romish Priests to return to their flocks.

"It appears from a letter of the Honourable Court of Directors† "of Amsterdam, to the Government of Cochin, dated 8th April,

---

* *Secret orders,* of the Batavian Government. *Government Records.*

† *Memorial of Governor Moens,* M.SS. p. 308, *Cochin Government Records.*

"1698. That in consequence of a request of His Majesty, (the "Emperor Leopold,) and his promise of allowing the free exercise "of the Protestant religion in his dominions, permission was granted "to Mr. Peter Paul de Palmá, Archbishop of Ancyres, Privy Coun-"cillor, and Envoy extraordinary to the Courts of Persia and Ethio-"pia, by letters patent, to send a few Priests of the order of the "barefooted Carmelites, (any other Romish Priests excepted,) to "these countries, as was hitherto practicable, whose number is fixed "at 6 or 8. On condition, that the aforesaid Carmelite Priests, "should be *Dutchmen*, *Germans*, or *Italians*, and liked by the Ho-"nourable Company. And moreover, that they should make them-"selves subject to every order and regulation of the Company, as "every other of their inhabitants does."

The Dutch have not left many records of the Christians in Malabar, when under their rule, for they interfered but little in their ecclesiastical concerns.* The Syrians applied to them to obtain a Bishop from Babylon, but they declined; at last, a Jew, Ezekiel, was induced to procure one. In 1747, he arrived from Bussorah, but was very much disliked, so a few years subsequently, was re-shipped, to return to his own country. Another was sent for, and landed the same year, from a Dutch vessel, together with three Metrans, and two Priests. Twelve thousand rupees, were demanded for their passage. Angry communications ensued, until at last the painful scene was witnessed, of a suit lasting years, in Travancore, in which a Christian Government were the plaintiffs, and a Christian people defendants; and the subject, the amount of money at which a passage for a Bishop and five Priests was valued, whilst a Hindu Court of justice, was the place chosen, for the arbitration of this unseemly strife.

The Churches according to *Moens*, "under the Company were, "the Church at Vypeen, Crusmilagri, Balarparte, Palliport, Cranga-

---

* They were however jealous of foreign interference; thus in 1740, when the *Moravian United Brethren*, attempted to establish a Mission in Ceylon, the Clergy opposed the project so virulently, that the Governor, *Van Imhoff*, was obliged to order the Missionaries to settle inland, beyond the Dutch limits. At the end of that year, Van Imhoff was promoted to Batavia, and the Moravians, in October were expelled the Island.

"nore, Paponetty, Chetwye, Vendoorty, Angikaimul, (this last "Church originally belonged to the Syrians, it was subsequently "given over to the Romanists, for the use of the Topasses and "Christian Peons, so is under the protection of the Company,) "Muttencherry, Sande with its chapel (two miles south of Cochin), "the Church is called that of "Senhora de Sande," and its chapel that "of "St. Janquebrado," the Church of St. Louis, and its chapel of "St. Jago, at Castella, one mile south of Jews' town. That of St. "Andrew, and its chapel of Tangie (now called Attingal, or St. An- "drea), of Tombolie (close to Allepey), Catoorty (north of Allepey), "and Manikoorde. The Topass Priests were taught in the Semi- "naries of Verapoly, and Pootencherra (Cranganore), and the Cata- "nars in that of Candanatty (Candenaad.)" '

Amongst the accounts of the agreement between the Rajah of Cochin and the Dutch, respecting the Native Christians, the most complete summary is found in the Memorial of Governor *Van Angelbeck*, dated 1793.

After observing that in the treaty dated March 20th, 1663, the Rajah of Cochin consented to become a vassal to the Dutch. He continued, that constant disputes had taken place with the Cochin Rajah, respecting the "Inland Christians" over the Roman Catholic or Romo Syrian (but not the Syrian) portion of which, they claimed authority, in accordance with article 3 of the treaty of 1663.

When discussions arose upon this subject, respecting the Canarese, and lasted two years, up to about 1789, Mr. Powney the English Commissioner, observed upon a difference which existed between the Rajah's Malayalim copy of the treaty, and the Dutch one. In the former, the Dutch were given authority over all *Moondoocars*, (persons wearing white clothing,) located near the town of Cochin, and those living along the coast. The Dutch copy after the word Moondoocars, had added, "viz., all Christians," words absent in the Rajah's copy. The Rajah and Mr. Powney insisted, that by the term "Moondoocars," only the fishermen were meant: but Mr. Van Angelbeck, got the Carmelite Priests of Verapoly, and other persons well acquainted with the language, "who declared, that it included "all who followed the Latin ritual, and not only the fishermen, but "also the Lascorins (peons), land cultivators, and handicraftsmen,

" (if Christians), as well as Topasses." He added "that by a con-
" vention completed in 1785, it was clearly defined, that not only
" fishermen, but all the others, classes before mentioned, were includ-
" ed in the term " Moondoocars."

To prevent *Mr. Powney* from knowing anything of the result, the matter was settled with the Rajah, without being committed to writing. *Van Angelbeck* stated, that the former conceded everything, and apologized for having listened to Mr. Powney's advice.

Reverting to earlier times, Van Angelbeck observed, that one Dutch right was, that all Christians should be tried by them. This the heathen subjects of the Rajah often took advantage of, and when they had committed crimes, were baptized in order to be freed from the Rajah's jurisdiction. But they were frequently handed over to the Native State, in order that it might not be considered, that Christianity afforded a refuge, from the punishment due to crimes.

The second right was, that the Rajah was unable to impose new demands on the Christians, or increase their taxes above what was paid by their forefathers.* But it was added, in the treaty of February 25th, 1664,—" That the subjects of the Rajah who have been
" accustomed to contribute head money, and other demands, shall
" not be freed from their obligations, by becoming Christians." Any claim the Rajah had on the Christians, had to be made through their Commandant, who alone could attach their houses, or gardens, or imprison them. If lands could be proved to have formerly belonged to heathens, or by the convention of 1785, should Christians purchase, or rent lands from the heathen, they were liable to imposts, which the purely Christian lands were exempt from. In 1762, when Hyder made heavy demands on the Cochin State, the Dutch admitted the justice of the Native Christians, contributing their share of the expenses.

* Land disposed of, either by the Government of Cochin, or by that of Travancore, had certain conditions or obligations attached to the transfer. Sometimes they were rent free, or on a very reduced rate, or tax, on condition that the holder should perform some particular service, such as beating out a certain quantity of paddy in the year, carrying a certain number of loads from one place to another, or supplying a certain quantity of articles, such as milk, oil flowers, &c., at stated periods.

Van Angelbeck observed, that "the Company however, deriv-"ed no advantage from these vassals, by their protection, either "in the way of income, or personal work, and their Commandant had "really nothing, but daily trouble with His Highness' Court."

Many Romo-Syrian congregations, attempted in 1709, to join the Syrians: in 1773, they declared themselves under the Latin Church, and in 1777, sent to Romo and requested that a Romo-Syrian Bishop might be attached exclusively to them. In 1787, they tried to shake off all connection with the Carmelites of Verapoly, but were reduced by force, for which purpose, Mr. Van Angelbeck, the Governor of Cochin, lent his assistance, and wrote several times to the neighbouring Rajahs, requesting them to help the Carmelites, by force if necessary.

In 1770, the Travancore Minister wrote to the Roman Catholics at Verapoly, announcing to them, that they were declared henceforwards, free from all Public burdens whatever. Four years subsequently, a petty officer, tried to reimpose them, but on the occasion of the presentation of a letter from the Pope to the Rajah of Travancore, the Delegates took the opportunity of bringing all their grievances to notice, when they were rectified, and an instrument granted to the Missionary establishment, giving them immunity in future from all imposts whatsoever. In 1783, some of the Latin clergy fined certain Christian congregations of fishermen in Travancore, who complained to the Rajah, who decided on separating 75 Churches from the Diocese of Cochin, and placing them under the Verapoly Mission, but this was never carried out in full. The Roman Catholic Bishop seems to have been treated with civility by the Dutch, and *Moens* states, that when once he paid him a visit at Cochin, "he "thought it but right to show him due respect, and on his return "had a guard of honour drawn up, who saluted him, and nine guns "were fired from the battery." But his successor, *Van Angelbeck*, observes, that when the Bishop at a later period visited him, he did not receive him with any honours. A letter was received by Governor Moens, from Pope Clement, dated July 23rd, 1772, thanking him for the support, which the Roman Catholics had received from the Cochin council.

The English at this time, held but little territory in Malabar, and had scarcely commenced to be a political power. The first scheme of the Church Missionary Society, appears to have been organized in Calcutta, by Messrs. Grant, Brown, Chambers, and Udory: the first mentioned of these (a Bengal Civilian,) agreed to give Rs. 300 a month towards supporting a Missionary, who it was proposed, should go to Benares, to learn the Sanscrit language, and native manners and customs, before attempting to argue against a creed, the leading features of which he might otherwise very possibly not understand. This plan unfortunately failed, but not from any want of support, amongst the lay members.*

In 1793, *Mr. Wilberforce* carried a series of resolutions in the House of Commons, pledging it, that Christianity and education should be extended in India. The Court of Directors considering, that their rights were being encroached on, and unfair reflections passed upon themselves and their actions, assailed these measures, and thus opposition was engendered, where conciliation only was needed. Wilberforce's party were in too great haste to commence the evangelization of India, an event no less desired by the Court of Directors than by themselves, although in a less impetuous and safer manner.

In 1714, two Bishops ruled the divided Syrian Church of Malabar, Mar Thomas a Jacobite in the south, and Mar Gabriel a Nestorian in the north. In 1751, the Patriarch of Antioch was no longer able to send a Bishop, and for many years subsequently, the Syrians elected and consecrated one from amongst themselves.

During the remainder of the eighteenth century, but little was done in religious matters in the Cochin territory. The Dutch were swept away by the British, who at first were too much engaged in temporal arrangements, to occupy themselves with the requirements of the Syrians. In 1806, the Rev. *Dr. Claudius Buchanan* visited these Churches, and interested himself warmly in their behalf: but

* It must be a subject of regret, to the well wishers of a Christianity of peace and love, to perceive the virulent declamations, of some Protestants, against those in authority, whom they denounce as passively, if not actively hostile to religion. The chapter on the Dutch, shows how Christianity flourishes under hot house cultivation: and the present lamentable paucity of Protestants, in the Cochin and Travancore States, the subsequent result of such a plan.

he was rather of a head strong disposition, and effected little good. He requested the Carmelite Vicar Apostolic of Verapoly, not to offer any objections to the circulation of the Scriptures in the Malayalim, and Syriac languages, amongst his congregations, a request also strongly urged by Col. Macaulay, and at once acceded to. Up to within the last few years, Protestant publications were freely received, but unfortunately one of the Missionaries, who was unable to obtain converts from the Roman Catholics around him, published a tract in Malayalim, a portion of which endeavoured to prove, that *the Roman Catholic feasts, were as bad, or worse, than those of the Hindus!* In consequence of this unfortunate production, which was distributed gratuitously, all Protestant works have since then, until just lately, been strictly prohibited. The Roman Catholics are now removing this prohibition, and surely it will be unwise, to cause any further irritation.

For some years the worship in the Churches under Romish sway, continued much in the same manner as formerly; *Captain Swanston* speaking of them about the latter period of the Dutch rule says, "The Christian religion has degenerated in the Roman Catholic "Churches of Malayala, into the most abominable superstitions: "which are equal to many, if not to all the disgusting ceremonies, "of the monstrous worship of Brahma." But since then a partial improvement has become visible, and many rites which a few years ago were countenanced, are now almost unknown. Still the native Roman Catholic, seldom enters a Portuguese Church: and the Romo-Syrian, goes to neither of them. Thus Churches may be seen standing side by side, belonging to persons who acknowledge the same creed, but are unable to worship in the same building. Four distinct castes also exist, which sever these congregations still more widely. The Inquisition at Goa, after for nearly three centuries practising the most inhuman barbarities, and enacting the most disgraceful and revolting crimes, finally ceased its blood-stained career, in 1816.

In 1796, according to *Paoli,* the Cochin and Travancore States, contained 64 Nestorian Churches, 32 Jacobite, 75 of Mucuas and Paravers, and 20 belonging to the Latin ritual: in all 181 congregations, apparently without including the Carmelites. In the year

1861, the following numbers were returned,* as being in the Cochin, Calicut, and Travancore States, under the authority of the Syrian Metropolitan See, 105 Latin Churches,† 62 Parochial Churches, with 246 chapels attached to them: and 139 Carmelite Parochial Churches, with 168 Chapels attached, one quarter of which are Latins, and the remainder Romo-Syrian.‡ The Protestant Church Missionary Society, have 10 Churches in the North, and the London Missionary Society 7 in the South.

The Travancore census shows 1,91,009 Native Christians, and that of Cochin 72,631: or a total of 2,63,640 in the two States. Out of the above 10,336 have been baptized into the Protestant faith: 1,38,337 into the Roman Catholic: and the remainder 1,16,483 are Syrians.

In 1813, Major Munro, the British Resident of Travancore and Cochin, circulated a series of questions to the various Syrian Churches in these States, and the replies proved their depression to be extreme. When they separated from the Romish Church, they became exposed to the attacks of numerous enemies, with no one to protect them. The Roman Catholics persecuted them as apostates, and rebels, the Brahmans and Nairs domineered over them, and the Officials of both States plundered and insulted them at discretion. Their books

* Trevandrum, *Government Almanac*, 1861. Some Churches which have been incorrectly included, have been here expunged.

† The Churches have been divided in the following manner: The *Roman Catholics*, and the *Romo-Syrians*, are under two distinct Missions.

The Romo-Syrians and the Latin Churches, were originally under the authority of the Portuguese. The Archbishop of Cranganore, receiving his instructions from Goa, and having under him the two subordinate Bishops of Cochin, who were removed in 1663 to Quilon, the Churches under the latter were considered to be all *within sight of the sea*. In 1709, they wished to join the Syrians.

The Romo-Syrians, or at all events some of them, obeyed the Carmelite Vicar Apostolic, or the Verapoly Mission, which receives orders from Rome. In 1773, they erected schools for the instruction of Romo-Syrian Priests, and began to encroach considerably on the Latin Churches, then acknowledging the authority of Goa. The *Syrians* are ostensibly under the Patriarch of Antioch, and are Monophysites, or Jacobites, with some slight differences.

‡ Their return of Christians professing their faith, is about 228,000, but this is obviously erroneous. Their native clergy are 30, and Romo-Syrians 332.

had been almost all destroyed, their pastors were destitute of instruction, "they had lost in their union with the Jesuits, the "pure system of religion and morals, and the high spirit by which "they were formerly distinguished: and the Dutch fomerly in posses-"sion of Cochin, whose policy was marked by perfidy and meanness, "abandoned them to their fate." Still many virtues were to be perceived in this interesting sect, and an attempt was therefore very properly made, to bring them to a purer faith.

Major Munro* ascertained that there was great dissension amongst them, that the Bishop under whom they were at that period, had been irregularly consecrated, and was altogether unfit for such an office. There was therefore a large body of the clergy and laity antagonistic to him, and opposition was rife on all subjects. But this Bishop died shortly afterwards, and was succeeded by the Ramban named Joseph, a good and pious man, by whose assistance, a little more unanimity was brought about, and the Resident was enabled to make arrangements for the erection of the Syrian College at Cottayam. But now it was found that an educated English Clergyman would be a requisite, as the Syrians themselves were far too deficient in energy, knowledge, or ability, to effect much good, in the way of training up youths, in a more enlightened manner. An application was then made to the *Church Missionary Society* for their assistance, the Resident proposing to endow the College for the support of a certain number of students, and masters, to teach English, Syriac, and the Scriptures, and to raise up efficient Native Priests and Catanars, to officiate in the Churches, as well as schoolmasters to diffuse learning throughout the country. He also proposed erecting a printing press.

It was not originally intended to alter the Syrian form of worship, in any way, but merely to educate the people, and trust that in time they would be enabled to see their errors, and themselves commence the work of reformation. It was simply suggested, to raise up this prostrate Church, and assist it in endeavouring to follow the right course.

---

* In 1808, three thousand star pagodas were given by the Syrian Metropolitan Mar Thomas to the British Resident for investment in Government securities at 8 per cent, interest for charitable purposes.

In April 1816, Mr. Norton, a Missionary, arrived at Allepey, to assist in the above purpose: and in the July following visited the Metran Joseph, at Cottayam, where he found he was regarded with some suspicion. This ancient Church, had in former times, suffered too much from false friends, not to be cautious how they formed connections with strangers. But this feeling soon wore away, and Mr. Norton's advent was hailed with joy.

In 1816, the Travancore Government, made the Syrians a donation of 8,000 Rupees, to enable them, "to prosecute the study of the "Holy Scriptures, according to the custom of their sect, * * by "means of the dissemination of the Bible, and other religious works "in the vernacular tongue, amongst the Syrians in general." Colonel Munro observed, that "the principal object of the esta-"blishment of a College in Travancore, *was* to instruct the Catanars "and officiating Priests amongst the Syrians, in a competent know-"ledge of the *Syriac language,* in which they were apparently too "generally deficient: * * with the study of the Syriac language, "would of course be combined that of the Scriptures, and other "religious books, written in that tongue."

The Ranee of Travancore, acting under the advice of the British Resident, gave the timber for erecting a Church at Allepey; in addition to this it cost 4,155 Rupees. It was opened on July 18th, 1819, but was subsequently pulled down, to build a larger one, which is now in a ruinous, and almost deserted condition. The Ranee also endowed the Syrian College at Cottayam, in 1818, with Rupees 20,000, as well as the ground on which it stands. The College was intended to accommodate forty or fifty students, and the money invested in land as an endowment, for the support of the College. The title deeds were drawn up in the names of the Syrian Metropolitan, and one of the Missionaries. "The object of this endowment "was, the political, moral, and religious renovation, of the whole of "the Syrian people, through the instruction of English Missionaries." Shortly afterwards, the Syrian Bishop died, and his coadjutor Philoxenus, who had (according to the usual custom since 1751,) been ordained, "cum spe successionis," succeeded him.

At first all went on smoothly at Cottayam, with a resident Syrian Bishop at the head. The Protestant Missionaries acted under his orders, and the Scriptures were translated into Malayalim. But after a time, when the novelty wore off, the result of this was found of a less favourable character, than was at first imagined. The Natives having Europeans under their authority, became exacting, and often overbearing; whilst the latter, not liking their position, were perhaps too ready to look upon common occurrences, as intentional insults. After a time, when the Protestant Missionaries had become more fully acquainted with this Church, they reported that the spiritual worth of the Syrians, had been formerly much over-estimated, that the people were careless about true religion, the Priesthood unconverted, formal in their service, and too much occupied in looking after their pecuniary gains, to care for the welfare of their flocks. That in fact, the whole body, was lifeless, and cold. Disputes about their various creeds, and tenets, then ensued: the Syrians denounced those taught by the Missionaries, who in their turn asserted that the Syrian doctrines were not evangelical.

The Bishop of Calcutta then addressed a letter to the Syrian Metropolitan, who in 1836, held a conclave of his clergy, and drew up an answer stating, that they were Jacobites, under the Patriarch of Antioch, and that if the Missionaries wished to preach the doctrines of the Jacobites in their Churches, they were at liberty to do so. The Metran after the signature of this document, imposed a solemn oath on the clergy, not to have any intercourse with the Protestant Missionaries in future, whilst the Metran prohibited Deacons, from again attending the Syrian College. Thus ceased the connection between these two Churches, which had been in existence since 1816, and the Protestant Missionaries were from that period, to divide themselves from the Syrians, "as converts in Bengal, or Tinnevelly, "separate themselves from the heathen."*

Now dissensions respecting money matters arose, and the Syrian Metropolitan, complained that the box containing the title deeds, and the copper plates, had been abstracted from the Church, during service time; a person having broken into its place of security, by means of a crowbar. Fortunately the box just at this time, came into the possession of the Missionaries, who preserved these impor-

* Mullen's Missions in South India, page 130.

tant documents from destruction. In 1838, a Government Commissioner was sent to arrange matters, consequent on the separation of the Syrians and the Missionaries, and he directed the lands to be sold, and the money deposited in the Travancore treasury. (Munro Island was not disposed of.) In 1840, three arbitrators were nominated by the Travancore Government, the Missionaries, and the Syrian Metropolitan, finally to arrange the division of property. Some of the moneys and deeds were then returned to the Syrians. But with regard to Munro Island, it was decided, that as its rents were to be employed for a specific purpose, in which the assistance of the Missionaries was necessary, and the Syrians in Synod assembled, had broken off all connection with them: they thereby resigned their part of the trust, leaving its duties to be executed by the remaining party.

At the time that this amalgamation took place, the orders of Priesthood were as follows in the Syrian Church: a Bishop styled *Metropolitan*, who had a coadjutor, whom he consecrated as his successor, in the event of his death: Doctors of the Law, or *Malpans*, who were instructors of youths, and those intended for Holy Orders, Priests or *Catanars*, and Deacons.

The Metropolitans had been elected from amongst the Malpans, and consecrated in readiness, from the year 1751, when it was found extremely difficult, or almost impossible to obtain foreign Bishops, as heretofore. The election took place in a general assembly of the Clergy, and elders of the Church, who ratified or rejected, the choice of the person previously selected. If there were several candidates, lots were drawn by them, and the result regarded as decisive. It should be mentioned here, that until the year 1751, *the office of Archdeacon* was hereditary, in the family of Palikommatta, because it was believed, that the first person who held that post, was chosen by St. Thomas, from that family. When Bishops came from Antioch, they were expected to give up all authority into the hands of the Archdeacon, the Portuguese on this account, used every exertion to convert the whole of that family to their faith, and finally succeeded in doing so. Many years since, the Palikommatta family became extinct.

The Priests could be admitted into minor orders, as early as seven years of age, unless anything very unusually bad could be brought against them. They were not under the necessity of observing a life of celibacy, but such had become the custom, and gained them higher favour with the people. The Ranee of Tranvancore offered Rupees 400 to any of them who would marry, but only a few accepted the inducement.

In 1814, when the Governor in Council revised the regulations of Cochin, it was brought to his notice, that the Christians in the Native State, were under British controul, and consequently treated with harshness and injustice by the Officials of that State. They were regarded by their fellow subjects with suspicion, and ill will, and that in spite of all efforts to ameliorate their condition, no good could be effected, whilst there remained this distinction between them and others. It was suggested, that this irritation might be removed by allowing them to be tried in the Rajah's Courts, to each of which a Christian Judge was appointed, the whole being under the supervision of the Resident. This course was accordingly pursued, and the result has exceeded all expectations, the feeling of dislike and jealousy with which they had been formerly regarded, soon passed away, and they are at the present time, as thriving a community as any other in the State.

In the year 1825, the long interrupted intercourse with Antioch was renewed, and the Bishops who had for such a length of time been Natives of the country, now lost their power of consecrating. The Patriarch of Antioch hearing flourishing accounts of this distant Church, despatched a Metropolitan named Athanasius, and a Ramban or Archdeacon, named Abraham, to Malabar, quite overlooking the existence of Philoxenus, and his coadjutor Dionysius. These new arrivals had several interviews with Bishop Heber in Bombay, who subsequently enjoined the Missionaries, to take no part in the dissensions, he saw their advent must occasion amongst the Syrians in Malabar.

The new Metropolitan Athanasius, commenced by excommunicating Philoxenus and Dionysius, who on the other hand obtained an order from the Ranee of Travancore and the British Resident, forbidding the new arrivals to exercise any functions in that State. The majority of the congregations appear to have wished to place themselves under the strangers, and great dissensions arose. Bishop

Heber proceeded towards Malabar, in hopes of being enabled to bring about some amicable arrangement, but unfortunately he expired on the journey. Soon afterwards, Mar Athanasius and his Malpan, sailed from Cochin.

But his departure, only gave the Syrians a short respite from incessant disputes, as a succession of claimants to the Metropolitan See arose. The Bishop who legally bore that title, resided at the Cottayam College, and received from its funds, Rupees 600 a year for his maintenance.

In the year 1848, the Patriarch of Antioch had five Bishops in Malabar, each denouncing the other four as intruders. When there were only three, the Patriarch sent a fourth, to supersede the others, with orders to transmit his dues to him punctually: but instead of obeying, this last followed the example of his predecessors, and commenced collecting for himself. A fifth was then despatched with the same orders, but he too flew upon the spoil, leaving the unfortunate Patriarch, vainly clamouring for his rights. It was impossible to decide which amongst these five Bishops was the real one, and therefore none of them were recognized by the Travancore and Cochin States. But without the legal sanction of these States, they were powerless to correct abuses, or exercise any authority. Each consequently did as he liked, and ordained as many Catanars as he pleased, without reference to anything, excepting whether the fees were forthcoming. Thus an immense number of Catanars were ordained, from seven years of age and upwards, who were in every respect, unfitted for the ministry. These scandalous disputes and dissensions, have continued since that period, and at the present time the Church is thoroughly disunited.

In 1856, two Catanars, and twenty one Syrians, provided with the necessary funds, and letters, left Cochin, and proceeded to Mosul, to endeavour to induce the Patriarch, Mar Yoosuf, to consecrate a Bishop for the Syrians of Malabar, as was done in 1825. They succeeded in their embassy, and in May 13th, 1861, a Bishop arrived at Cochin. It is said that Mar Yoosuf was imposed upon, and did not exactly comprehend, what their intentions were.

The Bishop Apostolic of Rome in Mesopotamia, finding that Mar Thomas had been consecrated as Metran of Malabar, forthwith excommunicated both him, and the Patriarch, as well as every one who had taken part in the consecration. Thus another schism, and cause of discord arose, in this divided Church.

Hardly had the new Bishop landed, when as always has been the case, a large party joined him, and many Romo-Syrian congregations, placed themselves under his authority, and wished to hand over the Churches to him. Riots in many places consequently ensued, until Mar Thomas, an infirm sickly old man, began to think it time for him to leave such an unruly set of people, and in March 1862, he finally left Cochin.

At the present time there are still three Bishops remaining, two of whom claim equal rank and power, both having been consecrated by the Patriarch of Antioch, the third admits his inferiority to the other two.

The crown of Portugal which has up to the present year claimed ecclesiastical jurisdiction over the Roman Catholics of Malabar, has now received orders to resign that pretension in British territory. A concordat has consequently been entered into, and the Bishop of the Cape de Verd Islands, has been appointed Archbishop of Goa, and Primate of the Catholic Church in India, thus bringing the Verapoly Mission, and the other Churches in the Cochin and Travancore States, under one head.

There can be no doubt, that each succeeding Christian sect, has obtained less power in Malabar, than those which preceded them, which may be accounted for in the following manner. The *Syrians* before the advent of the Portuguese, appear to have confined their attempts at conversion to Brahmans and the highest castes of Sudras (Nairs,) in the country. The *Portuguese* obtained converts from any classes they could, and these were consequently looked down upon by the higher castes, as the greatest proportion were fishermen and slaves.

The architecture of the ancient Syrian Churches was always the same, and it has been calculated, that none of them could have cost less than half a lac of Rupees, and some double that sum. The one at Paroor, is capable of containing 15,000 persons. They were formerly built long and narrow, with low entrances, having buttresses supporting the walls, and sloping roofs, and were easily distinguished from those of any other sect, by having the chancel end always higher than the nave, instead of being lower as with us. The façade had small columns, but these were never carved with emblematical figures externally, as some of those of later erections are. No bells were permitted to be rung from the belfreys, as the Hindus asserted, that their gods in the neighbouring Pagodas, were disturbed by the noise.

Inside these Churches, there were galleries corresponding to our organ lofts, for the residence of unmarried Priests. There were numerous crosses in various parts, and one on the altar, opposite which, at the entrance to the chancel, a lamp was kept burning night and day.

Gradually some of these ancient forms have changed, both with respect to worship, architecture, vestments, and the method of performing the services, a summary of which is as follows. The more modern Churches are built in a style something similar to those erected by the Jesuits, with pointed arched windows, circular and fretted ceilings over both the altar and choir, whilst the beams are exposed to view. No images are allowed within them, but some of them are adorned with paintings, which are *said* to be simply for ornamental purposes. There are three altars (or as they are termed *thrones*,) in each Church, the largest being at the east end and within the chancel, and one on each side just without the entrance of the chancel, covered with a white cloth, having a cross on it. The chancel is raised two steps higher than the body of the Church. Before it hangs a veil, so that if necessary it can be concealed from the congregation. Near the chancel are the bells used in honour of the host. Crucifixes are placed on the altars, and in various other parts of the buildings, some of them being plain, others adorned with, or composed of gold, silver, wood, or stone.

The Bishop when no great state is necessary, wears a long dark purple silk vest, but when officiating, he wears a long yellow muslin robe, thrown over his other garments: a large golden cross hangs from his neck, on his finger is a ring, and on his head an episcopal mitre, whilst in his hand he bears the crozier, or pastoral staff. The Priests at their ordination, engage to observe the canons of the Council of Nice. When not employed in religious ceremonies, they wear loose white shirts, over a pair of wide trowsers, either white or of some black material. On occasions of ceremony, a white gown is worn, in addition to an embroidered collar and waistband, and narrow sleeves. They have a crimson scarf, and a long white cotton cord passing around the shoulders, and fastening in front with a waistbelt, meeting there like a cross. Their hair is cut in the form of a tonsure, and their beards are sometimes of great length.

Their means of support are principally derived from the fees they receive, especially from those for prayers for the dead. Attached to each congregation, is a small Court, consisting of the Catanar, and four lay elders, who meet in the Church, and punish wrong doers, by admonitions, fines, or excommunications. Each parish, or rather the boundaries of each separate congregation, are divided off by land marks, and the names of persons belonging to it taken down, who must all receive the sacraments within their own Parishes. Before leaving their district for another, they must obtain a testimonial from their Catanars, of having conducted themselves soberly and steadily. A residence of twelve years in one Parish, is necessary before a person can become an elder.

The Syriac liturgies are numerous, this Church maintains the doctrines of Trinity in unity, and that of the atonement, but does not wholly admit justification by faith. Transubstantiation is now part of their creed, the Priests pray for the quick and the dead, and also separately and distinctly for the dead. They supplicate the intercession of the Virgin Mary, worship her with many prayers, and fast in her honour. They also worship the Saints, the altars, and the Host. The prayers are in the Syriac tongue, a language believed to have been used by our Lord, and his Apostles, but not understood by the Syrian congregations of the present day. The Clergy claim the power of cursing, and thereby destroying the souls and bodies of offenders. They have extreme unction, and auricular confession. God the father is represented in their Churches, and incense is burnt, but there is no exposition of the Scriptures. The practice of blessing holy water was commenced amongst them, about the 7th century, it is generally mixed with a little earth from St. Thomas' Mount, near Madras. The excommunicated murderer, is never absolved, not even after death.

The altar is twelve by eighteen inches in size, and is consecrated at

Easter, after which it must not be touched by unconsecrated hands. The services are chanted by the Priest, in a loud tone of voice, the oldest Catanar present, always officiating. During the service, the Priests at intervals pray in a low tone, accompanied by frequent crossings and prostrations: the congregation being in the mean time, occupied with their own devotions. When the Priests chant the words, "peace on earth, good will towards men," the Catanars take the right hand of the officiating Priest, between both theirs, and so pass the "peace" to the congregation, each of whom takes his neighbour's right hand, and salutes him with the word, "peace." The women are seated apart from the men. At the conclusion of the service, the senior Priest present, stands at the door, and as the congregation passes out, each individual member receives his blessing, unless guilty of any act, considered sufficiently bad to deprive him of it: in former times, its being withheld, was regarded as a very severe punishment.

During Lent, and other great fasts, service is performed three times a day, at morning, evening, and midnight, at the two former no one fails to be present, to receive their blessing, and offer vows of peace and obedience, which is done by taking the Priest's hands between their own, raising them on high, and then kissing them. On Sundays, service is performed twice a day. On the first Wednesday in Lent, they anoint the head with holy oil, which consists of olive oil made from the branches of olive trees, that were blessed before the fruit was formed, for doing which there is a peculiar ceremony. At this period, the Roman Catholics use ashes, and it is probable this custom has originated the use of oil by the Syrians, as also the theatricals performances, which take place a few weeks before Lent, and may be styled a species of carnival. During Lent which with them lasts fifty days, they abstain from flesh, fish, eggs, milk, butter, and spirituous liquors. They also fast in Advent, on the Assumption of the Virgin Mary, from the first to the fifteenth of August, and in commemoration of the Apostles which begins after Pentecost and lasts fifty days, and at the Nativity of our Saviour for twenty-five days before Christmas, and also on every Wednesday and Friday, commencing at sunset the preceding day, and lasting 24 hours. All these fasts must be kept, under pain of excommunication.

At the celebration of the Eucharist, the cup is placed on the East end of the altar, and the plate on the West, close to two others, one containing a sponge to wipe the Priest's fingers, the other a dish and spoon, the whole being covered with a white cloth. The cake is circular, and composed of wheaten flour, like a pie, in a silver dish, of leavened bread made during the service. Some portion of it is invariably kept until the communion following, and mixed with the next baking, and thus they believe that they have retained some of the bread, which was used at "Our Lord's Supper." This cake is stamped with the figure of the crosses of St. George, and St Andrew, with a square in the centre, exterior to which are two circular lines, and between each line of the crosses is a smaller line in the same direction, converging to the centre. Consequently each quarter of the cake has a perfect cross, and three lines or twelve in all, signifying the twelve Apostles. When the Priest consecrates the bread, he raises it, on which tom-toms and cymbals strike up, and the curtain is drawn, shutting the Priest out from the gaze of the congregation. He then prays alone after which the curtain is drawn aside, and he advances holding the bread in his right hand, and the wine in his left, and chanting a hymn: he then turns round to the altar, and receives the elements, the music again strikes up, followed by silence, during which the Priest says a short prayer to himself. Three Priests celebrate the Eucharist at the same time, at the three different altars. The Clergy receive the elements separately every day, the Laity only three times a year, with the difference, that for them the bread is dipped into the wine, which is not the case with the Priests.

Love feasts are still held. Large quantities of sugar-cane, rice, honey, and flour, are collected, and stored up for the occasion. When the time arrives, cakes are baked, and plantains, &c., procured, the feast being celebrated in a room adjoining the Church. The various portions are distributed with a blessing by the Priests. The guests are seated in rows, each provided with a plantain leaf on their knees, to serve instead of a plate: silence is then commanded, and the Church Overseers walk down the rows, to see that no one is omitted, and that all share alike. What is left may be eaten by the heathen.

Other feasts are held, not so harmless in their character. In one of their Churches, both Syrians and Heathen meet, and worship the image of St. George, and in many of them songs in praise of the heathen Deity Rama, are permitted. It is difficult to distinguish between Syrian feasts, and those of low caste Hindus. On a hill near Maleatur, there is a mountain sanctuary called Crucemah, or Cross Hill, on the rocky summit is a cross, believed to have sprung miraculously from the rock: both St. Thomas and Xavier, are reputed to have visited it, and pilgrimages are annually made to this place at Whitsuntide. Penances are endured there, and vows carried into effect. Penitents crawl up the hill, and roll themselves down along any parts, sufficiently level to admit of their doing so. Booths are erected, in which liquors, cakes, and sweetmeats may be purchased: music enlivens the scene, which somewhat resembles an English fair, and certainly there are no outward signs, of the endurance of any very painful penances. Beggars flock in from the surrounding country, jugglers exhibit their arts, and fireworks dispel the midnight gloom. At Palliport some of the Virgin Mary's hair is believed to be preserved, and an annual feast is held there in her honour, and celebrated much in the Hindu fashion.

Marriages amongst the Syrians take place at a very early age, and are negotiated for by the family, whose business it is to provide what they consider an eligible alliance for the children. The bride receives her dower, which she takes to her husband, but subsequently obtains nothing else from her parents. Mr. Van Angelbeck endeavoured ineffectually to alter this custom, which the Syrians refused to agree to, as they said it had been established, in order to obviate the sub-division of estates into small portions. The bride is dressed in white, with a muslin cloth over her head, and a jacket with a red stripe down the front, and sometimes worked round the sides and neck with yellow silk. She is loaded with jewels, generally hired for the occasion, strings of gold coins round her neck, large gold ornaments in her ears, with bangles on her arms and ankles. A large red silk umbrella, usually with green fringe, is carried over her head. The bridegroom wears a gold frontlet, with bangles on his arms, and occasionally a silver belt. The ceremony always takes place on Sunday, and is generally celebrated in the Church, the bridegroom throws a cloth over the bride as a symbol of her having bound herself to blind obedience to his commands, he then ties a golden cross attached to a silken cord round her neck. The party then adjourn to the bridegroom's house, at the entrance to which, they are met by a near female relative, bearing a lighted lamp, behind her are more women, some carrying water to symbolize purity, and others rice to denote plenty. The first female touches the various articles with her finger, and then applies them to the forehead of the young couple, who make obeisance to her. They are then conducted inside the house, placed on raised seats of honour, and fed with sweet rice. The friends then partake of some betel nut, and separate. On the following day a feast is held, either in the house, or under a pandall erected for the purpose, at which a considerable sum of money is frequently spent, pork is one of the principal articles of consumption in these repasts.

After the birth of a son, the mother may not enter the Church for forty days, but if the child be a girl, not for eighty, at the end of which time, she presents herself at the altar, and offers the babe to God, and the Church. Baptism is generally celebrated on the eighth day after birth, but in some instances not before the forty-first, although it is occasionally left until a more advanced period. For a boy there is one Godfather, and for a girl one Godmother. The sign of the cross is made in oil, on the eyes, nose, ears, and mouth of the infant, consecrating all these senses to God.

Members of the congregation are often buried inside the walls of the Church. Bishops close to the altar: and the laity in the body of the Church: no coffin is used, and no particular service is employed, with the exception of a few chants. Deaths are bewailed with loud lamentations, wax candles are carried in procession, incense burnt, and masses celebrated for the soul, if for that of a rich man for forty days, but for a poor man only one day. The Metropolitan is buried seated in a high wooden chair, dressed in his robes, with a wooden cross suspended from his neck, another held in his right hand, and in his left his pastoral staff. The chief mourner shuts himself up for about a week, or ten days, at the end of which time, he receives his friends' condolences, and gives them an entertainment, when one of his nearest relatives presents him with a new turban, which he puts on, and thus ends the mourning.

The Syrian costume does not essentially differ from that of the surrounding Hindus, a piece of cloth descends from the waist to about the knees, the quality of which depends upon the wealth of the wearer. When out of doors, or on occasions of ceremony, they wear a square handkerchief either of coloured silk, or white cotton, on their heads. They shave their beards, but allow the hair on their heads to grow to a great length, which they tie up behind in a knot, and fasten with a cross, either of gold, silver or some other material. The women have bangles of silver, brass, or copper, on their legs : a cross suspended from their necks. A jacket reaches from their necks below the waist, and a cloth descends from thence nearly as low as their ankles. When they go to Church, or visit their Priests, they cover themselves with a long white muslin scarf, which is put over their heads, and reaches to the ground, leaving only their face visible.

The Syrians are for these parts a fine race of people, lighter in colour than the other inhabitants, and in most respects very superior to the surrounding heathen. Their manners are rather ceremonious, but full of simplicity, at times even amounting to rudeness. They are generally speaking an honest race, but exceedingly superstitious, placing their principal dependence, on soothsayers and omens. They are inquisitive, devoted to their Priests, and suspicious of any interference. Their pursuits, principally relate to agriculture and trade. The Romo-Syrians are rather inferior to the Syrians, more given to intoxication and quarrelling, and not quite so honest, but exceeding them in civility. The Roman Catholics are taken from amongst quite the lower grades of the population, and are as a rule in consequence the least honest race.

The Syrian women are modest and retiring, and keep themselves respectable in the midst of Hindu immorality, and vice. If they have no children, they occasionally adopt those of their servants. The men stand uncovered before their superiors, and hold their right hands before their mouths. When two of them meet in the road, the inferior uncovers his head, and inclines his body a little forward, and this mark of respect is always shewn the clergy.

The Protestant Missions require a short notice, but not having existed anything like the length of time in Malabar that the other

Christian sects have, they may be said to be still in their infancy, and will probably so continue, until a sufficiency of Native pastors have been educated, and placed in charge of the various congregations. Any religion in Asia, which requires a resident European Clergyman, can never take root in the country, and will only last, as long as the white races who are its exponents, continue there. Thus when the Dutch left India, their creed disappeared with them. Far different is it with the Roman Catholic faith, the Clergy of which have with great wisdom, educated very many Native Priests. The Dutch found that the fact of their driving away the European Pastors of that faith, scarcely affected the numbers of the converts. Europeans may be necessary to teach in the first instance, until they have raised up Natives, competent to carry on the work: and they may also be advisable, as a species of Bishop, to supervise the Priests, and their congregations, in large tracts of country, until the Natives have acquired more self-reliance. The head quarters of the Church Missionary Society, has since its separation from the Syrian Church, been fixed at Cottayam, where there is a printing press. About half the Missionaries belonging to that Society, reside within a radius of only a few miles from the above town. In the Cochin State there are three stations, at Trichoor, and Kununkulum respectively, presided over by European clergymen, and one in the town of Cochin, under the superintendence of a Native Minister.

The tenets and mode of Church Government, are the same as elsewhere. Education is used as an adjunct to religious instruction. The question of caste in the Romish Church has already been alluded to. The Danish Missionary Schwartz, divided the congregations of converts into two parties, the highest castes being seated on one side, and the lower on the other, and at the celebration of the Eucharist, a separate cup was used. It was subsequently arranged, that if the Pariahs would agree not to eat offal, they might use the same cup, after the higher castes had been served. It is not thirty years since, that it was authoritatively ordered, that caste distinctions should cease once and for all, in the Protestant Missions, of the Madras Presidency.

In the year 1808, the Court of Directors made the following observation, in an official despatch. "When we afforded our countenance and sanction to the Missionaries, who have from time to "time proceeded to India, for the purpose of propagating the Christian religion, it was far from being in our contemplation, to add the "influence of our authority, to any attempts they might make: for on the "contrary we were perfectly aware, that the progress of each conversion would be gradual and slow, arising more from a conviction of "the purity of the principles of our religion itself, and the pious "examples of its teachers, than from any undue influence, or from "the execution of authority, which are never to be resorted to in such "cases.* * *

"We shall content ourselves at present, with remarking that *Dr.* "*Buchanan*, as well as other Ecclesiastics, who promulgate the doc"trines of Christianity in India, and who bestow such just and "merited encomiums on the conduct of the Missionary Schwartz, "would do well to adopt it as the model of their own; and would "always recollect, that discretion and moderation in their language "and actions, are more consistent with the mild spirit of our reli"gion, and are indispensably requisite, for those who are employed "in prosecuting the laborious work of conversion."

The *East India Company* endeavoured to raise the moral and religious character of their servants in the East, as they rightly considered, that he who not only professes to be a Christian, but acts as such, must greatly influence those around him, and acquire esteem even from the heathen. Such a man spreads religion, much more than could be done by controversial arguments, he becomes a star in his sphere, and an object of respect to the surrounding Natives, who although possibly unable to comprehend the theory of the Christian faith, are perfectly competent to understand its practice.

CHAPTER VII.

THE HINDUS.

Origin of Hindus—Their ancient faith—Its Indian corruptions—Vedas—Laws of Menu—Puranas—Origin of Hindu triad, and Hindu pantheon—Devil worship—Feasts and fasts—Births—Marriages—Deaths—Funerals—Suttee—Good and evil souls—Hindu protest against religious intolerance—Origin of castes—Namboorie, Imbran, Putter and Konkanie Brahmans—Umbalavassies—Schatriyas—Vysias—Sudras—Nairs—Chogans or Illovers—Mucuas—Kanakas—Paravers—Cunnians—Velluns—Carcarlans and Niecomars—Soil slaves—Hill races—Mulchers, Kardars, and Niadis—Sicknesses—Funerals—Inheritance.

Cochin is an exclusively Hindu state, where the Brahman has flourished, since the legendary Parasu Rama, obtained from Veruna, the gift of the country, from below the waters of the ocean. Here the Brahman still holds partial sway, and proclaims to a credulous population, that his creed is unalterable. In this Native state, Europeans obtained their first permanent settlement in India; amongst this people, the Arab and Moplah dwelt in peace, and traded in amity. Here the New St. Thomas's Christians, the Romo Syrians, the Roman Catholics, Protestants, and Jews, have obtained an amount of freedom of discussion, unaccorded to them, in some more civilized countries of Europe.

The Hindus are generally acknowledged, as sprung from one of the branches of the Arians. In *Bharata*, or Punyabhumi "the land of virtues," subsequently termed Hindustan, "the land of the Hindus," or from the Sancrit word *Sindhu*, "ocean," a name first transferred to a river, and then to the country, colony after colony spread over the peninsula. They assert that their national existence had continued unaltered, a great number of centuries, before the commencement of the Christian era, in the countries lying between the Himalayas and the Vindhya mountains. Their dominions were extended under two dynasties, south and east. Whilst the Bactrian race spread towards the west, perhaps carrying the Druidical system to Europe, in all its varied forms.

The Hindu faith in its ancient purity, was not idolatry, but great changes have come over it, requiring a short sketch, before passing onwards to the various classes or *castes*, into which all its professors in the Cochin state, (excepting the out-castes,) are now divided.

On their first entrance into India, their religious works owing to the art of writing being unknown, appear to have been handed down by tradition, from generation to generation, in a series of compositions termed the Vedas, this period is therefore commonly designated the Vedic age. Oral traditions alter by time, and as might be anticipated, certain differences were observed in the Vedas, as known in different places: and it has, and probably correctly been surmised, that most outlying Hindu tribes, included amongst their Vedic hymns, some which were addressed to the Gods of the countries which they conquered, perhaps to obtain favour in the eyes of the inhabitants, and assist in persuading them to enter the new sect. Universal conquest no doubt was aimed at, and maybe an universal religion hoped for.

Some period before the Christian era, the Vedas which up to that period had been handed down by tradition, and symbolical representations, were collected and inscribed; they consist of four, *the Rig Veda,* whose origin was said to have been from fire, and the hymns of which are amongst the most ancient of records. The *Sama Veda,* derived from the sun, in which hymns from the Rig Veda are arranged for worship. The *Yagur Veda* which gives later hymns as well as some new reading of old ones: and the *Athavarna* or fourth Veda, consisting of formularies. The Puranas have also been called a Veda. The four Vedas are commonly known as the *Great Shastras,* or "books of sacred ordinance," from *Shas,* "to govern," or as it signifies in this case, "by divine authority."

Each Veda is a collection of prayers, and precepts, the former termed *Sanhitas:* in the Puranas it is observed, that there are sixteen Sanhitas in the Rig Veda: eighty-six in the Yagur Veda, increased by a second revelation to one hundred and one: not less than one thousand in the Sama Veda: and nine in the Athavarna. But different versions, or *Sakhas* of the Vedas exist, which reduce the Sanhitas of the first Veda to five, and of the second including both revelations to eighty-six.

The Vedas have become greatly altered in the course of time, which is thus expressed in the Puranas,* "the tree of science spread abroad its numerous branches." The Rig Veda is said to have been taught to *Paila*, who in his turn communicated it to two disciples, Bahcala, and Indrapramati. The first of these wrote a Sanhita, or collection, which branched into four schools: whilst Indrapramati taught his son, and also Vedamitra, each of whom gave his own version to the world, which was improved upon by his successors.

The Yagur Veda, having been communicated to *Vaisampayana*, he taught it to twenty-seven pupils, and then instructed Yajnyawalcya to teach it to other disciples. Subsequently Vaisampayana accidentally killed his sister's son, and asked Yajnyawalcya to go shares in the guilt incurred, which he declined doing: so Vaisampayana, directed him to cease teaching, and return what he had learned. He obeyed the order, and disgorged the Veda in the form of food. The disciples were ordered to pick it up, and to do so were changed into partridges. This Veda being so soiled, was termed "black" also "tittiri," from the name of a partridge, now known by Europeans, as one of the filthiest feeding of Indian birds.

Yajnyawalcya went to the sun and bewailed his loss, when this luminary obtained for him a new, or second revelation, termed the *white*, or pure, in contra-distinction to the first or black. He taught this to fifteen pupils, each of whom originated a school.

The Sama Veda, having been learnt by *Jaimini*, he instructed his son in it, who founded a separate school, from which sprang two others, and they branched off into one thousand more.

The Atharvana, was taught to *Sumantu*, who divided his knowledge between two others.

Each Veda consists of two parts, the *Muntras* or prayers, the

* Colebrooke *Asiatic Researches*, Vol. 8, p. 383.

complete collection of which is termed a *Sanhita:* and the *Brahmanas* or precepts. The first differs but slightly in the numerous texts, the latter so considerably, that what is taught in some schools, is rejected in others. The argumentative portion, entitled *Vedanta*, is contained in tracts termed *Upanishads*.

The Brahmanas of the Vedas, instituted full directions for official duties, detailing those for each. The priests were divisible into four classes, the *Adhváryus* who according to the Yagur Veda, prepared the places for the ceremonies, the materials for offerings, and muttered invocations. The *Udgátris*, who sang the sacred hymns according to the Sama Veda. The *Hotri*, who recited in loud clear tones, the whole of the Rig Veda, its holy texts, its prayers, and invocations. The Brahmans who superintended the whole, had titles of honour, conferred upon those who were most learned in the Vedas. The priests were divided into two great divisions, the secular, and the regular clergy. A Brahman may be an householder, and also officiate as a priest, such belonged to the former class: but one who had gone through the prescribed devotional exercises, was of the latter.

Probably 600 years before the Christian era, many discussions arose concerning the correct reading of texts, the authenticity of certain hymns, and the authority for some of the practised rites: so it was proposed, to collect and inscribe the Vedas, which were accordingly written down, in the smallest possible space, in the form of aphorisms, and called *Sutras*. Consequent upon the mode in which they were written, from the first explanatory commentaries were necessary, which were many in number. The Brahmanas were likewise condensed into the *Kalpa Sutras*, which were so plain, that many preferred the study of the easier condensation, to the more abstruse Brahmanas.

Owing to the form of the collected Vedas, disputes arose as to their meaning on various points, and different schools of Hindu philosophy obtained places. Three great systems became pre-eminent. The *Sankhya* which is said to have been written by Kopila, one of the seven Rushis or penitents. In it nature without a god may be said to be advocated. The *Nyaya* attributed to Gautuma, which asserts the existence of a supreme Deity, and that everything consists of indestructible ultimate atoms. The *Vedanta,* the composition of Bádáráyan, or Veda Vyása, which attributes all to Brahm.

The *Sankhya* (reason, or judgment,) is amongst the earliest works of the philosophic age: it may be said to be, the Vedas examined by reason, in contradistinction to Brahmanical assertion. For many years it was considered heretical. It has two divisions, differing as to the existence of the Deity.

Kopila taught, that there were two agencies, substance and spirit: that each existed in a dormant state from all eternity, and would continue undestroyed to the end of time. That the two were separated, but at length through the assistance of nature, they became re-united: and thus twenty five secondary products were formed. All evil to the soul, was caused by its union with the body, or substance by which it came into communion with the material world, consequently the great wish should always be for the soul to be freed from the body, and its transmigrations to cease. Whoever learnt the Sankhya, it was said would attain to this most desirable end. From this it appears probable, the Buddhist sect arose. The Yoga doctrine added, the existence of a Supreme Being, Aum, which performed the part assigned by Kopila to nature, and declared that intense devotion to him, would cause transmigrations to cease.

The *Nyaya,* advocated the existence of a Supreme Deity, it is divisible into two parts, the first consisting of an enquiry into truth, the second into objects existing in the universe. It asserted, that everything was sprung from atoms, or ultimate particles, that were indestructible, and consequently eternal.

Perfect beatitude, or the restoration of the soul to its original state of rest, by a cessation of its transmigrations, and its union with the body being no longer sustained, was said to be only obtainable by a perfect knowledge of truth, which embraced many topics. The soul was divided into two kinds, the animal, and the supreme.

The *Vedanta.* The design of this system, was to exhibit the scope of the Vedas in a classified form. They were considered to consist of eleven Upanishads or inspired writings, learning was said to be reserved for the twice born.

Aum was given as the Supreme, "when there was neither day "nor night He was, who is without darkness, and pure goodness alone." The Hindu notion of Aum, is thus beautifully rendered,* "perfect truth: perfect happiness: without equal, immortal, absolute unity: whom neither speech can describe, nor mind comprehend: all pervading: all transcending: delighted with his own boundless intelligence: not limited by space or time: without feet, moving swiftly: without hands, grasping all worlds: without eyes, all surveying: without ears, all hearing: without an intelligent guide, understanding all: without cause, the first of all causes: all ruling: all powerful: the creator, preserver, transformer of all things: such is the great one."

This Supreme Aum,† or Brahm, is considered to pervade all space. "If God leaves the system of man which he pervades, then what of it can remain. Not through their vital powers, do mortals remain alive: they live through him, by whom those powers are themselves sustained." At death the speech of the dying Hindu, and his exterior faculties, (said to number ten,) are believed to be absorbed into the mind, which along with the other vital functions, retires into the breath: the breath recedes into the soul, which attended by all its faculties, retreats into a rudimentary body composed of light. This spirit with its frame of light, remains intact, during all its transmigrations, until the dissolution of all things, when it merges into the Supreme Aum.

Thus the spirit of all, is a portion of the supreme spirit at the first, and merges into it at the last. The followers of the *Vedas*, according "to the theology which is explained in the *Vedanta*, considering the human soul as a portion of the Divine and universal mind, believe that it is capable of perfect union with the divine essence: and the writers on the *Vedanta*, not only affirm that this union and identity, are attained through a knowledge of God, as by them taught: but have hinted, that by such means, the particular soul becomes God, even to the actual attainment of supremacy."‡

Men are said to be born in ignorance, "living in the midst of

---

* *Sir Wm. Jones* Vol. vi. p. 418.

† The three mystical letters AUM are said to mean, the Creator, preserver and destroyer: and like the mystical name of the Deity, HVH, amongst the Jews, is never pronounced aloud.

‡ *H. T. Colebrooke*, Asiatic Researches, Vol. ix, p. 289.

"ignorance, and believing themselves to be wise, fools frequently are "led astray, through crooked paths, like a blind man led by a blind "man." Man's consciousness is asserted to be a delusion, until the soul is freed from which, it must undergo a series of transmigrations, the cessation of which is the commencement of true happiness.

There is an inferior liberation of soul, obtainable by religious merit, sacrifices, and ceremonies; or by faith. "He who performs "his actions for ME, intent on ME, devoted to ME, free from interest, "and from enmity towards any being, comes to ME."

A superior liberation of soul, is affected by a true and complete comprehension, of what Brahm is, and man's relation to him: this must consist, in understanding that all is Brahm, who is the only real thing in the universe: this must be weaved into the believer's nature, embraced by his inmost soul. To obtain this, profound meditation is necessary, and the mode is pointed out. Man must understand, the non-existence of his own individuality, as apart from Brahm. His proudest wish, his chief thought, should be, to discover that he has no separate existence.

There are three degrees of rewards held out. Those deserving of the least go to Indra's heaven, where having expended their good works, they are born again into the world. The second go to Prajapathis, or Brahma's heaven, where they enjoy without the power of action, and after a time are born again, and carry their good works with them. The highest rewards are kept for him, who has learnt wisdom, and obtained a distinct understanding, that he is a portion of Brahm. This may be obtained in this world, and after it is attained, good and evil are to him unknown. "He can do "neither good, or evil." "He does not become greater by good deeds, "nor less by evil ones." Now his passions may have free vent, now his vices or his virtues may hold unlimited sway, for at his death, he will be at once absorbed into Brahm, transmigrations will be to him unknown. "As rivers flowing go into the sea, and lose their "name and form, so the wise freed from name and form, gain him "who is supreme, perfect, and splendid."

The *laws of Menu* (who has been asserted to be either Noah or else the son or grandson of Brahma,) are the production apparently of fourteen distinct persons, commencing about nine centuries before

Christ, and extend over a long period of years, marking a progressive era.* *Sir W. Jones* states, that many learned Hindus, consider some of these laws, were only enacted for the earlier stages of civilization in the world, and are now obsolete. *Namboories* do not hesitate to say, that Hinduism in Malabar, in many of its great essentials, differs from the rules laid down in the Shastras. In the laws of Menu, are regulations for the treatment of conquered nations, who were to be kept roaming about from place to place, not allowed any settled residence unless as perpetual slaves, shunned by the higher classes, and only permitted the possession of pariah dogs, and asses. They were obliged to execute all criminals, for which they received the culprits' clothes, bedding, and ornaments. Even their apparel was to be that of deceased persons, and their ornaments only of iron.†

Hard again are the laws of Menu upon the lower castes, "the "impure can never be relieved from bondage, though he may be "emancipated by a master. How can he whom God has destined to "be the slave of the Brahmans, ever be released from his destiny by "man?" Though an inferior killing a superior suffered death, a Brahman slaying another had his property confiscated, his head shaved, he was branded on the forehead, and banished. Should he slay a Schatriya, he was fined one thousand cows, and a bull. A Vysia's life cost him one hundred cows, and a bull. A Sudra's ten cows, and a bull; but pariahs and out-castes, were not mentioned. A Sudra was valued at the sixteenth part of a Brahman.

Towards their close, these laws most distinctly repeat, that there is but one God, "the principal object is, to obtain from the Up-"anishad, a true knowledge of one Supreme God." No mystical union of a triad is alluded to, and though respect is directed to be shewn to idols, their adoration is reprobated, whilst offerings to them, are not even alluded to. Still there is this great difference between the Vedas, and the laws of Menu: for in these latter,

* The ages of the world, are divided into the *golden*, when men lived 400 years: the silver, when they lasted 300: the brass, when they had sank to 200: and the iron, when a further reduction to 100 occurred.

† This may be one reason, why the castes in Malabar, below the Nairs, call their silver, copper: their copper, iron, &c.

it is asserted, that *the substance of the Creator* was the efficient cause, in the formation of all things: whereas the Vedas distinctly state, that they were all created by *the will of the Creator*. It must be here distinctly mentioned, that no Hindu questions in the sligbest degree the truth of the Vedas, but merely the construction placed upon them.

The age of the *Puranas*, or eighteen legendary poems, which may be fairly considered the worst period of the Hindu religion, now began: and it is surmised, continued between the eighth and sixteenth centuries, of the Christian era. Then the principle of one Supreme God was neglected, other divinities were by degrees introduced,* mortals became canonised and deified, sects were created by priests for their own benefit, and the sanctity of their order for their own aggrandisement. The doctrine was advanced, that faith in saints or deified mortals, was more efficacious than good works, and ceremonial observances, than a well spent life.

Some of the heavens mentioned in these poems, can hardly be deemed a place in which decorous, or even slightly respectable persons would desire to find themselves, for there deeds of the most abominable description are asserted to be of common occurrence.

The world is said to have lain in embryo in the mind of Brahm, until the creation: when he spoke, light appeared: from himself came the inert matter to fill up space: water was condensed from around, seeds appeared and vegetated.

Again Brahm spoke, and on the surrounding water, floated a golden egg, in which were three emblems, of wisdom, power, and destruction, or birth, increase, and death, in the forms of the gods, Brahma, Vishnu, and Siva: or the first of the nature of earth, the second of water, and the third of fire. The symbols are, red for Brahma signifying matter, blue for Vishnu signifying space or water, and white for Siva in contrast to the black night of eternity.

* *Paterson* gives the three first symbols of the Deity as follows: To the *Swan*, on which Brahma rides, he attributes purity, justice, and truth, it being a pure unspotted fowl, that swimming amongst the waters of the world, is distinct from, and unsullied by them, however filthy they may be. The *Garuda* of Vishnu, is the full blaze of day, the dazzling truth. The *Bull* of Siva, has a virtue in every joint, his three horns are the three Vedas, and his tail ends, where injustice commences.

The shell of the egg is said to have burst into 14 fragments, seven flying upwards formed as many superior worlds, the remainder passing downwards, were converted into an equal number of inferior ones.

Another version was, that Brahm having created nature in the form of a material woman, *Bowaney* the mother of the gods, she produced three eggs, which enacted the part of the one just mentioned: having done this, she became resolved into three female forms, thus creating a wife for each.

A third mode was, that Brahma created Viraj, who either continued the work of creation, or created Menu to do so.

The Vishnuites assert, that as Vishnu lay sleeping on the ocean, from him sprang a lotus, which gave birth to Brahma. Or else that Brahma, Siva, and all the minor gods, were created from his substance.

However these three gods were created, it is admitted, that forthwith Brahma and Vishnu, commenced a strife concerning which was the eldest. As they were quarrelling, Siva suddenly appeared, and affirmed that he was older than either, but would willingly resign his right, to whichever of them could find the crown of his head, or the soles of his feet. Brahma at once ascended, and although he discovered nothing, returned, declaring that he had found a cow, and likewise produced some of the screw pine, which he asserted he had gathered there. Sivà became very angry, at hearing this untruth, and prophecied that Brahma would never have sacred rites performed to him: at the present day, he is said to have only one temple raised to him throughout Hindustan, whilst the screw pine, is never used in religious ceremonies.

The disciples of Brahma assert, that as he burst from his shell, or else at a later period, he was directed to continue the work of creation. That above him grew the blue expanse of sky, whilst below sprang the earth. He ordered the waters to recede, and dry lands appeared. He peopled the world with men, into whose breasts he implanted discrimination between good and evil. At the same time, he endowed these mortals with good and bad passions, and five senses were added, for the purpose of connecting their internal faculties, with the external or material world.

Such were the three first Hindu gods, whose origin is thus accounted for by *Paterson*,* and others : viz., that the most ancient Brahmanical religion, simply attributed to the Deity the wonders that filled the surrounding space : due to his creative, protective, and destructive powers. To make this more plain, they attempted in time to explain these attributes by hieroglyphics, maybe letters had not then been invented, or that signs and emblematical figures, were better understood by the mass of the people. Thus it occurred, that three figures representing the three great attributes of the Divinity, became respectively known, as Brahma, Vishnu, and Siva : the Creator, Preserver, and Destroyer for the purpose of renewal.

As years rolled on, the images† became considered more than mere emblems of the attributes of the Deity, and the mass of Hindus, believed them to be representatives of three distinct divinities. Sects then became instituted, some of which took one for their immediate object of adoration, whilst others preferred another. After a time the followers of Vishnu, and those of Siva, invented new symbols, as descriptive of the special attributes of their particular Deity.

Then arose contentions for pre-eminence, and at this time the worship of Brahma became suppressed, whilst the followers of Vishnu temporarily succumbed to those of Siva. But soon religious crusades raged amongst these two sects. The *Sunnyassies* fighting for the superiority of Vishnu : the *Vairagies* or Bairagies for that of Siva. Sometimes victory attended one, sometimes the other, and bloodshed, destruction and misery, overspread the Hindu lands.

Returning to the three gods, *Brahma* is usually represented dressed in white, having four heads, arms, and hands, symbolical of earth, air, fire, and water, holding the Vedas of which he was the author. He has a ladle, to pour out holy water for religious ceremonies : a rosary to count prayers upon : and a chatty for ablution. He is generally seen riding upon a swan. Sometimes he is represented with three hands, due it is said to Siva having cut off one, and ordered his worship to cease, because when the Brahmans were van-

---

* *Asiatic Researches*, Vol. 8, page 44.

† "The Brahmanical worship is generally divided into the *Narganey Pooja*, "and the *Sarganey Pooja* : or the worship of the great invisible God, and "the worship of idols."

quished, he refused to acknowledge it. He is reputed to have originally possessed five heads, and the first was amputated by Siva, in the following way. The Gods having invented intoxicating liquors, all became in a state which must have been peculiarly obnoxious to sober persons. At this time they committed actions too disreputable to detail, and too disgusting to insert. Brahma boasted, that he was as great as Siva, who threatened to cut off one of his five heads. At last Brahma uttered a curse upon whoever should drink intoxicating liquors, so Siva and he became friends. Subsequently when he asserted his superiority, Siva actually carried his threat into effect and cut off one head. Bloody sacrifices are never offered to Brahma.

Vishnu the preserver, is considered an emblem of goodness, and is the Deity which the majority of the Cochin Hindus, more especially pay their vows to. He has about one thousand names, and is generally represented as a comely young man, of a dark azure colour, dressed as a king, and crowned with a Royal diadem. Or else reclining on a coiled seven headed cobra, or hooded snake, *(Ananta,)* which expanding its hoods over him, forms a canopy shielding him from the sun's rays. Or he may be perceived riding on the eagle *garuda*, a compound of a bird and a man: or on a Brahmanee kite.

Vishnu is represented with four hands, in one he holds a shell of the genus *Buccinum*: in the second a quoit, or wheel, which emits flames on being thrown: in the third a mace, his emblem of civic authority: in the fourth a lotus, either designating the flower from which Brahma sprung, or else typical of water. Before his image no animals are killed, only fruit, flowers, vegetables, milk, honey, and incense, are offered up: whilst his followers *profess*, never to eat animal food. There are no festivals to Vishnu, but there are to his incarnations.

Vishnu is the Hindu Avatar, nine times has he been incarnated, and descended on the earth, at his tenth advent, all things it is said are to be consummated, and the world resolved into himself. These incarnations no doubt are mere symbols, thus disciples of religious teachers were formerly termed their spiritual sons, or are even mentioned as their incarnations. Vishnu's nine incarnations, were as follows:

The *first* was a fish *(Matsia)*, which he assumed when the Supreme

Creator sent a flood which covered the earth: to his pectoral fin was bound a vessel, wherein a holy man and seven persons found refuge, along with pairs of the various animals which inhabited the earth. The holy man was *Menu Vaivaswata,* or the sun-born, who with seven other sages, disembarked after the subsidence of the flood, upon the holy mountain Meru,* from whence their posterity descended into the plains of India. Whilst the earth was submerged, a bad spirit *(Hayagriva,)* stole the books of the Vedas from Brahma, who was asleep, and flung them into the flood, whence Vishnu in his fish like form, rescued them.† It has been asserted, that it was not the substance of the god, but merely his spirit, that was within the fish-like body.

The *Second* was a tortoise *(Kachyapa,)* which form he took, when he perceived the world's foundations giving way, and sinking into a sea of milk, when he supported it on his back. Another version of this is, that after the world's destruction by water, the *Soors* or good genii, assembled on the summit of the golden mountain Meru, to meditate upon the best means of discovering the *Amreeta,* or waters of immortality, or as others have believed, the "reanimation of nature as an indestructible whole," after the desolation of the deluge. It was first considered necessary to agitate the ocean, by the rapid rotation of the mountain Mandar. The genii asked Vishnu's advice and assistance to help them in their task, which was accomplished in the following manner:

The great serpent Ananta, wound itself around the mountain, which was placed upon the body of a tortoise: the god Indra taking the serpent by the tail, used him as a rope is employed in a churn. The churning of the ocean was tremendous, the harder Indra pulled Ananta's tail, the more rapidly revolved the mountain Mandar. Every thing having life was destroyed, from the beast on the earth, to the fish in the ocean: and from the tree, to the sea-weed. The result of this great destruction of life was, the creation of a milk-like

---

* The exact situation of the mountain Meru, has not been defined, but it is generally believed to be located to the north of Hindustan.

† Some believe that Vishnu did not rescue the book of the Vedas, or *Sacred laws,* from the flood, but restored the *law of nature,* and the natural order and connection of the elements, which the flood had subverted.

juice, which arose from the ocean, and was the much wished for Amreeta, or waters of immortality.

The *third* was a boar, *(Varaha,)* which form he took when he found the giant Hirinacheren, had rolled the earth into a shapeless mass, and carried it to the lower regions, or a muddy abyss. Lifting it out with his tusk, he replaced it in its proper position.

The *fourth* was a monster, *(Narasingha,)* in which form he came to destroy a brute who ruled the world. Originally this tyrant had received Brahma's blessing, on account of his religious austerities, with the promise that he should neither die in the day, or night time: in earth, or heaven: by fire, water, or the sword, nor fall a victim to any mortal. Relying on this blessing, he commenced a series of wars and conquests, until he became the tyrant of the world: and besides all this, he had a son whom he wished to destroy, but whom Vishnu had promised to protect.

One evening between day and night time, standing under the droppings of the thatch, (Hindus denominate such a place "without "the world,") the tyrant asked his son where his friend Vishnu resided? everywhere was the answer. "Then" said he, "he must "be in this pillar, and if so I will kill him." Forthwith he struck the pillar, when from it emerged Vishnu, in the form of the monster Narasingha, half a man and half a beast, who at once killed him, and subsequently became intoxicated on his blood.

The *fifth* was a dwarf, *(Vamana,)* which form he took, to rid the world of king Balee, who was oppressing mankind. To obtain this king's favour, he served him most faithfully, and the monarch became so pleased, that before all his nobles, he told him to choose his own reward. "Give me" he replied, "as far as I can stride in "three steps." This was immediately acceded to. His first was half way round the world, his second brought him to his original starting point, and nothing being now left, he claimed to place his foot on the king's crown, whilst he was wearing it. This he did with so much force, that he pressed him down into the bottomless pit, where he still reigns.

The *sixth* was as a priest *(Parasu Rama,)* also called Rama of the battle axe. He came in this form to destroy the Schatriyas, who had declared themselves opposed to sacrifices, and the worship of idols.

He had numerous adventures, and as already mentioned, (page 38), obtained Malabar, from the depths of the ocean, as a place for Brahmans to reside in.

The *seventh* was as a prince, *(Rama)* of the moon or bow. He destroyed the giant of Ceylon, Ravana, who possessed ten heads, and twenty arms. He had carried away Rama's wife Seeta, with whom he safely arrived at Ceylon. Rama pursued Ravana, but first entered into an alliance with a monkey king, who sent his monkey general Hunaman, to discover where Seeta was.

Hunaman, began searching for Seeta, whom he discovered was in Ravana's garden in Ceylon. As Hunaman was enacting the spy, he unfortunately was made a prisoner, when as a punishment, his tail was oiled, and then set fire to. Attempting to blow out the fire, his face became singed, and permanently blackened, so all his tribe, had their physiognomies turned the same colour, which should any one doubt, they have only to examine the Hunaman monkey, *Semnopithecus entellus,* which with its black face, may to this day be found along the western Ghauts.

On Hunaman with his blackened face, returning to Rama with the intelligence of where Seeta was to be found, they immediately departed for Ceylon. But Rama was unable or unwilling to swim over to the Island, so the monkeys under Hunaman, collected large stones from northern India, and throwing them into the sea, formed stepping stones, over which Rama proceeded to Ceylon, where he destroyed Ravana,* and recaptured Seeta.

It has also been alleged, that when sufficient stones had been deposited in the sea, the line of monkeys who were bringing more, received an order to cease their labours, when each at once threw down his

---

* After Vishnu in the form of Rama had killed Ravana, the wife of the latter came and prayed for a blessing, and he promised she should never be a widow. Then discovering to whom he had made this promise, he directed Hunaman to constantly heap up wood on Ravana's funeral pyre, which he continues until the present time. Until the fire goes out, Ravana's body cannot be considered to be consumed, and until it is, his wife is not a widow. Should a Hindu be asked for a proof of the truth of this, he directs one to place a finger in either ear, when the noise of the fire still burning may be distinctly heard.

load where he stood, and thus the long line of the western Ghauts was formed. It is a little unfortunate for this legend, that in his previous incarnation, Vishnu was said to have inhabited these Ghauts, perhaps the monkey army increased their elevation.

The *eighth* incarnation was *Kristna*, a man of very bad morals, and an especial favorite with the female part of the population. The less said of his doings the better, what would now be called murders, were amongst his lesser crimes. His bones are believed to rest within the wooden image of Juggernaut, which is triennially renewed. The bones are then most respectfully taken from the old idol, and deposited inside the new one. The officiating Brahman never sees the bones, for whilst removing these precious relics, he covers his eyes, as a sight of them it is asserted, would cause his instantaneous death.

The *ninth* was a warrior *Buddha*, distinguishable by his long asinine ears, and curly hair. He taught that it was sinful to take the life of lower animals, steal, tell untruths, drink intoxicating liquors, or indulge in other evil propensities, but his especial object is said to have been, to abolish human sacrifices, believed to have been enjoined by the Vedas.

The *tenth* unfulfilled Avatar, is to be an avenger, or Judge, *Kulkee*, with seven crowns upon his head, whilst in his hand he will carry a sword. He is to destroy the wicked, burn up everything, and then re-create a new world, having no wickedness in it.

Vishnu under different names, is the god of Malabar. In Travancore, he is termed "Palmanabha Sawmy," and the Hindus assert, that to him belongs the country. Every new Rajah of Travancore, before commencing his reign, goes to the Pagoda, and receives the high title, of Sre Palmanabha Dausa, or Vishnu's head servant. He is given a sword, whilst a belt is put over his shoulder, and having received a cloth, and some rice, he henceforth reigns, as the Deity's viceregent, promising to return him the country, whenever he shall personally come to claim it!

Vishnu is said to have as wives, *Lutchmee*, the goddess of prosperity, and *Surwasvatee*, the goddess of learning. At each of his incarnations, his wife is supposed to be also incarnated, and although their forms are represented in mortal shapes, their heads are the same as those of the animals on which their Lords came, as of a lion, an elephant, &c., or those on which they rode, as a bull, swan, eagle, &c. These goddesses, appear originally to have been intended to typify a female or passive energy, attached to each god.

Siva is the third god, of the Hindu triad, and has as many aliases as Vishnu, some of the best known being, "the enemy of demons," "the moon crested," "the Lord of devils," "the conqueror of death," "the bearer of the tiger's skin," "the Lord of the hills," and "the Lord of the moon." He is the destroyer with a view to renew, and is believed to have been taken from Adam. He is thus described in the Puranas. "He wanders about, surrounded by ghosts and "goblins, inebriated, unclothed, with dishevelled hair, covered with "the ashes of a funeral pile, ornamented with human skulls and "bones, sometimes laughing, and sometimes crying."* He has three eyes, representing, past, present, and future: a trident in one of his four hands, which may typify heaven, earth, and the lower regions, and signify that he rules three worlds: in the second a cord, wherewith to strangle the wicked: his third is bent downwards, as if inviting petitioners towards him: his fourth is raised as if in blessing. Round his neck, is sometimes seen a string of human skulls, signifying his destructive powers, as regards the generations of mankind. In his ears are serpents, representing immortality.† Sometimes he holds a ray of lightning in his hand, as a symbol that fire is under his control. He is occasionally represented, riding upon a dog, and is then designated, "Regent of Benares," the holy city of the Hindus.

Siva divides with Vishnu the adoration of the millions of Indian Hindus, still the orthodox worshippers, do not address their exclusive prayers to one Divinity. It has been asserted, that Siva having been poisoned from drinking the waters which first arose from the ocean when churned by Auanta, the good spirits became alarmed,

---

* *Kennedy's Researches*, page 291.

† The serpent appears as a type of the evil one, to have always had altars raised for his service, to deprecate his anger. As this reptile is long lived, and yearly changes his skin, it after a time became to be considered, as almost immortal, and employed to typify immortality.

and the evil ones filled with triumph, hoping that he would die. But *Doorga* took him in his arms, and by the aid of incantations, restored him to health. This is the first place, where the efficacy of incantations are alluded to, for the purpose of destroying the power of poisons. Although Siva recovered, an indelible blue mark was left on his throat, which is the reason, why he is sometimes called the "blue throated God." It is to Siva the Vairagies perform their abominable rites, and before one of his numerous aliases, or those of his wife Kali, persons torture themselves, to carry into effect, vows already made; as piercing the tongue, or swinging by means of hooks fixed into their flesh. These persons have attained so sublime a state, that when death occurs, their souls are believed to go direct to a superior world, and to be exempt from transmigrations.

Other minor deities exist, but their numbers render them too numerous to name. They preside more immediately over the sea, air, fire, and water, the sun, the moon, and such like: whilst the goddesses are equal in number to the gods. *Lutchmee*, is the wife of Vishnu, who is usually mentioned, and *Doorga*, or Kali, that of Siva. To this last malevolent spirit, robbers pray before commencing their deeds of violence and bloodshed.

The Saktis, or evil spirits, are very numerous, presiding over all misfortunes, accidents, sicknesses, and crimes: new ones are constantly coming into being, and old ones sinking into oblivion. Some are considered to be the souls of those who have committed suicide, or died from such diseases, as preclude their either reaching heaven, or descending into the worlds beneath. In company with devils, they haunt mankind, striving to render them as miserable as they are themselves. To keep them quiet, propitiatory offerings are made. One of these evil spirits, most dreaded in the Cochin and Travancore states, was Palaveshun, a Maraver of a low family, but whose numerous murders and robberies, had become celebrated, and at the latter end of the last century, he was feared even as far as Madras. To propitiate him, thousands of infants received his name.

As the Supreme Being it is considered, can never be the author of evil, or cause pain to mankind, his worship is not deemed essential, like that of evil spirits, the originators of all human miseries, consequently offerings to the latter, have in many places totally superseded those to the former. The same principle is carried out with regard to their earthly masters, for the kind and indulgent one, is not so well served, as he who is severe and strict.* The first the Hindu says, " is a good man, he will not hurt me, the latter a severe " one, he may punish me."

During the rebellion in Travancore in 1809, a Captain Pole was mortally wounded. After his death, he was buried about 20 miles distant from the field of action, in a sandy waste: a few years subsequently his worship was established by the Shanars, not because they feared his spirit, but that it might drive away the wild animals from that part of the country, where whilst alive he had been a most successful sportsman. Brandy, or arrack, and cheroots, were there offered up, but such have been discontinued during the last few years, as owing to extensive clearings, the wild beasts have diminished.

Offerings are made, that diseases may be cured, or limbs preserved healthy. Thus should an arm, eye, or ear, be diseased, a representation of the affected member is made of silver, and offered up. Iuppen is believed especially by the Chogans and lower castes, to roam the jungles: and in order that he should preserve them from harm, wooden representations of limbs, &c., are left in his domains, large heaps of them may sometimes be found in the jungles, and it is expected that they will not be removed by passers by. Many tales are current regarding the punishments inflicted by Iuppen, upon those who have interfered with these offerings that have been made to him; one gentlemen is now said by the natives to be lame, owing to his having contemptuously spurned a heap of them with his foot, and asked some Hindus who were present whether they imagined their god could avenge himself. Unfortunately owing to some cause, his leg subsequently became affected. Skulls of animals,

---

* This may be one reason, why ill governed Native states, are preferred by the inhabitants, to the well ruled British possessions. Natives appear better satisfied if kept in order by force, and bullied into reason, than if treated by kindness, and ruled with forbearance, which is synonymous amongst them, with cowardice, fear, or foolishness. So it is in magisterial matters, he who decides all cases upon their merits, without allowing bribes to sway him, has the epithet of "silly fellow," or "fool," affixed to his name!

such as cows or dogs, are placed in cultivated fields, and gardens, to prevent "the evil eye."

The good spirits are believed to hover around those of their relatives and friends, who remain behind them in this world: whilst their Rushis, obtain almost as much veneration as their Deities.

The Hindu adores nature in all its forms, from the sun in the sky, to the stone on the earth: the oxen and implements of agriculture are both alike venerated, as are also the kite soaring in the heavens, the monkeys in the trees, and the snakes on the ground: whilst killing a cow, has been considered as deserving of greater punishment, than slaying a low caste man.

The foregoing is a very brief and imperfect summary of the Hindu laws, and the objects of their adoration, from which it must be evident, that in olden times gods now recognized, never polluted the lips of the Hindus. The change has been gradual, and owing to symbols having by degrees become to be considered as real substances, and figures signifying attributes for real persons, first made into idols, and now termed gods.

The demon worship of the Aborigines of India, and also of the Buddhists, is absent from the old Hindu code, but exists everywhere in the Cochin state. Two Genii are supposed to be attendant upon every person, one recording his good actions, the other keeping a history of his bad ones. These accounts are finally to be examined by the Supreme Judge.

The Hindu *feasts* are frequent, but differ very considerably from those held elsewhere, the chief ones are as follows. When the sun commences its southern declination, the night time in Meru, the supposed abode of the gods begins, and in March, the feast of *Baranee* is held to Siva's wife, in most parts of India designated Kali, but in Cochin commonly known by the name of Bhagavadi or Bargawutti. This goddess has no symbol of time, but as the world is occasionally destroyed and renewed, her necklace of skulls denoting "destruction," is still perceived. She is a hideous idol, symbolical of bloody sacrifices, holding a veil to cover over the sun, and leave the world in impenetrable darkness. An account of the various ceremonies which are performed to avert her anger, it is needless to detail. Originally animals were typically held as deserving of destruction, signifying that man should destroy and root out his evil passions, each of which was typified by some beast. The multitudes took these symbolical representations as realities, and instead of destroying their bad passions, they slaughtered innocent creatures, and thus bloody sacrifices in time became offered up. As the Hindu religion extended itself, new nations saw the reality, ignorant of its being (or rather that it ought to be,) a symbol: therefore considering blood would be acceptable, increased the horrors, by offering up human victims. The Cranganore or Kodungaloor pagoda, is the most celebrated place, where the feast of Barance is held, and thousands resort thither, each carrying a live cock, whose head is cut off, and the blood poured forth in honor of Bhagavadi, whom the suppliants implore to protect them from diseases and misfortunes, throughout the ensuing twelve months.

The feast of *Vishoo*, or of the "Astronomical new year," is held in April, and appears to have many characteristics, in common with the Hoolie. This was one of the periods, when subjects in Malabar, were expected to bring their new year's offerings to the ruling Prince, or authorities under whom they were placed. The British Government finding this a great burden on the people, obtained a promise from the native Princes, that the exaction of presents, should be discontinued from 1790. It is consequently, now shorn of much of its ancient splendour.

The *Ohnam* is the great feast of the year, and occurs in August or September, on the day of the new moon. During the first fortnight of the latter month, usually about the tenth, the rains cease, nature is considered renovated, it is the return of the Malabar spring. Hindus now supplicate for a fruitful year, and pray for plenty. Every one now puts on new clothes, and employers are expected to make a present of a new cloth, to each of their yearly employees. Many throw away their old clothes, and toss their chatties out of their houses, which they adorn with flowers, and make as smart as possible. Games are played by the men; in the evening bon fires are lighted, and the sounds of music are heard from almost every quarter. It is believed that at this time, the god Vishnu, is wandering about in a variety of forms, for the purpose of ascertaining how his people are thriving, whether they are contented and happy, or are tyrannized over by their temporal Princes. Therefore each vies with his neighbour, to appear as happy and contented, as well as, as wealthy, as he possibly can.

The fast, or funeral rites, of *Putta* or *Bhutta Thanam,* (gifts to learned Brahmans,) is held at Tripoonterah, in the month of August. It is a ceremony of expiation, and was instituted in the time of a Rajah, who died in 1775, in memory of his mother, who expired in 1769.

The *Cocoanut Feast,* is held on the new moon of the month Chingum, or between August 15th and September 15th. At this time the south west monsoon is supposed to have terminated, cocoanuts and other fruits, are therefore taken to the sea, and launched into it. After this ceremony, the coast is considered open for country crafts, from Bombay southward.

The feast of *Pooja Wipoo,* known elsewhere as the "Dusserah," or ten days' feast, occurs about the end of September, or beginning of October. It was after this feast, that in olden times, the Pindarees "took the auspices," by trying to annex their neighbour's dominions, or to assist themselves to their property. Robbers and murderers did the same, and all looked upon it as a species of religious duty, with one proviso attached, that it was incumbent upon them to give a portion of their booty to the Idols. In the Cochin state, it is now held in a more peaceful manner, the Tailor takes his needle, the Scrivener his style, and all Artizans implore a blessing, upon the means by which they obtain their livelihood. The Rajah of Travancore commemorates this feast, by going to Curramunay, where a plantain tree and another are bound together, and into them he shoots a golden arrow. It is commonly said that this is done as a symbol of hunting, in pursuit of which he trusts that his implements of the chase will be blessed, but it is questionable, whether this custom did not in reality originate, in commemoration of Parasu Rama's famous shot with the long bow.

After the celebration of the Pooja Wipoo, there is another feast called the *Maha Murtiya Teyum,* or the "Feast of burnt sacrifices to the great Siva." Clarified butter is cast into the sacred fire, as an offering to the god, and the Deity is invoked to bless the country, and protect the Sovereign. This ceremony should properly speaking be performed once every twelve years, but owing to the great expense which it entails, it has of late been neglected, and is now only held, when considered from some causes absolutely necessary. It was celebrated in 1862, for the purpose of extending the life of the present Rajah. It lasted forty days, during which time Namboorie Brahmans from all parts were fed, and received also gifts in money. The expense has been estimated at about Rs. 20,000.

The *Tiwalee* or *Diwalee* festival, is held with great honour in October or November, and is celebrated by nocturnal illuminations, in honour of Carticeya.

Numerous, as are their feasts, Hindus show their sense, in this depressing climate, in having few fasts excepting for the Brahmans. One of the greatest of these occurs in March, and is hardly symbolical of politeness, as it is held, in commemoration of Siva's marriage.

When there is a deficiency of rain, an order is sent round to the various head men of villages, and the communities under them have to raise money, to pay the Brahmans to perform the necessary devotions, (viz., the *Jella Jebbum*, or "water prayer,") for rain. Should a stranger view some of these holy devotees, patiently standing up to their necks in a tank of water, hour after hour, he may rest assured, that there they, or some of their fraternity will remain, until rain descends upon the earth.

There are several sects of Holy men, or Ascetics, whose austerities are believed by the Natives to be great, their filth is certainly so. They ought to mortify the flesh, and be indifferent to hunger, thirst, heat, or cold: they should neglect no ceremonies, reproach no Brahmans, and destroy no life. Two or more Sunnyassies, live at Trichoor, who are said for years, not to have moved out of their huts, excepting to go to the Pagoda. As a rule, this class worship Vishnu, and the Bairagies or Vairagies, Siva.

Hindu idols, may usually be known by their representing monsters, with partly brutal heads, or hands. The Buddhist temples are semi globular at their summits, and their idols are seated cross legged. The Jains have twenty-four figures without a pyramid. All Hindu temples face the east, and as they have no windows, the aroma within, is as may be imagined, much too strong to be agreeable. The lingum is sacred to Siva.

In some places, where the Brahmans are occasionally dissatisfied with the amount of offerings they receive, they give out that the Deities are in chains for debt, and show them in this state to the devotees. Or else they are sometimes said to be seriously ill, owing to their affliction at the manifest decrease of piety amongst their worshippers, and to have determined in consequence, to abandon this ungrateful country, and remove to other parts, where a more religious population will render them due honour. But they are subsequently appeased by offerings, which are regarded as a symbol of renewed devotion.

The idols are consecrated by Brahmans, who commence their proceedings, by invoking the Deity, to take up his abode in the image: prayers are then muttered, and the ceremony terminates, by their pouring oil and ghee over it. Subsequently if the figure is touched by any person not a Brahman, or by any lower animal, (with the exception of a cow,) it is defiled: the extent of the pollution, being in accordance with the degradation of the being who destroyed its sanctity. The spirit is believed to take flight, and the image is no longer regarded as a god. If the idol be of clay, it must be thrown away as useless, or if of more valuable materials, it must be re-consecrated, the expense of doing which, depends upon the extent of the defilement sustained.

The religious observances of the Hindus are numerous, and appear to exist for every possible and impossible emergency, but as they are so many, they cannot be gone through by any devotees. Everyone therefore takes credit for what he has done, and deems the religious services he performs, sufficient for the purposes of devotion.

Should a child be born under an unfavourable constellation, it is considered to be illegitimate, but this reproach can be removed by a Brahman, on the receipt of a fee. As soon as it is born, its horoscope is drawn, for everyone is believed to have his doom written upon the crown of his head, where the coronal suture runs, the digitations of which are considered the writings of the Deity, and consequently a person's fate is said to be inscribed on his skull in bony characters, before his birth. Parents always desire sons rather than daughters, for " by the former they are reverenced, whilst the latter are only raised for others."

Marriages are performed, partly in the following way. The Bridegroom is received in state in a room by the Bride's father, according to the rules of the astrologers. " The jewels and other presents intend-"ed for him, are placed there: a cow is tied on the northern "side of the apartment, and a stool or cushion and other furniture "for the reception of the guests, are arranged in order. On his "approach, the Bride's father rises to welcome him, and recites a short "prayer, while the Bridegroom stands before him. After the com-"pletion of many ceremonies, presents suitable to the rank of the "parties, are then presented to the guests. At the marriage cere-"mony, the Bride is formally given by her father to the Bridegroom, "in this stage of the solemnity according to some rituals, but later "according to others. The hospitable rites are then concluded, by "letting loose the cow, at the intercession of the guests."

"Many more pages of ceremonies then follow, which lead to one "of more consequence, when the Bridegroom puts his left hand un-"der the Bride's hands, which are joined together in a hollow "form, with *cusa* grass, and then taking her right hand in his, he "recites the six following texts. *First,* I take thee for the sake of "good fortune, that thou mayest become old with me thy husband. "May the generous, mighty, and prolific sun, render thee a matron, "that I may be an householder. *Second,* be gentle in thy aspect, "and loyal to thy husband: be fortunate in cattle: amiable in thy "mind, and beautiful in thy person: be mother of surviving sons: "be assiduous at the five sacraments: be cheerful, and bring pros-"perity to our bipeds, and quadrupeds. *Third,* may the lord of "creatures, grant us progeny, even unto old age: may the sun "render that progeny conspicuous. Auspicious Deities have given "thee to me. Enter thy husband's abode: and bring health to "our bipeds, and quadrupeds. *Fourth,* Oh Indra, who pourest "forth rain, render this woman fortunate, and the mother of chil-"dren: grant her ten sons, give her eleven protectors. *Fifth,* be "submissive to thy husband's father, to his mother, to his sisters, "and to his brothers. *Sixth,* give thy heart to my religious duties:

"may thy mind follow mine, be thou consentient to my speech. "May Vrihaspati unite thee unto me."*

Then follow many other ceremonies, and the husband places the Tali, around the Bride's neck: upon the Tali is engraved the image of the Deity, held in most estimation by their caste. The string is composed of 108 fine threads, dyed yellow with saffron, and the knot once tied, is in most parts of India indissoluble; it will presently be shown, why widowhood is almost unknown in Malabar, owing to the peculiar customs which obtain there.

On the fourth day, the Bridegroom takes the Bride to her new abode, where matrons are waiting to welcome her arrival. That is to say, if she is not too young, for marriages frequently take place before the age of ten years.

When so ill that recovery appears impossible, they have a species of "extreme unction" with Ganges water, or that in which the idol in the pagoda has been washed. At this period, presents of some description, especially cows, made to the Brahmans, will ensure a comfortable transmigration: whilst *scape goats*, are also permitted. Every one it is believed has to pass the burning river, over which those who have given a cow to the Brahmans, are assisted by one of those animals. Brahmans can become sureties, for the sins of the dying Hindu in the world to come. The sick man lays his hands on the Priest's head, and the latter repeats the following words, "I hereby take this man's sins upon me." Having said which, the scape goat Brahman, flies the house and country, for he has now become a most infamous out-caste, and even his life would probably be unsafe, from those of his former sect. A Brahman having received extreme unction, and absolution, in the belief that he is about to die, should he recover, becomes an out-caste as his spirit appears to have been rejected. Brahmans can expiate the sins of deceased persons, by swallowing portions of their burnt bones. *Scape goats* are sometimes made use of, to atone for the sins of persons or communities, when visited by sicknesses. The goat is invariably a black one, and covered with a black cumblie, garlands are placed around its neck, and after prayers and invocations have

* Colebrooke. *Forbes' Oriental Memoirs*, Vol. II, p. 310.

been muttered over it, it is led to the confines of a neighbouring jungle, to the sea shore, or the limits of the place, and there turned loose. Should it return, such is a very bad omen, but the Oolahders, the wild beasts, or the fishermen, generally prevent such an occurrence.

When *death* at last lays his tribute on a Hindu, and he pays his debt to nature, he hopes to be remembered in this world, by the works of utility which he has constructed. As the shadow follows the body, so good deeds are believed to accompany the soul, consequently canals, wells, bridges, and other works, are frequently spontaneous gifts from pious Hindus, for the benefit of their race. Death should not occur in doors, as the spirit is believed not to take its departure, with the same ease it would, were the dying person in the open air, and besides this, the house becomes defiled. The sick man should expire on the ground, as if death overtakes him on a bed, or mat, his spirit will be encumbered with them in the next world.

Amongst those who have regular wives, the female should just before her husband's death, dress herself, and as soon as he is no more, be convulsed with grief, for she is esteemed, in a ratio corresponding with the amount of her lamentations.

After death, but little time elapses before the *funeral ceremonies* commence. The body having been placed on the funeral pile, is set fire to by the eldest son or by the nephew, should he become head of the family, whilst he offers up the obsequies to the manes of his dead relatives. Beating of drums, and noisy music, rarely occurs, unless at the funeral of those below the caste of Nair. Ceremonies for the dead are gone through, on the anniversary of the death yearly, in accordance with the lunar calendar: whilst on the new and full moon, offerings are made on account of the departed.

During *the ceremony of incremation*, the Brahmans address the elements much in the following way. "Oh earth! to thee we com-
"mend our *brother:* of thee *he* was formed: by thee *he* was maintain-
"ed: and unto thee he now returns. Oh fire! thou hast a claim
"upon our *brother*, during *his* life *he* subsisted by thy influence on
"nature: to thee we commit *his* body: thou emblem of purity, may
"*his* spirit be purified on entering a new state of existence. Oh air!

"while the breath of life continued, our *brother* respired by thee: "*his* last breath has now departed; to thee we yield *him*. Oh water! "thou didst contribute to the life of our *brother:* thou wast one of "*his* sustaining elements. *His* remains are now dispersed: receive "thy share of *him*, who has now taken an everlasting flight."*

A death in a family causes pollution to the head of it, thus Brahmans are defiled 10 days: Schatriyas eleven: Vysias twelve: Sudras (including Nairs) thirteen. The first *visit of condolence* after a man's death is to his mother, as his widow is unrecognised, excepting in a few classes, and even then she comes after the mother. *Pollution* is of many varieties, too numerous in fact to detail. Should one of the higher castes touch, or in some instances approach one of the inferior classes, he must go through certain ceremonies, before he loses the effects of the pollution.

One of Siva's wives, named *Suttee,* is said to have died of grief, upon hearing her husband spoken badly of, and her name is now too well-known, to pass over in silence. Up to within a recent date, Suttee, or the burning of widows on their husbands' funeral pile, was considered one of the highest works a woman could perform, whilst in the next world, she would be permitted to live with her husband, the same number of years, she possessed hairs on her head, generally computed at 38,000,000. The Schatriyas are believed to have originated this rite, which was especially employed by the Rajpoots, amongst whose wives it became so fashionable to poison their husbands, that it was introduced by the men, as a law of self-preservation. It was believed that if a woman's hopes of earthly happiness ceased with her husband's life, she would be more likely to interest herself in his preservation, than in his destruction.

Under the same circumstances which in Europe preclude Capital punishments being carried into effect, Suttee was not allowed. Should a widow refuse to be burnt with her husband's corpse, she was considered disgraced, and had to devote her life as a dancing girl in the service of some Deity, or have her head shaved, was allowed to eat no betel, use no saffron water to colour her face, wear no coloured clothing, attend no joyous ceremonies, but was kept

* Forbes' *Oriental Memoirs.* Vol. II, p. 132.

in a state of servile degradation in her husband's family. Subsequently the Vysias followed this custom of the Schatriyas.

At the commencement of the present century, strict prohibitions against Suttee were promulgated by the Indian Government, and every succeeding year they became more stringent, until it was enjoined, "That should any woman feel disposed to burn with the "corpse of her husband, notice should be given to the Magistrate: "and should it be sanctioned, she must gather the firewood herself, "and prepare the pile without making any fence to it, and it should "be done in the presence of the Daroga. After putting a slow fire "to the pile, she must voluntarily get on it, and should any person "be found assisting, advising, and encouraging her in the horrid "deed, they should be prosecuted. As the flames touch her body, "should she wish to get off the pile, nobody should prevent her, and "should any person be found threatening her, in order to keep her "in the flames, that they should be prosecuted as murderers." On December 4th, 1829, Suttee or the burning, or burying alive of the widows of Hindus, was finally abolished in Bengal by Lord William Bentinck, and in Madras two months subsequently, whilst in Bombay within a year, by Sir G. Malcolm.

As already observed, the wish of the Hindu should be, that his spirit should in a future state be incorporated in the essence of the supreme Brahm. The spirit of the Brahman is nearest to this desirable re-union, and should he have been a good man, at his death, his desire will be accomplished. Should he have been an evil one, his soul goes to a place of torment, and after a certain purgatorial or expiatory process, it re-ascends to earth to occupy the body of some animal, for the period of torment is not eternal, but in accordance with the owner's demerits, and the soul must be cleansed in a body of affliction. Buddha had to wander 999 times: Vishnu 10: and Siva innumerable. All the bad spirits are under the inspection of the vigilant Yama, or Shahadeva, the "god of lamentations."

The origin of *transmigrations* is said to have been, that when some of the angels rebelled against the supreme god, he condemned them to eternal torments. After a time, at the intercession of the faithful angels, they were released, on promising amendment, and admitted to a state of probation. Worlds were created, and mortal bodies prepared for these apostate spirits. First animated in the bodies of lower animals, after a varying number of transmigrations, that of human beings was attained, when if the spirit failed to reform, it again had to pass backwards, through the lower grades.

By a process of transmigration of the soul, it gradually re-ascends until it again enters a Brahman's body, whom we will charitably suppose, will be a good man this time. Tumraj, is the appointed final judge of men's lives, or the judicial Deity, and is assisted by a secretary Chuttergopal. Good persons at each transmigration, are advanced one step onwards, towards the immortal Brahm : bad spirits, go one or more steps backwards. There are certain exceptions to this rule, thus if a Hindu dies at Benares, there is no need of becoming a Brahman before being rejoined to Brahm, consequently from many parts of India, good Hindus are always flocking in that direction. There is an account extant, of a certain wicked Brahman, whose soul was taken to a place of torment, but when his body was burnt, a crow flew away with one of his bones, and dropped it into the Ganges. Hardly had it reached those holy waters, when the culprit's soul was perceived emerging from the lower regions, in a splendid chariot, and evidently on its way to celestial bliss.

Some religious works of the Hindu's state, "he who steals rice "will go into Hell, at his next birth he will become a crow for 18 "years, afterwards a heron for 12 years, and then a diseased man. "He who kills an animal, or laughs at the reading of the Puranas, "will, after enduring excessive torment, become a snake, then a "tiger, a white heron, a crow, and lastly a man having an asthma. "He who steals alms will sink into Hell, and afterwards be born "blind, and afflicted with consumption. He who lives in affluence "without communicating of his substance to others, will be punish-"ed in Hell 30,000 years, and then be born a musk rat, then a "deer, and then a man whose person emits an offensive odour and "who prefers bad to excellent food."*

Good souls leaving their tenements of clay, proceed through beautiful paths, having silver streams murmuring along either side. Over-

---

* Weitbrech's *Missions in Bengal.*

head they are shaded by fragrant and luxuriant trees, which at every step shower down flowers on the passing spirit. Hymns and sweet sounds resound in the otherwise still atmosphere, and angels' melodious strains, are heard in the distance.

Bad souls having in pain parted from the body, pass naked, weary, parched with thirst, and covered with blood and dirt, through dark and dismal roads, sometimes under hideous trees, from out of which evil spirits appear in terrible forms: again emerging from these dark passages, they have to proceed over burning sands, or sharp cutting stones, which wound them at every step. Occasionally showers of red hot coals, or burning ashes, are rained down upon them. Shrieks and wailings are heard overhead, whilst imagination must conceive, what they will find when their journey is completed.

The Hindu satisfied with the religion of his forefathers, is disinclined to enter upon any arguments respecting that of others. He does not deny that either Christianity or Mahomedanism are true, he merely believes them unsuited to himself. Should miracles be adduced, he closes discussion by bringing forward greater. He points to Malabar as having been created for the Brahmans, or talks of the bridge to Ceylon erected by Hunaman and his monkey army. He placidly performs his rites, and keeps his festivals, without interrupting the observances of others, so long as they leave him in peace to perform his own.

The institutes of Menu say, that the Supreme Being selected man, the centre of knowledge, to have dominion and authority over the remainder of creation. Having bestowed on him comprehension and judgment, he gave him supremacy over the world, as far as its extreme limits, and when he had placed in his hands the controul and arbitrary disposal of all affairs, he appropriated to each tribe its own faith, and to every sect its own religion. Having introduced a variety of castes, and diversity of customs, he views in each different place, the mode of worship appointed to it.

A Hindu addressing Aurungezebe, complaining of his intolerance, said. "If your Majesty places any faith in those books by distinc-
"tion called Divine, you will there be instructed, that God is the God
"of all mankind, not the God of the Mahomedans alone. The Pagan
"and the Mussalman are equally in his presence: distinctions of

"colour are of his ordination: it is he who gives existence. In your "Temple to his name the voice is raised in prayer: in the house of "images where the bell is shaken, still he is the object of adoration. "To vilify the religions and customs of other men, is to set at "naught the pleasure of the Almighty."

The remarkable *institution of castes* amongst the Hindus, is perhaps a result of their early fondness for symbolical representations. It is probably a cunning invention of an unscrupulous Priesthood, who lusting for temporal power, altered the meaning of the symbols, and whilst giving themselves the pre-eminence, were also careful that it should be hereditary.

Man at first in a savage state, became as years rolled on, more and more civilized: luxuries were more general, and employments, trades, and professions multiplied. Different offices must have fallen to the lot of different classes of persons: some were Priests fattening on the credulity of their fellows: some subsisted by physical force as soldiers: some by cultivating the soil: and others by trades or manual labour. What more rational, than symbolically it should have been represented, that the Priests who expounded the law, and were considered the wisest of the people, should have derived their existence from Brahma's mouth, from whence the Vedas sprung? That the man of war, living by the strength of his arm, and ruling his fellows by the law of force, should be typified as created from the god's shoulder? That the agriculturist, who by tilling the soil provides sustenance for himself and others, and gives strength enabling man to stand fatigue, should be shown as coming from the divine thighs? Lastly, that those who subsist by manual labour, as artificers, servants, and slaves, to the higher classes, should be shown as coming from the feet of Brahma, they being the servile races?

These four classes, or *castes* denominated, *the Brahmans: the Schatriyas: the Vysias:* and *the Sudras*, are the divisions of which Hinduism now consists, whilst the out-castes are the Pariahs, a name derived from the Sanscrit word *Pari*, "abandoned," separated, having no part or lot with the Hindu sect. It is said by the Brahmans, that when Brahma created men, he asked each as he appeared what he wished to be, and received the answer, "Whatever duty we may be ordained to, that will we faith-

"fully perform:" and the four castes were directed what office each was to assume. The word *caste* is of Portuguese origin, (*Casta*, "a breed.") The native word *Varna*, means either caste or colour, and it is asserted, that the Brahmans were created white, the Schatriyas red, the Vysias yellow, and the Sudras black.*

The trivial word "caste," is one of most momentous import, a loss of it signifies a moral, and in olden times a civic death also. The share of the out-caste's inheritance, (if living in the Native State,) passes away, his funeral ceremonies are performed by his friends, who recognise him no more. Father, mother, wife, and children, loathe him: his mere presence contaminates those, who were previously his nearest and dearest friends. If he dies funeral rites are denied to his remains. He has become a thorough out-caste, and must so continue, unless he is below the caste of Nair, in which case, he can be purified by a slight ceremony, which will be alluded to further on.

The three superior Hindu castes,† are designated the "twice born," and as such are invested with the sacred thread, and may hear the reading of the Vedas, which privilege is denied to the Sudras, and the

---

* Castes existed amongst the Egyptians, Medes, Persians, and others. Castes are maintained amongst some Roman Catholic congregations in Malabar to this day. (See page 231.) Caste distinctions were observed in the Tanjore and other Protestant missions, from the time of Schwartz and Gerické, it was only July 5th, 1833, that Bishop Wilson declared, that the Native Christians had not followed the *advice* given by his predecessors for its discontinuance, that "in short under the name of Christianity, half the evils of Paganism are retained," and, that it "must be abandoned, decidedly, immediately, finally." In Tanjore the reading of the circular, "was received by the Native Christians with great displeasure, and they showed their views, by seceding in a body."—PERCIVAL, *Land of the Vedas.*

† In every place the above rank of castes does not hold good, thus a Nair who is a Sudra, would consider himself polluted, eating with an Oonee, who is an Ambalavassee, and wears the sacred thread. That caste is the cause of many of the evils of India, the *Abbé Dubois* declares to be a mistaken notion. Without caste, he believed the natives of Hindustan, would rapidly degenerate into a barbarous state: thus he held the Pariah who is without caste, as an example of how the want of it would act. The Abbé asserts, that a nation of Pariahs left to themselves, would speedily become worse than the hordes of Cannibals, that wander over the African deserts.

inferior classes. In speaking *generally* of Malabar, there are only two castes left, the Brahmans, and the Sudras: for the Schatriyas are very few in number, and Vysias very sparingly distributed.

It has been already mentioned, that Vishnu is the presiding Deity of these parts, though Siva's marks are more commonly perceived upon the people. Whilst painting on caste marks, prayers are muttered to the Deity in whose honor they are being applied. Some are made with red sandal wood, some with ashes, rice meal, earth taken from a sacred river, or the vicinity of some consecrated spot; sandal wood, saffron, and ashes, are more especially consecrated to the fire, sun, moon, or planets. Whilst earth, and rice meal, are usually only employed by the worshippers of Vishnu, and Lutchmee.

Caste marks are printed upon the forehead, breasts, or arms, and demonstrate devotion to some Deity, or sect. The trident on the forehead, is generally a distinctive mark of the followers of Vishnu, and horizontal white lines across the forehead, chest, and shoulders, those of Siva. But there are exceptions to this rule, the round mark which in some parts of India denote the worshippers of Siva, here usually distinguishes those of Vishnu, or of one of his incarnations, and the red dot those of either Rama, or Krishna, separately, or of the two conjoined. The marks in honour of Siva, are as a general rule, composed either of ashes, or cow dung.

The Brahmans divided Bharata, now known as Hindustan, into two divisions, the northern portion, or that extending from the Himalayas to the banks of the Nerbudda, where one division of them called Panjacowdars resided: and the southern, or that part between the Nerbudda and Cape Comorin including Ceylon, where the other division of them termed Panjadravadals were located. These were again sub-divided into three principal divisions, subject to an almost endless sub-division.

In the "Mackenzie Manuscripts," (No. 17, counter-mark 910,) there are stated to be fifteen different tribes of Brahmans in Malabar. In the Cochin state, they are often divided into five, the Dravada, Telinga, Carnatic, Mahratta, and Guzeratta. The common division is, the *Namboories** or those of the country, who are said to be an inferior

---

* The term Namboorie, is said to be derived from *Namboo*, "a paddle,"

race, and consequently are peculiarly proud and arrogant: the *Imbrans*, from Mangalore; the *Putters* or foreign Brahmans, who come generally from Coimbatore: and the *Konkanies*. The Ambalavassies, (who are not Brahmans,) are attached to the Temples, and act as Levites, they thread the flowers, tend the lights, &c.

Many of the feasts, and the days on which they are held, differ considerably from those in other parts of the Presidency, and even from those in the neighbouring state of Travancore. Much of the creed, and the customs, which obtain in Cochin, are not in accordance with the laws laid down in the Shastras. The very names of the castes differ from those in other places, thus a Pariah from the eastern coast, may approach quite close to a Namboorie Brahman without defiling him, unless he actually touch him, because he bears here the title of a Paandee. Consequently it will not be extraordinary, if many of the following remarks upon the Hindu castes of Cochin, appear strange to the dwellers in other parts of India.

The *Brahmans*, are regarded as emblems of the Deity, or of knowledge. They are a priestly, and dominant race, whose words are esteemed laws, and whose decrees are believed to have the power of condemning persons, to torment in a future state. Their office is stated to be to teach, preach, perform religious ceremonies, and make, or expound laws. They are said to owe the origin of their seven divisions, to the *seven Rushis*, who were saved by Vishnu, at the general flood, and after giving the example of a holy life on earth, were translated into Heaven, and are now visible, in the form of the seven stars, in the constellation of the "Great Bear," each of the brilliant luminaries of which, represent one of these lights of the sublunary world. As these illustrious individuals, existed before the Vedas were transcribed, the origin of the worship accorded to the stars in the firmament, might possibly be traced to their translation into the heavens.

The lives and persons of Brahmans, were protected by the most severe laws, for the punishment of offenders in this world, and the

---

which is used in this part of India, to steer boats with, and is believed to signify, that these Priests can steer persons, free from the shoals and quick sands, on which others less favoured are wrecked.

most awful denunciations of what they would suffer in a future state. They themselves are exempt from capital punishment, (in the Native State,) and their offences are treated with the utmost lenity, whilst transgressions against them are punished with the greatest severity. In ancient times, their religion directed austerities, and enjoined them not to engage in schemes of aggrandisement and ambition. But this system was of short duration, Kings were then advised, to take Brahmans for their confidential councillors, and all judicial authority not vested in Royalty, was entrusted to them. Thus they became in time the exponents of all laws, whether human or divine, and liberality to them became the first duty incumbent on all monarchs, whilst every religious ceremony, implied feasting the Brahmans, and making them handsome presents.

The *Abbé Dubois*, gives the following as being some of the reasons which preclude the possibility of the Brahmans having any esteem, or regard, for Europeans, and his observations are well worthy of consideration. The European eats the flesh of the sacred cow, whose destruction they look upon as worse than manslaughter, and eating the flesh of which, they esteem more horrible than Cannibalism.* He admits Pariahs as his servants, a class of persons whose very shadow causes defilement to the Brahmans. Sometimes they see him intoxicated in public, and drunkenness they regard as one of the most infamous vices. And again, he admits females to society, where they even dance in public, whilst in their opinion, all those who thus "amble and caper," are only fit for the lowest depths of degradation. European dress shocks them, and the use of leather causes the greatest disgust.

Unsatisfied with their enormous powers, desirous of extending the sphere of their gains, penances for sins became enjoined, but commutable by paying fines to the Priests. The same vein of legislation was perceptible in all their laws, thus should a Brahman discover a treasure he might keep it, any one else had to deliver it to the King, who usually divided it with the Priests. When heirs failed in any

* The Abbé also tells us, that in Mysore, the internal arrangements of a Hindu, are under the control of his spiritual guide, who in cases of grave delinquency, such as eating a porcupine, a snake, or an onion, has the power of expelling him from his caste.

class except the Brahmanical, property reverted to the Rajah, but with Priests to their caste. Exempt from taxation, if poor they had to be maintained by the King. They were, and are, prohibited from accepting offerings which have been made to Siva, but that law is now partially evaded.

So jealously are their Vedas guarded, that the Brahman may not read them even to himself, should a Sudra be present. If he assisted one of the servile class in sacrificing, taught him the law, or how to expiate his sins, he was condemned to the lowest depths in the next world, but now this law appears partially obsolete. If starving, a Brahman may accept dry grain from a Sudra, but should never receive any other gifts from him. The Nairs being rich people, are often looked upon more favourably by Brahmans, than is enjoined by their sacred laws.

Were the Brahman to live according to the precepts laid down in the Vedas, his life would be passed in the most severe austerities, laborious study, and close retirement. But taught from his infancy to believe, Malabar to be his lawful inheritance, and that to him alone pertains any right to its soil, he looks with contempt upon all those beneath him, and becomes the type of a thoroughly selfish man. Pity for his inferiors is to him unknown, and compassion for the starving slaves worthy only of his supreme contempt, expecting kindness and attention from all as his by right, he repays it to none.

A young Brahman should receive from his spiritual teacher, the sacred string, or "sacrificial cord," *(Poonool,)* when he is seven years of age, but as the ceremony is an expensive one, it is sometimes deferred to the ninth, or even to the fourteenth year, but should the investiture not take place, then the child becomes an outcaste. Until he has learnt the prayers, he wears a band of leather twisted with the Poonool, this is made from the skin of the spotted deer, as that of the unicorn, of which it aught properly speaking to be manufactured, cannot be procured. Before the investiture, he is said only to have been born once, viz., when he entered into the world, but the cord gives him a second birth, and he is subsequently known as, a "twice born" and allowed to read the Vedas. After marriage, or at least as soon as his wife resides with him, he becomes a Grihasta. When he marries, he twists his cloth in the same way as his Poonool, viz., over the left shoulder, and under the right, where it meets over the right hip. The Poonool consists of three threads, each of which is composed of three others. Should his thread be worn out, or destroyed, he can obtain another. The heads of all Brahmans at their first or third year, are shaved, excepting on the upper and forepart, where the hair is allowed to grow in a long lock, called a cudumi. The first quarter of a Brahman's life, ought properly to be passed in retirement, and in the study of the Vedas, during which period, abstinence is enjoined, and implicit obedience to superiors, with various species of self-humiliation, strictly enforced. The second quarter of his life, he is permitted as a married man to spend in his own home, where he may employ himself in bestowing alms, receiving gifts, &c., but the most honourable occupation, is considered to be teaching : whilst he is warned against living in a city governed by a Sudra King, or receiving a gift from such a person. A Brahman should not trade, join in popular conversation, music, dancing, or any thing else inconsistent with a grave deportment: he ought to shun temporal honours, to perform three great actions, read their sacred books, have a son, and offer regular sacrifices: after which, he may in due time, make over his duties to his son. They are not unfrequently expelled their caste, for heinous, and even trivial offences: the ceremonies which are elsewhere employed on this occasion, are here unpractised. A Namboorie woman who is sentenced to lose her caste, is sent to Tripoonterah, where a stage is erected, on which she stands, holding an umbrella over her head. The Dellawah then reads the sentence to the assembled people, declares her expelled her caste, and taking her umbrella, breaks its stick in two pieces. Persons willing to take the woman may now do so, on giving a written promise, to support her whilst she lives.

At a Brahman's *birth*, a great feast is held, and the constellation under which he was launched into existence duly considered, and inquired into, and from its character, and position, his future destiny is foretold. The younger sons of a Namboorie Brahman are not obliged to marry a woman of their own caste, unless their elder brother has no son, thus the inheritance is kept in the family, but they are permitted to form temporary alliances with Nair women, their children being of the same caste as the mother. This arrangement is considered very honourable to the Shudramah, sometimes called a Nairchee, and to elevate her in the social scale!

A Brahman wishing to marry, goes to the high Priest, *Videum*, from whom he obtains a license, and to whom he pays a fee. Parties generally keep a register of such occurrences in their houses, adding a leaf to their Kerula Ulpati, on which all important family occurrences are noted down. On the marriage of a Brahman, many ceremonies are gone through. He should not, if it be his first marriage, be above twelve years old, when it is celebrated, whilst the Bride is even younger. If the nuptials do not take place at this time, the parties are in some places considered as lying under the displeasure of the Deities. But the ceremony is expensive, and some are unable to afford it at that early age, Brahman women therefore occasionally marry as late in life as twenty, or thirty years of age. If the family is too poor to give the Bride a dower, they apply to the Rajah to do so for them, and he rarely refuses.

The Bridegroom meets the bridal party at the gate, dressed in old clothes, saturated with water, in which charcoal has been washed. All then adjourn to the tank, where they bathe, and re-dress, after which they return to the Bride's abode, preceded by music, and continue the various ceremonies. As soon as the Tali is tied around the girl's neck, she is declared to be married, and it is not removed until after her husband's death, when it is burnt with his body.

On leaving her home, the Bride cuts down a plantain tree, and the sacred betel vine, and places her foot upon the curry stone, signifying that she no longer needs a parent's sustaining care. On arriving at her new home, she first plants a small cocoanut tree, which she has taken from her father's house. She is allowed to eat with her husband on the day of her marriage, in a certain fashion, but never subsequently, as it is her duty to wait, until he has finished his meals, before she commences hers. The ceremony of eating together is performed, in the following manner. As soon as the Tali is tied, a plate of boiled rice is brought, out of which the husband helps himself, and then places his right hand on the top of the rice, the wife next imposes her right hand upon his, the man now withdraws his, and the woman finishes the food. As a wife she remains in strict seclusion, no stranger being ever admitted within her abode,* and she must never even pronounce her husband's name during his life-time.

A Namboorie woman is called an *Argieoolloothoo*, and has about four Nair females attached to her, each being known as a *Pnow.* Three out of four of the Nair divisions, are slaves to various Illums, and their wives consider it an honour to serve a Namboorie woman, from whom they merely receive their rice, and sometimes come in for a share of what is left at the pagodas. When an Argieoolloothoo goes out, one female attendant precedes her, and one follows her, whilst they continue to shout to keep low caste persons at a distance. They have two styles of dress, the one indulges in very little clothing, but carries a very large umbrella: the other is clothed from the head to the feet, and her umbrella is comparatively small. An unmarried or widowed Namboorie woman, wears no ornaments, but the married ones do not keep to this rule.

An European on witnessing one of their entertainments, would hardly consider their hospitality great, as the hostess serves out the ingredients, and each cooks for herself. The men of this caste are, even worse off than the women, as on going a journey, they are expected not only to cook enough for themselves, but also for their Sudra servants.

The Namboorie Brahmans may be divided into two, those who pass their time almost solely in religious exercises within the precincts of their sacred Temples, either studying the histories and legends of their Deities, and saints who have passed away, or diving into the mysteries of astrology and medicine. Their duties render them benevolent, and they preach kindness to the whole animal kingdom. The second division of Namboories, dwell in towns, and hold situations under the native Government. Some as the *Moosahtha* are doctors, and they do not perform religious ceremonies, but

* The house of a *Namboorie* is called an *Illum*, the ground on which it stands is freehold property. That of a *Putter*, is termed a *Muddum:* of a *Nair*, a *Veedoo*, unless a Dewan, or Judge, should be a Nair, when it is called a Muddum: a *Christian's*, a *Peediga:* a *Chogan's*, a *Cotikul:* a *Churmur's*, a *Chahlá*: an *European's*, a *Bungalow*.

they can eat with their Priestly brethren, as they have not lowered themselves in their caste.

Arrogant and oppressive, vindictive and grasping, these Brahmans will turn aside sooner than tread on a worm or any other insect, but think the murder of a slave no crime, should he provoke his death by too near an approach to one of their bigoted race, or by showing them any impertinence. They raise Temples in which to feed animals, but will let a Churmur die sooner than give him a morsel of food to save him from starvation. When they walk along a road, runners always precede them, to drive away all low caste persons: in olden times, certain roads were exclusively appropriated to them. Every one must alight from his carriage, or horse, before passing into a temple, which is usually surrounded by a wall.

Namboories* of late years, have become much more particular respecting their food than they were formerly, and they subsist exclusively on vegetables, ghee, &c. Near their houses they generally have a sacred grove, where snakes are an object of adoration.

In the Cochin State, the Namboorie Brahmans only are permitted as a right, to perform the duties of the Pagodas, or *Umbalams*, which are of two classes, those belonging to the Sircar, and the property of the native Government, and those appertaining to the various villages, called *Oaraulum devassom.* A description of the internal arrangements of one of these buildings will suffice for all, as they are identical, or nearly so. The Namboories are divided into four classes. First, the *Brahman Ootamun*, who may perform all the ceremonies. Secondly, a class who are able to officiate in all but one, provided a Namboorie of the superior class is present. The third class may only hear the prayers. The fourth is merely a nominal Brahman, and may only see the ceremonies, it is this last class alone, (with one exception), who have Illums in Travancore.†

Brahmans losing their caste, as for instance by having their cudumis cut off, or by being compelled to eat beef even if by violence, cannot regain it. A knowledge of this, enabled Hyder and Tippoo, to commit many enormities in Malabar.

* A Namboorie rarely gives a decided answer, this is said to be owing, to his being very fearful, lest he should state what is not exactly the truth.

† Any Namboorie woman going south of the Quilon river, loses caste.

Belonging to each Pagoda, are two officiating Brahmans, termed Shanties, who are allowed a small salary, and their food. They remain some years in each Pagoda, after which they are generally transferred to another. Some Shanties are hereditary, *(Thuntrees,)* and only attend occasionally. As a rule their duties are, after performing their ablutions at day-break, to proceed to the Pagoda, and open the windows of the rooms, where the Sawmies are kept, remove all faded flowers which remain from the previous day, and then commence the daily ceremonies, *(Poojah.)*

Shanties live either in the Pagoda, or in an adjacent house, and are not permitted to speak to any woman, during their term of duty. They walk to the Pagoda with their eyes fixed on the ground, and no one is allowed to approach them, for fear of causing pollution. There is a manager attached to every Pagoda, assistant Shanties varying in number in accordance with the work for them to do, an Accountant, a Cash-keeper, a store Maistry to attend to the lights, sweepers for the interior, and Nair women to sweep around the exterior of the building, besides Peons, Umbalavassies, and sometimes Elephants. Dancing girls are occasionally kept, or otherwise men musicians, as five times a day, the Temple resounds with their sacred tunes. Sandalwood is kept constantly burning, to perfume the Temple.

Offerings differ according to the occasion on which they are presented, and the individuals who give them, thus sick or maimed persons, offer representations in gold or silver, of the limb or organ believed to be affected and those who wish for protection against reptiles, figures of snakes, and jewels. Offerings made to Siva, the Namboories will not touch, they are given to the Umbalavassies. There are occasionally treasure chests in the porch of the Pagoda, in which persons may deposit their offerings. They are only opened at stated times. The Temples generally have gardens attached to them, where the *Occimum sanctum,* or Holy Basil, is grown, the fragrant purple flowers of which, are sacred to Vishnu, and constantly in bloom. The roots are made into beads, and worn as necklaces by the Vishnu Brahmans. *Orme* states, that these Brahmans sometimes devote themselves to death, and effect it in the unpleasant mode, of eating until they actually expire of surfeit!

The *Umbalavassies* already alluded to, are persons employed within the Pagoda, many of whom wear the sacred thread, they are in fact a species of Levite, attached to the Temple, who as a rule take precedence of Nairs, they are said to be descended from Namboorie fathers. There are several sub-divisions of them, 1, *Numbuddie,* who are accountants, wear the poonool, are superior to the others, and have no duties to perform, 2, *Prishardie,* 3, *Warrien,* 4, *Pushputtoo* also called *Nambier,* these three string flowers for the idols, but only the first wears the sacred thread. Nambiers are said to have been originally descended from the head men of villages, and to have received this distinctive title from an assembly of Namboories; 5, *Poodoowaal,* who are sweepers, 6, *Mootoodoo,* 7, *Moostoodoo,* who are the Brahman's barbers, but can also act in that capacity for other persons, 8, *Oonee,* who wear the poonool, act as accountants, cultivators, in fact in almost any capacity, and are held in but little esteem. 9, *Maraan,* or tom-tom beaters, called also *Shedeean* when they perform ceremonies, for the Nairs. Many of them are not attached to Pagodas, but at feasts most of them are fed before the Sudras.

Imbrans are a tribe of Brahmans, who are not Namboories, but have come from Mangalore, and are permitted as a great favour, to officiate in the Namboorie Pagodas; at Cranganore they even have an Umbalum of their own.

The *Putter** Brahmans frequently subsist upon charity, they are all foreign Brahmans, in fact all those in the country excepting the Namboories, and Konkanies. They amount to about 6000, and often reside in a room of a Nair's house, they are mostly worshippers of Siva, their females are termed Amieers. During the ceremony of marriage, the Bride is yoked to the Bridegroom, by a miniature representation of a plough, and thus coupled, they are driven round the room. It is curious that this ceremony should obtain amongst Brahmans, who never till the soil.

The *Konkanies* in the Cochin State, are nearly twice as numerous as the Namboorie Brahmans. They are not allowed to officiate in the Temples of the latter, or the Namboories in theirs, whilst many deny

* *Potie,* is a name given in Travancore, to all Brahmans.

them the title of Brahmans, to which they are undoubtedly entitled. They originally came to Malabar, from the Concan, from which their name is derived.

The arrogant Namboories, and jealous Nairs, assert that this tribe were originally fishermen, and that Parasu Rama finding that no Brahmans would live on the western coast, and consequently there was no one on whom to bestow his alms, invested some of this race of fishermen with the sacred thread, thereby constituting them Brahmans. As a proof of this, they point out that the Konkanies eat fish,* and drink spirits, and also affirm that at their marriage ceremonies, the Bride and Bridegroom have to catch a fish with a net, out of a tub of water, which is placed in the centre of the room. Following out their arguments by stating, that as the true Brahmans increased on the western coast, the Konkanies gradually sank into insignificance and became traders.

The *Konkanies* in Cochin are not strictly speaking Canareens, but they frequently designate themselves so, they are sub-divided into four grades, the *Tuttans*, or goldsmiths : the *Wunnears*, or oil merchants : the *Chetties*, who are shroffs, and general merchants : and the *Cudumis*, who pound rice, and perform inferior offices. They are not bound to continue in the occupation of their fathers, many of the Tuttans are now trying to give up their trade, which they consider degrading. They have a Temple of their own in Cochin, and once a year they give their idols a grand entertainment, by the side of the public road. According to the *Mackenzie Manuscripts*, the Konkanies emigrated from the Concan into Malabar, in consequence of some disturbances, and prevailed upon the Rajah of Cochin to permit them to settle and build Temples in his dominions. The four sub-divisions of Konkanies, were under the protection of the Dutch Company, and amenable to their laws, until 1772: since which period, authority over them has been claimed by the Cochin Rajah.

The following is their account, of the origin and history of their present Chief Bhimmum, or idol. Up to A.D. 1589, they possessed in Cochin a small metal idol, and in that year their High Priest,

---

* The *Konkanie* denies that he eats fish, true he is seen constantly carrying them to his house, but he declares it to be *only for the cats.* It is curious that all affirm, that they keep many of these four legged animals.

Coombaconum Madum Swamiyar visited the place, bringing with him a Bhimmum, before which he performed his private devotions. Having remained about six months, he prepared to depart, but at every attempt to leave became seriously ill. Alarmed at this, the Soothsayers were consulted, and they discovered, that his little god had taken such a fancy to Cochin, that he declined to leave the place. The Swamiyar then offered to give up the Bhimmum, provided he were given as many Venetian gold sequins, as would cover the image, when placed in a large salver. This was acceded to, but as fast as they heaped up the money, the higher grew the idol's head, until all the sequins in Cochin were expended. Again Soothsayers were consulted, and they discovered, that although the Bhimmum wished to reside in Cochin, he had an aversion to lose sight of his former master, and his family, so a contract was drawn up, in which the Pagoda worshippers stipulated, that they would always obey the Swamiyar, or one of his family as High Priest, and that his descendants should have the right to perform three days' devotion yearly, in the Pagoda.

The Bhimmum therefore remained peaceably in Cochin until about 1719, when it miraculously disappeared, and was found on the sea beach, and taken to the house of the Dutch Governor. He saw nothing but a little misshapen figure, apparently composed of an admixture of gold, silver, and other metals : and thinking it of little value, gave it his children as a plaything. But hardly had it reached the house, when the Governor's wife was attacked with severe colic, which did not cease, until the idol had left their roof, and obtained shelter in the house of a native Doctor. The poor man, as well as his family, were tormented with illnesses, for seven years, when it was fortunately discovered, that the idol was the cause of his misfortunes, and was the long lost Bhimmum. Again it reached the Pagoda, where it rested quietly until 1791, in which year the Rajah of Cochin, directed the Pagoda to contribute a large quantity of sugar-cane jaggery, towards a feast at Tripoonterah. The trustees refused, one of them being Dagwars Kinni, and the "Dagwars Kinni war," as it is termed, ensued. About the third week in September, two of the Rajah's Eurasian Officers, accompanied by a Ragiadoor, went to Dagwars Kinni's shop, and stated that they required some silks; but while serving them, he was murdered, his head cut off, and carried away to the Rajah; whose troops made a rush upon the Canarese Bazaar. The priests hearing the uproar hastily deposited the idol and its jewels in a box, and sought refuge under the guns of the Dutch fort, inside which, the Bhimmum was placed for safety. Fearing it might be given up by the Dutch, they the next day sent it by a canoe to Chellana, and about a month subsequently to Allepey, where the Travancore Rajah permitted it to be placed in an Ootooparrah, where it remained securely guarded for many years.

As soon as British supremacy had caused tranquillity, it was proposed to build a large Temple at Cochin, and again install the Bhimmum there. They believed that it was owing to the good will, manifested by the idol that Cochin had become a prosperous place, still they agreed, that if a Pagoda were built at Allepey, and lands yielding Rupees 12,000 yearly given as an endowment, they would let it remain there, and these terms were acceded to by the Rajah of Travancore. The importance of Allepey is now decreasing, which is attributed by the Hindus, to the Cochin Pagoda, having regained possession of the idol, owing to the Bhimmum having been conveyed out of the Allepey Pagoda, in the bread basket of a Cochin Brahman, and thus reached its old abode. It is usual after the Brahmans have been feasted, inside the Pagoda, for the remainder of the food, to be carried outside in long baskets, where persons are awaiting their shares of the precious morsels. In February 1853 after a feast, a Cochin Brahman concealed the god in one of these baskets, and thus it was conveyed out of the Temple, and was soon placed in a boat, and rapidly propelled to Cochin. Early the following morning, great was the dismay at Allepey, the image had disappeared, and the Travancore Government protested that the Cochin people had robbed Allepey of its chief treasure. Communications at last led to angry recriminations, and in 1856 troops were ordered from Quilon, to march towards Cochin, and compel the restitution of the highly prized idol.

The Cochin Dewan now offered to return it, this was acceded to, a day was chosen, on which to receive it and a portion of the Nair Brigade was in readiness to meet it with all honours at Allepey, at last, on January 28th 1857, the boat hove in sight, and the Priests met it at the landing place. Having broken a cocoanut the chief Brahman making profound salaams entered the cabin, but soon in wrath and disgust re-appeared, declaring the image was a spurious one, dressed up in the true jewels. Having deposited it in the verandah of the Pagoda, another letter was despatched to Cochin, and another idol declared to be the true one, was sent on January 31st, 1857, but was as false as the first. Finally in 1859, the Madras Government settled this important question, by deciding that as the idol had originally deserted from Cochin, and had now returned to that place, there it was to remain: whilst the Travancore officials are said to have finished the business, by resuming the lands they had granted, for the idol's support.

The *Schatriya*, (*Tirripard* Mal.) or royal caste, is that from which His Highness the Rajah of Cochin has sprung. This caste is said to have emanated from Brahma's shoulders, and to have been launched into existence with orders to rule the world, with justice, tempered by mercy. It is divided into two great divisions, the Solar race who came from Brahma's right shoulder, and the Lunar race who issued from his left. These are again sub-divided.* The female is termed an Umbattahree.

The ceremony of coronation has not been performed for many years, as the Temple in which it is obliged to be celebrated, is at Ponany, and some reason has militated against the Rajahs of Cochin visiting this place. The Schatriyan caste, were almost extirpated by Parasu Rama, as previously alluded to. It is now principally represented by the Rajpoots of Oude. Kings of this caste, may wear gold rings on their toes, and ankles, but no inferior member of it, is permitted this privilege. Inheritance in Malabar, descends through the sister's children. The Schatriyas are allowed to read the Vedas, but not to comment upon them, or place any interpretation of their own, on the various passages.

* The whole of the Hindu races, are divided into the northern and southern sects, said to have been by the direction of Kali, who delivered the order on copper plates at the Conjaveram Pagoda, but the plates cannot now be found. As a rule, those of different divisions do not inter-marry. The Syrians are also similarly divided.

Schatriya Rajahs, such of those of Cochin and Cranganore, possess the privilege of re-admitting to their caste, all beneath Nairs, who have forfeited it. A small fee is necessary. The individual who has lost caste, appears before the Rajah, who holds a copper or brass vessel containing water in his hands, some of which he sprinkles in the out-caste's face, and then hands him the vessel, contact has thus occurred between them, and the Rajah then calls him by his caste title, after which he is no longer an out-caste.

The *Vysias*, are a mercantile and agricultural caste, said to have been derived from Brahma's thighs, for the purpose of providing for the Brahmans. They are divided into the Boo Vysias, the Gho Vysias, and the Dana Vysias, each of which is again sub-divided. They believe that about the end of the sixth century, a King reigned, who re-modelled the castes, and formed eighteen classes, each of which had a distinct trade: but that the invasion of foreigners, disturbed all these rules.

Vysias are not allowed to read the Vedas, but they may listen to them when read by a Brahman. There are so few of this caste in Cochin, that a further account of them is unnecessary. They are required in certain ceremonies, but if unprocurable, Umbalavassies take their place.

The *Sudras* are considered as sprung from Brahma's feet, and their office is to serve the Branmans. This caste, and the Pariahs form more than half the population of the Cochin State. Sudras do not belong to the twice born classes, and may not wear the sacred thread. They are prohibited from either reading the Shastras, or hearing them read. In olden times if they infringed this regulation, they were punished by having boiling metals poured into their ears, and were even occasionally executed. All the irregular offspring of the three twice born classes, sink into Sudras, who are in their turn quite as intolerant of those beneath them, as the higher grades are. In modern times, they have been divided into the right hand, and left hand castes. The first includes many landlords, great agriculturists, dhobies, and others: whilst the second, is principally composed of artizans.

A Sudra is directed to endeavour to become a Brahman's servant, as in that case, his transmigrations will probably be happy. If he cannot procure employment with a Brahman, he should try and obtain it with a Schatriya, failing which, he may apply to a Vysia.

Sudras it is asserted, cannot pass from a lower grade to a higher, but the Rajahs of Travancore are always manufactured into Brahmans, on ascending the musnud, an important part in this transmigration, being sometimes played by a golden cow, at the mouth of which, the Rajah enters a Sudra, and having crawled along its interior arrangements, emerges under the animal's tail, as one of the twice born: otherwise he bathes in a golden lotus. The gold figures are subsequently divided amongst the officiating Brahmans. During the last century two Travancore Brahmans visited England, thereby of course losing their caste, which was only restored, by their passing through the sacred yoni, made of the finest gold, which afterwards with many other valuable gifts, were presented to one of the Temples.

Formerly if a Sudra abused his superiors, the punishment was slitting his tongue, if he seated himself next a Brahman the offending part was gashed, and if he presumed to offer him any advice respecting his religious duties, hot oil was poured on his tongue. The penance for killing a Sudra, was little more than that for killing any lower animal, excepting a cow which of course was far above him. Nairs were not subject to these punishments, and appear in many ways to have held a superior position to any other Sudras. They may all perform sacrifices, but must omit the holy texts.

The Nairs form about one-fifth of the whole population of the Cochin State, and although Sudras, in fact termed Shudrum *par excellence*, hold the highest position amongst them, and are generally admitted to be the nobility of the country; as there are so very few Schatriyas and Vysias, they may be said to be only divided from the Brahmans, by the Levites, or the Umbalavassies, who are the intermediate link.

The question of who these Nairs are, is one open to considerable discussion. It appears probable, that the Sudra race were originally formed of the aborigines, and those Hindus who had lost their caste none of whom were permitted to wear the sacred thread. But it is admitted by the Namboories, that in Cochin there are four castes, the three twice born, and the Nairs: all below these, being summed up under the term, *addira jardee*, Mal, who are regarded, (by the

Namboories,) as out-castes. Perhaps when the Hindus first overran Malabar, they found that the nature of the country formed such a barrier to their further progress, owing to the ghauts in the rear, the sea in the front, and the numerous streams by which it is intersected, that they were convinced that they could only conquer it, with the assistance of the aborigines, or of some portion of them. It may therefore be surmised, that certain classes were for this reason taken as soldiers, and given privileges, which as a rule were not accorded to Sudras elsewhere.

The Nairs are a proud and warlike race, arrogant to inferiors, subservient to superiors, profuse in promises, and slack in their performance. They occasionally officiate as accountants, but their statements must be received with caution, and additional testimony is generally advisable. Their security is always requested in writing, otherwise it cannot be greatly relied on. They are not uncleanly in their habits, but certainly have no superfluity of clothing. Their complexion is remarkably clear, in a foreign country they soon pine away, and die.

This tribe is variously divided in different places, and the customs in North Malabar, differ considerably from those which obtain in Cochin. Everywhere they have certain work to do in the Pagoda, so their presence is a necessity. They are divided into four classes, each of which is sub-divided into at least four more. 1, *Paniaputtoo Shudrum*, supplies oil and grass for the Pagoda, and are slaves to an Illum. 2, *Vellalun*, a class only employed when the others are absent, and can then perform any work, they are not slaves to an Illum. 3, *Pullichan*, also called *Kirüt*, or *Villüt*, and many other names, according to the locality in which they reside; they are bearers; and slaves to an Illum. 4, *Wutticara*, who are too low to perform any work for the Pagodas.

The Nairs may procure materials for meals, and collect what is required, but cannot cook. A very low-caste of them *Vellicarturra*, are barbers, to the Brahmans. The barber to the Nairs, is termed *Umbatan*, but he is very low in the scale of caste, and works for anybody.

Vishnu is their Deity, but they often wear the mark of Siva on their foreheads. The Namboories act as their Gurus, but will not be present when they offer bloody sacrifices to Kali, and other Deities, consequently the greater part of their feasts are performed by a race of Priests of their own caste, called *Ellada,* who are said to have been originally Brahmans, who were degraded, in consequence of their having performed religious rites for Sudras.

The Nairs were in olden times the Militia of the country, and held their lands in military tenure, being liable to be called out at any time, for active service. The Rajah of Cochin was the head of these Militia, in his own country, and under him were Namboorie commandants. When each man was of age to bear arms, he presented the Rajah with a nuzzer, who in return gave him his weapons. They were trained to warfare from infancy, but were "more inclined "to use their weapons for the purposes of assassination, or surprise, "than in the open field."

Nairs may receive the title of *Menon,* from the Rajah, an honour which may also be purchased, and of which there are two kinds: one hereditary, and the other only for a life-time: the last of these costs at the lowest rate about sixteen fanams, (13 annas, 4 cash.) When the Rajah intends to confer this honour, he salutes the person to whom he means to give it, by the title of Menon prefixed to his name, and should two other persons present, immediately address him in the same terms, the title is confirmed, if not he does not receive it. After becoming a Menon, he is called a Tumbaran, previous to this a Prakkulloo. They have also an hereditary title, of *Kooroopoo.*

Should a Chogan, a Mucua or one of a lower caste, dare to pollute a Nair by approaching nearer than the prescribed distance, he was formerly at liberty to cut him down. It is curious to observe two of them coming along the road in opposite directions, each is afraid of being polluted by the other, and shout out to clear the way, and if this is not done, they themselves turn aside. The only soldiers in olden times were Nairs, and it was considered a great breach of etiquette, to bring Tiers or those of any other lower grade to fight against them, it was only in the latter end of the last century, that this rule was broken through, previously the lower castes had been employed, only as coolies and menials.

The Nairs are at the present time, rather a superior race. Most of the men and women can read, but of course being Sudras are prohibited from opening the Shastras. They eat venison, goats, pork, fowls, and fish, and are excessively addicted to intoxicating liquors.

It cannot be doubted, that the Nairs of Cochin, are much less moral, in the European sense of the word, than those living in North Malabar. On the death of an owner of property, the landed estate is looked after by the eldest competent male member of the family, but each individual has a right to his share of the income. The mother manages the family, and after her death the eldest sister takes her place. All the brothers generally live under the same roof, but should they leave it, one of their sisters usually accompanies them.

The law of succession to property is as follows, it "goes to a "man's sisters: sister's sons, sister's daughters: sister's daughters' "sons, and daughters: Mother: Mother's sisters, their children; "then to his maternal grandmother, her sisters, and their children. "Failing these, and their stock, in the same way of descent, it goes "as in other parts of the Presidency, to a man's disciple, and fellow "student, and then escheats."*

The females who are termed Amahs or *Shudrunmars*, are nominally married, between the ages of six months and ten years, but rarely if ever at a later period. The mode in which the Bridegroom is chosen, is according to the constellations, as both parties must have been born under the same. The consequence is, that although two persons born at the same time may thus be united, it also acts, that the husband may be 60 or 80, and the bride a baby: still there is no necessity for their ever meeting subsequent to the ceremony. The Bride lives in her mother's house, where she has separate rooms, and indulges in indiscriminate polyandrism, with any of her own caste or of a higher grade: but should she receive the visits of a man of inferior caste to herself, she becomes an out-caste. The infamy and shame, which in most other parts of India, attends an erring wife, and extends to her family, is here unknown. Such deeds can be no subject for vituperation against the Shudrunmar, for in Malabar no

* Strange, page 67. Civil Law.

disgrace attends them. Until a change in this system occurs, this portion of India can hardly be said to be advancing in civilization. Some ignorant writers, unacquainted with the Hindu laws, view this idea as puerile, and denounce it, as "pious declamation," they have yet to learn, that *it is not* in accordance with the Hindu religion, and is directly antagonistic to their Shastras.

The Nair is very particular respecting his dress, and is evidently anxious to make an impression on the softer Shudrunmar. Until the last fifty years, on going abroad he always carried a firelock, or sword, and should he consider himself a very valiant individual, he armed himself with two. In his more amorous campaigns, the richest suitor presents the Shudrunmar on his first visit, with some ornaments and a cloth, he also whilst on terms with her, provides oil for her head. When she returns him the cloth, it is a sign he must cease his visits. It must not be concluded that the lady has only one favoured visitor. Each of these gentlemen friends, provides her with something, such as rice, &c., and thus the Shudrunmar lives, and indulges her own inclinations, unfettered either by domestic ties, or social observances. These fugitive connections, are as easily dissolved as formed.

Formerly if a Nair was too intimate with a Chogan woman, he was put to death, and the female was sold to the Moplahs; or if he had been too friendly with a slave girl, both were doomed to destruction.

The succession in this caste, is that best adapted to a military people. Their property, &c., descends to the eldest of their sister's children, as it would be almost impossible for fathers to know their own. Thus having no family in which to interest themselves, denied the right of adoption, (even of their own sons could they point them out,) excepting by the Rajah's special permission: unable either to will away their family property, or to give any away, (unless personally their own savings, they have no ties of kindred, and no occasion to save money like other men. But the time when military Nairs were a necessity has now passed away; and it is to be hoped that ere long, some great philanthropist will arise amongst this large and influential class of natives, who will reform some of the melancholy and vicious regulations now in force amongst them. It may be trusted that the time is not far distant, when parents can recognize and maintain their own children, when marriage will be no longer a misnomer, but a reality; and husband and wife be permitted to share the same home. Instead of squandering their money on their personal appearance, they would then take an interest in their property, and the State would be as great gainers as the persons themselves. But this work of reformation must be commenced by an influential member of their own caste, and he who effected such, would be a public benefactor to his race, and one whose name would be always revered by the Natives of Malabar.

The Nairs burn, and but seldom bury their dead. Suttee of course could never have been carried out, as owing to the peculiar customs of this caste, widows are unknown. They believe that good men go to Heaven, but that bad ones suffer transmigrations. A death in a family causes pollution for fifteen days, during which time only the Shedeeans, who are Maraans, and perform their funeral ceremonies, can go near the mourners, over whom they pour milk and water, mixed with less cleanly substances, on the fifth, tenth, and fifteenth days, after the death; on the last occasion, they are considered purified.

Nairs live in detached houses, surrounded by gardens, and usually of a rather superior description. They are raised off the ground, and have white washed, laterite, or mud walls, generally forming two sides of a square. The entrance to their compounds, *(dèsas,)* is at some little distance from the house, and consists of a door, in the centre of a strong gateway. These domiciles in former times, were frequently like little fortresses, a necessary precaution, when violence and assassination, were rife in every direction. Nairs who have once lost their caste cannot regain it.

The *Chogans,* also termed *Chagowans,* and *Illovers,* appear to have been one of the aboriginal tribes, and to have derived their designation, from the Sanscrit word Sevagum, "a servant," whilst the term "Illover," is supposed to be from Ceylon, which was formerly called Izoowen Dirpa, or Izoowen island, from whence they are believed to have come. They are nearly identical with the Teers*

*Teers in Travancore, *are said* to have purchased the title of Shanars, the latter assert that previously, the Teers had stood in the same position to them,

in the north, the Shanars in the south, and the Cinnamon pruners of Ceylon. Their females are termed *Choties.* They say that they are descended from the impure race called *Panchamas,* and are supposed to have been the slaves of the Brahmans, Nairs and Syrians, for whom they cultivated dry crops, took care of their gardens, and tended cattle: receiving in return, a rather uncertain remuneration. Nearly fifteen hundred years ago, it is said many classes were emancipated from serfdom to the Brahmans, but this boon did not extend to the Chogans, or those beneath them, and their lot remained unaltered, whilst others commenced paying rent to the crown, and obtained the privilege of residing and renting land where they pleased. They are now mostly known as toddy drawers, this laborious occupation is carried on by the poorer classes, who as soon as they possess sufficient means, purchase trees, and let them out to others. They also manufacture coarse sugar *(jaggery,)* from toddy, distil arrack, make country vinegar, act as cultivators: and in jungly places, as collectors of firewood. In the native State, they are prohibited from milking cows; (although in most places these laws are now obsolete,) from possessing calves with red horns; with a white mark on the forehead; or twins: these ought all to be sent to the nearest Pagoda or to the house of a high caste man, as also a Chogan's cow should it have a calf, when it rarely happens that the young animal is returned to its owner. The produce of their gardens, also is in some places considered fair spoil. They are not permitted to express oil from their cocoanuts, as the Syrians and Romo-Syrians claim the monopoly of this trade.

The Chogans are an industrious people, coarse in their manners and customs, covetous in their dispositions, and in their religion devil worshippers, or rather propitiators of evil spirits: their offerings consisting of bloody sacrifices, for a cock, hog, sheep, or goat, are generally considered acceptable to the Deity, who has also no objection to ardent spirits. They, and the classes below them, must not enter Hindu Temples. Their barbers *Cooroopoo,* are their Priests, and are held in very low esteem. The head men of the villages, who have received their titles from the Rajah, have charge of a

---

that Nairs do to Brahmans, but there appears no foundation for this statement. Teers, Chogans, and Shanars, will all eat together, but do not inter-marry.

certain number of houses, and decide when certain ceremonies are necessary, which without their sanction, are null and void. Their imagination peoples the forests with demons, and the wilds with vengeful spirits, especially the ghosts of their ancestors; they frequently have recourse to charms, some of which consist only of the leaves of jungle trees. Their Temples if they can be called such, are merely pyramidal pillars of mud, six or seven feet high, constructed with their faces towards the cardinal points, and frequently in the vicinity of a tamarind tree. In front of this idol, is a small raised flat surface made of mud, on which sacrifices are offered up. Bloody sacrifices, and dances, are essentials to the Demon worshipper. The person who conducts these ceremonies, is known as the *Vellichapard,** or *Rotator of the Demon*, and is most commonly one of their own caste, but any person, even a Nair, may officiate. The animal to be sacrificed, is ornamented with red ochre, and usually adorned with flowers, the head is severed by one blow of the sacrificial knife, and the trunk held up over the altar, that the blood may be poured out on it. Subsequently those who have presented the offering, cook and eat its flesh. In some cases, the Vellichapard must drink the blood of the sacrifice, and during the time of the ceremony, he appears like one possessed, and jumps, or rather rushes through the fire, cutting himself with knives, or other sharp instruments, until he is covered with blood: altogether the sight appears more like what might be conceived of a pandemonium, than anything else.

The Chogans are a people despised by the higher castes, such as the Nairs, and Brahmans, who nevertheless in former times whenever they required money, invariably looked to these classes from whence to obtain it. They have thus been rendered suspicious, whilst they have not advanced with an advancing age. Always destitute of literature, both sacred and profane, they are not apparently solicitous for education. Fearful of losing money, even in British territory, where little fear need exist, they often bury their savings in some secure place, by which means considerable sums must annually dis-

* This person is believed to be moved by a spirit, and his words to have a significance none should neglect. Even women are at times supposed to be possessed with spirits, and able to foretel future events.

appear, from the currency of the empire. This class, suspicious of not obtaining justice from the laws of the realm, formerly resorted to ordeals, and even at the present time, have frequently recourse to the decision of punchayets, or umpires, chosen by the consent of both parties. They are not permitted to enter within a native court of justice, by the laws of caste they should remain thirty-six paces from a Brahman, and twelve from a Nair, the latter class generally become their paid advocates, in these *Courts of Justice!*

Chogans in the Native State, were not permitted to wear any clothing above the waist, whether they were males or females. This prohibition was enforced throughout Malabar, until about the commencement of the present century, and in Travancore, until 1859: whilst in Cochin, it has always been strictly observed, up to the present time. Even in British territory, where they can dress as they please, they manifest no desire to change their style of clothing, a proceeding which would probably occasion them expulsion from their caste.

Chogans, may like Nairs, receive titles from the Rajah of Cochin, that of *Tundaan* is purchaseable, and gives a person the right to be the head man of the village, as well as of his caste in the place. He can wear a gold knife, and style, may walk before a Nair with a cloth on his head, ride in a palanquin, or on a horse, carry a silk umbrella, and have a brass lamp, *coalloo vellakoo*, borne before him. For each of these privileges, he pays separately.* A Tundaan is prohibited from doing any cooly work, ploughing, or going up cocoanut trees, &c. There are also inferior honours, such as *Punnikans*, *Ponumbans*, &c. Chogans may not use horses' bones for tapping trees, so they employ those of the Buffaloe, or the Sambur loaded with lead. Those of horses, are said to increase the amount of toddy procured from the trees.

They are divided into two tribes, who do not inter-marry, the first is called the *Mukkutti*, and their property descends to their own children. In all cases of dispute, they have a council of 31 persons, of their own tribe, who decide on the subject. The second is known

* If any persons use these privileges, who are unauthorized to do so, they lay themselves open to the Native *penal code*, and they would probably be punished by hard labour on the roads.

as the *Murri Mukkutti*, amongst whom the descent goes through the Nephews, they have a council of 61, to decide disputes. Some of both these divisions marry, but the majority merely form fugitive connections.

Widows cannot re-marry, those who have acted improperly are not divorced, but merely flogged. At the marriage, some money is presented to the girl's mother, a piece of cloth to herself, and food to her relations. Many of the women have no husbands, and as they are considered handsome, they are unfortunately exposed to much temptation, especially in sea port towns, which they hardly ever resist. In olden times, if the seducer were a Namboorie, his eyes were put out, and the girl and all her family, were either put to death, or sold to the Moplahs.

They do not appear to be quite so much addicted to intoxication as the Nairs, in fact they are prohibited from drinking the toddy which they draw. They believe in a future state. They bury their dead, always facing the east, and generally at the threshold of their houses, almost invariably in their own compounds. They daily cross over these tombs. If they die in a hired place, the body must be removed, because its interment gives the family of the deceased a species of claim to the ground.

The *Cunnians*, or Astrologers, are a low but learned and distinct division of the Chogans. If one of them approach within 24 feet of a Namboorie, he causes pollution, whilst his touch defiles a Nair. They are permitted to read the Yogi Shastra, which contains no prayers. The ignorant refer to them, to learn the best time for sowing seeds, or if they are sick, to discover from what evil spirit their disease is due, and how it can best be got rid of. They also pretend to cast out evil spirits, and are regarded with great awe. They pray both to Siva and Vishnu, and appear to offer sacrifices to every divinity in the Hindu calendar.

They employ themselves in cultivation, making umbrellas, and similar occupations. They believe in a future state, and hold that the spirits of the good, will remain with God: and those of the bad, occasion trouble on the earth. They eat animal food, and drink spirituous liquors. Their marriages are conducted in the same manner as those of the Chogans, and may be dissolved at pleasure.

Property descends to their children, some burn, and others bury their dead.

There are many classes of Artificers, the various distinctions and customs of whom might fill volumes, but space does not admit of even giving a slight sketch of them here.

The *four-joined-in-one* race, consist of 4 distinct classes, all of which are said to have had one common descent. They are as follows; 1st, the *Arjarree* (Carpenters), should one of these enter an Illum, it is defiled, unless he carries his chisel and his rule. He can even if thus armed, enter a Nair's cooking house. 2nd, the *Moojarree*, (Brass founders). 3rd, *Perincolun* (Smiths,) a Blacksmith* entering an Illum, must have a hammer, a pair of tongs, or some of his tools with him, and be very careful that they are not all absent from his hands at the same time, in which case the house would be defiled. 4th, the *Tuttans* (Silversmiths). All these four believe that they had one common origin, but as their numbers increased they divided into four trades, which their descendants are bound to follow. In performing ceremonies, all four unite, and they also eat together, whilst if one of them forms a temporary alliance with a woman of one of the other three divisions, he does not lose his caste. Still there are two sub-divisions of the Carpenters and Smiths, who must not be included in the above, as they are esteemed of an inferior position: amongst the first are the *Tuckhuns*, who as they make ploughs, and cut firewood for burning the dead, are looked down upon by the Arjarrees: amongst the latter, are the *Parricharcoluns*, who besides working in iron, will manufacture leather sword belts, or even shoes, and are consequently thought very inferior by the Perincoluns. The *Cullens*, are workers in granite, but owing to their propensities, their synonyme is equivalent to that of a rogue, or a thief: the *Pündarrans* or popadum makers, are a working class: whilst the *Cunnaains* are Braziers.

All the above are esteemed superior to the Chogans, but there are many others, such as the *Tarrogans*, (Weavers): the *Cunnya Cooroopoo*, (Schoolmasters,) who are Astrologers, who are equal to them:

---

* A Blacksmith may obtain a Poonool from the Rajah, but only rich men can afford the luxury, subsequently they cannot make plough shares, carry firewood, or perform many other important offices.

and some far inferior as the *Cojawuns*, (Potters), a word often used to designate a foolish fellow : the *Chucklers*, (Cobblers,) a foreign race : and the *Parnuns*, (Necromancers). Besides these, there are many more castes.

The *Arrians*, and *Vahluns*, appear identical castes, the first invariably fish in the sea, the latter always in the backwater. They both claim superiority over the Chogans.

The *Mucuas* or *Muckwas*, are an inferior tribe to the Chogans, and live along the sea coasts, rarely going inland. Until within the last fifty years, they were not permitted to travel along the inland roads, but were compelled to keep to the sea beach. They act as boatmen, palanquin bearers, and in some places also cultivate cocoanut trees. Many of those a little to the north,* have become Mahomedans, and some also in the Cochin State, but the majority are Christians. *Paoli* speaking of these people anterior to 1788, says that at that time, they had to pay "net money," which amounted to six poothens, or five annas, yearly. The following remarks refer only to the Hindu Mucuas, and not to the Christians, who are called *Marggacarers*, or "people having a law." The females are termed Mucattees.

Some amongst them marry, the ceremony consisting merely of a feast, without the aid of any religious exercises, and in this case a woman can only be divorced for infidelity. But another, and a simpler union is more prevalent, which leaves both parties able to separate at pleasure, the children always accompanying their mother.

They are not particular as to their food, excepting with regard to the exclusion of beef. Their Deity is Kali, who is represented by a log of wood, placed inside a hut. They must sacrifice a cock to her, four times a year. They must not enter within the precincts of any Temple, although they sometimes send offerings by the hands of those of superior castes, especially for recovery from sickness. They are quite ignorant of any future state, but are convinced of the exist-

---

*At *Chowghaut*, the Mucuas dissatisfied at having no religious observances like other people, and feeling the want of them, whilst they are aware that they cannot ascend in the Hindu scale, are rapidly decreasing in numbers, as it has become the custom, for one son in every family to become a Mahomedan Moplah. This class are known as the *Pooddia Islam*, or the "new Mahomedans."

ence of bad spirits, who inflict pains, losses, and other evils on mankind. They bury their dead.

The *Perdana Kanakas*, are a tribe who act as boatmen, float timber, make chunam, and bear the same relation to the inland rivers, as the Mucuas do to the sea. They are fishermen, but also act as cultivators.

The *Parravars*, reside along the sea coast to the south, and formerly were employed in the manufacture and dyeing of cotton articles. At page 99 is an account of their having sent an embassage to Cochin, seeking assistance against the Moors.

Vaillun is a tribe of Washermen, who cleanse clothes for all castes, from Namboories downwards. They also collect medicines. They are a necessity for many ceremonies, and often finding such to be the case, make their terms accordingly: thus a child must go through a ceremony on a certain day after birth, for which the Vaillun must have a cloth ready, and if it is not forthcoming, both mother and child are put out of caste. After the birth of a child, a woman must for twenty-four hours wear a cloth, which is the property of a Vaillun.

There are two castes, who are said to have arrived about the time of the Mysore invasion, both of which can only contaminate a Namboorie by contact. They themselves however, do not appear to care about even being touched by a soil slave. They are the *Carcarlans*, or Jugglers, who also do a little tailor work, such as making bedding, &c., and the *Nicomars*, who are the Tank diggers, they also make dams, and do similar work. They catch and eat field mice, jackalls, &c. It is said that none of this tribe have ever been either imprisoned, or brought up before a Magistrate, on any charge. They never drink spirits, and acknowledge that the Chogans are their superiors in caste.

The *soil slaves* are sometimes called *Churmurs* as a whole, and are rather a numerous race. The term "Churmur," appears to be an abbreviation of the word Cherrimuckull, (*cherri*, "a dam," *muckul*, "children") as they always are born and live on dams, and cultivate fields. Although nominally emancipated in 1854, such has never been carried out in its entirety. At the present day it is by no means rare, for persons to speak of their slaves, whom they consider dependent upon them, in old age, or sickness. Some there are no doubt, who when those in their employ fall sick, immediately remember the emancipation act, and dismiss them their service, especially in cases of leprosy. Other hard masters are accused of refusing to feed them, whilst unable to work, but these cases form the exceptions, not the rule. Slaves generally speaking, are terrible thieves, and great drunkards, this perhaps is mainly owing to their condition: they even teach their children to drink toddy. Education, is of course unknown amongst them. They are divided into four classes *Pellians, Pariahs, Oolahdurs* and the *Kanakas.*

They are pre-eminently a degraded race. When speaking of their bodily members, such as an eye, or an ear, to a superior, they (as must also Chogans, and those inferior to them,) prefix it by the epithet *old,* such as "old eye," "old ear." They are obliged to call their children "calves," their silver "copper," and their paddy "chaff." They commence speaking by saying, "your slave has received permission to observe." Nairs they must call "Kings," and Brahmans they may not approach: they are not allowed to draw near a Temple to pray, and must leave the public road to permit those of higher caste to pass undefiled. However the philanthropist may desire it, they can never as a class be elevated by legislation, as the first step must be to raise them in their own estimation, and until this is gained, they will make no real advance in civilization.

Amongst the highest division of this tribe, when the word is not taken for the whole race, are the *Churmurs, (cherra,* "a dam,") also known as the Pellians. These poor creatures, usually reside in the paddy fields, where their miserable little huts, may be seen raised upon the dams, which keep the water at its proper level. They are employed in cultivating fields, in cleaning and watering the cocoanut trees, and picking the nuts, but in some places must use no knife, as these trees rank too high in the social scale, to submit to the indignity of being cut by a Churmur. They also tie hedges around the trunks of the trees, to prevent unauthorized persons from trespassing, tend buffaloes, look after the crops, and separate the rice, from the husks.

This tribe is divided into several families, all of which may intermarry and eat together. They acknowledge no hereditary chiefs, but have assemblies of the elders, who settle disputes. The Pellian rejects carrion, but will eat animal food, and drink intoxicating liquors. They are a debased, ignorant race, and seem as timid as hares, at the approach of any human being. An European can scarcely ever succeed in coming near them, as their eyes and ears always appear watching for strangers, and they rush away in spite of every attempt to induce them to stop. They rarely go along a public road, but if they do, they keep looking about, to see if any person of a higher caste is near, in which case they dare not proceed. Whilst on, or near a road, they shout to give warning of their approach, as their presence within a certain distance, causes pollution to those of superior classes. When defiled by the touch of a Pariah, they have to bathe in 5 separate places, and take a drop of blood from one finger.

The slave castes, appear as a rule, never to have worn the Cudumi, but latterly many of those to the north, have commenced to do so. They wear the Tali, but the marriage ceremony is very simple. a man brings a woman to his master, and states that he wishes to keep her as his wife, subsequently she receives her allowance of rice, but she may leave her husband when she pleases, and is not particular in changing one spouse for another. The husband's master by the old law, maintains his wife and children, until they are able to work, when the eldest son becomes his property, and the others that of the mother's master.

They worship a goddess which is merely represented by a stone, raised on a mound in the open air. Their Priest is one of their own caste, and at the commencement of the new year, offers up fowls, fruits, and spirituous liquors. They believe that after death, the spirit exercises an influence in terrestrial affairs, those of the good being the most powerful, but offerings are made to both species. They do not recognize the Brahmans as their teachers. Their dead are burnt.

The *Pariahs* are a lower caste of slaves, and eat carrion, even that of cows. They cultivate paddy fields, clean ponds, and till the ground, but will not use buffaloes to assist in this purpose, as if they touch these animals, they are defiled, they have however no objection to bullocks. They also skin animals, make baskets, bamboo mats, umbrellas, and such like. The males alone were saleable, the females who according to tradition are believed to be descended from Brahmanee women who had forgotten themselves, could not be disposed of. After death, good men are believed to resemble gods, and bad ones demons. They have small huts, in which the Deity is represented by a rude stone. They make offerings, and pray to both good and evil spirits.

The *Oolahdurs*, are said to have derived their name, either from *Ooladana*, "it is true," being the answer given by a Brahmanee woman, to a grave accusation, by which she became an out-caste, and the progenitor of a class of slaves. Or else from the two words *Ool*, "within," *Adana*, "runs," or a person who runs into the forest, evidently when any of a higher caste should approach. They are, the lowest class of soil slaves, and are unable to approach any of the other tribes, even the Mulchers. They live more especially around the base of the Ghauts, and may collect bees' wax, gums, &c., from bushes or shrubs if within reach of the ground: but they must not climb trees, as that would necessitate their driving pegs into them, which could not be permitted. They may not touch water, and if they do so, must fast for a day. Their clothes are usually merely leaves, their filthiness is extreme. They snare birds, and small game, and watch crops by night.

Their marriage ceremony is very simple, but it is also employed by some of the other inferior tribes, at certain times, although quite contrary to their rites. A large round building is made of leaves, and inside this the Bride is ensconced. All the eligible young men of the village then assemble, and form a ring around this hut. At a short distance, sits the girl's father, or nearest male relative, with a tom-tom in his hands, and a few more such musical instruments, complete the scene. Presently the music begins, and a chant which may be translated as follows, is sung by the father,

"Take the stick my sweetest daughter,
 Now seize the stick, my dearest love.
Should you not capture the husband you wish for,
 Remember 'tis fate, decides whom you shall have."

The young men each armed with a bamboo, commence dancing round the hut, into which each of them thrusts his stick. This continues about an hour, when the owner of whichever bamboo she seizes, become the fortunate husband of the concealed bride.

A feast then follows, the ceremony is now complete, whilst there is no divorce.

The *Mulchers, Mulliars,* or *Malasirs,* derived their name apparently from *Mala,* "a hill," and *Kaira,* "to go up," for their present designation, appears to be an abbreviation from "Malakaira," or "Malaira." The high caste natives, affirm that they, and the Kardahs, are identical races, but that the Mulchers originally lived on the Malabar, or western side of the ghauts, and the Kardahs on the Coimbatore, or eastern. The Mulchers are a tribe, who are not considered slaves: their nature partakes both of that of the Aborigines, and of the Hindus of the plains, above whom they are found in a topographically ascending, but a socially descending scale. Each Mulcher believes that both himself, and his neighbour, have many spirits at their command: consequently if one offends another, his bodily health may suffer, or even his life fall a sacrifice; thus it is, that should a quantity of bees' wax be perceived on a tree, the Mulcher first well examines the bark, to see if one of his tribe has been before him, and left his sign manual there, should he have done so, nothing would induce him to touch it, for fear of the consequences which might ensue, from his offended neighbour's demon. They do not believe, that their spirits have any power over the white races.

The Mulcher language, is a compound of Tamil and Malayalam, with some words of their own added, and a most curious pronunciation. They bury their dead.

The Mulchers live in small villages, situated on the skirts of the Hills, or part of the way up them, but between them and the Kardahs is a species of neutral ground, which is trodden on by neither tribe. In appearance they are superior to the slaves, or to the Kardahs. They are defiled if touched by one of the latter tribe. Men wear a string of beads around their necks: whilst the women, have also strings of large red and white beads, bangles on their arms, and sometimes rings on their fingers and toes. There is a head man over each community, who receives a certain amount of the sums they collect, and arranges their barters for them. When they have nothing to exchange for rice, they subsist on wild yams, *Dioscoreas,* but they cultivate small spots of Rali, *Cynosurus corocanus,* Avaray, *Dolichos Lablab,* and Tonda, *Ricinus palma christi.* They will fell timber and firewood, collect honey and bees' wax, and are good beaters for game, or trackers in the jungles. They are very fond of arrack, brandy, and toddy.

They take wives from their own village, and the girl's father is particular that the husband is such a one as he would be satisfied with. During the wife's life, they do not take a second. Marriages may be dissolved for infidelity on the woman's side, on which occasion the people of the village assemble, and should the case be proved to their satisfaction, she is returned to her parents. The husband does not again receive her, but any one else who wishes to marry her, may do so, if she accedes, but this is a very rare case. On the occasion of a marriage, the boy's father gives a feast to all the relations, a certain sum to the girl's mother, and a present to the daughter to buy a new dress. The Bride and Bridegroom, now proceed to a new hut, which has been erected for their future residence. The Bridegroom's parents, continue to live with the youngest son.

Their god called Mallung, is merely in some places a stone, surrounded by a wall, but more generally a collection of stones, each of which represents one of their forefathers, whose spirits they supplicate, to protect them from harm. In April they sacrifice honey, and sometimes goats, in the belief that should they neglect this duty, tigers and elephants, would be sent to destroy them. The Mulchers do not acknowledge any dependence upon the Brahmans, in their religious ceremonies.

Their diseases are numerous, and at times cholera sweeps their villages, but in their own locality, they are said very seldom to be attacked by malarious fevers. They are famous snake charmers, and assert that they possess the knowledge of some tree, the green leaf of which taken internally, as well as applied externally to any part, bitten by a venomous snake, is an infallible cure.

Along the highest range of the Hills in the Cochin territory, are found a race of true jungle people, known as the *Kardahs*, (*Kardah* "a jungle.") The most numerous division of them, live at Nelliampuddy at the summit of one of the highest mountains, on the Annamullies, and Kollumkode. Their villages are collections of small hovels, composed of the branches of trees, covered over with leaves

They are a very lazy race, and appear to greatly dislike manual labour, but are excellent trackers in the jungles, or collectors of wild produce: they are also useful in finding out the proper trees for felling, when timber is required.

The Kardahs are a short muscular race, of a deep black colour, with thick lips. Their language is Tamul, but their dialect such, that few Tamul persons can understand them. The women wear dark coloured clothes, and beads, bangles, rings, and charms. They have a head man, who decides all questions for them, and acts as a sort of Priest. He is entitled to the proceeds from certain large trees, and rocks, and a certain percentage of all honey and wax collected. Their Temples are small huts, in which rude stones painted over with red, represent their Deities, who are believed to protect them from tigers, elephants, and misfortunes; once a year at the time of the feast of Vishoo, they as well as the Mulchers, visit the low country; they pray to any image they see, but have nothing to do with the Brahmans. They dislike the Mulchers to come too near them, and if they encroach on what they consider their domain, they drive them away.

They subsist upon animals they are able to trap, wild yams, seeds of the bamboo, and other productions of the jungle; whilst they also receive a certain amount of rice, for collecting honey and bees wax. They obtain the latter in the following manner; around their waist, they carry a bundle of sharp pointed pegs of bamboo, that have had their points hardened in the fire, and over their shoulder is swung a basket, containing a mallet, and an additional supply of pegs, in case of their being required. Having driven one of the pegs into the trunk of the tree, in which the bees' nest is situated, they mount it, and insert another higher up, continuing this proceeding, until in about half an hour, they have succeeded in ascending the highest tree. But the prize is not captured until night, when armed with a lighted torch, they ascend, and the flame scares away the insects. Should the nest be on the face of the precipice, or rock, another expedient is resorted to. Having obtained some large and very long rattans, they split off the outside of this species of creeper, and fasten them together, so as to form a long rope ladder which fixed from the overhanging ledge, reaches the nest, and they climb down this. The Mulchers and Kardahs, both of which tribes, collect honey in this manner, are quite as susceptible to the stings of bees, as other people. In eating wild yams, they cut them up into small pieces, and leave them to soak in a running stream, for three days or more. This effectually removes all poisonous particles.

Men are only permitted one wife, and never take one who is related to themselves, on the male side. A swain who wishes for a wife, leaves his own community, and goes to another, where he works from six months to a year, by which time he will no doubt have made his choice: he then returns to his village, to obtain the consent of his family, and having gained this, he re-visits his Bride elect, and works in her community for a year, for her dowry. The lover presents the girl's mother with some cloth, and iron tools, and the marriage ceremony consists of a feast. After which the pair return to the husband's village. Should a woman have formed any fugitive connection, the tribe assemble, and oblige the paramour to take her as his wife, and should she be a married woman, she has to pay her former husband a fine. Widows are allowed to re-marry.

This people suffer little, if at all, from fever so long as they continue in their native jungles, but not so when they descend to the plains. They attribute all their diseases to witchcraft, and the exorcist carries on a thriving trade. They bury their dead.

The Mulchers and Kardahs, are let with the hills on which they live, they collect the produce, especially arrowroot for their winter food: they keep the last of the honey, and mix it with an equal proportion of pounded arrowroot. They then place the whole in a hollow bamboo, which they sink into the floors of their houses, where it becomes hard, and is considered capital eating.

The last tribe that space will allow any mention of, are the *Niadis*, a wandering out-caste abject race, so impure that hardly a slave will touch them. Roving about in small companies, or dragging out a miserable existence in wretched hovels, they live by watching crops, and protecting them from wild animals. They also howl at passers by for charity, which they must not advance to receive. They positively refuse to perform any manual labour whatever, though they do not object to act as beaters for sportsmen.

They collect roots for their ordinary sustenance, but have no knowledge of snaring birds, or animals. A tortoise sometimes comes in their way, when they kill and eat him, and occasionally they capture crocodiles by means of hooks and ropes, these they consider great luxuries.

The Niadis from continually howling for charity, have most unnaturally loud voices. Their habits are of a very filthy description. They worship a female Deity, and in March sacrifice a cock to preserve them from evil. They have no marriage-ceremonies, and bury their dead. This tribe as long as they continue in Malabar, will be useless to others, and will exercise no good influence in the country. *Dr. F. Buchanan*, proposed that they should be removed bodily to some place, where they would be compelled to labour for their subsistence.

Amongst the Hindu castes of Malabar, it cannot be denied that marriage to a certain extent does exist, as the eldest son of every Brahman goes through this ceremony, which is binding. But the marriage tie according to European ideas is unknown, polyandrism being the rule, not the exception. Perhaps the people's ideas are accustomed to this, and do not perceive the monstrosities of their proceedings, for were one half of the extent to which this prevails, and the mode in which it is conducted detailed, the writer's statements would not be believed, and his book would be unfit for respectable persons to read.

Sicknesses are usually treated by exorcisms and charms, for the power of evil spirits is admitted by all, the more ancient the tribes are, and the nearer they approach to the Aborigines, the greater seems their fear of these evil spirits. The Kardahs believe that they are bewitched by the Malabars, and *vice versa* ; whilst the Chogans extensively spread over the land, are most determined devil-worshippers, and offer sacrifices to demons, to keep them in health ; or drive away disease. The Hindus also offer sacrifices to Kali, in which they are joined by the Syrians, and some of the Romo-Syrians.

Burials as already mentioned, with the tribes in the Cochin State, are effected in three modes. Some bury their dead, as the Aborigines always used to do, this custom more especially prevails amongst the Kardahs, on the highest Hills, and the Mucuas of the sea shore.

Others burn their dead, these are the true Hindu castes; and others again employ both these methods.

Inheritance descends as a rule in Malabar through the sister's children, who are the legitimate representatives of the family. But there are some exceptions as amongst the Brahmans, and a few other castes already alluded to, with whom it descends to the children of the parents.

CHAPTER VIII.

JEWS.

Census of Jews—Their various communities—Jews town—Synagogue—Division into two classes—White Jews—Costume—Copper plates—Translations—Date of its grant—Black Jews—War between Black and White Jews—Circumcision—Marriage—Death—Burial—Sabbath—Day of wailing—Feast of Tabernacles—Similarity of Jewish and Hindu tabernacles—History of Jews of Cochin—Early settlement—First rulers—Destruction of Cranganore—Total defeat of Jews by the Moors—Migration to Cochin—Dutch—English.

Scattered about in various parts of India, are small families of Jews, some interesting communities of whom, reside in Malabar, and especially in the Cochin State. Around the town of Cochin, they have several settlements, the largest, *Jews town,* situated a little more than one mile to the South East, contains 419 of this peculiar race.* At Ernacollum to the East, on the mainland, 353 reside : and at Chennamungalum, twenty-five miles inland, 65 more. In the town of Cochin, there are also a few Half-caste and black Jews, who have removed there, for the purpose of more easily obtaining employment, as well as in consequence of certain privileges being denied them elsewhere.

Jews town may be reached, either by water, or by going along the Culvetty and Muttencherry Bazaars, passing a Roman Catholic Church and the Rajah's Palace, the wall of which divides his residence, from the Jewish Synagogue. It has been asserted, that the Jews

* The census of these places, was taken by order of the Dewan, *Vencata Row,* in 1857, there were 1,790 Jews in the whole of the Cochin State. The Rev. *Claudius Buchanan,* in his enthusiastic manner, computed the Jews of Cochin, at 16,000 !

came here from Cranganore, to escape from Portuguese tyranny: not a very likely migration, were they thus suffering, for it is hardly probable they would leave the vicinity of the smaller station of Cranganore, to come into the Cochin fort, and reside there, whilst they were erecting a town for themselves hard by: and that all this should be accomplished, to escape from the Portuguese. Had oppressions caused them to migrate, they would have removed inland, or even to Ernacollum, or Chennamungalum, or to some distance from their oppressors: but the Jews were traders of note in those days, and their presence was useful to the Portuguese.

Jews town is about ⅛ of a mile in length, and is situated close to the banks of the backwater, commencing from the southern wall of the Rajah's Palace, and terminating at a stream which divides it from the Arab and Moplah sailors. The bazaar is situated along the southern half of the town.

The houses are of the same description as those in Cochin, being constructed of laterite, mostly two storied high, having tiled pent roofs, and running in the form of one long narrow street. Various representations may be seen on the walls of the houses, either graven on the stone, or formed out of the chunam with which they are covered. They consist of peacocks, sometimes two or three, being on one house: double headed eagles: in one instance, two cocks fighting: in another, a man on one knee presenting a sword with his right hand against a tiger, which, is rushing upon him: a deer with huge antlers is on one house, a non-descript animal, something resembling a crocodile, on another. The interior of these houses, are of exactly the same description, as the usual style of those of Portuguese construction within the fort of Cochin, from which they were no doubt copied; the windows have the same kind of seats, and shutters, and are glazed in the same manner, whilst the walls are as thick, and as crooked, and the doors as strong, as those in Cochin. In the door posts, of every room the Jews according to the Mosaic command insert small tubes of tin, or bamboo, in which are portions of Deuteronomy, and the name of Jehovah, written upon very thin leather, or vellum. On leaving their houses, or even on simply going from room to room, they kiss this tube, bow to it or touch it with their fingers, which they then kiss.

There are two chief Synagogues, one at the northern end of the town, close to the wall of the Rajah's palace, and only used by the white Jews. Another at its southern extremity, which is used by the black, also termed slave Jews. There is a third smaller one.

The chief or northern Synagogue, is about 40 feet long, and 30 wide, and by no means a fine building. Tawdry brass chandeliers, hold numerous tumblers of oil for lights. The reading desk, is in the centre, facing the Books of the Law to the west where they are kept in a cupboard behind a curtain, and consist of five copies of the Pentateuch, most beautifully written in Hebrew characters, on vellum. Having no altar, they have no sacrifices, and the yearly oblation of a cock, said to take place in Europe, does not do so in Cochin, where no bloody sacrifices are made. The flooring of the Synagogue, is of blue and white China tiles. The women's gallery, is screened from the body of the Church, around which are benches for the men.

On passing inside the gateway, through the first court yard, where four ostrich eggs are suspended, the porch of the Synagogue is arrived at: here the Jew leaves his shoes, before he enters within the house of prayer. There is an iron safe, for the reception of alms for the poor, fixed against the outer wall of the building.

A person visiting the Synagogue during the service, cannot draw the conclusion, that he is surrounded by a devotional people: as children are running about all the time, talking, laughing, and playing tricks upon one another. The service commences by a Rabbi, who with his head covered by a tallith, or veil, thrown over his turban, chants a prayer from the reading desk. This faces the West, is raised two steps above the floor, and surrounded by a railing, outside which are seats. The Rabbi generally covers his face whilst reading, but this is not done in the feast of the Tabernacles. He turns towards the west, whilst the congregation continue swaying their bodies incessantly backwards and forwards, and bowing towards the Tabernacle. This is interrupted, by their suddenly bursting forth with an electrifying response, to the Rabbi. Although before entering the Synagogue, the Jews remove their shoes, which they leave in the outer Court, (Exod. iii. 5. Josh. v. 15.) some of the better classes, wear stockings, which they retain. When inside the building, they advance a few steps towards the Books of the Law, place the two first fingers of their right hands on their lips, incline their bodies, and then proceed to their seats.

The Jews are strictly divisible into two classes, but there is also an intermediate one. The two former are the white, or Jerusalem Jews, whose blood has never been mixed with that of the surrounding people: and the black Jews, who are pure Natives, 500 of whom are said to have been purchased by the first Jewish settlers, and the present race are believed to be the descendants of these slaves, and of other Natives of Malabar, who were converted to the Jewish faith. These last, are said to call themselves Beni Israel. The white Jews inhabit the sea coast, but the black Jews* generally live more in the interior of the country. Besides these, there is the intermediate race, known as half-caste Jews, whose denomination sufficiently denotes their origin.

The white Jew retains the peculiar characteristics of his race; his religion, manners, and customs, are unaltered either by time, or distance: and if his contempt of the Nazarenes is as great here as in Europe, he does not show it in his manner, which is very courteous: he shakes hands with those who enter his house, and is by no means shy, or ill at ease. The Jews are naturally very much annoyed, if persons present during their religious services, ridicule or laugh at them, and in consequence it is said, of the uncivil behaviour of certain sailors, they have latterly become averse to strangers visiting their Synagogue, and endeavour to mislead, respecting the days of their feasts.

The complexion of the white Jew, is fairer than that of most Europeans, and his features in many instances, but not in all, bear the true Jewish stamp. He is usually good looking, intelligent, and agreeable. Many of them have flaxen hair, and light blue eyes, which singularly agrees with the following remark, made by *Miss Martineau.* "Here," (Hebron) "at Jerusalem, and elsewhere, we "saw many Jews with fair complexions, and light hair." Time appears to improve the personal appearance of the Jew, who even in old age, retains his handsome features, whilst his long white beard,

* It is curious that it has been asserted, and still is repeated again and again in Europe, that these black Jews are a distinct race, instead of Natives of the country, converted to the Jewish faith.

gives him an imposing and patriarchal appearance. It is curious to visit one of these communities of an evening, and to watch them in a Hindu State, in their long flowing robes, wending their way to the Synagogue. Their waist-coats are buttoned up in front, and the robe is on Sundays composed of materials, of whatever hue they prefer, and full white trowsers complete the costume. Their heads are shaved at an early age, leaving only one lock in front and above both ears, they wear a scull cap on ordinary occasions, but occasionally a turban.

The Jewesses do not like being seen by strangers, or walking in the streets. They are seldom visible, excepting at weddings, and great festivals, and their language is said not to be such, as is generally approved by ears polite. They have fine figures, but there are but few pretty faces amongst them. The attire of the middle aged women, is by no means so graceful as that of the men, as they have copied the jackets, and scanty skirts, or cloths, worn by the surrounding Natives. The cloth is fastened round the waist, by a gold or silver belt, from whence a bunch of gold or silver keys, are suspended. They are usually very plainly dressed, but for grand occasions, they have some magnificent costumes, composed of cloth of gold and silver, but these they seldom wear, after the first few years of their marriage: one of them has a white muslin Malabar dress, bordered all round with sovereigns, and a stomacher made of little gold fish, intermingled with jewels. Sometimes the skirt is made of silk, but more commonly of printed calico. They wear a square head dress, with a white veil, which falls over their shoulders, as low as the waist. The necks are perfectly loaded with chains of coins, mostly Venetian sequins, and other curiously fashioned golden ornaments. When the black Jews, commonly called by the white Jews, "the slaves,"* became more opulent, they began to wear dresses and ornaments of coins, and necklaces, like the white division. This gave great offence, so about 1860, the Bagdad dress was adopted by the young white Jewesses. Another reason assigned for this change of costume, is that young Jews from other places

* The Jews of Cochin, do not appear to have strictly kept to the Mosaical law, of manumitting their slaves, after a certain number of years: or boring their ears against the door post. A person now in Cochin who was a slave, but manumitted himself, states that his father, grandfather and himself, were kept slaves, whilst he is not the only instance of this having been done.

who were unaccustomed to the ugly Malabar style of dress, disliked it extremely, and in consequence rarely took Brides from amongst their country women in Cochin. The more elderly married women, not caring so much for personal appearance, have retained the costume to which they are accustomed.

The Bagdad dress consists of a scanty skirt, of rich cloth, satin, figured barege, or muslin, made in one piece, from the neck to the ankles, gathered in behind, fastened up in front, and open from the throat, nearly as far down as the waist, showing a white handkerchief or stomacher. Their hair is usually very untidy, and the older women appear to take very little trouble in personal adornment. Married women after the birth of their second child, generally leave off their jewels, and dress plainly. In mourning, they wear either white clothing edged with black, and white or black ornaments: or dresses of a deep blue colour.

After marriage, they always cover their heads, either with a handkerchief, or on grand occasions, with a little gold coloured cap, with a long golden tassel. In the Synagogue, all the females have their heads covered, some of them by long muslin or net veils.

As age creeps on, the Jewess rapidly loses her good looks, and at thirty may be considered quite passée.

The white Jews possess three copper plates,* looking as if they had been taken from a ship's side, $\frac{1}{4}$ by $\frac{1}{8}$ of a yard in size. The outer one has no inscription. The translation has been declared by those competent to judge, to be identical with that of the Syrian Plates. *Governor Moens* obtained three different translations of these plates, the substance of the three being the same, although the wording was different. He gives the following as the most correct version.

"With the help of God who formed the world, and establishes
" Kings, and whom we honor, we, Erawi, Wanwara, emperor of
" Malabar, in the thirty-sixth year of our lucky reign, and in the
" fort, Moidiricotta, (Cranganore,) give this deed of rights, to the

* The *Rev. C. Buchanan*, states that the original plate was of brass, and engraved on both sides. He had facsimiles made from it, on two copper plates, which he deposited in the University of Cambridge. The carving of the original, is said to have looked very old, that on the present plates, certainly does not do so. If the plate at Cambridge is of brass, and engraved on both sides, it may perhaps be concluded, that Dr. Buchanan returned the new plates to the Jews, and kept the old one.

"good Joseph Rabaan, that he may use the five colours, spread his "religion amongst the five castes, have all honour offered him, "have guns fired, be allowed to ride on elephants and horses, to "proceed in state, have his honours proclaimed before him, have "lights used by day, have all kinds of music; also he may employ "a large umbrella, walk on white cloth spread on the road, "have the stick play played before him, and sit under a stately "canopy. These rights give we to Joseph Rabaan, and to 72 Jewish "householders, with the government over their nation, who are "directed tc obey them, and their heirs, so long as the sun shines "on the face of the earth. This deed is given in the presence of the "Kings of Travancore, Teckencoor, Baddakencoor, Culli Quilon, "Aringoot, Samorin, Paliat Achen, and Colastria: written by the "Secretary Calembi Kelapoor, in the year 3481, of the Cali Yuga."

The difference in the other two translations, was as follows:—

1st.—In them the year of the Cali Yuga is not given.

2nd.—The witnesses in the 2nd translation are:

1st.—The Chief of Wanaud, named Comaraten Mataandoon.

2nd.—The chief of Wanaa-Odea, named Codie Chericanden.

3rd.—The chief of Eraala, named Maana Bepalamaan.

4th.—The chief of Walonaddu, named Irawaren Chaten.

5th.—The chief of Neddoowaloor, named Cody Irawi.

6th.—As also the chief of the minor princes of Coosapadi, heir of Moorkom Chaten, and named Kelokanden.

Written by the Secretary named Gunawende Wanasen Nayer Kisapa Kelapa, signed by the emperor.

In the 3rd translation, the differences are,—

1st.—That the granter's name is Erwi Barmen.

2nd.—The witnesses are,—

1st.	The King of	Travancore,		5th.	The King of	Palghautcherry	
2nd.	" "	Berkencoor,		6th.	" "	Colastria,	
3rd.	" "	Samorin,		7th.	" "	Corambanadu.	
4th.	" "	Argot,					

Written by the Secretary Kellapen.

Also in the last two translations, the grant is made only to Joseph Rabaan, whereas according to the 1st translation, it is made to him and the 72 families.

Moens makes the remark, that although this grant was made, yet the sovereignty remained with the sovereign of the country, and the Jews were not exempted from taxes, &c., their chief being empowered, to take notice, only of trifling civil cases.

It was not until after the last of the Permauls had ceased to reign, in A. D. 378, that the various Rajahs enumerated above, were in independent possession of their territories. The Jews assert that this plate was granted to them by Cheraman Permaul, and if the translation be correct, such must have been the fact, as he was the only Permaul who ruled more than 12 years. The text of the grant states, that it was made in the 36th year of the reign of Cheraman Permaul, or A. D. 377, but the date on which the plate was engraved, or completed, is given as 379, the witnesses being the various Rajahs, amongst whom the extensive territory of Cheraman Permaul was evidently divided, and it was only at this period of division, or in the year subsequent to the death of this powerful monarch, that when settling their respective claims, A. D. 379, they could all have been present at Cranganore. It may therefore be concluded that Cheraman Permaul conferred the rights, A. D. 377, and that all these chieftains were aware of the grant, but that it had not been committed to writing, consequently when a settlement of their respective shares had been effected, they all agreed to the rights given by Cheraman Permaul to the Jews, and these were then engraved on metal plates, and thus the date given, viz., A. D. 379, may be accounted for.

These plates therefore become another link in the chain of collateral evidence, respecting the date when the last of the Permauls divided his kingdom, whilst he is known, to be the only one of them who reigned 36 years.

The *Rev. Claudius Buchanan*, collected most of the old, and valuable M.S. records, from the black Jews' Synagogue. The manuscripts some of which almost every collector tries to obtain, may be procured without much difficulty, as a good store appear to be usually kept, ready for sale: but none of them are ancient, whilst the printed books are mostly from Amsterdam, and according to the Flemish ritual. When the Books of the Law are too much worn to be of service, they are said to be buried, never burnt. Buchanan states, that the most ancient M.S. that he obtained from the black Jews, was a copy of the Pentateuch, written on a roll of 37 goatskins, dyed red, 48 feet long, and 22 inches broad, (a Jewish cubit,) it was incomplete, as Leviticus, and a great part of Deuteronomy were absent: its original length must have been about ninety feet. The deviations from the common Hebrew text, printed in Europe, were very unimportant. The half-caste Jews, may belong to the congregation of the white Jews. One community of this class, has settled in the town of Cochin, and have obtained the sanction from Bagdad, which permits one of their number to slaughter fowls for food, and to perform the requisite ceremonies. They separated themselves from the remainder of their community in Jew's town, about 15 years since, partly on account of an ill-feeling at that time prevalent, in consequence of their women not being allowed to dress themselves in the golden chains, and ornaments, worn by the higher classes. In the British town, they can now do as they please, and dress in any way they like, but should they return to Jews' town, these privileges would be immediately, and forcibly, taken from them.

The *Synagogues* belonging to the black Jews, have nothing remarkable about them.* These people, distinctly show their native origin. The Jewish caste of features is apparent, in those of rather a light complexion, demonstrating the race from which they are sprung. Some of the darkest coloured of these Jews, are so like the Natives of Malabar, as at once to convince the most sceptical observer, that they must have originated from amongst the surrounding population. Some of them are converts, and others the descendants of slaves, purchased by the Jews, in the time of the Portuguese, and Dutch, and converted to the Jewish faith. They act as inferiors to the white Jews at some feasts, but have never paid any tribute to them, still being an inferior race, they are not allowed to sit down in their presence. The white Jews are traders, and merchants, whilst the black Jews gain their livelihood, by practising various handicrafts, and are sawyers, blacksmiths, carpenters, bricklayers, book-binders, tailors, fishermen, servants to the white

* Although the Black Jews perform their own religious services, should a White Rabbi enter their Synagogue, they must give place, and allow him to carry on the Service.

Jews, &c., they travel about the country for these purposes, nearly as far as Bombay: three quarters of them, are vendors of household necessaries. During the last few years, a manifest improvement has taken place in their circumstances.

Many years ago, the black Jews claimed equal rank with the white Jews, and demanded the same privileges, especially the right of inter-marrying with them; but as they would not listen to any proposals of this nature, the black Jews refused to recognise their authority, setting the dictates of the head man at defiance. A war ensued, in which the white Jews are said to have been nearly extirpated, but a Native prince coming to their assistance, the rebels were reduced to obedience, and since then, the two races have totally separated.

The *rite of circumcision* is performed on the eighth day, and usually takes place in the Synagogue, at the same time the child also receives his name. When old enough, he is sent to a Priest, to be instructed in the rudiments of religion, and as much secular knowledge, as his spiritual teacher is able to impart. There are very few of either sex, who are unable to read, and write.

When a child attains the age of thirteen, his parents are no longer considered responsible for his sins, and the sabbath after he has attained that age, a species of "confirmation" is held in the Synagogue, when he is invested with the phylacteries, or little boxes which contain inscriptions on parchment, taken from the law: they are bound around his head and left arm, during his devotions.

Sometimes as early as sixteen, or seventeen years of age, the young Jew is betrothed to a Jewess, several years younger than himself: and about twelve months afterwards, the marriage is celebrated with great pomp, unless it occurs whilst the parents are in mourning. On this occasion, if the family is wealthy, a grand feast is generally held, to which most of the European inhabitants of Cochin are invited. When the parents of the Bride are wealthy, she is loaded with jewels, which are a portion of her dowry, but should her parents be poor, they must not be taken from the house, but are kept for the use of the younger sisters. Dr. Buchanan mentions, that at the commencement of this century, the women at marriages, "were covered with gold and silver Dacca and Surat "muslins, that being the costume on such occasions, from time im-"memorial." As previously mentioned, the younger females have now changed this dress.

When the death of a member of the white community is expected, some of the elders of the Church are sent for, who receive the invalid's confession, and directions as to the division of his property, and sometimes as to his own obsequies, which take place about three hours after death. All male relatives and friends usually attend, as a last mark of respect to the remnant of mortality. His nearest blood relatives, then entreat the corpse to pardon them anything which they may have done to offend him, during his life time.

The burial ground, which is designated the "house of the living," is to the west of the town, surrounded by a dense tope of cocoanut trees, and in this cold damp spot, the dead are deposited, usually without coffins, in graves which are dug north and south, there to await, the resurrection morn.

The Jews desire sons, nearly as much as do the surrounding Hindus, as they have much the same duties to carry out, which can be performed by no female. Twice a day for eleven months after a father's death, his son ought to pray in the Synagogue. The anniversary is always held as a fast, and certain ceremonies must then be performed. During the whole of this period, a lamp is kept lighted.

The *Jewish Sabbath*, their *feasts*, and their *fasts*, commence at 6 P. M. on the evening of one day, and are computed by the succeeding twenty-four hours: the same mode of reckoning is employed, as previously given for the Syrians, (p. 259). Before their Sabbath commences, everything in the form of work for the succeeding day must be completed, food is prepared, even the tables laid, whilst all remain ready dressed, for the Sabbath when they "do no manner of work." The fires in every house are extinguished, even smoking is prohibited, until the evening, when a light is procured from the Synagogue, where one is always kept burning. The Sabbath is considered a time of rejoicing, prayers are said at stated periods, but the remainder of the day, is spent in visiting one another, playing cards, and other games.

As a rule, every day is commenced by prayer, both at home,

and in the Synagogue, repeated about three in the evening; and again at sun set.

On one day in the year, in commemoration of the destruction of Jerusalem, they hold a very strict and solemn fast, from 3-30 one day, until 7 P. M. on the following. They clothe themselves in deep mourning, and bewail the desolation of their parent city. The Jews in their Synagogues, and the Jewesses on the floors of their houses, all appear to be weeping for some great calamity, and mourning the loss of some dear object.* The great day of atonement every year, is kept very strictly, and the males are dressed in the same white flowing robes, that will after death, form their shrouds.

The *Passover* is strictly kept, and very few Europeans have had an opportunity of observing its celebration. Every one is dressed as for a journey, the kid is divided in accordance with the Mosaic order, and is eaten in haste, but the blood is *not sprinkled* upon the door post and lintel.

The *feast of the Tabernacles*, is observed with more pomp and ceremony, than any of the others, and then the women appear in public. Attached to every house, is an open flat roof or space, on which some cadjan leaves are raised, so as to form a sort of covering, and here in the open air, all take their meals. Cups of oil are kept lighted at the doorways of every house, whilst opposite the Synagogue is a large stand, filled with oil lights. On the last and great day of the feast, the congregation assembles in the Synagogue, at about half-past one, and the service commences at two. Persons of both sexes and every age, congregate in the house of prayer, which is decorated, for the occasion: square pieces of coloured tinsel hang from the ceiling of the porch, whilst within, the walls are hidden from view, by cloths of various colours, some of which are spangled with silver. Around the reading desk, is a string of the white flowers, of the Indian Jessamine. The five books of the law are seen in the tabernacle, in their silver cases, each being surmounted by a golden crown, the two

---

*The observer acquainted with the cause of this great mourning, must on entering the Synagogue of the black Jews, experience a mixed feeling, of pain and absurdity. The former at witnessing the mournful aspect, and doleful lamentations around him; and the latter on remembering, that they are all Natives of India, alike ignorant of history, or geography.

external of which, differ, in that they have a sort of turret at either extremity. All the oil lights, which are in brazen vessels, or else in glasses with brass supporters, are seen alight, every one is in holiday attire. The flowing robes of the Jews are crimson, plum colour, bronze, amber, orange, green, yellow, or even shawl patterns : whilst the turbans wound around the white skull caps, are often exceedingly handsome. The women in their gallery,* have dresses of the same bright colours, as those of the men, also dark blue, light blue, primrose, pink spotted, and barege.

A little after two o'clock, all the male congregation advance towards the Books of the Law, the three centre ones are taken down from their position, and borne towards the door, in the midst of chants and songs of praise ; at every step members of the congregation press forward to salute them. Having arrived at the Court, they are carried around the building, commencing from the northern side. All join in singing, whilst those in front, and around the books, commence dancing and jumping about. When the Jews have left the building, the Jewesses come down from their gallery, and kiss the two remaining books. In the meantime, the three others having been carried as described, three times around the building, the Synagogue is again entered, and the two remaining volumes are taken out, to join in the last round.† In the Synagogue of the black Jews, rose

* Women are not a portion of the congregation, their presence being merely tolerated in a gallery, which is hardly considered a portion of the sacred building. It is said, that Jews offer up daily thanks, that they were not born of the female sex !

† The *Rev. J. Roberts*, (Journal Royal Asiatic Society,) observes upon the similarity of this feast, to that obtaining amongst the Hindus when they take their principal Deities out in procession, in their tabernacles, preceded by priests, singers, musicians, and the dancing girls of the Temple. This is done to demonstrate from which god they considered they are deriving protection, or else to honour him, in hopes that he will dissipate some sickness, or avert the evil eye. The Hindu tabernacle, is properly speaking borne by priests, (although it is now mostly taken on wheels forming a car) whilst that of the Jews is directed to be carried by Levites : or should none such be present, by the highest in rank, amongst the members of the congregation.

The Jews, *Amos* v. 26, were told, that "ye have borne the tabernacle of your "Moloch, and Chiun, your images, the star of your god, which ye made to "yourselves." This Chiun, has been by good authorities, surmised to mean

water is sprinkled from a silver bottle over the books, and the people, but with the white Jews, it is only made use of at the door.*

This peculiar people, this nation within a nation, have been occasionally persecuted and oppressed, but still they throve. In the time of the Dutch they reached the highest point of their prosperity, but when the British took Cochin, they gradually but surely declined, and decreased in numbers, power, and opulence. During the last few years, they have again been more prosperous, their trade has increased, they have become more wealthy, and altogether a decided change for the better, is perceptible amongst them. In their formerly great and remunerative trade, which in the time of the Dutch they almost monopolized, they are now supplanted by Europeans, Parsees, Moplahs, and others. The women now principally employ themselves in making coarse lace, and embroidering caps, which meet with a ready sale in Bombay, amongst the Parsees.

Basnage supposes it not improbable, that the first Jews who arrived on this coast, came in Solomon's fleet. Their own legends affirm, that about A. D. 68 after the destruction of the second temple, about one thousand Jews and Jewesses came to Malabar, where three fourths of them settled at Cranganore, and the remainder in other places, and that in the year A. D. 379,† just the year after Cheraman Permaul's death, the Jews at Cranganore received a copper plate,

---

Chiven, or Siva of the Hindus, the idol they mostly carry in procession; whilst Moloch, appears to be Kali or Bhagavadi, Siva's wife (see page 283.) The star in the knee of Gemini, is termed Siva's star, and is painted on his car.

In the fragment to Calmet, it is said. "It will no doubt be observed, that "the Chiun of Amos, is a term used many ages after the event to which the "prophet refers, which are thus connected with the history of Balaam, *Numbers* "Ch. XXII and the term in Numbers, is not Chiun, but Baal-peor." Thus Amos calls Baal-peor by the name of Chiven, or Siva, which "Israel joined himself to."

* In the *Romo-Syrian* church at Shallacooddee, there is a representation over their figure of St. George, said to have been of *Jewish origin.* It is a triangle inside which is an eye, surrounded by a halo, or Unity in Trinity. The Vicar stated it owed its origin to a Jewish legend, that Moses on Mount Sinai was only permitted to see one of the Almighty's eyes.

† This is the date given in the Jewish translation, received from the Senior Rabbi at Jewstown, who in 1861 had charge of the Jewish plates. The most

giving them the privileges, as already translated in full, and according to their own account, they had a head man of their tribes Suranum Moplah.

Van Reede, who took a great interest in this people, stated in 1695, that they were of the tribe of Manasseh, a portion of whom were carried away by Nebuchadnezzar, to the eastern extremity of his vast empire, from whence they migrated into Malabar, carrying with them the silver trumpets, made use of in the time of the Jubilee, and on which were inscribed the ineffable name. The number of persons composing this emigration, has been variously estimated, at from 18, to 80,000, but common sense precludes the possibility of so large a number of persons as that last mentioned, arriving at the same time. Even at the present day, notwithstanding all the modern appliances of steam, &c., moving such an enormous army, would be a fearful undertaking. However this may have been, the Jews increased rapidly in Malabar, and in course of time, having become wealthy, they were able according to some accounts, to purchase Cranganore. But this may much more probably be understood to mean, that they purchased the right of living tax free, being under the Government of their own people, and trying and punishing their

---

extraordinary legends concerning this people are extant, and for the verification of many of them, the shade of Cheraman Permaul is invoked, even hundreds of years after he had paid the debt of nature, A. D. 378. For this event various authors have indulged in dates of their own, without advancing any argument whatever, tending to prove them correct; for instance, *Moens*, gives A. D. 426. *Dr. C. Buchanan*, 490. *Bishop Middleton*, 508. *Mr. Lawson*, 750. *The Rev. T. Whitehouse*, 825! *Paoli*, the tenth century; and the *Jews* themselves, A. D. 379, making a trifling difference of 446 years, between the date given by them, and that by Mr. Whitehouse. It appears that the original date, or rather that given on the copper plates by the translator, is one year subsequent to Cheraman Permaul's death, whereas the text of the grant, states it to have been made in the 36th year of his reign, or the year before his demise, viz., A. D. 377. If the translation is referred to, it will be seen that the grant was made in the 36th year of his reign, but *written* in A. D. 379. The Syrian plates are identical with those of the Jews, which has given rise to the idea, that both, or at all events one of them, must be spurious, but quite an opposite construction may be placed on this similarity. If they were both granted at the same time, and conferred the same privileges, it is but natural to suppose, that similar words and expressions might be used, where the witnesses were the same, and the same Secretary drew up the grants,

own race, by their own laws. They then chose two brothers, who were members of a family which had long been esteemed, for wisdom, intelligence, and wealth: and elected them to govern their small commonwealth, conjointly. But dissensions are said to have arisen, and at length one of the brothers, invited the other to a feast, and took advantage of this opportunity, to murder him, that he might reign supreme. His triumph however was of short duration, as he in turn, was slain by the son of his victim. The community then lapsed into democracy, and anarchy, and gradually but surely declined in importance, wealth, and character.

These early dates, are very difficult to settle definitely, but according to Jewish traditions, about 1,000 years after their arrival at Cranganore, dissensions arose amongst them: at all events before the arrival of the Portuguese, there had been a great dispute between the white Jews and the black, said to have been occasioned, by the latter claiming the privileges of the former, and demanding the right of inter-marriage with them. The former appealed to a Native Prince for assistance, (to whom they were probably vassals, very possibly the Paliat Achen, at Chenotta,) who thoroughly destroyed the settlement. The number of Jews were thus considerably decreased, and although since that period, they have seen many vicissitudes, they have never enjoyed the same power and opulence. The desolation of Cranganore, was likened to a miniature destruction of Jerusalem, and has often been laid to the account of the Portuguese. *Zeirredien* the Mahomedan historian, states that in 1524, the Moors engaged in a most barbarous war against the Jews at Cranganore, when all who could be captured, were massacred without mercy, whilst their houses and Synagogues were burnt. In this, the Portuguese could not have been concerned, because they and the Moors were at that period in a deadly feud, and Zeirredien continues, that on the following year, the Moors having retired to Calicut, joined the Samorin's forces, and assisted him to destroy the Portuguese factory there, killing or driving away all of that nation. The Portuguese themselves give an account of this, (p. 104), but assert, that they drove away the Natives, although they found it advisable subsequently to evacuate and blow up the fort.

After the destruction of Cranganore, prior to the arrival of the

Portuguese, many of the Jews were probably carried away to Chenotta, or Chennamungalum, where a colony of them still exists. There were no Jews in Cochin, when the Portuguese arrived there in 1500, but at Cranganore there were a few, in a miserable state of destitution, who were probably a remnant of the former community, who had either returned, or escaped from servitude. It is only natural, that they should after this, wish to quit the scene of their former power, and grandeur, which had now passed away, and in 1565, when the Samorin, and his Moorish Allies, assisted by one of the petty Rajahs, again invaded the Cochin State, these people were probably again severely treated, for the Samorin's party were victorious, and the Cochin Rajah, and two Princes, were slain in battle on January 27th, 1565,* whilst the succeeding Rajah, met with the same fate, fourteen days later. Some of the Portuguese, were no doubt present, with the Cochin party, and as they were worsted, had no time for oppressing the Jews, who in this very year, (probably after the occurrence of the above events,) obtained refuge in Cochin, during the time they were building Jews town, under the walls of the fort. In this year also, the Portuguese were obliged to enlarge and strengthen the fortress, at Cranganore,† evidently against the Samorin's party. All that appears to be now known, is, that in 1565, the Jews fled from Cranganore to Cochin, and erected their present settlement of Jews town.

A want of space, precludes the possibility of giving the numerous Jewish legends, which vary in different places, and may be said to be simply their own surmises, some of which are founded on actual occurrences affecting themselves, and others on those concerning either the Syrians, or some of the other sects around them.

On the capture of Cochin by the Dutch in 1663, the Jews were much depressed, owing to the punishment which had been inflicted

* This battle was celebrated in Malabar verse, the poem is still extant, and enters fully into the details of the defeat, and death, of the Rajah of Cochin, and the two Princes.

† From the above it would seem probable, that the statement of *Mr. Whitehouse*, in HISTORICAL NOTICES OF COCHIN "That in 1565 the Jews to escape the "persecutions of the Portuguese, left Cranganore, and put themselves under the protection of the Cochin Rajah," is an error.

upon them by the Portuguese, for having assisted the Dutch, in their first attack upon Cochin. But after this date prosperity again dawned upon them, and a leading member of the community had the title of Modeliar conferred upon him, whilst one rich family, (Ezekiel,) acted a very important part, in contracting their treaties with the Samorin, the Travancore or Ram Rajah, and others. The better class of Jews, were received in the best society of Cochin, where the wealthier possessed houses. In 1685, an immigration of White Jews occurred from Amsterdam, and subsequently others joined them from Palestine, Persia, Bagdad, Egypt, England, Poland, Germany, especially Frankfort, and Spain.*

It may be asked, what the British since their advent to Cochin have done for the Jews? First came the Rev. C. Buchanan, who interested himself greatly, both in the people and their records, many of which last he obtained, and removed to Europe, where they are still regarded with wonder and interest. In his "Christian Researches," may be found an account of all he gleaned respecting them. At the Black Jews' Synagogue, he found many manuscripts written on parchments, goat's skin, and cotton paper, many of these he purchased, or rather procured, notwithstanding the resistance of the greatest part of the Jews, and their disinclination to part with the legends of their forefathers. But he managed to escape from Jew's town with his prize, and by the aid of money, and the assistance of the Magistrate, it was finally agreed, that he should retain many of them.

* Observers have remarked upon the White Jews, having existed many centuries in the Cochin State, and have argued, that this affords a proof, that European blood, *unmixed with that of the Native races*, can be continued through many generations. But it is nothing of the sort, it is the best test that could be adduced to the contrary, (admitting them to be pure Europeans, which they are not.) The pure White Jews have never been able to continue their race without the aid of immigrants from other places, and before this question was ever mooted, *Governor* Moen's remarked, that the White Jews were continued, owing to constant admixture with new blood. So it is now, none of upwards of three generations, born in the country, of pure white blood on both father's and mother's side, can be detected. The plains of India are unsuited for permanent colonization by the white races, if we are to draw conclusions from bygone facts, or reason by analogy with what is daily perceptible around.

Missionaries have been sent to the Jews, with very little effect. *Buchanan* states, that one of this sect translated the New Testament, in order to refute some arguments adduced by the Syrians, but instead of that, he himself embraced Christianity. It has subsequently become a belief, that any person who translates the whole of that portion of the Scriptures, will inevitably become a convert to Christianity, by the power of the evil spirit. Occasionally they even now obtain converts to their faith : but they have a rule, that no woman becoming a Jewess can marry a Jew, although a male embracing their tenets may be united in matrimony to a Jewess. The Jews do not like to enter into any religious arguments respecting our Saviour, and if questioned as to the meaning of certain passages in Isaiah, they always declare that they refer, to the good king Hosea, and if pressed further, they grow sullen, and refuse to continue the conversation.

CHAPTER IX.

THE MAHOMEDANS.

Mahomedans in the Cochin State—Mahomed, his rise, teaching, and death—The four Caliphs—The Imams—Sheeas—Soonees—Rise of various schools—Creed spreads to India—Division of Indian Mahomedans—Hindu rites become engrafted on new creed—Caste distinctions commence—Origin of Moplahs—Persecutions of Portuguese—Beebee of Cannanore—Hyder—Tippoo—English—Priests—Rites—Feasts—Marriages—Unlucky days—Seclusion of women—Dirty race—Burials—Fast of Mohorram—Ramzan.

The Mahomedans in the Cochin State, comprise about 1 in 20 of the entire population, but they appear to be rapidly increasing in numbers. They are distinctly divisible into two portions, the *true Mahomedans* who live in small communities, and exercise the tenets of their faith as in other portions of the South of India: and the *Moplahs,* who though also Mahomedans, are to a great extent distinct from them, and form a bigoted and intolerant sect of their own.

A summary of the rise of Mahomedanism is necessary, in order to explain as shortly as possible, the origin of its numerous divisions.

Mahomed, the founder of this religious sect, was born at Mecca; A.D. 569, and on his father's death, whilst he was still very young, he found himself the head of a small Arab family, one of the branches of the tribe of Korésh, and the owner of one slave and five camels. His mother Amina, is said to have been a Jewess, converted to Christianity, by the Syrian monk Sergius. His Grandfather took care of the orphan, but on his death, the charge fell to his uncle, who treated him as one of his own children. At the age of thirteen, he accompanied his uncle into Syria, and at the fair of Bosra, is thought to have met Felix, or Sergius Bahira, who is believed subsequently, to have assisted him in the composition of the Koran, a word derived from *Karaa* "to read," at all events, most of it seems, to be a new reading, of the Jewish and Christian sacred books, then current in the East, intermingled with the traditions and fables of Arabia, and some Persian Mythology. Many Mahomedans assert, that the Koran was in existence from all eternity, and written upon tables, which were kept before God: that these Mahomed was permitted to see once a year during his life, and in the last twelve months of it, twice. Some sects however deny the authority of the Koran altogether.

Mahomed in the course of some mercantile transactions, became the agent and factor, of a rich widow, named Kadijah, who was so pleased with his appearance, manners, and address, that she gave him her hand in marriage, when he was 25 years of age. Thus at one step, Mahomed rose to the first rank in Mecca. His nation at this time, worshipped the stars of Heaven, and many gods subordinate to one supreme Deity: in short, neither their religion, nor morals, possessed any check, and all acted as suited their convenience, or as their imagination dictated.

Some Jewish and Christian tribes, having settled in his locality he is thought to have learnt from them, that there was a purer faith than that held by his countrymen, which aroused in him an ardent desire, to introduce a better creed amongst them.

Then he remembered the teachings of Sergius, and if he did not long for his presence, (which it is said he obtained,) still he wished for the words of his Holy Book: and his cousin Warka-ben-naufel, is believed to have procured him a copy of the Scriptures, translated from Hebrew into Arabic. Naturally of a contemplative mind, he passed one month in every year on Mount Hira in solitude, studying the mysteries of the Jewish and Christian faith. He found the writings of both enveloped in fables, and Jewish legends, and his mind shrank from adopting either creed, wherein man, unsatisfied with the teachings of infinite wisdom, had superadded the compositions of his own finite ideas. These solitary musings led to great nervous susceptibility, his dreams took the form of realities, until his reason, unable to bear the stretch, tottered on her throne. Insanity or excitement were the only courses now left open to him, he chose the latter, and his reason was preserved.

He disclosed to his wife, that the Angel Gabriel had appeared to him, and given him a divine commission, to reform the religion of his countrymen : and like a dutiful spouse, she at once declared her belief in the truth of his mission. In his fortieth year, he left the recesses of Mount Hira, and seeking the busy haunts of men, announced himself as the Prophet of the Most High. He enunciated this fact at a large feast, when he publicly expounded his creed, and ridiculed idolatry, requesting to know, what advantage could be expected from trusting in images of wood and stone, and wound up his most forcible speech, by exclaiming that, " there is but one God, " and should there be any amongst you, who wishes to be my Vicar, " as Aaron was to Moses, let him now proclaim himself." His nephew and son-in-law Ali, at once accepted the post. This occurred in A.D. 609, and for ten years Mahomed endured persecutions and insults, but at this time his uncle and protector died. Persecution was then redoubled, fanned by the zeal of bigots, which ended as such always has done, by giving renown, to what would otherwise soon have quietly disappeared, in the legends of things gone by.

The Priests of his tribe Korésh, perceiving the eminence to which Mahomed was attaining, and fearing the loss which might accrue to their temple, were a new religion to gain the ascendancy, as they were aware that it would cause the downfall of their idolatrous worship, persecuted him greatly, and so vehement was their animosity after his uncle's death, that he was compelled to leave Mecca, and take refuge in Tayef, three days' journey distant. But the people would not be convinced of his divine mission, and after a time he returned to Mecca. At first he resided there quietly, but soon commenced enunciating his religion, to the Pilgrims who resorted thither.

At this time, many persons came from Yatreb, who listened attentively to the new doctrine, for circumstances had occurred, which rendered it of great interest to them. Their city had been inhabited by Jews and Arabs, who fought for supremacy, and the first were reduced to slavery : in this degraded condition, the Arabs frequently heard them praying, that the Messiah would come. Now at Mecca, they found one who announced himself as the Prophet of God, they enquired whether he was the Messiah, of whom they had heard, and on his replying in the affirmative, they became greatly interested in his doctrines.

Mahomed then finding that his disciples were augmenting, and his creed taking root, changed his teaching, which up to this time had inculcated maxims of peace, and submission to injuries, and insults, for the sake of religion : and now declared, that peace was good, until God gave them opportunities to destroy their enemies. During this stirring time, his wife and most of his offspring died, and the fiery and unquenchable spirit of the enthusiast, had no check.

The chiefs of Mecca attempted his destruction, but he fled to Yatreb, A.D. 622, where he was received with enthusiasm and the name of the Town was forthwith changed to *Medinet-al-Nabi*, or the "City of the Prophet," commonly known as Medina. This is the *Hégira*, or period of flight, from which the Mahomedan era is computed. New forms of worship and rituals were then devised, and the first Mosque raised. Now Mahomed's mildness changed to ferocity, his former gentle nature to that of the tiger, he became the head of a warlike sect, and the leader of a band of marauding freebooters, who were the terror and scourge of the surrounding country.

At first no doubt Mahomed was sincere in his pretensions, but now he found frauds necessary, to support his assertions, and sank from a religious enthusiast, to an eminent impostor, successful hypocrite, and intolerant bigot. First he only declared war against his enemies, now he included in that category, all who denied the truth of his sacred mission. His nation espoused his assertions, they spread his doctrines by the sword, and were determined to conquer for the creed which they believed to have emanated from God, or die fighting in His cause.

As victories crowned his arms, and his empire extended, his toleration decreased, and his love of blood augmented. At last the time of his decease drew nigh, and he directed his followers to be very careful on three points, viz. to abolish idolatry, receive any proselytes, and observe prayers at stated times: and then after having cursed the Jews, he directed that no one should be permitted to attend him in his last hours, but his favourite wife Ayesha. He died on June 8th, A. D. 632, aged 63 years, and according to his own request, was buried where he drew his last breath. No son continued his name, he left only one daughter Fatima, as the survivor of eight children. It is curious that with him did not die his sect, and that along with him did not perish belief in his doctrines. His creed was carried by force of arms towards Europe, and when checked in that direction, found new channels to the Eastward.

He is believed to have nominated his nephew and son-in-law Ali, his daughter Fatima's husband, as his heir, but his widow Ayesha declared, that he had named her father, Aboobukur. Now arose disputes, an ambition to rule seized his late submissive chieftains, and dissensions ensued as to whether his temporal power was hereditary, which all admitted his spiritual one must be. *Aboobukur* was chosen as first *Caliph*, and was succeeded by the coarse and fiery *Omar;* this latter designated himself, "Commander of the faithful." After reigning eleven years, "conquering 36,000 cities, towns, and castles: "destroying 4000 Christian, Magian, and Pagan temples: and "erecting 1,400 Mosques," he was assassinated by a slave. On his death bed, he nominated a council of six, to meet after his demise, and decide upon his successor. At the end of three days, should they not have agreed, all were to be executed. But this latter part, was not found necessary, as they were unanimous in choosing *Othman.*

This third Caliph, had been Mahomed's Secretary, and one of his sons-in-law. Although above eighty years of age, his vigour was great, and under his direction, the Moslem empire extended to the confines of India. He revised the Koran: during his reign, however luxuries began to be indulged in, new sects to arise, and Ali's partisans daily acquired more power. Othman was slain, A.D. 661 by his troops, on a Friday, whilst he was fasting, and reading the Koran. Horror and consternation were universal, and during the confusion which ensued, *Ali's* partisans obtained for him the fourth Caliphite. He commenced by deposing all Governors, and elevating his own friends in their place: his enemies then asserted that he had been foremost in conspiring against his predecessor, and one of the chiefs whom he had deposed, Mowaveeah, the Governor of Syria, claimed the Caliphite. Three fanatics determined, that the cause of the Mahomedan divisions was the existence of Ali, Mowaveeah, and his friend Amru, so they determined to assassinate all in one day. This they attempted, but were only successful in murdering Ali, and thus terminated the reign of the last Caliph, in whom was united, both the temporal sovereignty or Caliphite, and the Iman or spiritual power. The first from this period fell to Mowaveeah and his successors, the latter to the descendants of Ali.

Hassan, Ali's eldest son, was proclaimed Caliph, as well as Imam,* but Mowaveeah compelled him to resign the first dignity, A. D. 669, and nine years subsequently, he was poisoned by his wife. His brother *Hossein*, was second Imam, and when Mowaveeah died A. D. 679, and was succeeded by his profligate son Yezid, Hossein attempted to obtain the Caliphite, but was surrounded by Yezid's troops, and mortally wounded. He staggered to his tent, and lifted up his infant to give it his last blessing, when an arrow pierced the child's breast, and its life blood flowed over its agonised father, who rushing amongst the foe, soon fell a victim to their fury. All his family, excepting his son Ali, 12 years of age, and two sisters, perished at the same time, but his murder was fearfully avenged. The anniversary of Hossein's martyrdom, is kept as the Mohorrum, both in India and Persia.

There were altogether twelve Imams, although some Moslem sects acknowledge only one, others seven, whilst it is considered, there will be no legitimate Sovereign upon earth, until Mahomed the last Imam, or his spirit, re-appears.

The Mahomedans are separated into two great divisions, the *Sheeas* of whom the Persians are the chief representatives, and the *Soonees* amongst whom the Turks form the largest division. They are in most places very rancorous against one another, and have separate Mosques, or should a member of one sect attend the house of prayer of the other, it is mostly to cavil, whilst each dooms the other to eternal condemnation in the world to come.

The *Sheeas* call themselves lovers of justice, and assert that Ali was Mahomed's lawful successor, and therefore the three other Caliphs

---

* Some sects assert, that the spirit of one Imam was transmigrated into that of his successor: whilst others even believed them to be incarnations of the Deity.

were merely usurpers. They pray with unclasped hands, mourn deeply the martyrdom of Hossein, curse his enemies, and doom Ali's opponents to the lowest depths of condemnation. Some of them consider Ali equal to Mahomed, and that the authority of the Koran has been rendered void by tradition. This class are mostly found amongst the Persians, form a large portion of the Tartars, and comprise some of the Indian Princes.

The *Soonees*, follow the Soonut, or "traditions," and believe in the equally divine mission, of all four Caliphs. Mahomed they call the last of the Prophets, and Ali the first of the Fakeers. They speak highly of Omar, whose assassination the Persian Sheeas celebrate as a festival, and assert that the traditions merely explain the Koran. This sect is mostly represented by the Turks, Egyptians, and Arabs. They clasp their hands in prayer, shave the middle of the Moustache, observe the fast of the Ramzan, go on pilgrimages to Mecca, read the Koran, assemble for public prayer, believe in the resurrection and consider it unlawful to make the image of Hossein's tomb, the taboot, at the Mohorrum, and to read the funeral eulogy, or beat the breast at that time, but they may shed tears. They ought never to take intoxicating drinks.

Predestination is firmly believed in. It is alleged that as soon as the body is laid in the grave, the two examiners Monker and Nakir, enquire into the works of the deceased, during his life time. The bridge from Earth to Heaven, is said to pass over the centre of Hell, (a burning fiery furnace,) and being finer than a hair, and sharper than a razor, the good souls are assisted rapidly across, by guiding and protecting spirits, whilst the wicked who attempt to follow, fall down into the abyss below. After the consummation of all things, the bridge will be destroyed, and communication cut off. The chief punishment, is to be denied the sight of God; there are eight degrees of beatitude, varying according to the proximity to Him. Hell is not considered eternal, but after a certain period of expiation, the cleansed soul arrives at Paradise.

After Mahomedanism had flourished some time, disseminated by soldiers, and enunciated by military Chieftains, men began to discover, that something more was necessary, and that now scholars were required who were deeply versed in the doctrines of the new religion, irrespective of whether they were or were not skilled in martial exercises. Thus after it had existed above a century, a school was formed in Bagdad, traditions were collected and examined, and a class of religious teachers raised up. Then arose four sects, the *Hanifites*, the originator of which was a strict partisan of Ali. They call themselves the "followers of reason." The *Shafites;* the *Malecites* who accept every thing, according to its literal meaning; and the *Hanbalites*, who consider the Koran to have been eternal. Each of these sects derives its name from that of its originator. They were established by four Doctors of the law, who flourished at various times, and are highly venerated, whilst it has been declared, that to slay a Persian Sheeah, is more acceptable to God, than to destroy seventy Christians.

When the religion of the Crescent had existed some time in India, the Sheeas and the Soonees, began to lay aside their animosities, so *Acbar* in 1556, aimed at a new religion, embracing Mahomedanism, Hinduism, the belief of the followers of Zoroaster, the creed of the Christians, and that of the Jews. It failed, and from a curious circumstance, viz., from his directing its adherents to leave off wearing beards! Interference in their faith they could tolerate, alteration in their ritual they would permit, but cutting of their beards was a most intolerable insult.

The divisions of Indian Mussalmen are the *Syeds*, who are descended from Mahomed, and held in the highest esteem. They may take their wives from either of the other divisions, but will not allow their daughters to intermarry with either of the other three, and are exceedingly jealous respecting their genealogy. The *Sheiks* who may be sprung from any class, such as Hindus, or converts, the women wear petticoats instead of the flowing trowsers. The *Moguls*, or Persians, and the *Pathans*, who consist of the Rohillas, and the Afghans. Each of these tribes has numerous sub-divisions, some higher, some lower than the other: whilst those who perform pilgrimages to Mecca, are called Hadgees, or if their father also went there, the term is repeated twice before their names. Many are the ship loads yearly passing Cochin, proceeding to, or returning from Mecca.

Acbar possessed in his Seraglio, the beautiful lady *Donna Juliana*

*Diez,** who had been captured by a Corsair, on her voyage to Terceira, and came by purchase into the possession of the Sultan Selim. The grand Seignor, sent her as a present to Acbar. Having won that Emperor's affection, she applied herself, and with success, to promote the interests of her country, and religion, in India. She it was who shook his belief in his faith, and had the Romish priests given him the Bible without adding legends to it, probably he might have embraced the Christians' creed. As it was, he attempted a religion of his own composition, and from that day, Mahomedans have been unable to assert, that their's is the *only* true faith, but can only call it, one amongst the many.

Thus Hindu rites became engrafted into the Mahomedan ritual, and as in Chapter VI we have seen, that Syrian Christians have not rejected Hindu feasts; in Chapter VII, how Hinduism in India, became altered, and amalgamated with the religion of the aborigines: and in Chapter VIII, how identical many Jewish and Hindu forms are: so now we may perceive, how greatly Mahomedanism sank from its contact with Hinduism, until even caste formed a part of the Moslem's creed. Saints and Martyrs were received into its Calendar, and offerings at their shrines exceeded those made at the Mosques, divisions became subdivided, until at last they numbered at least 72 sects, differing in their belief, from true Islamism, to downright atheism.

Caste goes by birth, in the same way as amongst the Hindus, but it does not compel each son, to follow the exact occupation of his father. The Fakeers live near tombs, where they meditate and pray, subsisting on voluntary offerings. Amongst the devotees some deny the divine mission of Mahomed, and others the sacred character of the Koran, or even the existence of a God.

Imam was their ancient battle cry, the exulting shout of the victor, and the defiant cry of the vanquished. It is one that the conquered have often heard with such varying feelings, well knowing that where it was triumphant, mercy to the fallen was unknown. Imam was the name of their religious creed, their old faith, but in India it is now no longer heard, calling their followers to arms, or encour-

* Major Jervis, *Memoirs of the Konkun*, 1840.

aging the charging cavalry, for as their practices changed, they altered the cheering word to *Deen*, (religious practice,) which now urges on their sectaries, to victory, or defeat.

The first advent of Mahomedanism to India, in any force, occurred at the beginning of the tenth century of the Christian era, when the Sultan Mahomed of Ghuznee, invaded Northern India, and annexed territory, from the Indus to the Ganges. Wave after wave of the followers of the Crescent then appeared, and rolled over Northern India, from whence they swept the riches of the country. When the Mahomedans first conquered cities in India, all males above 17 years of age who refused to embrace their faith, were slaughtered, whilst those below that age, were forcibly converted, and spared, as were also the women.

Subsequently they consented to receive tribute, and to allow the Native sovereigns to retain possession of their dominions. In later times, the Brahmans were again permitted to erect temples, and 3 per cent of their former revenues, were continued to them. After eighteen Princes of the Ghuznee dynasty had reigned in India, they were subverted by other conquerors of the same creed from Khorasan, who made Delhi the seat of their power. But in 1206, their Sultan was assassinated, and their empire divided: and 83 years subsequently, their dynasty terminated, when the Afghans became the dominant race.

Timor, a Mogul Tartar, in 1398, overthrew the Afghans, but did not remain permanently in India; and in 1526, Baber the Sultan of Cabul, erected his throne at Delhi, and founded a compact empire. Shah Jehan commenced his reign, in 1627, and under him the Moslems reached the summit of their Eastern glory. During the reign of Aurungzebe, the Mahrattas under Sevajee, became a very powerful body, whilst the Afghans, revolted, and established a separate kingdom, and the Mogul empire subsequent to his death, showed symptoms of decay.

Some of these Mussalmen spread to the Western Coast of India, and their descendants now form the division, already designated as the "true Mahomedans:" but the larger class known as "Moplahs," or "Jonnaga Moplahs," will be more especially dwelt upon. They were a sect hated by the Portuguese, detested by the Dutch, and in their turn very inimical to the British, by whom they consider that they have been slighted, and not shown that favour, they believed themselves entitled to. Although still as a class, a type of vindictiveness, they appear to be improving, and are at present less blood-thirsty than they formerly were, and the sphere of their mercantile transactions is increasing.

Traditionary accounts of their origin exist in abundance, and differ materially from one another. Some of them are said to have settled on the Western coast in the seventh century, where they established themselves under Caliph Valid, and were believed to be a portion of the posterity of Hashem, expelled by Mahomed for cowardice in his battles, against the partisans of Abu Jakeel. In the seventh century, a Mahomedan merchant named Malek Medina, accompanied by some Priests, are stated by *Moens*, to have settled in, or near Mangalore. But the Mahomedans obtained no great footing, until the ninth century of the Christian era.

Many legends respecting the origin of the Moplahs may be found in the *Mackenzie* M. S., one of which, stated to be taken from a copy of the Kerala Ulpati, observes that Buddhists, (see note p. 44) came to Cheraman Permaul's (not the last of that name,) country, and converted the monarch, who directed the Brahmans to follow the tenets of that sect. But the Brahmans remonstrated, and proposed a public discussion on the subject, in which they contrived to vanquish their opponents, when according to a previous agreement, the tongues of the Buddhists were cut out. The monarch was then dethroned, and his son, (nephew?) installed in his place, and an oath taken, by which they bound themselves, never to allow any persons, not of the orthodox Hindu religion to obtain public sanction to reside in the country. The Mahomedans did not arrive until after this oath had become obsolete, but even when it was in force, the Arabs were allowed to trade along the coast.

The above is probably founded on fact, as it appears likely that one of these Kings did turn Buddhist, and was dethroned. By degrees both Jains and Mahomedans were included in the above term, as they both came from Arabia, and it became a common saying, that Cheraman Permaul became a Buddhist, and went away to Mecca. At the present time, no Jains trade to India, and their only remaining representatives, are the Mussalmen, still called Buddhists, consequently it is commonly reported, and believed, that Cheraman Permaul became a Mahomedan. But as he, (the last of that race of rulers,) died A.D. 378, and Mahomed was not born, until A.D. 569, it appears impossible, that any of that race, could have embraced Islamism.

A rich Mahomedan came from Arabia, A.D. 1489-90, and having ingratiated himself with the Samorin, obtained leave to build additional mosques in the country, consequently before this period, they must have had temples in Malabar.

Many towns along the Malabar coast, have a large proportion of their inhabitants, composed of Moplahs, (termed Lubbays in the South, and on the Madras side.) They no doubt are descended from Arab fathers, who traded to this coast, and formed fugitive alliances, with Teer or Chogan women: for ideas regarding the marriage tie, are rather peculiar in Malabar, (see page 317.) The children never appear to have been claimed by the fathers, in fact the very word Moplah, is said to have been derived, from Mother, *Ma*, and child, *pilla*, showing to whose care, the offspring fell.* These *Mother's Children*, now known as "Moplahs," could not be considered Hindus, neither were they pure Mahomedans, by whom those with a "bar sinister," are regarded as a disgrace. Thus the Moplahs, rejected by both Hindus and Mahomedans, formed communities and churches of their own, combining the superstitions of the former race, with the intolerance of the latter: looked down upon and despised by others, they became morose and bigoted, and as their wealth and importance augmented, so did their jealousy against all interference with them. The "old Moplahs" assert, that being of Arabian extraction, they consider themselves of better birth than the Tartar races of Northern India. Their written characters are peculiar to themselves, and very different from the present Arabic:

* The term Moplah, is not used by those of that sect, who call themselves Mussalmen, or Mahomedans. *Duncan* says, that a Cazee derived the name from *Ma*, "mother," and *pilla*, "a puppy:" as a term of reproach. *MacLean* considered that the word came from *Maha*, or *Mahai*, "Mocha" and *Pilla*, "a child, and therefore translated it, "children, or Natives, (perhaps outcastes) of Mahai, or Mocha." *Asiatic Researches*, Vol. 5, Page 28.

their language is likewise such as is not found elsewhere, being a combination and corruption of several tongues.

Before the arrival of Vasco de Gama, the Moplahs had increased the trade of the cities on the Malabar coast, and the people were in a flourishing condition though having no Emir of note, they submitted to Pagan laws. But none of their race were ever executed, until those of his sect, first confirmed the judgment.*

In the foregoing pages, it has been shown that they invariably joined against the Europeans, as well as the many sources of irritation they encountered. In the last chapter, it has also been stated that they massacred the Jews, a people accursed by Mahomed; whilst they persuaded the Samorin, to expel the Syrian Christians from his territories, which was the principal reason of their seeking refuge in the Cochin and Travancore States.

The Mahomedan author Zeireddein, writing about two centuries and a half since, gave his version of the manner in which this sect was treated by the Portuguese. He was naturally as much biassed against the latter people, as their authors were against the Moplahs. He says that because the Mussalmen sinned so, God sent the Portuguese to punish them, by oppression, and cruelty, that they beat and derided them, sunk or stranded their vessels, spit in their faces when they met, prohibited them from making voyages to Mecca, plundered their property, and burnt their houses and Mosques. That they also endeavoured to persuade the followers of the crescent, to embrace the cross, and offered pecuniary rewards to those who would accede. Hadjees and others were put to cruel deaths, Mahomed was publicly reviled, and his followers, sold as slaves, or else led about loaded with irons, and large ransoms demanded from their friends, and until these were obtained, they were confined at night time, in dark, noisome, and hideous dungeons: beaten with slippers, tortured by fire, and had the most severe tasks imposed upon them. The Cochin Rajah he observes, refused to debar the Mahomedans from trafficking in his country, when requested to do so, by the Portuguese.

The Beebee of Cannanore, may be considered as the chief of the

---

* *Tohfut-ul-Mujahideen* translated by Rawlinson.

Moplahs, she purchased that fort of the Dutch; and is believed to be descended from a young Hindu lady, who fell in love with a Moplah, and married him: subsequently when they became possessed of land, and afterwards of a fort, they became looked up to, as the head of their sect. Of course succession, went through the female line. Even now, the Beebee keeps up the remembrance of her Hindu relatives, and mourns three days, when a death amongst them occurs, sending rice, and other presents, to the bereaved ones.

Hyder when he took possession of the Malabar coast, gave the Ady Rajah of Cannanore, extensive powers, but some of this race, even fought against the Mahomedan conquerors, and joined their forces in the field to those of the Hindus. In 1785, a powerful Moplah, of Munjerry in Ernaad, north of Calicut, rose in rebellion against Tippoo's Government, and was with great difficulty subdued. In 1789 even the Beebee of Cannanore, requested leave to enter the English Fort of Tellicherry, to escape Tippoo, but in the following year they arranged matters, and again became firm friends. It was the Moplahs, who murdered the Chief of the English Factory at Anjengo, and his suite, whilst on a visit to the Queen of Attingal. Whilst in the ascendant, they despoiled the Hindus their former masters, who when they again became rulers, "considered it no "crime, to put a Moplah to death."

At the end of the last century, when Malabar was distracted by wars, and desolated both by those who called themselves its friends, as well as by its avowed enemies, the Moplahs were divided into two distinct classes, those residing along the sea coast, who were traders or large farmers; and those inland, called "jungle Moplahs," who lived by rapine, murder, and kidnapping children, some of whom they sold as slaves to the supercargoes of vessels, but the greater part to the French at Mahé, and the Dutch in Cochin. The jungle Moplahs defied Tippoo's troops, and not unfrequently plundered his inland treasuries, and defeated those in charge of his property. When they took any spoil, they immediately divided it, and dispersed. Their houses were like small fortresses, surrounded by strong walls, with loop holes for musquetry.

A *succession tax* was levied in Malabar, under the native Princes on the estates of all Moplahs who died leaving heirs, and varied from $\frac{1}{6}$th to $\frac{1}{20}$th of the amount bequeathed. The origin of this impost, is lost in obscurity, but legends assert it to be, coeval with the advent of the Arabs to the coast, although it was occasionally held in abeyance. The English abolished it in 1792, and in the following year; made many fruitless attempts, to quiet this unruly race.

Moplahs in the native state, receive much more consideration from the petty and village Officials, than do the native Christians. They are never kept waiting for hours, and then probably directed, " to come to-morrow." Every Mahomedan Moplah, if only a convert of a few days' standing, will be received with civility, and if kept waiting, have a seat given him.

During the Mahomedan rule, thousands as already stated, were forcibly converted to this faith : and strange to say, they became as bigoted and intolerant in their new religion, as if they had always belonged to that sect. They or their descendants, and those latterly converted are now known, as the " new Moplahs," in contradistinction to the old races. They could not again become Hindus, unless by greatly sinking in rank, and importance, so they embraced the new sect, and spread it as widely as they were able. At the present time, they are purchasing young children, and bringing them up in their faith, and thus this sect, is rapidly increasing. They also convert many Christians, though they themselves are apparently never converted to any other faith. Near Calicut, the late *Mr. Conolly*, a Collector, (who was murdered in his house by Moplahs,) established a colony of *Niadis*, (see page 333,) and gave them ground to cultivate. After a time, Government handed the experiment over to the German Mission, who sent them a resident schoolmaster, and thus succeeded in converting, and baptizing, three of them. The Moplahs then determined on proselytizing this set of people, and suddenly all but the three, who had been baptized, left the Mission village, and were received into the Moplah community, where they speedily became converts to Islam.

The small communities of true Mahomedans in the Cochin State, are Sheeas and Safis ; whilst the Moplahs, are Soonees, and Hanafites, still they agree very well. They increase rapidly, and it is remarkable, what a much finer race they are, than their Hindu brethren. This perhaps is due, to their eating meat, (with the exception of pork,) and partly probably, to their indulging in spirituous liquors in private. Their countenances, show the play of their minds, more than do those of Mahomedans elsewhere.

The Koran* is written in Arabic, which few but the Priests understand, it is held in great reverence by some sects, and never carried lower than the girdle. In education, a smattering of Arabic is taught in their schools.

Their *chief priest*, whose office is hereditary, is called a Tungel, he usually resides at Ponany, but is now a transported felon, for inciting his caste to insurrection, and the commission of murders.

The head Priest in each Mosque, is also called a Tungel, and another an Imam, these inferior clergy, are supported by their congregations. They are jealous of any one, even approaching their mosques, and are so unsociable, that they will not assemble in any numbers to pray. Their prayers should be recited five times daily, and on Fridays, should be repeated at the musjeed. Boys are named about the seventh day after birth, when their heads ought also to be shaved. They may be circumcised at any age, but generally are so, before ten, this rite is not essential to the Mahomedan religion, but is universal in India, amongst those of this creed. Their ears are never bored : from an early age they carry a sheathed knife, as the terrible Kydakathee, or Moplah knife, has been inter-

---

* It has been already shown, (Chap. VII) how the Hindus venerate the Vedas, and what care they take, to prevent their even being seen by the lower castes : how carefully the Jews preserve their Pentateuch, and the honour in which they hold it. It has been discussed, whether the Bible ought or ought not to be in the hands of all indiscriminately. The Roman Catholics consider that the former course would end in its not being respected, whilst on the other hand many Protestants think it would be advisable to use it as a class book in the schools. It may well be remarked, with what respect the Koran is treated by the Mahomedans. In a public discussion in Mysore, regarding the respective merits of the Christian and Mahomedan faith, the Missionary produced his bible, "but a difficulty arose about the Koran, for the Jury insist- " ed on its being produced. After much delay, discussion, and anger amongst "the Mussalmen, it was brought carefully folded in a handkerchief, and a "chair provided for its reception, * * as the Jury could not deface thes "books, or even touch them, they were carefully folded up in a handkerchief, "and the mark was put upon the knot, so that it could not be opened, but "by consent of the Jury."—Mullens' *Missions in South India*, 1854.

dicted, by order of Government. The Mussalmen wear turbans but the Moplahs do not do so, they have as a rule, a small piece of cloth around their heads, or wear Arab caps. Girls have holes bored in their ears, as a mark of affection, consequently the more they are *bored*, the greater their parent's love for them may be supposed to be.

In their *feasts*, their marriages, and their rejoicings, the forbidden music finds a place: in the processions, flags are carried, whilst the plantain and the cocoanut, the lime and the orange, are employed by them, in the same manner as by the Hindus.

It is essential for Moplahs to *marry*, and this rite is considered as a species of foretaste of their paradise, consequently they are particular, about the feasts and ceremonies connected with it. Mahomed advised those of his followers, who were too poor to marry, to retire from the world, and pass their days in devotion. The bride's family seek a husband for her, thus a father sends some persons to the friends of a youth, whom he considers suitable, and the bridegroom requires a present, in return for marrying the daughter, as well as her dowry. The Hanafites sometimes espouse brides under ten years of age, but the Safis do this more rarely. All preliminaries being settled, and a day for celebration of the betrothal fixed, the bridegroom attended by his friends, proceeds to the bride's house, where her father meets him, and sprinkles him with rose water, whilst some matrons anxious to avert the evil eye, advance with a basin, containing water, turmeric, cusa grass, and other seeds, which they whirl three times round his head. The party then proceed to a pandall, under which they sit on carpets, or mats, spread on the ground. Here they amuse themselves, by chewing betel, and some elder introduces the subject. Numerous questions are asked by both sides, at the termination of which, betrothal takes place, in the form of a contract, in which the amount to be paid is stipulated. Trays containing some of the money, are then brought in, together with some presents, and a gold ring, which is touched successively by each person present. The Priest then places the ring on the bridegroom's finger, and the bride's father gives the contract to the Cazee, to file amongst the records of the Temple. Betel is then distributed, and after the bride's father has rubbed sandal wood on the breasts of his guests, they withdraw.

The marriage often does not take place for some time ; in the intermediate period, care is taken to choose a lucky day, whilst in the unlucky months, espousals may be said to be almost prohibited. Also "on the third day of the new moon, as Adam was then expel-"led from Paradise: on the fifth, when Jonah was swallowed by a "whale: on the thirteenth, when Abraham was thrown into the "fire : on the sixteenth, when Joseph was lowered into a well : on "the twenty-first, when Job was afflicted with diseases: on the "twenty-fourth, when Zachariah was murdered: on the twenty-fifth "when Mahomed had his front teeth broken by a sling." Marriages are mostly celebrated in January, April, August, October, and November, excluding all the days having bad omens, as enumerated.

It is needless to detail the whole of the ceremony, the most important and concluding part of which is, when the Tungel goes into the inner room with the bridegroom, unites his little finger to that of the bride, and pronounces a benediction. A gold chain, or a string, sometimes of beads, in the form of a tali, is usually hung around the bride's neck at some convenient time, subsequent to the ceremony.

The richer and some of the stricter Mahomedans, rigidly seclude their women, who have to keep their faces covered, when going out, but these are exceptional cases. The Moplah women, are usually allowed to go about, like those of the Hindus. These Moplahchees are amongst the dirtiest people in India, wearing their clothes until they almost rot off them: even in chewing betel, they have the objectionable practice, of sitting outside their houses and spitting* inwards through the door. Their filth is said to be considered a sign, that they are good housewives. Their necks are often covered with strings of beads, their arms with bangles, as are also their ankles, whilst their ears are weighed down with ornaments.

Their *burial ground* is in Muttencherry. After death the feet of the corpse are tied together, as are also the hands, and the face is

---

* This practice is held in the greatest detestation by the Hindus, for doing such inside the house, is considered the height of filthiness. Hindus (if high caste) can hardly be induced to touch a letter closed with a wafer, as they believe it must have been touched by the tongue.

turned towards Mecca: a lamp is kept lighted at the head, and thus it remains, until the time of burial, whilst loud lamentations are made by the women. The body having been washed, is dressed and enveloped in a long shroud, reaching to the ankles, and is then wound round by a sheet: whilst males have on their usual head-dress, the true Mahomedans turbans, the Moplahs their caps, or a piece of cloth. At the time of burial, the corpse is first carried to the Mosque, where a prayer is recited by the Priest, and then it is taken to the place of sepulture. It is buried with its face downwards, and never enclosed in a coffin. Sometimes it is surrounded by planks, bound round by cords, but like the Jews, never secured together by iron nails. On the fortieth day, the relations go to the tomb, and place a white cloth over it, burn incense, and offer up prayers. The richer classes entertain the poor, on each anniversary. Tombs of females, are quite plain: but those of males, have a small round piece of chunam work at the top. In most of their burial grounds, are seen the custard apple, the guava, and the pomegranate, trees.

The fast of *the Mohorrum*, is kept by the Safis, who are Sheeas, but not by the Jonnaga Moplahs, who are Hanafites and Soonees: although these last, do not object to join in the procession, should they meet it by accident. The taboot which they bear down to the sea beach, consists of a wooden framework, covered with cloth, paper, and tinsel, and is rarely, if ever, mounted on wheels. Before it starts, the Mahomedans dance around a fire, shouting the names of the Imams, and that of Ali, and cursing his murderers, as well as the three usurpers. The fast has more the appearance of a feast, and instead of a time of mourning, appears to be held as one of rejoicing.

The Moplahs are strict in keeping the *Ramzan*, when they strictly fast for 30 days, bewail the sins of the preceding year, and give of their substance to their poorer brethren.

CHAPTER X.

PEOPLE, AND THEIR CUSTOMS.

Census— Ethnology — Language — Divisions of time— Birth — Horoscope — Children—Marriages— Deaths—Offences—Laws—Ordeals— Omens— Superstitions—Etiquette—Marks of distinctions—Letters—Poetry—Music—Theatricals—Nautches—Amusements— Dress—Ornaments—Umbrellas—Houses —Furniture—Hospitality—Food.

The inhabitants of the Cochin State, in the year 1857, numbered 399,056 : out of which, 123,037 were engaged in agriculture. The *Christians* of all denominations, were 88,920 : *Mahomedans* 18,496 : *Jews* 1,790 : and the *Hindus* 229,950 : of these last, 4,101 were Namboories, and Imbran Brahmans : and 10,882 other Brahmans, this includes 5,810 Konkanies : 422 were Schatriyas : Vysias not even mentioned : and the remainder Sudras,* out of which 51,305 were soil slaves. Thus giving an average, of 352¾ individuals, to every square mile of territory.

In the Town of Cochin, and the British territory, the population which is a floating one, was in 1861, according to the census, 11,449: of these, 205 were Europeans, and Eurasians : 6,569 Native Christians : 3,455 Hindus : 1,186 Mahomedans : and 34 Jews.

Without asserting the perfect accuracy of these figures, it will be sufficient to observe, that they were taken from official sources, and are consequently a nearer approach to the truth, than any mere suppositions are likely to be. Certainly the census papers, do not place the number of the population, at so high a rate as is generally believed : but the country in accordance with its physical aspect, must be thinly populated. A large portion of it is covered with uninhabitable forests : a considerable amount with water, and marshes : and much with inhospitable scrubby jungle, or stunted grass, growing, or rather existing, on a laterite bed. These localities, are of course almost destitute of human beings.

* By Sudras is meant, all castes not wearing the sacred string, including outcastes.

An examination of the old *census returns*, shows a marked increase in the population. That of the *Native State* in 1836* was taken at 288,176 which in 21 years, would show an increase of 110,880 persons, which is simply impossible: unless accounted for by extensive immigration. The reason of the apparent increase is probably, that many of the lower castes, which may have been formerly omitted, now find a place. But that the population does augment, much more rapidly than in olden times, cannot be doubted: the frequent and sanguinary wars, the daily murders, and the annual export of thousands of slaves, are all things of the past, which it is to be hoped will in future be unknown. The tranquil pursuits of peace, have superseded those of warfare: and at the present time, there are probably more ploughs, than swords, to be found in the Cochin State.

Among such a very varied population, it would be difficult as well as tedious, to give a detailed account, of the Ethnology of each separate race, with the manners of each tribe, and the language of each people. A general summary of the indigenous Hindu population, will only therefore be detailed, with whom the Native Christians, black Jews, and Moplahs, have many general features in common.

The following figures, give the average height, and size of limbs, in four classes of the people.

Caste.	Age.	Height.	Head.	Neck.	Chest.	Arm.	Thigh.
Nairs............	26·5	63·9	22·3	14·2	33·4	10·7	18·6
Chogans........	34·6	64·1	21·4	13·2	32·7	10·1	18·8
N. Christians..	28·0	62·4	21·6	13·2	31·4	10·1	17·6
Moplahs........	35·7	63·5	20·4	13·9	32·3	10·4	18·0
Average............		63·4	21·4	13·6	32·4	10·3	18·2
Average on the east coast.†...		64·8	20·8	11·9	31·3	8·9	16·1

* Returns of Lieutenants Connor, and Ward. *M. S. S. Official Records.*

† Short.—*Madras Medical Journal*, vol. IV. page 103, 1862. Ethnology of Chingleput.

It will be seen by the above, that although the Natives of the Eastern Coast at Chingleput, are taller than those of Cochin, the size of their heads, and extremities, are considerably smaller. Much of this increased muscularity, is probably due to harder work, as, this is a sea port town, in which considerable manual labour is required from some Castes: whilst the limbs of the Chogans, are of course rendered very muscular, by their occupation, which consists mostly in climbing Cocoanut trees.

It is difficult to say, why the Chogan should be taller than the Nair: and it is questionable, whether this would be the case, if the examination were made, of the inhabitants of a considerable tract of country. The circumference of the head is largest amongst the Nairs, and it must be conceded, that they are as a race, very superior to the other classes. Even on the eastern coast, it is perceived, that the circumference of the Brahman's head, is greater than in any of those belonging to other Hindu castes.

The personal appearance of the people of this coast, is as varied as in Europe, or elsewhere. Their heads are well formed, and the animal developement of the African, is rarely seen amongst them. Their shoulders are often broad, hands small, but joints rather large: feet mostly flattened, and legs a little bowed. They reach their prime, about their thirtieth year, and generally weigh from seven stone five, to seven stone ten. Their complexion is of a lighter brown, or rather of a more copper coloured tinge, than that of those on the eastern coast: and the higher the rank and station, the lighter is the colour.

They are able to carry considerable weights, but cannot lift them with impunity, although they are well adapted for traction, and propulsion.

The women differ much from the men in appearance. The Brahmanees are often uncommonly beautiful, their hair being of a shining black, and their eyes either of the same colour, or of a dark hazel. Their dress and ornaments have been already described. They are exceedingly cleanly, (which certainly cannot be said of their low caste sisters,) performing their ablutions twice a day, and once a week anointing their bodies with Cocoanut oil, or the white of eggs. There are tanks near every Pagoda, in which the higher castes can bathe, before performing their devotions; the richer classes have them, also inside their own houses. In some Pagodas, these tanks, or cisterns, are of granite, and of beautiful workmanship. After the age of thirty, the women of the higher castes, arrive at the downward path of life. Cooly women are broad across the shoulders, and strongly built for work; loud in wrangling, and usually possessed of inharmonious voices. As they grow old, they certainly do not delight the eye by their beauty.

The people of Malabar as a whole, appear to enjoy a most passive state of existence, and are delighted to make any excuse for obtaining a holiday. No matter of what caste, or creed, they may be, indolence seems to constitute the acmé of their happiness, and a quiet swing in the verandahs of their houses, or a lounge under a tree chewing betel, is much preferred by them to any active pleasure, which entails exertion. Their meditations do not disturb their tranquillity, they reflect not on the past, and whilst they have sufficient for to-day, they are indifferent as to the wants of to-morrow. The pay of workmen, and coolies, during late years, has risen greatly, and now having no fear of the heavy exactions, of the rapacious Governments of former days, many are able to subsist in idleness for a week, on the work of one day. In promises they are equally profuse, with their forgetfulness in performing them. Their expressions are florid, and often interspersed with high flown similes. They are very good-natured, especially the Romo-Syrians: but very inquisitive, although suspicious of being questioned themselves, and averse to giving a correct reply: they are also extremely vindictive in their animosities. The Nairs (more especially,) are rather lavish in their expenditure, and have not so much of that sordid disposition, frequently found in Hindus of other parts of India. The inhabitants of Travancore, and Cochin, are celebrated amongst neighbouring tribes, as being great proficients in the black art, and even possessing the power of destroying their enemies.

The Malayalim language extends from Mangalore to Cape Comorin, and is one of the Dravidian family group, which includes "the Tamil, Telugu, Canarese, Tulu, Tuda, Kota, Gond, and Ku." The roots of their principal words are either identical or allied, whilst the idiom in all has the same peculiarities. This Dravidian language, appears to have been that of the dwellers in India, before the advent of the Hindus, and it has been surmised that it originally came from central Asia. As the Hindus bringing the Sanscrit language extended from the North West, the Dravidian races appear to have been driven Southwards, or partially incorporated amongst those of the conquerors, perhaps forming the Sudras.

As the Hindu races firmly seized upon the land, Sanscrit words became introduced into the Dravidian language; thus amongst the Kardahs of the Cochin forests, trades and occupations have sanscrit designations, but the language is of the true Dravidian family. Probably until the Hindus arrived these occupations were unknown, and that whilst communicating a knowledge of them to the Dravidian races, the latter retained their sanscrit nomenclature.

If the usually adopted rule, that the languages of people, give a clue to the national character be remembered, that of Cochin, would hardly tend to raise a very high idea of the inhabitants. On asking a favour, the phrase is, "*you must give,*" "*you had better give,*" or "*it will be best to give.*" If the petition is granted, thanks are considered quite superfluous, indeed there is no word in which to express such: thanks, patriotism, and some others, have no synonyms. The same may be observed in their religious ceremonies, their prayers are long and frequently repeated, but even when they believe their petitions to have been heard and favourably received, thanks are exceedingly rarely offered up. Still if patriotism does not exist, a strong affection for their Native land, is found firmly rooted amongst the Natives of these parts: they can rarely be induced to leave it for any length of time, and should they do so, they rapidly pine away, and generally before long, die in a foreign land.

Natives of other parts of India, when wishing delicately to insinuate, that a person is not telling the exact truth, often say, that such and such a statement, "is about as true, as the word of a Native of Malabar."

Time is reckoned by the era of Parasu Rama, divided into cycles. For astronomical purposes, they use the Chaldæan mode, or a cycle of sixty years, being a portion as they believe, of a period of 24,000 years, which is necessary "before the whole of the heavenly host, "together with the fixed stars belonging to them, can perform their "revolution, from East to West."* The year is 365 days, 12′ 30″. The astronomical new year, commences in April, when the sun enters under the sign of Aries as at that period it is believed the world was created. At this time a great festival is held, offerings are made, and some Brahmans amongst other ceremonies, are said sometimes to strangle a ram, consecrated to the sun, and the planets, in the hope of inducing the genii, to give them good fortune, during the ensuing year.

The months of the solar year, in 1862, were as follows, *Madum*, "the Ram," April 12th till May 12th or 31 days. *Eddavum*, "the "Bull," till June 12th or 31 days. *Methunum*, "the Twins," till July 14th or 32 days. *Cacadaum*, "the Crab" till August 14th or 31 days. *Chingum*, "the lion," till September 14th or 31 days. *Cunny*, "the Virgin," till October 15th or 31 days. *Toolam*, "the Scales," till November 14th or 30 days. *Vrecheecum*, "the Scorpion," till December 13th or 29 days. *Dhanoo*, "the Archer" till January 11th or 29 days. *Magarom*, "the Goat," till February 10th or 20 days. *Coombhum*, "the water bearer" till March 12th or 30 days. *Menum*, "the fishes" till April 13th or 30 days. The civil year commences with the 1st of Chingum, or about the middle of August.

In their calculations, the days of the new and full moon, are not taken into account, but they reckon those of the increase and decrease; thus they speak of the first day after the new moon. A lunar month is computed from the new moon to the new moon, and appears to consist of 27 days, each of which is named after the constellation in which the moon is on that day. To adjust the lunar to the solar year additional months are inserted. The portion of a month from new to full moon, is called the "black moon:" from the full to the new, the "white moon."

Sunday, Nyaraicha, (*Nayar*, the sun.) *Monday*, Theengulaicha, (*Theengul*, the moon.) *Tuesday*, Chowahaicha, (*Chowah*, Mars.) *Wednesday*, Bhoodunnaicha. (*Bhoodunn*, Mercury.) *Thursday* Weeahsaicha, (*Weeahshum*, Jupiter.) *Friday*, Welleyaicha, (*Welley*, Venus.) *Saturday*, Sheneeaicha, (*Shenee*, Saturn.)

The twenty four hours are divided into sixty Nazigas, as follows:

---

* Paoli. Page 348.

eight *Nody*, one *Mathran:* four Mathran, one *Gunnidun:* ten Gunnidun, one *Vinahligay* : six Vinahligay, one *Naziga:* sixty Nazigas, are one day. Thus the day consists of sixty Malabar hours, each containing twenty-four minutes.

During the last ten days in the month Carcadaum (August) high caste Hindus, will neither receive nor pay away money. Should it be necessary to receive payment for a debt, they depute some one else to undertake the office for them. These ten days are considered very unlucky. They also have no money transactions on their sabbath, (Thursday): but Sunday is esteemed a most propitious day for commencing an undertaking, buying land, starting upon a journey, or beginning to build a house.

When a child is expected, the friends and neighbours, flock to the house, and crowd the rooms. The men remaining in an outer apartment. Should the little stranger be a monstrosity the probability is, that some poor wretched creature will be accused of having bewitched the mother.

The directions for drawing horoscopes are very full, and there are guides, or manuals of instruction, to the table, which is like a chess board, with sixteen squares, but the four centre ones, are not employed, thus reducing the number of the squares, or houses, to twelve.

12 Mercury, 1 year.	1 Mars $1\frac{1}{2}$ months.	2 Jupiter 1 month.	3 Venus 1 month.
11 Saturn $1\frac{1}{2}$ years.			4 Moon $2\frac{1}{4}$ days.
10 Saturn $1\frac{1}{2}$ years.			5 Sun 1 month.
9 Mercury 1 year.	8 Mars $1\frac{1}{2}$ months.	7 Jupiter 1 month.	6 Venus one month.

Each day as previously mentioned, consists of sixty Nazigas, of

24 minutes each. The *sun* is supposed to commence at the division marked No. 1 or on the 1st day of the 1st month of the Malabar year and daily travels through every compartment of the horoscopic table. In No. 1 he remains $4\frac{1}{2}$ Nazigas : in 2, $4\frac{3}{4}$: 3, $5\frac{1}{4}$: 4, $5\frac{1}{2}$: 5, $5\frac{1}{4}$: 6 and 7, 5 : 8,$5\frac{1}{4}$: 9,$5\frac{1}{2}$: 10,$5\frac{1}{4}$: 11,$4\frac{3}{4}$: 12,$4\frac{1}{2}$. On the second day the sun commences ten minutes earlier, from the house No. 1 ; on the third day, twenty minutes : and so on, every day : on the thirtieth day, he remains at home, only ten minutes, and then goes on.

The *moon* remains $2\frac{1}{4}$ days in each division of the table, and commences according to the star, at the time of the new and full moon. It is thus 27 days going round.

Besides the Sun, Moon, and the Planets named, which travel respectively from No. 1, to No. 12, at various rates of progression, marked on the table, there are two other very wickedly disposed reptiles, who have an influence, on the good or bad fortune, of the newly born infant's future life. They are called the black snake, *Rhagu*, and the red snake, *Khadu* ; bad as the first is, the second is much worse. As might be anticipated, they travel backwards, from No. 12 to No. 1, and they loiter one and a half years, in each house.

When one of these snakes is calling at No. 1, the other is paying his respects at No. 7, and thus when Raghu visits No. 2, Khadu has progressed to No. 8.

The reputed characters of the tenants, of these houses, are as follows: the sun is tolerably good, though sometimes bad. Saturn and the two snakes, are infamous, and without any redeeming qualities. The remainder, are all reported as passably good. To draw out the programme, of the infant's future life, two blank tables are constructed, like that for the horoscope; on the first, the sun, moon, planets, and snakes, are placed at their proper position at the exact moment of the infant's birth. On the second, the numbers of the houses of the child's future are examined. No. 1, is the birth place, and from whence he derives his education, good looks, and fine person. No. 2, if the omen be good he will possess cattle, a well behaved family, and will also become rich, and a scholar, every comfort in fact depends upon this house: if a bad spirit be in it, and he be born in that bad spirit's abode, he will have good fortune. No. 3, bodily strength and bravery. No. 4, his mother's house, and if his own compound and his cattle will be good. No. 5, the affection of his children, and a quiet conscience. No. 6, if he is to be subject to robbery, or a robber himself. Whether he shall be healthly, or the reverse. No. 7, what sort of wife he will have. No. 8, length of his life, and time of his death. No. 9, length of his father's days. No. 10, ceremonial performances of parents. No. 11, no harm occurs in this house, but future gains. No. 12, the same as No. 8 and No. 6 combined.

From a comparison of these tables, the astrologer predicts the various events, which will befal the child. These are frequently stated in a very vague manner, as for instance, " if the child lives over the fifth year, it will live until it is ten," or that, " in such and such a year, a great misfortune will happen to it."

There are various ceremonies to be performed at an infant's birth, and subsequently numerous others at betrothals, marriages, and funerals, some of which have been detailed in the preceding chapters. As a general rule, marriage occurs at such an early age, that it may simply be called betrothal. Girls below the twice born class who have arrived at maturity, without having a husband to claim them are considered as to a certain degree, lying under a curse, but this is not regarded with such horror here, as in many other parts of Hindustan: for the females of most classes, indulge in polyandrism, which is sanctioned both by law and custom. Amongst the Native Christians, and Syrians, morality in the European sense, is much more observed, and the marriage tie is considered binding. Still the Hindu Custom, of a girl being betrothed at an early age, obtains amongst them. The bride remains in her father's house, for two or three years, and then with many ceremonies is removed to that of her husband. The Verapoly Mission, is now energetically attempting to stop these early marriages, and should they succeed, they will have conferred a great blessing on their people: but unfortunately, their failure is too probable. A single girl of the lower castes after eighteen, is looked upon as a disgrace to her family, which indeed she generally is, or soon becomes, owing to the ill-treatment, and abusive taunts, she constantly receives.

Wrede states, (Asiatic Researches, vol. 7, Page 367,) that when the Portuguese, arrived, the Syrians lived in villages, in stone houses, and mostly in North Malabar, and that their weddings, were celebrated with great pomp and ostentation. They maintained the privileges given them by the Permauls, viz. "of the Bride and Bridegroom, "riding on elephants, having their hair ornamented with flowers "of gold, of different musical instruments playing before them, as also "of flags of various colours being carried in front of them. They "also wore swords and targets, and some of them had firelocks." The girls were precluded from all inheritance, even if there were no sons in the family, the property going to the next male cousin, or uncle on the father's side. A Syrian law, exactly contrary to that of Malabar.

It is directed in the Hindu Code, according to *Colebrook*, that a dying man, should be laid on a bed of cusa grass, if he be a Sudra either in the house, or out of it indifferently, but if of any higher caste he must be placed in the open air. A Brahman's corpse should be carried out of a town by the Western gate, a Schatriya's by the Northern, a Vysian's by the Eastern, and a Sudra's by the Southern.

After a death in a family the room in which it occurred is supposed to be haunted by the spirit of the departed, and amongst wealthy families is generally not used again, until that generation has passed away; the successor occupying another set of apartments, at all events for the first twelve months; the principal ceremonies for the happiness of his soul, are performed by the nearest male relative of the deceased.

Amongst the Schatryas, the chief mourner, does not shave for twelve months after the event has occurred, whilst amongst others, as for instance some of the Putter Brahmans, they keep their hair (with the exception of the cudumi,*) and even their eyebrows shaved off for a year. When the Rajah dies, all the Natives in the place must leave off their turbans for ten days, as a sign of mourning, and fishermen are debarred from following their avocation for three days, for fear they might capture one of the finny tribes, in which the soul of the departed, has obtained a dwelling.

* On seeing a Christian child wearing a Cudumi, the parents were asked the reason: they replied that it was not done for caste purposes, but to keep the head warm and protect the fontanelle. Some of the Natives who dress as Eurasians, shave the back of the head and wear a skull cap.

The crime of infanticide is unnecessary in these parts, and almost unknown. The domestic lives of the people, appear to be less disturbed, by quarrels and jealousies, (because they have no one to be jealous of,) than in most other portions of India, with the exception of the Brahmans, who are very suspicious of the fidelity of their wives.

In times of famine, mothers sometimes dispose of their children, frequently with the hope of being able to redeem them in more prosperous times. The Hindu Laws, contain a provision for these cases, directing, that whoever should during a famine, have sold his liberty for food may in better times regain his freedom on returning the amount he had received, and giving two head of cattle.

Many of the laws and maxims of the Natives, are good, were they followed out. In former times a person convicted of telling an untruth,* was tortured, or very severely punished, were this not obsolete, the courts of justice would have sufficient employment, as veracity is a virtue, unfortunately not too prevalent amongst the Natives of the low country, but in the wilder parts they are more truthful. It appears that the further they are removed from cities, and communication with the external world, the more their word, may be relied on. This can scarcely be wondered at, subject as they have been for centuries, to tyrannical rule, where the law of the most powerful, has by force of circumstances, been that of the country, and each official has had, (and truth must admit many still have,) their price; dissimulation has thus become necessary, and fraud been so thoroughly engrafted into the Native Character, that many a long year must elapse, ere it can be eradicated.

It is a curious anomaly, that this race, who think it no crime to cheat a white man, but on the contrary rather a meritorious action,

---

* Mr. Muller, a German missionary, mentions appealing to a Hindu's conscience, with respect to the future rewards of good and evil. The Hindu answered by a story. A butcher bought a cow, whilst taking her home, she broke her rope and escaped. Going in pursuit he met a veracious Hindu, who informed him which road the cow had taken. Proceeding a little further asking a mendacious Hindu, he told him the wrong road, consequently the cow escaped. After death, the one who by telling the true road, whereby the butcher was able to pursue the cow with the intention of slaughtering her was adjudged to be gnawed by worms for twenty lifetimes. He who by telling an untruth had saved the cow's life was adjudged to be born twenty times a king.

and would pilfer as labourers, are as a rule to be trusted as coolies, with valuable property, to carry long distances; very rarely does the cooly, ever abscond with his load, although he may leave it in some safe place, if from sickness or other cause, he is unable to proceed with it. And the same applies to Bills of Exchange, given by Natives, scarcely one of which, was ever known to be dishonoured. There is a strong underlying vein of honesty in the Natives of India, which is much to be admired, and esteemed.

But at the present time, perjury is unfortunately very frequent, a devil-worshipper would as soon swear anything falsely, as state it so; as an oath is neither binding on him, nor on the Hindu idolater, it was therefore ordained, that in trying doubtful cases, ordeals should be permitted, the same as at the present day, in some Christian countries, lots are drawn. Natives when remonstrated with for swearing untruths on the Ollahs, reply that they are obliged to do so or they would obtain no justice.

In some of the greater crimes such as dacoity, murder, (especially those of children for the sake of obtaining their ornaments,) and incendiarism, the people of this portion of India have evidently undergone a change for the better, as they are less frequent here than in many other localities. Suicide is also very rare. The curse of the country, is the universal love of law suits, in which men do not mind ruining themselves, provided their opponents are involved in the same catastrophe.

The following are some of the *Ordeals*, which were prevalent in olden times. That of the Crocodile, is said to have been tried in the Cochin state during the last fifty years. Ordeals very clearly demonstrate, the superstitious character of the people by whom they are employed, or rather their belief in the efficacy of a direct, and personal appeal to the Deity, for his decision in difficult cases. In 1759 *Akbar* forbade this method of trial in his dominions, greatly to the disgust of the Brahmans. Several forms of ordeal were made use of, up to the middle of the last century, some in the commencement of this, and others at the present time, still obtain. Only the most common forms, are detailed here. In all instances, when the accused came off scathless, the accuser was fined.

The water Ordeals, were of several descriptions, that of the Crocodile being the most terrible, near Palliport, the Backwater is very full of these creatures, but formerly it used to swarm with them. The prisoner was first taken to a small temple in the vicinity of the place, where he took the most solemn oaths, as to the justice of his cause, and called upon the gods, not only to permit, but to direct the Crocodiles to eat him, were he not telling the exact truth. This ceremony over, he was obliged to wade across the water, which was eight hundred paces wide, and then return to the place he started from. Multitudes awaited the result, and if the Crocodiles were lazy, or not hungry, and the man escaped being devoured, his safe return was hailed as a certain proof of his innocence; and the contrary, if he fell a victim to the jaws of these ravenous monsters.

Another water ordeal, consisted in the accused standing up to his waist in water. A Brahman holding a stout stick in his hand, being stationed near him. A sepoy on the shore then shot three arrows from his bow, when a man was sent to bring back the arrow which had gone the farthest; as soon as he had picked it up, another person was despatched for the middle arrow, and when brought, another for the nearest; as soon as this last was picked up, the accused grasped the Brahman's foot, or the end of his staff, and dived under water. If he raised his head, or body, above the water, before the arrows were brought back, to the Sepoy, it was considered a clear proof of his guilt.

A mode still employed, sometimes even in the houses of Europeans, and giving rise to much unnecessary misery, is often thoughtlessly practised. When an article has been stolen, and there is no clue as to the robber, a person writes the name of every one in the house, enclosing each piece of paper in a ball of wax and other materials. These balls are then tossed into water, and that bearing the name of the guilty individual, is said always to float on the surface, Natives believe implicitly, in the truth of this trial.

Another common mode in criminal cases, was for the accused to take three draughts of water, in which some Hindu Deity had been washed for the purpose: if he remained quite well, for fourteen days, he was considered innocent, but if any sickness or internal pain occurred, he was proved guilty.

In some places, in civil cases, both Plaintiff and Defendant, or their Advocates, tried who could remain longest under water, holding on by some stakes, which were placed for that purpose, in sanctified spots. Whoever remained the longest, was considered in the right. The last case ended, in both the Advocates being drowned, and as both could not have been wrong, this method fell into disrepute.

Fire ordeals, or by heated substances, were those most commonly employed; in cases where the person was accused of a capital crime, they were as follows. Some days before the trial, the prisoner's right arm and hand were enveloped in wax cloth, and sealed up. When the day of the trial came, a cauldron was filled with cocoanut oil, and a fire placed beneath; a rupee, or some bright substance being inside, as the fire gradually heated the oil, the accused and accusers stood round, and the Brahman invoked the Deities, to show by the result, the guilt or innocence of the accused. When the oil boiled, the latter having first invoked the fire to declare the truth of his statements, by its effects on his arm, thrust it into the cauldron, and drew up the rupee. The arm was immediately swathed up in bandages, and sealed with the judge's seal, the man was then removed to prison. At the end of fourteen days, the seal was publicly removed, and the arm inspected, when if no scars were perceptible, he was held guiltless, and acquitted. It was supposed that if highly paid, the Brahman contrived to rub some substances on the arm to prevent any scalding taking place. But no doubt in many cases, the immediate and total exclusion of the atmospheric air, from the surface, would tend to heal the arm, without leaving any, or at all events, only a very slight scar.

Another method consisted, in holding a red hot piece of iron. The accused stretched out his hand, and seven leaves of the Peepul tree were placed upon his palm, and above them the red hot iron, and he had to walk backwards and forwards thus, for a certain length of time. Sometimes molten lead was poured over the palm of one hand, or at others the accused walked over a fire, made by burning Peepul wood.

Another ordeal, was that of *the balance*. The accused and a Pundit fasted 24 hours. The first then bathed in sacred water, and the second having presented oblations to the Deity, the prisoner was weighed. The Pundit now prostrated himself before the scales, and having written the accusation on a piece of paper, fastened it to the man's forehead. He was then after six minutes had elapsed, re-weighed, and if his weight had decreased, he was considered guiltless, if it had increased, guilty : and if the same, he had to be weighed again. Should the balance break, it was never doubted, but that the weight of the guilt of the accused, had caused it to do so.

Ordeals by poison, were of two kinds ; in the first, the Pundits performed their oblations, and then having mixed three barley corns of a poisonous root, or of white arsenic, in thirty-two times its weight of ghee, the accused was obliged to eat it from a Brahman's hand. If it had no injurious effect, he was declared innocent, otherwise as certainly guilty. The second consisted in placing a cobra, in a deep earthen chatty, into which was thrown some coin, or other small substance : if he could take this out, without being injured, he was proved to be innocent of the crime, imputed to him.

Another Ordeal consisted, in giving a number of persons suspected of theft, some rice to chew, and it was believed, that from the mouth of the guilty one, the grain would come out dry. Fear of detection, often caused this trial to prove correct.

Another was more especially, consecrated to the God of Justice. An image was made of silver, and another of iron or clay, they were then thrown into a jar of water, if the accused brought out the silver one, he was adjudged innocent.

Each of the different castes, are said to have had appropriate ordeals. The Brahmans by the balance, the Schatriyas by fire, the Vysias by water, and the Sudras by poison : but this had in very early days fallen into disuse in Malabar, and only those below the rank of Nairs, were usually subject to ordeal trials.

The lower classes of Natives, thoroughly believe in the possibility of the transmigration of evil spirits by witchcraft, into persons' bodies.

It is thought that evil spirits can be placed in charge of fields and gardens, and if a person should steal any of the produce and eat it, he would be afflicted with most terrible internal pains, which can be only removed by the sorcerer, or the person from whom he stole the fruit. It is also believed, that a sorcerer can produce such intense pain in the thief's body, that he will be glad to make an immediate confession, in hopes of getting cured.

It is also believed that a sorcerer besides afflicting a person with disease, can remove them altogether from the world. If a true account of the murders, which a belief in sorcery has occasioned in the form of revenge could be obtained, a most horrible revelation of atrocities, which have occurred in the Cochin State, would no doubt be brought to light.

The Native Christians, and Hindus, have many charms against the evil eye, amongst them jewels, and tiger's claws, set in silver, with which they load their children. The Mahomedans also suspend charms from the ceiling for the same purpose. Whilst, the Jews put figures on their houses. Women were not allowed to undergo the trial by water, or poison, but were not exempted from the other forms of ordeal. There was rather a curious one employed in Trichoor not many years ago, a husband suspicious of his wife's conduct, had her sewn up in a sack, and carried to an upper window, and thrown out: her guilt was judged of, according to the injuries she received.

Amongst a people given to trials by ordeal, sacrifices to evil spirits in every form, and who firmly believe that ghosts and hobgoblins are everywhere around them: amongst a race many of whom even worship the first animal they meet in the morning, a tree, or a block of wood, auguries are of course regarded as most important, and many a great undertaking is postponed, solely because some anticipated good omen, is not forthcoming. No one would think of continuing a walk, should a black cat happen to run across the road soon after he started. If a Namboorie setting out on a journey meet another Namboorie he invariably returns home, and if possible postpones his journey, but if this is impracticable he remains at his house half an hour and then makes a fresh start, meeting a jackall or two Namboories are good omens. If a lizard chirp upon the wall the conversation is at once changed. In some parts of India no answer is returned by the father to a proposal of marriage for his daughter until the lizard has made itself heard, and the position of the sound, its loudness, and other equally important differences, determine the tenor of the reply. Thursday is an inauspicious day. Hawkers consider it very unlucky should they not sell any article at the first house they visit in a day, and would rather dispose of something at a loss, than part with nothing.

The Syrians are as superstitious in their way, as the Hindus. One of their most extraordinary ceremonies, consists in poking out the eye of Judas Iscariot. On good Friday, a cake on which is a representation of an eye, is placed in the midst of the family circle. Each person is armed with a knife, and in succession makes a dig at the eye : after this is satisfactorily destroyed, the cake is cut up, and distributed.

One sect were said not long since, once a year, to have had their sins written out on a piece of paper, by a Catanar, and then placed inside a loaded bamboo gun, and discharged in the midst of a great feast : the uproar thus effectually dissipating, and destroying, their year's accumulation of misdemeanours. It is not unusual to perceive the skull of an animal, raised on a stick in a Christian's paddy field to avert the evil eye, in the same way as in those of the surrounding Hindus; and very many of their superstitious rites, are identical.

Of course atmospheric disturbances are viewed with great awe, an eclipse is believed by the vulgar to be one of their two bad spirits, swallowing the sun or moon. A comet, is supposed to foretel disasters, a dear season, or a frightful sickness : and lightning with its attendant thunder, is believed to be the gods waging war in Heaven, or elsewhere, whilst the Mahomedans assert, the shooting stars to be missiles, discharged by angels, at evil spirits, who are listening to what is going on in Heaven.

Etiquette is a subject deserving of a few remarks, those in power have at various times attempted to break through its regulations, but unsuccessfully. He who disregards its observances, is liable to be disrespectfully treated in public, and laughed at in private. Although to many Europeans, it may appear absurd to insist upon Natives, from a Prince to a Cooly, removing their shoes when entering an European house,* still all who understand the Native character, must admit its necessity ; they themselves originated the

---

* In some places, Shroffs, have been excepted from this rule.

custom, in the same manner as Europeans, have the removal of the hat as a sign of respect.

There is first the etiquette of caste, which has of late years been broken through to a great extent, up to the last sixty years, low caste Natives, and all Europeans, were compelled to keep to the road along the sea beach, those inland being reserved for the Nairs, and those of superior castes, for none of these classes approached the sea, excepting at certain seasons of the year when it was necessary for them to do so, to perform certain ceremonies of purification.

On certain ceremonies, the town gates were closed for several consecutive days, and none of the inferior classes were allowed to enter. Only a few years since, the Dewan of Travancore at the instigation of the Brahmans, forbade Native Christians, the use of some of the public roads, but the Court of Directors of the East India Company, *advised* the withdrawal of the prohibition, and it was consequently withdrawn. Missionaries were permitted to carry large umbrellas, which secured for them the use of the prohibited roads, provided they kept clear of the Pagodas.

The rules respecting the distances, which were always maintained between persons of the various castes, and subdivisions of such, do not appear to have been distinctly laid down, but formerly they were enforced by custom much in the following manner. A Nair was allowed to approach, but not to touch a Brahman: a Chogan remained 21 addi, or feet from him: and a Pullien above twice that distance: a Pariah, Oolahdur, or Niadi, 64 addi. A Chogan dared not approach within twelve paces of a Nair, if he did so in olden times, the latter was considered justified in cutting him down. A slave could not go nearer to a Nair, than he could to a Brahman, whilst he might not touch a Chogan.

The result of all this now is, that there exists overweening arrogance on the side of the higher castes, and cringing servility on that of the lower. From continually calling out from a distance, to be heard by persons of the higher orders, the majority of the natives have no idea of modulating their voices, but shout as if they were speaking to a deaf person. It is very amusing to see the Rajah's Sepoys, armed and dressed like those in the British service, and going out in charge of convicts; as being Nairs, they cannot approach their prisoners, for fear of pollution, and consequently keep a long way, either in their front, or in their rear.

Persons of the hightest rank, such as the Rajah, have obeisance made to them by Sudras, in the following manner. The palms of the hands are first brought together, and then usually raised to the forehead, or should it be intended to be particularly respectful, they are elevated above the head : but if only slightly so, the thumbs stop about the tip of the nose. The hands are then lowered to a level with the chest, from which a space of about six inches divides them : and then rapidly folded across the breasts, which expresses a hope that the good pleasure of the great person, will fall upon his servant. The number of times this ceremony is repeated, depend upon the rank of the person addressed, who in return joins his hands and holds them as if in the act of receiving something, thus showing that he accepts the salutation. Even the highest native will not sit down, in the presence of his mother, until she has granted him permission to do so: for great respect and attention, is always shewn to elders, and instructors.

A low caste man, respectfully addressing a superior, places his left hand on his breast, and his right over his mouth, and whilst speaking, continues to hold it only a short distance in front of it, for fear his breath may pollute the air, he is generally frightened, and anxious to get away.

Natives of the same rank, address each other as "Brother." A Brahman is called by inferiors *Tiroo-manasu*, or "man of a holy disposition." A Nair is addressed as *Tambaran*, or Lord. When calling each other, the natives hiss, if within a short distance, or beckon with the hand if far off: the palm being turned downwards, and moved in the opposite direction, to that employed by Europeans. In walking along the roads, the wife is always a few paces behind her husband. Natives are very much afraid of going out after dark, if compelled to do so; they shout as loud as they can, or sing to show their courage, and frighten off evil spirits.

A late Surwaddy Cariacar, who had been useful to the British, in the time of Colonel Macaulay, received a pension of two hundred rupees monthly as well as the privilege of entering the Huzzoor

Cutcherry with his shoes on, and the high honour of being allowed to chew betel there. Many a time in the middle of business, were a pair of wooden soled shoes, heard stumping up the stairs, and many a look of disgust, did the Hindus cast upon the ground, after these unwelcome visits.

The Brahmans are regarded by the Hindus, with greater deference than any other caste; in fact superstition has placed the priestly class, in most religions, foremost in the social rank. Next no doubt, are those from whom temporal honours are derived, and in a graduated scale, corresponding with their rank, pay, and official position, is difference shown to all. Without any official post, the next persons looked up to, are either those whose money commands them respect, or whose treatment of the natives, obtains it from their good will.

There are numerous proverbs, a few of which are as follows.

"Should one swallow a live coal, it turns into charcoal." Thus should a man be accused of having done a rash deed for the good of a friend, he replies as above; implying, he is resolved to suffer a little, for what he has done.

"Of what use is study, unless to learn knowledge which is true "wisdom."

"Why do we live in Towns, instead of forests, unless our object "be, to enjoy friendship, do good to others, and receive the wanderer, "and the stranger."

"He who revenges an injury, enjoys his triumph for a day, but "the man who forgives one, has a life-long satisfaction."

"It is a foolish deed, to burn your house for the purpose of destroying the rats."

"Politeness to a rude man, is as lines drawn upon a stream "of water."

"Modesty is becoming to every one, but is a particular ornament "to the rich and learned."

A person writing to a superior, sits down with his face to the rising sun, and commences his letter, on a piece of a palmyra leaf, termed an "*ollah*." First, for good luck, he praises the gods, and having cut off this scrap, begins with many high flown compliments, and an enumeration of all the titles, which he can conceive the person he addresses, to have any claim to. When the Rajah sends a letter by a messenger it is his duty to place it in the hands of the person to whom it is addressed, and not to entrust it to any third party. Wafers are never employed as saliva causes pollution.

In giving a letter to a Native of superior caste, it must not be handed, as that would cause contamination : but it must be thrown, the short transit through the air, breaking the line of contact to the superior. A letter is received with an amount of respect, varying in accordance with the relative rank of the recipient, to that of the writer. It is considered a great compliment to an European when the Rajah sends him some dishes prepared in the Native fashion, and etiquette requires him to taste a little of almost all; but as they often number as many as thirty, and are of the most varied description, he is frequently none the better for the honour done him.

Natives as a rule, on New Year's day, wait upon those under whom they are serving, and dressed in their best clothes, usually bring the children, a couple of limes,* some sweetmeats, or flowers; the Baker sends a cake, and the other petty trades-people, send or bring some trivial offering. Limes are on all occasions, indispensable for this purpose. It is also usual for the under servants, to make a present of sweetmeats to the butler, and head Ayah, on the first of the Malabar year.

The Rajah of Cochin, has the power to confer titles on his people, when he is presented with a nuzzer it is generally tied up in a square piece of silk, of a red and yellow colour. As silk is one of those substances, which does not convey pollution by touch.

The Rajah's personal guard of honor carry Pikes, bound around that portion, where the steel joins the handle, with a tuft of white feathery substance. Silver sticks are in attendance on him and persons to fan him both with a yah's (or Thibet cow's) tail, and with a fan surrounded by peacock's feathers.

---

* The presentation of a lime, has not with Europeans the signification it had amongst the native in times gone bye: it was in fact, the genteel way of giving a bribe, *the gift being inside the lime.* Bribery was so common, that at last no inferior ever came to ask a favour of his Native superior, without presenting him with a lime, this custom in Ceylon was so usual, that in time, *Bennet* states, they had a proverb, "*first look at the lime, and then open the mouth.*" Rajahs give visitors as marks of civility a shaddock, but in vain may he look for aught but fruit within.

Young persons may not sit in the presence of their elders, or inferiors in that of their superiors, until permission to do so has been received. This deference to seniors, forms part of their education. The village school, consists of an assembly of half dressed children, placed in rows, in an open room, in the verandah of a house, an open shed, or even under a tree. They are taught to trace letters on the sand, and are educated according to their station in life and the future occupation intended for them. After leaving this elementary school, they enter another, where they commence learning to write on palm leaves with an iron style, these leaves have a hole at one end, and are strung together like a book, between two boards. When the teacher enters this school, the pupils all prostrate themselves on the ground, and never speak until they have received permission to do so. When they can write, they proceed to learn accounts, and then other sciences, and branches of education : such as poetry, botany, medicine, law, logic and fencing: the art of playing at ball, chess, tennis, and especially silence. This last difficult art, is taught at Trichoor, to youths destined for the Brahmanical profession, who must remain inside the temple, for ten years, without speaking. Geography is not taught, as they do not wish to understand anything of other countries, and Anatomy and Surgery are unknown, as they must not either touch dead bodies or shed blood.

Nearly all the females, amongst the higher classes, especially the Nairamahs, learn to read and write, but they are not taught either needlework, or dancing, the former being considered a menial employment only fitted for tailors, and the latter a sign of a decidedly base character.

The literature is not abundant. The *Kerula Ulpati* a species of legendary history of Malabar appears to be the only original Malayalim work, but there are several versions of it. Their other writings, are free translations from the Sanscrit, such as the *Ràmàyana* or the history of Rama and Seeta, the *Baghavada* or the history of the incarnations of Krishna, &c., girls above the Nair caste, are never permitted to go out, except under the protection of their mothers, or aunts. Boys in their ninth year, are initiated into their father's caste.

Poetry such as it is, is much admired by the Natives, and even the boatmen, time the stroke of their oars to extemporary verses which are not invariably of the most reputable description, and consequently, will not bear translating. They have songs in honour of their gods, of great persons, and of noble deeds.

In olden times, only three kinds of poets were permitted, the historical who chanted history as they understood it, the genealogical who praised the ancestors of great persons and traced back their descent from the gods, and thirdly those who sang the praises of the king, wishing him and his family long lives, happiness and prosperous reigns.

The various kinds of voices, are said to be six, each bearing a curious name, as the peacock voice, the elephant voice, the ox voice, the sheep's voice, the bird's voice, and the horse's voice. Their instruments for warlike music, or for celebrating the deeds of Bacchus, are the large drum, the small drum, two clarionets, a kettle drum beaten with two pieces of iron, two copper or brass basins, and a pair of cow's horns. Those for pastoral tunes, are the guitar, the spinet, the flute, and a species of lyre.

Dramas in celebration of the Pagan gods have been copied by the Syrians in former times, and for many years have been inveighed against by Romish Priests unsuccessfully. Roman Catholic theatricals are enacted during the last few weeks before lent, when they become the rage, and a species of carnival is held, and old and young of both sexes, meet every night at about nine o'clock in the evening, to witness these performances, which generally continue until nearly daybreak. The theatre is on some open piece of ground, and in front of it are some temporary booths for the accommodation of the better classes, the poorer being in the open air. The stage is about six feet from the ground, and thatched with matting. The overture, and close of every scene, is enlivened by the most discordant music. The plays are generally selections from the sacred writings of the Portuguese, and are said to portray passages in the lives of some of their saints. The costumes are varied, and grotesque. Emperors and Princes hop about like mountebanks, whilst Queens and Princesses look like so many attempted representations of monkeys. The parts are sung with numerous choruses, in which there is no pretence of keeping time. As literary productions, they are below farces, and as representations they may be taken as caricatures, whilst the language is bad, and the acting worse. When all are wearied, the finale represents the punishment of vice, and the reward of virtue.

Nautches are also popular amusements amongst Natives, and consist in women of a light character, dancing in a listless manner, to a monotonous tune, which they sometimes accompany with their voices. The room is generally strongly impregnated with otta of roses, flowers, and various other kinds of perfumes. It is a mystery, how European ladies can allow themselves, even to be asked to such entertainments, but it is still more surprising, how they can ever frequent them: the taste is evidently a bad one, although Natives consider an European ball room much worse.

The amusements of the various races of Hindus, are much mixed up with their religious customs. Manly exercises are not much in vogue, those of a sedentary character being substituted. Games of cards, made of ollahs, are employed for gambling purposes: and lines are formed in the sand, for playing a species of draughts. Chess occupies a good deal of time, in the life of the Namboorie Brahman; and is played in the following manner, "The ground is smoothed "and checquered with chunam, and the pieces cut out of plantain "stalks, the Queen and Bishop alone differ in their moves, and "value, from ours. The queen or "*Wazeer*," moves diagonally back-"wards, and forwards, on one square, taking like a pawn. The "Bishop clears over everything within its range, but taking, and "checking, only on the second square, diagonally. The castle is "thus the only piece, which can move, and take from one end of the "board, to the other."*

Johnson writing in 1611 of the Nairs, who were then trained to arms, says, "at seven years of age they were put to school, to learn "the use of their weapons, and to make them nimble and active: "their sinews and joints were stretched by skilful persons, and "anointed with gingelly oil, by which they became so light and "nimble, that they could wind and turn their bodies, as if they had

* Colonel Welsh's "*Military Reminiscences*," vol. 2, page 86.

"no bones, casting them backwards, forewards, high and low, to the "astonishment of the beholders. Their continual delight was in "their weapons, persuading themselves that no nation went beyond "them, in skill and dexterity." This description, certainly does not tally with the mild and delicate looking Nair, of the present day. At the end of the last century, *Forbes* mentions, that in the festival of the new moon, in September, the Nairs drawn up in two divisions, held a tournament, in which it was considered a great honour to be killed. Persons who were so, were said to have sacrificed their lives for glory. At the present time, a more peaceful festival is celebrated.

The dress of the Natives, varies according to their religion, caste, and sex. That of the Arab, is the same as is worn in his Native country. The White Jew wears the long flowing garments of his race: but the black Jew clothes himself more like the Hindu from whom he is sprung. The various races of Christians, are distinguished by the men not wearing turbans, or caste-marks and by the women having jackets instead of the usual cloth. The dress of the Hindus, does not differ very materially, except with reference to the absence of turbans, from that of those in other parts of India. The Mussalman Moplahs, are much the same as those elsewhere. The Portuguese, or Topeecara, or people who wear hats, and trowsers, were always considered a distinct race, although there is no necessity for their having any European blood in their veins. The Moondoocars, or people with white clothing, may be either Christian fishermen *(Mucuas)*, cloth dyers, *(Paravers)* or others, who were first under Portuguese protection, and subsequently under that of the Dutch.

Clothing is amongst children, almost totally disregarded, however some mothers, who are very particular tie a string round their waists, and in rare instances they may be seen with a small scrap of cloth, a piece of a plantain leaf, or the representation of a fig leaf in silver, worn as Adam and Eve, are supposed to have adorned themselves.

As they grow older, a slight advance is made in the clothing department, but still there is never any superfluity of drapery, and the religious mendicants are extremely indecent, as they seem to consider, caste marks made with a preparation of sandal wood, as almost sufficient clothing. Native sailors, also are certainly not dressed in a manner admitting their entrance into European places of resort.

The turban perceived on Hindus, in large towns, is said to have been an imitation of that of the Mahomedans. Wherever the Hindu is most conservative of the customs of his ancestors, there the turban will not be found, neither will it amongst the pre-Hindu tribes. In the Cochin state, where the Mahomedans have never been stationary conquerors, the turban is not a common head dress: whilst inland, it is almost, and amongst the Hill tribes, quite unknown. Consequently wearing no turban, is not an insult in the Hindus of Cochin, as it would be amongst the Mahomedans. Besides the turban, another article of dress, has in many places, been borrowed from the Mussalmen, viz., the long white jacket, or rather coat, worn by Hindu, and other servants, who tie it on the left side, in contradistinction to the Mahomedans, who fasten it on the right.

The Arabs certainly, have rather an unprepossessing appearance, many of them visit the Port, during the shipping season, and some remain through the Monsoon. As a rule, they are strongly built men, and wear long beards: their clothing usually consists of an exceedingly dirty shirt, and trowsers, or rather drawers which were at some long antecedent date, of white cotton. They may be found smoking pipes, in the bazaar, and drinking the juice of the forbidden tree, some however appear to take their sherbet, and in several shops, coffee may be seen, provided expressly for them.

In India, the Manchester merchant would find but a poor mart for his manufactures, in comparison with the number of the population: a piece of cotton cloth, twisted around a man's waist, and descending to the knees, (about 1 yard, by 2 feet,) is sufficient for his daily wants, and perhaps another piece of the same size as a turban. At night time, they serve as coverings, when he curls himself up in a corner, stretches himself on the floor, or lies down on his cot, or mat, in the verandah to sleep. The higher castes, wear fine transparent white muslin cloths, and the richer, of even some of the lower classes, use fine white cotton. The Christians have a common pocket handkerchief, or a piece of muslin over their shoulders, and on grand occasions, or when they go out of doors, put it on their heads.

The dress of the Rajah, when at home, is of the same elegant simplicity, as that of his people,* being a thin muslin cloth, from the waist to the knees, a magnificent necklace of pearls, with a diamond clasp, no turban, but caste marks. When receiving strangers, he has on a most beautiful head dress of precious stones, and a long white muslin dress, edged with gold. On Durbar days, he is likewise dressed in white muslin, with gold lace, and a turban adorned with jewels: around his right arm (sometimes also on both) is a bangle of splendid diamonds, which are cut flat, and very thin, according to the Native fashion. His fingers are adorned with beautiful jewels, and on his second toe, is a gold ring. On each side of him, stand two Peons, one fanning him with the tail of the yah, the other with a white fan, surrounded by peacock's feathers. Next to him is seated the Resident, and the Princes either on his left hand, or below the Resident on the right. The Dewan or Prime Minister stands behind him, and many turbanless Brahmans in their single cloths, either behind, or on one side of him.

If the Rajah receives the visit of another Prince, at Muttencherry the following is the etiquette. The Rajah generally passes the preceding night at the palace, which is about one hundred paces from the water's edge, the whole distance from which, is covered in by a long pandall. On each side, along the entire length, are plantain trees in splendid bearing, tied to each of the pillars, that support the pandall. The Rajah's body-guard of Sepoys, are drawn up in two lines, the guard of honour armed with pikes, surmounted by white ostrich plumes, are in waiting. A drummer, a few fifers and fiddlers, are ready to strike up, and two small six pounders, are loaded at the water's edge.

When the boat of honour is approaching, the Elliah Rajah, or first Prince, attended by the Dewan, the officials, and others, proceed to the landing place, to receive the strangers. After they are landed,

* Natives cannot understand, why Europeans clothe themselves to such an extent in India. A Namboorie visiting at the house of an European gentleman, after meditating for some little time suddenly pointed to a wine bottle, which had on a worked cover, and exclaimed, "well you are a curious race "of people, not only do you clothe yourselves from your head to your feet, "put cloths upon your wooden tables, but also petticoats on your bottles."

they walk hand and hand towards the Palace, preceded by music, and dancing girls, who strew the ground with handsful of parched rice. At the top of the Palace steps stands the Rajah, who shakes his visitor's hand, and leads him into the room of state, which is a long apartment of Portuguese architecture having a deeply carved ceiling and small windows. The musnud or silver throne, is placed under a canopy of crimson velvet, at the West end of the room.

At a reception, as soon as a letter from the Governor or any other great personage has been read, the guns fire, the troops give a volley, and the Rajah after having been introduced to any strangers present, rises, as do all the assembled guests. Two gold trays are then brought forward, one covered with necklaces of Jasmine, the other with bouquets of the same species of flowers, arranged on artificial stalks. The Rajah then places one of these necklaces around the Resident's neck, a chain around each arm, and then presents him with a bouquet, which he sprinkles with otta of roses. The Elliah Rajah does the same to all the remaining guests, after which the Rajah takes the Resident's arm, and hands him to the door, standing there to shake every body by the hand on leaving, and address an appropriate word to each.

Hindu women addressing superiors, uncover as low as the girdle, as a mark of respect: Christian women, on going to church, put a white scarf over their heads, in accordance with the injunction that they should not go with their heads uncovered. On ordinary occasions, they wear only a white close fitting jacket. The termination of the under cloth is generally finished off in a plaited fan shape, commonly known as a "Cochin tail." The females of Quilon, usually fasten their cloths in front, and are consequently destitute of caudal appendages.

Many Cochin girls before marriage, dress like Tamil women, but subsequently change to the plainer Malayalim costume.

One division of Brahmanee women, (page 305) wear a piece of fine cotton cloth, about 5 yards long, by one and a half wide, fastened round the waist, without the assistance of pins. A piece of muslin, is thrown over the upper part of the body, passing under the right arm, and over the left shoulder.

The Nairamah, wears a loose separate upper cloth, thrown over the shoulder.

The Mucua women, have a coarse upper cloth, which covers up to the arm pits, but does not go above the shoulders, or hide the arms. The Shanar women in Travancore, have since July 26th 1859, been permitted to wear either the same jacket as the Christians, or dress in any other manner they like, so long as they do not imitate the costume of the females of the higher classes, which all those of a lower caste are strictly prohibited from copying.

The Topeecara or Potuguese class of women, who are in many instances, descended from the converted slaves of the Portuguese and Dutch, have a costume of their own, viz.—a long loose jacket made either of white or coloured material, and reaching as low as the knees, the lower cloth is generally a coloured one. In the Eurasian class, the poorer persons have scanty skirts, without petticoats. Some of them wear beautiful lace veils out of doors, instead of bonnets; the advance in style is gradual, according to means and position, and many are seen in the gayest European fashions.

Men who go about begging, sometimes use a cocoanut shell split in its long axis, as a head dress, as it serves two purposes, to protect the head from the sun, and also as a box to hold out for the reception of alms. The boatmen have large wide shaped hats, very like umbrellas, made of palm leaves, the same as are worn, higher up the coast.

Ornaments are much more profusely employed in eastern countries than in Europe. The ears undergo great punishments, and in some cases when a woman wears a Tamil dress, the corner of the nose, is also perforated by the Barber. Rings adorn the fingers and toes, the fore arms are covered with bangles, as are also the legs, whilst necklaces of gold coins, are often seen, where those of Rome and Venice; are placed next to those of Egypt, and the English St. George and the dragon jostles its Australian relative. The materials of which ordinary native ornaments are manufactured, are of the most varied description. Rings of copper, iron, and lead, and bangles of painted glass and wood, are made in imitation of more valuable metals, and precious stones. Necklaces are often composed of strings of beads, the threaded seeds of trees, or those turned from its roots, some are scented, others not so.

Almost every Native, carries in his waist cloth a small silver, tin' or brass, box fastened with many complicated screws and turns, and in this he deposits his poothens and other small valuables. The areca or betel nut with chunam, spice, and betel leaf are usually also secured in a small silver box suspended by a chain. Even the Nairs, according to Herbert, about 1627, although they usually went about armed, would not abate one jot of the common ornament of these oriental parts, which was to beautify, or rather load their arms and necks with silver bracelets, ropes of pearls, and other ornaments: in passing through crowds, they struck their sword upon their targets, and called out, both to make known their dignity, and also quickly to obtain a clear passage.

The Malabars do not wear nose rings, which is a peculiarity, as the Tamils consider it a great ornament, however they make up for this deficiency, by loading their ears: well might an ancient traveller, have spoken with astonishment of the bored ears of the inhabitants of Malabar. When children are a year old, or even less, their ears are pierced, and a small quill inserted in the lobe: as the irritation subsides, a bit of lead is substituted, and subsequently, when this has enlarged the hole, a piece of plantain leaf is rolled up, and put in: this is gradually increased in size, until the entire lobe is expanded into a circular hole, capable of containing a large round plug of wood, the circumference of which is often as great as the top of a wineglass: sometimes the flesh is torn away, but by care the part is healed. The appearance of the two black wooden ear rings, with circular flattened tops in front of each ear, certainly does not enhance a woman's beauty. This enormous orifice is made to enable it on her wedding day, to contain a gold ornament of about the size of a hen's egg, or even of a turkey's: sometimes a number of smaller ornaments, of a crescent shape, are fastened in. These are never worn before marriage, and are afterwards taken out, and rarely re-inserted. In some instances however they are retained, until the birth of the first child. The Mahomedan Moplah girls, have a succession of holes pierced, in each of which a ring is fastened, dragging down the ear by their weight, whilst the other fashion, expands it from the centre. There is little to choose between the two modes, as both occasion tumours, and other diseases.

All dowerless Roman Catholic, and Romo-Syrian girls, in olden times, were portioned by the congregations to which they belonged: the amount being raised by fines from the richer members. All female orphans, belonging to each congregation, had their names registered, and the Church Overseers, were obliged to provide them with husbands. On the wedding day, the gold ear rings are not the only ornaments put on, for the first and probably for the last time, as a head dress is also worn, made of pasteboard, and wound round with chains of gold, silver, or precious stones, to which smaller ornaments are also often attached, the weight of the whole being excessive.

Hindu women, after the birth of their first child, invariably remove the bangles from their arms and occasionally their other ornaments also. Native Christians, sometimes follow this custom but it is not the rule.

The women have hair of the deepest black, which reaches down as low as the waist, they are very proud of it, and keep it profusely oiled. It is coarse in texture, and differs from that of the African. They are fond of false tresses, and nearly all, even those of the poorer classes, wear them.

Cutting off the hair, or shaving the head, is considered a great disgrace. On festivals, or grand occasions, it is adorned with flowers, or silver ornaments.

Umbrellas* were formerly only carried over the great and noble: but all this is changed under British supremacy, although a remnant of the old idea, of the distinction of carrying it, still remains, and is enforced by law in the native state. The Rajah on ceremonial occasions, has a crimson one, with silver mountings carried over him, and a similar one shades the Hindu gods, from the rain or sunshine, when taken out of the Pagodas. At Christian weddings, the Bride and Bridegroom, also each have one carried over them; it is always a mark of honour. The size of the umbrella, was formerly in proportion to the rank of the person, over whom it was carried. Common umbrellas are usually made of the dried leaf of the Talipot palm which is occasionally tarred.

* *Cope* mentions, that when he was in Canara about 1714, no man was permitted to ride on horses, mules, or elephants, but Troopers, or Officers of State, although Europeans, were allowed to ride on oxen or buffaloes. Neither might umbrellas be carried over them by servants, but if the sun or rain offended them, they might carry them themselves. Page 300.

Native houses are of most varied descriptions. That of the Rajah is termed a Colgum* from *Col* "a sceptre" and "agum" "a house." It also means a distinct branch, or house, of any of the regal Hindu dynasties of Malabar. In building for those of the higher castes, great care is necessary, as a piece of wood, clothing or drapery will convey pollution, from the lower to the higher castes: as will also coir matting should it contain even one thread of cotton upon it although it is of itself unpollutable, a piece of new cloth may be thrown to a high caste person, who can look at it and toss it back without having been defiled, but should it be old it causes pollution. Floors must be made of chunam, stone, or earth, which are non-conductors, and not of planks: and for the same reason no carpets or mats can be spread. The checquered black and white chunam floors, are therefore usually seen, in the houses of the higher castes. Natives prefer houses situated in the centre of large compounds, many of those belonging to the nobility are two stories high, before the lowest of these there is a verandah, in which visitors are received: when the reception room is not in a separate building. In the upper story, the family sleep, study, or transact business.

When the Portuguese arrived, few Natives were allowed to live in anything but thatched huts, with mud or bamboo leaf walls. Traders such as the Moplahs, were allowed to build stone walls around their compounds, and even stone storehouses, in consequence of the risks they were otherwise exposed to. Princes and Priests had stone houses, and Pagodas were allowed the privilege of tiled roofs. Whole villages could thus easily be burnt down, if the inhabitants refused to pay their taxes, or their evacuation were necessary.

The miserable huts of the Churmurs, are dotted along the raised banks of paddy fields, and those of the Niadis may occasionally be seen perched like baskets, or birds' nests, up in jungle trees, into which they crawl at night time. The situation of the generality of houses, may be said to be damp, either from the places in which they are built,

* Wherever the Rajah has a Colgum, the Paliat Achen possessed an Illum. District courts go by the name of "the gate of the palace," therefore should the Rajah be hearing any case in the courts, he is "sitting in the gate of the palace."

or in consequence of the number of trees surrounding them. Their appearance is pretty, and no doubt the vegetation, breaks the force of many of the prevailing winds, but still sickness is very rife.

The domiciles of the Brahmans, and Nairs, are as a rule cleanly, as are those of the Syrians, and Romo-Syrians, but those of the lower castes, and of the Roman Catholics, can lay no claim to cleanliness, whilst those of the Mussalmen Moplahs are dirty in the extreme, as they live amongst filth and vermin, and their compounds if they have any, are the receptacles of the house sweepings. The women of this class, pride themselves in excelling their neighbours in filth, as they labour under the impression, that "a filthy garment is "a sign of a thrifty housewife!"

A very small amount of furniture is necessary for these houses, no table is required, as Natives sit on the floor, and the lower orders rarely employ bedsteads, but sleep on the ground: the better classes, use common coir roped cots, which with a few chairs also, and some brass cooking pots, complete the establishment. The wealthy appear to have a preference for European furniture, especially easy chairs, mirrors, and lamps. Plates, and dishes are unknown, the plantain leaf being a substitute for both, whilst a small cocoanut shell, with a wooden handle, answers the purpose of a ladle, or a spoon.

A brass or iron lamp suspended by a chain, is usually seen in the centre of their rooms, this can be elevated, or let down as required. There is always a large stone, or wooden mortar, for pounding unshelled rice. Numerous prints, and pictures, or rather caricatures, adorn the walls, as the Native idea of drawing, is very primitive, and the needy portrait painter, the photographer, or the dauber in colours, find an easy prey in Native Princes.

It is considered a good deed, to give large feasts to the poor, and at Tripoonterah, the Rajah of Cochin, on many occasions, yearly feeds some hundreds of persons. This is the more acceptable, from the fact that the rice is generally boiled by Brahmans. On recovering from an illness, it is sometimes customary to give a large feast which elevates the convalescent in the eyes of those around. No Malabar rivers are venerated, although some ceremonies are performed at the Alwaye, Shallacoodee, and some other streams. Those who construct tanks, and reservoirs of water, will it is believed be rewarded in a future state; it is therefore the ambition of the people of Malabar to have a tank, a well, or a choultrie named after them. Hospitality is much lauded, but of course is confined to persons of the same caste.

The usual mode of travelling, is by the Moncheel or Palanquin, carried by bearers, each of whom receives 4 pie a mile, by bullock or buffaloe carts, which are paid at the rate of one anna nine pie a mile, and by boats of every description, from the comfortable cabin to the little snake boat, which can go up very shallow streams.

Letters in the Rajah's territory, are conveyed by Ungil, free of charge, as are also small parcels. Before the inland roads were open to Europeans, the post office runners were permitted the use of them.

The food of the people, is as varied as their castes and creeds, the Brahmans of the country, (the Namboories,) are a very bigoted sect, who disdaining to touch animal food, or rather perhaps having a religious aversion to it, eat their vegetables alone, and grow fat on their milk and ghee. The amount of sugar* they consume, is only limited by their means of procuring it. The criterion by which one Native judges of the wealth and respectability of another, is his size, a stout man is therefore held in much greater esteem, than a thin one. There are certain feeding houses, Ootooparas, already alluded to, in the topographical chapter of this work, where this pampered Brahmanical class are gratuitously fed, the cost being defrayed by the taxes of the country, thus they can always be supplied with a meal.

As every Native, no matter what his property may be, would rather be fed at Government expense, than at his own, there is no dearth of applicants at these houses. The cost of this, is reckoned in the official records, amongst that for public works, of which this *good work*, absorbs a very large portion.

The Schatriyas, are as particular about their food as the Brahmans,

---

* The late *Rajah of Travancore*, had a private museum, in which "bonbons," and "jujubes," held a conspicuous place. One day an advertisement in a Madras newspaper caught his eye, announcing the arrival of a consignment of "Jupons." Concluding that they also must be something nice to eat, he ordered a number by post. In due time they arrived, and great surprise was manifested when the contents were discovered to be steel crinolines. Their use was unknown, but they were placed in the museum!

who will eat in the same room with them, if the food be perfectly distinct, and separate. The number of curries, made for each meal, is enormous. The Vysias are too few to require notice.

The Nairs, are not particular as to their food. If asked, they declare that they never touch, either beef, pork, or ardent spirits, but respecting the last, this is by no means the fact. Some there are, who wishing for a favourable transmigration, are as particular as any Brahman, but their caste does not exact this. Many are notorious drinkers of ardent spirits, in excessive quantities, and one of the favourite repasts of the lower division of Nairs, is a fine pig. Respecting the diet of the people, volumes might be written, and much still remain untold.

A Native generally commences the day, by having about a quarter or half a pound of pounded brown rice, boiled in a pint of water, to which some sugar is added, and if he can afford it, a little buttermilk. From this time, he rarely takes anything, with the exception of smoking tobacco, opium, or bhang, until eleven or twelve o'clock, when he expects his wife to have prepared his breakfast. Some classes however continue without food, until three or four in the afternoon. This meal consists of a pint, or more, of brown rice, carefully boiled, and thus augmented to about twice the first amount. Should he reside near the sea coast, it is made more palatable, by the addition of some fish, fried in cocoanut oil, or curried. The Native Portuguese, invariably add country vinegar, whilst some of them, eat white rice, instead of brown, as do also the Tamils, or most of them.

The wife, having prepared the food, and placed it on plantain leaves, the husband (who if a Brahman may not eat off anything else, although tin vessels may be used for cooking,) having previously bathed, and if a Brahman, exchanged his cloth for a silk handkerchief, seats himself on his mat, with his feet crossed under him, and commences his meal. No Hindu woman can eat in the presence of, or at the same time as her lord and master, excepting on the day of her marriage, (as described page 304) such being considered, as both indecent, and disrespectful. If they can afford it, some soup made of vegetables, herbs, fruits, pepper, and other pungent articles is placed in a vessel, with which they moisten the rice, from time to time. Buttermilk, ghee, and herbs that have been fried in oil, or curried, are also eaten. The man never touches his food with his left hand, such being considered impure. The rice ready for consumption, is heaped up into a mound, with a depression on the top, in the centre of which is an amalgamation of various other articles; he then opens his mouth, and throws the food into it, in the form of little balls, and when thirsty, pours hot water, or ginger water, into the same receptacle, without letting it touch his lips. Sometimes he has a dessert, of betel or tobacco leaves. Having finished his meal, he goes outside the door, where water is poured from a brass vessel, over his hands, after which he retires to a tank, to perform his ablutions, attended by his wife, and family.

Natives of the highest classes, are sometimes very much pleased at being invited to the dinner table of Europeans. The host is expected to hand in the illustrious stranger on his arm, as if he were a lady, but questions are frequently asked respecting the ingredients of the various dishes, to which it is necessary to give guarded replies, thus beef is never mentioned, and is usually called ham, whilst of course eggs must not be admitted, to form any part of a pudding. During the entertainment, they appear to feel, much as a visitor to the Zoological gardens, when seeing the lions and tigers fed, and they would be equally likely, to join in the repast.

There are many articles, fit for human food, procurable in almost every locality, and the Native is a much greater adept at discovering them in his own country, than the European. The Poonac, or oil cake the refuse of the cocoanut after the oil has been expressed, is usually given to cattle and poultry, but still the poorer classes eat it: a great luxury is the pounded seeds of the Bamboo, mixed with equal quantities of honey, placed in a hollow Bamboo, then surrounded with clay, and baked. Yams of many varieties, flourish all over the country: arrowroot is found wild in numerous places, and vetches and pulses, may be seen growing both on the dry land, and in the paddy fields. A flour is prepared from the seeds of the Lotus, Talipot Palm, and other plants. The fruit of the Jack, the apple of the Cashew nut, the various productions of the numerous fruit trees, give some of the greatest delicacies of the country. The roots of the sweet potatoe, and other plants, are eaten: vegetables are raised for the table, and the leaves of many trees are used for seasoning, whilst the Areca, the betel, and tobacco, are in constant request.

But animal food also is abundantly supplied ; all marshy places, and paddy fields, contain quantities of Ampullariœ, Unionaceœ, and Paludinœ, which are all employed as human nutriment. During the rains, when out-door work is almost impossible, when the land is a swamp, and the atmosphere saturated with moisture, animal life abounds, and the component parts of a repast, may be found almost everywhere. Dried fish ought to have been saved, as food during this time, but the people are too improvident to provide for the future, and the salt tax is very oppressive. No fresh sea fish can be obtained, as the water is too rough, to admit of deep sea fishing. The same may be said, of the mouths of the large rivers. But fish may be found in every small stream, whilst the climbing Perch, the Verrarl, and others, come forth from the over-crowded ponds, and find their way into wet ditches, and irrigated paddy fields, but as the ghauts are approached, the character of these fish alter, until they become actually unwholesome.

The laws of caste, also prevail regarding food. The Churmurs, and even sometimes the Chogans, will collect and eat the marsh snails, (*Paludinœ*) which become abundant inland, as the *Ampullariœ* decrease. The large *Potamides*, (*terebralii telescopium,*) are also abundant near the mouths of estuaries, and in paddy fields along the coast. But these crawling molluscs, are considered only fit food for slaves, and are consequently not eaten by those of any higher caste, who only collect and eat those, which do not crawl, and are not so common, as the fresh water mussel, *Unionidœ* and some of the *Cardiadœ*.

Mutton also during the South West monsoon is unprocurable, excepting by the wealthier classes. Cows are of course not killed, in the Native state, although if they die, slaves are allowed to eat them. Pigs are considered luxuries by Native Christians, and Nairs, whilst even the Mussalmen Moplahs, are known to eat them under the name of *Mutton*. The lower castes, are fond of eating squirrels, porcupines, large lizards called iguanas, flying foxes, deer, all birds excepting reptorial ones, (and even some of these,) mice, and frogs. Some castes delight in the flesh of the crocodile, and will even eat a tiger if they can get him. The dog is usually spared, but not so his enemy the cat, of which the tank diggers are so fond, that at Trichoor, no tabby is safe, and even in Cochin, they are not unfrequently killed, and their livers eaten as a remedy for asthma. Amongst the Nicomars, the Bridegroom on his marriage, invariably kills and eats a cat, in which he is assisted by the Bride. The Bridal feast of the tank diggers, consists of a fox.

When the South-West monsoon closes, the ground dries up, the fisheries re-open, and food of all descriptions is abundant: the North East monsoon, scarcely decreases the fishing, and there is then plenty of work.

The Hindus and Native Christians, drink with their food, large quantities of hot water, or ginger water. Much opium is consumed, but less bhang than in other parts of India. The consumption of arrack, and toddy is very great, and French brandy finds an enormous sale.

The Native of India, has been generally held up as a model of sobriety, and good health, from abstemious living: whatever he may be elsewhere, he certainly is not this in Cochin. Drunkenness is a prevalent vice, amongst all excepting the twice born classes: he is a martyr to dyspepsia, immoderate in his eating, gorging himself at his meals, and takes strong condiments to assist his appetite. He is also an habitual consumer of narcotics, (Brahmans, and Slaves excepted,) so it is not surprising, that he is a great sufferer from visceral affections, and short lived.

CHAPTER XI.

CLIMATE AND DISEASES.

Climate—Temperature—Monsoons—Rain fall—Land winds—Sea breeze—Hail storms—Offensive emanations from the sea—Native ideas of disease—Cochin Dispensary—Fevers—Natives able to produce it themselves—Native Practitioners—Small pox and vaccination—Consumption—Cholera—Feasts to avert Epidemics—Curious remedies—Rheumatism—Elephant leg—Leprosy and Leper house—Fits considered to be the effects of evil spirits—At Births Astrologers consulted—Witchcraft—Enchantments—Hill deity—Novel mode of curing all diseases.

THE climate of Malabar, is moister and more sultry, than that which prevails on the Coromandel coast, and it consequently has a very different effect on the health. The seasons of the year are divisible, into the hot, wet, and cold months. The thermometer rarely rises above 92° in the shade, at any period. In the commencement of March, the hot weather begins, and the oppressiveness of the atmosphere increases, and then the inhabitants of the town of Cochin who are able to do so, usually proceed to Alwaye, where they can enjoy the luxury of river bathing. During this month, the mean temperature (in the shade,) is about 80°, and it rarely falls below 68° or 69°. In April it may be estimated at an average of 2° higher than it was in March. During the first part of May, the temperature keeps up to the average of April, but during the latter part of the month, the heat is diminished, by frequent showers. In June the wet season commences, and a sudden fall in the temperature occurs. As the South West monsoon breaks, about the first of the month, rarely later than the fifteenth, vast masses of clouds appear in the horizon, to the S. S. W., whilst towards evening, the sky becomes lowering, accompanied by vivid flashes of lightning, and loud peals of thunder. The thermometer about this time sinks down to 77°, and the usual monthly averages, may be considered as follows, during July, August, September, October, and November, 76°. In December, the temperature decreases to about 75°, and remains about the same in January. In February it rises about 4°, and in March about 1° more.

The word *Monsoon*, appears to be derived from the Persian term "Monsum," a season, and is now generally applied to the rainy months. *The South West Monsoon*, is that most severely felt on the Malabar coast. In Cochin the average yearly fall of rain, is about 108 inches, although sometimes it reaches 120, or even more. Between 70 and 80 inches, are sometimes gauged in the South West Monsoon. The amount which falls at night time, exceeds that during the day. This Monsoon ceases about the middle of August, but the weather remains unsettled, until September, and even then the sea is still rough.

During this period, vegetation springs up very rapidly, and nature appears renewed. The intervals between the showers, are very oppressive. Owing to the porous nature of the soil, water rarely continues long on the ground, but is soon absorbed. Even in the full height of the Monsoon, there are usually a few hours daily without rain, and about twenty days after the first burst, there is sometimes a cessation for a fortnight.

Whilst the rains continue, the resident suffers great loss, in all property liable to spoil from the effects of moisture. Steel and Iron rust, clothing especially woollen articles become damp, mildew, spot, or are destroyed by the fish insects, moths, cockroaches, or crickets: colours also fade, silks spot, gloves become rotten, the bindings of books lose their colour and strength, and furniture its polish, whilst if fastened together by glue, it falls to pieces. Even writing paper becomes damp, if glazed greasy, and unpleasant to write on. Collections of Zooloogical specimens, are almost destroyed, the Butterflies by small insects, and mildew: Birds, by the moth; and fish, especially those of the salt water species become very damp, as if they had again just arrived from their native element. In fact during this season, there are very few things, that escape injury of some kind.

Reasoning by analogy with other places, it might be expected that at this time, the whole country would swarm with animal life, but this is not the case. The birds retire to some drier locality, and the insects are not more numerous. The rains are too heavy, and the moisture too great, for animal life to thrive, small creatures are destroyed, and the larger unable to obtain food, migrate to more genial climes.

The *North East Monsoon*, or as it is sometimes called, the Madras Monsoon, is very slightly perceptible in Cochin, it occurs in October, and lasts partly into November: the fall of rain is not great. Coughs and colds, with feverish attacks, are at this season very prevalent.

The *cold season*, if it can be so designated, commences about the beginning of November, at the termination of the North East Monsoon.

The *average rain fall*, excluding unusual years, has been as follows, January 0¾, February 0½, March 3¾, April 7½, May 10½, (in 1859, 50 inches fell during this month,) June 29½, July 10½, August 10¼, September 7½, October 14½, November 4, and December 1¼ inches.

The perceptible heat of the atmosphere, does not depend entirely on that registered by the thermometer, for the movements of the air, also sensibly affect the feeling; the heat at night time, all the year round, is not in a ratio corresponding with what occurs during the day. Generally in October, or at the latest in November, the low lands around the bases of the ghauts, and for some distance from them, commence to be covered with dew, and fogs hang about the wooded hills. All low country people, are at this time obliged to leave the Jungles, fever increases in intensity, and sleeping in the woods, would almost certainly be followed by an attack of Jungle fever. This dangerous time continues until February, or the end of March, but cases contracted in December, and January, are most dreaded, for the type is then of a sthenic character.*

The *land winds*, or those from the North East or East, are exceedingly variable, for whilst in October they may be severe further North,

* These observations have been made, amongst the Kodachayree Hills, and Jungles.

—as for instance at Trichoor,—they are but slightly felt in Cochin, where they generally commence in November, and reach their maximum strength, about the middle of December, or the commencement of January. They are very irregular in their continuance: generally in the town of Cochin, setting in about 7 P. M., and usually last 12 hours, but it is by no means rare, for them not to cease, till 11 or 12 o'clock in the next day. Immediately the land wind stops, the sea breeze usually commences, occasionally the force of the former, decreases towards the full of the moon. This deleterious wind, is the heated air from Mysore and the higher table lands, conjoined with that from the Coimbatore district, which rushes through the Paulghaut pass, towards the sea; in its course it travels over a jungly and highly feverish country, and is consequently very unhealthy. The land winds were in 1862, perceptible in the month of May in Cochin, but they generally cease in February.

The strength and continuance of these winds, are proportionate to the severity of the Monsoons. If the fall of rain has been very great, saturating the Malabar side of the ghauts, filling the tanks, and flooding the swamps, the evaporation during the succeeding months becomes great. The air is thus partially cooled, and the rush of the heated air from inland, displacing this which is cooler, causes the wind from the land towards the sea, to become impetuous, but it reaches different places along the coast, at different hours, depending greatly on their distance from the ghauts. At Trichoor between the Paulghaut gap and the sea, the land winds are excessive, and blow continuously day and night, with great violence. The travellers' bangalow at Kurriapudnam, placed upon a high spot of ground, is remarkably free from these winds. From about the middle of August, until October, or even later, strong breezes set in from the N. N. W., or North West and are unhealthy, but perhaps not so much so, as the land winds just described.

The *sea breeze* continues irregularly throughout the year. Before the South West Monsoon sets in, strong winds come gradually round from the North, to the West: and at last to the South West increasing in severity, whilst the noise overhead, is a sure criterion, that the Monsoon is setting in: it comes with a rushing sound, something like a flock of wild ducks passing. In the commencement of March, strong cold sea breezes, generally occur, rendering the sea rough: should persons remain in them whilst perspiring, fever is frequently the result; during April and May, thunder and lightning become severe, the flashes being very vivid, whilst the claps appear close: sometimes the shipping in the roads are struck, trees are frequently knocked down, and some fatal accidents to coolies working out of doors usually take place, especially to those preparing the paddy grounds, for the Monsoon crop. As the downpour becomes more decided, the thunder and lightning gradually disappear, and cease by the middle of June. In the North East Monsoon, there is usually a return of this electrical disturbance.

Hail storms are of very rare occurrence: one occurred in Cochin in May 1862, and was looked upon by the Natives, with extreme wonder.

At various periods in the year, very *offensive effluviæ* arise from the sea, the backwater, and the banks of the Alwaye river. These exhalations from the sea, during the last three years, have been especially apparent, on June 14th and 15th, 1861: July 22nd, 23rd and 24th, 1860: and August 8th, 1862. Whilst in "November, and "December, 1836, the state of the sea at this station, (Calicut,) and "Tellicherry, was very unwholesome, it sent forth a strong stench of "putrifying matter, and deposited a black mud on the sand. For many "yards from the shore, the water was covered by dead fish, and on the "beach they were lying in large heaps: the effluviæ arising from which "extended over the station, and almost every person was more or "less ailing,—fevers, headaches, and nausea, were the general complaints."* In this last instance, the state of the sea, could not be owing to the admixture of fresh with salt water, as such was not then occurring, whilst the state of the sea appears to have *caused* the destruction of the fish. In Cochin when emanations arise from the sea, they also do so from the backwater, showing from whence the odour is derived. Still it seems as if the smell is augmented, when the unsavoury water from the backwater, reaches the sea, and many of the finny tribe, and sea snakes, are often perceived at this time lying dead on the shore.

---

* *Medical Topography of the Madras Presidency,* Malabar, and Canara, page 84.

Offensive emanations from the backwater, and river, are by no means confined to the Monsoon months. One cause is, that immense numbers of cocoanut shells are buried in the mud, within tidal influence,—in order to separate the fibres, and thus form coir. When these deposits are opened, the effluvia is most horrible, and the river is polluted for many miles. Another cause is the water which has been retained in paddy fields, in which vegetable matter is allowed to putrify for manure; and when let out into the river, or overflowed, it renders the river water very offensive. Thus it is, that when the Monsoon rains cause the rivers to overflow their banks, all decayed matter is carried towards the sea, which is thus rendered semi-putrid. The cause of this effluvia in the sea, during the hot months, is difficult to determine. *Benett** considered that in Ceylon, it arose from the presence of vast numbers of the Arum fœtidum.

Cochin though called healthy by its inhabitants, is much dreaded on account of its numerous diseases, as a place of residence, by the Natives of other parts of India. The mortality is about one person yearly in every twenty-four inhabitants, or excluding epidemics, such as Cholera and Small Pox; one in thirty-three individuals. Natives are not generally speaking long lived, whilst their mode of stuffing themselves at meals, drinking large quantities of intoxicating or hot fluids, and eating opium, renders them martyrs to dyspepsia.

All diseases are considered to be more or less due to demoniacal influence, and consequently a belief in the efficacy of spells, is deeply rooted. Charms as a rule, are more relied on than drugs, and a piece of peacock's feather tied round an arm or leg, than the appliances of a Medical Practitioner. The Brahman, the Priest, and the Exorcist, rank about equal: and the decapitation of a cock, as a sacrifice to the goddess Kali, is believed incomparably superior to vaccination, as a preservative against Small Pox. The presentation of an umbrella to a Brahman, it is believed will protect the donor from the injurious effects of the sun: giving him shoes will prevent his feet being blistered on a journey: whilst presenting him with some aromatic spices, will preserve him all his days, from offensive smells,

* Ceylon, and its capabilities.

and foul exhalations: consequently, the benefits of a sanitary commission are not much esteemed, by pious Hindus.

The European Surgeon, is thoroughly trusted in all cases requiring surgical operations, most accidents, and in some few species of disease: but in the common complaints of the country, the Natives prefer their own nostrums, and die under the treatment of those of their own caste.

Since May 7th, 1817, the British have maintained a Civil Surgeon at Cochin, for the purpose of attending Government Servants, and the Prisoners in the Jail, as well as to afford aid to the poorer classes who may apply for it.

At the present time, the duties of Medical Officers, are strictly confined to Medical affairs, but the Dutch employed a variety of persons, but few of whom had been educated in Europe, and whose chief occupation appears to have consisted, in tasting cinnamon, and applying themselves to other mercantile occupations : whilst it does not appear that inside Cochin, that nation ever had Hospitals, available to the sick native community, who were not servants of the Company.

On June 23rd, 1847, the inhabitants of Cochin addressed a Memorial to the *Marquis of Tweeddale*, Governor of Madras, drawing his attention to the miserable objects of disease, which might be seen in every street, to the general poverty of the inhabitants, and the absence of medical aid within an Hospital, and praying for the establishment of a Government Dispensary.

Many a family as the Memoralists observed, were dependent for the means of support on the labour of a father, or brother, who when falling sick, if properly treated, might soon be restored to health, instead of probably succumbing to disease. Owing to the absence of Medical assistance, mortality amongst able bodied labourers had become very great, and numerous families were thus left burdens on the community, whilst the Friend-in-Need Society, which was only established in 1845, for the relief of the necessitous poor, could not afford to feed all pauper sick, whilst under treatment.

On July 23rd, 1850, a public meeting was held, and another Memorial addressed on the same subject, to *Sir H. Pottinger*, then

Governor of Madras. In the intermediate time, the Rajah of Cochin, sensible of the benefits to be derived from a Dispensary, established one for his own subjects, at Ernacollum, and placed it under the supervision of the Civil Surgeon of Cochin.

A favourable answer was returned to this second petition, and the erection of a Dispensary finally sanctioned. The inhabitants of the town, subscribed 1768 Rupees, and Government contributed the remainder: the total cost of the building, being 4,517¼ Rupees. In the interim, a house was rented, and employed as a Dispensary, being opened for the reception of patients, on December 14th, 1850. The new building was situated in a central locality, easily accessible from every part of the town, and the sick were removed there, in the end of January 1853.

Patients rapidly increased, severe accidents and cases of disease were brought from many inland places, and still continue to be so. The expense of maintaining paupers, gradually augmented as years rolled on, until at last the number of those who dieted themselves as In-Patients, was much less than those fed by Government as paupers. In 1861 it was therefore decided, that for the future, Government would provide Medical attendance, European drugs, and Hospital servants, and in addition Rupees 50 a month, towards dieting paupers, finding lights for the building, and country medicines, leaving the inhabitants to subscribe the remainder.

Besides the Cochin Dispensary, a Lazaretto for incurable lepers is maintained by the British Government at Palliport. There is, likewise a staff of Vaccinators, spread throughout the country. The whole of these establishments, are under the immediate control, of the Civil Surgeon of Cochin.

The climate of Cochin is very enervating, and may be described as a dilatory one, inducing persons of all classes, to defer until to-morrow, what should be done to-day. The nervous system becomes greatly depressed, and it takes long, to rally from the effects of a severe illness. It is curious, that sun stroke is almost unknown. Both Natives and Europeans are constantly troubled with nervous twitchings, even when asleep at night time, in various muscles, to an extent rarely observed elsewhere. The lower animals also do not escape nervous affections, thus startings, *paralysis agitans*, (?) frequently affects dogs and cats, whilst horses go weak in the loins, which has been attributed either to their eating the *Lathyrus sativus* or analogous vetches or else to their being exposed to a draught of cold wind when freely perspiring. Person's teeth become extremely brittle and are very apt to break when brought in contact with any hard substance.

The Monsoon rains when heavy are productive of irritation of the intestines, consequently diarrhæa and dysentery are then very prevalent.*

When epidemics of cholera or Small Pox are severe, evil spirits are believed to be roaming about after dark, through the towns, villages and highways, consequently as soon as it begins to get dusk, all doors are securely fastened, to prevent their entrance. This superstitious belief, is apparently prevalent, amongst all creeds and castes.

Malarious fevers, (*Puney*, Mal.) in the form of *dumb agues,* are amongst the most common diseases in Cochin, and are rather fatal in their effects, especially if contracted in the jungles. It is curious to observe, that the further south a locality is on the Western Coast, the less frequent are the attacks of this disease.

During the dry cold months of the year, namely December, January, and February, the number of attacks is below the average, but the mortality exceeds it. The virulence of the malaria, however decreases in the three succeeding hot months. With the mangoe showers in March, the jungles and some other localities, become feverish, whilst in the plains, fevers become very severe, until the Monsoon has well set in, when they begin to decrease. Different localities in the Jungles, apparently suffer from fever at slightly different times, whilst the most sickly period in the hilly ranges, is not the same as that in the plains. In August the unhealthy North West long shore winds, are frequently perceived, and cause fevers, colds, and dysenteries.

* For a detailed account of the diseases of Cochin, which is unsuited to these pages, the reader is referred, to the *Madras Journal of Medical Science,* Vols. 1, 2, and 3. Out of upwards of 20,000 admissions, into the Cochin Civil Dispensary, in five years, ending 1861, they were as follows: malarious fevers 9·7: eruptive fevers 3·5: lung affections 5·5: liver 0·3: intestines 28·8: brain 1·2: cholera 0·1; dropsies 2·3: rheumatism 5·8: lock hospital 4·4: abscesses and ulcers 10·1: wounds 10·4: eye 2·4: skin 7·1: other diseases 8·4.

Every change of temperature is felt by a feverish subject, such as thunder in the air, a storm of wind or rain, which increases the number of attacks, whether on the hills, in the jungles, or in the plains.

In October should the land winds have set in, the frequency of cases of fever combined with coughs and colds becomes very great. A gentleman who has a plantation in the Cochin State, has observed, that every cooly standing in a tank of an evening, for the purpose of drawing water, for the young coffee plants, invariably has an attack of fever by the next morning. Drinking the water of the wells, or rivers, has also the effect of producing fever: so the natives in those jungles always drink boiled water, mixed with green ginger.

Natives are able to produce a paroxysm of fever, when such may be deemed necessary. For this purpose after having bathed in cold water early in the morning, they eat a large quantity of cold rice, and buttermilk, followed by the fruit of the Narga, *Calyptranthes Caryophyllifolia*, Swartz. When the sun rises, they lie down in its rays, and fever almost invariably ensues. Persons who are not in the habit of bathing in warm water, and anointing themselves, frequently get fever from doing so, and it has been observed, that should those unaccustomed to bathe in a river, such for instance as that at Shallacoodee, do so whilst the water is muddy, from the washing of the ghauts, owing to heavy rain, fever almost invariably occurs. But Natives who usually bathe several times daily in the river, do not find that the changes in the purity of the water affects their health.

In some Europeans, attacks here as elsewhere, may be induced by sitting under a punkah, eating some kinds of fruit, especially plantains, or even drinking large quantities of milk. The effects of the cold sea breezes, and the land winds, have already been alluded to, as occasioning this disease.

The Native Practitioners are very ignorant, consequently they are badly paid, which prevents a better class of persons, from studying medicine. *Paoli* mentions, that in his time, (before 1790) the people " were accustomed, never to pay the physician, until they " were completely freed from their diseases" and that " when a Ma- " labar Physician failed of a cure, the patient gave him a certain pre-

" sent, according to the trouble he had had." Reasoning by analogy with the present time, the unfortunate Medical Practitioner, must have been badly paid indeed. If no cure ensued, it seems to have been the rule to give no pay. Whilst it is proverbial, that persons when sick, are profuse in promises, which when well, they are slack in performing.

Some Native Practitioners at the present time, receive so much a day, whilst attending, and a reward which has been agreed upon before hand, when the person has recovered. In the jungles, where any cooly can practise, Natives agree to give him a certain sum, if he can cure them.

The Hindu and Mahomedan treatises upon Medicine, are voluminous, and their ideas of many diseases, very absurd: they have a few good simples in use, but very many of the valuable drugs growing around them, they are quite unacquainted with. There are several Herbalists' stalls in the Muttencherry Bazaar, and they are curious to examine, whilst some useful drugs may be procured at them. But the purchaser should not trust the seller, as to the properties of the drugs, as in that case, he runs a great risk of being poisoned: whilst owing to the careless manner in which they are dried, and preserved, no two samples are of the same strength.

The Native remedy for fevers, consists of a compound of numerous herbs, which should be collected fresh, but as this often takes from five to forty days, the grass is sometimes growing high above the patient's grave, before the prescribed drugs have been collected, from the various and distant localities in which they are alone supposed to grow. The fame of quinine is now spread throughout the country, but arsenic appears to be quite as beneficial.

Small Pox is greatly dreaded. The yearly sacrifice to Kali, to avert its onslaught, has been alluded to; when the disease breaks out, the avenging deity is supposed to be sowing the seeds far and wide, and each pustule is considered as the germination of a single one. Then relatives forsake their smitten relation, the husband flees in terror from his wife; the mother from her child, and no ties of consanguinity are for the time regarded.

In the interior of the country, relations sometimes fix a hollow bamboo through the roof of the hut, and twice a day pour rice down it, for the sick person's use: otherwise if they can afford it, or the neighbours are generous enough to subscribe, a nurse who has had the disease is procured. In this case, a cock is first sacrificed to Kali, and the blood occasionally rubbed over the patient's body; a branch of neem, *Azadirachta Indica*, the symbol of purification, is hung over the bed: or leaves of this tree, sacred to the Goddess of small-pox, are thrown over the patient.

This disease is most severe, during the first three months of the year. The mortality amongst natives protected by vaccination, is about six per cent.; but amongst the unprotected, as high as forty-six per cent. Exclusive of the direct mortality caused by small-pox in unvaccinated persons, many have their constitutions so shaken, that they subsequently fall victims to consumptions, dysenteries, dropsies, or other diseases.

Should Hindus die of small-pox, they are believed to be accursed, but it is not the Hindu alone who succumbing to the dire effects of this disease, receives no funeral rites. There is a prevalent belief, that individuals may be attacked by seven different species of eruptive fevers, but as there is no discrimination between each, it is a common saying, that persons may have small-pox seven times.

Vaccination is most inert, in the hot dry months. This operation, cannot be said to be a success in India. The Hindu will rail at the folly of his neighbours, not submitting to it, and when pressed, will promise his family shall undergo the operation, at an early date. But it ends in the promise, for the performance is but rarely permitted.

Some are apathetic, but not actively hostile: others submit through fear, but immediately subsequently rub warm woodashes over the place, to prevent its being effectual. A notion at one time prevailed, that the indelible mark of vaccination, was placed on person's arms, in order that at some future date, when the individual was grown up, he might be distinguished, to send as a slave to the Mauritius, or some island beyond the sea: or else that he might be known, for the purposes of taxation.

Certain causes must always be at work, to counteract the spread of vaccination. High caste Hindus, wish for vaccinators of their own grade, and that the lymph should be only taken from a person of the same caste. Then again a high caste vaccinator, will not touch a low caste man, much less vaccinate him: consequently as the majority of the Natives are of low castes, the vaccinators are usually taken from the same class. Compulsory vaccination cannot be employed, because such would enable the low caste man, to threaten those of a higher caste than himself with pollution, and either bribery or force would naturally be the result.

The very small pay which the Vaccinators receive, and the many obstructions they experience in carrying out their duty, render them idle and discontented.

Some years since, a Magistrate on a tour of duty in Malabar, made some enquiries of an acting Native Vaccinator, respecting the amount of work he was doing; the answers not being quite satisfactory, he was asked how he procured his lymph. The man with a profound salaam at once replied, "I use, your excellency, the white "juice of a tree, which grows in the neighbouring jungles."

Consumption (*Chayun*, Mal.) Is by no means rare, and the best remedy is considered to be the blood of the Hanuman monkey, *semnopithecus entellus.* As much should be drank as the patient can swallow, and subsequently he must run a mile, to assist digestion. The flesh of this animal, is also prescribed for persons with this disease, whilst that of the flying fox, *Pteropus Edwarsii,* is recommended in all cases of cough, (*Choammi*, Mal.)

Cholera is designated the *Nurruppoo denum,* Mal. or jumping and catching disease, as the bad spirit is thought to spring out at times at the person attacked. This disease is also attributed to the influence of the land winds, and to eating unhealthy fish. It is popularly believed to have been sent to India, as a curse by the goddess Kali, because a British force, in 1817, looted a Pagoda dedicated to her.

It is much less common on the Western coast, than in many other parts of India, and this immunity appears to be due, to the sandy formation of the country. The locality where there is least alluvial deposit mixed with the sand is that most free from outbreaks of cholera, but should cases occur, they are of a very fatal type. This portion of India, was formerly regarded as the birth place of cholera. Eating the flesh of the foul-feeding swine, and drinking arrack, may possibly conduce to its origin.

During an epidemic of this disease, the Hindus hold fasts, sacred to Kali ; and the Native Christians, [Roman Catholics, and Syrians,] to St. Sebastian, to implore them to grant, or obtain, a cessation of the plague.

The *liver* is not frequently affected, and the popular belief that inflammation of that organ is due to excess in drinking spirituous liquors, appears to be a fallacy here at least ; drunkenness being exceedingly common, and attacks of liver equally rare. Still cases of abscess of that organ are occasionally perceived, and are commonly attributed to witchcraft, the evil spirit being supposed to have devoured the affected part. Bilious persons are recommended to eat the flesh of the black crow, *corvus culminatus*, and also that of the grey headed one, *corvus splendens*.

Although acute *madness* is not very frequent, idiotcy is by no means unusual.

Dropsies (*Neeroo*, Mal.) may be said to be the most prevalent cause of death, but then it must be remembered, that most fatal cases in Natives of India, if of long duration, terminate in dropsy. It is curious to observe, that this disease decreases gradually up the Western Coast; whilst on the Eastern, exactly the reverse obtains, the most Northern stations of the Madras side of the Presidency, being the most affected by it.

Accidents very frequently occur, and arise from various causes. Sometimes a crocodile seizes a person in the backwater, at others Fishermen are wounded by Sharks, Rays, or by Saw-fishes. Carpenters and coolies are often seriously injured when working amongst the shipping, or in the Merchants' yards either by heavy blocks of wood falling on them, or other causes.

In most places there are Natives who are able to reduce dislocations of almost any joint, and by rubbing and other means, they prevent the patient from suffering much pain. Severe wounds are also sometimes caused by the spines in the fins, of two species of fish, one a *Bagrus*, and the other a *Silurus*, which are found in the various tanks and swamps.

In the moonsoon time, toddy drawers frequently fall from cocoanut trees, and receive severe and often fatal injuries. The leaves are of course at this period very slippery from the rain, and few and insufficient precautions are taken to guard against the occurrence of accidents.

A few years since, the Natives of Malabar were stated to be much averse to undergoing surgical operations, that objection no longer exists, but on the contrary there is probably no part of India, in which Natives are more willing to submit to the knife, than in Cochin, where they understand, and fully appreciate the benefits of chloroform. Operations also succeed better amongst Natives in Cochin, than amongst Europeans in Europe.

Eye diseases are not so frequent, as in the hot sandy plains. Night blindness is a very common affection: colour blindness is treated by eating goat's liver.

Skin affections are very prevalent, one commonly known by a designation gained from its frequency in the northern portion of the British Isles, is here called "the Malabar:" the Moon is believed to exercise some influence in this complaint. Persons should be careful in using ointments, or oily substances to the skin, as they are liable to be attacked by small ants, who not satisfied with merely the appliances, also bite the subjacent cuticle.

Rheumatism is not nearly so common, in the moist damp climate of the Western Coast, as on the Eastern, which is much hotter and drier. The variations in the seasons, do not appear materially to affect the numbers suffering from this disease. The Native doctors usually give preparations of mercury internally, with mercurial baths, and marsh mallow fomentations externally. A house remedy is, either sleeping on the skin of a goat, tanned with the hair on: or the application of a fresh Jackall skin, to the affected part.

There are two species of discolouration of the skin, the tawny, and the black: the first is regarded as a pleasing variety in the complexion, or a species of beauty spot: but the second is dreaded, as it is supposed to foretel disaster.

The great disease of Cochin, is *Elephantiasis* (*Mundookarl,* Mal.) often denominated Cochin leg. As many as 5 per cent. of the entire Native, and Eurasian population, appear to be affected by it: and many more, suffer from it in a masked form. Males and females are about equally attacked, and children as young as four years of age, though it is unusual before 15 or 16. It is regarded as a family disgrace, and much dreaded.

The Natives assert, that should the roots of the screw pine, extend themselves into a tank of drinking water, it becomes poisoned, and all who use it are speedily affected with Elephantiasis: this idea is strongly impressed upon their minds, by the fact, that the root-stock is always thickened, and in appearance resembles a Cochin leg.

Another theory is common on the Eastern coast, viz., that St. Thomas the Apostle, whilst at prayer near Madras, was accidently killed by a low caste man, who was shooting at a peacock: as a retribution, his leg swelled up, until it became nearly as thick as his body, and his descendants have all been afflicted with Elephantiasis.

This disease though it may attack any part of the body, is most commonly seen in the lower extremities, which become by degrees, rounded, shapeless masses, hard and unyielding to pressure. The limb may remain in this state for years, and the health may or may not suffer, according to circumstances, and though it may be as large round as the person's waist, it still continues useful for progression, unless there be excessive pain. Each increase in size, is ushered in by fever, and generally great pain.

Should the disease be of recent occurrence, the swelling may suddenly disappear from one part, and show itself in another; thus leaving the leg, in a few hours it may be found in the arm, and vice versâ.

The range in which Elephantiasis is endemic, may be geographically mapped out, it extends along the coast, but not farther than ten miles inland, decreasing rapidly in severity, as the distance from the sea becomes greater. Natives and Eurasians from other parts of India, where this disease does not exist, after a time become amenable to its influence.

Persons of all occupations, and castes, whether strictly vegetarians, partakers of mixed diet, or mostly consumers of fish, are indiscriminately attacked. The indigenous Black and the White Jew, the Indo-European, and the Native, appear equally liable to it, and although the poverty stricken classes are the most frequent sufferers, the richer do not escape. It may be partially hereditary, but often affects a person in whom no such taint could exist. Sometimes it may show itself after the receipt of an injury, or again without any such exciting cause. It appears due to some deleterious property in the drinking water, and therefore in the time of the Portuguese, Europeans commenced supplying themselves with that necessary commodity, from the Alwaye river, and this plan has always been continued, up to the present time.

Persons who are attacked with Elephantiasis, often quite lose the disease, by going on a sea voyage, or removing beyond the local influence of the complaint: but on their return to the infected locality, it usually reappears. Others again find great benefit, in abstaining from toddy, and bhang, for which they substitute opium.

The removal of an affected limb, rarely eradicates the disease, which usually returns at some subsequent date.

Goitre is sometimes seen in Cochin. This affection so alarmed Shah Jehan, and his suite in Bengal, that it not only prevented his settling in Padshah Mahal, which he had previously decided on doing, but its frightful appearance, scared himself and his court, into precipitate flight. What would he have said, to an elephant leg, or to limbs larger round than the waist?

Leprosy is closely allied to Elephantiasis, and very prevalent. A Lazaretto exists at Palliport, a few miles from Cochin, in which lepers are received. Over the door way of this building, is a stone, bearing the following inscription, *Lazarus huss*, A. D. 1728, which date being in the time of the Dutch rule, at first gives the impression that they were the founders of this benevolent institution. But on further inquiry, it appears probable, that they only restored it, and that the Portuguese originally established it as a Syrian College in 1587. It is a tiled stone building, situated on a strip of land, facing due east, towards the backwater, and having the sea about half a mile to its rear.

Inside the entrance to the Lazaretto, is a yard 29 feet wide, from around which the wards have been removed, to promote free circulation of air. Into this front yard, two others open at right angles, either being flanked at the Northern and Southern aspect, by a lofty range of eight rooms, each twelve feet four inches square, and occupied by two lepers. The Northern yard is inhabited by the women, and the Southern by the men. One ward in the women's yard, is employed as a Roman Catholic Chapel, in which the lepers themselves officiate; the walls present a curious appearance, being ornamented with pictures of railway carriages, and similar productions.

This institution, appears in the time of the Dutch, to have been under the direction, of four Church Deacons, and collections were made in the Church every Sunday, for the maintenance of the lepers. At the commencement of each year, the Commandant and Senior Surgeon, visited every house in the town, to ascertain whether any of the slaves were afflicted with this loathsome malady, and if so, had them immediately transferred to the Lazaretto. It is probable that each person who placed any one belonging to him in this Hospital, was obliged to pay for his maintenance, as the Dutch Government did not subscribe to its support.

At the present time, the lepers receive from the British Government, one and a half annas a day, (two pence farthing,) with which they find themselves food, and fuel. Clothes and bedding, are also supplied to them.

No Europeans in Cochin, appear of late years to have suffered from leprosy, but, East Indians occasionally fall victims to it, although it more particularly affects the Native community.

The leper as long as he can procure money, is not expelled from the society of his fellow creatures, who live in the same house, partake of the same food, and even intermarry with him. But as soon as money fails, he is driven forth to subsist on charity, until death mercifully relieves his sufferings.

In the Levitical law, the leper was directed to bathe in the running stream; which the Hindus consider much more efficacious, than a tank, or standing water. In olden times, in Bengal at least, the leper used to be immolated on the Suttee, buried alive, or drowned in the Ganges.

The colour of the skin in leprosy, is generally speaking darker than that in a healthy native. It is only when ulceration has destroyed it, that the scars are of a white colour. The nature of this disease, renders the unfortunate sufferers, extremely obstinate and morose, they drink spirits, eat opium, smoke gangah, in fact do anything, to wean themselves even for a short time, from a recollection of the past, a view of the present, or a thought of the miserable earthly future before them, as they all believe the disease incurable.

Leprosy is frequently hereditary, sometimes missing one generation, and attacking the succeeding: it may commence at any age, from the infant in arms, to old persons on the brink of the grave. A fish diet seems to have some influence in its production.

It is remarkable, that in Norway, leprosy augmented as the fisheries increased in extent; that in Sweden, and the Faroe Isles, it disappeared when the fish left, and the fisheries were discontinued: and that precisely at the time of the arrival of the fish on the Bergen coast, leprosy commenced amongst the people.

One form of this disease, attacks locally the smaller joints, as the fingers and toes, which ulcerate, and gradually drop off, until the poor leper, crawls about on the stumps of his hands and feet. Occasionally he also loses his eyesight, and is almost covered with ulcers: in these cases, when death terminates the sufferings of these miserable beings, it must be regarded more as a cause for congratulation, than either pity or regret.

The other form is even more repulsive, as the face and body are covered with tubercles. The Shastras which so strictly enforce the necessity of burning the dead, make an exception as far as lepers are concerned, and direct their corpses to be thrown into a forest, or river, "like a log of wood," without any funeral rites, or ceremonies.

A curious disease, not unknown in other parts of India, is found in Cochin, namely, burning in the hands, and feet. There are two forms of this affection, the moist variety, when the extremities are in a constant state of perspiration; and the dry when they crack, and are never humid. Should fever be of constant occurrence, death frequently ensues; this is a most dangerous, and insidious affection.

Ulcers are very prevalent, though perhaps not so common as in some inland stations. The scars which remain, are usually white, and deficient in sensation, apparently from a leprous taint. It is commonly believed by the natives, that should a wall lizard, *gecko*, be divided down the centre, and bound to a person's body, in twelve hours it will have produced an ulcer, with every appearance of having existed for a month. The earth-worm, *Iulus*, certainly causes great irritation, if trodden on, and occasionally obstinate ulcers are produced thereby. The favourite native application to these complaints are spider's webs, whilst dirt and other irritating substances, are kept from the sore, by tying over it leaves of the Portia tree. Should there be much discharge without pain, they often wash the part twice a day, with an infusion made by soaking the leaves of the Tamarind, in hot water. It is believed that a harmless snake, (*Chera*, Mal.) is attracted by the smell of foul ulcers.

In *Hooping Cough*, which is frequently epidemic, the flesh of the crocodile is given, or pieces of its bones are tied round the patient's neck, and considered a very efficacious charm, in driving it away.

Scrophula is not uncommon, amongst the more drunken and diseased classes, but some very respectable Eurasians, also suffer from it.

Hysterical fits frequently affect Eurasians of both sexes. Natives labour under the idea, that persons in this state, are possessed by an evil spirit, which requires immediate exorcism : if this has no effect, a cudgel is brought into action, and the malignant spirit is exorcised by club law.

Curvatures of the spine, are often perceived. In one instance, the patient, a woman, asserted her belief, that it was caused in herself, by demoniacal influence. She was then thirty years of age, and stated that when about eleven years old, she was walking alone in a narrow lane after dark, when the Demon came behind her, and struck her a violent blow on the back, thus occasioning the curve, which had continued from that time: and that even then, unless she propitiated it by occasional offerings, she experienced similar attacks.

Guinea worm is very rarely seen in Cochin, and then only in persons who during some period in the previous twelve months have been in Madras, Coimbatore, or other places, where it is endemic. The laterite soil of Cochin, appears to be exempt from this entozoan, as it is never found in any one who has resided there for more than a year. It has been frequently asserted, and still maintained by many, that guinea worms, and the fiery serpents, which were so destructive to the Israelites, in the vicinity of the Red Sea, are identical.

Intestinal entozoa, are exceedingly common, and one species is very easily cured, by santonine. It has lately been recommended, to employ a fungus, as a vermicide, but it is scarcely a remedy adapted to Hindus, as Yama now the Judge of the departed, has declared, that " those who eat mushrooms, whether springing from the ground, "or growing on a tree, equal in guilt the slayers of Brahmans, and "the most despicable of all deadly sinners."*

Cancer of the mouth, and lips, is very common, and incorrectly attributed to chewing chunam, and smoking tobacco. It is a curious coincidence between Native and European ideas, that this is often thought to be caused in Europe, by smoking clay pipes.

Tetanus or lock jaw, may occur at any season of the year, either from the effects of severe injuries, or simply from slight ones, and is generally fatal. But there is a severe chronic type of this distressing malady, which occurs during the months of October, November, and December, and is usually curable.

Hydrophobia sometimes occurs. Whenever there is a suspicion of a mad dog being at large, a reward is offered for the dead bodies of any stray animals of the canine tribe: large numbers are then killed, and all who wish to preserve their favourites, must tie them up, until the order for this general massacre, is cancelled.

When a child is born, an Astrologer is usually seated in the next room, in readiness to draw out its horoscope: this is a very difficult process; if it is desired very exact, the situation of the stars at the moment of the infant's birth, must be ascertained. Natives have the most implicit belief in the fulfilment of all predictions in their horoscopes, and the confident anticipation of death at a certain date, frequently produces such injurious effects on their health, as indirectly to cause it.

Should a child be born in any unnatural form, it is supposed to be the incarnation of an evil spirit, or else of some deceased enemy, and it is immediately destroyed.

Should a woman suffer from convulsions after the birth of a child, a fowl is divided in half down the centre, and a portion bound on each side of the patient's head.

When native married women, do not become in the state which it is generally expected they should be, some very extraordinary remedies are employed, for the purpose of effecting a change. A mole cricket, [gryllotalpus,] is caught, and she must then swallow it whole, and if possible alive; this is difficult, as its appearance is most repulsive, and if it does not go down the throat at once, it

* Sir W. Jones, vol. 5, page 160.

causes great pain. At all events, she must neither bite it, nor kill it, some other person having performed this kind office, she bolts it whole, head foremost, and the effect is said to be marvellous!

Poisoning appears to be most commonly affected by Datura, but it is more frequently the result of accident, than of design. It is a very common practice, to rub the inside of chatties with datura juice, for the purpose of causing effervescence in the arrack, with which they are subsequently filled: this increases the intoxicating effects of the spirit, and also unfortunately, is too often the cause of accidental poisonings.

Personal deformities are very frequently perceived, especially in families in whom there is a leprous taint.

Natives are usually very impatient to recover from attacks of sickness, and expect the European Medical Officer, to cure an illness of months, or even years duration, in the course of a few days: if not well in a week, or even less, they frequently get extremely indignant, and maintain that inferior drugs are being administered to them.

Few and simple are the Native preservatives against disease. The Portia tree is planted round their houses, to prevent malaria from penetrating to their dwellings. Hindus very rarely sleep for any length of time, with their heads to the North, or West; the East is their favourite direction, but they do not object to the South. This custom is stated to have originated, in one of the eighteen Puranas.

Witchcraft is occasionally combined with medicine, by Native Practitioners. One man of the Teer caste, now living in the Cochin State, is believed to have a hundred spirits under his control, whom he lets out by the year, for one rupee, one anna, [two shillings, and one penny half penny.] The Wizard must be first informed for what purpose the spirit is required, and after he has made the necessary arrangements for parting with him, prayers are then said to the spirit, and a feast, in his honour must be held when arrack, toddy, eggs, salt fish curry, fruits, cocoanuts, rice pounded and raw, flowers, oil, ghee, betel, burnt chunam, sharks and other flesh, fowls, incense, &c., must be offered up to it, each article being separately placed on a plantain leaf, and individually worshipped. Then another prayer ensues, and the figure of the person to be bewitched, is made out of mud, the name being written upon it, with both the words and letters placed backwards, a number of curious ceremonies succeed, before the spirit is permitted to take its departure, with its new master.

There are eight species of enchantment, said to cause death, to drive persons from houses, to produce love, and so on.

Europeans if in good health, can go out at any time during the day, if their heads, temples, and the backs of their necks, are well protected from the sun: but if fatigued, or feeling unwell, they should not expose themselves to its rays. Sleeping in the land wind, or cold sea breeze, is very dangerous, and even the soft mild sea breeze may injuriously affect a feverish subject. The effects of the climate are very depressing, and tea-totalism is injudicious.

If compelled to travel through the jungles in the malarious months, Europeans should only drink water which has been boiled,* and it is preferable to add a little spirit to it. He should bathe in warm water, and take one or two drops of Fowler's solution of arsenic, and two grains of quinine, in a cup of coffee, every morning. Sleeping under musquitoe curtains at night time, assists in keeping out the malaria.

The Hindu Deity of one of the hill coffee plantations, is said to be Iuppen. There is an altar raised there to him, consisting of a quantity of stones, and an iron trident. The Hindus state, that if this Deity be not propitiated by offerings, they will be inevitably destroyed by him, if they remain in the place more than two days. In one instance, a Native timber cutter from Chittoor, refused him the customary offering, and the very next day, whilst engaged in felling a tree, by some mischance it went in the wrong direction, and literally smashed the poor man to death. This so frightened the coolies, that now none venture to remain there a day after his arrival from the plains, without presenting a cocoanut, from which they have drank the milk, in front of Iuppen's shrine.

Another sect when ill, not many years since, almost invariably went to their Priests, who wrote down their diseases on a piece of paper, with a supplication for their speedy removal. This paper was then burnt and the ashes mixed in water, and drank by the patient. The efficacy of this treatment, was believed to be marvellous.

* Natives frequently poison wells, by throwing in leaves of the milk hedge.

CHAPTER XII.

MAMMALS.

Monkeys—Bats—Tigers—Legends respecting them—Cheetahs; curious method of destruction of one of them—Jackalls—Wild Dogs, their mode of hunting—The Mongoose—Encounter between two Bears—Orange species of Porcupine—The Gour or Bison—The Malabar Ibex—Massacre of Europeans in consequence of their killing a Cow—Elephants.

No portion of the Continent of India, is more replete with animal life, or has a more diversified vegetation, than the Western Coast, especially in the Southern part of it. The more dense and lofty jungles, which cover the ghauts, are dangerous, owing to the numerous tigers, cheetahs, elephants, and bears, by which they are infested: whilst in the open country, the dismal howl of the Jackall, may be everywhere heard.

Amongst the *Mammalia*, and the Monkey tribe, several species are found, residing on the well wooded ghauts, but few, if any, are located near the sea shore. They are divided into communities, each having its own domain, which is rarely invaded by those of other species: or should such occur, a battle for territorial sovereignty ensues. The predominant tribe of Monkeys, are of the long tailed, *Semnopithecidæ* family.

These animals are exceedingly mischievous, and are believed by the Natives, [in common with the ignorant of some other countries,] to be capable of speech, but not exercising that power, in dread of being compelled to work. It is said that in Ceylon, natives frequently revenge themselves on their enemies, by sprinkling rice over the roofs of their houses, thereby attracting the Monkeys, who in their efforts to obtain the grains, pull off the tiles.

One of the commonest species, which is by no means averse to take up its quarters near the public road, is the *Hunaman* or Long

Jaw Monkey, *Semnopithecus entellus*, Duff. This is considered by the natives, as the representative of Rama's Monkey allies. They are very common at the base of the ghauts, where large vegetation exists.

The Hunaman Monkey is of considerable size, but slender make, its colour is ashy grey, lightest underneath, the hands and feet of a deep brown colour, and the tail of great length. When young it is very gentle, but with advancing age, it becomes sullen, and vindictive : whilst its mischievous propensities increase. Communities of these Monkeys, are generally about a score in number; in the early morning, some of them may often be seen on the tops of the highest trees, either sunning themselves, jumping or swinging from bough to bough: whilst others act as sentinels, and warn their companions of the approach of strangers.

On the arrival of an intruder, the Monkeys either remain perfectly still, or else rapidly make off gesticulating, and uttering cries of warning, to their more distant friends. The mother may be seen fleeing with one, or more rarely two, little ones clinging round her neck : and sometimes, the old male, will even turn at bay, and attack the intruder. When Monkeys perceive a tiger, they generally follow him for some little distance, jumping from tree to tree, and making a peculiar warning noise.

In cocoanut plantations, amongst plantain trees, and in cultivated rice grounds, they commit great devastations. Their food in the jungles, consists of roots and fruits, especially those of the various species of wild fig trees, more particularly the *Ficus excelsa*, and the *F. religiosa*.

This species of Monkey, is believed by devout Hindus, never to die a natural death,* whilst should a house be inadvertently constructed, over the bones of one of them, the domicile is doomed to certain destruction, and its inmates to misfortunes.

In some parts of India, and occasionally also in the Cochin State, children delight in playing tricks with Monkeys, a common one being, to obtain an innocuous snake, and rolling it up with some rice in a

* It is a common Hindu saying, that he who has seen a straight cocoanut tree, a dead Monkey, the nest of a paddy bird, or the depth of a woman's deceitful heart, &c. will live for ever.

plantain leaf, to tie it up securely into a small parcel, and then throw it to an old Monkey, who deliberately unties the string, and opens it, when to his horror out comes a snake. He immediately seizes it by the neck, and rushing off to the nearest stone, grinds its head to pieces, maliciously grinning, and grimacing all the time at his victim. When satisfied that it can no longer do any injury, he either throws the body away, or gives it to his young to play with.

A favourite cage monkey, is the Malabar Wanderoo, *Silenus venter*, Linn. (*Chingala*, Mal.) which is smaller than the last named species, and of a black colour with white whiskers. It is rather a wary creature, and consequently not so frequently seen, as the Hunaman: it is also found in a higher range, and in steep, and almost inaccessible fastnesses. Its tail is short, and terminates in a tuft, which has gained it the designation of the Lion-tailed, or pig-tailed Monkey. Natives consider it very lucky, to look one of these creatures in the face the first thing in the morning, and they are often kept tame for this reason. A peep at the physiognomy of the large black Monkey (*Kurring korungoo*, Mal.) does not appear to be so efficacious. In Trichoor the common brown Monkey, *Macacus radiatus*, Geoff. (*Kurungoo*, Mal.) is the only one found, it is also extensively spread along the base of the ghauts. It appears to be the favourite species for taming amongst both Europeans and the Native Sailors who frequent the coast. But when fully grown, it becomes very vindictive, and is by no means a desirable pet for children.

Should several young Monkeys of this species be domesticated together, the elder appear to take great care of the younger ones. In 1859, three young Monkeys were taken on board a ship in the Cochin river, and when the evening approached, the two eldest ascended into the main top, to pass the night. The smallest being unable to climb up, or perhaps too frightened to make the attempt, remained below crying in great distress. The largest of the two elder monkeys then descended, and carried the little fellow in his arms, up to their sleeping place.

The next evening, the same scene was in part renewed, but this time both the larger Monkeys descended, on hearing the little one cry, and one taking it by the hand, dragged it up the rigging, whilst the other beat it from behind. Subsequently there was no more trouble.

Monkeys though worshipped in the form of Hunaman, who is believed to be still wandering in the ghauts, are sometimes eaten by the lower classes, if other persons kill them. Beaters will even not unfrequently propose, that Sportsmen returning from shooting, should kill them some monkeys, but such a cruel proposition is rarely acceded to. If a young one is killed, the grief of the parents is most distressing to witness, sometimes they even follow the Sportsman, holding up their dead infant as if imploring that its life might be returned. If a mother has been shot, the young frequently remain by her side, apparently ignorant of the loss they have sustained.

When a Monkey is wounded, its comrades advance, and each peer into the wound, inserting their fingers, and trying to drag it open, apparently out of mere curiosity. An injured Monkey is a most painful sight, and most persons, who have not some object in effecting the destruction of these mischievous animals, carefully avoid hurting them.

Many Natives, who would be glad to rid their neighbourhood of a troublesome Monkey, and should an opportunity occur of asking an European to shoot him, would not hesitate to do so, nevertheless raise a great clamour, if the creature is killed without their consent. Distinct Monkey communities, are very tenacious in keeping within certain localities, and not permitting the intrusion of strangers: thus in Bangalore, the Pettah, and the Fort, are merely separated by a road, but in each there is a distinct family of monkeys, although the species is identical: a few plantains thrown down between the rival states, occasion a most determined battle, and great commotion.

Some years since, a complaint was made to a Collector, of the depredations committed by the Monkeys, in a certain locality: after a long consultation as to the feasability of such a proceeding, it was settled that they must be deported, by being carried across a broad river, and thus forced to locate themselves on the other side: but as may be imagined, this was rather a difficult undertaking. At length it was effected, in the following manner: numerous chatties of boiled rice were placed in their haunts, the mouth of each chatty being made so small, that although a Monkey's open hand might be inserted, it could not when closed be withdrawn. These creatures never let go any food which they have once obtained hold of, so, when they had clutched the rice, as they were unable to withdraw their closed hands, they were caught by the chatties, and some hundreds of them were thus taken and transported.

The Loris, or slow paced Lemur, *Stenops Pardigradus*, Linn., is found in the dense jungles of the ghauts, but is rare even there.

Bats are seen in large numbers, from those which measure several feet in expanse, to those of only a few inches. Of an evening they flit about in all directions, and during the day reside in old buildings, unused rooms, under the eaves of houses, in old caves, passages, and hollow trees. They are frequently attracted into rooms by lights.

The Flying Fox, *Pteropus Edwarsii*, Geoff., (*Barvaloo,* Mal.) is a large species of Roussette, or bat with a dog like head. These creatures measure four feet, or even more, in the expanse of their wings, and may be seen in large flocks of an evening, wending their way towards their feeding ground. In their diet they are exclusively frugivorous, and they do very great injury to Cocoanut plantations, and Mangoe gardens. Their habits are very intemperate, and they often pass the night, drinking the toddy from the chatties in the cocoanut trees, which results, either in their returning home in the early morning, in a state of extreme and riotous intoxication, or in being found the next day, at the foot of the trees, sleeping off the effects of their midnight debauch. The wild almond, *terminalia catappa,* when in fruit, is one of their favourite resorts at night time, they sometimes carry off the almonds into the verandahs of houses, where they extract the kernels, and in so doing frighten nervous people into the belief, that robbers are endeavouring to effect an entrance. They are also very partial to wild figs.

It is anything but pleasant, to reside near a plantation or field, which at night time is guarded from the depredations of these animals, as persons are kept shouting continuously, and throwing stones, or cross sticks, by means of strings, to immense distances, which make a disagreeable rushing noise. As this uproar is commenced at sunset, and kept up uninterruptedly until day-break, any unfortunate European in the vicinity, finds his night's rest sadly disturbed. Clappers in trees, or lights suspended from a bough, will sometimes keep these bats away.

It is curious to see innumerable flying foxes asleep, hanging in long rows, by their hind claws, to the leafless boughs of trees.

One little species of bat, (*Nurrachilloo,* Mal.) is inferior in point of size, to many butterflies, and moths.

Both the large Flying Fox, and the smaller species of the bat family, are eaten by the lower classes of natives, as well as by the so called Portuguese, and they are also employed medicinally.

The Tiger, *Felis tigris,* Linn., (*Coudouah,* Mal.) generally called the Royal Tiger, in contradistinction to the Cheetah, which is usually denominated the Tiger: is by no means a rare animal, but those which indulge in human food, are scarce. At times when irritated they attack persons, and occasion much loss amongst domesticated cattle. A reward of from ten to twelve Rupees, is paid for the skin of each tiger.* They are generally shot at night time by Sportsmen, who conceal themselves in trees, and watch for them, either at some tank, or near a dead animal.

Natives assert that a new lobe grows on to the liver of a Tiger every year it lives, and therefore by an examination of that organ, the animal's age can be accurately ascertained.

Man eating tigers, are said to be very often without hair, or in other words mangy, after they have killed their first victim, they are believed to be quite safe from all attacks, as the spirit of the murdered person rides upon their forehead, and guides them from every danger. If a tiger swallows any clothing it frequently causes his destruction : and this is perhaps the reason, why he prefers the Native in his undress, to the well clothed European.

Evil spirits are supposed to have the power at times, of changing

* The Dewan of Cochin, has kindly furnished the following return, of animals, for the destruction of which rewards have been disbursed by the Cochin Sircar during the last five years, viz., 10 Tigers, 67 Cheetahs, and 6 Crocodiles, at a total cost of Rupees 408½. The skins of the first two mentioned animals, are forwarded to the Cutcherry at Ernacollum, but owing to the difficulty in obtaining the rewards, and the deductions for expenses, very many no doubt are shot without their skins being brought forward, and are therefore not included in the accounts,

men into tigers, such being subsequently distinguished, by having no tails.

The claws, and even the teeth of the tiger, are used as charms against witchcraft, and the evil eye. They may frequently be seen set in silver, and worn round the necks of children. Tigers' whiskers, have also the same efficacy, against demoniacal influence. The flesh is eaten as medicine, and a favourite remedy for deafness, is the skin of this animal burnt with gingelly oil, and dropped into the ear.

The Cheetah or Panther, *Felis pardus*, Linn. (*Pouli*, Mal.) sometimes called a Leopard, is both a very common, and a very dangerous animal. At night time it prowls around houses, carrying off goats, dogs, and even smaller game. If very hungry however, he is not contented with this uncertain means of obtaining food, but penetrates into villages, and carries off animals, and even children. There is a black variety, *Felis melas*, Peron. (*Kurring pouli*, Mal.) which is not nearly so numerous, one of them may sometimes be found in a den of three or four young cubs. There is also another dark coloured one, intermediate between the other two, but they are all of the same species. The black one is said to be both the most timid, and the most dangerous.

In the Cochin Jungles in 1859, during the working season, a Cheetah took up his abode, inside a small hut, used as a store house for the workmen's rice. The Natives were in a great state of alarm, and numerous expedients to make him decamp were ineffectually tried, until at last it was suggested, to obtain the assistance of some Elephants, and after they had thrown down the hut, to endeavour to kill the animal with the only weapons they could muster, viz. spears, hatchets, and carpenter's tools.

Several Elephants were therefore collected from the various working parties, and one rather young animal charged the hut, and knocked it down; when out sprang the Cheetah. But an old Elephant rushed at him, and before he had time to rally from the shock, impaled him on his tusk, causing instantaneous death.

The best Cheetah skins, are nicely tanned, and employed by the Brahmans as mats, on which they pray. The inferior ones are used as bags for the Post Office runners, the belts of Peons, &c.

The Native Cheetah trap, is a large cage, divided into two rooms: in one of these a live dog, or goat is placed, which at night time attracts the Cheetah, who enters by the open door of the empty division, which is so contrived, that it immediately falls, and encloses him. Shooting them by ambuscade at night time, is the most common mode of destroying them.

The Toddy cat, *Viverra Indica*, Geoff. (*Murruputti*, Mal.) is very common in this part of India, and commits great depredations amongst the fruit trees, pulling down the cocoa, and destroying cocoanuts. Thorny briars, are consequently placed around the trunk of all fruit trees, to prevent the ascent of these animals.

They inhabit houses, pursue the rats and mice, destroy the poultry and their eggs, and make such a disturbance at night time, that they are far from being welcome guests. They are so cunning, that the Natives assert, that they disappear, immediately an order is given to re-roof a house, where they may have taken up their abode. They have however the credit of killing snakes.

One day whilst passing up the backwater, a tame cat,* was seen out on a travelling excursion. The monsoon had set in, and the paddy fields were small ponds: on reaching one of these, pussy paddled along, until she arrived at a deep drain, when without any hesitation she plunged in, swam across and pursued her original course.

The Hyena, *Hyœna Striata*, Zimm. is not rare, and descends into the plains: whilst the Jackall, *Canis aureus*, Linn. (*Curuken* also *Nurree*, Mal.) by his unearthly howlings, disturbs the quiet of the night: the noise of these animals has been likened to many things. An old saying is that one Jackall calls out, " Here's the body of a dead

* The Egyptians held cats in such great estimation, that when one died in the house, the owner of it shaved his eyebrows, and mourned as if for a child. The body was embalmed, and taken to a particular city for interment, where it may be said, there was many a cat-a-wall-in. Killing a cat was considered a heinous offence, and was punished by a fine, the amount of which depended on the Priest's verdict. Even in Wales we are told, that in olden times, a Prince included a law for the preservation of cats, amongst the code by which he regulated his kingdom. A kitten before she could see, was estimated at the value of a calf, after her first capture her price was doubled, and a regular mouser was valued at four calves. However in those primitive times, a calf might be purchased for a penny.

Hindu," when the eager cry arises from all quarters, "where ? where ? where ?" followed by the response, "Here ! here ! here !"*

The Wild dog, *Cuon primævus*, Hodg. (*Chennai*, Mal.) is sometimes seen in the higher regions, hunting in small packs. When there are a number of them, they are asserted occasionally to kill wild boars, or even tigers. *Dr. Francis Buchanan*, mentions that these animals, are said to surprise a tiger by springing out suddenly and fastening on his neck, and so killing him. Having twice had an opportunity of seeing packs of wild dogs hunting, once in the early morning, and once in the evening, a remark on the subject may be deemed interesting. On each occasion, they were five in number, their size just between a jackall and a wolf, the tail of a rusty colour above, and greyish yellow below. In hunting one appeared to take the lead, casting about for the trail, whilst the others were all together. The noise made by them, has been well described as a barking whistle. The pack sometimes advances on its game, from different quarters, but this is not always the case.

Wild dogs when hunting do not appear to be such very timid creatures as they are frequently represented. They are said to kill Sambur, and other species of Deer, Tigers, wild Hogs, Hyenas, Jackalls, Bears, Porcupines, and Quails.

The Fox, *Vulpes Indicus*, (Hodgs.) is very common in some places, occasionally they have horns on their foreheads. It is said, that the fortunate possessor of one of these, will be able to cheat and swindle with impunity, they are consequently in great request, and spurious ones are not unfrequently disposed of.

Amongst the genus *Herpestes*, the Mongoose, *H. Griseus*, Geoff. (*Keerree*, Mal.) is found in almost every clump of thick bushes, and is very useful, in clearing the ground of snakes and rats : but unfortunately it sometimes also attacks poultry, and in one night may destroy a large amount, as it merely sucks the blood of its victims. In the higher ranges, the larger and much more beautiful chestnut coloured Mongoose, *H. Elliottii*, is still more destructive.

* A Missionary in Tinnevelly informs us, that Jackalls catch crabs, by putting their own tails into the crabs' holes, and when they feel a bite, drawing that appendage quickly up. The Cochin Jackalls, do not appear to have such a sporting turn of mind, as their Tinnevelly relatives, at least, they are not reputed, to go fishing with their tails, in crabs' retreats !

The gall bladder of the Mongoose, combined with that of the peacock is one of the numerous Native antidotes used for snake bites.

The Water Dog, *Lutra Nair*, Cuv. (*Neernai*, Mal.) is found in the Backwater, but is not very numerous. In some localities the skins are collected, and they are said to be employed in the manufacture of hats.

The large Bear, Ursiform Sloth, *Melursus lybicus*, Meyer, (*Punni curroudee*, Mal.) is very common, and if interfered with, extremely dangerous, it is much dreaded by the Natives. When in confinement, it will eat animal substances, but such do not appear to be its natural food. In the Jungles, it has been observed to be very fond of honey, white ants, common ants, beetles, and the sweet fruit of trees, especially the pods of the *Cassia Fistula.*

Some friends when out shooting, procured the skins of two fine bears, in the following manner. Perceiving a Cheetah, and a bear, coming down the slope, of a hill at the same time, both were simultaneously fired at. The Cheetah escaped, but the bear being desperately wounded, turned back into the neighbouring jungles, from whence loud growls were heard. The party having re-loaded, advanced, when two bears were seen fighting furiously, and both were thus killed. It appeared probable, that the wounded bear, not seeing from whence his injury emanated, and knowing that his companion was behind, imagined that he had attacked him, and had therefore returned to avenge himself.

These bears are frequently trained by Jugglers, to dance and play various tricks.

The Porpoise, *Platanista Gangetica*, Gray, (*Cuddapunni*, Mal.) is exceedingly common, about the mouth of the Cochin river, as well as in the backwater. The Dugong, *Halicore Dugung*, Cuv. is very frequently seen along the coast, and the skulls of both species, are often found, especially near the Narrikal mud bank.

A small species of rat, *Mus providens*, Elliott, which is of a brownish colour, lives in burrows, in which it stores up grain. The tank diggers, Corravers, eat this animal, and plunder its supply of grain. They also eat another species of rat, *Mus Languiosus*, Elliott, which at times commits great havoc, amongst the corn fields. There are several other species of rats, and mice, which infest the fields, the ghauts, and the houses; in the last the squeak of the Musk rat, (*Cundeli*, Mal.) is heard with great aversion. It is a curious fact that this little animal by simply running over beer or wine bottles which are corked and sealed, imparts such a disagreeable flavour to the liquor as to render it unfit for consumption. Even dogs and cats, have apparently a great dislike to touching one of these rats.

The Brown Rat, *Mus Decumanus*, Pallas, is the most common species in Cochin, but the large Bandicoot, *Mus Bandicota*, is by no means rare, undermining the walls of houses, and committing extensive depredations. In the Monsoon time, when the burrows are filled with water, they take up their abode in houses, and are a great nuisance. One night a number of them got on board a ship which was lying attached to a wharf in Cochin, and before morning, they had entirely destroyed a complete set of new sails.

Cats will very rarely attack this large species of Indian rat, excepting when they are quite young.

The little striped squirrel, *Sciurus Palmarum*, Linn. (*Unnun*, Mal.) is never found in the town of Cochin, and is not very common in the surrounding country. It is a very pretty little creature, and a great favourite as a pet, but unfortunately it is exceedingly destructive, and bites very severely.

The Jungle Squirrel, *Sciurus Maximus*, Schrel. (*Malaunnun*, Mal.) is a very handsome animal, and a favourite pet. Although generally very sociable, its sharp pointed teeth, render it a formidable antagonist, when irate, and it is therefore not well adapted, as a playmate for children. It is apt to be rather spiteful if aroused from its sleep, as once having curled its beautiful tail around its body, it does not like to be disturbed from its slumbers. The centre of its back is a chestnut colour, and the remainder of a deep black. The skin is useful for some purposes, thus sportsmen who use a flint and steel gun, prefer it to any other, for a covering over the pan. Several other species, including the *S. Elphinstonii*, Sykes, and the *S. Macrourus*, Forst, are also found.

Two species of Flying Squirrel, *Pteromys*, are also seen, but the grey variety is the most common.

The Hare, *Lepus Nigricollis*, Fr. Cuv. (*Moillou*, Mal.) is very numerous in some places. In cases of Scrofula, natives often drink the blood of this animal, and regard it as a very efficacious remedy. The Rabbit does not thrive in confinement, and here as in other parts of India, it is unknown in a wild state. The little Guinea Pig, is kept domesticated.

Two species of Porcupines, (*Moullun Punni*, Mal.) are found, viz., the common black and white, *Hystrix Leucurus*, Sykes, and a smaller but much handsomer species, at present apparently undescribed which is Orange and Black, both are equally destructive in gardens.

Having kept both species, at different times for some months in the house, a short sketch of their respective characters, may not be uninteresting.

In 1855, having obtained a common Porcupine, *Hystrix Leucurus*, at Mercara in Coorg, it was kept domesticated for eleven months, when it met with an accidental death. At first it was very shy, but as it grew older, it became tame, excepting to strangers, and appeared regularly at the breakfast and dinner table with the dogs. At first all lived amicably together: but as the Porcupine's strength increased, it became more exacting, so if not fed quickly, would jump up and put its paws on the chair, scratching until attended to. As this was not permitted, he soon learnt to sit up like the dogs, and beg quietly until his turn came. Sometimes when hungry, on seeing one of the dogs served first, it became very indignant, and with all its quills erect, rushed at its canine companions and drove them all out of the room. It had an intense aversion to water, and if some were thrown over him would immediately run away. It usually allowed itself to be led out by a chain with the dogs, but sometimes strayed away in the compound, when the dogs were turned out in pursuit, and always found it again. It was a destructive, and rather unsavoury pet, and very fond of gnawing tables, chairs, &c. Its diet was omnivorous.

The Orange Porcupine, *Hystrix Malabaricus*, is found in the Western Ghauts, in certain localities mostly near Trichoor, and generally in subterraneous abodes, in the laterite rocks. In size it is smaller than the *H. Leucurus*, and the epicurean Native prizes its flesh more highly. To obtain a specimen alive, it must be smoked out of its den, where its presence may be detected, by its offensive aroma, which is considerably worse than that of the common variety. A pit-fall is dug in front of one hole, while brushwood is heaped up and set fire to at the mouths of all other entrances; but they endure smoking and starvation for an extraordinary length of time, before they will venture out, the usual period being about three days; on one occasion, a very fine one, driven to desperation, rushed from his hole, and falling into the pit-fall, was impaled on the quills of two others, who had been previously precipitated down.

At no period of their lives, is the orange colour absent from all their quills, but certainly it becomes much less, when they are in ill health, or in confinement. In some specimens, the quills in those places where they are white, in the common variety are of a deep reddish orange. After death, the colour fades considerably.

Having obtained a pair which were half-grown, they were placed in a wooden cage, which at night time was taken inside a room for security, but in a few hours, they had gnawed their way out, and regained their liberty. The house was then aroused to endeavour to catch them again, as it was feared they would make their escape from the room, by gnawing through the venetians. This was a difficult undertaking, and one in which the natives declined assisting as they believe the wound made by a porcupine's quill, to be very venomous, and often fatal. Having seized the female by the top-knot, she struggled so desperately, that she actually escaped, leaving her scalp and attached crest behind. They were however at length captured, and a barred wooden cage subsequently constructed, in which the wood was covered with tin, but notwithstanding these precautions one night the male managed to escape, and could not be recaptured. The gnawing propensities of the remaining animal occasioned constant trouble, until the plan of cutting its teeth, once a month, was adopted, which was effectual for the time.

Although it allowed cats, and dogs, to steel its rice, it became extremely indignant one day, when a little tame Mongoose looked into its cage, both parties prepared for war, and had not assistance been at hand, the poor Mongoose would soon have come to an untimely end.

The Manis, or Scaly ant-eater, *M. Pentadactyla*, Linn., is found in the Ghauts, where it performs essential service, in destroying the

White Ants' nests. It is very difficult to keep it in a box as it inserts its long nose under the lid, and forces its way out in spite of enormous pressure.

The Gour, *Bos Cavifrons*, Hodg. (*Kartoo Poathoo*, Mal.) is very abundant in the jungles, along the whole range of the ghauts, where it is generally known as the Bison. The male stands as much as 6 feet 1 inch at the shoulder. Its hump is very small, and the body of a dark colour, with white legs, and its eyes are of a curious light blue. It is a timid animal, and when alarmed rushes madly away through the bushes, never turning to bay, unless either desperately wounded, or having no other means of escape. The Natives are greatly alarmed when it thus turns, as they assert, that it will root up a stone from the ground, and discharge it with a snort, with fatal effect at its adversary. In Ramghur, the Natives never attack it, as they believe it to be so vindictive, that should it pursue them, and they take refuge in a tree, it will watch around the base, until they fall down from the effects of starvation, or exhaustion, when it immediately destroys them. It is very fond of young bamboo shoots. It has been suggested that this animal might advantageously be introduced into Europe, but it appears to have been overlooked, that although it is large, it grows very slowly. Whilst in the low country, at Salem, and in their haunts on the Shevaroys, attempts to domesticate them have proved unsuccessful. Some few calves have lived up to three years of age, but none are recorded as having survived that period.*

Its skin is employed for covering shields, and also for the soles of shoes. Its horns take a very beautiful polish, they should first be filed and scraped, until quite smooth, and then rubbed with the leaves of the *Ficus aspera:* subsequently being polished by strong friction, with a soft leather, or cloth covered with charcoal and grease, or oil.

---

* Mr. Elliot, in the *Madras Quarterly Journal*, gives the size of one measured by him most accurately. Height at shoulder 73½: at rump 65: length from nose to insertion of tail 114½: of tail 34: of dorsal ridge, including hump 40: height of the same 4½: girth behind fore legs 96: breadth of forehead 15½: between points of horn 25: circumference of neck 52: skin of neck, shoulder and thighs about 2 inches thick.

Domesticated cattle do not thrive in this portion of India; the cows are small and few in number, oxen are used for ploughing, and as beasts of draught and burden, as are also the country ponies. The reason of this deficiency in cattle appears to be due to two causes, first to the difficulty in procuring pasturage, and secondly to the heavy monsoons, which are so destructive to the health and life of large ruminant animals.* The idols and great people are fanned with the tail of the Thibet cow, *Bos gruiens.*

The Malabar Ibex, *Capra—?* may be identical with the Neilgherry species, although in some respects it appears to differ. The length of the male is about 5 feet 4 inches, from the base of the horns to the tip of the nose, which last is aquiline, the horns are 14½ inches in length, and 5¼ apart at the tips. The general colour is a greyish brown, with a greyish ash coloured saddle across the loins; it is also grey at the sides and base of the neck, and has a black streak from the occiput to the tail, the legs are black with a spot of white on the forelegs, an inch above each knee. The skin, is of the same thickness in every part of the body. It is good eating, but inhabits rocks and other almost inaccessible places, with the exception of Maliatur, where, as already mentioned, it is, curious to say, perfectly tame. Sometimes it may be seen almost as shaggy as the Cashmere goats, with hair almost touching the ground.

Sheep (*Ardou,* Mal.) may be said to be unknown in Cochin, but are brought into the country from Palghaut, and are long legged, ugly, red, brown, and black creatures.† Although very thin, the mutton is usually pretty good, but small goats thrive much better, and are more numerous in the interior of the country. When brought into the town, they multiply rapidly, but do not give much

* In the memoirs of the *Missionary Weitbrecht,* it is stated that Hindus believe coal, to be the remains of horses, of which as many as 5,000 were frequently sacrificed to the gods, by their kings in ancient times. The tar in the coal is supposed to arise from the ghee, poured on the sacrificial fire.

† Krishna was an especial favourite with the Shepherdesses, of whom he had a large number under his protection. On hearing of his death, they are believed to have drowned themselves in the pool at Dwárka; in commemoration of which, the caste marks of the Vishnuites ought to be made of the mud from that pond.

milk, and this is said never to be used for butter, it is certainly injurious to some young children, even causing dysentery.

The Bull cut in granite, is a well known emblem of one of the Hindu Deities. It is related that the Cottayam Brahmans, requiring money, represented to the Dewan that their idol had a severe boil on its thigh, and forwarded an estimate of the amount of money, that would be required to purchase drugs. The money was sent them, with, at the same time, an intimation, that *it was expected the animal would be permanently cured.*

The reason why cows are objects of veneration to Hindus is a very difficult question, but it appears more than probable that it first arose, from a legislative enactment, to prevent their being tortured, as in some parts of Africa they are to this day, by having portions of flesh cut off them for steaks when alive. Perhaps failing in legislation, priestly assistance was called in, and the animal made sacred. The worshippers of Siva sometimes abstain from working their cattle on Monday, as that day is sacred to the bull. Amongst the ancient Jewish laws, the ox was declared clean, and frequently used for sacrificial purposes. Also amongst the Egyptians it was venerated, and had divine honours paid to it. Possibly it was in imitation of these last that Aaron made the golden calf.

Ignorance of the troubles likely to arise from killing this sacred animal, was productive of many injurious occurrences to the concerns of the early settlements of the Honorable East India Company. An English Captain of a vessel on one occasion presented a Bull dog, to the Commandant of a small factory, containing about 18 persons at Batacola near Onore. However the animal almost immediately on its arrival, unfortunately perceiving a cow, fastened upon it and could not be taken off, until it had killed it. The Hindus believing the dog to have been instigated by the Europeans, rose, and massacred all of them. Natives imagine that milch cows will never give milk unless they see their calves, therefore when these last die, they often stuff them with straw, and bring them forward, whilst the mother is being milked. Large herds of cattle are constantly allowed to roam into the forests in search of food, and one would imagine, that they would be apt to stray away, and become wild. But this is not the case, as they dare not remain there during the night, for fear of wild beasts, but invariably either return to the plains, or congregate together in open spaces, where should they lie down, they are very careful that their horns shall form a circle externally, in readiness to meet an enemy.

The descendant of the Zebu, or Indian Ox, is said to lose the hump, on being crossed with other cattle, and is considered to be the originator, of the Eurcpean stock.

Buffaloes, *Bubalus buffelus*, Blum., appear to thrive pretty well, and are kept principally for their milk, from which a kind of cream cheese is made; to Europeans these animals always appear to be in a half savage state. They are sometimes employed in ploughing, in deep wet soils, and may occasionally be seen in carts. During the day, they delight in remaining in the water, with only their noses above the surface. They thrive in many moist places, fatal to the Indian Ox.

Donkeys are not used in the town of Cochin as beasts of burden, but they are so in Trichoor. In olden times, these animals were employed for punishing women, who had committed certain offences; after their heads had been shaved, they were compelled to ride through the Bazaar, with their faces to the animal's tail, probably it was found necessary subsequently, to destroy the poor creatures, for fear they should be overworked.* Riding upon an Ass, was in the time of the Jewish Judges, considered a great mark of distinction. Solomon was the first to introduce the horse, in the place of the more patient Ass.

The Sambur, *Rusa equina, Cuv.*, grows to a large size, and though not esteemed good eating by Europeans, its horns are fine, and its marrow bones are an Indian delicacy.

The spotted Deer, *Axis maculata*, Gray. (*Pulliman*, Mal.) is very numerous, and its horns form an article of export. The animal is sometimes killed to procure them, but at the time of shedding, they are collected in large numbers in the jungles. The young horns are rough, but the older ones are much smoother, as the animals before

* The authoress of "Delhi" says, Natives believe that "If you pass between two donkies, you will lose your religion, but if you touch them both, you will get it back again, and keep it"! if so easily lost, it might be added, "as long as you hold on by the animals' tails."

shedding, finding them irritable, are in the habit of rubbing them constantly against the trees. Its flesh is very good eating, and when young, it makes a pretty and interesting pet, but as it gets older, it generally becomes very vicious.

Dogs of every nomenclature, and of many nondescript varieties, exist in large numbers, and occasionally produce Hydrophobia in the inhabitants. Amongst European dogs, the Bull dog appears to thrive the best, and the Spaniels and Lap dogs the worst, if their livers are affected, and the skin turns yellow, there is probably nothing which can preserve their lives.

The Elephant, *Elephas Indica*, Linn. (*Ahna*, Mal.) is by no means rare in the thicker jungles, and at times causes great devastations in the paddy fields, in plantations of sugar cane, and in palm gardens, they also beat down the betel palm to obtain the cabbage on the top. As their tusks if wild, are the property of the Native State, there is little inducement to kill them. When encountered in numbers, they generally run away, but a single one, who has been deserted by the herd, is extremely dangerous. The Elephant was an emblem of the Rajahs of Mysore, before Hyder's time, and may still be frequently seen on their coins.

When Elephants fix their quarters near cultivated lands, and carry their depredations into plantations, and paddy fields, the inhabitants endeavour to frighten them away, by lighting large fires at night time, beating tomtoms, sounding horns, and making various other discordant noises. They ravage the low lands, mostly in the rainy season.

Elephants are usually captured in pitfalls, which are covered over with green boughs of trees, but this method occasionally destroys their efficiency. When captured they alarm the forest with their outcries, they are generally left there several days, when two or more tame elephants are employed, in dragging them out of their prison by ropes and chains, subsequently they also assist in taming them. When properly broken in, they are employed by the Native Government, to drag timber down from the Hills, and they are also let out for Rupees 6 a day. They are very clever in piling logs, and assist with great decorum at the various Hindu ceremonies, some of them being entirely set apart for this purpose.

Elephants occasionally at certain times become very excitable, and unmanageable. In 1861, a magnificent animal which was a great favourite of the Rajah's, killed its keeper, and escaped in this mad condition. But instead of betaking itself to the jungles, it haunted villages and inhabited places, causing great loss of life, and much destruction of property. No one dared destroy it, as the Rajah was most anxious to have it taken alive. At last it chased a cow, which took refuge in a neighbouring Pagoda, into which the Elephant followed, and to the great horror of all pious Hindus, killed the sacred animal within its walls. A large sum was subsequently paid for purifying the temple.

The numerous tales recorded, proving the wonderful sagacity of this animal, would fill volumes, but it is rarely that they have proved themselves good detective police. An instance however occurred at Nagercoil, a few years since. An Elephant was sent there for the purpose of piling timber by the Dewan, who requested the wife of a Missionary residing there, to be good enough to see the animal fed, and thus prevent its keeper from abstracting its food. It was therefore brought to the house daily for this purpose, and at first all went on correctly: but after a time it was suspected that the amount of rice was getting smaller, and smaller, so one day the keeper was remonstrated with, and of course protested against the imputation of having taken it, adding in true Native phraseology, "Madam, do you think I could rob my own child?" The Elephant looked on most sagaciously, and at this stage of the proceedings, quietly threw his trunk around his keeper, and untied his bulky waist cloth, when the missing rice fell to the ground.

It is said that in some parts of India, when a Rajah or a great man wishes to ruin a friend, he presents him with an Elephant, which of course he cannot subsequently part with, but whose keep is so expensive, that unless very wealthy, his owner soon finds himself reduced to poverty. In Cochin, such would have quite the contrary effect, the hire of one of these animals being Rs. 6 a day, the person who uses him also paying all expenses. They commence work at about 19 years of age, and are at their prime, until thirty. A good Elephant costs about Rs. 1,100, but a very fine one has been known to fetch as much as Rs. 2,300. It is many years since any of these animals captured by the Sircar authorities, have been trained for work. Large numbers die of actual starvation, in consequence of the attendants neglecting to feed them. Sambur and Bison frequently fall into the Elephant traps, but should a Tiger be caught, information must be immediately sent to the Rajah, when if he does not require it, it is shot.

The Wild Hog, *Sus scrofa*, Linn. (Variety) grows to a large size in the jungles. The finest hog hunting in Malabar, was formerly at Chetwye. The flesh is very wholesome.

Pigs (*Punni*, Mal.) appear to be very great favorites,* and are kept by many of the Native Christians, and others, as well as by the lowest castes of Hindus. They may be seen running around the houses, and are by no means clean feeders, whilst the fish that they are frequently allowed to eat, renders their flesh very unwholesome. In the neighbourhood of an oil mill, they generally get fed on Poonac, or the refuse of the cocoanut, which is very fattening. Pigs are killed for almost all wedding feasts amongst Native Christians, and even Mahomedans are not unfrequently found, who eat this unclean beast, under the denomination of *Mutton*.

* The occupation of Swineherd, is stated by Herodotus, to have been deemed most vile and contemptible, and the Egyptians refused persons who followed this occupation, admission into their temples, whilst they were spurned even by the very dregs of the population.

CHAPTER XIII.

BIRDS.

Tribes of birds found in different times of the year—Period of nidification—Legend concerning the nest of the Brahmanee kite—Origin of the Owl being termed the "one legged carpenter"—Bulbul drawing off attention from its nest—Destruction of young Larks by ants—Nest of the Tailor bird—nest of the bottle nested sparrow—Mynah acting as a house dog—Impudent Crows, origin of their being considered accursed by the Hindus—Sun bird, and its nest—Water fowl.

THE birds of India, form a most elegant and charming division of its zoology, and have their representatives in almost every tree, on the sandy plains, the muddy marshes, on the sea, and in the backwater: some being nocturnal, others diurnal in their habits.

The same tribes of birds as a rule, range for their food, and find their homes, from the most northern to the most southern portions of the continent, but the time of year in which they prefer a residence in one place to that of another, differs. The towns are full of Crows, *Corvus splendens*, whose audacity makes one wish them less common, but the chirp of the house Sparrow, *Passer Indicus*, is seldom heard in the Cochin state. The banks of the backwater are dotted with groups of Herons, and flocks of Terns.

During the prevalence of the S. W. Monsoon, there is a remarkable paucity of birds, even the waders forsake the coast, the Herons and Egrets are rarely observable, and paddy birds are scarce, whilst Terns, Gulls, and Ring Dotterels are entirely absent, and do not return until November or December. The common Sandpiper disappears, but the green one is occasionally seen. The Snipe also retreats, but the Brahmanee kite becomes more numerous, although the common Kite is rarely preceived. In the depths of the Jungles of the western ghauts the stillness appears to be only broken by Monkeys, and Squirrels, still an occasional Woodpecker, Nuthatch, or Hornbill, may be heard, or perceived.

Nidification appears to take place at any period between October and June whilst some birds such as Crows, seem to be building nests, or rearing young, all the year round. Birds are in their most elegant plumage either in the months of October, November, or in March and April.

Amongst the order of birds of prey, *Raptores*, and the family of Vultures, is the large and certainly most disgusting species, the Indian Vulture, *Gyps Indicus*, Scop. which though less frequently perceived within the limits of the town of Cochin, than further inland, still is not rare. Unburied bodies, are a feast for these carrion birds, whose odour owing to the nature of their food, renders them objects to be avoided, but they are of great benefit to mankind, in freeing the air from putrid animal substances, which should mark them out as worthy of preservation.

These large sad coloured birds, may often be approached when gorged with food, as then they sit upon the naked branches of trees with their wings half opened, or stand upon the ground too lazy to move.

It is curious that the Ægyptian Vulture, *Neophron percnopterus*, Sav., so common and widely distributed in India, does not appear to visit the town of Cochin, though an occasional pair may be perceived further inland : their white colour, and large size, rendering them conspicuous objects.

Amongst the falcons, is the common Kestril, *Tinnunculus alaudarius*, Briss., which devours lizards, young birds, and insects. The natives sometimes keep it domesticated. The elegant Peregrine falcon, *Falco peregrinus*, Gmel., occasionally comes to Cochin, but merely as a passer by, during his sojourn he visits the dovecotes, carrying away pigeons, and sometimes condescends to capture small chickens. The Sultan falcon, *Falco peregrinator*, Sund., is also seen at intervals, and both species appear fond of parroquets.

The most common Kite is the pariah, *Milvus Govinda*, Sykes, which is present all the year round, but least common in the South West monsoon. It is useful in removing the remains of animal substances from the drains, and around the cook rooms : it is also fond of reptiles, and may even be seen catching winged ants, whilst flying. When it is wished to capture it, a piece of meat is placed in the centre of a thin cumblie, (Native blanket,) and when it dashes down on the bait, its claws become fixed in the cumblie, and it is unable to rise. Another plan is, to put some raw flesh on the ground, with numerous horsehair springes around, in which it is caught when swooping down.

The Marsh Harrier, *Circus æruginosus* is of very common occurence, and may frequently be seen sitting by the side of marshy places, apparently watching for frogs.

The Sparrow Hawk, *Accipiter nisus*, Linn. (*Paranda*, Mal.) is occasionally seen. Amongst the Eagles, is the very handsome Brahmanee kite, or Pondicherry Eagle, *Haliastur Indus*, Bodd, (*Kristnasawmy*, Mal.) sacred to Vishnu. It is also called Siva's or the Washerman's Kite, and is an object of veneration, both to Hindus and Mahomedans: the great day for its worship amongst the former being Saturday. Its gall bladder and contents, are frequently mixed with other ingredients, and used as an antidote to poison, as it is alleged, that this bird is at enmity with all venom, especially that of the cobra.

This species of Eagle, is most commonly engaged in hovering over shoals of small fish, now and then darting down, and usually reascending with one or more in its talons: or else it may be seen, sitting at the top of a fishing stake, with its white chest and neck glancing in the sun: it is found all the year round.

There is a common legend, that should the nest of a Brahmanee Kite be found, one of the young should be attached to it by a string; and as the squab becomes strong, it breaks away, generally leaving a portion of the line attached to the nest. This nest which is formed of sticks should then be thrown into a running stream, when if any of the sticks that compose it, float *against the current*, they will on being applied to any fetters, cause them immediately to fly into a thousand fragments.

The Owls are extensively distributed, from the large species, *Bubo orientalis*, Horsf. (*Moonah*, Mal.) in the neighbourhood of the ghauts, where its moaning cry disturbs, the midnight solitude, to a diminutive species, which issues forth of an evening, or may even be seen in the day time, when it is worried by Crows, and other birds.

The Owl which is an emblem of wisdom in Europe, and the Goose that of stupidity, completely change their respective places in the East: the former becoming a symbol of stupidity, the latter that of wisdom.

The Owl's inharmonious voice, heard at night-time, has in all parts of the world, and in all ages of time, been considered ominous of evil, and consequently much dreaded. In Cochin it is generally believed that their hootings betoken an impending calamity, or even the death of some individual near to whose abode they are uttering their lonesome cry: so the dwellers in the neighbouring houses, at once turn out, and drive them away.

In some places, the Owl goes by the name of the "one legged carpenter," in commemoration of the following legend. One evening a carpenter who had been working all day in the Jungles, was proceeding howewards, when he discovered that he had left his axe behind, and therefore returned to fetch it. But whilst searching for it, he unfortunately came across a concourse of demons, feasting on a human corpse. At first the evil spirits were scared, but subsequently they surrounded him, and demanded why he had dared to invade their domains? He replied, that he only came in search of his axe; but his captors having consulted together, announced to him that he must die, and that they would then eat his body. The prisoner however protested against this, declaring that he had had no intention of playing the spy upon them, and in fact would much rather not have seen them at all, but as it was, that he would swear by all that was holy, never to divulge what he had seen or heard, if they would release him.

The demons then consulted again, and at last agreed, that he might return home, but that should his tongue ever play him false, the original sentence was to be executed. The carpenter then ran off to his house, delighted at his escape; but his wife who had been kept waiting, enquired why he had been so long absent, and the reason of his down cast looks? "Do not ask me," he replied, "for I must not tell." On being further pressed, he assured her that he believed an answer would cost him his life. But woman's curiosity was now fully aroused, and she suggested that he might be mistaken, and promised that if he would only tell her, she would keep his secret inviolate. At last he consented to confide in her, and commenced giving an account of his adventures; but when he came to speak of the demons, an awful sound was heard overhead, and the carpenter taking the form of an Owl, uttered an unearthly screech, and flew towards the window : but his wife seized him by one leg, which came off in her hands, and away he flew across a river. It is still thought a very bad omen, to hear his screech across water, for such is believed to fortell some dire calamity.

It is said that whilst the white Owl, *Strix Javanica*, Horsf., utters its harsh shrill cry, " drops of blood are forced from its bill, and " should any of these fall upon the backs of cattle, they become weak in the loins." The small Owl, is called *Natthu*, Mal.

Amongst the second order of perchers, one which first strikes the eye, is the Bee-eater, *Koalee killee*, Mal. the larger variety of which, *Merops badius*, Gmel., gives place about the month of March, to the smaller green species, *Merops viridis*, Linn., whilst both forsake Cochin during the South West Monsoon. Their habits are the same, they are usually perceived in small flocks, and sitting either on a branch of a tree, or the wire of the Electric Telegraph, they dart upon any passing insect, after capturing which, they return to their original seat: in the hot months they may be seen hawking for insects, in much the same way as the Swallows.

Swallows are by no means uncommon, particularly the Panayan, but the Daurian is not rare. At the commencement of the South West Monsoon, the Sand Martin Swallow, *Cotyle riparia*, Linn., is the most frequently perceived species of this family, still the Panayan, appears never to be entirely absent.

The Goatsuckers, are very common, noiselessly flitting up from a path, or sandy place, in the dusk of the evening, or if disturbed during the day time, flying up, but almost immediately seeking shelter under a neighbouring shrub, they are known to every one. The most common species, *Caprimulgus Asiaticus*, Lath., lays its two purplish veined eggs, upon a lighter coloured ground, $1\frac{2}{10} \times \frac{6}{10}$ inches, under a bush, without any nest.

The Kingfishers, *Halcyonidæ*, (*Meen koathee* or *Poumán*, Mal.) are extremely numerous. Persons arrive annually from the Coromandel Coast, to snare them for their plumage, which is said to be exported to China. The Indian species, *H. fuscus*, Bodd, is seen in pairs, often at a distance from water, and sometimes perched upon trees, or even houses. It lays its round white eggs, $\frac{19}{25} \times \frac{16}{20}$ inches, in holes in banks, and remains during the whole year. The most common species, is the beautiful little Indian Kingfisher, *Alcedo Bengaliensis*, Gmel., a diminutive representative of the European one. Sometimes on a stone, a bank, a piece of upright stick, or bough of a tree overhanging a stream, this little speck of emerald green, may be seen, then suddenly shooting through the air, it is perceived dashing upon a passing fish. It is a very tame bird, and easy to approach.

The most common of the large Kingfishers inland, is the black and white one, *Ceryle rudis*, Linn., they are generally seen in pairs, mostly close to the water, but often hovering above their prey and then suddenly darting down upon it. It is said, that this species if once foiled, never makes a second attempt, until it has settled again.

It lays its white eggs about October, in holes in a bank, without any nest, they are $\frac{18\frac{1}{2}}{20} \times \frac{17}{20}$ inches. It generally returns to the same place, year after year.

Besides the foregoing species, the rare and beautiful black headed Kingfisher, *H. atricapillus*, Gmel., is sometimes seen; and the strong as well as handsome Gurial Kingfisher, *H. leucocephalus*, Gmel., is found near the ghauts, it is very wary, and its flight greatly resembles that of the *A. Bengaliensis*.

Amongst the family of Flycatchers, vast in extent, and elegant in form, the Sultana Bulbul, or Paradise Flycatcher, *Tchitrea Paradisi*, holds a prominent place. Though most frequent at the foot of the ghauts, or along the margin of the inland rivers, it is widely distributed, and is even occasionally seen inside the town of Cochin.

The male and young birds, are of a deep chesnut brown, with greenish black crested heads, but their most prominent feature, is two long central tail feathers, from two to three times the length, of any of the others. Darting amongst the trees after its insect prey, it is an object to arrest the attention of the most incurious passer by, but in beauty of colour, it is surpassed by the females, which in their second year, become of a pure milk white colour, having black markings on some of the feathers, and the same green black crested heads, as the males.

Three species of Flycatchers, having more or less crimson about them, (*Pericrocotidæ*) are spread through the jungles, but are no where common.

Amongst the Shrike family, *Laniadæ*, especially in the sub-family, *Dicrurina*, some well known species exist; first the common Kingcrow of India, *D. balicassius*, Vieill (*Kaka tumbrattee*, Mal.) also called the Cutwal, because it is a terror to the insolent Crows, the adversary of the Kites, and the tormentor of the Owls. When it is very clamorous, it is said to be a certain indication of rain. It remains throughout the year.

The wary long tailed Shrike, *D. retifer*, Lan., the outer feathers of which terminate on each side of the tail in a long hair, with apparently a round ball at the end, is seen at the base of the ghauts, or even as far as Shallacoodie. They are favorite cage birds, and able to imitate the songs of any others they may hear, which has obtained for them the name, of *Huzar dustan*, or the bird of a thousand songs. They become very tame when in confinement.

The family of Thrushes, *Merulidæ*, though far inferior as songsters, to those in Europe, still possesses some, who have sweet toned voices: whilst the beauty of their plumage, is unsurpassed, by that of any other birds.

The Bengal Pitta, or the nine coloured bird is a most elegantly blended combination of the brightest colours, far different in appearance from its relative, the plain Grey Thrush, *Malacocircus griseus*, Gmel., which is very common, and seen in small families, hopping about around the roots of trees, and bushes. Its nest consists of fibres, very plainly woven together and generally contains four deep blue eggs, $\frac{16}{20} \times \frac{11}{20}$ inches in size.

The common Bulbul, *Pycnonotus pygæus*, Hodgs., is by no means rare: when two males of this species are placed together in a cage, they engage in a most vehement contest. It sings very sweetly, and also imitates the notes of other birds. One morning one of them was seen tumbling out of a tree as if wounded, and then fluttering along the ground, as if its back were broken: seeing it look much distressed, and having followed it a few yards, surprise was great at perceiving it suddenly fly up into a mangoe tree, and utter a short triumphant song.

The next morning at the same spot, a similar scene was enacted conjointly both by the male and female birds. On instituting a search, their nest containing four young ones, was detected in a Rangoon creeper, *Quisqualis Indica,* which encircled a verandah pillar.

The yellow Mangoe birds, (*Magnakli,* Mal.) or orioles, are exceedingly common, the most frequently perceived species, being the black naped one, *Oriolanus melanocephalus.,* Linn., but the common Indian golden Oriole, *O. kundoo,* Sykes, is by no means rare. Their deep golden plumage renders them easily perceptible, as they usually resort to trees with dark coloured leaves such as the mangoe, and jack fruit.

Another species of this family, known as the Fairy blue bird, *Irena puella,* Lath., well deserves its name; its shape is most elegant, and the male is superbly marked, with a black chest, and most lovely blue back. Its sweet song might well entitle it to the honor of being a cage bird, but it does not appear ever to be kept in confinement.

Larks are not plentiful, but are no where rare. In October 1861, a pair of these birds, *Alauda Malabarica,* Scop., were seen flying about in a very excited state, and apparently in great distress. On carefully examining the surface of the ground, their nest was discovered, in which only one little one remained, who was writhing in agony, from the bites of numerous dark coloured ants, *Formica timida,* Jerd., who swarmed all over it, and were eating it alive. The parents unable to rescue their offspring, were thus compelled to see them devoured piecemeal. Ants no doubt besides clearing away dead animals, and used up vegetable productions, prevent too great an increase, in other races of the animal kingdom. This species of Lark delivers its song like the English Sky Lark whilst soaring in the air but it is inferior in melody.

The Indian Robin, *Copsychus saularis,* Linn., (*Boomi koolleki,* Mal.) is a very common, and well known bird; it may be seen hopping about under the low bushes, and occasionally jerking up its tail, and warbling a short song. Its colour is much the same as that of the Magpie, [black and white,] otherwise it might easily be mistaken for its English namesake. It is often kept tame, on account of its sweet though very short song; two of these birds can however rarely be caged together, on account of their pugnacious habits.

The Tailorbird, *Orthotomus longicanda*, Gmel., which is often found in the gardens of Cochin, makes its nest by sewing leaves together, sometimes a living to a dead one but generally joining those which are green and thus forming the external case, which effectually screens the nest from observation, the inside is mostly lined with horse hair. The bird itself, appears to spin the thread he requires for this purpose. It is a curious little creature, and may be seen creeping about in bushes, and thick trees, just before, and during nesting time: the male occasionally flies up into a tree, and utters a few short but sweet notes, it appears to forsake Cochin only during the very wet and stormy weather, of the S. W. Monsoon.

The Pied Wagtail, *Motacilla Madraspatana*, Briss., is very similar to its European relative, frequenting streams in the same manner, but the single white stripe above the eye, and side of head, sufficiently distinguishes it. It runs about for short distances, jerking its tail and catching flies, and insects: it arrives about October, and remains until May. The Grey species, *M. sulphurea*, Bechst., is that most frequently seen; between October and February, it visits the small patches of green inside the town. At the end of the year when the ground becomes parched, it retires.

The House Sparrow, *Passer Indicus*, Jardine, which elsewhere so impertinently intrudes into houses, is almost unknown in Cochin, as is also the Mountain Sparrow, *Passer montanus*, Linn., which is so common in Burmah. All birds appear to give way to the Crows. Proceeding up the coast, the House Sparrow first comes into anything like notoriety, at Tellicherry, although occasional specimens may be seen at Calicut. Further north at Cannanore, they do not appear to be so plentiful as at Tellicherry. A yellow necked, or Jungle Sparrow, *Gymnoris flavicollis*, Franklin, is occasionally seen, four or five are generally together, but their visits are few and far between.

In some places, more especially along the banks of the Backwater, are seen the hanging nests of what is commonly known as the Bottle nested sparrow, or Weaver bird, *Ploceus Baya*, Blyth., (*Olamari*, Mal.) They appear like long necked bottles, made of grass, having the smaller end upwards. The little architects, commence building from above, and gradually extend their domicile, to the size required, it is divided into two compartments, by an open partition, thus the bottom part has two openings, one of which is filled up from the inside, by the nest with its white eggs; the other being the door, into the antechamber, which leads through the partition wall, into the place where the eggs are. These birds put two fireflies on the walls of their house, sticking them on with mud, and making use of them as lights during the dark hours of the night.

The jungle Mynah, *Eulabes religiosa*, Linn., (*Malachittray*, Mal.) is a very favourite cage bird, but unless caught when very young, is wild and untractable, and not nearly so amusing as the common Mynah, (*Chittray*, Mal.) which is easily taught to talk, imitate the mewing of cats, and in fact is preferable to the European Starling, although it is not considered necessary to slit its tongue to conduce to its garrulous propensities.

Its eggs are larger than those of the Brahmanee Mynah, being $1 \times \frac{8}{10}$ inches in size, and are of a blue colour. When it talks well, it obtains the name of *Chittray killee*, Mal. or Mynah Parrot: one of these small birds, was kept loose in a gentleman's house, and guarded the door like a watch dog. Some classes of persons he allowed to enter, but others he had apparently a great aversion to, and would sometimes fly at a Native's uncovered feet, and hold on like a bull dog, even until he drew blood. Should the person thus attacked, lift it up to put it in its cage, it would cry out, "go away, go away," and as soon as its enemy had left, it uttered its note of triumph, spread out its tail, erected its crest, and chuckled with delight.

The elegant little Brahmanee Mynah, *Temenuchus Pagodarum*, Gmel. (*Vella Kahrah*, Mal.) or Pagoda Starling, with its black crest, and brown body, is by no means uncommon. Though it has a very sweet short song, it does not seem to be a favourite cage bird. Its eggs are of a light blue, $\frac{8}{10} \times \frac{6}{10}$ inches, and are mostly found in June. The White headed Mynah, *T. Blythii*, Jerd., inhabits the lofty forests, and has a very melodious note.

The pretty Rose coloured Pastor, or Cholum bird, *Pastor roseus*, Linn., arrives in large flocks in the Cochin territory, about the end of January, or the beginning of February, but they do not remain long, as at the commencement of March, only a few stragglers are to be seen. The name Cholum, is derived from its being so very destructive in fields of that grain, *Andropogon sorghum*, watchers are obliged to be constantly kept, to frighten them away. These birds roost in enormous flocks, often in bamboo trees, and so closely packed, that dozens may be killed at a shot: they are very fat and good eating.

The family of the Crows, brings itself more into notice, than any other. The Indian Carrion Crow, *Corvus culminatus*, Sykes, (*Undun Kaka*, Mal.) is the species most frequently seen in the country, but excepting during the South West Monsoon it almost forsakes the town: its eggs are bluish, with darker spots, $1\frac{6}{20} \times \frac{19}{20}$ inches. The common Grey Headed Crow, *Corvus splendens*, Vieill. (*Kaka*, Mal.) is very numerous, and troublesome. If windows are left open unwatched for a few minutes, a Crow is almost sure to walk in, to see if there is anything he can find to eat: not satisfied with this, he carries off any small articles which may be lying about, and destroys flowers in vases, as if for pure mischief. Even the presence of persons sitting at the table, will not always deter these impudent birds, from darting down, and seizing anything they can carry off. They appear to be mating nearly all the year round.* The eggs are blotched all over with bluish brown, on a blue ground, $1\frac{1}{10} \times \frac{8}{10}$ inches in size. An instance occurred near Cochin, in which a little boy was eating a piece of bread and butter, when a large Crow darted down to take it from his hand, but the little fellow held it tightly, when the Crow determined on getting it, wounded him severely with his strong bill on the hand.†

Crows are very wary; the sight of a pellet bow, will scare them

---

* A writer in the *Calcutta Review*, mentions a " curious fact, of two Crows' " nests being found, entirely and very neatly constructed, of the wires used " for fastening down, the corks of soda water bottles."

† *Lieutenant Burgess* mentions the following anecdote, which well illustrates the manners of these birds. " Some Crows had been sitting near a young dog, " watching him whilst engaged with a bone. Having apparently concerted the " plan, one of them alighted, stepped up, and took a peck at the dog's tail; the " dog irritated, made a snap at the bully ; on which a comrade who appears " to have been ready, made a dash and went off with the prize." A Cochin dog before turning round to snap at a Crow puts his paw on the bone he is eating.

away. If one is killed, the others make a most uproarious noise. They are very destructive in gardens, especially amongst creepers.

The black plumage of the Crow, *Corvus culminatus*, has rendered him an object of aversion, to many classes of persons, even the Hindu Puranas, give the following legend, as one of the reasons of its being an accursed bird.

Chanacya,* caused eight royal brothers to be murdered, but subsequently when his conscience smote him, he applied to the Brahmans, and requested to know how he could atone for his sins, which they informed him was impossible. Subsequently as the gods and holy men were assembled in Indra's presence, they were conversing on this subject, and one of the sages enquired of the god, what mode of expiation was necessary. Indra replied, that certain severe religious austerities, and expiatory ceremonies must be employed, after which Chanacya should sail in a boat with white sails, when if they turned black, it would be a sure sign of the remission of his sins.

A Crow was present during this conversation, who from his friendly disposition, was named *Mitra kaka*, and it immediately carried the welcome news to Chanacya, who performed the necessary rite, (the Carshagni,) and went to Heaven. But the Crow was cursed for its indiscretion, and it and all its tribe, were forbidden ever to enter Heaven again, and doomed whilst on earth, to subsist on carrion.

It may be mentioned here, that the rite of Carshagni is performed at the present day, although the expense of a boat with white sails, is not generally incurred, an earthen pot being now considered sufficient, for carrying the sins of a Hindu. This is sent adrift on the Ganges, loaded with the suppliant's misdemeanours which are expected to be either carried away, or covered by the waters of that holy stream.

A cruel experiment has been sometimes tried, of salivating, or rather mercurializing Crows, by feeding them every day with pieces of bread, in which calomel is secreted. In a few days, the poor birds' heads begin to droop, whilst their feathers get dull, and fall off,

* Wilford, *Asiatic Researches*, Vol. 9 page 96.

leaving their heads bald; but they soon become suspicious, and resolutely refuse all overtures of bread.

But Crows are also occasionally a nuisance at night time, as well as during the day, for they sometimes appear to assemble in large numbers, when all respectable birds are sleeping, and fly about in every direction, cawing and making a great noise.

There is one little animal, that Crows appear fond of, when food is scarce, but find great difficulty in catching: viz., the little striped squirrel, *Sciurus palmarum* (*Unnun*, Mal.) One day a full grown squirrel, was observed in a Casuarina tree, *Casuarina muricata*, Roxb., trying to evade the pursuit of two Crows, who were doing their best to catch him. He ran round and round the tree, dodging them, but at last was caught by the tail: he then commenced running about as fast as possible, dragging the Crow after him, until at length the tail gave way, and the latter being thoroughly tired out, gave up the pursuit, and the squirrel escaped.

The common Mynah, sometimes attacks Crows, probably in consequence of their having plundered his nest. In one instance, when two Mynahs were seen furiously attacking a Crow, he suddenly turned round, and seizing one of his assailants by the neck, immediately killed him.

In Cochin a Crow one day flew into a room, and aimed a blow at a full sized guinea pig, which was running about, and only just escaped his powerful bill. They also attack and eat Lizards. During the commencement of the South West Monsoon, the bull frog, *Rana Malabarica* abounds: and appears to form their principal food.

The pretty Rufus Tree Crow, *Dendrocitta rufa*, Scop., (*Woalun Narrain*, Mal.) comes into gardens, and is not afraid of the vicinity of houses, but is more commonly seen near the high jungles, and gradually increases in numbers, as these are approached.

The Indian Rolla, or Blue Jay, *Coracias Indica*, Linn., (*Tourtoo Poata*, Mal.) is remarked at once by its gorgeous hues of blue. Though not very numerous, it is nowhere rare. It is generally difficult to approach, and wary of the Sportsman, whilst its harsh clamour disturbs other game, so it is at times considerably in the way. It is more common north of the Beypore river, than it is to its south.

It is usually to be seen on the bare bough of a tree, or in the middle of a ploughed field, but does not appear to remain long on the ground, at one time. It may be found at any period of the year in Cochin. Its blue colour is said to have been occasioned by standing on Siva's neck at the time he was poisoned, and as the blue line showed itself on the Deity's throat, the colour of the Rolla also acquired a blue tinge.

An old traveller in the East, has often been accused of a wilful perversion of facts, because he asserted that he had seen a bird with two heads: but no doubt he meant one of the Hornbills, *Homraius bicornis*, Linn., (*Veshambel*, Mal.) which are sometimes seen flying about in the Malabar forests. It is called the Garuda, and is sacred to Vishnu, holding the same position with some tribes of Hindus, as the Brahmanee Kite, *Haliastur Indus*, does with the generality of the worshippers of that Deity. The male bird, in order to insure the female's not quitting the nest, during the period of incubation, blocks up the opening, into the hollow tree, in which the nest is constructed, leaving only a small cavity, through which he feeds her. Hornbills are believed to feed with impunity on the poisonous seeds of the *Nux vomica*, which abounds in the Cochin territory. *Paoli* mentions, amongst his observations in Malabar, that it devours snakes.

The Pied Hornbill, *Hydrocissa coronata*, Bodd., is the most common species found here. One was observed in confinement who always when a plantain was given him, threw it up, caught it again lengthways, and swallowed it whole.

The tribe of Climbers, *Scansores*, are very numerous, beautiful and interesting.

Parrots (*Thatta*, Mal.) are amongst the most common of all Indian birds, and are caught in large numbers for sale.* The Rose Ringed Parrokeet, *Palæornis torquatus*, Briss., the Blue Winged Parrokeet, *P. Columboides*, Vigors, the Plum or Blue Headed Par-

* Amongst the *Psittacinæ*, or short square tailed true parrots, the Indian species are not loquacious: none could compete with the following pair which belonged "to a serious old lady, one of which (a recent acquisition,) having bestowed "some hearty forecastle curses upon his mistress, the other, whose education "had been better attended to, immediately followed with the pious response, "'We beseech thee to hear us, good Lord.'"

rokeet, *P. cyanocephalus*, Linn., are all found here, and also the Alexandrine Ring Necked Parrokeet, *P. Alexandri*, Linn., although more rarely. This last obtained its specific name from being the first of its tribe imported into Europe.

A Golden or Canary coloured Parrokeet is occasionally caught, but only at long intervals, they are considered great curiosities. One was brought round Cochin for sale, and no one would purchase it for some time, as it was believed to have been painted yellow. It is supposed to be a "lusus" of another sort, but nothing has been proved respecting it.

A very pretty little Lorikeet, or Dwarf Parrot, which is red under the tail, *Psittaculus vernalis*, Sw., is found in the high jungles, occasionally it descends in large flocks into millet crops, or where food is abundant.

The Woodpeckers and their allies are very numerous. The green Barbet, *Megalaima caniceps*, Frank, comes into Cochin. It is quite a mistaken idea that this bird confines itself to the forests, it is curious to observe that the usually common Indian Barbet, *Xantholæma Indica*, Lath., is much the most rarely seen of the two. The Indian Barbet though small, is a well known bird, owing to the singular noise it makes, like a copper-smith at work hammering, whilst its beautiful crimson forehead, and zone round its chest, renders it an object of remark to every passer by.

The handsome Royal Indian Woodpecker, *Chrysocolaptes Sultaneus*, Hodgs., is by no means rare in the jungles, its crimson crown and pretty plumage generally induce sportsmen to aim at it, but even when shot, it is a very difficult bird to secure.

The Crow Pheasant or Chestnut Cuckoo, *Centropus rufipennis*, Illig., is very common, and certainly bears a resemblance to the English Pheasant, especially when perceived running amongst bushes. The note it utters is very similar to that of a monkey. It devours lizards, insects, and even snakes, and is a very harmless, stupid bird. Some natives eat it.

The Coël or Eastern Black Cuckoo, *Eudynamys Orientalis*, Linn., is not rare, and from its being fond of stealing pepper, it has obtained the Malyalim name of *Mullagoo Poathee* (pepper eater.) This bird on finding the nest of the Grey Headed Crow, and more rarely that of the Black, is said to turn out the whole of the eggs belonging to the original occupant, and lay one of its own in their place. As the Crow always attacks this Cuckoo, whenever it finds it near its nest, it is probably suspicious of its intentions. The natives assert, that as soon as this bird has discovered what sort of a chicken it has hatched, it drives it away to seek its own food, and the old Coël being on the watch, takes charge of its progeny.

Perhaps one of the most beautiful birds on the Malabar Coast is the fasciated Trogon, *Harpactes fasciatus*, Gmel., which, though rare, is occasionally procured by the sportsman, but more commonly by the native Shikaree. This is a most difficult bird to obtain good specimens of, as its very thin skin, and easily detached feathers, renders skinning it far from being an easy task.

The Hoopoe, *Upupa nigripennis*, Gould., is not uncommon, it may be seen running about in search of food, or sitting on an elevated place uttering its single note, and raising its elegant crest. It generally comes about October, and is rarely seen after April or May.

One of those birds, which at once reminds persons of being in a tropical country, is the pretty diminutive purple Sun Bird, *Arachnechthra Asiatica*, Lath., looking like a bright green beetle. They may be found, although not very commonly, from April (or sometimes only from June) to January. The most numerous species is the *A. lotenia*, Linn. (*Aruckka*, Mal.,) which remains all the year round: they may be seen hovering about over flowers, into which they insert their curved, and comparatively long bills. In the month of October, its beautiful nest containing a pair of eggs, $\frac{11}{20} \times \frac{7}{20}$ of an inch in size, and speckled with dirty white near the larger end, on a white ground, may be found in every garden.

The nest hangs from a small twig of a tree; of two taken in one day, one was from a nutmeg tree, and the other from an acacia. Its shape is generally oval, with a portico hanging over the entrance, evidently as a protection from the rain, and is composed of grass and horsehair, lined with feathers. Some moss, cobwebs, and other materials, are placed outside, for the sake of concealment, and so arranged, as exactly to resemble the bough of a tree. In both instances mentioned above, the nests were hanging over pathways, and one only about 7 feet from the ground, but their colour had screened them from observation.

The Cochin territory must be considered as very well supplied with Fowls and Pigeons, though the Spurred Partridge, *Francolinus Ponticerianus*, Gray, also called the Scavenger Partridge, is not abundant, the latter name is very applicable as regards its habits. The Rock Pigeon, *Pterocles exustus*, Temm., the Painted Rock Pigeon, *P. quadricinctus*, Temm., and the Painted Partridge, appear unknown.* But the Peafowl, *Pavo cristatus*, Linn., the Jungle Fowl, *Gallus Sonneratii*, Temm., (*Kattucoli*, Mal.) and the Spur Fowl, *Francolinus spadiceus*, Lath., are very numerous. The Peafowl, (*Miloo*, Mal.) in the jungles, often warns sportsmen of the vicinity of tigers, as when several of these birds are congregated together, one of these animals is seldom far distant.

Different species of Quails, *Coturnix*, (*Cada*, Mal.) though small, afford good sport, when larger game is unattainable. The pretty little Button Quail, *Ortygis Dussumierii*, Temm., is occasionally to be procured.

Pigeons, (*Prow*, Mal.) as might be anticipated, are very numerous, and when the cashew nuts begin to ripen, they come in flocks from the ghauts, to feast on them. Perhaps the most beautiful species is the Imperial green variety, *Carpophaga œnea*, Auct., (*Cuila*, Mal.) which is about a foot and a half in length. It may be killed in the beginning of September at Trichoor, but does not appear in any numbers, until November or December. The Green Pigeon, *Vinago mililaris*, Jerd., (*Choola*, Mal.) is very common in some seasons. It comes in September, the smallest variety with the purple on their wings, first making their appearance. The common Blue Pigeon, *Columba œnas*, Linn., is very numerous, and often shot when perched on the top of one of the Travellers' Bungalows. The prettiest dove is one with bronze wings, Imperial Dove, *C. Tavanica*, Jerd., which is very common inland.

---

* The Painted Snipe is found in considerable numbers, on a large tract of land, near Tellicherry, but appears rarely to go further south. It is by no means common around Cannanore. The Shikarees say that it remains all the year round. It is also found at Palamcotta.

The elegant Demoiselle Crane, *Anthropoides Virgo*, Buff., is sometimes perceived in small flocks, or flying in long lines. When struck by the Peregrine Falcon, its mate is said to come to its assistance. It fights with its sharp beak and inner claw.

The European Heron, *Ardea cinerea*, Lath., is very frequent on the banks of the back-water. The Purple Heron, *A. purpurea*, Auct., is very common, and at the commencement of the year may be seen, towards evening, flying in flocks of some hundreds, in an irregular line, towards their feeding ground.

The beautiful milk white Egrets are most prominent objects all along the back-water from October to June. The larger or yellow billed Egret is very common, *Egretta flavirostris*, Temm., but the smaller black billed one, *E. garzetta*, Auct., is by no means rare. They may be seen running about at the sides of streams, and pieces of water, catching fish, and other articles of food. Natives believe that the powdered bones of this bird, employed in cooking fish, render their bones soft, and capable of being easily and agreeably eaten. The Green Heron, *E. Tavanica*, Sw., and the little Chesnut Heron, *Botaurus cinnamomeus*, Gmel., are both occasionally seen along the banks of the back-water, where there are a few overhanging trees. The white necked Stork, *Ciconia leucocephala*, Auct., is not uncommon, and breeds in the deep jungles, where a species of Marabout is also obtained; its feathers are collected, but are only in season, during the month of September, as the most delicate parts soon got rubbed off. Most of these families quit Cochin during the monsoon, whilst the Spoonbills and Flamingos, so common in most parts of India, do not visit it at all.

Besides the birds frequenting the sides of the back-water and rivers, other tribes are found on the tanks, which rarely intrude elsewhere, but remain throughout the year. The tank runners, *Parra Indica*, Lath., the Purple Coot, *Porphyrio smaragnotus*, Temm. the Bald Coot, *Fulica atra*, Linn., the blue throated Rail, *Rallus gularis*, Horsf., and the Indian water hen, *Gallinula akool*, Sykes., are all pretty common; the last is most prevalent in the dry months, when morning and evening it may be seen wandering about in the paddy fields and roads, sometimes far from any water, in search of food.

The varieties of Snipes and Sandpipers, are very great, and the representatives of each, are common.

The Snipe, *Gallinago stenura,* said to be the same as the European, one *Gallinago scolopacinus,* from which however it differs most essentially, comes to Cochin about December, and remains until April, single specimens may be procured inland as early as September. Its flight is by no means so rapid as that of the European species, and the fact of its having from twenty-four to twenty-six tail feathers, at once proves it to be distinct. Its European relative is said to be very common in Bengal, but does not come so far south as Cochin.

The little Sandpiper, *Oollee,* Mal., is frequently seen, especially in the cold season, but rarely if ever in the rains; it generally arrives in September and at once pairs. The green Sandpiper, and Redshank, are by no means rare, whilst the Curlew, *Numenius arquata,* Briss., and the Whimbrel, *N. phœopus,* Briss., are both found.

The common Ringed Plover, *Charadrius zirreah,* is to be seen not only by the sea side, but also in sandy plains, dried up dusty paddy fields and where there is grass, from June until December it is absent. The yellow wattled Lapwing, *Vanellus bilobus,* Gmel., is by no means rare, its call resembles that of a Pee-wit, and it remains all the year round.

Amongst the Ducks, (*Warthoo,* Mal.) the Whistling Teal, *Dendrocygna awsuree,* Sw., a few remain all the year round, but it comes in flocks in October, as also the numerous common species *Nettipus Coromandelicus,* and the Garganeys, *Boschas circia,* Linn., whilst amongst the flights, several other species are occasionally obtained. The average price is about two poothens each (one anna eight pie.)

A Cormorant, *Carbo cormoranus,* Linn., formerly stationed himself on the buoy in the outer roads, during the month of February, arriving daily at 10 A. M., and remaining until the evening. None of the Darters, *Plotidæ,* visit this part of India.

The Gulls, *Laridæ,* are not common, but the Terns, *Sternidæ,* are very numerous: they leave during the monsoon months, and return at the end of October, or in the commencement of November.

Cochin is celebrated amongst the neighbouring stations for its poultry. The large Christian population in the villages rear it, and the Jews, as a rule, purchase it from them, to supply Europeans. The trade is a very profitable one, and the risk small.

Turkeys (*Cullukkoo*, Mal.) succeed very well, full grown ones, excepting near Christmas time, cost from twelve to eighteen rupees the dozen, and very large ones two and a half or three rupees each. They are cheapest in August, when half grown ones can be obtained for about 8 annas, because the paddy is then ripe, and they stray into the fields, where they commit much damage, and are consequently killed by the Ryots. Fine fowls (*Coaree*, Mal.) for these parts, may be procured at four or five annas each. The introduction of a better breed, is a great desideratum.

The numerous sheets of water, streams, and tanks, which abound, render ducks very easy to rear, at a trifling cost. They are cheapest about October, when very good ones can generally be obtained for Rs. 2½ a dozen. Geese also thrive pretty well, but they are frequently difficult to dispose of, and therefore comparatively seldom reared by natives.

This bird, according to Cæsar, was held sacred by the ancient Britons, whilst *Mills* states, that the first Crusaders which issued from England, France, and Flanders, adored a goat, and a *goose*, which they believed to be filled by the Holy Spirit.

There is an amply sufficient supply of poultry for Cochin as well as for all the sailors in the harbour, and for the neighbouring stations. Some of the fowls have black bones, or more properly speaking, the covering of the bones (periosteum) is black. They do not look well on the table, but are the best kind for soups. The Schatriyas (Tirripards,) consider their houses polluted if a fowl enter them, and immediately destroy all the cooking vessels.

Large quantities of poultry are also shipped to Ceylon and Bombay. From December to April, a disease, apparently chicken-pox, occasionally breaks out amongst them, and within twenty four hours, fat turkeys fit for the table become mere skeletons, and perfectly useless. The disorder is contagious, and birds thus affected, generally die within a week or two, and those which apparently recover, take a very long time to fatten again.

CHAPTER XIV.

REPTILES.

Reptiles in Cochin State—Colossal tortoise of ancient times—Hawks-bill turtle and mode of procuring tortoise shell—Crocodiles—Accounts of its seizing human beings—Its enormous size—Sacred character—Mode of capture—Lizards—Snakes, objects of adoration—The cobra—Snake charmers—Evil spirits in the form of snakes—Sea snakes—Frogs and their reputed evil effects.

Reptiles are of course well represented in such a country as Malabar, having a tropical climate, low lands intersected with rivers and back-waters, hills covered with scrubby brushwood, and ghauts with forests. In addition to a propitious climate, and a favourable locality, many of the tribes of reptiles are held in veneration by the Hindus, which renders them to a great extent, protected from hostile attacks.

There are several species of land Tortoises, to be found in almost every part of the country. They are partial to wallowing in the mud, and by following the beaten tracks made by these creatures in the Galapagos Islands, the Spaniards are said to have been directed from the sea shore to fresh water inland. The tortoise is declared unclean in the Mosaical law, and the Mahomedans strictly regard this prohibition.

In olden times, colossal Tortoises wandered over Hindustan; Messrs. Falconer and Cautley, discovered in the Sewalic Hills, the remains of one, which must have measured eighteen feet, perhaps a degenerate descendant of the enormous one, on the back of which, in the ancient Hindu writings, the world was recorded to have been supported. (p. 278.) The lyre is said to have been invented by Mercury, who found a dead tortoise on the banks of the Nile, and having hollowed the shell of its back, fitted it with strings, and formed a musical instrument.

Turtles are not uncommon, the Green species, *Chelonia Midas*, is captured in numbers whilst sleeping on the water, it is a large one, that weighs above sixty pounds. Its flesh is good, but its shell is considered useless, and barnacles are frequently found attached to it. The Hawks-bill Turtle, *C. imbricata*, (*Ammah*, Mal.) is likewise captured, and Tortoise shell obtained from this species, is largely manufactured into boxes and other articles. This animal visits Cochin only during the South-west monsoon, when it may be bought alive for about eight annas, or even less. The size of all of them is usually the same, about 2½ feet long, its snout bearing some resemblance to the bill of a hawk, has obtained for it its specific name. The beautiful plates of tortoise shell, with which it is covered, are manufactured into various useful and fancy articles, there are five scollop shaped plates along the centre of the back, and four more on each side, the second being the longest. Its white under horny surface, is also employed for making boxes.

In Ceylon the following cruel process is employed for obtaining tortoise shell. A number of these animals having been captured, large fires are lighted, and the captives' feet having been securely fastened together, a bamboo pole is passed between them and the breast plate. Thus the unfortunate creature is suspended over the fire, until the dorsal plates start from its back, and then the whole thirteen are torn off. The tortured Turtle, in this denuded state, is allowed its liberty, and permitted to regain the salt water.

Turtle in Cochin, though constantly eaten, does not appear to occasion symptoms of Cholera, attributed to the effects of this food in Ceylon. If killed immediately it is caught, its flesh is bitter and should be washed in beer before being cooked, to remove its disagreeable aroma. It should be fed on cocoanuts and rice for a week before it is killed, by which time both the bitter taste, and offensive smell, will have vanished : and it will then be found good for soups, steaks, roasting, stewing, or curries.

The Saurian class is very extensive in this portion of India, whilst the size of its members, varies from the gigantic Crocodile infesting the backwaters, rivers, and tanks, to the little wall Lizard, that runs along the sides of the rooms, across the ceiling, or pays its visits to the dinner table. Whilst amongst the great curiosities of the East, the Chameleon, and flying Lizard, are not the least prized.

Some of this class, such as the Crocodiles, are venerated by the Hindus, and were formerly employed in ordeals, (page 385) for the detection of crime, and the punishment of the criminals: whilst the little harmless Brahmanee lizard, is held in great awe, and its bite is believed to be inevitably fatal. Others of the Lizards, are execrated by the Mahomedans, who consider their constant bobbing, or bowing motion, with their heads, as intended to mock the true believers. There is also a legend, that once when Mahomed was hiding in a well, a Spider spun its web over the top, which would have effectually concealed him, but a Lizard would look down on his place of security, and continued such a constant chirping, that it drew the attention of his pursuers to the spot, and he was discovered.

The Crocodile, *Crocodilus porosus*, Schn., is generally termed the Alligator, or Mugger, and may be frequently perceived basking in the sun, on muddy banks, or with its nose just above the water, or else lazily reclining on the top of a rock in the centre, or to one side of a river. When at rest it appears like a log of wood, and often requires an experienced eye to detect its presence. If disturbed, it quietly sinks its huge body into the water without a splash, and almost without a ripple. At times Crocodiles become men eaters, and seize bathers, fishermen, and persons who go to draw water.

Accidents sometimes fatal, are of frequent occurrence around Cochin from these animals, a few of those which have occurred during the last three years, will be now alluded to. In one instance a fisherman in the early morning, went to visit the nets, from which shortly afterwards awful shrieks were heard, but owing to its still being dark, nothing could be seen: many fishermen being near, they raised a great shout, and by the time they reached the nets, they saw their comrade in the jaws of a Crocodile, which became so alarmed at the noise that it let go its prey. The poor man was so terribly bitten that he died the same day. Another day two lads were fishing, with hooks and lines, and hooked what appeared to be a large prize, but with their united strength, they were unable to lift it into the boat. They cried out lustily for assistance, and a man came to their aid, who seized the line with one hand, and ran his other down it, to catch the fish by its gills. But unfortunately the prize proved to be a Crocodile, which seized the man's forearm, when the boys with great presence of mind, cut the fishing line, and the animal carried off the hand, but the man did not lose his life.

Within the space of a month, two girls were separately pursued by a Crocodile, the first he caught by the forearm, but before he could secure his prey, some men hearing her cries ran to her assistance and she was rescued with the loss of an arm. In the second instance, the girl escaped altogether, and within a few days, the Crocodile was taken and despatched.

The size of this animal is often very great, and though personal observation is limited to 18 or 20 feet, the natives declare that it grows to 30. In the British Museum, is a skull of one of these creatures, 26 inches long, which the gentleman who presented it, stated was taken from the body of one 33 feet in length. Another skull in the same collection, is 3 inches longer. At any rate its strength is so enormous, that it has been seen to carry a full grown Buffaloe across a piece of water. As might be anticipated, such enormous animals, are difficult to capture.*

The Crocodile is in many places considered sacred, as it was also in Egypt, where it was reputed to have 365 teeth. In Malabar although one hears nothing about the number of its dental appendages, it is a common belief, that it swallows a stone every year of its life, and thus after its death, the number of seasons it has seen, may be reckoned up from the stones in its stomach. Representations of this animal's head, are seen adorning the balustrades of the bridges, leading to the Rajah's palace at Tripoonterah, which is curious, considering that in Rangoon, before it was bombarded in 1852, the same

---

* In Africa *Mr. McGregor Laird*, states that Natives run a spear through Crocodiles tails, *when* they can catch them asleep. The captor holds on to the spear, whilst the captive twists around as if on a spit. Now a second Native rushes to the scene of strife, and endeavours to despatch the game. In India this plan would hardly succeed, as the Crocodile's tail is too well protected to be securely pivoted through, besides he is not a sound sleeper, whilst his strength is too great to be held by a spear, thrust through into the ground, and merely pressed down by the weight of one man.

embellishments adorned the bridges, leading to the great Buddhist, Shoe Dagon Pagoda.

When it has been decided to attempt the destruction of a dreaded man-eater, a spot near his haunt is chosen, and here 3 or 4 coir ropes are securely fixed to trees, or strong stakes, whilst to the other end is a large iron hook, to which a dog or a goat is attached. There is generally no difficulty in hooking the game, for he usually swallows the bait on the first night, but as he at once takes to the water, his final capture is not so easy.

As soon as a large Crocodile is reported as hooked, two jungars, (page 27) each capable of accommodating 20 or 30 men, are brought close to the spot where it is intended to drag the game to the surface of the water. Each is supplied with heavy stones for anchors, strong ropes, and boat hooks. The men are armed with guns, spears, and harpoons, as are also other persons in small boats, who are intended as the attacking party. Two ropes are now passed over the original line, to which the animal is hooked, in the form of running nooses, one is affixed to one jungar to the right of the hooked game, and the other to the left. The shore line is then hauled up by people on land, and the monster's head soon appears above the surface of the water, when attempts are made to pass the nooses over it. This is a most difficult task, as he is snapping his huge jaws at everything within reach, still in time with the assistance of the boat hooks, the two lines are securely passed around his neck.

The monster on this becomes furious, and generally makes for one of the jungars, which if he can reach he at once attacks, the people in the further jungar then endeavour to drag the game in their direction, whilst the occupants of that which is attacked, try to harpoon or otherwise wound it. If the three lines can simultaneously be made tight, harpooning is not very difficult, but not only its jaws, but the lashing of its tail, have to be avoided. The shouting on all sides is deafening, every one yells for a different course to be pursued, and this continues for sometime, and it occasionally takes three days to complete the work of destruction.

When the Crocodile is dead, each of its legs are fastened to harpoons, which are stuck into his body like skewers. Thus it is carried in triumph round the country on a cart, and subscriptions are raised to reward the captors.

Resorting to the banks of the same rivers, where the Crocodiles reside, as well as in the wood, and in the nests of the white ants, is a large dark species of Lizard, generally termed the Iguana, *Lacerta Iguana,* it is considered very good eating by the Natives, and is commonly about three feet or more in length. Its enormously long and forked tongue, gives it the power of reaching some distance into ants' nests, and securing many of its prey at a time, on that sticky organ. Its bite is very much dreaded, and it is a common belief, that it occasionally causes death within 24 hours. When pursued on land, it runs speedily to its hole, or if far distant from it, takes refuge in trees: sometimes it is hunted by dogs, and when tree'd, the sportsman must get upon a branch above it, and knock it down with a stick. If near water, it at once takes to it, and generally escapes, as it is very expert in that element. It can also rapidly make its way in the sand, as its claws are both sharp, and powerful.

Amongst the thick tongued group, the Bloodsuckers, or Galeotes, *Calotes,* so termed from the blood red colour of their heads are familiar to almost every one in Cochin. They attain a great length, due more to the extension of their tails, than to the size of their bodies. Two placed together, will wrestle, fight, and bite. Persian cats are very fond of capturing reptiles of this family.

Perhaps the prettiest, as well as the most extraordinary lizard, is the flying dragon, *Draco volans,* which lives in the forests, on the Ghauts. Its first six false ribs, are extended outwards, to support a membrane, something like a wing, or more properly speaking a parachute, which assists the animal when jumping from bough to bough. Its colours are bright, and appearance engaging.

The wall lizard, or Gecko, takes very good care, that it is not overlooked. Towards evening, it generally emerges from under the eaves of houses, or from dark corners, and makes itself useful, by destroying mosquitoes, flies, moths, and cockroaches, as well as eating the eggs of these last, which it scratches out with its sharp claws, as soon as the egg cases begin to open. Active in its habits, but repulsive in appearance, this little creature often gets destroyed, its usefulness being forgotten, and its sociability overlooked.

Its brown colour, and the little tubercles over its body, more especially on the tail, give it a disagreeable appearance, but its bright and comparatively large eyes, and the silvery colour of the pads of its toes, looking underneath like a silvered leaf, (to be seen as it runs upon glass,) are very pretty, or just appearing at the sides of each toe, as it runs along, makes it look as if it had frosted edges. It is a very active little creature, running up the walls, or across the ceiling, and if caught by its tail, leaves that appendage behind it, but reproduces it before long.

If undisturbed, it soon finds its way to the dinner table, where it eats crumbs, and gradually becomes bolder in its incursions, eventually returning every evening, for its accustomed supply. On observing appropriate food, the brown colour of its inferior surface, changes to a silvery shade, with a purplish tinge underneath the throat, when it rapidly rushes at it, and almost instantaneously swallows it.

Many superstitions have originated, with reference to this little inoffensive and useful creature. If a Lizard chirps upon a wall, the Hindu, or Syrian Christians, believe there is some latent meaning, so the subject of discussion is changed, but should the chirp be again heard in the same position, further conversation ceases. It is said that a Lizard divided down the centre, and bound to a person's body, will within twelve hours, produce an ulcer, having every appearance of being of a month's standing. The Mahomedans catch Lizards, for the purpose of feeding their hawks with them, of which they keep many, in this part of India.

The *Chameleon* is too well known to need description, it crawls about slowly, looking as if the two sides of its head had originally belonged to two distinct bodies, and had been joined together, or that it had lost one of its sides, and had stolen that of another to supply itself with, it is neither active, nor graceful in its movements. Its colour changes, but not to any great extent, and appears influenced by its feelings, or perhaps by its nervous system.

Snakes are not very numerous within the town of Cochin, where fatal effects from their bites are rarely heard of. But in the Native State, and in the Ghauts, their numbers and venomous properties are great. It is not an uncommon belief, amongst the Hindus, that a person who has died from the effects of the bite of a snake, will come to life again in fourteen days, provided certain ceremonies are performed by the Brahmans. An antidote as a preservative against the venom of these bites, is said to be the seeds of the nux vomica, one of which should be swallowed daily. Whether it is possible for this immunity to be purchased by drugs, is still a question open to doubt. The Mongoose appears to escape with impunity, when bitten, which has been attributed to his eating the leaf of a plant, which counteracts the effect of the venom, but of this there does not seem to be any proof, and it is a more probable supposition, that the bite of a venomous Serpent, exercises no influence on its deadly enemy the Mongoose, whilst the venom is certainly innocuous, to slugs, and leeches. Those who have had the curiosity to taste this secretion, (which is harmless should there be no wound, or sore on the mouth, or tongue, or on any part, where it can touch,) declare it to be oily.

There is no question, but that the effects of the bites of these reptiles, are at some periods more deadly than at others, depending both upon the part of the body bitten, and whether they have or have not lately discharged the contents of their poison sac, which takes time to be again secreted. Snake charmers aware of this, sometimes make them bite some article such as a bit of red rag, to evacuate the venom. The lower classes of Natives, have no objection to capture Snakes, but appear greatly tantalized, if they chance to see one of them, put into a bottle of good arrack, to preserve it, and sometimes loudly exclaim, against so much good spirit being wasted!

Serpents are in some places emblems of destruction, and have therefore rites performed to them, to deprecate their anger, or mitigate their vengeance. Hindus for this purpose, set aside a small grove in their compounds, where the reptiles are appeased by milk, and clarified butter. It is not considered obligatory to keep Snake Festivals, but if once kept, they must be continued, and there is only one Temple in Malabar, where a person can obtain a release from them, by undergoing a very expensive course of ablutions, and purification, which must be repeated for several days.

Besides the Tortoise of ancient times, there was also an enormous snake, Ananta (page 277) which was generally said to surround the world: this appears to have been the *Annulus Platonis*, a symbol of life and death, or the revolution of all things, which idea it has been supposed that Plato borrowed from India. We are told, that in the Wilderness, the children of Israel, when bitten by the fiery serpents, immediately recovered their health, if they looked up to the brass figure of a snake raised upon a pole (Numbers xxi. 89.) Moses also when sent to Pharoah, had his rod turned into a Serpent, as a symbol of his divine mission, (Exod. iv. 2, 3, &c.) and subsequently, the Jews were told that they had "changed the glory of "the incorruptible God into an image made like unto corruptible "man, and to birds, and to four footed beasts, and *creeping things*."

Kristna is said to have destroyed a Snake, that was poisoning the waters of a river, so he is sometimes represented, either with a monstrous Serpent coiled round his body, or placing his right foot on the neck of one. An analogy has been drawn, between this figure, and the prophecy, "I will put enmity between thy seed, and her "seed, it shall bruize thy head, and thou shalt bruize his heel." (Gen. iii. 15.)

There are numbers of exceedingly venomous Serpents, but a large majority of harmless ones. Many inhabit the salt or fresh water, others again prefer houses and outbuildings, some live amongst the stones, and grass, or in the woods, whilst others inhabit the ground. Some are accused of attacking persons in the water, others of giving venomous bites, some of jumping at the eyes, and others of throwing themselves backwards at the object of attack, but the most curious is a species of *Amphisbœna*, which is believed to be able to progress equally well either backwards or forwards, and is generally said to have a head at each end of its body, the appearance and markings, about the tail being so very similar to those of the head.

One of the snakes most dreaded, is the Cobra di capella, or spectacle snake, *Naija tripudians*, (*Nella paamba*, Mal.) the bite of which is often rapidly fatal. Its colour varies greatly, according to its age, and the locality in which it resides, some are of a light clayey brown, whilst in others the tint is black. It is capable of expanding the skin of its neck, in the form of a hood over its head; on it there is a black mark, like a pair of spectacles. When exasperated, it raises itself, hisses and darts at its enemy. It has a deadly antagonist in the little Mongoose, and Monkeys will destroy Snakes, whenever they get an opportunity.

The Cobra is generally used by the snake charmers, who sometimes remove the poison fangs, but frequently omit to do so. On hearing music, it raises the front portion of its body from the ground, and sways itself backwards and forwards marking the time. The instant the music stops, the creature ceases its movements. Many persons imagining, that because these animals allowed themselves to be handled so quietly by the snake charmer, their venom must have been removed, have foolishly allowed themselves to be bitten by them, and have lost their lives for their temerity. A few years since, a Snake charmer who was considered very clever at tricks with Snakes, was accustomed to swallow a Cobra, holding it by the tail, and when nearly out of sight, pulling it back again. But one day he unfortunately lost his hold, when the reptile slipt down his throat, and his death ensued.

If Snakes are fed, they will return to the same house every day to receive milk, but they are very averse to strong scents, and the fumes of sulphur, will generally cause them to leave a place. Natives who had secret rooms constructed, in which to deposit treasure, used frequently to place very poisonous Snakes in them, to deter plunderers from taking their goods.

A little innocuous Snake, (*Tevi*, Mal.) of a brownish colour, is very common in the houses, and it is asserted, that when one of them dies, or is killed, all its relatives come to its funeral, consequently Natives are very averse to its being destroyed.

A long thin snake like a whip, (*Coombarree Mookan,* Mal.) or branch climbing Mookan, has obtained its name from the belief, that it is the incarnated spirit of a departed enemy, or some demon employed by an enemy, for the destruction of an adversary. After having bitten a person, it is said to climb up into a tree, and creep to the extreme end of a branch, where it most attentively watches the ground on which bodies are burnt. If it perceives an incremation taking place, it is supposed that its malevolence is appeased, as it labours under the belief, that its venom has effected the object it had in view. On the other hand, should no smoke arise from the burning place, it is believed that at some future date, it will renew its attempt, on the object of its malevolence.

The beautiful little innocuous green snake, so common in gardens, is frequently caught, and killed, as it is considered a good remedy for headaches, when bound around a person's temples.

A very common harmless snake of an olive colour, *Coryphodon Blumenbachii* (*Cheera*, Mal.) is frequently seen near moist places, in paddy fields, and often as the monsoon sets in, by the side of the public roads, it grows to a very large size. It hits its captors with its tail, and wounds so inflicted, are said to be very difficult to cure. Sometimes in the monsoons, some of these reptiles are swept down by the rivers, to the islands between the backwater and the sea. The Rock Snake, *Python Molurus*, Gray, in the ghauts, grows to a very large size.

Sea snakes are exceedingly numerous, though there are only five common species. None are reputed to be venomious. One day a specimen was brought, with a bone protruding through its side, which however was not apparently causing much distress. On dissecting it, the bony protrusion was found to be the spiny ray of a *Bagrus*, or sea cat fish, as it is sometimes termed, which it had swallowed.

The Frog (*Towallay*, Mal.) in Egypt, was considered sacred, and looked upon as an emblem of the sun, or Osiris the first object of their adoration. In Malabar, it should be considered an emblem of rain, for as the first showers of the S. W. Monsoon commence, the croak of the large Bull Frog, *Rana Malabarica*, is at night time heard in all directions. Silence may sometimes reign undisturbed, when suddenly the croak, almost bleat, of one of these batrachians is heard, and others answer from all sides; the concert however terminates as rapidly as it began, to be recommenced after a short interval.

The Bull Frog frequently extends to eight inches in length, and is of an olive colour, with yellow underneath. It may be found in every moist place, and swampy bit of ground, in the morning long lines of them may be seen near the sea beach, but when disturbed, they at once make landwards. The leaps they take are enormous, as well as the height to which they jump.

The Crows are very much attached to these reptiles, and feed almost entirely on them whilst they continue about the place, as do also the Brahmanee kites, and other birds, as well as snakes. When these last seize a frog, it struggles most violently, and makes a loud and extraordinary noise for help. The aroma from a dead Frog, is most exceedingly unpleasant, and extends to a very long distance. Natives have an idea, that in one night the brown Frog turns green, the same as they assert that the tree Frog is born from the leaves of trees.

The brown Well Frog, is hardly inferior in size to the Bull Frog, and is esteemed very useful in keeping the water pure in wells, in each of which one of them is usually found. They are considered very good eating, but there are few natives who will permit their destruction.

One small brown Frog has a very bad character, as it is asserted that should it jump upon a child, it will cause it to become ricketty. The fat of the Frog, rubbed over the hand, is said to be a preservative against burning, and it is asserted, that any part of the body thus protected, may with impunity be touched with a red hot iron.

The active and pretty little Tree Frog, *Hyla leucomystax*, is sometimes seen inside houses, most frequently in the bath rooms. Out of doors, it is most commonly found under the leaves of plantain trees. It is very active, and as it has suckers at the under surface of each toe, it can attach itself to the wall, to wood, or even to glass.

CHAPTER XV.

FISH.

Numerous fish in Cochin State—Fishermen—Modes of fishing—by nets—Hooks and Lines—Trolling—Shooting—Labyrinths—Poison—Fish emblem of—Carnivorous fish—Mackerel Shoals, and mode of cure—Lancet fish—Climbing perch—Walking fish—Legend of fish—Tame ones in river—Sardines—Sharks—Saw fish, its extraordinary eye—accidents from fish—Economic aspect of Indian fisheries.

THE Fish which find their homes in the ocean that bounds the Cochin State, as well as those which populate the enormous expanse of Backwater running parrallel to its shores, and those inhabiting its numerous rivers and tanks, afford objects of extreme interest, to several classes of persons. To the Fishermen by the employment they give him, the Community in the food they supply, the Merchants for the Fish oil obtained, the Shopkeepers for the salted provisions procured from them, and the Naturalist for the variety and interest of the numerous families, composing this tribe. Whilst the Artist values them, for their beautiful and ever varying tints, and the Medical man is interested, in ascertaining the effects of a fish diet, upon the health of the general population.

The number and variety of forms which exist, the beauty of some species, the extraordinary habits of others, render fish one of the most interesting divisions of the animal kingdom, perhaps enhanced by the difficulty in ascertaining their individual peculiarities.

Fish are generally considered cold blooded animals, but this must be admitted with a reservation, as for instance, some species can reside in hot springs, whilst in Northern Europe, they have been found apparently quite frozen, and resuscitated by thawing. As a rule it appears probable, that those tribes which swim near the surface in the Tropics, such as the Mackerel and other allied species, have a high standard of respiration, and a low degree of muscular irritability, whilst having a great necessity for oxygen, they die almost as soon as removed from their native element, and taint almost immediately after death. Those tribes which live in deep water, have a low standard of respiration, a high degree of muscular irritability, a less necessity for oxygen, live long after their removal from water, and remain fresh some time subsequent to their demise.

The castes of natives fishing along the sea coast, besides the Christians are the *Arrians* and the *Mucuas*, Mal., who have always been considered inferior races and as such were in former times precluded from travelling along the public roads, and obliged to keep to the sea coast. When the Portuguese power first became predominant in the East, the Romish Missionaries particularly turned their attention to the conversion of these poor degraded Fishermen, and at the present time, the majority of them acknowledge the Roman Catholic religion. It should be mentioned that by becoming Christians, they were elevated in the social scale, and that by relapsing into heathenism they again become outcastes. Formerly on the death of a prince of Malabar, all fishing was temporarily prohibited, and only renewed after three days, when the spirit of the departed, was supposed to have had time to choose its own future abode without molestation, and this law is not yet abrogated.

The modes of fishing, vary according to the seasons of the year, and may be divided into those employed in the deep sea, along the coast, and in the river and Backwater, these again may be subdivided, into several different methods, a short description of some of which, may be deemed interesting.

At some periods of the year, boats leave for the deep sea fishing, about four o'clock in the afternoon, and having remained out all night, may be seen returning with their captures, at about 7 o'clock the following morning, when the purchasers meet them as they land. At other seasons, they leave at daybreak, and return about 4 in the afternoon, and sell their cargo on coming to shore, either in lots or as a whole. Should the weather appear stormy, no boats go out to sea, and fishing with nets, excepting in the river, or backwater, is unknown, consequently, the loss of fishing vessels, with all hands on board, is of very rare occurrence.

Nets are generally made of cotton thread, and when the large wall nets are employed, they are as a rule the joint property of several persons. Meshes of three sizes are used, according to the class, or rather the power of the fish it is intended to capture. One share, which is a distinct piece of netting, and usually belongs to one person, is about five yards square : and a large one sometimes consists of about forty of these pieces, fastened together. These wall nets, are employed for catching large fish, and also shoals of small ones. The larger ropes, are invariably made of coir.

The Mackerel net is generally a single wall net, about one hundred yards long, by eighteen feet deep, floated by hollow cocoanut shells at the top, and weighted below with stones. When a shoal of Mackerel is perceived, a heavy stone is affixed to one end of the net, which is thrown into the sea, and the boat to which the other end is attached, is rowed quickly round the shoal.

This same species of net, about half a mile in length, is also occasionally employed when shoals of fish come near the shore, one end is kept on shore, and the other carried round them, and thus enclosed they are dragged to land.

When round nets are required, two boats must be used. In the centre of the net is a long funnel, otherwise it is much the same as that employed in taking Mackerel. The funnel is first thrown into the sea, and then the two boats to each of which one end of the net is attached, are rowed rapidly through the shoals.

Cast nets are employed from the shore, by a number of fishermen, who station themselves either in the early morning, or in the afternoon, along the coast from 50 to 100 yards apart. They keep a careful watch on the water, and on perceiving a fish rise sufficiently near the land, rush down and attempt to throw their nets over it. This is not done as in Europe, by twisting the net round and round the head, until it has acquired the necessary impetus, and then throwing it : but by the person twirling himself, and the net, round and round, at the same time, and then casting it ; he not unfrequently gets knocked over by a wave. When fish are caught, they are buried in the sand, to prevent their tainting.

In the wide inland rivers, fishermen employ cast nets, in the following manner. Each man is in a boat, which is propelled by a boy, with a bamboo. The fisherman has a cast net, and a small empty cocoanut shell, this last he throws into the river, about twenty yards before the boat, and it comes down with a splash, said to be done to scare away the Crocodiles. As the boat approaches the place where the cocoanut shell was thrown, the man casts his net around the spot. This method is only for obtaining small fish, and as many as fifteen boats at a time, are to be seen thus employed in one place, one following the other in rapid succession, some trying the centre, others the sides of the river.

Double rows of long bamboos, firmly fixed in the mud, are placed at intervals across the Backwater, and on these nets are fixed at the flood tide, so that fish which have entered, are unable to return to the sea. Numbers of very large ones, are occasionally captured in this way.

A species of Chinese nets, are used along the river's banks, they are about 16 feet square, suspended by bamboos from each corner, and let down like buckets into the water, and then after a few minutes drawn up again ; a piece of string to which is attached portions of the white leaves of the cocoanut trees, is tied at short intervals along the ebb side of the net, which effectually prevents fish from going that way.

As this mode of fishing is continued all through the monsoon, (excepting on very stormy days,) it affords an excellent criterion, of the tribes and species to be found in the rainy months, and renders Cochin the best place along the Western Coast, for making observations on this subject : owing to this, the Icthyologist can continue his enquiries, (with occasional intervals,) during the boisterous, as well as the quiet months of the year, although the sea netting may be quite suspended. Fish thus caught, are sold at the nets.

A plan somewhat analogous, is employed on a small scale for catching crabs, a net three feet square, is supported at the four corners, by two pieces of stick, fastened crosswise : from the centre of these sticks where they cross, is a string to pull it up by, or let it down, and a piece of meat is tied to the middle of the net, inside. This is let down from a wharf, left under water for a few minutes, and then pulled up again, and crabs coming to feed, are thus caught.

Fishing with a line, is seldom attempted in the deep sea, excepting for sharks, rays, and other large fish. The hooks employed are of two descriptions, the roughest although perhaps the strongest, being of Native manufacture, the others are of English make, denominated China hooks.

The hook is fastened to a species of fibre, called *Thumboo,* said to be derived from a sea weed, but more probably from one of the species of palms, it takes the place of the silk worm gut in Europe. For very large fish, a brass wire is attached to the hook; on one of these two substances, the lead for sinking the bait is placed.

The lines are either hemp, cotton, or the fibre of the Talipot Palm, *Caryota urens,* which is obtained by maceration. But although very strong, these lines, are if a little dry, apt to snap, when suddenly bent. In Europe, they are called "Indian gut."

Trolling from the shore, at the river's mouth, is only carried on of a morning, or evening, during the winter months of the year, when the sea is smooth. The line is from 80 to 100 yards in length, and held wound round the left hand, the hook is fastened to the line by a brass wire, and the bait is a live fish. The fishermen after giving the line an impetus by twirling it round and round his head, throws it with great precision, from 50 to 60 yards. A man is always close by, with a cast net, catching baits, which he sells for one quarter of an anna each. This mode of fishing, is very exciting sport, but is very uncertain in its results, and therefore usually carried on by coolies, either before their day's work has commenced, or after its termination.

Fishing with a bait, continues all day long in Cochin during the monsoon months, when work is almost at a stand still, and five or six persons may be perceived at each jetty, busily engaged in this occupation. The Bagrus tribe is then plentiful, and as it bites readily, large numbers are captured.

Fishing in small boats, appears at times to be a dangerous occupation, the small canoe only steadied by the paddle of one man seated in it, looks as if it must every minute be swamped. Very large fish are sometimes captured in this way, should one be hooked too large for the Fisherman to manage, the man in the next boat comes to his assistance, and receives a quarter of the fish for his trouble.

This is carried on all through the year, and the size of some of the *Bagri* thus caught is enormous.

Night and day lines, are not much in vogue, which is rather strange, as the returns would probably be great. Fly fishing in the rivers of Cochin, does not afford large sport ; but small fish may be caught in numbers, and it is certainly a pleasure again to cast an English fly, and land a fish, however small the prize may be.

Fish are shot in various ways, by a Chittagong bamboo, which is a hollow tube, down which the arrow is propelled by the marksman's mouth. This mode is sometimes very remunerative, and is followed by persons who quietly sneak along the shores, either of sluggish streams, or of the Backwater, sometimes they climb up into trees, and there await a good shot. Or during the monsoon, the sportsman quietly seats himself near some narrow channel, that passes from one wide piece of water into another and watches for his prey.

Other Fishermen shoot with bows and arrows, and again others with cross bows, the iron arrow or bolt of which, is attached by a line to the bow, to prevent its being lost.

But netting fish, catching them with hooks, or shooting them with arrows, are not the only means employed for their capture. Bamboo labyrinths, bamboo baskets, and even men's hands alone, are called into use.

Persons fish for crabs* in shallow brackish water, provided with baskets like those employed in Europe for catching eels, but open at both ends. The Fishermen walk about in the mud, and when they feel a fish move, endeavour to cover it with the larger end of the basket, which is forced down some distance into the mud, and the hand is then passed downwards through the upper extremity, and the fish taken out.

Another plan of catching them by the hand, is by having two lines to which white cocoanut leaves are attached, tied to the Fisherman's two great toes, from which they diverge: the other end of each, being held by another man a good way off, and some distance

* As the Zoological portion of this work, is intended more for popular reading, than as a scientific treatise, the manner of catching crustaceæ, has been placed in the chapter on Fish, and amongst the various methods of fishing, instead of amongst the radiatæ.

apart. On these lines being shaken, the fish become frightened, and strange as it may appear, cluster for protection around the man's feet, who is able to stoop down, and catch them with his hands, by watching his opportunity.

Bamboo labyrinths are common all along the backwater, in which a good many fish, especially eels, and crabs, are captured. These labyrinths are formed of a screen of split bamboos, passing perpendicularly out of the water, and leading into a larger baited chamber. A dead cat is often employed as a bait for crabs, a string is attached to its body, and after it has been in the water some days, it is pulled up with these crustaceæ adherent to it. Persons are often surprized at crabs being considered unwholesome, but their astonishment would cease, if they were aware what extremely unclean feeders they are.

Fish are obtained from the inland rivers by poisoning them, but this can only be done when the water is low: a dam is thrown across a certain portion, and the poison placed within it. It generally consists of Cocculus Indicus pounded with rice: croton oil seeds, &c. The fish when captured, are either sent away for sale, or dried and then sold.

A fish is an emblem of Vishnu, in commemoration of his first incarnation. It is also one of the symbols of the Kings of Madura, or as they were formerly called Kings of Pandia, whose standard was called a *Meen kodah*, or Fish standard, which fact alone would almost prove them to be Hindus, and Vishnuites. The fish is also found on Buddhist seals. As these kings exacted tribute from the ancient Travancore Rajahs, many cash with fish on them are found in that State, and even as far north as Cochin, although it would puzzle a very good Icthyologist, to decide to which family they belong.

The tribes of fish caught during the South West Monsoon, in the Cochin river, depend upon the amount of the freshes, and the consequent saltness, or the reverse, of the water. Thus if the estuary is very fresh, fish are few in number, for instance on July 23rd, 1862, the fishermen refused, even to try their nets. The most prevalent species at this period, are the bagri, serrani, and white bait, whilst the Hemiramphus becomes very rare.

The Epicure would not regard the finny tribes of Cochin, as of superior quality. They have at times a muddy taste, there being no rocks in the ocean, or backwater around, and a great paucity of sea weed, but the mud bottom of the sea, and the Narrikal mud bank, within a few miles, appear to be good feeding and breeding places. Higher up the coast, where smaller rivers open into the sea, and there is therefore not such an accumulation of mud, whilst the shores are rocky, the fish are far superior in flavour.

It appears that owing to the smoothness of the sea about the Narrikal mud bank, and the great width of the backwater, fish proceed there to spawn: hence the roe for which Cochin is famous, and which is generally very plentiful, although scarce on other parts of the coast.

As is the case in all divisions of Zoology, those tribes which voraciously prey upon their neighbours, such as the sharks, and perches, are more numerous in India than the more peaceful tribes, such as the mackerel, sardine, &c., but of course the individual numbers of the last, are much the greatest.

It is remarkable that many fish are prevalent during the whole year, which are generally said to feed on sea weeds, and around rocks; this cannot however be invariably the case, as such places and food are unattainable around Cochin.

The Perches both in the sea and the backwater, form a very numerous group, some few families are also found in the rivers, tanks, and swampy places. The finest of them is called the Soldier fish, from its bright red colour, *Holocentrus ruber*, (*Chemboollay*, Mal.) it grows to about a foot and a half in length, and is esteemed good eating, although seldom procurable, until the South West Monsoon has commenced, when it becomes plentiful. Other perches of great variety are found, but the number is much too large for enumeration, they are of every shade, from a bright golden, to a dull brown: some spotted, others striped with gold, and again others plain.

The *Ambassis* genus, are found in all the backwaters, and rivers, beyond the influence of the tides, and even in the ponds. These diaphanous fishes, are very numerous, and though it is said that in the East they are made into anchovies, such does not hold good in

Malabar. They are very bony, but are eaten by the Natives. There are several species, if a slight variety in the number of the fin rays may be taken as a distinctive mark.

Amongst the curious fishes, may be placed the *Nandus marmoratus*, C. V. which has an olive green body, marbled over with brown, and fins also streaked with the same colour. It has a brassy reflection, when fresh. Its lateral line is interrupted in the posterior third. Its long protrusible mouth, does not add to its beauty, but no doubt is very serviceable in catching its prey.

One of the prettiest fishes, although rarely found, is a small yellow *Upeneus*, with longitudinal gold and chesnut stripes. The *Mullus* family is interesting on account of the great esteem in which one of the species belonging to it was held by Epicures of ancient Rome. Thus a fish of six pound's weight, is said to have been worth an amount equivalent, to £48 sterling, a large one as much as £64, whilst on one occasion £240 were given for three large ones.

Of the Maigre family, the *Sciœnidœ* are common, both in the fresh backwater, and in the sea. The *Otolithus*, and *Corvina* generœ, have several species along the coast, and a beautiful *Umbrina* is also found, but as they are rarely eaten by Europeans, further notice of them is unnecessary.

There are numerous species of *Pristipoma*, and *Scolopsides*, whilst some very interesting ones are found amongst the Sciœnidœ, in the fresh and backwaters. A species of *Etroplus*, of a deep green colour, with six vertical deep green bands, and an inky black base to its ventral extremity, is found to above nine inches in length. This species may be the *Etroplus maculatus*, C. V. which also exists in the same localities, but does not appear to grow to the same length, and the colouration is a little different, but in both, the lateral line is absent in the posterior half of the body.

The colours of living fish, cannot be accurately determined by the examination of dead, or dried specimens, the latter invariably change, as also do fresh fish, kept sodden in water.*

* It should be stated, that preserved specimens of every species of fish here mentioned, besides many others, are kept for transmission to Europe, by an early opportunity; when the new species, several of which are included amongst them, may be named.

The beautiful little *Etroplus Coruchi,* C. V. (*Pulluttay meen,* Mal.) which rarely exceeds three inches in length, is very common in every little stream of water, and even in the mud of the paddy fields. Its general colour is yellow, with 17 horizontal lines, of bright golden spots, along its back and sides. The fins are stained with black, and some black blotches are seen along the sides. This small, pretty, but pugnacious animal, keeps amongst plants, which grow in tanks and streams. It avoids nets, by diving down into the mud, but may be easily taken by ground fishing. It defends its eggs, and drives off all intruders, but if several are placed together in an aquarium, they seem never tired of fighting.

There are several genera, and species of the scaly finned family, they appear most common during the South West Monsoon, but are on the whole less numerous, than on the Eastern coast. One bat species, *Platax vespertilio,* C.V., which is frequently found on the Eastern coast, as far as Ceylon, does not appear to have extended its range to Cochin.

The Chœtodons, are not very plentiful, but several species of them are found, amongst which is one of a lavender colour. They are rarely above four inches in length, and are never eaten by Europeans. With the South West Monsoon, a beautiful little species comes into the river rather abundantly. Its general colour is grey, one long white line passes completely around it behind the eye, and two others in front of it. The tail is of a scarlet colour, excepting the last half, which is snow white. The posterior part of the dorsal fin is edged with white, having a red border on each side. The prettiest species is an elegant little Coachman, *Heniochus macrolepidotus,* C.V. about two inches long, of a pearly white colour, dashed with lavender, and two wide dark purple ventral bands. Its compressed oval form, and bright appearance, gives it much the resemblance of a pretty butterfly. Its third dorsal ray, is extended to about the same length as its body, which has obtained for this genus the designation of the coachman, they are rare at all times, but particularly so during the dry hot weather.

The Mackerel family, *Scomberidæ,* are extremely numerous. Amongst them are some which are very highly esteemed. The Indian mackerel, *Scomber karagurta,* C. V. (*Ila,* Mal.) is very abundant along the Western, and Southern parts of India, as well as around Ceylon, but appears not to be found on the Eastern Coast. It rarely exceeds ten or eleven inches in length, and appears to be usually of the same size. It is most common in April and May, and is very excellent eating, the flavour being the same as in the European species, S. Scomber. Natives recognize two sorts, one being smaller than the other but with a larger eye, this they call the *Cunny ila*, Mal. It does not venture within two miles of the shore, or into the backwater. During the hot weather, great exertions are made to salt this species of mackerel, and from 20 to 50,000 of them, are frequently landed daily at Vypeen, where the salting process is carried on, either by the natives, or by persons who come over from Ceylon for that purpose, as well as to assist in capturing them.

The first process consists in a cooly making one cut with a sharp knife along the back bone, from the head to the tail, and then a second down its ventral surface, exposing the intestines. It is then thrown over to a woman, who having removed its inside, tosses it into a basket with two handles, which when half full, is carried by two men to the sea shore, where the fish are washed without being removed. When clean, they are thrown on some leaves, and the salting commences. Women and children, rapidly put some black salt into each cut, and throw the fish into a boat close beside them, (on the shore,) in which there is brine, there they remain for a few hours, and are subsequently spread out in the sun, dried and packed in square bundles, of 1000 each, and usually sold for export to Columbo.

The Seir Fish, or Indian Salmon, *Cybium*, abound off Cochin, and have at least four varieties. They grow to a large size; most of them are captured from October through the cold months. The Fishermen denominate the four sorts according to their size and shape. The largest is called *Arrakeeah*, and is said to grow to four feet or even more in length. The second is the *Varee meen*, it is broader than the first and does not exceed three feet in length. The third is the *Chumbum* which is never above two feet long, and the smallest the *Poodtha Chumbum* is rather less. They are commonly said to be the best of Indian fishes, but although good, a large common mullet, is in no wise its inferior, and perhaps might even claim superiority.

The Scad or Horse Mackerel, *Caranx*, is rare on the Western Coast, but amongst the shoals on the Eastern side of the Peninsular, *Mr. Jerdon* mentions, having procured at least 23 species.

The Pomfret of both varieties is found; the white, *Stromateus candidus*, C. V. (*Vella Arwoolee*, Mal.) and the black, *S. Niger*, C. V. (*Kar Arwoolee*, Mal.) The first is the most numerous, and held in the greatest estimation for eating, it is like a small turbot, but of more delicate flavour, occasionally the latter comes in large quantities. They are most commonly found during the South West Monsoon, but may also be procured in the succeeding months.

Amongst the ribbon shaped fishes, Tœnidœ, two species of hair-tail, *Trichiurus naumela*, C. V. and *T. savala*, are exceedingly common, and much esteemed by the natives for food.

The Lancet Fish family, *Theutyes*, has one species of Acanthurus, which is not uncommon. It is rarely above five inches long, and of a flat oval form. Its general colour is a dull brown, with deep brown longitudinal stripes, having bluish margins. At the side of its tail, is a lancet shaped spine, capable of being either elevated or depressed, within a kind of yellow sheaf. When irritated, it can inflict a severe wound, by striking sideways with its tail, and hitting a person with this little weapon. There is a *Siganus* and other armed fish, which will be subsequently mentioned.

The family of fish having dilated and hollowed superior pharyngeal bones, peculiar to tropical countries, are well represented. The most extraordinary, although generally speaking true accounts of this tribe which have been given to the world, have been but too commonly treated as subjects for ridicule, or incredulity, it will therefore demand more space, than would otherwise be necessary. They are able to remain from a few hours, to above a day, out of fresh water, to live in the mud, and crawl over dry land, therefore their apparently miraculous presence, in newly formed ponds of water, during the Monsoon, has given rise to the belief, that they must have fallen from the sky.

Perhaps the most extraordinary of these is the climbing Perch, *Anabas Scandens*, Daldorf, (*Kurroopoo*, Mal.) also denominated, Panieri, or climber of Palmira trees, by the Tamuls, although there is no such distinctive term in Malayalim, Lieut. Daldorf mentions having witnessed one of them, five feet from the ground; and as it is well known, that the leaves of Palmira trees come down close to their roots, it is not impossible that it might have climbed up there, provided its walking, and leaping powers, were proved.

Having procured some living specimens from a tank, they were placed upon the ground, and they certainly progressed for some distance, this they effected in two different modes, either by lying on their sides, flapping their tails, and moving their pectoral fins, in fact by almost gliding along; or in another way, which was still more curious, and much more dignified, principally managed, by the aid of the pectoral fins, which were moved like wrists, one being first advanced, and then the other, whilst progression was assisted by the caudal fin.

There is scarcely a fisherman, or even a Native, who during the Monsoon time, has not seen the climbing Perch proceeding in large numbers, from one tank to another. To aid him whilst on land, his pharynx is hollowed, and possesses a spongy bone, in which water is carried, with which he moistens his fins and gills. Having personally tried to ascertain the length of time, this fish can in the hot weather live out of water, from 24 to 26 hours, appears to be the maximum.

Having thus shown its powers of progression, and that it can live out of water, the next question is, whether it is capable of leaping. Its spinous gill lids, have been considered to be the instruments, with which it holds on when climbing up a tree, and certainly they are very sharp: its scales even, are all very rough, and it appears able to elevate them at pleasure, whilst its spinous fin rays, renders it a very unpleasant fish to lay hold of. Nevertheless without denying its climbing propensities, or its holding on by its gill fins, until it gets higher up, such certainly appears doubtful. A Native suggested, that perhaps a kite might have dropped the fish into the position in which it was seen by Daldorf. But it is known that a climbing Perch can jump, and its Tamul name is a curious, and probably, an expressive one.

It is impossible to keep this fish in a vivarium, unless there be a cover on the top, or the water is a long distance from the glass: one which was a foot in height could never keep them in.

This fish has an interrupted lateral line, its colour is dark green, and some have a spot near the side of the tail, only perceptible when in the water: others are barred transversely, and they do not appear to be the same species.

As the Monsoon sets in, the *Anabas Scandens*, and the *Ophicephalus*, are found in every place, where there is water, they appear generally to creep over land, from the full stocked tanks, to those newly created by the fall of rain.

There are several species of *Ophicephali*, (*Verrarl*, Mal.) which might well be termed walking fish, they have also labyrinths in their pharynx, but not of nearly so complicated a description, as in the genus last mentioned. The largest, *O. striatus*, Bloch., grows to nearly 3 feet in length, and is perhaps the most esteemed of all fresh water fishes inland. For the greater the distance from the sea coast the more indigestible the fish become, with the exception of those of this family.

This fish is of a lengthened form, and rather slimy, of a dusky greenish colour above, and white underneath, with stripes or spots: it will jump out of water, but by no means as high as the climbing perch. When on the ground, it never throws itself on its side, but remaining in the same position as when in its native element, helps itself along by means of its pectoral fins.

Further inland is another small species, *O. punctatus*, Bloch., which is said never to exceed 6 or 7 inches in length. It has two short cirri on its upper lip; their habits are similar. The most beautiful is the *O. marulius*, Buch., of a rifle green with orange stripes, and pearl white spots, it grows to a very large size. All this family may be at times seen in soft muddy places, where it would apparently be almost impossible, for a fish to remain, but the testimony of all classes of Natives, and also of some Europeans, afford reliable evidence, of these fish having been dug up alive. Personal observation cannot be brought forward to support this, but it is without doubt, a well authenticated fact.

The Mullets, *Mugilidæ*, are the most numerous of the larger fish, and certainly as good as any for eating. About the middle of October or commencement of November, they begin to swarm into the river, and backwater to deposit their spawn. They are then to be procured in great numbers and their roe is much sought after. By February they begin to get scarce and by April are almost unprocurable.

Mullets take surprising leaps, and should one spring over a net, others follow. Whilst sleeping at night in a cabin boat, on the backwater, persons' nerves may be, and often are upset, by the grey Mullet, *Mugil Capito*, C. V., jumping in at the window, and coming in contact with the sleeper's face. Fish frequently jump into boats, and are thus captured.

Several species, of Mullets (*Cunnumboo*, Mal.) are distinguishable in Cochin, and some of them correspond with the *Mugil Capito, M. Chela*, or *M. Curtis*, of great Britain. Certainly a good Mullet, *M. Cephalotus*, C. V. (*Mahlah*, Mal.) yields the palm to no fish as far as its table properties are concerned, although abundant and wholesome, it is not esteemed so much as it deserves to be.

Amongst the small Eel shaped fishes, having very long projecting snouts, the *Mastacemblus Marmoratus*, C. V., is found inland, in large quantities.

The Goby family, or sea Gudgeons, *Gobiodæ*, are exceedingly numerous, not only in the backwater, but also in the tanks and rivers. First in the rivers come the Blennies, and one little tufted species, is by no means rare.

The true Gobies, which have been celebrated from the time of Aristotle, for building a nest, and watching their spawn, are very common, and grow to a great size. They are a curious genus, in that the ventral fins, which are distinct one from the other, in most fish, are joined together in the true Gobies, in the form of a rounded disc, or sucker, the use of which does not appear to be well known.

One small species of this family, *G. Viridipunctatus*, C. V., is occasionally taken. Its brown body, has numerous spots of a beautiful emerald green, dispersed over it. When young, these fish are without the spots, which are also lost when they are dried. There are several species of *Eleotris* in the sea, the backwaters, the rivers, and the tanks.

The Wrasse, or Rock fish family, called by Europeans, the "old wives of the sea," has its representatives: amongst them the genus of Julis, though small in size, holds a conspicuous place, on account of its beauty.

The pipe mouthed fish, *Fistulariæ*, are extremely curious in their appearance, and two species are occasionally obtained; they are called tobacco-pipe fish, from their jaws being elongated, and only opening at the extremity.

Amongst the most interesting fish, are those which are mostly inhabitants of fresh water, some of which in the beauty of their colours, vie with those from the sea. The *Systomus filamentosus*, V., when alive is white, when dead and preserved in the usual way, it becomes of a carmine colour.

A very pretty species of *Systomus*, exists in the rivers, it is generally about four inches long, with two tendrils on the upper jaw, the colour is dusky greenish black, sides and ventral surface whitish, black diffused spot on lateral line near the tail, caudal fin deeply lobed, its centre third of a deep scarlet, its posterior third deep black, and the other fins white. There are many other species in this family, but with neither beauty of colouring to bring them to notice, nor size sufficient to recommend them a place at the table of Europeans.

There are several species of *Barbus*, *Systomus*, and *Leuciscus*, &c., which are invariably to be found in all rivers and ponds.

At Erritara Carvee, nearly eight miles North East of Shallacoody, is an Umbalum, situated upon the river's bank, where the fish receive a supply of food, every week, and it is believed that whoever kills any, will certainly die within the year. There is a tradition that a Portuguese Priest ridiculed this idle legend, and started in a boat with the intention of catching some: after having vainly attempted to obtain the assistance of the boatmen, he fired his gun at one of the fish with fatal effect, and it instantly sank. He then directed his servant to dive down and bring up the game, but he declined: so the Priest went down himself, where according to the Native account, he found a lot of Demons, who however vanished when he made the sign of the cross. He then seized his prey, and ascended into the boat, but hardly had the fish touched its planks, when it miraculously disappeared. The Priest returned home and died in two days.

Setting tradition aside, the place is sufficiently remarkable, it is a deep river, about 500 yards wide, well wooded, and removed from houses, or dwellings, (no one resides in the Umbalum) and hundreds of carp flock up, to receive rice from the passer by. They vary in size, from three feet, to 8 inches in length, and are so tame, that they will take food from a person's hand. It is no use attempting to capture them with the hand, in some instances a finger may even be inserted in their mouths, (this tribe have no teeth,) but they cannot be held, as they are too slippery to drag out of the water. No assistance can be obtained from the boatmen, who are afraid of hurting them. It is said, that should any one visit the place with the intention of capturing them, he will see none, but personal experience does not carry out this theory. Some species brought from another place, but said to be the same, were the *Barbus Malabaricus*, Jerd.

A little Loach, *Cobitis rubripimus*, Jerd., may be seen in any irrigated paddy field, generally in company with some species of *Ophicephalus*, and the little *Etroplus coruchi.*

Amongst the Pike family, the genus *Belone*, (*Coplah*, Mal.) affords more than one example. Their jaws are extended into a long beak, their colours are bright green, white underneath, and a black spot on the tail. The species found in the rivers, is the *Belone Graii*, Sykes. (*Morrahloo*, Mal.) They are considered good eating by Natives, but not so by Europeans, on account of their bones. It is said that in whatever part of the world there are Jews, these fish are to be found.

A common little fish, is the *Hemiramphus*, (*Morrul*, Mal.) which much resembles a small Belone, and appears as if its upper jaw had been cut off, as the lower one extends far beyond it. It is rare during the South West Monsoon, at other periods very numerous. Of this family, there are several species, one of which is found in the fresh water. It is very highly esteemed for eating by the Natives.

The flying fish, *Exocetus nigripinnis*, C. V., is found in the deep sea and rarely comes near the land. It is curious to see them springing out of the water, apparently to escape from some unseen enemy. They do not appear exactly to fly, but jump and skim along, whilst their long pectoral fins remain moist: but as soon as they are dry, they again drop into the ocean; if a wave touches them, they seem able to skim further along. They jump to a great height, and frequently come on board large vessels. They are good eating.

In the family of *Siluridœ*, or Sheat fish, is found a species, which is greatly dreaded by the Natives. With something the appearance of an Eel, it has eight long cirri growing from round its mouth, which has sometimes caused it to be designated the cat fish. Its power of mischief exists in a very strong saw-like bony ray, situated in its pectoral fin, with which it strikes severely, inflicting a very jagged wound, believed by some to be poisonous, and by others to be very irritating, owing merely to its jagged nature. Its colour is black, it lives in the tanks and stagnant water, and is esteemed good eating, it is called the *Kahree meen*, Mal. *Silurus voalis* (?) Buch. Immediately after catching it the Natives break off its offensive spine.

Another species, *Silurus Malabaricus*, Bl., is also found farther inland, but is not so common, and its wound is not feared. Its colours are very much lighter, and its underneath surface of silvery white.

Another tribe of fish, which is nearly as much dreaded as the Siluridœ, is the *Bagri*, (*Cooree*, Mal.) which swarm not only in all the fresh water, but also in the backwater. Their pectoral spines inflict severe wounds. The species are very numerous, and some are of a large size, and frequently salted.

The Herring Family, *Clupeidœ*, yield some very important fish, requiring especial notice, which are apparently much more numerous than on the Eastern coast of India: still in Cochin, their prevalence during different years varies greatly. The oil Sardine, *Sardinella Neohowii*, (*Karlay*, Mal.) which not long since yielded 40,000 gallons of fish oil in twelve months, does not appear since then, to have come in any numbers. In another few months, shoals may possibly return even larger than any that have preceded them. Nothing appears certain in this family, as they are very capricious both in choosing and leaving localities. Another species is recognised, from its never being so fat as the oil sardine, and consequently useless for oil, it is called the *Cutthee karlay*, Mal.

An Anchovy, about 5½ inches long, *Engraulis albus*, C. V., comes in enormous quantities, and is caught even in the parallelogram nets at the mouth of the river. It is very good eating, but Indian ingenuity has not yet attempted preserving Anchovies, as is done in

Europe, for which purpose the Cochin would be as good as the Mediterranean.

There are many other genera of this vast family, that come in large quantities, and are extensively employed as food, but none appear to be preserved or salted.

The flat fish, or Flounder Family, Pleuronectidœ, are not numerous, still they are not unknown, whilst they are excellent eating.

There is a very curious fish the Remora or sucking fish, *Echeneis*, called the *Puttoo moday*, Mal., or "catching mouth," with reference to a sucker having 23 plates on the top of its head, whereby it holds on to any smooth object. It is usually found attached to the back of a shark, from whence it is said to extract its vital fluids: but it cannot be considered common.

In ancient times, its powers were considered very great, and at the battle of Actium, Antony's ship was said to have been held motionless by a large Remora. The sailors pulled, but the remorseless fish would not permit them to advance: other equally circumstantial accounts are in existence, but in the present age, persons are not credulous enough, to attribute so much power to a fish of about a foot in length.

The Eels do not appear to be rare anywhere, and some of them are very interesting. There is one species, *Dalophis Orientalis*, which is easily caught, and affords great amusement to boys, as if thrown on the moist sand, it buries itself, tail foremost, with the greatest rapidity. It is much more numerous a little to the South, than in Cochin.

In the backwater, canals, and other places, a large Eel, *anguilla*, is found, which does not quite agree with the recorded species. It is excellent eating. Whilst a deep brown coloured *Synbranchus*, blotched with black, and slightly tinged with greenish, exists in the Fort Ditch, and other places.

The sea Porcupines, *Tetraodons*, (*Kurramah cutchee*, Mal.) are very common, and may often be seen thrown up by the sea, and lying inflated on the shore: they are very tenacious of life, and are able to elevate little spines, all over their bodies at pleasure, they croak something like frogs. The natives occasionally eat them, but they often cause indigestion, whilst others call them sea frogs, and will not touch them, they are given in cases of consumption. Though much differing in appearance, still belonging to another division of the same family, is a class of fish, *Balistes*, with hard granulated skins, bright colours, and very extraordinary looking spines, or horns firmly attached to the body. In the *Triacanthus* (*Mootarree*, Mal.) one horn, extends upwards from the back of the head, and two downwards, in the position of the ventral fins. These fish are most common about the cold months of the year, and the termination of the South West Monsoon.

Passing onwards to the Sharks, and Rays, we find many varieties, of which curious tales are told, the appearance of some of them is very extraordinary; whilst the uses they are put to, are varied, and the fear they instil into the fishermen, is very great.

There are several species of Dog fishes, *Scylliidœ*, and Sharks, *Carcharidœ*, (*Choorawoo*, Mal.,) which destroy fish, and tear the nets, should they become entangled in them; the large species is very common, and will even carry off men. A man eating shark is of very rare occurrence. For several years, only one instance has occurred of a person being taken by a shark near Cochin.

A fisherman who had been out all night, in January 1862, wished for some toddy, but as the remainder of the men objected to landing, it was agreed that he should swim ashore, obtain what he required, and then return to the boat. But he had scarcely left the boat's side, when a large white shark was seen in pursuit: it seized the unfortunate man almost immediately, and bit a piece out of him, but dropping this, it turned again upon its back, and carried off its prey, who was never seen again.

The most frequent accidents arising from sharks, occur either after the fish has been hooked, and brought into the boat, or else when it has become entangled in a net, and the Fishermen either attempt to seize it, or to cut the meshes to let it go.

Sharks are generally caught by lines and hooks, and take a bait, if their guide is not with them, which is a variety of the Pilot Fish, *Naucrates ductor*, that appears never to lose sight of its friend the shark. It has been observed to keep it from swallowing a bait, and even to hold on by its tail, after it has been hooked, to prevent its being drawn out of the water. The ancients believed that the pilot fish, went with their vessels, until the desired haven was reached, when it left them. Its darkly striped sides, makes it easily perceived from the deck of a vessel, and when captured, it is good eating, as it belongs to the Mackerel family.

A shark is rather a valuable acquisition, its flesh is esteemed very nutritive, and though rarely eaten fresh, it is salted in pieces, and then is believed to be very good, especially for women who have young infants. Its native name, of *Pāl Soora*, Mal., or milk producing, refers to the powers attributed to it. The hammer headed shark, grows to 12 feet, or even more in length,* it is not esteemed so nourishing, as the other species.

The Saw Fish, *Pristis semi sagittatus*, Shaw., is certainly more to be dreaded than the sharks, and accidents are more commonly seen caused by its snout, which is extended like a sword, and toothed like a large saw; a very formidable weapon of offence, and one it is very fond of making use of. The eye is very curiously formed, the yellowish coloured iris, which has a very fine black margin, instead of possessing a circular hole in its centre, commonly called the pupil, may be said to be entire, and an oval flap made of its upper and lower half. These flaps appear to be easily raised, depressed, or expanded, thus partially or completely excluding light as required. The habits of this fish are too little known, for any assertion to be made regarding the use of this peculiar iris, but as neither eyelids nor nictitating membranes could act owing to external pressure under water, analogy would favour the belief, that this fish traverses some peculiarly bright spaces, where the light would be too strong for its optical apparatus, and that consequently it has the power of excluding as much of it as it pleases, by means of these curtains formed of the iris. The lens is peculiarly soft. Their flesh is equally good with the sharks. The fins of all these species, are salted, and generally sent to China. Their skins are used for sword belts, and rubbing down rough surfaces.

The Skates, *Raiaidæ*, are very numerous, and of great variety,

* The Natives give most exaggerated accounts of the size of these fish; the hammer headed shark, they say is often from 40 to 60 feet in length, and the white variety much larger, but they cannot catch them, owing to their enormous size!

both in colour and form. They are considered as nutritious as the sharks, all are used if captured in the Monsoon time by the fish oil manufacturers. A species of Eagle Ray, *Myliobatidæ*, also known as a Whip Ray, from its long tail, which is often three times the length of its body, is very common from October to February. It is generally perceived jumping, or as the Natives express it flying out of the sea, or Backwater, at which period, they are believed to be spawning. Their large size renders them conspicuous objects, even as far as a distance of three miles. When jumping they turn round, and their white under surface, is more apparent than their darker backs, which in some are marked all over like the skin of a Cheetah.

Natives are from experience, very cautious in handling these fish, until quite dead. The spine on their tails are employed as weapons of either offence or defence, as the case may be. By twisting their tail around a person's hand, or arm, they inflict a most severe wound, by a dragging motion. In 1861 a man came to the Dispensary, with his right forearm mortified, from a wound of this description, and amputation was obliged to be resorted to.

One day on the backwater, a few miles from Cochin, an Eagle Ray nearly 6 feet in length, from the end of his tail to the tip of his nose, was seen gyrating about, close to the cabin boat. No difficulty was experienced in coming up to him, but the question then arose, whether he was only playing a trick to induce some unwary individual to try and capture him, and then after giving him a wound with its tail, to swim away triumphant. But accidents will happen, a boat hook was at hand, the prize was captured, its tail cut off, and its evil powers destroyed.

This tail has in it an evident power of evil, whilst the fish is alive, but after its death, it is supposed to have equally excellent virtues. The fortunate possessor of it, being effectually protected against charms, and able to face the evil eye with impunity.

There are many other species of Rays, one of which (*Therrundee*, Mal.,) would be exactly like a Bat, were its long tail removed, all appear aware of the possession of this powerful weapon, and Fishermen almost invariably cut it off, as soon as the Fish is caught, to prevent its injuring them.

Some species of Electric Rays, are found farther down the coast, but they do not appear to be captured at Cochin.

The Fisheries are now unrestricted, but in the time of the Dutch, every fisherman was either obliged to pay a certain amount, or give a proportion of his gains as a sort of royalty, to the officials of Cochin.

The foregoing glance at the enormous numbers, and varieties of fish, must give rise to the thought; what use are all these bountiful gifts of Providence turned to? Or are the Shark and the Perch allowed to prey upon their smaller neighbours, and the weaker to be destroyed by the stronger, whilst man is starving in the vicinity? It is unfortunately, but too evident, that year after year, the horrors of starvation are not unknown amongst the population, and a want of nutriment is of common occurrence. The Hindu of Bengal may exclaim, that those of his religion will not eat fish, but such is incorrect, in Malabar most of the twice born classes refuse to do so, none of the Sudras and those beneath them.

The reason why large quantities of salt fish are not exported from the Native States, is a question for the Politician to solve, but heavy taxes on salt, and enormous almost prohibitory duties, cannot conduce to the success of this trade. In Europe from very early ages fisheries were protected by legislative enactment, not so in the Native States of India, where neither protection, free trade, nor encouragement, is afforded the low caste fisherman, to enable him to extend his occupation, to the curing and exportation of fish.

CHAPTER XVI.

INVERTEBRATE ANIMALS.

Molluscs—Cuttle fish—Shells—Articulata—Insects and when found—Beetles—Rose Beetles—Cocoanut Beetles—Carpenter Bee—Wasps—Ants—Butterflies and moths—Mosquitoes—Fleas—Ant lions—Dragon flies—White Ants—Earwigs—Cockroaches—Mantis and St. Francis Xavier—Walking leaves—Walking sticks—Mole crickets and uses to which put—Locusts—Bugs—Cicadœ—Fish insects—Centipedes—Spiders—Scorpions—Crabs—Spider crabs—Cray fish—Hermit crabs—Sea Mantis.

The Molluscs have many representatives, inhabiting both the salt and the fresh water, the running streams, and the stagnant tanks, as well as the surface of the earth, although more sparingly. A certain deficiency in variety, is compensated for, by the enormous numbers of some of the existing species.

During the South West Monsoon, and subsequent to it, there are many long oval plates on the sea beach, which although fragile, are easily recognized as shells: being the internal, or dorsal plate, (gladius,) of the Cuttle fish, *Octopus*, which are thrown up by the violence of the winds and tides. They are so numerous, that they are collected for cleaning windows, and similar domestic purposes.

The common species, has a convex back, of a shield-like form, whilst the skin covering it is loose, and of a rich purplish brown, shot with other colours. It can apparently change its hue at pleasure, or through fear, when touched it frequently becomes of a silvery white. The shell of its back is shaped very much like a dog's tongue, and is from 4½ to 5 inches in length.

This most voracious Mollusc, has a head surrounded by eight arms, or appendages, of about equal length, all of which are furnished with suckers on their inner surface. Its mouth is armed with brown horny jaws, resembling a parrot's bill, excepting that the short mandible is the upper one: whilst round this organ are two rows of suckers. Its ink bag, from the contents of which, a rich tint of sepia may be procured, it employs to discolour the water around it when pursued. It swims with rapidity or crawls along the bed of the river, or sea, in search of crustaccea, or its finny prey.

Wonderful tales have been told of the enormous size to which this creature grows, navigators have asserted that they have seen it with arms sixty feet in length, with which it has embraced and dragged down passing boats, and one of them mentioned in Scandinavian legends, was able to lay hold of, and remove Islands!

Passing on to the gasteropods, we reach that beautiful division, which both charms the eye by the colouration and form of its shelly covering, and pleases the Epicure, by the delicacy of the food afforded by its tribes.

The family of *Muricidæ* are not well represented, as but two species are apparently found, and those only during the violence of the South West Monsoon. One is a spiny murex with a long beak, the other a frog shell, (*Ranella*, Lam.)

Along the shore as the tide recedes, are perceived many varieties of the Auger shell, (*Terebra*, Lam.) their colours varying, from pure white, to bluish purple, whilst some are striped, others plain.

The Cones are not common, occasionally a dead money cowry, *Cypræa moneta*, may be found on the shore, but it is not improbable that such may have been dropped there. But still as they form a large article of commerce in the neighbouring Maldives and Laccadives, they may not be merely visitors here. Cowries are not employed as small change for money in Cochin, as in the Deccan and other inland places, but occasionally a favourite bull may be perceived, with a string of them around his neck.

Amongst the Potamides, the *Terebralia telescopia*, is very common at the mouths of rivers, and within the influence of the tides. A number of specimens which were obtained from the canal during the hot month of November, and placed in an ant's nest were removed in the end of January, in the expectation that the animal substance would have been cleared out: but when they were put into a basin of water, preparatory to their being cleansed, after two or three hours the animals commenced emerging from the shells, as healthy as ever. No doubt they *hybernate,* if it may so be called, in the heat, and as in the ant's nest they had no means of subsisting, they retreated into their shells, which they firmly closed with the operculum at the external aperture, and waited for a damper state of the weather, and a time more congenial to their requirements. The little *Cerithidea obtura,* Lam., is seen lying in thousands along the muddy banks of the same places where the Potamides are found, these last are collected in great numbers, and burnt with other shells for lime.

A species of undescribed marsh snail is found on the coast, it is "a variety of the *Paludomus Parva,* of Edgar Layard, and differs from the Deccan and Bombay species." The little *Melania tuberculata,* is common in every stagnant piece of water. Two varieties of *Turritella* are exceedingly numerous on the sea shore, the one being light, (*T. imbricata,*) the other slate coloured.

Amongst the family of *Paludinidæ,* there are many known species, the river snail is very abundant: in localities not far removed from the sea, the light brown, *P. melanostoma,* Benson, is most prevalent, but inland the larger olive coloured and striped, *P. Bengaliensis,* appears to take its place. Together with this last, is an angulate variety, which is of rather a lighter colour, and has been obtained from Burmah and Bundelcund. These snails are employed as articles of food, by some of the lower classes.

Ampullariæ, or apple snails, are very abundant, and some of them grow to a very large size. The average diameter of the aperture of four of these taken from amongst a number collected for eating, was $1\frac{1}{2}$ by $\frac{4}{5}$ inches, whilst one of them, (*A. Malabarica,*) held $1\frac{3}{4}$ ounces of water. Natives assert that in the month of January very much larger specimens may be obtained.

Nerites or sea snails, and Trochi, are occasionally found on the shore, but are neither so common, nor so large, as further south where there are rocks. Of the Cup and Saucer Limpets, (*Calyptræidæ,*) there is one small species exceedingly numerous along the shore, as well as a Tooth shell, (*dentalium.*) There is one fresh water Nerite, (*Neritina crepidularia,* Lam.) which is common.

The Helicidœ, or Land Snails, said to exist wherever there are trees, is not unknown in Malabar, but it is most difficult to obtain fresh specimens. In the hot months, dead ones may be perceived under shrubs, and amongst bushes, but living ones are rarely to be found.

In tanks, the Pond Snail, (*Lymnœa lateola*, Lam.) is very common, as well as the little *Bithinia Travancorica*, and the *Planorbis Indicus*, Benson. On examining dried up tanks at the end of the cold season, as in March, numbers of specimens of the Planorbis are seen, in all of which the Mollusc is dead. The same observation holds good in respect to Ampullariœ, many dead shells of which are everywhere apparent in the scorched up paddy fields at this time, and when they are irrigated in January and February, enormous numbers of dead Ampullariœ and Palludinœ, float about in the water.

In the fresh water tanks, there are a great quantity of a bivalve, somewhat resembling a dark brown cockle, (*Cyrena*, Lam.) it grows to some size, and is employed for food, whilst its shells are burnt for lime. The *Corbicula striatabla*? Desh., is also found in the sandy inland rivers, in company with what appears to be the *Mya-radiatus*, Ch., as "in form it approaches that figure in Wood's Index." The fresh water mussel, which "has a salmon nacred shell, is apparently identical with the Chinese, *Unio consobrinus*, Lea." It is very numerous in ponds, and moist paddy fields, beyond the influence of the tides, but a long and patient search, has failed to detect pearls in them. It is esteemed as food, as is also a smaller variety, which usually inhabits the same, or contiguous localities. The *Cythereœ*, Lam., are much used for food, in spite of their size not being great: the rather ugly brown, *C. casta*, is generally the largest, but the *C. ovum*, Var., *C. meretrix*, Lam. Jun., and *C. fusca*, (?) are amongst the most common species. A beautiful bright blue green mussel, is found in the sea, both North and South of the Cochin state, and the pretty *Cultellus politus*, Wood., is occasionally thrown up by the waves.

Space will not permit the enumeration of the various shells procurable, even were such possible, but it must be observed, that enormous numbers of *Mytilidœ*, *Arcadœ*, *Cyprinidœ*, *Veneridœ*, and other bivalves, are collected on the sea beach, for the purpose of making chunam.

Oysters are exceedingly numerous, and are procured in large quantities by divers, in about ten feet water. They are very large, and at times unwholesome, occasionally little pearls are found in them. As there are no rocks to which they can attach themselves, they affix themselves to any object within reach, and may frequently be seen clinging to one another. Both the singular cock's comb Oyster, *Ostrea crista galli*, and the curious Anomia, are also found along the coast. The Pearl Oyster, *Meleagrina margaritiferœ*, is not found, but it might be worth while to try the experiment of importing it, as in such a locality as the Narrikal mud bank, it might possibly thrive.

The Articulata division of the animal kingdom, is very largely represented and is divisible into the true articulated animals, and the worms. The insect class claims much of the attention of the residents on the Malabar coast. Many of its tribes are gorgeously arrayed, and the brilliant colours of some of them as they flit about from bush to bush, give a charm to the scenery, which motionless objects could never afford. The Centipedes are dreaded, from their venomous bites; the Thysanoura, for the family of the fish insect which they contain, so destructive to clothes; the Suctorial tribe for the irritation caused by its fleas, the Beetles for the spoliation and consumption of trees, food, and clothing: the Orthoptera, for the disgusting cockroach, the still more frightful looking mole cricket, and the numerous locusts. The Hemiptera for its brilliant, but too odoriferous bugs; the Neuroptera for the white ants, the Hymenoptera, for its biting and stinging insects, and its numerous bees, and wasps: even the beautiful class of Lepidoptera, furnishes the moth, which is so destructive to clothes and furs: and the Diptera contains the unfortunately but too well known mosquitoe.

Insect life is comparatively deficient during the rains, but after their cessation, and the commencement of the cold weather, the varied food most suited to the tastes and habits of each, abounds; and insects come forth from their retreats, enlivening the scenery with their gorgeous colours, peopling the air, the water, the grass, the high lands, the plains, and the woods, furnishing their destroyers with food, and the lover of natural history, with most interesting and ever varying wonders.

Besides the seasons, other causes are in operation, regulating the distribution of insects; thus, amongst the Beetles,* the great mass of Cicindelidœ are found along the sea shore, and the Scorpion beetle, (*Anthia 6-guttata*) prolific on the mountainous ghauts, is unknown in the plains. This Geographical limitation, is perceptible in many other forms of insect life, and though many species have a most extensive range, there are others with a most circumscribed distribution.

The Beetles, *Coleopteræ,*† form a numerous family, not only on account of the number of their generœ, but also in respect of the infinity of individuals belonging to each. Some are employed as medicine, others as food, some are admired for their brilliant colours, and again others are dreaded for the mischief they occasion, especially amongst the Cocoanut trees, which form much of the wealth of this portion of India. Whilst some destroy the rice which is being kept for human food, or the Ginger in readiness for export to European markets, others again clear away dead animal substances, and thus prevent much of the unwholesome taint, which the atmosphere might receive therefrom. Cocoanut beetles vary in different localities. In Ceylon‡ the dreaded Cocoanut beetle, is of the Long Horned species, *Longicornia*, and in South Travancore a Longirostral *curculio*, is accused of causing the mischief, but in North Travancore and Cochin, the *Heliocopris midas*, has the credit of it. But it must be remembered, that some species attack the stem, and cause it to become rotten, whilst others attach themselves to the leaves, and others again fix themselves to the summit of the tree, and destroy the portion known as the cabbage.

Along the sea shore, a beautiful and most numerous species of *Cicindela*, (*C. Biramosa*, Fab.) may be found, its long legs assist it in jumping about most actively, whilst its bright purple under-

---

* A large collection of Coleopterœ, has been personally made in Malabar; amongst which are specimens, of every species named in these pages.

† Amongst much valuable information on insects, and shells, kindly furnished me by *W. H. Benson, Esq.*, and included in these pages, I am also indebted to him for the knowledge, that *Cajeput oil,* is the best preservative in collections of insects, against the depredations to which they are so subject, especially within the tropics. A few drops on a piece of sponge, renewed every three or four months, in each tray will be found to be most efficacious.

‡ Sir Emerson Tennent, Ceylon.

surface, greenish red chest, and reddish back with black markings, renders this little Tiger beetle, a prominent object on the sands of the sea shore.

The Scorpion beetle, *Anthia 6-guttata*, as it is generally called, on account of the venomous wounds it inflicts, is found on or near the Ghauts, but does not descend to the plains, it is also common on the table land of Mysore, the Deccan, and the Neilgherries, and is every where dreaded. It is about 1½ inches long, and black with six large white spots, which renders it a very conspicuous object. Several species of water beetles, *Dyticus*, and Whirligigs, *Gyrini*, are recognised by strangers, as closely resembling their European relatives.

Amongst the Serricornes, is the Rose beetle, *Sternocera Chrysis* which is found in great numbers, both on the Ghauts and inland. Its under surface is a glossy green, with wings either of a deep chestnut colour, or of a bluish green, whilst its head and chest are of a golden green, in little pits, even the Natives notice this beautiful beetle. When taken it tries to throw itself on the ground, where it is slow in its movements, although its flight is very rapid. Children affix a string round it, between the chest and the wing cases, which part it can close with great force, squeezing anything which may get there severely. The Hector butterfly, *Papilio Hector*, is also frequently fastened to a piece of cotton in a similar manner, and played with by children. The wing cases of this green species of beetle, are collected in large numbers, and sold in the Bazaar, either for exportation to Bombay, or for Native actors and mountebanks, to adorn their dresses. There is a beautiful green gold species, of the *Buprestis* family, *B. Chrysochora*, and another rare species of the same family, which has its wing cases and thorax pitted in lines, and coloured with green and gold. This has been also found at Saugor, but appears to be still unnamed.

A curious family, known as skip jacks, *Elateridæ*, furnish some very gorgeous beetles, and few in India can surpass the colourings, of the *Campsosternus Stephensii*, Hope. Its wing cases are of a golden green colour, whilst the thorax which is expanded transversely, is of a chesnut colour in the centre, and surrounded by a beautiful blue. This appears however to be very rare, the single specimen here referred to, was caught at Trichoor. A small but very beautiful little bronze coloured Elater has the credit of eating clothes, and evidence is strongly in favour of such being the case.

The Scarabeides, give some large species which are not looked upon with favour, owing to a great extent to their scavenger duties, and to the want of brilliancy in their colouring, but to this last, there are several exceptions ; one large black species, *Copris molossus*, has a horn on the summit of its head, and each of the front and external corners of its chest, are carried forward into overarching projections. Another nearly allied species of copris is smaller, and of a brown colour ; one very rough brown beetle, has wing cases like the bark of a tree, or perhaps something like a toad, it does not appear to have been described, but is to a certain extent similar to the *Trox granulatus*, which is found in the Doâb, and elsewhere. One small species of Scarabeus, is of a burnished blue green colour, *S. Onthrophagus*, it is mostly seen in sandy places. A Bull horned dung beetle Anthrophagus — ? is very beautiful, it has two horns in front, like those of a cow, and another small one in the centre, its head and chest are of a bronze green colour, whilst its wing cases are brown, it is 1½ inches long.

Amongst the stag beetles, is one enormous species of *Lucanus*, three and a half inches long, by one inch wide : its mandibles are large and strong, and it is altogether a formidable looking creature. Its colour is brown, and it is not uncommon about the monsoon time.

A very handsome Curculio is found, but more frequently in Travancore than in Cochin, its general colour is a reddish chestnut, with a heart shaped black mark in the centre of its wing coverings, which are sulcated, and one round black spot on either side : its under surface has also some chestnut markings. One deep purple colored Elephant beetle, so named from its prolonged snout, is rather handsome, it is the *Rhyncophorus ferruginœus*, Fab. An exceedingly curious beetle which is rather rare in Cochin, but common further south in Travancore, is a species of Paussus, *Platyrhopalus, Mellii* : each of its antennœ terminate in a flattened knob, giving it at the first glance the appearance of having two heads, its wing cases are of a deep brown colour. It emits a yellow fluid, having an offensive smell, that lasts for a day, and the stain of which should it get upon a person's hand, continues for nearly a week. It has a nasty squeak when captured. One placed with an Earwig in a glass, was devoured by the latter insect.

The Long horned beetles are very numerous, the finest is the *Lamia Roglii*, or a closely allied species, nearly 2 inches long, of a brownish colour, with four reddish white round spots on either wing case. Occasionally the hardened white cases looking like eggs, within which are the perfect insects, may be found inside soft trees. Some obligingly sent by Mr. Kohlhoff from Trichoor, measured $1\frac{8}{10} \times \frac{8}{10}$ inches. As a number of them often exist in the same tree, the timber is of course rendered comparatively useless. In some places it is said, that even after furniture has been made up, these unwelcome visitors are occasionally perceived, emerging from the interior.

The Cassididœ are numerously represented, one little species looking like burnished gold, may be seen of an evening in the cold months of the year. Another is of a light green and gold, whilst a third is smaller but of much the same colours, although differently marked, and there is also a large unnamed species, certainly bearing a strong resemblance to a miniature Tortoise. The Lady Birds, (*Coccinellœ*) cannot easily be mistaken, either in their appearance, or their smell, one lovely little species is of a beautiful blue green colour.

The Hymenopterœ, or membrane winged insects, call for especial attention, as the Hindus highly venerate the Bee, and some species of Ants, believing that the spirits by which they are animated, are favoured of God, and their intellects more developed, than in most other forms of insect life. Amongst this tribe are the Carpenter Bees, (*Xylocopa latipes,*) the deep blue species, is sacred to Vishnu, and there is another smaller one with a yellow thorax. Both are very destructive as they bore into wood. The Honey Bee which exists in large swarms in the jungles, furnishes large quantities of honey, and wax, not only to man, but to bears and other wild animals.

The solitary Wasp, is a frequent visitor into houses, where it forms its nest consisting of single mud cells, in which it deposits its eggs against the door posts, venetians, or any other suitable places; day after day, or every second or third morning, it increases the structure, by adding one more room within each of which it encloses a caterpillar. The Social Wasps as they are termed, construct a little delicate nest, as if made of paper, divided into cells, and hanging from the ceiling by a fine stalk.

Many and exceedingly interesting are the vast family of Ants, which come to the notice of the traveller, on account of the virulence of their attacks, to the resident for the damage they do to his goods and stores, and to the Sanitary Officer, supposing one to exist, for the service they render, by removing animal substances, which without their assistance, might remain to taint and poison the atmosphere, giving rise to various and fatal diseases.

The common Black Ant, *Formica compressa*, Fab., does not reside in this portion of India: but a species which is quite as virulent is found, viz., the Rufous tree ant, *Formica smaragdina*, nearly half an inch in length, it forms its nest of leaves, especially of the Mangoe, whilst they are growing on the trees. After having drawn them together, it unites them with a fine white web, and numbers of them reside within this nest. Should any person take hold of one of these domiciles, in mistake for a bird's nest, he will repent his capture, as the inmates at once sally forth, in defence of their dwelling, and woe to him whom many of them simultaneously attack.

A Gentleman wishing to examine one of these Ant's nests, directed his servants to procure one, and place it on his table. This was done, but on his return home, he found his visitors had become so irate, that no one could venture into the room, in which they were located. In the North West Provinces, these ants are employed to free houses of wasps which sometimes take up their abodes within, and they speedily destroy or drive them away, but subsequently become so irritated, that they attack all the inmates indiscriminately. They are by no means averse to animal food, and may frequently be perceived upon bamboo fences, catching small Black Ants, *Formica phyllophila*, Jerd., by their backs, and carrying them away for a meal. But in doing this, they are obliged to be careful, as should the intended prey exude a certain secretion, which it has the power of doing, it produces most injurious effects on them.

A minute ant, which is more frequently noticed by persons who rarely leave their houses, has a light buff coloured chest and legs, with a dark brown body, *Atta destructor*, Jerd. It clears away anything that comes in its way from crumbs of bread, to large pieces of flesh. In fine weather, in the cold months of the year, colonies of these ants, may be seen passing along the walls of houses. Soon after a number of neuters issue forth carrying eggs, and then some females, about three times the length of the neuters, show themselves. Each of the last appears to have a driver behind her, and other assistants on either side, to convey her to her new home. Should a female fall off the wall, a great commotion arises, and some of her personal attendants, immediately proceed in each direction, in search of her, and reconvey her into the proper road.

An ant having found a piece of bread, or any other substance, suitable to its requirements, and of a proper size, seizes it with its jaws and straightens it with its feet and antennœ. When progressing, the antennœ project on either side of the object, to steady it. When several ants are simultaneouly dragging or rolling an object along, some are frequently underneath it.

A very beautiful bright blue stinging fly, *Stilbum splendidum*, West. is seen in almost every house, it is very active, and is captured with difficulty. Sometimes it has a spot of scarlet on either side of its body, this may be a distinct species, and much resembles the *S. oculatum*, of Westwood.

The Lepidopterœ, are most common during the cold months of the year, and are of all colours from the most sober, to gorgeous red, blue, green, or golden. Their size varies, from six inches in the expanse of their wings, or even more, down to less than one third of an inch. Whilst in the Larva State, as Caterpillars, they do much damage, and the period passed in their transformations, varies with the family to which they belong, and the time of year in which such occurs.

The Butterflies are most gorgeous, and vie in beauty with the little Sun-birds, as both flit in the sunshine from tree to tree, and from one flower to another. One of the largest of the Diurnal Lepidopterœ, (*Ornithoptera darsius*, Gray.) appears during October, and is seen from the early morning, to the evenings, as late as February, or March. Its upper wings are of velvet black, its lower mostly satin yellow, whilst their expanse is rarely less than six inches. The beautiful black and red *Papilio Hector*, Linn., is never uncommon, and appears to take very long flights, being frequently perceived crossing the backwater, when at least a mile from land. Where all are more or less beautiful, and species so varied, it is difficult which to specify.

Moths are as numerous as Butterflies, and some most delicately marked and coloured species exist, specially amongst the Noctuœ, which are most easily obtained by spreading a sheet out of doors of an evening and placing a lamp in the centre of it. The white *Lithosia Sanguinolenta*, Donovan, with the front edge of its fore wings, of a crimson colour, and the posterior pair spotted with black, occasionally shows itself in considerable numbers. The *Taragama ganesa*, Lafeb., is curious on account of its dropping down as if dead, when touched.

The Gnat tribe is not wanting. Its representative the Mosquitoe, *Culex molestus*, which is never absent, becomes most common about a fortnight after the rains have set in. In the cold months, these pests are comparatively few, but as the hot season begins, they increase. To some persons their buzz as they fly around, is as irritating as their bite is to others. The Flea, *Pulex irritans*, becomes most common in the hot months of the year.

If a house is closed for any length of time, on being re-opened it is found swarming with these little pests. If a fowl is sick they attach themselves to it. Between its eye and bill, there are generally large communities, so closely packed that a pin cannot be inserted between them.

The second sub-class of insects *(Hemimetabola)* are very numerous, and some of them very attractive, owing either to their elegant or curious forms, whilst others on the contrary are very disgusting, not only in their appearance, but owing to the articles upon which they feed. Some again are very destructive, without external beauty to offer as an excuse.

The nerve winged insects *(Neuropterœ)* are exceedingly numerous. Amongst the *Tricopterœ* are an enormous number of the Phryganeidœ family, and their larvœ may be found enclosed in various materials, such as bits of stick and grass. Amongst the flat winged *(Planipedes)*, there is a very interesting species, of Ant Lion, *(Myrmeleo)* which is however by no means so common in the town of Cochin, as in many other localities, such as Trichoor. The little pits which they form in the sand, may be seen at the side of paths, and sandy spots of ground, and should an ant or other small insect fall in, it instantly disappears in a shower of sand, discharged at it by the hidden occupant of the trap. It is said that in order to obtain a satisfactory answer to any request, the internal administration of an ant Lion is a capital specific, given to the party from whom the benefit is required.

Amongst the net winged insects, (*Dictyotoptera*) are the beautiful Dragon Flies, *Libellulidæ*, they may be seen in all directions, of most varied and gorgeous hues, which however decrease in brilliancy after death. Some have crimson bodies, some blue, or yellow, and others orange, or yellow and blue, in fact there is scarcely any shade of colour of which they may not be perceived, whilst the size of the species, is very varied.* One of the most destructive of Indian insects, is the Termite, or White Ant, (*Curriaan*, or *cheddel*, Mal.) it is found in British Cochin, but owing to the sandy nature of the soil, its communities do not erect the large nests, which are common in the Native state and elsewhere. As they never work in the light, they prefer rooms which are kept dark, especially if the floors are made of mud, and they destroy everything they are capable of masticating. They construct their nests of mud prepared in their mouths, and covered with a sticky secretion: and form covered passages along which they reach any object they intend to consume; or else they glue boxes or other objects to the floor, and then commence their destruction. They ascend trees in the same manner, removing the bark, and destroying their vitality. It is not uncommon to see one of these raised galleries, commenced in the centre of a floor, and carried up as much as a foot from the ground, and then forsaken: it appears that they sometimes raise these, in hopes of finding some edible substance, but failing in doing so forsake them, and retire to some more favourable locality.

Although white ants may occasionally destroy boxes, and articles, left upon the floor, in one night, such is of rare occurrence, as they are generally at least twelve hours in glueing objects down, with their gummy fine sand, before they commence eating them: thus

* Dragon flies in confinement soon die. Col. Pringle states that a specific for this is to cut off their heads.

furniture which is moved once every 24 hours, will very seldom be injured. There are certain substances to which they have a great aversion, such as oils, indigo, teak, iron wood, and more especially the oil of the cashew nut.

On examining a living mangoe tree, the stem of which was covered by these termites, the first thing perceived, was their great dislike to light, which evidently induces them to form covered passages, leading to their works of depredation. The bark of the tree was bitten into grooved channels, and small galleries of a strong character, were evidently set apart, for the reception of the eggs. Many little black ants, *Formica Phyllophila*, Jerd., were inside these galleries, but what they were doing it was impossible to conjecture, the instant the eggs were exposed to the light, these little black attendants, seized them with avidity, and carried them away to darker places. Not far distant, were a number of large brown ants, *Ponira sculpta*, Jerd., apparently watching, but not for the purpose of affording protection, as immediately a termite appeared, they seized it, and carried it away for a meal.

The Orthopteræ are largely represented, first comes the Earwig, which in Malabar does not appear to have obtained the credit of taking up its abode in people's ears, but is said to eat bugs. The Cockroach, *Blatta Indica*, is of such an enormous size, and so common, that its presence cannot be concealed : it infests houses, and outbuildings, eats clothes, especially if made of woollen materials, or stiffened with rice conjee, as well as both the outside and inside of books, and almost any animal, and most vegetable substances. On the approach of damp weather, it flies about the rooms of an evening, and becomes very active. Its egg cases are found adherent to the panels of doors, window frames, tables, and in almost any situation, but they are frequently detected, and destroyed, by the wall lizards. The Cockroach forms a favourite repast of a large spider. It is looked upon with great disgust, as in common with some species of ants, it devours the face and extremities of the dead. The best animal to keep in the house for its destruction, is the mongoose.

Several species of Mantis, (*Mantinæ*) are found, their slow steady gait, and the praying attitude of their front limbs, gives them an appearance of solemnity, which has gained them the appellation of the

"Malabar Parsons," amongst Europeans, whilst the Natives for the same reason, designate them, *Parasu Rama's poochee*, or "Parasu Rama's insect."* It is believed to be always praying for rain to descend on the earth. It is most prevalent at the commencement of the monsoons. In the sixteenth century, when *St. Francis Xavier* came to Malabar, he is believed to have required a choir, to chant upon a certain occasion, and not having one, he asked a Mantis, (the species is not recorded,) to sing the praises of the Deity, on which without any hesitation, it broke forth into a beautiful canticle. After such an excellent character, it is unfortunate to be obliged to add, that its actions do not correspond with its devout attitudes, as it is of a very pugilistic disposition, and when two of them are placed opposite one another, they immediately engage in a most determined combat. One of the most curious species, (*Empusa Gongyloides*,) is of a dark brown colour, with a leaf like head, and a large expansion over each joint.

The beautifully delicate walking leaves, *Phylliidæ*, are not unfrequently seen, but are more abundant in the jungles, they are as elegant in their structure, and as captivating in appearance, as any of the tropical insects. The curious walking sticks, or spectres, *Phasminæ*, are also numerous. Natives most positively assert, that the first is merely a leaf, to which life has been imparted, and the latter a vivified piece of stick, and no arguments can convince them to the contrary.

Amongst the jumping, (saltatorial,) section of the orthopteræ, is the *Mole Cricket* (*Gryllotalpa.*) It is a constant visitor indoors, of an evening, more especially during the North East Monsoon and the cold months. This horribly ugly insect, was formerly employed for purposes of torture, as it has a strong saw like apparatus, on the outer surface of its front legs, to fit it for burrowing. Wherever it may be, it tries incessantly to work its way out, by means of these front legs. Should a person have refused to pay his taxes, one of these insects used to be placed on some tender part of the body, and covered by a cockle shell, which was kept in its place by a piece of cloth: the pain caused was so excessive, that this refined piece of

---

* See Chap. ii. origin of Malabar.

cruelty, was usually very efficacious. If it did not succeed, the insect was subsequently placed over *the eye!* It is denominated the *Poolla Poochee,* Mal., by the natives, and married women who are childless, are advised to swallow a dead mole cricket which they must first have killed themselves, and this recipe is vulgarly considered very efficacious. There are a large variety of House and Field crickets.

Locusts are much more common than Grasshoppers, *Grillinæ,* but the elegant green species of the latter is seen everywhere. Natives who keep birds, may often be observed in the early morning, hunting about in the grass, to find insects of these families, for tame Partridges, Mynahs, or Bulbuls, which they either carry with them, or else have running about near them, ready to come and receive the captured prize, immediately on being called. In Persia and Arabia, Locusts are used for human food, they are first fried, until their legs and wings drop off, and then mixed with rice and dates, sometimes flavoured with spice and salt.

Amongst the Hemiptera, several species of both Water Bugs, (*Hydrocores*) and Land Bugs, (Geocores,) are found. In the Land Bug group, and the family of *Scutatæ* are some very large and brilliant species, even rivalling the colouring of butterflies. One beautiful but very unpleasantly odoriferous species, *Raphigaster incarnatus,* West., is bright scarlet or yellow, and may be seen of every intermediate shade, it is extremely common in some localities. The smaller yellow Bug, spotted with black, *Pentatoma cruciata,* West., is still more numerous, and more extensively spread. The common Bed Bugs, *Simex lectuarius,* must not be omitted, still in this portion of India, and especially for a sea port town, Cochin may be said to be remarkably free from them. The popular belief appears to be, that they have been devoured either by the enormous numbers of cockroaches, which swarm everywhere, or by the ear wigs, which are also accounted amongst their greatest opponents. Pounded Bugs are prescribed for intermittent fevers, and convulsions, and if their flavour is anything similar to their smell, the remedy must be a strong one. One species of *Nepa,* nearly 2½ inches long, is found in the old fort ditch, and in most stagnant pools of water, and moist muddy places.

Amongst the Homoptera, the first family calling for notice

is the Chirpers, (*Stridulantiæ*) amongst which is the *Cicada*, often from two, to three and a half inches in length. All the year round, excepting during the South West Monsoon, it enlivens the stillness, with a noise resembling the winding up of a multiplying fishing reel, or the grinding of a knife upon a stone wheel. Anacreon composed an ode to its happiness, which according to another poet, is augmented from the fact, that "*all have voiceless wives*," the female being mute. Amongst the *Cicadellinæ*, are the Frog Hoppers, which number a great many species, and small ones may be perceived of an evening on tables, where there is a light. They are little triangular insects, the most common species being green, or green and black; on being touched, they take long hops. Some of them have extraordinary forms, looking almost as if they were monstrosities, or else that nature had indulged in some freak. These last are most frequently perceived just before the South West Monsoon, and in inland situations.

In the family of Plant Parasites, (*Aphides*) are seen several little species, which the Black Ants are so fond of milking, that they have received the name of "the Ants' milch cows." These are the larvœ, and pupœ, in which state they are covered by a white flaky secretion, and exude a sweet gummy substance. That generally seen upon the Bamboo, looks like a dark spot, surrounded by a yellow circle, but with the exception of the rainy season, Aphides may be perceived all the year round on the Mangoe, the Bauhinia, and many other trees. Should an Aphis, from which an Ant has been sucking the sweets, be suddenly removed, and the Ant on his return find it gone, a great tumult ensues. Other ants assemble, and all join in a search for the missing cow, which the natives assert is every night penned up by the Ants, and taken in the morning to the tree in which it lives during the day. Amongst the Coccina group there is one species which produces the gum lac, on various trees.

The third sub class of insects, contains some very common, but no less disgusting house parasites, some of which make themselves at home in the hair of their hosts, without leave being either asked or obtained, whilst others destroy clothes.

In the order *Thysanura*, exists one of the greatest pests to the possessor of books and clothes, the silvery grey Fish insect or Lepisma,

L. niveo-fasciata, Temp., which is particularly active in the monsoon time: inland a darker variety, *L. Niger*, Temp., is more common, but not less active in its depredations. These insects are exceedingly destructive to books, in which they bore small circular holes, and cutting laterally, remove pieces of the leaves. Clothes are eaten by them in numerous little slits, as if snipped with a pair of scissors, but in this process, a small elater bears its share. They appear to be remarkably fond of country paper, on which no records intended for preservation, should ever be written: they do not destroy either French, or English foolscap, to any great extent. It is said (but no doubt incorrectly,) that the Portuguese introduced these little creatures, but the species found in the old Portuguese Fort of Cochin and at the houses at Kurriavanoor, and other places, are not the same. The best preservatives against them, are camphor wood boxes, and turpentine, perhaps the oil of cajeput might also succeed. It is said that placing leaves of the neem tree, between some of the pages of books, will keep them away, but this certainly is not invariably the case. The Spring Tails, *Poduridæ*, are perceived principally in moist places. The Wool devouring *Mallophagæ*, and the unarmed tailed *Anopluræ*, order of insects, are common amongst birds' feathers, the fur of animals, or as parasites, and although some are troublesome, none are very attractive in their outward forms.

Amongst the Myriapods, the Centipedes, are exceedingly numerous, but not very venomous in the town of Cochin. They are not frequently seen, as they live under stones, and in other congenial spots, or enclosed within the folds of shawls, &c. Their bite causes severe pain, which often continues for some hours. Swarms of the Iulus, are perceived in the moist cold months, in communities of hundreds at a time. When bruized in vinegar, they are regarded as irritants, whilst their other ill effects have already been alluded to.

The Arachnidæ, or Spiders, and Scorpions, are very numerous, both in the sub-classes, and divisions. The Spiders are a class which require working out, as tribes hitherto undescribed* would reward

* It would be most desirable if Spiders could be safely transmitted uninjured to Europe for examination. But they loose their colour in spirit, or Glycerine, and then their interest is much diminished. The numbers instead of being enumerated by tens, and twenties, would be found to consist of *hundreds*.

the inquirer, whilst the immense number and beauty of the species is very great. It is not improbable, that a nearer relationship will be found to exist, between the Pedipalpi and Dimerosomata, than is afforded by the Thelyphonidœ and the Araneidœ.

Spiders are all carnivorous creatures, and though one species of Mygale has been reputed to catch small birds, the report has been received with incredulity by many, although believed in by others. A specimen of the *Mygale fasciata*, 7 inches in diameter, was placed under the same finger glass, with a small Gecko, where they lived together quite amicably. But the Mygale had no intention of remaining on similar terms with a Cockroach, which was subsequently put underneath the glass. On seeing the latter, it commenced cleaning its mandibles, and then rushed at its victim, which it quickly seized, and turning it over, caught it by the throat, holding its head and chest fast by aid of its antennœ. After having killed it, the spider let it go, apparently to see which was the best part to begin eating, or perhaps to allow it to get tender. It then again cleaned its mandibles, and commenced its repast, the Lizard in the mean time, looking quietly on. A Mole Cricket was afterwards introduced, who foiled the Spider when it attacked it, and the encounter was not renewed. On the following day, the Cricket died, but the Mygale would not eat it, and it also refused to touch the body of a dead Cockroach, which was given it for food. But it very soon killed and ate a live green Mantis ; and a House Spider, which was put into the glass to keep it company, soon shared the same fate. This spider appears to choose its lair, and to remain there day after day, watching for its prey.

The Mahomedans regard the Spider with respect, because they believe that it concealed Mahomed from his enemies, by spinning a web over the mouth of a well, in which he was hidden. The Jews also assert that when David was concealed in the cave of Adullam he remained undiscovered, because a Spider wove its web over the entrance. Some species form long burrows in hedgerows, and similar places, in which they make their nests. They are most wary, and although seen at the entrances, are rarely captured.

Some Spiders of the Lycosidœ family, live in trees, holes, and out of the way places, and run down, or jump out upon their prey : others such as the Araneidœ, as a rule spin nets, in which to capture their victims, and although in this portion of India, these are in the minority, still the varieties are numerous. The webs of some species are reputed to be good anteperiodics, and natives apply them to cases of ulcers.

The Scorpions are by no means rare, especially a brown house species, *Scorpio australis*, and the common flat one, *S. linearis*, the effect of their sting is not severe, and although during the last few years, many instances have occurred, none have been serious.

The large black Scorpion, *Buthus afer*, is found in the town, although only rarely, but it is much more frequent in the interior of the country. Its sting is very severe, it lives under stones, by the river, in moist places, and is able to swim, it is thus oftener seen by sportsmen in the jungles, than in houses. It is curious to see the skin of a person who has been stung by one of these creatures, as a profuse perspiration is generally perceived around the injured spot, which is probably an effort of nature, to discharge the poison. A naturalist placed a Scorpion and its young under a glass, when the mother destroyed all her offspring, with the exception of one, which got on her back and revenged its brothers and sisters, by killing its parent. Surrounded by burning spirits, Scorpions unable to escape are said to sting themselves to death.

The Decapoda, include an enormous number of species, amongst which the Crabs rank first, and form a vast and interesting family. One of the prettiest of them which is much esteemed for the table belongs to the stalk eyed family, (*Podophthalmus.*) The two last joints of its hind claws, being converted into reddish coloured paddles. Its body is reddish brown, with three purplish spots like eyes, on its dorsal surface. Though its front claws are pink, the last two joints are of a beautiful light blue colour. Crabs are to be found everywhere along the shore burrowing in the sand, and living within the influence of the breakers: in the backwater, or paddy fields, or else along the margin of canals; the little red and black, Calling Crabs, exist in thousands, and if alarmed suddenly disappear. They have only one claw developed, the other remaining quite rudimentary. Whilst running they carry their large claw over their back, and if several are placed together in a small space, they fight most

T 2

desperately, and some will soon be killed with the red claw of their neighbour, fixed into their black bodies. One of the great difficulties in collecting good specimens of this family, is the facility they possess, of shedding their claws. During the months of October, November and December, they are sometimes poisonous, and occasion symptoms like cholera.

The little Spider Crab *(Maiada)* living in the deep sea, requires a passing notice. It has a round or oval body, rarely larger than a nut, covered with spines, to which are attached bits of grass and stick, evidently for the purpose of concealment. Numbers are captured in the sea fisheries, during the cold months of the year, but no use is made of them.

Cray fish are very common, and various species are caught all the year round, both in the sea and in the backwater.

Amongst the Anomurœ, is found a Hermit Crab. Having collected a number of large Terebralia telescopium, from the canal, and left them forgotten for some days in a chatty, a curious appearance was presented when they were turned out. First a few small Hermit Crabs were perceived, and on examining more closely, green feet like those of a large spider, were seen projecting from two of the shells, but on being touched or the shell being moved, they immediately retracted, and disappeared. The length of the body in six specimens, averaged four inches.

Whether they had as is usually believed, merely taken up their abodes in empty shells, or whether as seems more probable, they had first dispossessed the original tenants, is open to doubt.

Amongst the mouth footed insects, *(Stomapoda,)* the Brown Sea Mantis *(Squilla,)* is often caught by the fishermen, though frequently overlooked, it is usually 3 or 4 inches in length. It has long bifurcated antennœ, and other appendages about the head, amongst which its satin green eyes, situated on long stalks, are not the least interesting. It has a pair of foot jaws of large size, which give it somewhat the appearance of the common mantis. Its three pairs of legs are followed by five more pairs of fin like organs, each of which bears gills. Its posterior extremity or tail, is composed of flat expanded plates, terminating in sharp pointed spinous extremities. Its general colour is brown, tinged with blue, and each segment of the back is terminated on either side by two raised spines, whilst down its centre, is a pair of smaller ones.

Amongst the Isopods, a wood boring species claims attention, it is more especially seen in the rainy season, in boats, and crawling amongst the stones, and about the wharfs, whilst in the warm weather it is always found in moist places. It is about two inches long, of a light brown colour, whilst each of its tail filaments, are again sub-divided into two. It is principally owing to the destructive properties, of this creature, that the wooden piles of the wharfs have to be renewed every third year. After climbing above the copper, it commences destroying the wood, and high tides enable it to complete the work of destruction.

The Wood Louse, (*Oniscus,*) and several species of the same family, are not uncommon, but an insect of this order, which deserves attention, is one of the Natatorial Isopods which appears generally to be found as a parasite, about the heads and mouths of fish. Its claws are furnished with hooks, enabling it to take very firm hold.

Amongst the creatures with feet and heads in one, (*Cirrhopoda,*) both the Barnacle, and the Belanus, are found, this last making the bottoms of vessels very foul.

The Annelides, and the worms are well known, both to patients and Medical Practitioners, from the Leech, which swarms in the paddy fields, but is difficult to capture, unless when the water is low, to the Parasitic Worms, that infest the interior of the Human body. The Tape worm and Guinea worm, unless imported, are unknown, but other species are numerous.

The Medusœ, are common excepting during the cold months of the year, and are seen making their way against the current in the Backwater by aid of their tentacles.

Where such vast numbers of families exist, with almost infinite divisions of species, and when at nearly every step, something new in Zoology strikes the eye, bold would be the individual who attempted a description, of all that exists in Malabar. Volumes might be filled by simply enumerating the species. The foregoing is only intended as a brief summary, of some of the more common and interesting tribes, to be found in British Cochin and in the neighbouring Native State.

CHAPTER XVII.

BOTANY.

Relationship of Botany to wealth, beauty, utility, and health of a country—Water kept pure by weeds—Grasses rare—Oil producing plants common—Fruit trees—Cocoanut, its origin, and uses—Plantain—Tamarind—Jack fruit—Mangoe—Vegetables—Shumach—Cork tree—Casuarina—Wild almond—Flowering trees—Pepper—Talipot palm—Maroti—Cashew nut—Bamboo—Banian—Teak—The Poon tree—Blackwood—Ebony—Sappan—Cotton—Coffee—Lemon grass. Van Reede's Hortus Malabaricus.

Much of a country's wealth, depends upon its vegetable productions which in their turn, are influenced by soil, climate, and elevation: whilst a great effect, is reciprocated upon climate, by the vegetation, or more properly speaking by forests. Trees which flourish in the dry plains of India, would wither, and die, on the Malabar coast: whilst were the vegetation of the Western Ghauts, transplanted to the arid plains, the same results would doubtless ensue.

The Cocoanut tree of Travancore and Cochin, thrives along the Western shores, as far as Calicut, but further North its size and productiveness steadily decreases, whilst a few miles inland, the crop is comparatively valueless. The Coffee tree, flourishes from 2500 to 4500 feet above the sea level, on the Wynaad, and elsewhere, and although it grows and produces its important berry at the sea level, it is with a corresponding diminution of productiveness. The Teak or Indian Oak, so magnificent and so hard, when taken from the high forests, runs to a mere pole, on the stony laterite low lands, where the Blackwood hardly grows at all.

The beauty of countries, much depends upon their vegetation; the traveller from the interior, cannot but be struck with that of Malabar, as he glides along the Backwater in his cabin boat: whilst if long from Europe, it will give him pleasure, to see the shrub *Dilivaria ilicifo-*

lia, which so much resembles the English Holly, growing on its alluvial banks. Or should a visitor arrive at Cochin by sea, in the earlier part of the South West Monsoon, the appearance of the Flamboyante tree, *Poinciana Regia*, must strike his attention, as it appears covered with a scarlet mantle of flowers, interspersed with green feathery leaves. Little less beautiful is the *Lagerstrœmia Reginæ*, Rox., (*adamboe*, Mal.) which is obtained from the jungles. Its large bunches of flowers, are of a lilac or purplish rose colour, whilst it continues in blossom, from April to July. It can be at a distance compared to nothing better, than a large English Lilac tree, in full bloom. It is much prized in gardens, and looks excedingly well by the side of the Flamboyante. Smaller in size is the Persian Lilac, which is however nearly as pretty as the Adamboe, whilst there are many other trees equally striking. Along the tanks and ditches, the screw pine, *Pandanus odoratissimus*, Linn., with its Pine apple looking fruit, arrests the attention of the passer by. The Hindu refuses to admit its flowers amongst those suited for religious purposes: and even the Termites shun it owing to its strong aroma: but the devil-worshippers consider it indispensable in their ceremonies. The whole of the jungles from May to July are magnificent, owing to the beauty and variety of the flowering trees and shrubs, which require to be seen to be properly appreciated.

The utility of a country, is often directly in respect to its vegetable wealth, whether as a corn or rice producing and exporting land, or a timber field, which the interior of Cochin undoubtedly is. Here the Teak grows to perfection, a worthy substitute for the English Oak: and but little inferior to it, is the Anjely wood, whilst the forests have always been celebrated, for their Poon Spars or Masts for vessels. To vegetation we must look for building materials, as well as for those for fencing, conveyances, furniture, and ornaments: it is therefore a great pity, more care is not taken in preserving these forests, and keeping up a proper supply of timber.

The healthiness of a climate may be impaired by irregular destruction of forests, thus the Kumari or Punam cultivators, who burn down the jungle, in order to raise their crops of grain on the rich debris, cause the death of the larger trees, as well as of the smaller brushwood. But after two or three years, vegetation again commences to raise its head, and a small scrubby feverish jungle takes the place of the former one. Large forest trees do not appear to be unhealthy *per se*, but low stunted vegetation undoubtedly is so, whilst climate is modified by trees, and the healthiness of a place, is frequently improved by judicious planting and thus screening off prevailing winds, whilst trees partially mitigate the intensity of tropical heat, and create or improve the soil. The amount of rain fall is in places increased by trees, whilst they keep the surface of the ground cool, thus to a certain extent preventing the drying up of the springs ; consequently felling trees that cover the summits and sides of mountains, diminishes not only the fuel, but also the water of a place. Mountain forests, especially on ridges, attract and also condense the clouds, and besides diminishing the local temperature, are supposed to give rise to electric action. In the Cochin state, although the large timber is in places being felled, perhaps injudiciously, still no considerable clearance of forest lands has yet taken place, probably owing to the want of forest roads, otherwise no doubt all the best trees would soon be sold.

The water in the various tanks and ditches, is kept sweet by the growth of a weed, *Pistia stratiotes*, Linn., on its surface, which keeps off the sun's rays, preventing both its too great evaporation, and its becoming putrid. It ought never to be removed, until its leaves and roots begin to decay.

Grass is a very rare production, of the low lands of the Cochin State. In the Town itself, owing to the vast amount of alluvial deposit, and debris existing there, it thrives well : but sandy or laterite formations, are unsuited to its growth. This occasions much distress in feeding cattle, which are, as already stated, a poor diminutive breed. There are some important wild grasses, from that producing the lemon grass oil, to other species employed in Hindu customs and ceremonies. Thus biting a blade of grass, is considered a token of submission, and may possibly be the origin of the European expression " biting the grass." In religious ceremonies again, the Brahman is not always present to officiate, but an efficacious and excellent representative, for the absent priest, is found in a bundle of 50 blades of cusa grass.

The proper season, for felling timber, is an important consideration.

The Natives of Cochin, and all Europeans who have anything to do with the forests, agree that trees should be felled when the sap is least in quantity, which in those with deciduous leaves, is known to be at the period of the fall of the leaf. Timber and bamboos, also last much longer if cut when the moon is on the wane, than when on the increase.

There is probably no part of the world where there are more oil producing vegetables ready to the hand of man, than in Malabar, much is certainly collected, especially from the Cocoanut tree, but the cashew nut appears to be left to the Pigeons, (more especially the Imperial variety,) which come in flocks to feast upon its fruit: and the ground nut falls to the share of the wilder animals, whilst the maroti is more commonly left to decay.

Fruit trees of many and varied sorts, and esculent vegetables, are common. In different species, fruits, leaves, or root stocks, form articles of diet. But the Natives are mostly ignorant of modes of graft-ing; the wild mangoe continues the same, and they are careless respecting improving it. Satisfied with the trees they possess, although thankfully receiving better ones as a gift if they cost them no trouble, they do not concern themselves about obtaining them. All is left to nature, and as their fathers lived, so the sons are satisfied to subsist.

Pre-eminent amongst the trees in the town of Cochin and towering above all others along the sea shore and sides of the Back-water, are the Cocoanut Palms, *Cocos nucifera*, Linn., every portion of which, from their leaves to their roots, may be turned to some useful purpose.

Hindu tradition informs us, that Kusi Rajah, being a strenuous worshipper of one supreme God, and rejecting the custom of offerings to inferior divinities, became in course of time, almost equal to the gods, and made many of the grains now in common use. As his powers increased so did his ambition, and he meditated creating another species of human being very superior to anything existing in the world. But after he had completed its head, the demi-gods became alarmed, and prevailed on him to cease his work. The head was therefore transformed into a Cocoanut tree, which was henceforth to be one of the most useful of all trees in the vegetable kingdom: and was dedicated to *Ganesha*, the protector of sciences, and learned men.

The cocoanut tree flourishes best along the sea coast, and thrives in the sandy and alluvial soil of Cochin. Salt appears almost essential to it, consequently a few miles from the sea, it becomes less luxuriant, and not so prolific.

North of Calicut, where the laterite rooks extend down to the sea, it is less productive, and its appearance is more stunted. In Ceylon there is a saying, also applicable to Malabar, that "this tree will not grow further than a man's voice can extend from his dwelling." This very truly demonstrates, the amount of attention that is necessary, for its successful cultivation.

It commences to bear, about the sixth year, sometimes before, sometimes after, and reaches its prime when nearly a quarter of a century old. For about fifty years it continues prolific, but by the time it has attained the ripe age of a century, its bearing powers have ceased, its work is done.

It is unnecessary to enter upon the cultivation of this tree in its various phases, it requires a moderate amount of water, and occasionally manure, amongst which, could it be afforded, salt would form a good staple. When age has rendered this tree useless, and the place it occupies is required for younger ones, a plan is successfully adopted, which not only clears away the roots, but also manures the soil. The stem is cut off a few inches above the ground, and allowed to dry thoroughly, charcoal or firewood is then heaped round the stump, and the whole set on fire. It is remarkable, that this smoulders away until the whole of the fibrous structure has been consumed. The young tree which has been raised from the nut is then placed over the same spot, some time before the commencement of the South West Monsoon. Cocoanut trees are planted about 20 feet apart if near the sea, but if farther inland, at a greater distance.

The Cocoanut has been called "the great nut of India," and more than one author has pointed out, that it is sufficient to build, rig, and freight a vessel, with bread, wine, water, oil, vinegar, sugar, and other commodities.

The tree is valued at from half a rupee to five rupees when in full bearing, and is taxed according to its productiveness: the profits from large plantations are considerable, especially if they are the property of a Native, and still more so if he also is the cultivator. The Toddy Drawers, whose especial duty it is to climb these trees, to remove the produce, cut steps about one foot apart, on each side, up which they carefully ascend. The slave castes may tend the trees, and tie thorns around them, to keep off thieves, but they are not permitted to cut them, with any sharp instrument.

"Of all the trees which Providence has bestowed on the Oriental world, the Cocoanut tree most deserves our notice. In this single production of nature, what blessings are conveyed to man! It grows in a stately column, from thirty to fifty feet in height, crowned by a verdant capital of waving branches, covered with long spiral leaves; under this foliage, branches of blossoms, clusters of green fruit, and others arrived at maturity, appear in mingled beauty. The trunk though porous, furnishes beams, and rafters for our habitations, and the leaves when plaited together, make an excellent thatch, common umbrellas, coarse mats for the floor, and brooms: whilst their finest fibres, are woven into very beautiful mats for the rich. The covering of the young fruit is extremely curious, resembling a piece of thick cloth, in a conical form, close and firm as if it came from the loom, it expands after the fruit has burst through its enclosure and then appears of a coarser texture. The nuts contain a delicious milk, and a kernel sweet as an almond, this when dried affords abundance of oil; and when that is expressed, the remains feed cattle and poultry, and make a good manure. The shell of the nut furnishes cups, ladles, and other domestic utensils, whilst the husk which encloses it, is of the utmost importance, it is manufactured into ropes, and cordage of every kind, from the smallest twines, to the largest cables which are far more durable than those of hemp. * * * The Asiatic celebrated either in verse or prose, the three hundred and sixty uses, to which the trunk, the branches, the leaves, the juice, and the fruit, were skilfully applied. Many of the trees are not permitted to bear fruit, but the embryo bud from which the blossoms and nuts would spring, is tied up, to prevent its expansion, and a small incision being made at the end, there oozes out in gentle drops, a cool liquid called toddy, the Palm wine of the poets. This when first drawn is cooling and salutary, but when fermented and distilled, produces an intoxicating spirit (arrack.)"*

* *Forbes*, Oriental Memoirs. Vol. I. page 12.

The web-like texture, from around the fronds, where the branches expand, the Toddy Drawers employ for straining the toddy through; it is also used for coarse cloths, and bags, or as a torch after it has been steeped in oil and lightly rolled up.

Should epicures desire, a substitute for a good cabbage, or a nice pickle, they may obtain it from the cocoanut cabbage, or the terminal bud, at the summit of the tree.

Some very useful purposes are served by the leaves, which are first divided down the centre of the midrib into halves, exposed for two or three days to the sun, then soaked for about the same period in water, and subsequently plaited into baskets, or thatch for huts and houses. Owing to the amount of potash the leaves contain, they are also burnt by the Dhobies, and the ashes mixed with the water, in which the clothes are soaked. The wood of the tree is strong and hard, and is susceptible of a very fine polish; it is known as the porcupine wood, from its black and white veins. The stem is employed as rafters of houses, bridges, beams, small boats, &c. The nuts are used as cups, and small lamps, they are also cut and polished, carved as baskets, and into many pretty and curious ornaments. The midribs of the leaves are employed as paddles for small boats. In olden times they also formed an instrument of torture. A few pieces about four inches in length, were cut jaggedly from the midrib, and four of these were lightly bound around the prisoner's thumb, with a piece of strong whip cord. When the circulation was completely arrested, and swelling had taken place, each of these four pieces were in succession slowly dragged out through the congested skin. The torture was declared by the victims to be excessive. The root of this palm is chewed by Natives, as a substitute for the areca nut.

In Cochin the piles employed for jetties, are very commonly made of Cocoanut trees, and although it would at first sight appear probable that they would last many years, experience shows that five is as much as may be anticipated. The Carpenter Bees, *Xylocopa latipes*, and *X. tenuiscapa*, do not appear to wait until the tree is dead, before commencing their destructive attacks upon it, whilst immediately that it is driven into its position, some species of Isopods commence their inroads, these are probably the most destructive animals, small though they be, which infest the Cochin river, destroying the boats, and woodwork.

The Cocoanut tree when hollowed, is commonly employed as large pipes for drains, whilst a single tree is both an ordinary Native bridge, and when notched at the sides, an useful ladder.

A tree which is often seen amongst the Cocoanuts, and other trees, but more commonly in gardens by itself is the Plantain or Banana, *Musa paradisiaca*, Linn. (*Vella*, Mal.) This useful tree which forms such a common staple of food, appears to thrive from the sea level, to five thousand feet, and even more: it is considered an emblem of fertility, and plenty, by the Hindus, and always takes its place in marriage ceremonies, and other grand occasions, whilst amongst the Princes of Malabar it is a symbol of sovereignty.

The wide-spreading leaves, which diminish the circulation of air, also tend to keep the ground moist, and consequently houses surrounded by them, are damp. On the under surface of their leaves, is often seen the little tree frog. There are many varieties of this tree, one garden at Trevandrum, is said to contain forty species: as an article of diet, it is hardly inferior in nutritive properties to the potatoe. From the fibrous texture, especially of one species, *M. textilis*, is obtained a kind of flax, from which a delicate cloth is manufactured. The whole of the tree is so fibrous, that from plantain tribes, almost any amount of fibre could be obtained for export. If the best sort is taken, and the fibre well cleaned and prepared, all the sap having been quickly removed, it bears immersion in water well, and is said to be of about the same strength as Russian hemp.

Besides many other properties, it should not be omitted, that the leaves are employed as caps and bags by the Chogans, and are also very useful to the Medical practitioner. They are commonly employed, in dressing blisters. If their upper surface be applied to the blistered part, the healing process soon takes place, on the contrary should it be desirable to prevent the sore from rapidly skinning over, the under surface of the leaves act as the necessary irritant. If manured with the weed (*Paiiloo*, Mal.) *Pistia Stratiotes*, it is said to bear more plentifully and to have larger and better tasted fruit. To ripen plantains, a little lime is smeared on each one.

The slow growing dark green Tamarind, *Tamarindus Indica*,

Linn., is found in Cochin, sparingly spread over the country. The large amount of acid properties contained in this tree, renders it unadvisable for travellers to encamp in its shade, as should a shower of rain occur, and the drops fall from its leaves, it will most assuredly rot the tent. Even the damp weather will destroy tents under this shelter. Natives will never sleep beneath it.

Probably amongst the most beautiful of trees, is the Bread-fruit, *Artocarpus incisa*, which grows exceedingly well in the soil of Cochin, but does not thrive inland, on the laterite formation. Its growth in congenial soils is rapid, and it often commences to bear by its third year. Its spreading branches cover rather a large space, but the tree is rarely above 40 or 50 feet high. About March the fruit from which it takes its name is ripe. The size varies from that of a child's head, to three times that circumference. It is said to resemble bread, but the similarity is very slight. After being cut and baked, the outer rind is removed, and the interior or bread, is very like dry pith, with little or no taste, it is sometimes curried. The sap of this tree dried in the sun, and subsequently boiled, forms an inferior substitute for pitch. The tree is propagated by shoots or layers, taken from its roots.

The Jack Fruit, *Artocarpus integrifolius*, Linn., is a far more useful tree than the foregoing, to which its fruit in outward appearance, bears considerable resemblance. The wood is of a light colour, but after a time, if regularly cleaned, assumes a darker hue, approaching that of mahogany, it is much esteemed for tables and furniture, as well as for general purposes, such as doors and buildings.

This tree which grows on laterite soil, where the Bread-fruit and Cocoanut do not thrive, is a monopoly of the Sirkar, and yields an annual tax, the size of the fruit, which is much prized by Natives, is sometimes enormous. The seeds are either roasted or curried, and taste like very dry broad beans: its juice is sometimes employed as birdlime.

The Mangoe, *Mangifera Indica,* grows to a very large size, but its fruit is of a very inferior description, apparently owing more to want of proper cultivation, than the incompatibility of the climate. Fine trees exist at Cannanore, and even at Calicut, from which good mangoes are obtained. There is one curious tree in the Town of

Cochin which although it never produces much fruit at a time, still rarely passes a month without bearing some. Mangoes are generally ripe in the month of May, but they have mostly disappeared by June.

As a timber wood, it is soft, easily decays, and does not stand moisture, but is good for fuel. This tree should be propagated by grafting. In some parts of India, no Hindu would think of tasting the fruit of his Mangoe grove, until a marriage of trees has taken place. The Tamarind is generally chosen as the Bride. The Brahmans attend these ceremonies, and derive considerable profit from them, as they are conducted with much pomp.

There are many other trees, grown in gardens, which are useful for food, and prized for their ornamental appearance. The Pomegranite, *Punica granatum*, Linn., has a pretty bright red flower. Its fruit is celebrated, but great disappointment is usually experienced, on first tasting it. The Bullock's-heart or Soursop, *Annona reticulata*, Linn., is found in gardens, and its fruit is esteemed one of the best in the place. It grows to several pounds weight, and tastes like the Custard Apple flavoured with geraniums. In the West Indies, an excellent liqueur is made from this fruit. Its leaves attract bugs.

The Red and White Guavas, *Psideum pomiferum*, and *P. pyriferum*, Linn., are also found: the fruit of both are rather too strong for the table, but make good puddings, and excellent preserves. The Limes, *Citrus bergamia*, Briss., are acid but useful.

The Papaw Tree, *Carica papaya*, Linn., is liked for its fruit, which is esteemed for puddings, and also eaten raw; the Bilimbi, *Averrhoa bilimbi*, is also a favourite with those who are fond of acid fruit, or preserves. There are also other trees, the fruits of which are held in esteem, the Lobi lobi, and the Marson, are both found, and are probably importations from Ceylon.

There are many other useful trees, amongst them may be mentioned the Nutmeg, *Pyrrhoria Horsfieldii*, Blume, (?) which grows well in Cochin, when sheltered from violent gusts of wind, and strong sea breezes. The Cashew nut, *Anacardium occidentale*, Linn., grows well, and bears abundantly, even as early as February. The roots of the Horse Reddish Tree, *Moringa pterygosperma*, Gœrtu, form an excellent substitute for the real article as a relish for beef

The Shaddock, or Pumplemose, *Citrus decumana*, Linn., is not a common shrub. This large species of orange, is much liked, but is more suited for making into Marmelade, than for eating in its raw state, whilst its fruit makes excellent jam. The Citron, *Citrus Medica*, Linn., also bears in Cochin, and good Marmelade is made from it. The small China Orange, the fruit of which is hardly larger than a pea, thrives well, and makes excellent jams, or puddings, as well as answering the purpose of good gum on an emergency. The Mulberry grows well, but does not appear to bear fruit. It is said that in olden time, the silk worm flourished here, but this is not well authenticated, and is probably incorrect.

Other useful trees must not be omitted. The soap nut tree, *Sapindus laurifolius*, Vahl. (*Purmaji*, Mal.) which is suitable for the sides of roads, has a saponaceous berry, which is used as soap for washing the hair, and other purposes. From its wood, harps and combs are made. The Shumach, *Cœsalpinia coriaria*, Willd., known also as the divi divi, grows well if properly attended to, when young. When large it is a beautiful tree, and most valuable for its pods, which contain about 50 per cent. of Tannin, the price of which varies in Europe, from £8 to £13 a ton. In its native soil, the produce of one tree is about lb. 100.

It germinates well from seeds, and if the side branches are trimmed off until the tree reaches ten feet in height, and the stem is properly supported, it will in a few years form quite a fine tree, the cultivation of which it may be imagined would pay as a commercial enterprise.

Vegetables, and some seeds, succeed pretty well, but the situation is too low for potatoes, which however are procured from the Neilgherries, or Palghaut, at about an average rate of Rs. 2 for 30 lbs. weight. The following grown in the place, are most esteemed, the Aghaty kai, *Coronilla Grandiflora*. Willd., Red Pumpkin, *Cucurbita hispida*, Thumb., which is very common, and the white variety, reputed to be extremely strengthening, and therefore seldom absent from the meals or feasts of rich Natives. The Brinzal, or Egg Plant, *Solanum melongena*, Linn., Bandakai, *Hibiscus esculentus*, Linn., Cucumber, *Cucumis sativus*, Linn., (*Mullen belleri*, Mal.) Onion, *Allium cepa*, Linn., Pineapple, *Ananas sativus*, Schult., (*Pooreethee*,

Mal.) Melon, *Cucumis melo*, Linn., Water Melon, *Cucurbita citrullus*, Linn. Several species of Yams, *Dioscoreæ alatæ; D. bullifera; D. pentaphylla;* and *D. triphylla*, Linn., Sweet Potatoes, *Convolvulus batatas*, Linn., (*Kappa Kalenga*, Mal.) Arrowroot, *Curcuma augustifolia*, Roxb., (*Kooa*, Mal.) Pepper, *Piper nigrum*, Linn., (*Molago-codi*, Mal.) Betel, *Piper betle*, Linn., (*Vetta*, Mal.) and many others.

The pretty Cork tree, *Bignonia suberosa*, Roxb., does not thrive in Cochin, and consequently is unadapted for avenues, it does not flower well, and its sweet scent is almost unknown. The Neem tree, *Azadirachta Indica*, Ad. de Juss, likewise merely runs to a small pole, and is unadapted for ornamental planting. It is an emblem of purification, and sacred to Kali. The timber is beautifully marked, and suitable for cabinet making. The Portia tree, *Thespesia populnea*, Lam., grows very well, if properly attended to, but if propagated by boughs, they are apt after a few years, to break at the points, from which the branches sprout off. The heavy rains appear to weaken this part, never strong, and the high breezes complete the mischief. Its leaves being deciduous, render the ground very untidy, at the fall of the leaf; and the same may be said, when its yellow or buff coloured blossoms fall.

The Casuarina, *Casuarina muricata*, Roxb., grows well and rapidly, but unless the tops are occasionally cut off when young, it runs too much to a weedy head top, and becomes unfit for avenues. Its wood though extremely hard, is brittle and easily broken off in high winds.

The finest and strongest tree, and consequently that best adapted for ornamental planting, is the Indian almond, *Terminalia catappa*, Linn. Its dark thick foliage, is very handsome, and shows to advantage in the months of March and April, when interspersed with purplish flowers. Its seeds are very much like those of the true Almond, and its kernel has much the same taste. The Flying Foxes, *Pteropus Edwardsii* are very fond of them, and are often a great nuisance at night time, fighting over the spoil.

Oil may be expressed from the nuts, the fruit being gathered, dried in the sun, and the kernels cleaned, they are bruized in a mill, when six seers produce three pucka seers of oil. The oil cake is considered good for feeding pigs. It is like English Almond oil, but so badly prepared, that it soon becomes turbid.

The smaller ornamental trees, which are grown either for the beauty of the flowers, their bright tinted leaves, or their curious appearance, are by no means few, considering the small amount of space, available for such purposes, in the town of Cochin.

The Persian Lilac, *Melia azedarach,* Linn., though not growing to any height, may be seen covered with magnificent clusters of purple flowers, quite loading the tree during March, April, and even in the beginning of May. The beads, are bored and strung by the Roman Catholics. The timber is hard and handsomely marked.

The purple species of Bauhinia, often variegated with brown and yellow, is a handsome and ornamental tree. The Silk Cotton tree, *Bombax Malabaricum,* D. C., with its prickly trunk, branches springing at right angles from the stem, and palmate leaves, grows in the town. The deep red flowers, blossoming from February till April, are looked upon by the Natives as a cause of sore eyes, as it is said that whoever looks at them, will be affected with ophthalmia. Its seeds are embedded in a silky cotton, the staple of which is too short to weave, but is most useful in stuffing pillows and mattrasses.

Holding a conspicuous place amongst the smaller flowering shrubs, is the Rose tree, which flourishes and blossoms most luxuriantly, in small courts, where the free circulation of air, must apparently be almost unknown. Where there is a little more space, the Exile, *Thevetia nereifolia,* Juss., may be found : this tree is a native of South America, but now naturalized in India, it grows from 12 to 20 feet high. Its milky juice is highly venomous.

The shoe flower, or China Rose, *Hibiscus rosa sinensis,* thrives in both its buff, and red varieties : the latter are employed on festive occasions, and the Nairs in olden time, made garlands of them for their cannon, and for hanging around their elephants, when going to battle ; the petals of the flowers, are employed for blacking shoes, and women use them for dyeing the hair and eyebrows black. When rubbed on blotting paper they leave a bluish tint, and render it a good substitute for blue litmus paper, for detecting the acidity of any fluid.

The deep crimson leaves of the *Poincettia pulcherrima,* Linn., give this shrub a very gay appearance, and it is consequently perceived in most gardens as is also the French Croton, *Croton variegatum,* which is grown for its beauty: as well as many other shrubs which it is unnecessary to enumerate.

The foregoing trees and shrubs, (unless otherwise stated,) from the Cocoanut downwards, may be found within the small space of British Cochin. But the great wealth of Malabar, partly arises from its Cocoanut plantations, its pepper, and other produce.

Pepper, *Piper nigrum*, Linn., (*Molago codi*, Mal.) has been from the most ancient times, until last year, a monopoly of the Sircar. It was formerly called "*Malabar Money*." The Cochin state produces but little of this article. It is propagated by cuttings, and commences to produce in about three years, it is trained up trees which have rough barks, and requires careful pruning and watching. The berries are red, but when dried become black. The best are grown in the vallies of the ghauts, where there is most moisture. When *black pepper* is required, the seeds are picked green, and when dried become black, with a corrugated surface. *White pepper* is the ripe fruit, in which state it is covered with a red pulp, which is washed off, and the white pepper corn beneath it, cleansed and dried, after which it is ready for the market.

The leaves of the Betel, *Piper betle*, Linn., (*Vetla*, Mal.) are most extensively chewed by the Native and Eurasian population, mixed with Chunam, and the nut of the areca palm. This practice is considered conducive to health and is a powerful stimulant to the salivary glands, and digestive organs, though if long continued it renders the mouth dry, and parches the tongue and fauces. It is said to diminish perspiration, but has an unpleasant sickly odour. This vine requires a rich moist soil, and is planted in rows, and trained up on poles or trees. The leaves must only be removed at certain seasons of the year.

The Areca Palm, *Areca catechu*, Linn., (*Adaka*, Mal.) is a most valuable, and at the same time beautiful tree. It thrives either near the sea, or even in high regions, at some distance inland. It produces about three hundred nuts yearly on an average, which somewhat resemble nutmegs. At ceremonial visits, as a sign that it is time for a visitor to take leave, they are presented in slices, mixed with chunam and cardamoms, folded up in a betel leaf, and secured by a clove. An inferior chewing betel in the presence of a superior, is at the least, taking a great liberty, and his conduct may well be considered, as an intentional impertinence.

The Fan, or Talipot Palm, *Corypha umbraculifera*, Linn., though perhaps better known in Ceylon than in India, is by no means uncommon a few miles to the North of Cochin, and not very far inland. It is numerous at Trichoor.

Its beautiful fan shaped leaves, their enormous size, and dark green colour, renders this tree a very striking object. It is said that only Royalty in Malabar were permitted to have a branch of the Cocoanut palm carried over them, but it does not appear improbable, that this is a mistake, and that in reality it was the leaf of the Talipot palm. In Ceylon only Royalty and Buddhist priests, could have "the talipot fan borne over them, with the broad end foremost." This tree is generally seen in gardens. The leaves are cut into proper sizes, and used as a substitute for writing paper, an iron style being employed as a pen: they resist the ravages of time, but unfortunately not that of insects. On this species of paper, all the records, reports, and correspondence of the Cochin Government were kept, until the year 1858, when paper was introduced into the Dewan's Office, but not into the Talooks. Its leaves are also used for thatching houses, and when properly dried, for umbrellas. The seeds are employed as beads by some Hindu sects, and are sometimes cut, dyed red, and sold as coral. Flour or a sort of sago, is prepared from the pith of its trunk.

Another tree which arrests attention, is the handsome Maroti, *Hydrocarpus inebrians*, Vahl., so designated from its fruit occasioning dizziness, its seeds are occasionally employed for poisoning fish. This tree grows wild in many places, but is more especially seen in gardens, where it is cultivated for its oil. The fruit from which this is extracted, is about the size of a small orange, of a brown colour, and a hard and rough texture.

The most favourite tree along the road sides, appears to be the Cashew Nut, *Anacardium occidentale*, Linn., (*Parunkimavah*, Mal.) from its truuk is obtained a gum, from its fruit a vesicating oil, often employed for putting over floors, and wooden rafters, to preserve them from white ants. The kernels are edible, as are also the apples from which they grow.

The Vomit nut, or Poison nut, *Strychnos nux vomica*, Linn., (*Cariram*, Mal.) is a very common, medium sized tree, its yellow fruit looks at a distance like oranges, and immediately attracts attention. Although the powerful irritant poison of Strychnine, is contained in the seeds, the Hornbill and some other birds, are said to live upon them.

The Bamboo, *Bambusa arundinacea*, Willd., although found in the vicinity of the sea, increases both in size and number, nearer the ghauts, on which it grows most luxuriantly. Its long feathery foliage, and delicate light green hue, renders it when waving in the breeze, a most attractive object. But it is not only for its beauty that this tree is valued, as being light but strong, it is useful for many economic purposes.

The seeds ripen, about April or May. It is said that this tree flowers only once in fifteen years, fructifies, then droops, and dies. The seeds are pounded, and eaten by the poorer classes, but are considered very unwholesome.

The rapidity at which this tree grows is something wonderful, "it attains a considerable height, some 70—80 feet, and has been "known to spring up thirty inches, in six days."*

The young shoots of some species are eaten as asparagus, the stems are "converted into bows, arrows, and quivers, lance shafts, "the masts of vessels, bed posts, walking sticks, the poles of palan-"quins, as floors and supporters of rustic bridges." They are sharpened and hardened in the fire, and thus form stockades, or the hollow ones are loaded as guns, to which slow matches are attached and left in long grass, to annoy Infantry. The uses to which they are put are most numerous, the partitions being destroyed, they form water pipes. "Of the Bamboo are made implements for weaving, "the post and frames of the roofs of huts, scaffoldings for build-"ings, portable stages for native processions, raised floors for grana-"ries, stakes for nets in rivers, rafts, masts, yards, oars, spars, &c., "in boat's decks. It is used for building bridges across creeks, for "fences, as a lever for raising water for irrigation, and as flag poles. "Several agricultural implements are made of it, as are also hacke-

* *Drury*, "Useful Plants of India," page 62.

" ries or carts, doolies or litters, and biers; the shafts of javelins or " spears, bows and arrows, clubs and fishing rods.

" A joint of bamboo serves as a holder for pens, small instruments " and tools. It is used as a case in which things of little bulk are " sent to a distance, a joint of bamboo serves the purpose of a " bottle, and a section of it, is a measure for solids, and liquids, in " Bazaars. A piece of it is used as a blow pipe, and as a tube in " a distilling apparatus. A small bit of it split at one end, serves " as tongs to take up burning charcoal, and a thin slip of it, is " sharp enough to be used as a knife, in shelling betelnuts. Its " surface is so hard, that it answers the purpose of a whet stone, " upon which the Ryots sharpen their agricultural implements."*

In the jungles, the vegetation changes from that found in the alluvial or laterite plains, and this alteration becomes more and more perceptible, as a higher elevation is attained, therefore leaving a further account of the Botany of the open country, that of the Jungles which is found most useful for building, railways, and other purposes, claims our attention.

Amongst the Jungle trees, is found the Elephant creeper, *Argyreia Speciosa*, Sweet., (*Samudra stogam*, Mal.) which in July and August, is covered with rose coloured flowers, something like convolvuli. It grows to an enormous thickness, often carried from one tree to another, forming a natural swing, or embracing large trees so firmly, as to arrest the circulation in the bark, and cause their death.

A well known tree, is the Banian, *Ficus Bengaliensis*, Linn. (*Peralu*, Mal.) common all over India, and celebrated in prose and verse, from the most ancient times. Large as it grows in the Cochin territory, it must pale before those mentioned in many other places. One at Mhow for instance is stated to have had 68 stems, and is computed to have covered a space, large enough to encamp 20,000 men. This tree is very destructive to buildings, old Forts, and monuments, as the seeds are frequently conveyed by birds, or in some other way, to various places, where they rapidly take root, and spring up. As it is regarded by the Hindus in a superstitious light, they will never pull it down, and the young saplin speedily inserts

* *Drury*, " Useful Plants of India," page 62.

its roots amongst the stones, and in time forces them out of their proper places: even after the head has been cut off, the root continues enlarging. Sometimes it germinates inside another tree such as the Palmyra, and the roots descending around it, by degrees entirely envelope it, with the exception of the head.

It constantly throws out roots downwards from its branches, which strike again as they reach the ground, and these descending portions become trunks, from which the same process is carried on. Hindus "consider its long duration, its outshadowing arms, and "overshadowing beneficence, as emblems of the deity:" and beneath them the Hindu philosophers often spend much of their time, in contemplation and solitude. Idols are often found at its base, Ganesha the Sylvan deity, being that in whose honour they are generally speaking raised.

The small red fig of this tree when ripe, is fit for human food, and is also eaten by monkeys, squirrels, and birds. Snakes, lizards, and other reptiles, seek a home amongst its roots, and even mice may be found under its sheltering protection.

Nearly allied to the above is the poplar-leaved fig tree, *Ficus religiosa*, Linn. (*Arealu*, Mal.) It is generally found near Hindu Pagodas, and it is believed that Vishnu was born amongst its foliage where the gods now delight to sit listening to its rustling, as its leaves tremble like those of the Aspen. Under this tree in village communities, suspected persons are sometimes taken to assert the truth of their statements, by taking one of the leaves in their hand, and invoking the gods above, to curse them, and all near and dear to them, if they speak not the truth. Hindus believe that did any one dare to assert a falsehood, in such a sanctified place, the wrath of the gods would assuredly descend upon him, and his family. The Syrian Christians assert, that the wood of the cross, was of this tree, in consequence of which, the leaves have never ceased trembling. The Buddhists affirm, that Buddha when on earth, delighted to recline under its shade, since which period the leaves have been in a state of incessant ecstatic motion. This tree does not extend itself by throwing down roots from its branches.

Another species of fig, *Ficus cunia*, Buch., (*Pernia teregam*, Mal.) is very common, and its rough leaves are very useful to Cabinet makers, who employ them like Shagreen, for rubbing down furniture, to a smooth surface, and thus preparing it for its final polish. It is also used for smoothing horns, before polishing, when they have been roughly filed.

The Teak tree, *Tectona grandis*, Linn., (*Tekka*, Mal.) is considered the oak of India, and the most useful of Indian trees, being very strong, and resisting to a great extent both the ravages of White Ants, and the rotting action of water. Its leaf is large, thin, and rounded, about ten inches in diameter; its branches of blossoms have been compared to hops, and its berries to grapes. A group of these trees when in full bloom, from a distance resembles a field of ripe corn, owing to which the Mulchers and Kardars, discover them a long way off. In ship building it is superior to any forest tree, and the best Malabar Teak, is reckoned better than that found elsewhere. Its growth should be slow, for that which rapidly comes to maturity, in rich soils, is not so good as that which takes from 60 to 80 years growing. It does not affect iron in any way, and does not shrink.

The oily nature of teak, enables it to resist the dry rot. Vessels constructed of this wood, do not warp, or become crazy, like those built of European timbers. But possibly teak being in its native climate in the Indian Seas, is not so susceptible to the injurious effect, either of the heat, or of the sudden changes of the Monsoons. However that may be, the vessels are certainly not so leaky, and the crews consequently more healthy. Ships are considered to last from 30 to 50 years, when constructed of teak. There are four sorts, or distinctions of this wood, known to Ship builders, brought from the Malabar forests. A small species, (*Coal Tekka*, Mal.) has a porous grain, and grows at the foot of the Ghauts, in valleys where the soil is rich, and deep, and along the banks of large rivers. This is rather small, but is adapted for planking and boarding. The largest but most inferior species, (*Oomi Tekka*, Mal.) grows on the hills and but rarely at the foot of the Ghauts. As a general rule, teak timber which is above twenty inches in diameter at the butt, has the heart shake from end to end, and consequently requires much care to convert it into use.

The superior kind (*Cullen Tekka*, Mal.) grows in the forests, where the soil is not deep. On the Ghauts, it is curved, hard and knotty, and very like the English Oak, its weight is greater than the above mentioned species, and its durability more considerable.*

Teak wood oil, from the inferior, (*Nee Tekka*, Mal.) may be used as a substitute for the Linseed, and makes a good varnish for paint. The number of these trees is rapidly diminishing, as the Cochin Government has no young ones planted, to succeed those which are constantly being felled. Up to 1814, the Cochin and Travancore Sircar teaks were excluded from the Bombay dockyards, and had to be sent to Bengal for sale, where there was a great demand for them.

Next in importance, and but little inferior in value, is the Anjelly wood, *Artocarpus hirsutus*, Linn. (*Ansjeli*, Mal.) a tree exclusively found on the Western Coast where three species are known. A large tract of them is situated about 40 miles South East of Trichoor, at an elevation of perhaps 3,000 feet. It is much prized by the natives for canoes, snake boats and house building, whilst from its hard texture, it is especially adapted for large sea boats, the boards of which are sewn together, as they are apt to give way: it is thought more durable than oak. It is also well suited for the bottom planking of ships, as high as the bends, but the fastenings if not trenailed, should be made of copper, as it corrodes iron very rapidly.

It is now getting scarcer, in the most accessible forests, and consequently the value is greatly augmenting. It appears to prefer the higher range of hills. At present the annual supply from the Cochin and Travancore forests, only averages 6,000 or 7,000 candies, not above one tenth of which, would be suitable for ship building.

Dr. Cleghorn advances, whether "it might be advisable, to form "plantations on the banks of navigable rivers:" but such would most likely not succeed, as the trees so situated would probably grow too rapidly, and the trunk thereby lose much of its density and consequent utility.

---

* The following is a list of the *first British Men of War*, built of this material.

Ships of the Line.—Minden, Cornwallis, Melville, Malabar, Wellesley, Ganges, Asia, Bombay, Calcutta, Hastings.

Frigates.—Salsette, Amphitrite, Trincomalee, Seringapatam, Madagascar, Andromeda, Alligator, Samarang, Herald.

Sloops—Victor, Cameleon, Sphynx, Cochin.

The Poon tree, *Calophyllum augustifolium*, Roxb., or Poon Pine, was formerly exceedingly common, and is well adapted for masts and spars. Drawing as it does to 70 or 80 feet in height, and from two to three in diameter, it has been cut down and removed from the most accessible places, and has consequently become scarce. Small Poon spars are believed to be made from the *Sterculia fœtida*, Linn., which is common in all the jungles.

The Blackwood, is one of the most valuable of the trees, and hardly inferior to teak. It is exported to Bombay, for the furniture makers, and is also used in Cochin, for the same purpose, many of the articles being sent to the Mauritius, and elsewhere. The two species which are botanically distinct, *Dalbergia latifolia*, Roxb., and the *D. Sissoides*, are both found in the forests, but there are three distinct varieties of wood, obtained from different species of these trees. The first in importance and value for exportation to Bombay, and certainly the handsomest when worked up into furniture, is the very dark wood, with deep black veins, (*Poo Viti*, Mal.) the next (*Chālur Viti*, Mal.) is more like rosewood, of a brown colour, very strong, and unsuited for splitting, which process is easy in either of the other varieties. The third is very black, with light reddish veins. (*Kurri viti*, Mal.) Blackwood is known in the market, as the Indian Rosewood.

Blackwood may be obtained of a great width, but two of the varieties are very liable to split, unless well dried. It is much esteemed for gun carriage manufactories. There is a species of wood, (*Coroo Murradoo*, Mal.) of which there are four varieties, which are like discoloured Blackwood, but the Carpenters rub some composition over them and the unwary are easily deceived, it is coarse, but does not split readily.

The Ebony tree, *Diospyros melanoxylon*, Roxb., is found in the Cochin forests, but it is far inferior to the Ceylon Ebony. It is of a deep black colour, and of enormous weight, but the size is small, being only found in the interior of the tree, the outside having to be first removed. It requires great care in drying, during which time, it must be placed under sheds, as otherwise it is very apt to split. Some of the species are variegated, with light brown lines, which deteriorate from the beauty of the wood.

The Sappan tree, *Cœsalpinia Sappan*, Linn., is much valued for its dye, and has a good export market. Some of the Moplahs on the birth of a daughter, sow a number of the seeds of this valuable tree, which come to maturity in 14 or 15 years, and form the infant's dowry.

Two of the most useful trees for common timber, are the so called Cedars: which are very plentiful in the Cochin forests. The White Cedar, (*Vella Uggul*, Mal.) shrinks in seasoning, about $\frac{1}{24}$. Its density is 4℔ per foot superficially. It decays if exposed to moisture. On account of its cheapness, [Rupees 4 per candy,] it is much sought after for beams, rafters, and laths, of houses, boxes and other common purposes. It is rather a favourite wood with the White Ants. There are certainly two species, one of which floats in water, whilst the other sinks at once.

The Red Cedar, *Cedrelacea* (*Choganmur Uggul*, Mal.) is not so common, its density is half that of the White Cedar, and the quality of the wood not esteemed so good. It is useful for common furniture, and takes a fair polish. There are two varieties.

A short summary may now be given, of a few of the most useful and pretty trees and flowers, found in the Cochin territory. The Indian Cotton Tree, *Gossypium Indicum*, Linn., is merely cultivated in gardens. This plant from its scourging the soil, can only be sown in rotation with other crops. The short staple is said to be the best for Native manufactures, and the strongest for their use. It is inferior to that grown in Tinnivelly, and Coimbatore.

The Custard Apple, *Anona Squamosa*, Linn., is said to have been introduced by the Portuguese, but does not attain the perfection arrived at in the Deccan. It is only found in gardens. The Cocculus Indicus, *Anamirta Cocculus*, W. A., is not uncommon, it is an article of export, and said to be used for making malt liquors still more intoxicating. The Black Dammer Tree, *Canarium Strictune*, Roxb., from which a deep red or amber coloured resin can be obtained, is found in the Trichoor forests.

The Cassia Fistula, *Cathartocarpus fistula*, Pers., with its fragrant and clustering blossoms, considered by the Hindus sacred to Vishnu, is seen every where: under its shade votaries to that god erect their altars, and offer their flowery sacrifices. The Catechu tree,

Acacia catechu, Willd., from which is obtained the Catechu, or Terra Japonica, is also found, as well as the Bastard Teak, *Butea frondosa*, Roxb., with its beautiful scarlet flowers, which are offered to the presiding deities of Hindu temples, and with which women, also bind their hair, on festive occasions. The Ringworm shrub, *Cassia alata*, Linn., is evidently an importation, but is found in many localities, both dry and marshy; its name denotes one of its principal uses. The Wild Liquorice, *Abrus precatorius*, Linn., is common, whilst the three varieties of berries which it bears, are collected for necklaces, and ornaments, but the crimson with a deep black spot, is generally the favourite. Each seed usually weighs exactly one grain.

The Wood Apple, or Jambo, *Eugenia Malaccensis*, Linn., is not uncommon, and its fruit is prized for the dessert table, as it possesses a delicate rose like flavour; it is much plundered by bats. The Bael tree, *Œgle marmelos*, Corr., is also found, its fruit when partially ripe, is very useful in cases of chronic scorbutic dysentery, whilst to render it more palatable, it can be made into a preserve. A species of Ixora, *I. coccinea*, Linn., is prized for its scarlet flowers, dedicated to Iswara. Coffee, *Coffea Arabica*, Linn., has been already mentioned, as thriving in this part of India. *Paoli* mentioned it before 1790, as growing wild, but stated that it was not cultivated, as the Natives attend to productions of more utility! The Indian Copal Tree, *Viteria Indica*, Linn., which yields the copal, or piney varnish, was always a favourite tree with the Rajahs, and forms excellent avenues.

The Colocynth, *Citrullus colocynthis*, Schrad., when its fruit is ripe, at once attracts attention, its bright orange coloured fruit, is perceived either in a long irregular row, trailing along the ground, or hanging from the branches of shrubs, into which it has climbed. A species of Gutta Percha tree, *Isonandria acuminata*, Lindl., grows very abundantly in the forests, and appears to thrive almost equally well, from the sea level, to 3000 feet above it. The wild Mangosteen, *Embryopteris glutinifera*, Roxb., is made use of by Carpenters, on account of the glue it contains. The Jasmine, *Jasminum sambac*, Ait., the fragrant white flowers of which, are considered sacred to Vishnu.

The little purple Chiretta, *Exacum tetragonum*, Roxb., which although a small annual, is most useful as a tonic, whilst the Indian jalap, *Ipomea turpethum*, R., which is grown in gardens for its flowers, is found as a weed in the jungles. The two species of Datura, are no where rare, and are employed for rendering intoxicating liquors still more inebriating. The purple variety is the strongest. It is said that when married women wish their husbands to remain quietly asleep at home, they add some of this drug to their evening meal.

The Wild Nutmeg, *Pyrrhosia Horsfeldii*, Blume, grows in the forests where the Wild Cinnamon, *Cinnamomum iners*, Rein., is also common : as well as some species of *Aristolochiæ*, which are celebrated all over the world, as antidotes for snake bites. The country Gooseberry, *Cicca disticha*, Linn., is cultivated in gardens. The Belgaum Walnut, *Aleurites triloba*, Fors., is found in the Jungles, its nut owing to the very large amount of oil it contains, may be burnt as a candle, and will continue alight for a long time. When dried, they are strung and used as bracelets, and other ornaments. The tiger's milk tree, *Excœcaria camettia*, Spreng., grows along the sides of the Backwater, and has received its name from the natives, as they assert that if its irritating white juice, penetrates into the eye, it will infallibly destroy vision. Good Caoutchouc, can be prepared from this secretion.

The castor oil plant, *Ricinus communis*, Linn., grows almost everywhere, but does not appear to pay, when grown in fields, so well as other crops. The Kamila, *Röttlera tinctoria*, Roxb., also exists in many localities, the red dye is much prized in Europe. It is known to the natives as the monkey faced tree, because that animal often amuses himself, by rubbing the dye over his physiognomy.

The beautiful creeper, *Gloriosa superba*, Linn., blossoms from August to October, during which period, its yellow and crimson flowers, may be occasionally met with in the jungles, or hedgerows. Its root is considered highly poisonous.

The Bastard Sago, *Caryota urens*, Linn., is found sprinkled over the country. Sugar and toddy wine, are obtained from it, and a species of sago from the pith, on which some classes subsist for some months in the year. Its fibres are made into fishing lines, and bow strings ; the fibres of the leaf stalk, yield ropes strong enough to confine elephants, whilst the seeds are used as beads by the Mahomedans. The sugar cane, *Saccharum officinarum*, Linn., is cultivated in many places, but its saccharine properties are insufficient in a commercial point of view, to remunerate for expressing the sugar. The Lemon grass, *Andropogon muricatum*, Retz., is also found in the Trichoor Jungles, its pleasant aroma is much prized, and it is used as fringes to punkahs, and tats for doors and windows. There is also one species of tree fern.

Much, very much, remains untold, of the magnificent botanical scenery, which exists in these parts, as well as of the rich timbers, the splendid flowering shrubs and trees, and of those productions suitable for the food of man. Should the reader be curious on these subjects, and wish for more information, he may well be referred to Van Rheede's *Hortus Malabaricus.* In conclusion it must not be omitted, that the tea plant (one species of which is said to grow wild in Ceylon) was introduced by Mr. Huxham, into Travancore, some twenty-five years ago, and has since then been successfully cultivated by the late General Cullen ; that the Cinchona raised at Ootacamund, by the skill of Mr. MacIvor, has been sent by His Excellency Sir W. Dennison, the Governor of Madras, as a present to the Travancore gardens, situated on the confines of the Cochin State. Whilst the introduction of the Chinese Sugar Cane, *Sorghum Saccaratum*, from the Mauritius, has been accomplished by the exertions of M. Regnaud of Cochin, and may in time perhaps, be successfully cultivated as food for cattle.

CHAPTER XVIII.

TRADES AND OCCUPATIONS.

Imports into Cochin—Exports from Cochin—Cocoanut oil—Fish oil—Coprah—Coir—Coffee—Settlers in land—Pepper—Timber—Native produce—Agriculture—Cattle—Fisheries—Houses—Chunam—Mercantile firms—Labour Market—Shoemakers—Canarese—Carpenters—Hawkers—Sailors—Vessels and boats—Coinage—Weights and Measures.

In the foregoing pages, a short account of the most common, useful, or curious forms of animal and vegetable life, found in this portion of India, has been detailed. It now remains to point out, which are most prized in commerce, and what are the various trades and occupations, of the Commercial, and Artizan inhabitants. The *Imports* and *Exports* for the last 5 years, have been as follows:—*

	1856-57	1857-58	1858-59	1859-60	1860-61	Average.
Cocoanut oil *imported*, Cwt.	975	163	72	223	1,515	590
Fish oil, „	1,498	7,968	1,370	4,416	8,890	4,828
Coprah, „ „	1,139	727	1,272	717	2,839	1,339
Cocoanuts, „ Thds.	43	95	141	162	49	98
Coir goods, „ Cwt.	4,411	3,979	3,928	841	1,712	2,974
Coffee, „ „	5,395	1,531	828	804	13,675	4,447
Pepper, „ „	„	402	„	„	3,214	723
Ginger, „ „	95	70	„	178	2,388	546
Cotton, „ „	1,543	6,174	1,082	1,247	4,079	2,825
Hides, „ Corges.	9,017	1,861	690	566	351	2,497
Rice, „ Robbins.	74,336	76,424	62,040	77,607	80,907	74,263
Horns, „ Cwt.	8	76	6	26	140	51
Bees' wax, „ „	6	94	90	55	130	75

Amongst the remaining goods imported, viz., piece goods of cotton, wool, or silk: Iron, Copper, Brass, Lead and Spelter, Sugar, Paints,

* Furnished by *the Manager of the Sea Customs.*

Tea and Canvas, some are of European manufacture, but the whole are so mixed up, that it is not worth while to give the figures.

The total *Exports* of Native produce, have been as follows ; of which much has been sent to Europe, and elsewhere ; the totals of which, will be found under each heading.

	1856-57	1857-58	1858-59	1859-60	1860-61	Average.
Cocoanut oil exported, Cwt.	1,60,982	1,83,048	1,51,228	1,22,070	13,543	1,26,174
Fish oil, exported, „	1,964	17,169	26,154	34,569	18,295	19,630
Coprah, „ „	24,864	13,842	16,688	31,181	79,642	33,243
Cocoanuts, „ Thds.	731	495	29,809	1,670	2,360	7,013
Coir goods, „ Cwt.	1,21,336	1,14,182	1,25,817	1,38,496	1,06,224	1,21,211
Coir fibre, „ „	„	4,558	5,562	4,368	4,488	3,795
Coffee, „ „	14,251	10,582	8,480	10,375	13,543	11,446
Pepper, „ „	10,575	18,723	5,104	7,832	4,887	9,424
Ginger, „ „	4,310	3,657	5,903	9,606	12,248	7,145
Cotton, „ „	1,790	5,401	466	903	2,366	2,185
Hides, „ Corges.	4,514	10,429	6,521	1,097	1,247	4,762
Rice, „ Cwt.	5,663	19,223	31,162	2,495	11,274	13,963
Horns, „ „	2,104	1,204	851	322	630	1,022
Wax, „ „	291	168	325	58	126	194
Croton seeds, „ „	141	146	198	223	348	211

By examining into the declared value of the articles of native produce, exported to various parts of the world, it is found that Europe obtains about 37 per cent., the Indian markets about 43 per cent., Ceylon about 14 per cent., the Mauritius and Bourbon nearly 4 per cent., and the remainder goes in small quantities to other places, such as Australia, America, China, the Malay coast, Muscat and Singapore. Out of the produce which finds its way to Europe, about 82 per cent. goes to England. Cochin may thus be considered more valuable in the capacity of a feeder to other Indian markets, than as an exporter to Europe on its own account. Nearly one third of the produce, appears to be taken in small country crafts along the coast.

The principal article is Cocoanut Oil, the export of which has averaged upwards of 126,174 cwt. yearly, 71 per cent. of which goes to the European markets. The selling price in London, has averaged about £46 per ton, and at the present time it is rising, not only there, but also in India. The average Bazaar price in Cochin has been about 73 rupees a candy. But although the *average* cost is merely set down at 73 rupees a candy, the Merchant rarely obtains it at that, as he seldom purchases until the end of August, or commencement of September, and the price has then advanced, and 78 rupees may perhaps be considered a fair average, although, it sometimes reaches nearly as high as 100 rupees. Considering the duties and other charges, the profits on the article, do not appear large.

Fish oil depends upon the number of Sardines, and other oil producing fish, which come to Cochin: this has been alluded to in the chapter on fish, where the mode of preparing it, has also been detailed. It is a good substitute for cod liver oil, but as it has been ably shown in Europe, that the amount of phosphorous and iodine in each species, depends not only on the mode of its preparation, but also on the time of the year, and the state of health of the fish: so no doubt, the same would be found in Cochin. Its value in the market is about Rupees 35, or 37, a candy.

Coprah, or the dried kernel of the cocoanut, is largely exported, in both its white and black varieties, and the average appears increasing, to the detriment of the amount of oil manufactured. Some goes to Europe, but Calcutta is the great market for this commodity, where it forms an ingredient in every Native curry. Cocoanuts are also exported in great numbers. As a general rule, toddy drawers have steps cut in the trees by which to ascend them, but the cocoanut pickers have a string passing from one great toe to the other, and sometimes a belt which goes from their backs around the trees.

Coir, or the fibrous covering, or rind of the nuts, is obtained by soaking them for a few months in brackish water. From this coir ropes are made, or the substance is exported in bales. Its strength, elasticity, and lightness, renders it one of the best materials for cables. A considerable quantity is exported to Bombay, where it is largely shipped, as broken stowage.

Coffee is grown in gardens, but the ingenuity of the fiscal arrangements of the Native states, (especially that of Travancore,) are apparantly those best calculated to check its cultivation. From the little place Alwaye, only 16 miles from Cochin, a duty of Rupees 12 a candy is now levied, which will be probably augmented, and in addition to this, the boats containing the produce, are detained at the small custom houses, and every impediment is thrown in the way of its being brought to the coast. The Cochin State, will be as great a loser by this Travancore process, as any one.

Fortunate will it be for Cochin and Travancore, when the at present unreclaimed Western ghauts, are dotted with plantations of coffee, and possibly tea. And when other minor productions, which are as yet untried, find cultivators in those magnificent, but feverish regions, where the tiger, the bear, and the elephant, find secure retreats, still untrodden by the foot of man. Every inducement ought surely to be afforded to settlers there, even as far as guaranteeing the land at a certain rate, and *permanently fixing the transit duties* to be levied on the produce.

Amongst the disadvantages enjoyed by a settler, who takes land in a Native State, for coffee plantations, is the facility with which any petty official, can stop his obtaining labour, unless he receives "Custom;" whilst taxes on produce may be increased, almost at pleasure.

Pepper since the removal of the monopoly, may be said to have been chiefly smuggled into Cochin, where it may be obtained at a certain rate. Ginger is not much grown, as though highly remunerative in some years, it is a total failure in others. It must be raised away from the sea. The largest quantity comes from Chernaad, in Malabar: whilst en route to Europe, it suffers greatly from the depredations of 2 or 3 species of Coleopterœ. It costs from 90 to 100 Rupees a candy.

The timber merchants consist of those who purchase from the Native State, the timber as it stands: and those who trade in it when cut.

Trade in timber mostly consists in Teak, Anjelly, Benteak, White cedar, Red cedar, Sapan and Sandal wood. The worm is very destructive.

The following articles of Native produce are those principally dealt in, Arrowroot, Bees' Wax, Cardamoms, Cocoanuts, Cocculus Indicus, Coffee, Coir rope, Yarn, fibre and junk. Coprah, Ginger, Kino, Hemp, Hides, Hogslard, Horns, Myrabolams, Nux vomica, Cocoanut oil, Fish oil, Poonac oil, and Gingelly oil, (which is used in Europe for the manufacture of Olive oil,) Paddy, Pepper, Rice, Croton seeds, Terra Japonica, and Turmeric.

The manner in which Parasu Rama obtained this country from the sea, and his method of peopling it, as well as the uses to which he devoted it, have been detailed in the second chapter. When the second race of Brahmans had obtained possession, and been instructed how to propitiate the snakes, they came to the conclusion, that agricultural pursuits were necessary, in order to procure agricultural productions, to sustain life. They accordingly addressed their patron,* stating that although the land was fertile, they were ignorant of the means of cultivating it; on which he is believed to have given full instructions on the best methods of proceeding. The work was divided into four parts, but as the directions were very full, and the present generation have become wiser than their ancient lawgivers, it will be unnecessary to detail them, and will answer a better purpose to enquire what course is now pursued.

In olden times the Agriculturists were merely the Slaves of the higher classes, and in return for their labour, received a certain amount of protection. War had few terrors for them, as only the Nairs and the superior castes, indulged themselves in the pleasures of fighting, and the cultivators were only employed as Coolies, for carrying the baggage, and throwing up earth works, as their caste was too low, for any one to kill them. In warfare, cultivation was always spared, the cocoanut plantations and the rice fields were as safe from the foe as the friend, and the Agriculturist might continue his occupation in peace, undisturbed by the proximity of hostile armies. The Portuguese appear to have been the first who introduced the practice of destroying the means of subsistence, when harassing an enemy's country.

It was formerly the plan, and may be said still to be so, to cultivate almost wholly the low lands, and those easily watered, as the Agriculturist was formerly almost unable to trade in grain, in consequence of the rents to the Sirkar being paid in that produce, and the supplies being sold to the Sirkar Officials, to whose agents this traffic was confined, even

* *Mackenzie, M.SS.* Book No. 3, C. 896. Section 3.

as late as 1810.* Thus there was no inducement to the Agriculturist to cultivate more than was required for his own family and dependants, as the small shops had even to pay a tax for retailing it. The tax on the Backwater is at present a great drawback to the conveyance of grain to other places, and many of the disastrous famines in Travancore, may have been partly ascribed to the rapacity of the Sircar under officials, and the discouragement given by them to traders and producers. There was, and still is, only one class unaffected, viz. the Brahmans, who fed at Government expense out of the produce of the land, fatten in idleness, and luxury, and are consequently averse to any change in the present system.

The methods of rice cultivation, are divided into three; the *Moondoowun*, which is the largest and principal crop, is sown in August, and reaped in January. The *Poonjah*, which is sown in January, in low moist lands, and reaped in April, the crop is small but profitable: and the *Birripoo*, which is a dry crop. It is only very rich lands, which will yield three crops, and the first and third, are those most usually produced. The Birripoo is grown on high dry lands, and is succeeded by gram. In fact rice is raised by three principal methods, dry or wet sowing, or transplanting. After the land has been prepared by ploughing twice a month for several in succession, the first sowing occurs, after a fall of rain. The fields are manured with ashes, prepared from burning the leaves of Cocoanut trees, or if procurable from the manure of cows. The seed is sown broad cast, about 2½ bushels being required for each acre, and it is hoed or ploughed in. A month subsequently, the ground is weeded, and more ashes put on, the banks are then repaired, and the water is confined to the field, or else raised and brought into it by the aid of either a Persian wheel, or a tread wheel.

The sprouted seed requires different management, the land is prepared to receive it, by being kept moist, and subsequently drained, until only four inches of water are left; and at every ploughing ashes are put into the mud, but rarely manure. The mud is smoothed by having a plank drawn over it by men, if the water is

---

* Official Reports to the Resident. *Lieut. Arthur.* 1840.

deep, but if shallow by buffaloes, which are preferred for this purpose to oxen. The water is drained off before the sowing commences, ten days after this two or three inches are allowed to remain upon the field, and as the crop grows, the depth of water is increased.

Transplanted rice is raised at the same time as the sprouted seed. The young plants are transplanted into the field in which they are to be reared. If many worms are seen amongst them, they are kept for three days, with their roots uppermost, in bundles on the banks, which separate the rice plots. They are planted in a field which has three inches of water on it, and this is increased on the fourth day to nine inches.

In irrigated lands, along the banks of the backwater, only one crop is obtained yearly, which is the second one, sown about September, for rice cannot grow in salt water, (whioh the backwater is,) and unless the fields are banked up highly, the tide overflows them, whilst even if well embanked, the strong tides are liable to break in and destroy the crops. In the Trichoor lake, in the Thaullapully district, and in the Northern parts of the State, two crops can be grown yearly, because the water is fresh and in some parts of Thaullapully, even three are annually produced.

The dry sowing is the least trouble, and if the early rains are copious, the crop is generally good. The transplanting process requires the greatest labour, but as it is the most remunerative, it is usually pursued at the second period.

Kumari, or Malavellamy cultivation, yields a large return: and is a species of jungle crop. A portion of the forest is appropriated for this purpose, and set fire to. The soil of course is rich, owing both to the vegetable debris, and to the ashes of the burnt trees. This ground is then ploughed, and the seed sown, from which enormous crops are usually reaped. On the following year, a smaller one is obtained, and on the third year also, provided the bushes have not risen too high. The cultivator then passes on to another portion of the forest, where all large trees are again destroyed by the action of fire. It is considered that this process may be repeated on the same spots, once in every ten years, but in some districts once in every seven.

The abundance of the crops, depends entirely on the amount of rain, for artificial irrigation is only employed very locally. Should the rain fall have been small, the rice becomes yellow and the yield is unremunerative: or if the South West Monsoon has been excessive, the crops get washed away bodily. Rice in full bearing, looks very much like an English wheat field. At intervals of about 100 yards, there are small sheds, in which watchers are located to scare away birds.

The implements of agriculture are of the most primitive description, the wooden plough scarcely deserves the name, and in dry lands does not turn up the earth for more than six inches in depth. In some of the gravelly districts, a hand hoe is substituted for a plough, and the dry grains thrive well on the slopes. The sickle for cutting rice, is like that used in England, but smaller. The stalk is divided about six inches from the ground, or should the paddy be growing in the water, the ear only is cut off. If rice is required for immediate consumption, the bundles or sheaves are taken by the stalks, and beaten against a block of stone or wood, until most of the seed is obtained. This seed is the rough paddy, which is soaked for one night, and the next morning partially boiled, after which it is dried in the sun, and the rice subsequently obtained by beating it in a wooden mortar, in fact a species of threshing. It is then winnowed, and the husk separated from the rice. If it is intended to keep the rice for seed after it is cut, it is at once dried in the sun without being boiled. Some of the grains are then broken through, to ascertain whether they are of a good quality for sowing, which is evidenced by their being quite white in the centre. Three or four days after the paddy has been threshed by the hand beating as described, the straw is placed in a room with a wooden floor, and muzzled oxen are turned in, to tread out any grains that remain. The straw is used for fodder. The rice may be kept for years, if it has been partially boiled before drying, but if not it becomes a powder. It must not be omitted, that the varieties of rice are very numerous, some are best adapted for one species of cultivation, and some for another, but an enumeration of each, would fill up much space, without being of any practical utility.

Millet, (Chāmay,) *Panicum Miliaceum,* Linn., is grown in considerable quantities in inland places. It is very easy of digestion, and esteemed wholesome food.

The Cocoanut plantations are those which occupy the principal place in the maritime districts, as wherever they flourish, other agricultural produce is generally neglected. The soil of the valleys and uplands of the State, consists of a tough clay, of a dark colour, which on the banks of the streams, is mixed with sand. In the low lands it has a brown stiff character, but changes in the higher spots, either to loose white sand, or to a gravelly earth. The higher the ground is, the larger is the proportion of sand, which also greatly predominates along the maritime tract, between the sea and the backwater. This just suits the cocoanut tree, as it receives salt from the air, whilst there is sufficient mould in the sand for its subsistence, and the soil is of the loose nature it delights in.

More inland, there are two other prevalent species of garden cultivation, viz., that of the Areka, and Sago Palms. Picking the Areka nut, is rather a dangerous occupation, as the man after climbing to the top of the first tree, and having picked the fruit it contains, does not descend, but swings the fragile tree on which he is, backwards and forwards, until he is able to take hold of some portion of the next in the row, which he then clings to, and lets go the first. After obtaining the fruit from this second one, he repeats the process to the end. But unfortunately the trees frequently break, and fatal accidents ensue, from this fancied saving of labour. When the nut is prepared for the inland market, it is sliced and covered with a thick coating of gum, which improves its appearance, and increases its weight. Spinning-tops for children, are often made of betel nuts, with a stick inserted through them.

The cattle which consist principally of oxen and buffaloes, vary in their comparative quantities, in different parts of the State. They are generally a very diminutive breed, and their appearance varies according to the district, and the time of year. During the South West Monsoon, they are in the best condition, as there is sufficient grass from about June to October, for them to subsist on. But as the dry hot weather returns, the vegetation becomes burnt up, and persons who have laid by straw feed their cattle upon it: but where no such provision has been made for them, the poor creatures roam about in search of food, and soon look miserable enough. The buffaloes appear to thrive better than either the cows or oxen, as they pass the heat of the day in the water. In some portions of the State, the cattle appear almost wild. Although goats are plentiful, sheep do not thrive, and though Agriculturists have frequently tried to introduce them, they have never succeeded in doing so.

The Fisheries have been previously alluded to, salt fish forms an article of export. One morning on visiting the deep sea fishing ground, 48 boats were perceived engaged, of which 34 were Ceylonese, who although idle and indifferent around their own fishing grounds in Ceylon, appear very industrious in Cochin : the waste of fish is lamentable, and a mitigation of the enormous salt tax in the Native States, in favour of the curers of fish, one might imagine would prove a beneficial, politic, and humane proceeding: but the poor fisher appears to have no friends.

Before entering upon the trades, a remark is necessary on the houses, in which produce was formerly stored. With the exception of Rajahs, Princes, Priests, and Foreign Merchants, no persons at the time of the advent of the Portuguese, were permitted to have stone houses. As the only buildings which will stand the climate, are those made of stone, the composition of the walls, requires notice. All were constructed of laterite, but the trade of the Chunam maker, appears to have been better understood in olden times, than in the present day. Whether the Bricklayers were superior, more jaggery was mixed up with the mortar, or any other reason existed for such being the case, it is now almost impossible to say: but the fact is patent. As houses are a necessity for all, the first occupations adverted to, will be those of the Chunam makers, and Bricklayers.

Buildings erected by the Dutch and English, as a rule are unsound, and not unfrequently fall down, whilst the great majority of those now standing in Cochin, are of Portuguese construction. Buildings in the interior, do not show this decadence, which is commonly attributed to the violence of the Monsoons, but in addition to this, the quality of the building materials, must exercise a great influence.

Many buildings no doubt fall down, owing to the superior description of laterite, not having been employed in their construction : or else its having been used, before exposure to the sun had rendered it sufficiently dry and hard. But these causes will not account for all the damage now going on.

As lime to make Chunam for mortar has to be brought from long distances, shells which are exceedingly common are burnt, and the lime thus obtained when slacked, is adapted for use. Salt, (Chloride of Sodium) as is well known exists in the sea, and is the principal cause of its saline taste. One of the many well known characteristics of salt, is to abstract moisture from the atmosphere, and any one remaining only a few days in Malabar, during the Monsoon time, has only to look at his salt cellar to perceive the great extent to which this is carried on.

Sand, as well as chunam, is necessary for building purposes, and those in Cochin who desire lasting walls, send to the Alwaye river, where it cannot be mixed with saline matter. When salt is present in mortar, owing to its absorbing properties, it keeps the walls damp, and perhaps occasions, or at least greatly assists their destruction. Of late years sand has been used, which has been collected during the Monsoon time, from the mouth of the river, where it empties itself into the sea, or in fact from the sea shore. As the freshes come down, they remove the taste of salt from this sand, but chemistry shows, that they do not carry away all its saline ingredients. Damp is thus drawn from the atmosphere to buildings, walls are weakened, and structures fall down. Sand should invariably be taken from a river, beyond the influence of the tides, or at least beyond that point to which salt water ever reaches.

There are four descriptions of shells, mainly employed for chunam: bivalves from the sea shore: Oysters from the backwater: large Potamides from the estuaries: and Cyrenœ, amongst which are often Ampullariœ, and Unionaciœ, from the fresh water marshes, and lakes. If the three first were thoroughly cleansed from salt, before they were burnt, no doubt they would be as good as the last: but all are burnt as found, and the fresh water species being commonest inland, is presumptive evidence in favour of their use, being one cause (conjoined with fresh water sand,) why inland houses stand the Monsoon the best.

There are several, probably too many, European Mercantile firms in Cochin. They have instituted a *Chamber of Commerce*, to which

Merchants and others are admissible. The Native traders, and petty Merchants, appear to be doing well, and the country coasters have a thriving carrying business. Contrary to what is the usual course elsewhere, it does not appear improbable, that the trade of the Europeans has reached its maximum, unless it obtains some at present unexpected stimulus, whilst that of the Natives will increase.

The first thing to be noticed in trade, is the labour market, for even procuring coolies is an occupation. Merchants have to keep a Moopa, to obtain men; and a Mooputtee, to engage women. Now as both the employer, and employee, have "*to give custom*," synonymous with a pecuniary reward, in the form of a salary from the former, and a percentage from the latter's pay, it follows that the middle man or woman as the case may be, has often a good time of it. This is said to be only contracting, and the fixing of the price of the labour market by Government to be a hardship. Matters are only changed in Cochin, instead of Government, the Moopas and Mooputtees are the fixers of the rate of pay for the coolies, out of which they obtain a percentage. Inland this is what is so unfair to the European traveller, however well it may act in sea port towns. The rights of the Native are said to be protected, but are not those of the European disregarded? The cooly, or the cart man, cannot now supply the traveller, without the sanction of the head of his department, (if it may so be called,) in fact of his Moopa, and the European is in his hands.

It is not here intended to argue respecting the law of supply and demand, but many theories true in Europe are misplaced in India, and even in England it is questionable, at what rate the Cab man, or Omnibus driver, untrammelled by law, would charge a stray passenger, almost ignorant of the language of the country. But when common bullock carts, going at the rate of 15 miles a day in Malabar, cost 4 annas or six pence a mile, (including tolls,) or the rate of a London cab, surely some alteration is called for, and some protection for the European traveller needed: for this is not competition, but combination. Likewise if unrestricted combination is permissible, for the purpose of augmenting the rates of land and backwater travelling in Malabar, (exclusive of the Native State,) why is it not allowed for sea boats? The theory if true for one, must be true for the other. But licensed boats only can ply for hire and then at a fixed rate, when engaged in loading and unloading vessels. *If the first is not a hardship to the European, the latter must be to the Native.*

The Shoemaking trade appears to be a lucrative one. *Governor Moens* stated in his *Memorial*, that Shoemakers were sent for from Tuticorin to Cochin by Governor de Jong, before 1731, and remarked that in 1781, they consisted of 16 families numbering 71 persons, some of whom had become Christians whilst others were Mahomedans. At the present time the majority of them are Eurasians. Skins of animals with the fur on, can be most beautifully tanned in Cochin.

The Cloth dyers according to *Moens*, were brought to Cochin about 1681 from Coilpatnam, near Tuticorin, and were introduced by a Canarese, named Baba Porboo, and were employed by the Dutch Company.

Amongst the traders of note, are the Konkanies, or Canarese, (page 309). They are astute in their dealings, and clever in their transactions. *Moens* stated, that "on the taking of Cochin, they " came under Dutch protection, and that boys of six or seven years " of age, were taught their trades. That they were up to every- " thing, had ingratiated themselves so with the high Officials about " the Rajah, and were so ready to barter anything for money, that " much required information could be obtained through them." The Banians he continued were originally identical with the Wunnears, and though they dabbled in all trades, were masters of none. To a Banian, *Moens* stated, the imports and exports of Cochin were rented out. The Tuttans or Silversmiths, do not appear to have been more celebrated in those times, for correct dealings, than they are now, for he says, " they were great rogues in making up trinkets, " and never worked in shops, but went wherever their services were " required."

The Carpenters compose a large portion of the working class, some of them carve well in teak or blackwood, but not so neatly or cheaply as those in Bombay. The Coopers likewise have a good trade, owing to the large demand for casks, in which oil is exported. Blacksmiths, and Brassfounders, are also clever at their respective trades. Tailors abound, and obtain excellent wages. The Dhobies are of two classes, the Christians, and the Hindus, the latter being Tamuls. They are by no means superior to those of their occupation elsewhere.

The Hawkers, some of whom are large shopkeepers, sell articles of attire, in fact of almost everything required in houses, excepting furniture. They always wish to dispose of something in the first house they go to of a morning, as it is considered a bad omen should they not do so. Hindus unless of very low caste, rarely trade on Thursdays, and many of the Hawkers are Konkanie Brahmans. Moplahs will do nothing on Fridays, until they return from their mosque, mostly about 3 P. M. Jews do not work from 6 P. M. on Fridays, to 6 P. M. on Saturdays. Syrians from 6 P. M. on Saturdays, to 6 P. M. on Sundays.

The next occupation which deserves attention, is that of the Seafaring Native, and the Ship builder. A short description of the various boats and vessels, which are made in, or trade to Cochin, is therefore given. In the early part of this century, some Frigates made of teak, were built in the port, but although their quality was excellent, their cost was great. The same may be said of merchant vessels, and a large one is now very rarely launched, the last, named the Allum Ghir of 800 tons, was completed in 1861. Small crafts and native vessels are not uncommonly built, but more frequently in the neighbouring Native State at Muttencherry, than within British territory.

Native vessels are as follows,* *Pattamars* which are employed in the Bombay coasting trade, and are amongst the best for stowing cargo in, as well as for sailing qualities. Owing to their construction, they are able to sail nearer to the wind, than any other description of vessel, whilst their speed is pretty good. They are "grab built," or with a prow stern, which is of the same length as the keel. They have two masts, the foremast raking forwards, for the purpose of keeping the ponderous yard clear when it is raised or lowered. The yard is slung at one third of its length. The tack of the sail is brought to the stern head, through a fixed block, and

* *Edge.* On Indian Vessels, *Journal Asiatic Society.* Vol. I. 1834.

a sheet hauled aft at the side. The haulyard is a pendant, and treble block, from the mast head aft to midships, thus acting as a backstay for the mast's security: there are also about two pairs of shrouds. The size of the large Pattamars, are about 76½ feet long: 21½ broad: 11 feet 9 inches deep: and of about 200 tons burden. They are planked with teak, upon jungle wood frames, and put together in the European manner, with nails, bolts, &c.; their bottoms are sheathed with inch board, and a layer of chunam, mixed with cocoanut oil and country resin, said to preserve the planks very effectually, against the ravages of insects. Some of the smaller Pattamars have their planks sewn together with coir, but these have only one mast.

The sailors are generally Mahomedans, and these vessels often come from Bombay, with salt and other cargoes, and take back coir, rice, cocoanuts, coprah, oil, timber, sandal wood, pepper, and other productions of the coast. Some occasionally bring passengers, but these are of a very superior description, with a fine cabin in the stern part, and a large pandall outside for servants, with a deck over the after cabin. The hold is divided, the large portion being sufficient to accommodate two ponies, and two cows. Pattamars are usually anchored every night, when sailing along the coast. The crews are generally honest, and trust-worthy, as well as civil and obliging, if their prejudices are not interfered with.

The *Arab Dows*, are vessels employed in trading between the Red Sea, the Arabian Coast, the Gulf of Persia, and the Indian coast. They are invariably manned by Arabs. Their size is generally from 150 to 250 tons burden by measurement, they are grab built, with ten or twelve ports. This description of vessel is occasionally constructed at Cochin. They have a great rise of floor, and are calculated for sailing with small cargoes. They are fully prepared for defence, with decks, hatchways, ports, poop decks, and in fact are adapted either for war or piracy. Many of them are sheathed on 2½ inch plank bottoms, with one inch board, and the same preparation of oil and resin, as is placed on Pattamars, is put between the planks and the sheathing boards. On the outside there is a coat of whitewash, to which resin and oil are added, which is renewed every year.

Dows have generally one mast, the yard is the length of the vessel aloft, and the mast rakes forward, for the purpose of keeping the ponderous weight clear, in raising or lowering it. The tack of the sail is brought to the stern head, and sheets aft in the usual way. The haulyards lead to the taffrail, having a pendant and treble purchase block, which becomes a backstay, to support the mast, when the sail is set: this with three pairs of shrouds, completes the rigging, which is very simple, and made of coir rope. Tippoo Sultan's fleet on the Malabar Coast, consisted of this class of vessels. Those which come to Cochin, generally bring dates, fruits, preserves, shiraz wine, and horses; and take back the productions of the country, as well as European articles, and have also been known to have carried off kidnapped women, to dispose of at Zanzibar. More Dows and Budgerows are said to be annually lost, than any other description of native craft, as they are very unsafe.

The *Budgerows*, or *Baggalas*, are Indian vessels, manned with Lascars, Arabs, or Natives of Cutch, who trade from the coast of Hindustan, to the Gulf of Persia, the coast of Arabia, and the Red Sea. The peculiar form, and extraordinary equipment of these vessels, is said to have remained unaltered from the time of Alexander the Great. They are armed with two guns on the after part, or right aft of the stern, as a defence against Pirates. Their poop deck has a round stern, they are very broad in proportion to their length, with a sharp rising floor. The stern is straight, and rakes very little more than the stern posts. The extreme length is about 74 feet: 25 broad: 11½ in the depth of the hold, and they are of about 150 tons burden.

These vessels are constructed with timbers and planks, which are nail and trenail fastened, in the rudest and most unsafe manner possible. They have one mast, with a huge yard, made from two spars: the small ends of which are lashed together. The tack of the sail goes to the stern head. The topside above the deck, is barricadoed with mats on the outside of the timbers, which run up to about 8 feet from the deck. If there is no cargo, these are removed.

The *Munjoo* or *Munjees*,* are very strong built boats, with something of a Grab prow, with no deck, but a sort of cabin astern. They convey produce from port to port.

* Col. Welsh, *Military Reminiscences*. V. II. p. 74.

The *Cargo Boats* are very safe, the whole length of the keel is sometimes constructed from one tree, to which planks are sewn by coir ropes. Underneath the coir rope, is a long piece of coir, which has been steeped in oil and resin, and which covers the seam from stem to stern. They are about 36 feet long, and 5 broad.

The *Fishing Boats* for single persons, are composed of hollowed trees, in which one man paddles about, in his piscatorial occupation.

Cabin Boats for backwater travelling, are of various descriptions, but vastly superior to the things called by the same name at Calicut. A first class one is from 4¾ to 5¼ feet broad, and from 34 to 38 long. A second class from 4¼ to 4¾ feet broad, and 32 to 34 long. A third class from 4 to 4¼ feet broad, and 28 to 30 long. But there are others even smaller. The largest take about 14 rowers, and a Steersman or Marakan, and the smallest 4 and the Steersman. In Cochin the hire of a first class boat a day, without rowers, is from 1¼ to 1½ rupees; of a second class 1 rupee: of a third from 8 to 12 annas. The pay of the coolies, differs considerably.

Baggage Boats vary, from those adapted to convey 1000 or 1200 Markals of paddy, to quite small ones, whilst the hire is in accordance with the size.

Snake Boats are more used as boats of honour, on either side of that of the Rajah, or of the Resident, on State occasions, than for travellers. The numerous paddlers, who use their paddles to the sound of a wild Malabar song, form a pretty sight, but in spite of their apparently rapid motion, they cannot keep up with a good cabin boat.

Having thus detailed the objects of merchandize, and the mode in which it is conveyed, the medium of exchange, as respects the coinage in use, claims attention.

The possessor of the old coins of a country, may be said to have its history for some centuries in his possession. From them the religion of its inhabitants may be gathered, whilst changes in its Monarchs, and especially in its Dynasties, are invariably succeeded by alterations in its coinage. These and the inscriptions on plates of metal, and on stones, are now the only data, of the ancient history of Southern India.

It appears probable, that the art of coining money, by the aid of dies, giving an inscription on both sides, came from the West, and was not introduced into India, until about two centuries before the Christian era. So slowly did the process spread, that south of the Nerbudda, it was not employed for coining precious metals, until the 5th or 6th century.

The earliest coins which are apparently now to be collected, are those of the Romans, some of whose gold ones, are occasionally found. They may have been originally received from traders, who came to the Western Coast. At Ponany, and near Coimbatore inland, the largest numbers have been found in one spot, where they had been no doubt secreted by some persons for security. This could not have been done by the original traders, as it is improbable that they penetrated far into the interior of the country, and they may fairly be considered to have been purchased of the Romans, by Natives, for the purpose of hoarding. Buddhist coins are also reputed to be occasionally found in the tombs spread over the country.

A good numismatic collection is still a great desideratum for these parts, and one for which there is ample scope. Parasu Rama's battle axe, may be said to be the type of the Malabar coins, and it may be traced in those found in Ceylon, until at last the convex coins of that Island, are perceived bearing this device. It is unnecessary to enter into any discussion here, as to when the Malabarians conquered Ceylon, and the people of India obtained such ascendancy there, that their coinage even superseded that of the island.

The hook, or fish money, termed *ridi*, was introduced by the Portuguese, and consisted merely of pieces of twisted silver, Ceylon was originally supposed to have been the country from which they emanated, but their Persian device has now proved their origin. The Dutch continued to use them during their supremacy.

The Portuguese historians affirm that on the arrival of their nation in Cochin, none of the native Princes along the coast, had the power of coining money, with the exception of the Samorin. It does not appear that the Portuguese coined any Indian money, whilst they retained possession of the country, but they certainly introduced European coinage.

Continuing the history of the coins of Malabar, we arrive at the time of Hyder's second conquest, (1774), when there appears to have been two species of gold fanams current, one termed the Cannanore, the other the Verary, the rate of the former being with the shroffs four fanams per surat Rupee, or 2½ Rupees to the nominal Hoon. After Hyder's Government had become established in Malabar, the Verary which alone was employed for Revenue matters, was stamped with the Hindustanee H on one side in allusion to his own name, thus constituting the Verary the Hyderie fanam, but its value remained the same. The Hyderie Hoon or Pagoda, was of 4 Rupees value. In 1786-87* Tippoo ordered the cessation of this coinage, and in its stead, introduced the Sultany, the value of which fell below that of the Hyderie coinage. In 1790-91, on the restoration of the Samorin, the old Verary Hoon was re-introduced. In 1793 the relative value of the Hoons had become as follows, 10½ new Verarys, were worth 10 Sultany fanams, and Hoons were at any rate worth Rs. 3 each, but in revenue matters, the British discovered that they were imposed upon by the Samorin's Minister, who valued them in the accounts, at Rupees 2½, thereby causing a loss of nearly Rupees 120,000 in one year.

The most common copper coins now current in the Bazaar, next to those of the English East India Company are those of the Dutch, which have a large V on one side, with an O on the right arm of the V and a C on the left. These coins have various emblems on the other side, generally with a crown surmounting one or more Lions, or a coat of arms. The only ones with inscriptions, are those of 1791 and 1792, on which are *Indeo est spes nostra.* The earliest date to be found on them, is 1731, but specimens of almost every year from that time, until 1792, may be procured. In 1757 a half

* "From Hyder's death, until the year 1200, A. H. all Tippoo's gold and " silver coins, are dated according to the usual calculation, the figures reading " from left to right. About this time however, with his well known love of " innovation, he introduced a new system of reckoning, which from some of " the inscriptions on his copper coinage, appears to have been reckoned from the " *Death*, instead of the flight of Mahomet, the figures reading from right to " left. This then will account for the space of eleven or twelve years, which " intervenes between coins struck in two successive years of his reign."—Hawkes. *Sketch of coinages of Mysore*, 1856.

cash appears, to have been coined, whilst some of those minted in 1746, are of the thinnest description. There cannot be a question, as to whether these cash are of European manufacture, as they have evidently been minted in Europe, and subsequently despatched to India. Antecedent to that date, good Dutch money cannot now be discovered in Cochin, but a curious specimen like lead, covered over with a brown amalgam exists, on which is the V O C of the Dutch East India Company, meaning *Vor Ost Indien Compagnie.*

The next most common coins, are the Elephant cash of Mysore, previous to the Mahomedan era of Mysore, the symbol was invariably an Elephant, with the usual cross lines on the obverse, subsequently a moon was placed over the elephant. Tippoo added dates and letters, or placed an Hindostani B, (Bangalore,) over the elephant, which is now known as the B elephant cash. When the present line of Mysore Rajahs returned, the copper coinage was altered, and a sun and moon placed over the elephant, to which in a few years subsequently, the figures V, X, or XX cash, in English characters, were added. Then the elephant and the cypher were discarded, and the tiger looking like a mangey cat was substituted.

Some of the copper coins have fish upon them, some deer, and in fact there are specimens to be met with, of all the neighbouring petty states, that coined money. Even one exists much corroded by time, which has a large cross on one side, and is apparently Portuguese, it is mostly dug up in the ruins of the old forts.

When the Cochin Sircar first commenced to coin, is not well known. Certainly they did not do so in the time of the Portuguese, and apparently not so whilst the Dutch sway was predominant. In 1812 it is said, the coinage was as follows, 1 doit, equalled 2 reas: 10 reas, one poothen: 19¼ poothens, one Surat rupee. Here a *poothen* first comes into notice, this is a Cochin coin, and its very name signifies "new."

It is considered, that 19¼ poothens equal one Company's rupee. It is a little ugly coin, without even good mintage to bring it into notice. Its materials are very impure, whilst it takes 32 to equal the weight of a rupee, thus supposing the purity of the two coinages to be equal, the receiver of the poothens loses 12¾ in every rupee. But even it has not purity to recommend it, a single poothen having only 6 pie worth of silver in it, it follows that about 9 annas 7 pie is a legal tender in the Native State, for 16 annas. At the Madras Mint, the charge for coinage, is 2 per cent. on silver, and 1 per cent. on gold, sending metal to Madras to be thus converted into poothens, at the present rate, ought to be a remunerative transaction.

The double poothen, has a Hindu god on one side, wearing a crown, and a snake emerging from either side of his chair, and meeting over his head. Round his neck is a string of skulls, in his left-hand is the wheel of fate, around each shoulder two circlets, and on each wrist two bracelets. On the obverse is a palanqueen. Formerly instead of the god Siva, there was a chank shell.

The British coinage is the same as elsewhere in the Presidency 12 pie, one anna: 16 annas, one rupee.

The weight and measures are peculiar to the place. Of course in the custom's house, the Presidency weights are employed, 1 rupee equals 1 tolah: 80 tolahs 1 seer: 40 seers 1 maund, or 82¼ English pounds.

One Dutch pound equals 42½ tolahs, or 1·0927 lbs. English. The usual Bazaar maund, is 30 Dutch pounds, 20 of which equal 1 candy, or 656 English pounds.

For iron or sugar, 25 Dutch pounds go to a maund. For oil, 75 Dutch pounds one chodana, 25 of which go to 1 candy. For wood, 24 borrels or 28½ square inch English, 1 tooda, 24 of which equal a candy.

FINIS.

CHRONOLOGY.

Year	Date	Event
B.C. 68		A great congress, *is believed* to have been held in Kerala, at which the rulers decided on sending to Chéra (Madura,) for a Permaul or Governor.
A.D. 52		St. Thomas, *is said* to have visited Malabar.
A.D. 68		An immigration of Jews into Malabar, *is stated* to have occurred.
325 (351?)		The Rajah of Cochin had the title of Raveeloke Sharajay given him.
341	March 24th.	Cheraman Permaul ascended the Musnud.
345		Thomas Cana, asserts that in this year, he saw the last of the Permauls alive.
350	(about)	Theophilus the famous Arrian Bishop, *is said* to have visited Malabar.
378		The year when Cheraman Permaul, was last seen alive.
379		The date of the Jewish and Syrian copper plates.
379		The succession of the Priesthood in India was cut off from the Primate of Persia, by the Metropolitan of Mosul,—on which the Primate threw off his allegiance to the Seleucian Patriarch.
829		Mar Sapor, and Mar Peroses, came from Babylon, and obtained leave to erect Churches in the territories of the Rajah of Culli-Quilon.
1341		Era of Poothoo Veppoo, or New Vypeen.
1496		The Wiwah-karah Mahlah, a code of Hindu laws, written by Mahesha Mungalum Nambuderi, an inhabitant of Parumanum, in the Cochin State.
1498	May 20th.	Vasca de Gama, anchored before Calicut.
1500	Dec. 20th.	Cabral's fleet arrived at Cochin.
1501	Jan. 10th.	The Samorin's fleet was descried off Cochin, on which Cabral pursued it, and did not again return to Cochin.
1501	Dec. 15th.	The Samorin's fleet, of about 180 vessels, arrived off Cochin, for the purpose of attacking the Portuguese.
1502		The Christians at Cranganore, sent a deputation to Vasca de Gama at Cochin, asking him to present a petition to the King of Portugal, that he would take them under his protection.

1503	March 1st.	The Samorin entered the Cochin territory, and attempted to force a passage by a Ford near Cranganore.
1503	Sept. 20th.	Francisco de Albuquerque, with six sail, arrived at Cochin, on which the Samorin's party fled to Cranganore.
1503	Sept. 22nd.	The Samorin's troops, were defeated at the Island of Vypeen.
1503	Sept. 23rd.	The Portuguese attacked, and took Repelim.
1503	Sept. 26th.	The foundations of the Portuguese Fort at Cochin were laid.
1503	Sept. 30th.	Alonso de Albuquerque, arrived at Cochin from Portugal, with three ships.
1503		The Portuguese obtained land from the Rajah of Cochin, and established a factory in Cochin.
1504	August 17th.	Pacheco defeated the Samorin's troops at Chetwye.
1505		Don Francisco de Almeyda, first Viceroy of India, arrived at Cochin.
1517		Alcacova was sent out from Portugal, as "Surveyor of the King's Revenue," or Finance Minister.
1521		The Samorin attacked the Rajah of Cochin, but was routed.
1523		Cranganore Fort was built by the Portuguese.
1524-25		The Mahomedans engaged in a barbarous warfare against the Jews at Cranganore.
1531		The Samorin, anxious to conclude a peace with the Portuguese, presented them with a piece of land at Chaul, on which to build a fort.
1538		Paichi Marcar, a Moor of Cochin, sent forces to Ceylon, to assist King Bhuwaneka Bahu VII against the Portuguese.
1539		Peace was concluded with the Samorin.
1542		Xavier arrived at Cochin.
1545		Albuquerque, Archbishop of Goa, compelled his soldiers to marry Native women, for the purpose of proselytization.
1545		The Bishop of Goa, sent a Franciscan Friar, to preach to the Syrians at Cranganore, and enquiries were instituted into the Syrian faith.
1550		The Portuguese built the Rajah of Cochin a palace at Muttencherry, or old Cochin.
1557		The Church of Santa Cruz, at Cochin, was made a Cathedral, by Pope Pius IV at the request of the King of Portugal. A Dominican was made Bishop of it.
1560		An order, promulgated by the Rajah of Cochin, soon after the arrival of the Portuguese, forbidding his subjects to embrace the Roman Catholic faith, was cancelled.

1565	Jany 27th.	The Rajah of Cochin, and two Princes, slain in battle.
1565	Feby. 10th.	Another Rajah of Cochin, killed in battle at Poodikavoo.
1565		The Jews left Cranganore, and settled at Cochin, whilst Jews town was being built.
1565		The Portuguese enlarged the Cranganore Fort.
1567		Jews town was completed, and the Jews removed into it.
1571		The Portuguese possessions in India and the East, were divided into three portions, designated India, Monomotapa, and Malacca.
1577		The Jesuits commenced publishing religious books in Cochin, in the Native languages.
1587		A College was erected for the Syrians at Vaipicotta, at the expense of Antonio Morales.
1591		Captain Raymond's expedition was fitted out, and left England for India.
1594		The "Bull of Crusade" arrived from Portugal, commanding the Portuguese to reduce the infidels of Malabar to the faith, by force of arms.
1594		Houtman organized the Dutch East India Company.
1595		Pope Clement, despatched a brief to Menezes, ordering him to enquire into the faith of the Malabar Bishop and his flock.
1597		Two Dutch vessels appeared off the coast of India.
1597		Mar Abraham, the Syrian Bishop of Malabar died, and Menezes nominated a Jesuit, Francisco, Vicar Apostolic of Malabar.
1598	Dec. 27th.	Don Alexis Menezes, embarked at Goa for Cochin, where he commenced enquiring into the faith of the Syrians.
1599	June 20th.	The Synod of Diamper, was held at that place.
1599	Nov. 16th.	Menezes returned to Goa.
1599		The Samorin first permitted the Portuguese to erect Churches, and forward the Christian religion in his dominions.
1600	May 31st.	The English East India Company of London, was established.
1604		A truce of 12 years was agreed upon between Holland and Spain, one of the articles of which recognized the right of Holland to share in the commerce of India.
1605		The See of Angamale was translated to Cranganore, by Pope Paul V., and the Prelate of the latter church made Archbishop.
1608	August.	The first English ship arrived at Surat, under Capt Hawkins.
1608	Nov. 16th.	The Samorin made a contract with Admiral Peter

		Willem Verhoeven, by which the former was compelled to besiege the town of Cochin, then under the Portuguese.
1634-35		A treaty was entered into between the British and the Portuguese, by which the English gained free access to the Portuguese Ports, and agreed in return to receive the people of that nation as friends in their factories.
1635		The English first exported pepper from the Malabar coast.
1642		The French East India Company established.
1653	May 22nd.	A tumultuous congress of Syrians was held at Alangatta, which ended in their formally separating themselves from the Roman Catholic Church.
1661	March 12th.	The date of an agreement entered into on board the Muscaatboom, between the Dutch and the Paliat Achen, who agreed to assist them against the Portuguese.
1661		The Dutch under VanGoens, attacked the town of Cochin, but the Rajah of Porca came to the assistance of the Portuguese, and the Dutch were beaten off. In this year the Dutch took Quilon, Cranganore, and Tangicherry.
1661		The Portuguese punished the Jews for having assisted the Dutch, plundered Jews town, attempted to destroy the Synagogue, and carried away the Pentateuch.
1662	February.	The Dutch attacked and took the palace of the Ranee of Cochin, and made her a prisoner.
1662	Oct. 25th.	The Dutch forces returned to Cochin under General Hustaart.
1662	November.	Van Goens joined the Dutch, who were besieging Cochin.
1662	December.	The Rajah of Porca, the Ally of the Portuguese, arrived at Ernaccollum, and threw supplies into the Cochin Fort, on which a bloody engagement ensued, between the Dutch and the troops of this Rajah.
1663	Jany. 8th.	Cochin capitulated to the Dutch. The garrison was commanded by Captain Pierre de Pou.
1663	Jany. 23rd.	Protestant service, performed in Cochin for the first time, by Dr. Anthonius Scherius.
1663	March 20th.	The Dutch concluded a treaty with the Rajah of Cochin, who consented to become their vassal.
1663		The Propaganda convent, the Jesuit college, and several Roman Catholic churches in the town of Cochin, were destroyed by the Dutch.
1665-66		The Vypeen church was built.

1667		The Dutch possessions in Malabar, and on the Western coast, were placed under the Cochin command, which included Quilon, Culli-Quilon, Cranganore, and Cannanore.
1668		The Jewish Pentateuch which had been taken away by the Portuguese, in 1661, was recovered.
1680		An attempt was made by the Dutch, to sell back or exchange with the Portuguese, those places where the Roman Catholic faith had taken such hold, retaining the town of Cochin for the purposes of trade.
1685		Immigration of some White Jews from Amsterdam.
1689		Adoption into the family of the Rajah of Cochin took place.
1691	Sept. 10th.	Chetwye was given to the Samorin by the Dutch
1697		The Cochin Fort was reduced one half. The Cranganore Fort was left with only the outer walls, and the Forts of Cannanore and Quilon reduced to only one tower.
1698	April 8th.	The date of a letter from the Court of Directors at Amsterdam, to the Government of Cochin, stating that permission had been given to the Archbishop of Ancyres, to send a few Carmelite Priests to Malabar.
1701		War commenced between the Dutch and the Samorin, which lasted until 1710.
1706		The Kodaychayree Kaimul, shook off the Samorin, and joined the Cochin faction.
1709		Many of the Romo-Syrian congregations, attempted to join the Syrians.
1710	January.	The Rajah of Cranganore was re-instated in the possessions he had held in 1691.
1714		A dispute occurred between the Dutch and the Samorin, respecting a piece of ground at Chetwye, which resulted in the Samorin taking and destroying the Chetwye Fort.
1715		The Samorin invaded and conquered part of the Cochin State.
1717		A peace was concluded between the Dutch and the Samorin, who was compelled to re-build the walls of the Chetwye Fort, to cede the whole of Chetwye to the Dutch, and to divide all his possessions on that Island, between the Rajah of Cochin, and the Dutch.
1738		Angria the Pirate, attacked the Dutch ship Noord Wolfsbergen, and the yachts Zeelands Wolvaren, and Magdalena, and after three days' fighting, captured the two last.

1739		The Rajah of Quilon died, and his country became blended with that of Culli-Quilon, the Rajah of which, was also Rajah of Pannapully.
1742		The Dutch Fort at Quilon, was attacked by 3,000 of the Travancore troops, who were beaten off.
1742		The Samorin's troops 1,000 strong, invaded the territories of the Cochin Rajah, but retreated on the English protesting.
1747		The Syrians obtained a bishop from Babylon, through the assistance of a Jew named Ezekiel.
1749		Angria's piratical fleet appeared before Cochin.
1750		The Nestorians ceased to preside over the churches of Malabar.
1753	Oct. 15th.	The Cochin Rajah met the Dutch Ambassador at Mavillicurray, when they attempted to negotiate a peace with Travancore.
1753		A peace was concluded between the Dutch and the Travancore Rajah by which the former bound themselves to a strict peace policy.
1757		Three hundred Europeans and 17,000 coloured troops, arrived at Cochin from Batavia.
1758		The Samorin attacked and took part of Chowghaut,—on which the Rajah of that country applied to Hyder for assistance.
1757-58		The Rajah of Cochin and the Dutch, formed an alliance to drive the Samorin out of the Cochin State.
1758		The Dutch relieved the Chetwye Fort, routing the Samorin's troops.
1761		The Travancore lines constructed.
1762		The Rajah of Travancore defeated the Samorin in the cause of the Rajah of Cochin, whom he reinstated in part of his dominions, (Chowghaut.)
1762		The Rajah of Travancore opened Allepey to foreign trade.
1762		The districts of Paroor, Alungaad, and Korutnaar, were made over to the Rajah of Travancore, by the Rajah of Cochin.
1766		Hyder conquered Malabar, from Cannanore to the State of Cochin, when that Rajah agreed to become tributary to him, if he would not invade his territory.
1766	April.	The Dutch Commissioners at Hyder's request met him at Calicut, and enumerated the various titles, &c., by which they held their factories, &c., under the Samorin.
1767	Feby. 20th.	Hyder's fleet of 28 sail, came into the Cochin roads, and two of them even entered the river, and anchored close under the walls. They left the next day.

1770		The Mahratta fleet of 30 sail came into the Cochin roads, and proposed to the Dutch to form an alliance with them,—they remained eighteen days, and then sailed northwards.
1775		The Travancore lines were improved, and the ground on which they stood purchased by the Rajah of Travancore, from the Dutch.
1776		Tippoo took Cranganore and Ayroor, the Rajahs of which had previously been under the protection of the Dutch.
1776	August.	Hyder's troops, invaded the Northern part of Cochin, and took the Fort of Trichoor.
1776	Nov. 12th.	The Dutch troops landed at Chetwye, but falling into an ambuscade, the advanced guard, were all either killed, or made prisoners.
1776	Nov. 13th.	The Dutch Fort of Chetwye was compelled to surrender to Sirdar Khan.
1778		The Fort of Cochin, was repaired by Governor Moens.
1778	Jany. 8th.	The Dutch stormed and took the palace of the Cranganore Rajah.
1778	Jany. 19th.	The Dutch were compelled to retreat to Cranganore.
1778	March 3rd.	The Mysoreans attacked the palace of Cranganore, and compelled the Dutch to retire to the Cranganore Fort.
1779		The Protestant Church at Cochin was renovated.
1784		Orders arrived from Batavia, to return the territories of the Rajah of Chetwye, to Tippoo.
1787		The Rajah of Cochin imposed a poll tax upon the Christians of St. Thomas.
1788	May 28th.	The Rajah of Cochin met Tippoo at Paulghaut.
1788	June 4th.	The Rajahs of Travancore and Cochin held a conference at Annanada, North East of Cranganore.
1789		The Fort of Cranganore sold by the Dutch to the Travancore Rajah.
1789		Chowghaut was taken by the British forces.
1789	August.	Cranganore and Palliport sold by the Dutch to Travancore.
1789	October.	Tippoo's army was encamped near Paulghaut.
1789	Decr. 28th.	Tippoo established his camp 6 miles to the North of the principal gate of the Travancore lines.
1789	Decr. 29th.	Tippoo unsuccessfully attempted to take the Travancore wall.
1790	April.	Tippoo received re-inforcements and effected a breach in, and took the Travancore lines.
1790	April 15th.	Tippoo's troops took the Monastery of Verapoly, the records of which were lost in the river, whilst the Priests were endeavouring to convey them away.

1790	May 7th.	Tippoo occupied Cranganore Fort which had been evacuated the night before.
1790	May 24th.	Tippoo hurried back to his capital.
1790		A treaty was concluded between the Rajah of Cochin and the English, in which the former agreed to pay the latter a tribute of Rs. 100,000 annually.
1790	Nov. 26th.	The British Commissioners let the Island of Chetwye to the Rajah of Cochin, for one year, at 40,000 Rs. rent.
1791		Lally, Tippoo's General, was driven out of Cranganore.
1791		The Rajah of Cochin was enabled by the assistance of the British, to throw off the Mysore yoke.
1791		The Rajah of Cochin loaded the Konkanies with new imposts, but was opposed by the Dutch, and eventually obliged to admit their right over this people.
1791		The above disputes occasioned the "Dagwar's Kinni" war, during which the famous Konkanie Bhimmum was removed to Allepey, by the Konkanies for safety.
1791		There was a subsidiary treaty between the British and the Rajah of Cochin.
1791		The Dutch presented Chetwye as a gift to the Samorin.
1793	March 1st.	Cochin was transferred from the Government of Bombay to that of Madras.
1794		Earthen ramparts were erected around Trichoor.
1794		The Reception Hall at Tripoonterah built by the Dutch.
1795	Feby. 24th.	The date of a letter received from the Stadtholder, by the Dutch in Cochin, ordering them to admit the British into their possessions.
1795	Sept. 6th.	Major Petrie, Mr. Stevenson, and Governor Van Spall, held a conference at Cochin, respecting giving up that fortress to the British.
1795	Sept. 10th.	A re-inforcement left Tellicherry, to join Major Petrie at Cochin.
1795	Oct. 19th.	The fortress of Cochin was captured by the British.
1796	December.	The Cochin prisoners of war were sent to Bombay.
1797		The Cochin prisoners of war received permission to go to Batavia.
1802		The people of the Cochin Rajah, arrested persons in British Cochin, so all subjects of his State were excluded from the town.
1802		A party of persons from British Cochin, presented the Rajah with a portrait of Napoleon.
1803	Oct. 6th.	Orders bearing this date, were sent to Cochin, di-

		recting the garrison to be prepared for foreign invaders.
1803		The Cochin Fort was blown up.
1808	Dec. 29th.	The Travancoreans entered Cochin, attacked the Resident's house, and set the prisoners in the jail at liberty.
1809	Jany. 14th.	The Travancoreans again attacked Cochin.
1809		The district of Irunaad, and Mooloorcurry, assumed by the Rajah of Cochin, in consequence of the Paliat Achen having rebelled against the British.
1809	Feby. 8th.	The date of a subsidiary treaty between the British and the Rajah of Cochin.
1809	April 11th.	The Resident took forcible possession of the Palace at Muttencherry.
1809	April.	The Christians in the Cochin State, petitioned to the British to protect them against the ill treatment they received from the Native Officials.
1810		The Cochin Zillah Courts were established.
1814		The town of Cochin was finally ceded to the British.
1814	Augt. 16th.	The English Government gave up all control over the Native Christians in the Rajah's territory, who were ordered to be henceforth subject to the Rajah's Courts of Law.
1817		The Zillah Court of Cochin was abolished, and the records were sent to Calicut.
1818		The subsidy from Cochin was reduced to two lacs, with the proviso, that should they not be forthcoming, Government would be at liberty to annex the country.
1820-21		Three British frigates were built in Cochin.
1823		The first coffee plantation was established in Malabar.
1832		Amaravady Chapel built.
1835		The Rajah of Cochin was in arrears with his kist, as the Dewan had misappropriated the revenues of the country, so the British Resident of Travancore and Cochin, gave the Rajah the option of either giving up his kingdom to the British, according to the treaty of 1809, or agreeing to receive a certain sum monthly, and being allowed to retain his title of Rajah, with the customary honors. The Rajah acceded to the latter course; the Dewan was put in irons, and all his property confiscated.
1836		The Bishop of Calcutta wrote to the Syrian Metropolitan, enquiring into the disagreements between the Missionaries of the Church Missionary

		Society, and the Syrians—on which the Metropolitan held a conclave of his clergy, and replied that the members of his faith were all Jacobites, and that if the Missionaries chose to preach those tenets in their Churches they were at liberty to do so. He then imposed a solemn oath on his clergy that they would have nothing more to do with the Protestant Missionaries.
1853		A Cochin Brahman stole the Konkanie Bhimmum from the Allepey Pagoda, and carried it to Cochin.
1853	January.	The Government Civil Dispensary at Cochin opened.
1856		A New Poor House was built in Cochin, in lieu of the old one which was destroyed by a previous Monsoon.
1859		The Telegraph established in Cochin.
1860		The detachment of troops previously stationed in Cochin was withdrawn and a Police Force organized in its stead.
1862	Oct. 1st.	General Cullen, late British Resident of Travancore and Cochin, died at Allepey.
1862	Decr. 24th	The Rajah of Travancore visited the Rajah of Cochin at Tripoonterah.

INDEX.*

* When two names appear in the Index, the second of which is in Italics, it is intended to designate the Native reading in Romanized characters. Having procured from the Rev. J. Maten and other Natives the words written in their own tongue, Mr. Garthwaite, *Inspector of Schools*, kindly undertook the translation of their characters.

† "In the translations of Malayalam names, the hard letters k-t-ṭ and p— "when not initial, and not *doubled* (thus kk, tt, ṭṭ pp,) are to be pronounced like "the corresponding soft letters, g, ḍ, d, and b—when commencing a word they "retain their usual hard sound. Thus in *Karmmam, Paniyan,* and *Tiyan* the "letters K, P, T, have the hard sound, but *Akam, Aṭé, Uteyan,* and *Lòpam* are "pronounced *Aḍé, Udeyan* and *Lòbam*. This rule is common to both Tamil "and Malayalam, two languages much more closely related, than for example, "English and Broad Scotch."—*Note by Mr. Garthwaite.*

Pages.

Pages.